Specific learning disabilities and difficulties in children and adolescents
Psychological assessment and evaluation

The assessment of specific learning disabilities and disorders (SLD) has long been controversial. Definitions, diagnosis, and treatments have been vigorously debated for decades, with the use of IQ tests attracting particular controversy. However, in recent times there have been many other new assessment tools devised for measuring intelligence and neuropsychological functioning, extending well beyond the scope of Wechsler's scales. In this cutting-edge survey, an international team of leaders in the field examines the available methods. Many of the contributors are themselves the developers of the most recent assessment tests.

The authors of each chapter evaluate the diversity of clinical applications of these new instruments in SLD, and their important implications for educational intervention. The historical context and the underlying neuropsychological and cognitive theory are also expertly examined. This book will be essential reading for any practitioner or trainee dealing with specific learning issues in young people.

Alan and **Nadeen Kaufman** are based at the Yale University School of Medicine and together have developed and published eight tests of intelligence, achievement, and neuropsychological functioning, including the Kaufman Brief Intelligence Test (K-BIT), the Kaufman Test of Educational Achievement (K-TEA), and the Kaufman Adolescent and Adult Intelligence Test (KAIT). They are world-renowned authorities in the area of neuropsychological and cognitive assessment for specific learning disabilities and disorders.

Cambridge Child and Adolescent Psychiatry

Child and adolescent psychiatry is an important and growing area of clinical psychiatry. The last decade has seen a rapid expansion of scientific knowledge in this field and has provided a new understanding of the underlying pathology of mental disorders in these age groups. This series is aimed at practitioners and researchers both in child and adolescent mental health services and developmental and clinical neuroscience. Focusing on psychopathology, it highlights those topics where the growth of knowledge has had the greatest impact on clinical practice and on the treatment and understanding of mental illness. Individual volumes benefit both from the international expertise of their contributors and a coherence generated through a uniform style and structure for the series. Each volume provides firstly an historical overview and a clear descriptive account of the psychopathology of a specific disorder or group of related disorders. These features then form the basis for a thorough critical review of the etiology, natural history, management, prevention and impact on later adult adjustment. Whilst each volume is therefore complete in its own right, volumes also relate to each other to create a flexible and collectable series that should appeal to students as well as experienced scientists and practitioners.

Already published in this series:

Specific learning disabilities and difficulties in children and adolescents

Psychological assessment and evaluation

Edited by

Alan S. Kaufman

and

Nadeen L. Kaufman

CAMBRIDGE
UNIVERSITY PRESS

PUBLISHED BY THE PRESS SYNDICATE OF THE UNIVERSITY OF CAMBRIDGE
The Pitt Building, Trumpington Street, Cambridge, United Kingdom

CAMBRIDGE UNIVERSITY PRESS
The Edinburgh Building, Cambridge CB2 2RU, UK
40 West 20th Street, New York, NY 10011-4211, USA
10 Stamford Road, Oakleigh, VIC 3166, Australia
Ruiz do Alarcón 13, 28014 Madrid, Spain
Dock House, The Waterfront, Cape Town 8001, South Africa

http://www.cambridge.org

First published 2001

Printed in the United Kingdom at the University Press, Cambridge

Typeface Dante MT 11/14pt *System* Poltype® [VN]

A catalogue record for this book is available from the British Library

Library of Congress Cataloging in Publication data
Specific learning disabilities and difficulties in children and adolescents/edited by Alan S. Kaufman
and Nadeen L. Kaufman.
   p.   cm. – (Cambridge child and adolescent psychiatry)
Includes index.
ISBN 0 521 65840 3 (pb)
1. Learning disabilities – Treatment.   2. Learning disabled children.   I. Kaufman, Alan S., 1944–
II. Kaufman, Nadeen L.   III. Cambridge child and adolescent psychiatry series
RJ506.L4 S644 2001
618.92'85889–dc21   00-064187

ISBN 0 521 65840 3 paperback

Every effort has been made in preparing this book to provide accurate and up-to-date information which is in
accord with accepted standards and practice at the time of publication. Nevertheless, the authors, editors and
publisher can make no warranties that the information contained herein is totally free from error, not least
because clinical standards are constantly changing through research and regulation. The authors, editors and
publisher therefore disclaim all liability for direct or consequential damages resulting from the use of material
contained in this book. Readers are strongly advised to pay careful attention to information provided by the
manufacturer of any drugs or equipment that they plan to use.

To Blanche Kaufman,
OUR MOTHER

> She loved us, and she listened.
> Hear our love and gratitude,
> For we are lonely without you.

Contents

Contributors

Wayne V. Adams
Professor of Psychology
Graduate School of Clinical Psychology
George Fox University
414 North Meridian Street
Newberg
Oregon 97132
USA
E-mail: wadams@georgefox.edu

Erin D. Bigler
Professor and Chair
Department of Psychology
Brigham Young University
1082 Kimball Tower
Provo
Utah 84602
USA
E-mail: erin_bigler@byu.edu

Colin D. Elliott
860 Fowler Avenue
Newbury Park
California 91320
USA
E-mail: Basdasman@aol.com

Raphael S. Feuerstein
International Center for the Enhancement of
Learning Potential
PO Box 7755
47 Narkis Street
Jerusalem 91077
Israel
E-mail: reuvenf@actcom.co.il

Reuven Feuerstein
International Center for the Enhancement of
Learning Potential
PO Box 7755
47 Narkis Street
Jerusalem 91077
Israel
E-mail: reuvenf@actcom.co.il

Gary Groth-Marnat
Senior Lecturer in Clinical Health
Psychology
School of Psychology
Curtin University
GPO Box U1987
Perth
Western Australia 6001
Australia
E-mail:
G.Groth-Marnat@psychology.curtin.edu.au

Alan S. Kaufman
Clinical Professor of Psychology
Yale Child Study Center
Yale University School of Medicine
PO Box 207900
230 South Frontage Road
New Haven
Connecticut 06520-7900
USA
E-mail: NadeenKaufman@msn.com

Nadeen L. Kaufman
Lecturer, Clinical Faculty
Yale Child Study Center
Yale University School of Medicine
PO Box 207900
230 South Frontage Road
New Haven
Connecticut 06520-7900
USA
E-mail: Nadeen Kaufman@msn.com

Sarah L. Kemp
1802 S. Cheyenne Drive
Tulsa
Oklahoma 74119
USA
E-mail: Doctorsally@comnpuserve.com

Ursula Kirk
Apt. 27B, 222 E. 93rd Street
New York
New York 10128-3759
USA
E-mail: uk12@columbia.edu

Marit Korkman
Professor of Child Neuropsychology
The Hospital for Children and Adolescents
Helsinki and Uusimaa Hospital District
Helsinki
Finland
E-mail: marit.korkman@skynet.be

Elizabeth O. Lichtenberger
Salk Institute of Biological Studies
6740 Tea Tree Street
Carlsbad
California 92009
USA
E-mail: drlizmike@aol.com

Nancy Mather
Associate Professor
College of Education – 409
Department of Special Education and
Rehabilitation
University of Arizona
Tucson
Arizona 85721
USA
E-mail: nmather@U.Arizona.EDU

Jack A. Naglieri
Director
Center for Cognitive Development
George Mason University
4400 University Drive
Fairfax
Virginia 22030
USA
E-mail: naglieri.1@osu.edu

Ralph M. Reitan
Reitan Neuropsychology Laboratory
2920 S. 4th Avenue
South Tucson
Arizona 85713-4819
USA
E-mail: Reitanlab@aol.com

Margaret Jo Shepherd
454 W. 46th Street
Apt. 4C-S
New York
New York 10036
USA
E-mail: mjs96@columbia.edu

Otfried Spreen
Professor Emeritus
Department of Psychology
University of Victoria
PO Box 3050
Victoria
British Columbia V8W 3P5
Canada
E-mail: spreen@UVic.CA

Elisabeth H. Wiig
7101 Lake Powell Drive
Arlington
Texas 76017-3517
USA
E-mail: ehwiig@krii.com

Deborah Wolfson
Reitan Neuropsychology Laboratory
2920 S. 4th Avenue
South Tucson
Arizona 85713-4819
USA
E-mail: Reitanlab@aol.com

Richard W. Woodcock
532 Creelman Lane
Ramona
California 92065
USA
E-mail: rww4m.ramona@worldnet.att.net

Preface

This book, *Specific learning disabilities and difficulties in children and adolescents: Psychological assessment and evaluation*, is devoted to the topic of *specific* learning disabilities, with a focus on their assessment. The terms 'learning disabilities' (LD) and 'specific learning disabilities' (SLD) are used interchangeably throughout the book. When a chapter author uses the term learning disabilities, it should always be interpreted as specific learning disabilities.

The field of learning disabilities assessment has long been controversial, and remains so as the twenty-first century begins. Controversies have raged over definitions, interventions, and instruments. Recent articles in the *Journal of Learning Disabilities* (by leaders in the field such as Linda Siegel, Keith Stanovich, and Frank Vellutino) have called for the elimination of the IQ–achievement discrepancy from the definition of specific learning disabilities, and some leaders are demanding the elimination of IQ tests from the psychoeducational assessment process. To some extent, these arguments are based on the continued use of Wechsler's scales for the diagnosis of specific learning disabilities. We deal with these controversies in the concluding chapter of this book. However, one of the reasons that we wanted to write this book in the first place was because of the many alternatives to the Wechsler scales that became available during the last two decades of the previous millennium.

There is now much more to intellectual assessment than Wechsler scales. This fact is probably obvious in the UK, where the British Ability Scales (BAS) and now its revision, the BAS II, have been commonly used (as have Wechsler scales) for evaluations of specific learning disabilities. The fact may be less obvious in the USA, where Wechsler scales (then the WISC and WAIS) surpassed the Stanford–Binet (then Form L-M) and established their supreme reign during the 1960s. The ascendance of the Wechsler scales at the time coincided, but not by coincidence, with the burgeoning field of learning disabilities, whose leaders demanded multi-score profiles instead of global IQs. The reign continued through the 'R' tests (WISC–R and WAIS–R) in the 1970s and 1980s and is still going strong with the third generation of tests (WISC–III and WAIS–III). However, it may be time for clinicians to re-evaluate or, at least, explore the diversity of options that are now available for specific learning disabilities evaluations. Many of these tests are theory based, with Luria's neuropsychological theory and Horn's fluid–crystallized theory of intelligence each forming the foundation of several new tests. In contrast, Wechsler scales, like the Binet before them, were developed from pragmatic, decidedly non-theoretical, frameworks.

In conceiving this book, we wanted to put on display the many new methods developed for the neuropsychological, intellectual, and language assessment of children, adolescents, and adults, with the chapter authors endeavoring to relate the tests to the diagnosis and treatment of individuals with specific learning disabilities. A number of chapters are written by authors who know the specific instruments intimately, namely the authors of the tests themselves. Among the new breed of tests, this dual role of test/chapter author was true for the Woodcock–Johnson Tests of Cognitive Ability–Revised (WJ–R) and WJ III (Nancy Mather and Richard Woodcock, Chapter 3), the Cognitive Ability Scales (CAS) (Jack Naglieri, Chapter 5), the British Ability Scales II (BAS II) and Differential Ability Scales (DAS) (Colin Elliott, Chapter 6), the NEPSY (Marit Korkman, Sally Kemp, and Ursula Kirk, Chapter 11), and comprehensive measures of memory and learning (WRAML and TOMAL) (Erin Bigler and Wayne Adams, Chapter 12). We did not go right to the horse's mouth for the Kaufman tests, because we knew that the horses would have their say in the final, integrative chapter (Chapter 13), but the psychologist we selected to write Chapter 4 on the K-ABC and KAIT, Elizabeth Lichtenberger, was clinically supervised and trained by Nadeen and has collaborated with Alan on several texts.

In addition to the chapters on new measures, there are three chapters that feature more established instruments, but that focus just as much on a specific *style* of assessment as on the tests themselves. These chapters, too, are written directly by the professionals who developed the featured tests and, even more importantly, innovated a particular style of assessment – dynamic assessment (Reuven Feuerstein and Raphael Feuerstein, Chapter 7), clinical–educational language assessment (Elisabeth Wiig, Chapter 8), and neuropsychological assessment (Ralph Reitan and Deborah Wolfson, Chapter 10).

The best way to understand where a field is headed in the future is to have a solid grounding on where it has been. The field of specific learning disabilities has had a colorful history and can trace its roots to both neurology and education. We believed that it was important to offer both of these historical perspectives, and enlisted experts who have witnessed the growth of the field of specific learning disabilities from its inception and have been dynamically involved with the directions specific learning disabilities and their assessment have taken during their evolution. Representing the educational viewpoint is Margaret Jo Shepherd (Chapter 1), with Otfried Spreen (Chapter 9) supplying the neurological perspective.

This book might have been organized in a number of ways, particularly because of the complexity of both of the fields we have merged, specific learning disabilities and assessment. Whereas education and neurology can appear worlds apart, they are intertwined for specific learning disabilities assessment, and it is difficult to separate them; indeed, it is not possible to write about the application of an instrument for specific learning disabilities assessment without blending biological bases and presumed brain dysfunction with academic deficits and educational intervention. We have chosen to organize the book in four parts. The first and last parts are relatively short, the middle two parts more extensive. We begin with history and tradition in Part I, encompassing Shepherd's education-oriented and practical-focused History lessons (Chapter 1) and Gary Groth-Marnat's treatment of Wechsler scales (Chapter 2). Part II presents alternative *cognitive* approaches to specific learning disabilities assessment and remediation, meaning alternatives to Wechsler scales, and includes a variety of new instruments in Chapters 3 to 6, as well as the Feuersteins' dynamic assessment approach in Chapter 7, and Wiig's clinical–educational approach to language assessment in Chapter 8. Part III features *neuropsychological* approaches to specific learning disabilities assessment and remediation, encompassing the historical foundations in Chapters 9, the old, established Halstead–Reitan in Chapter 10, the new NEPSY in Chapter 11, and tests specifically geared to memory and learning in Chapter 12. Part IV, composed solely of our concluding chapter, integrates the topics covered in the book, addressing contemporary controversies and illustrating how the scales and subtests discussed throughout the book can be hand-picked and reorganized to measure a diversity of key areas that are routinely assessed during specific learning disabilities evaluations, for example attention, reasoning, and motor coordination.

Because this book was edited by American authors, published by a British company, and targeted for a world-wide audience, we wanted to achieve an international flavor. Toward that end we have assembled an international cast that includes a number of American chapter authors as well as authors from Great Britain (Colin Elliott, currently living in the USA), Finland (Marit Korkman), Israel (Reuven and Raphael Feuerstein), Germany (Otfried Spreen, currently living in Canada), and Australia (American-born Gary Groth-Marnat).

We believe that this book will be of extreme value to anyone interested in learning disabilities or assessment. It is intended for graduate students and upper-level undergraduate students in education, special education, and psychology (e.g., school, clinical, educational, and counseling psychology; neuropsychology; psychometrics), and for practicing, academic, and research-oriented professionals in each of these disciplines. Neurologists, medical students, and others with a medical orientation should also find the topics informative and valuable.

Alan S. Kaufman and Nadeen L. Kaufman

Acknowledgments

We are extremely grateful to a number of people for their direct or indirect contributions to this book: to Dr James C. Kaufman, for his generous, swift, invaluable research and editorial assistance – not just with this book, but with all of our research, test development, and writing projects – and for his unflagging love, support, and friendship; to Dr Margaret Jo Shepherd, for serving as our mentor for more than a quarter of a century in the fields of learning disabilities and clinical inference, and for a close friendship that developed while collaborating on this book; to Dr Peter Melchers, of Cologne, Germany, and to Jan and Rüya Alm, of Uppsala, Sweden, who have enriched us with their knowledge of the international scope of dyslexia and clinical assessment, and who have demonstrated that deep friendships can easily transcend oceans and cultures; and to Kathy Howell and Shauna Cooper, who gave generously of their time and effort to facilitate the final preparation of this manuscript.

Part I

History and Tradition

History lessons

Margaret Jo Shepherd

Introduction

In April 1963, Samuel Kirk, a prominent psychologist/special educator, stood before a group composed of people whose children were in trouble in school and other people, in smaller numbers, who had a professional interest in the children, and said:

I know that one of your problems at this meeting is to find a term that applies to every child. Last night, a friend of mine accosted me with the statement, 'We're going to ask you to give us a term' (Kirk, 1963, p. 1).

A few sentences later, Dr Kirk referred to 'children with developmental deficits of one kind or another' and then, after pointing out problems with 'technical and complex labels' and arguing for behavioral descriptions of children's problems rather than etiological statements, said:

Recently, I have used the term 'learning disabilities' to describe a group of children who have disorders in development in language, speech, reading and associated communication skills needed for social interaction. In this group I do not include children who have sensory handicaps such as blindness or deafness, because we have methods of managing and training the deaf and the blind. I also exclude from this group children who have generalized mental retardation. This approach has led me and my colleagues to develop methods of assessing children, or describing their communication skills in objective terms (Kirk, 1963, pp. 2–3).

Dr Kirk concluded the speech with a detailed description of a test he was creating, the Illinois Test of Psycholinguistic Abilities, emphasizing the test's capacity to specify deficits and strengths in the psychological processes underlying spoken and, by implication, written language.

Subsequently, 'specific learning disability' was acknowledged in federal laws as a disability that entitled every individual so described to publicly funded special education and related special services and to protection from discrimination in education and employment. Simultaneously, professionals struggled to turn the idea behind the name Dr Kirk suggested into criteria for identifying the children. That struggle continues, and people who choose to read this book are at the heart of it.

Although the name 'learning disabilities' has a relatively short history, the ideas behind the name are older. I was asked to place these ideas and the identification practices they engender in historical perspective. At first, my task seemed easy, because the history is written (see Wiederholt, 1974; Kessler, 1980; Doris, 1986, 1993; Farnham-Diggory, 1992; Kavale & Forness, 1995; and Torgesen, 1998; among others). Using these texts, I planned to construct another history differing from those in print in the emphasis I would place on identification (more accurately named assessment) practices.

Following Lee Wiederholt's lead (1974), most histories are, understandably, chronological. These histories link work on acquired spoken and written language disorders with work on developmental written language disorders, and link work on acquired disorders of perception, attention, and mood with similar developmental disorders. Although there are variations in sequence, the people whose ideas relate to language disorders are usually considered first and those whose ideas are associated with disorders of perception, attention, and mood are considered second. Whatever the sequence, the implication is that ideas about developmental language disorders and ideas about perceptual and mood disorders and the clinical and research traditions each set of ideas spawned are part of a single history linked to the contemporary concept 'learning disabilities.'

I believe the historical story should be told in a different way. In agreement with others (Hallahan & Cruickshank, 1973; Kessler, 1980; Kavale & Forness, 1995; Torgesen, 1998), I believe that ideas about developmental disorders of perception are the influential ideas in the terms 'learning disabilities' and 'specific learning disability.' We should carry this analysis further, however.[1] Ideas about developmental written language disorders, originating in the work of James Hinshelwood and Samuel Orton, are not compatible with the ideas about developmental disorders of perception that originated in the work of Heinz Werner and Alfred Strauss. Developmental dyslexia and specific learning disability are different concepts and cannot be combined.

An illustration of this point should help. Because I think it is a clear statement about specific learning problems, I wanted to begin this chapter as follows:

Some children enter school without giving advance notice of trouble ahead and proceed to experience severe and persistent difficulty learning to read, spell, write or calculate. The struggle with learning that we see is restricted, initially at least, to this list of tasks and to specific tasks within the list. Some children have difficulty learning to read (reading, here, is defined as transcribing printed words back to speech) and spell; others have difficulty learning to write (writing, here, is defined as composing text) and spell. Still others have difficulty learning to use numbers and write (writing, here, is defined as forming letters, numbers, and words). The children's learning problems must exist, in some form, before they enter school, but we do not see them until the children confront reading, writing, or arithmetic. With help, correction and compensation occur, but the children carry the learning problems into their adult lives. These children and the adults they become are the topic of this book.

Hinshelwood and Orton are talking in this paragraph and Strauss and Werner's voices are silent. Consequently, I could not begin this chapter with this paragraph. I could not combine these two clinical and research conditions and tell an accurate story. Hinshelwood and Orton believed that brain damage or dysfunction could disrupt learning specific to reading and writing. They described children and adolescents who were considered intelligent by their teachers except in relation to reading and writing. In contrast, Werner and Strauss believed that brain damage could affect a specific mental activity, perception, and consequently disrupt learning on any task that required that mental activity. Strauss and Werner studied adolescents who were known to be mentally retarded and, presumably, struggled to read, spell, write, and calculate. Strauss and Werner and Hinshelwood and Orton cannot speak in the same paragraph. Their views about specific learning disabilities were different in the ways described above. And their views about remedial or special education were different, too.

Both views are presented in this chapter. I begin with the Werner/Strauss view because, as indicated earlier, several people who have studied this history believe that their view influenced the definition of 'specific learning disability' in federal laws and also influenced US public school practices. The Strauss/Werner view is introduced with a story told by a school psychologist who, with the other members of his assessment team, is trying to use the federal definition and criteria to identify students with 'learning disabilities.' The Hinshelwood/Orton view is introduced with a story about an adolescent who has a specific arithmetic and writing (penmanship) disability. I have a preference for the Hinshelwood and Orton view, and that preference is certainly reflected in the way I wrote this chapter. I do not believe that I have privileged knowledge, however, so in the end I leave decision and choice in your hands.

Though it will be repetitive to some of you, I will preface the psychologist's story with information about assessment guidelines in the federal special education law.[2] Remember, each state education agency develops regulations for the state that must conform with, but can exceed, the federal regulations.

Furthermore, most states give some latitude to local school districts. Consequently, there is not one way across all states and all school districts within a state to determine that a child has a learning disability.

'Specific learning disability' according to Federal Special Education Law

A definition of 'specific learning disability' was first incorporated into federal law when Congress amended Title V of the Elementary and Secondary Education Act to include The Children with Specific Learning Disabilities Act of 1969 (PL 91-230). This act authorized federal funds to support the professional preparation of educators, programs of research, and the creation of model education programs for children with specific learning disabilities. The same definition was incorporated into the Right to Education for All Handicapped Children's Act of 1975 (PL 94-142). Unlike the earlier legislation, however, PL 94-142 not only contained a definition, but also criteria for identifying learning-disabled students. The definition and identification criteria have been maintained, without change, through the various amendments to PL 94-142 and are currently in place in the Individuals with Disabilities Education Act of 1997 (PL 105-17). The definition reads:

'Specific learning disability' means a disorder in one or more of the basic psychological processes involved in understanding or in using language, spoken or written, that may manifest itself in an imperfect ability to listen, speak, read, write, spell, or do mathematical calculations. The term includes such conditions as perceptual disabilities, brain injury, minimal brain dysfunction, dyslexia, and developmental aphasia. The term does not apply to children who have learning problems that are primarily the result of visual, hearing, or motor disabilities, of mental retardation, of emotional disturbance, or of environmental, cultural, or economic disadvantage (Federal Register 42 [1977] p. 60 582).

Regulations then specify that a multidisciplinary assessment team can find a 'specific learning disability' if:

(1) The child does not achieve commensurate with his or her age and ability when provided with appropriate educational experiences, and (2) the child has a severe discrepancy between achievement and intellectual ability in one or more of seven areas related to communication skills and mathematics abilities (Federal Register 42 [1977] p. 65 083).

The severe discrepancy specified in the regulations may be found in one or more of these domains: oral expression; listening comprehension; basic reading skill; reading comprehension; mathematical calculation; and mathematical reasoning. As part of the assessment, one member of the team must observe the child in the classroom. A child may not be called 'learning disabled', regardless of discrepancy(ies), unless the team can exclude other disabilities and adverse environmental factors (see list in definition) as causes for the discrepancies. Members of the assessment team must also document a need for special education.

Federal law, then, specifies three identification criteria: discrepancy between a measure of aptitude and measure of achievement; exclusion of certain causes for the discrepancy(ies) between aptitude and achievement; and need for special education. Most state education agencies use the federal definition and eligibility criteria with only minor variations (Frankenberger & Harper, 1987). It may interest you to learn, if you do not already know, that 'specific learning disability' is the only disability for which federal law specifies identification criteria.

Now that we know the psychologist's task, we can hear his story.

One psychologist's story

New York State is beautiful in the fall. And you don't have to travel far from New York City to enjoy the beauty. One particularly pretty autumn day, not so very long ago, a friend called to ask if I would like to join him on, in his words, a 'fall foliage walk.' As we walked, our conversation turned to retirement and my friend asked when I planned to leave the faculty at Teachers' College. I replied to his question by saying that I enjoyed teaching and wanted to continue as long as I had reason to believe that my lectures were current and coherent. Hearing my reply, he stopped walking, turned to face me and, with a look on his face that would be difficult to describe, exclaimed, 'Jo, you teach about learning disabilities. How will anyone know if your lectures are coherent!'. He was teasing, of course, and he wasn't teasing, too.

He has reason to care. He leads a school-based assessment team whose members are responsible for assigning students to special education. In any one school year, they place more students in the category 'specific learning disability' than in all the remaining disability categories that entitle students to publicly financed special education combined. They do this, he says, despite the fact that they are dissatisfied with the way they make the decision. Subsequent to our 'fall foliage walk,' we talked about his team's concerns about assessment for learning disabilities. I report summaries of these conversations as though he is speaking directly to you.

He begins, 'A child is referred to us for assessment because of persistent learning and, frequently, behavior problems in the classroom. We are supposed to decide how to explain these problems and to determine if the child will benefit from special education. Specific learning disability is an explanation for learning problems that we can use to recommend special education. Federal special education law and state education codes give us a definition and identification criteria to guide or assessments.'

Drawing a breath, he continues, 'Here is our problem. We don't know how to define, let alone test for, the psychological process disorder(s) specified in the definition. We don't know if we are supposed to look for a disorder that is common to all of the symptoms listed in the definition or if we should look for a process disorder specific to each symptom: imperfect ability to listen, speak, read, etc. We thought we had this problem solved for reading disability with the evidence that a phonological processing disorder causes specific reading disability. We ordered new tests and began testing phonological processing skills to differentiate students with specific reading disability from other poor readers. Then we learned that phonological processing disorders are common to all children who have difficulty decoding print back to speech, including children who are mentally retarded.'

He pauses for a moment and continues, 'Since we don't know how to use the federal definition to guide our assessments, we are left with criteria that tell us to find a discrepancy between an IQ score and achievement test scores. We can select appropriate intelligence and achievement tests. Though we know that underachievement is a problematic concept, we have acceptable methods for determining expected achievement based on IQ and for determining if the distance between expected and actual achievement is significant. When we do this carefully, though, what do we have when we are finished? We have a symptom, only a symptom. After we exclude other explanations for the discrepancy, we are left with an unexplained symptom. Presumably, the reason for the discrepancy is the learning disability that we couldn't find in the first place. So we end where we began.'

Speaking a little faster, he says, 'I want to be sure you understand our concerns here. This would make more sense to us if we could find both the process disorder (i.e., the learning disability) and a significant discrepancy between IQ and achievement, but without the process disorder, the discrepancy does not make sense as a diagnosis. We are willing to use the discrepancy and exclusion criteria to justify the need for special education. But we do not like to label those students learning disabled without better evidence for a disability.'

This pause is longer than the first. Finally, he says, 'There is more to this story. Because we don't know how to treat this construct as a diagnosis, we often give tests and then put our data aside and place the student in the learning-disability category for reasons unrelated to our data. For example, we respond to teachers who need relief in their classrooms and to parents who either want their child in special education or want to protect a child from special education. Our decisions are always influenced by the resources for help that are available in our school. If a student needs help and a teacher needs relief and special education is all we have, we use it regardless of the message in the assessment data. I don't understand what I am about to say but I can feel it. The ambiguous definition and identification criteria that do not explain the problem paralyze us. We are reluctant, or, perhaps, afraid, to use professional or clinical judgment to guide our decisions. We are not happy with our role in this process. We feel trapped between the commonly held belief that "specific learning disability" is an explanation for learning problems in school and the fact that, as we use it, the name is nothing more or less than an unrestricted ticket to special education.'

'Wait,' he says, after thinking for a moment, 'I am not finished. I have one more thing to say. The identification criteria we are using tell us that we can find a specific learning disability if the student presents a severe discrepancy in one or more of two language and five academic domains What is so specific about a learning disability that technically can occur across all of these domains?'

Beyond one psychologist's story

My friend tells us that, for his assessment team, at least, the federal definition and identification criteria do not work. He says that the members of his team are not willing to create their own interpretations of a psychological process disorder and that, though they can minimize the technical problems in determining a discrepancy between IQ and achievement test scores and, thus, create a consistent criterion for special education placement, they are unwilling to call children 'disabled' on the basis of one unexplained symptom. He admits that they usually make decisions based on adults' needs and available resources.

This is one person's story. It is an important story, which certainly warrants our attention, if it is a common story. Although we have to draw inferences about practice from the data, we do have studies, conducted over several years and in different places, that describe the characteristics of students identified as learning disabled by the assessment teams in their schools. These studies indicate that other teams also have difficulty using the definition and identification criteria in federal law and state education codes.

The first studies (Kirk & Elkins, 1975; Norman & Zigmond, 1980; Mann et al., 1983) were conducted with students enrolled in the model education programs, called Child Service Demonstration Centers, funded under PL 91-230 (1969). As indicated earlier, these centers were created before the discrepancy and exclusion criteria were added to federal law. Thus, the definition of 'specific learning disability,' alone, provided the guidelines for identifying students to be served as 'learning disabled.' Data for the studies were obtained either through questionnaires or by visiting the sites and reviewing students' records. Summarizing results from all three studies, Zigmond (1993) concluded that, given a significant number of IQ scores below 85 concomitant with low-achievement test scores across academic domains, many of the students identified as learning disabled in these center programs could also be identified as mentally retarded or as slow learners. She reported that investigators for each study could not find evidence that the definition in the law authorizing the centers was used to select students. Notice that the first of these studies was published in 1975, revealing that the definition was problematic from the start.

MacMillan and Speece (1999) reviewed three studies (Shepard, Smith, & Vojir, 1983; Shaywitz et al., 1990; MacMillan, Gresham, & Bocian, 1998) conducted after PL 94-142 was implemented. Assessment teams identifying students whose case records provided the data for these studies were using regulations that included the definition and the discrepancy and exclusion criteria. In these studies, the investigators created identification criteria derived from state education codes and, using records' review, sought to determine the percentage of students identified by their school teams who also met the investigators' criteria as learning disabled. Across the three studies, between 52% and 70% of the students identified as learning disabled by their school teams did not meet the investigators' criteria (MacMillan & Speece, 1999). Shepard et al. (1983), for example, found records of students for whom English was a second language, records documenting emotional problems, and records indicating IQ scores low enough to meet criteria for mental retardation among the records of students identified as learning disabled. Conclusions reached by MacMillan and Speece confirm our psychologist's story:

Several observations about how the schools sort students with severe and persistent achievement problems into the LD category seem in order. First, LD in the schools is a *nonspecific category of children with absolute low achievement relative to school peers* (italics added). At present, school practices do not appear to consider aptitude and achievement simultaneously as the definitions and education codes suggest they should. Cases where the low achievement is consistent and inconsistent with 'expected' levels of achievement are not differentiated . . . Second, the classification of 'mental retardation' apparently is viewed as pessimistic in its prognosis, and LD appears to be a more acceptable diagnosis. As a consequence, the schools have evolved a practice of certifying most students with absolute low achievement as LD, regardless of whether the IQ is below the cutoff for mental retardation or whether the achievement qualifies as discrepant from expected level . . . Finally, the schools do adhere to the requirement of administering instruments and scales required for certification of children as eligible under the various state-sanctioned disability categories. Hence, individual intelligence tests, achievement tests, adaptive behavior scales, and processing tests are administered; however, this is done more to conform to requirements than to secure data on which a differential diagnosis is to be made (1999, p. 117–18).

Remember, these conclusions are not based on direct observations of assessment teams at work, but on the records that their work produces.

Our psychologist's story and conclusions from the studies cited here help us to understand data released by the US Office of Education in 1996. Between 1977 and 1995, the percentage of students identified as learning disabled increased from 1.8% to 5.8% of the total public school enrollment (grades kindergarten through 12). This represents an increase close to 200% in the number of students identified as learning disabled in less than 20 years. By 1995, students identified as learning disabled accounted for slightly more than 50% of all students enrolled in special education. Consistent with MacMillan and Speece's conclusions, during the period characterized by a dramatic increase in the numbers of students identified as learning disabled, the number of students identified as mentally retarded decreased by 41% and the number of students identified as speech and language impaired decreased by 15% (US Office of Education, 1994).

By now you should be prepared to understand the following quotation, taken from the first chapter of a book emanating from a symposium on learning disabilities convened under the auspices of the National Institute for Child Health and Human Development:

The field of learning disabilities has grown since learning disabilities were first recognized as a federally designated disabling condition in 1968 to represent almost half of all students receiving special education nationally. At the same time, learning disabilities remain one of the least understood yet most debated disabling conditions that affect children in the United States (Lyon & Moats, 1993, p. 1).

Similar statements, decrying the fact that psychologists and educators are placing students, in ever-increasing numbers, in a disability category that cannot be defined and that no one understands, appear continuously in the literature about learning disabilities. (To read particularly passionate criticisms of this practice and to see that the practice has been criticized for a long time, read Freeman, 1976, and Stanovich, 1999.)

How did this happen? Looking back from Samuel Kirk's speech, delivered, as you will remember, in 1963, helps answer this question. We look back to Alfred Strauss, Heinz Werner, and a colleague, Newell Kephart. We also look to William Cruickshank and, again, to Samuel Kirk. Please understand, though, looking back to the work of these people and to special education and its advocates does not provide a complete answer to our question[3]

From brain injury to specific learning disability

I make two historical points in this chapter. The first is that a study of history reveals two perspectives on specific learning problems: a perspective represented in the work of James Hinshelwood and Samuel Orton (who were not collaborators), and a perspective represented in the work of Alfred Strauss and Heinz Werner (who were collaborators). I claim, along with Joseph Torgesen (1998), that these perspectives, though they share some assumptions, are significantly different. The second history 'lesson' is that the Strauss perspective shaped the definition and diagnostic criteria for 'specific learning disability' in the federal laws. Others have made the same historical point: Kavale and Forness (1995) in particular. My purpose here is to develop this second historical point with the assistance of Kenneth Kavale and Steven Forness.

As we consider Strauss and Werner's work, it is helpful to use the name 'specific learning disability' and refrain from using the name 'specific learning disabilities.' Historical accounts of 'specific learning disability' usually begin with Kurt Goldstein, a German neurologist, because he was a teacher and mentor for Alfred Strauss. Goldstein studied the behavior of soldiers who recovered from head injuries sustained in combat. Based on the soldiers' performance on several experimental tasks, Goldstein described them as prone to perceptual confusion, distractible, disinhibited, perseverative, disinclined to abstract thinking, and given to extreme emotional responses that shifted quickly (Goldstein, 1942). Strauss was apparently interested in refining the diagnosis of mental retardation and felt that Goldstein's findings with brain-injured adults could be helpful.

Using Goldstein's experimental tasks and a group of mentally retarded adolescents (who, incidentally, were also adjudicated delinquents), Strauss and Werner claimed a behavioral distinction between mental retardation of familial, presumably genetic, origin and mental retardation caused by external insults to the brain subsequent to conception. According to Strauss and Werner (1943), mentally retarded youngsters without a familial history of mental retardation and with birth and medical histories suggestive of brain injury behaved with the experimental tasks like Goldstein's soldiers. Similar task performance was not noted among the youngsters with a family history of mental retardation. Werner and Strauss drew these conclusions from their studies: mental retardation caused by brain injury was different from mental retardation that was inherited; brain injury produced specific perceptual and behavioral consequences; brain injury could be diagnosed on the basis of (inferred from) those behavioral and perceptual consequences; and youngsters whose mental retardation was caused by brain injury might benefit from a special education different from the special education provided for mentally retarded youngsters who inherited mental retardation from their parents.

Working with Laura Lehtinen, an educator, Strauss designed a learning environment for 'brain-injured' children that eliminated, or at least controlled, opportunities for distraction and inattention and emphasized perceptual training. In Strauss and Lehtinen's words, 'the erratic behavior of brain-injured children in perceptual tasks might be explained by a figure-ground deficiency, and an approach to remedy such deficiency should be directed toward strengthening the figure-ground perception' (1947, p. 50). The special learning environment was designed to be remedial, that is, to correct or ameliorate the problems with perception and attention and, in so doing, remove obstacles to learning to read, write, and calculate. The implication was that, with effective remedial instruction, the children might leave their mentally retarded status behind them.

It was not long before investigations similar to those conducted with mentally retarded adolescents were undertaken with children of normal intelligence. William Cruickshank (Cruickshank, Bice, & Wallen, 1957) strengthened the claim that the disorders of perception, attention, and emotion Strauss and Werner linked to brain damage were, in fact, linked to brain damage by finding them in the performance of cerebral-palsied children with normal or near-normal IQ scores. Strauss and another colleague, Newell Kephart, extended the research to children whose performance on intelligence tests placed them above standard cut-off points for mental retardation, but who did not show clinical signs of brain injury (Strauss & Kephart, 1955). These men, Kurt Goldstein, Alfred Strauss, Heinz Werner, William Cruickshank, and Newell Kephart, established the concept of a learning and behavior disability, caused by minimal (i.e., not necessarily observable through standard clinical signs) brain injury that could be disassociated from mental retardation. Further, they had ideas about special education, remedial special education, that is.

Their message was important and appealing. Some difficult children are actually brain injured and their difficult behaviors stem from the brain injury.

The difficult behaviors are neither willful nor their parents' fault. More important, the brain injury causes specific deficits in perception and attention that impair learning on tasks that depend on perception and attention. These learning and behavior problems can be corrected, or at least controlled, through special education. Private schools were created to educate these 'brain-injured' children. These schools served as models for special education that emphasized training attention, perception, and perceptual–motor processes. By the mid-1950s, a few public school districts were providing special education classes modelled on the private school programs. In some states, children placed in these classes were called 'brain injured' or 'neurologically impaired.' In other states, the children placed in these new special education classes were called 'perceptually impaired.' To repeat, the curriculum in these classes, regardless of the name given to the children, emphasized perceptual and perceptual–motor education preparatory for academic education.

The emergence of local and state organizations, composed primarily of parents advocating publicly funded education, paralleled the emergence of publicly funded special education classes. As was true for the children enrolled in the special classes, advocacy organizations chose from one of several possible names. Advocates living in New York State named themselves The New York Association for Brain-Injured Children, whereas advocates living in California became the California Association for Neurologically Impaired Children. One state organization, perhaps the oldest, The Fund for the Perceptually Impaired, established in Evanston, Illinois, in 1957, chose to host a conference for the purpose of forming a national organization and selecting one name acceptable to delegates from each of the state organizations. As indicated at the beginning of this chapter, the name 'specific learning disability' became public property at that conference. Acting on Samuel Kirk's suggestion, members of the various state organizations voted to form a national organization named the Association for Children with Learning Disabilities.

In this move, a concept acquired a new name, but the concept did not change. Remember the concept, because it underpins the definition in subsequent federal laws: minimal brain damage, insufficient to produce classical clinical signs, can disrupt a specific psychological process typically defined as a perception, creating obstacles to learning across many tasks, most prominently speaking, listening, reading, writing, and arithmetic. Because the learning disability is specific and can be isolated, it can, perhaps, also be corrected or, at least, the impact can be ameliorated. Assessment designed to identify the psychological processing disorder should lead to special education based on a curriculum designed to correct the psychological process (read perceptual) deficiencies. Learning disability, a behavioral name, replaced brain injury, a medical name for the concept and the related assessment and instructional practices.[4]

Between 1963 and the enactment of the federal special education legislation in 1975, studies were conducted that challenged this concept and the assessment and educational practices that emanated from it. (For a comprehensive review of these studies, see Kavale & Forness, 1995). Some of the studies challenged the technical properties of the tests that were used to assess psychological processes. Others produced evidence that special education programs designed to remediate deficient psychological processes were not having the intended effects. (Later, Kavale and Forness would re-analyze Strauss and Werner's data and conclude that they had not, in fact, proved perceptual and behavioral differences between the two groups of mentally retarded adolescents: reported in Kavale & Forness, 1985).

It was evident that the concept 'specific learning disability,' in the form it had taken, could not be validated just as the name and definition were about to become law. An alternative to 'specific learning disability,' defined only as a psychological processing disorder, was needed and the aptitude/achievement discrepancy criterion was the alternative. Barbara Bateman may have provided the justification for the aptitude/achievement discrepancy criterion with the following definition:

Children who have learning disorders are those who manifest an educationally significant discrepancy between their estimated intellectual potential and actual level of performance related to basic disorders in the learning process, which may or may not be accompanied by demonstrable central nervous system dysfunction and which are not secondary to generalized mental retardation, educational or cultural deprivation, severe emotional disturbance, or sensory loss (Bateman, 1965, p. 220).

Specific learning disability or specific learning disabilities

The Strauss concept was based on a particular class of psychological theories, prominent in the early decades of the twentieth century, that assumed that intellectual performance was a composite of many specific mental abilities or faculties. Between these faculties of mind and within any of them, one might expect to find strengths and weaknesses. Assuming a weak faculty could be isolated, it might be strengthened with exercise, to the benefit of the whole mental system, in the same way that exercise strengthens muscles to the benefit of the body. Ann Brown and Joseph Campione provide a description of this theory in action:

A child is brought to a practitioner's attention because she is experiencing difficulty in reading. After she is subjected to a battery of diagnostic tests it is determined that she has particular problems with auditory memory and that this deficit is stable and reliable across situations and over time. Traditionally, the most likely prescription for remediation would be practice on tasks of auditory short-term memory presented out of the context of any academic task of which auditory short-term memory could be assumed to be a component (1986, p. 1060).

Assuming that auditory short-term memory could be strengthened, improvement in reading should follow. Given the theory, we might expect our young student to have difficulty with other tasks requiring auditory short-term memory. The specific learning disability, weak short-term auditory memory, might also create difficulty learning arithmetic.

Hinshelwood and Orton did not rely on these assumptions about learning. They observed children's failure to learn specific skills and reasoned from those observations directly to brain damage or dysfunction. A child's disability was a reading disability, a writing disability, or, by logical extension, an arithmetic disability, not a visual perception disability or an auditory disability. As we consider Hinshelwood and Orton's work, it is helpful to use the name 'specific learning disabilities' and refrain from using the name 'specific learning disability.'

The Orton/Hinshelwood perspective is reflected in the way learning disorders are presented in *Diagnostic and Statistical Manual of Mental Disorders* (DSM-IV; American Psychiatric Association, 1994). DSM-IV presents four learning disorders: reading disorder; mathematics disorder; disorder of written expression; and learning disorder not otherwise specified. Each is presented as a distinct disorder, identifiable as a discrepancy between the child's achievement and chronological age and measured intelligence.

Lisa, an adolescent with a learning disability in arithmetic, introduces the Hinshelwood and Orton perspective.

Lisa's story

Although children with learning problems specific to reading, writing, or arithmetic have been identified, described, and studied for more than a century, it has proven surprisingly difficult to construct reliable generalizations about them. For that reason, we rely on descriptions of individuals to confirm the existence of learning problems specific to these scholastic tasks. Lisa and her English teacher will help us this time.

Lisa looks away from the computer screen for a moment to think about the text she is creating. Voicing her thoughts, she says, 'Mrs Abbott told us to use words to make pictures in our readers' minds. Can I see my characters when I read what I have written?' Returning to the screen, she re-reads her text with that question in mind.[5]

I imagine myself sitting in a rocking chair, my husband's arm around my blue-clad shoulders: his other hand stroking my rough, bony old limbs. My snow white hair, the curls straightened by age, flies into my sunburned wrinkled face. I am dreaming of the days when I was young but my mind is old and worn and it is hard. The sound of my husband's heavy breathing brings me back to the present moment. 'Are you alright?' I ask in a raspy voice, no longer clear and beautiful.

He takes my hand in his. My hands, the only still young aspect of me, are petite, soft and smooth. I turn my head to the side to gaze at him and the expression of his love for me gleams through his eyes. There is no pain in my neck and I am relieved. Slowly I slip, once again, into a daytime reverie but this time I do not dream of the younger days I have left behind. Instead I dream of all the days ahead that my beloved husband and I will share together.

Satisfied that she is responding to the intent of her teacher's assignment, Lisa continues to work with her text.

Tomorrow, or the day after, Mrs Abbott, the eighth grade English teacher, will read Lisa's text. We can predict that at some point as she reads, she will look away from Lisa's text as Lisa looked away from the computer. Voicing her thoughts, Mrs Abbott will say something to this effect: 'This young woman cannot learn to read time from an ordinary clock. I have to suspend all of my beliefs about learning and intelligence to accept this text as hers. She struggles so with numbers, how can she write like this?'

Lisa's teacher is not the only person stunned by the contrast between her competence when reading, spelling, and writing (using a computer), and the absence of competence when she is performing arithmetic calculations, writing with a pen or pencil, and drawing. Members of the assessment team who worked with Lisa, though more knowledgeable about striking disparities in academic competence than Lisa's teachers, were also stunned by the contrasts. You probably will be surprised, too. Consider, for example, the contrasts in scores she obtained on standardized reading, spelling, and mathematics tests. Her reading scores (Gates MacGinitie, Form L) were at or slightly above the 50th percentile for her age; her spelling scores (Test of Written Spelling – 2) were at the 70th percentile for her age; but her mathematics scores (Sequential Assessment of Mathematics Inventory) were below the 10th percentile for her age. Similar contrasts were apparent in the standard scores obtained from the Wechsler Intelligence Scale for Children–Revised. On this test, Lisa obtained IQs of 102 (Verbal) and 64 (Performance), producing a Full Scale IQ of 81.

Members of the team responsible for the assessment remarked that it was painful to watch Lisa work with some of the assessment tasks, particularly tasks from the Performance Scale of the Wechsler. A brief report of scores obtained with the Wechsler is instructive. Lisa did not find missing details in pictures easily (Picture Completion 3). Among other problems, she did not have a systematic strategy for scanning the pictures. She had great difficulty with the simplest puzzles (Object Assembly 2). She usually did not realize when she misplaced a puzzle piece. One of the more striking examples occurred when she placed the horse's hoof under his tail. When asked if she was satisfied with the construction, she replied, 'The horse looks just fine to me.' Attempting the block designs, she placed the blocks in a row rather than trying to construct the pictured pattern (Block Design 4).

Think back to Lisa's text. She constructed a vivid picture of two elderly people using their feelings for each other to ease the pain of being old. But she seemed unable to construct mental images to guide the construction of the puzzles and block designs. Her teacher told us that she could not tell time from an ordinary clock, but she wrote a story about time. Her competence with language, as revealed in her text, is confirmed by scores on the Verbal subtests of the Wechsler (Similarities 13; Vocabulary 11; and Comprehension 13).[6]

Lisa's medical history is suggestive of neurological impairment. She was born with a congenital heart defect, had to be resuscitated a few days after birth when her heart stopped beating, and had corrective heart surgery when she was three. Her motor development, prior to entering school, was delayed. However, results from standard neurological examinations are unremarkable. Neurologic impairment remains an inference.

If we only knew Lisa's age and her mathematics and Wechsler Performance test scores, we would probably assume that she is mentally retarded. On the other hand, if, knowing her age, we were only given her story, and the Reading, Spelling and Verbal IQ test scores, we would not assume that learning is difficult for her.

I will refer to the critical features in Lisa's story as 'compass points,' acknowledging that, whereas we can set the compass, we cannot construct an exact map of her learning problems. As noted earlier, the most striking feature of Lisa's academic and cognitive development is the fact that she acquires verbal knowledge easily and struggles to acquire spatial knowledge. To differentiate Lisa's learning disability from a learning disability that involves all knowledge domains, we describe it as 'specific.' We assume a specific cognitive deficit that impairs learning to calculate and form letters, but spares learning to read and spell. We assume that the cognitive and academic deficits are caused by neurologic dysfunction. More exactly, we assume that neurological impairment is the primary cause of Lisa's learning disability. Assuming a neurologic cause does not, however, blind us to the fact that the symptoms of learning disability take form in a complex interaction between biology and experience.

Lisa's learning disability is one of three specific learning disabilities. Interest in these learning disabilities, conceptualized as difficulty acquiring the knowledge essential to reading, writing, or arithmetic, predates Strauss and Werner. As we shall see, there has been more interest, historically, in reading disability and spelling disability (dyslexia) than in writing and spelling disability (dysgraphia) and arithmetic disability (dyscalculia).

Dyslexia, dysgraphia, and dyscalculia

By the end of the nineteenth century, physicians in Great Britain, France, and Germany published descriptions of adults who lost the ability to read subsequent to trauma in certain regions of the brain. Surprisingly, the loss was often specific. An individual might, for example, lose the ability to read but retain the ability to write and spell. Reflecting the specific nature of adults' loss of a learned skill after brain trauma, Dejerine (1892) described a man, Monsieur C., who lost the ability to read subsequent to a stroke. According to Dejerine (cited in Kessler, 1980, p. 23), the man was still able to express himself fluently, understand everything said to him, remember minute details from conversations, and write without difficulty. He was, however, unable to name letters or even read what he had written.

A more recent example (Warrington, 1982) illustrates the loss of learned skills in mathematics subsequent to brain trauma. Warrington described an adult who, within two weeks after suffering a stroke, demonstrated a return to normal intellectual functioning, language comprehension, reading, and verbal memory. He could not, however, retrieve basic number facts. He could write numbers and specify the process needed to perform a particular calculation, but could not perform the calculation without counting and, even with the aid of counting, made frequent calculation errors.

The earlier observations about adults and reading soon became inferences about children. The first published description of such a child (Morgan, 1896) captures the essence of the learning problem. Percy F., aged 14, was referred to Pringle Morgan, a physician, by the headmaster of his school because he could not learn to read, 'despite laborious and persistent training.' Suggesting that Percy's problem was specific to reading, his headmaster is quoted as saying that, 'he would be the smartest lad in school if the instruction were entirely oral' (p. 1378). Morgan said about Percy, referring to his inability to read, 'This inability is so remarkable and so pronounced that I have no doubt it is due to some congenital defect' (p. 1378). Subsequent to Pringle Morgan's report, a clinical literature evolved describing children with specific reading and writing disabilities (Kerr, 1897; Morgan, 1914; Hinshelwood, 1917; Monroe, 1932; Orton, 1937). Early reports of learning disabilities in arithmetic (Schmitt, 1921; Guttman, 1937) appeared toward the end of the early history of reading and writing disabilities. All of these clinicians and researchers, except Marian Monroe, assumed a biological cause for the learning disabilities they described. Monroe acknowledged biology as one cause of reading disability, but considered other causes as well.

When you stop to think about it, the logical distance from brain-injured adults to, mostly normal, children is large. Obviously, procedures for studying brain function have evolved since Morgan and others started us on this path. We still do not have unequivocal direct evidence of a biological cause for the learning disabilities that we describe as 'specific,' however.[7] We do have evidence of genetic causation for some portion of all individuals with specific reading disability.[8] We also have indirect evidence of the influence of biology on these learning disabilities in the fact that some children show signs of a developmental language delay prior to developing a reading disability in school (Scarborough, 1990), and in the fact that reading and writing disabilities persist into adulthood despite remedial instruction (Snowling & Hulme, 1989; Olson et al., 1997; Bruck, 1998; Felton, 1998). However, we have not yet proven the historical claim that symptoms observed in adults known to be brain injured are the only evidence we need to assert brain dysfunction in children.

As was true for Strauss and Werner, physicians and psychologists interested in the study and treatment of reading, writing, or arithmetic disabilities recommended educational treatments. Hinshelwood and Orton illustrate the point.

In 1917, James Hinshelwood, a Scottish ophthalmologist with a bent for neurology, published a monograph, *Congenital Word Blindness*, describing children who appeared intelligent but struggled with reading. Hinshelwood, reasoning from brain-injured adults, attributed these problems to a congenital lesion in the left angular gyrus, which, he hypothesized, made it difficult to store and retain visual memories for letters and words. He noted that the disorder occurred more frequently among males than females and also noted its familial tendency. Parts of a case report from that monograph are worth quoting, because of insight we gain about Hinshelwood's approach to assessment:

A boy, 12 years of age, was brought in March 1902 to the Glasgow Eye infirmary by his mother, to see if there was anything wrong with his eyesight. The boy had been seven years at school, and there had been from the outset the greatest difficulty in teaching him to read . . . On examining him, I found that his reading was very defective for a boy who had been seven years in school. He could rarely read by sight more than two or three words, but came to a standstill every second or third word . . . The words he stuck at were chiefly polysyllables, but this was not always the case, as he often failed to recognize by sight even simple monosyllabic words . . . He read all combinations of figures with the greatest fluency up to millions. I made him do several sums up to compound addition. All of these he did smartly and correctly (pp. 49–51).

The next good clinical description of reading disorders was provided by Samuel Orton (1937). Orton called the disorder *strephosymbolia* (twisted symbols), highlighting reading errors that he believed were a constant feature of the disorder: difficulty reading and writing reversible letters (b and d, p and q); a tendency to confuse reversed words (was and saw; on and no); and a tendency to reverse paired letters, whole syllables, and words. These transpositions occurred intermittently, giving the impression that the children read from left to right sometimes and, at other times, from right to left.

Orton's assessments consisted of detailed family and school histories, and the administration of an intelligence test and tests of reading, spelling, and arithmetic. He also asked his young patients to write for him. He was interested in contrasts between scores on the achievement tests, assuming that students with a reading disability would have lower reading and spelling scores than arithmetic scores and that students with a writing disability would earn lower spelling scores than reading and arithmetic scores. All of Orton's patients had difficulty at school over the years and decades that he followed their lives. Many had speech disorders (speech delay or stuttering) and motor disorders (abnormal clumsiness) in addition to reading disorders. Males outnumbered females among his patients. He frequently treated several members of one family. Unlike Hinshelwood, who postulated brain damage as the cause of specific reading disability, Orton postulated a functional brain disorder, failure of one hemisphere to become dominant in the control of language.

Although Hinshelwood and Orton had different views about the cause of this disorder, they shared a common view about assessment and treatment. They assessed reading, spelling, and arithmetic skills. According to both physicians, the treatment of choice was intensive individual reading instruction teaching sound to letter correspondences (Hinshelwood) or letter to sound correspondences (Orton). Each physician urged his patients' teachers to refrain from using methods of reading instruction where words are learned without using sound/letter or letter/sound correspondences.

By the 1930s, neurologists were documenting the existence in children of arithmetic disorders associated with brain damage (see Cohn, 1961, 1971;

Badian, 1983; Rourke, 1989; for reviews). Dyscalculic children were shown to manifest the same range of symptoms as brain-injured adults who lost the ability to calculate. The children were shown to have difficulty learning number words and facts, forming numerals, aligning numerals in correct arrays for computation, and applying computational skill to problem solving. As with reading and writing disabilities, though, the cause was presumed to be biological and recommended treatments were educational.

Conclusion

If number of citations is an indication of influence, Lee Wiederholt's history of the people and ideas behind the term 'learning disability,' published in 1974, is the most influential history in print. Wiederholt divides the clinical and research traditions behind the term into three categories: disorders of spoken language, beginning with Gall's first publication in 1802; disorders of written language, beginning with Hinshelwood's publication in 1917; and disorders of perceptual and motor processing, beginning with Goldstein's first publication in 1927. To summarize this history, he presents a diagram (p. 105) indicating that each of these lines of work converged in the term 'learning disability' in 1963. I have argued for a different interpretation of this history. I will summarize that argument here.

First, I believe that the work on language disorders, spoken and written, and the work on disorders of perception and perceptual–motor processes does not rest comfortably in the same concept. Though people interested in both types of disorders believed in a biological cause and believed that developmental versions of these disorders could be diagnosed on the basis of behavioral signs only, similarities between these classes of disorders end there. Perceptual theorists were interested in mental traits, or faculties, that they believed could be isolated from each other and from the cognitive system as a whole. Consequently, they believed that the 'learning disability' (defective faculty) could co-occur with below-average, average and above-average intelligence. They also believed that the learning disability would be general in its effect. If the defective faculty was visual perception, any task requiring visual perception would be difficult to learn. Assessment, for these theorists, required a search for the defective faculty, and treatment was remedial training of the defective faculty. Clinicians and researchers interested in language disorders believed that brain damage or dysfunction could interfere with the acquisition of specific language skills and leave the ability to acquire other skills unimpaired. Assessment, for these theorists, required description of the impaired skills and those that had been spared; and treatment was direct language instruction. Differences between these two clinical and research traditions are substantial.

My second point echoes others (particularly Hallahan & Cruickshank, 1973; Kavale & Forness, 1995). If I were to construct a diagram similar to Weiderholt's, I would make 'learning disability' a direct descendant of the perceptual theorists, only. Let us return to Samuel Kirk in Chicago in 1963. Remember, he said:

Recently, I have used the term 'learning disabilities' to describe a group of children who have disorders in development in language, speech, reading and associated communication skills needed for social interaction (p. 2).

As indicated at the beginning of this chapter, Dr Kirk was working on a test to assess psycholinguistic functions in young children at the time. He also had, at earlier times in his career (1936, 1940), published influential books on reading and reading instruction. Surely he must have been thinking about aphasia and dyslexia when he spoke. Now, let us look at the first lines of the definition that guides practice once again.

'Specific learning disability' means a disorder in one or more of the basic psychological processes involved in understanding or in using language, spoken or written, that may manifest itself in an imperfect ability to listen, speak, read, write, spell or do mathematical calculations.

The disability in this definition is in a psychological process, and that is the Strauss orientation. If Orton were present in this definition, the disability would be the reading disorder. We would have seven distinct disabilities in the definition. That is not the way the definition or the regulations are written. Remember, the regulations allow discrepancies in several domains concurrently to be diagnostic of 'specific learning disability.'

If we are serious about the concept of specific learning disabilities, I believe the Hinshelwood/Orton perspective is the appropriate ancestor for contemporary clinical practice and research. To switch from the definition and guidelines in federal law to a taxonomy similar to the DSM-IV taxonomy creates a dilemma for practice, however. A perspective on specific learning disabilities that restricts the diagnosis to youngsters like Lisa will include fewer children. The guidelines for diagnosis in federal laws are, by design, I think, much more inclusive. To the extent that the diagnosis 'learning disability' turns failure into hope and gains access to entitlements that are helpful, who would be so callous as to try to take it away from any child. Do we want less inclusive diagnostic criteria?

Think about the children who are receiving special education because they are 'learning disabled,' though. Some of them are undeniably mentally re-tarded; others have behavior problems too serious to allow them to work in a classroom; others do not speak English; and others have very poor attendance at school. A few of them, perhaps one-third, resemble the Strauss/Werner and Cruickshank/Kephart idea of learning disability, and still fewer of them re-semble Lisa. It is hard to imagine a teacher working effectively with 15 students who present so many different problems. Perhaps it is time to clarify the concept, even if it means making it more exclusive. Others who have written histories about learning disability, John Doris, Sylvia Farnham-Diggory, and Jane Kessler, have been saying that for some time.

ENDNOTES

1 Joe Torgesen (1998) does this. He claims not only that Samuel Orton's work has a weak link to special education for students with learning disabilities, but also that perceptual theories of learning disability and language theories are different.

2 The current iteration of the law is the Individuals with Disabilities Education Act of 1997 (PL 106-17).

3 In the history that follows, I do not include two important facts documented by Lazerson (1983) and Tropea (1987), among others. Special classes for children with learning and behavior problems were created contiguous with the enactment of compulsory school attendance laws. Furthermore, administrators in urban schools created the first classes. People who write histories of special education that include all these facts usually embed them in the claim that public education for all children could not exist in the form it does in this country without an open, that is, subjectively defined, special education category into which school psychologists can easily place students whose rates of learning and/or behavior interfere with classroom work. For a particularly interesting version of this claim, see Richardson (1999). Richardson observes that school administrators named the open category first, calling it 'backward children.' When the responsibility for naming this category was transferred to psychologists, the first name was 'mental retardation' and then 'learning disability.' From this perspective, school psychologists, and other members of school-based assessment teams, are beholden first to the structure of the institution in which they work and second to the characteristics of the students referred to them for assessment.

  I place this note in this text because my friend's story and the studies that confirm his story show that 'learning disability' as used in schools has a broader meaning than disability. I place it as a note, however, because I do not want this claim to overpower the idea of biologically influenced specific learning disabilities – an idea that needs to be preserved and protected. You should know, however, that others (see Christensen, 1999, for example) would make Richard-son's claim the main text in an historical account of learning disabilities.

4 Samuel Kirk was particularly wary of medical explanations and names for educational problems (see Kirk & Becker, 1963).

5 Lisa's credibility as a student with a special learning disability rests in large measure with the authenticity of her text. These paragraphs are taken from a longer composition written in May 1991. Lisa's English teacher sent the text to the Child Study Center (now the Center for Educational and Psychological Services) at Teachers' College, Columbia University. Lisa had been referred to the Child Study Center for a learning disabilities assessment. She was 14 when she wrote the composition, and was preparing to graduate from the eighth grade at a private school in New York City. According to Lisa's teacher, these paragraphs represent a first draft of her text and have not been edited for grammar, spelling, or punctuation.

6 These scores were obtained from the psychoeducational assessment conducted in June 1991. Though late in the school year, Lisa's parents brought her to the Child Study Center at Teachers College for advice about a new school placement for ninth grade. By the time she took these tests, Lisa had worked with a special education teacher and occupational therapist for seven years. Lisa's education had taken place in private school. Her parents paid for occupational therapy and special education.

7 This is a large literature. A recent book (Duane, 1999) provides access to the larger literature. See also Bigler, Lajiness-O'Neill, & Howes (1998); Sternberg & Grigorenko (1999).

8 This is a large literature too. Duane (1999) and Sternberg & Grigorenko (1999) are relevant here, too. See also Pennington (1994).

REFERENCES

American Psychiatric Association (1994). *Diagnostic and Statistical Manual of Mental Disorders*, 4th edn. Washington, DC: American Psychiatric Association.

Badian, N.A. (1983). *Dyscalculia and Nonverbal Disorders of Learning*, Vol. 5, pp. 235–64. New York: Grune & Stratton.

Bateman, B.D. (1965). An educator's view of a diagnostic approach to learning disorders. In *Learning Disorders*, Vol. 1, ed. J. Hellmuth, pp. 219–39. Seattle, WA: Special Child Publications.

Bigler, E.D., Lajiness-O'Neill, R., & Howes, N. (1998). Technology in the assessment of learning disability. *Journal of Learning Disabilities*, 31, 67–82.

Brown, A. & Campione, J. (1966). Psychological theory and the study of learning disabilities. *American Psychologist*, 41, 1059–68.

Bruck, M. (1998). Outcomes of adults with childhood histories of dyslexia. In *Reading and Spelling: Development and Disorders*, ed. C. Hulme & R.M. Joshi, pp. 179–200. Mahwah, NJ: Erlbaum.

Christensen C.A. (1999). Learning disability: issues of representation, power, and the medicalization of school failure. In *Perspectives on Learning Disabilities: Biological, Cognitive, Contextual*, ed. R.J. Sternberg & L. Spear-Swerling, pp. 227–49. Boulder, CO: Westview Press.

Cohn, R. (1961). Dyscalculia. *Archives of Neurology*, 4, 301–7.

Cohn, R. (1971). Arithmetic and learning disabilities. In *Progress in Learning Disabilities*, Vol. 2, ed. H.R. Myklebust, pp. 322–89. New York: Grune & Stratton.

Cruickshank, W.M., Bice, H.V., & Wallen, N.E. (1957). *Perception and Cerebral Palsy.* Syracuse, NY: Syracuse University Press.

Doris, J. (1986). Learning disabilities. In *Handbook of Cognitive Social and Neuropsychological Aspects of Learning Disabilities*, Vol. 1, ed. S.J. Ceci, pp. 3–53. Hillsdale, NJ: Erlbaum.

Doris J.L. (1993). Defining learning disabilities: a history of the search for consensus. In *Better Understanding Learning Disabilities: New Views from Research and their Implications for Education and Public Policies*, ed. G.R. Lyon, D.B. Gray, J.F. Kavanagh, & N.A. Krasnegor, pp. 97–115. Baltimore, MD: Paul H. Brookes.

Duane D.D. (ed.) (1999). *Reading and Attention Disorders: Neurobiological Correlates.* Baltimore, MD: York Press.

Farnham-Diggory, S. (1992). *The Learning-disabled Child.* Cambridge MA: Harvard University Press.

Felton, R. (1998). The development of reading skills in poor readers: educational implications. In *Reading and Spelling: Development and Disorders*, ed. C. Hulme & R.M. Joshi, pp. 219–33. Mahwah, NJ: Erlbaum.

Frankenberger, W. & Harper, J. (1987). States' criteria and procedures for identifying learning disabled children: a comparison of 1981/82 and 1985/86 guidelines. *Journal of Learning Disabilities*, 20, 118–21.

Freeman, R.D. (1976). Minimal brain dysfunction, hyperactivity, and learning disorders: epidemic or episode? *School Review*, 85, 5–30.

Goldstein, K. (1942). *After-effects of Brain Injuries in War.* New York: Grune & Stratton.

Guttman, F. (1937). Congenital arithmetic disability and acalculia (Henschen). *British Journal of Medical Psychology*, 16, 16–35.

Hallahan, D.P. & Cruickshank, W.M. (1973). *Psychoeducational Foundations of Learning Disabilities.* Englewood Cliffs, NJ: Prentice-Hall.

Hegge, T.G., Kirk, S.A., & Kirk, W.D. (1936). *Remedial Reading Drills.* Ann Arbor, MI: George Wahr.

Hinshelwood, J. (1917). *Congenital Word Blindness.* London: H.K. Lewis.

Kavale, K.A. & Forness, S.R. (1985). *The Science of Learning Disabilities.* San Diego, CA: College Hill Press.

Kavale, K.A. & Forness, S.R. (1995). *The Nature of Learning Disabilities: Critical Elements of Diagnosis and Classification.* Mahwah, NJ: Erlbaum.

Kerr, J. (1897). School hygiene in its mental, moral and physical aspects. *Journal of the Royal Statistical Society*, 60, 613–80.

Kessler, J.W. (1980). History of minimal brain dysfunctions. In *Handbook of Minimal Brain Dysfunctions: a Critical View*, ed. H.E. Rie & E.D. Rie, pp. 18–51. New York: Wiley.

Kirk, S.A. (1940). *Teaching Reading to Slow Learning Children.* Boston: Houghton Mifflin.

Kirk, S.A. (1963). Behavioral diagnosis and remediation of learning disabilities. In *Proceedings of the Annual Meeting of the Conference on Exploration into the Problems of the Perceptually Handicapped Child*, Vol. 1, pp. 3–7. Chicago, IL.

Kirk, S.A. & Becker, W.C. (eds.) (1963). *Conference on Children with Minimal Brain Impairment.* Chicago, IL: National Society for Crippled Children and Adults.

Kirk, S.A. & Elkins, J. (1975). Characteristics of children enrolled in the Child Service Demonstration Centers. *Journal of Learning Disabilities*, 4, 6–21.

Lazerson, M. (1983). The origins of special education. In *Special Education Policies: Their History, Implementation, and Finance*, ed. J.G. Chambers & W.T. Hartman, pp. 15–47. Philadelphia, PA: Temple University Press.

Lyon, G.R. & Moats, L.C. (1993). An examination of research in learning disabilities: past practices and future directions. In *Better Understanding Learning Disabilities: New Views from Research and their Implications for Education and Public Policies*, ed. G.R. Lyon, D.B. Gray, J.F. Kavanagh, & N.A. Krasnegor, pp. 1–13. Baltimore, MD: Paul H. Brookes.

MacMillan D.L., Gresham, F.M., & Bocian, K.M. (1998). Discrepancy between definitions of learning disabilities and what schools use: an empirical investigation. *Journal of Learning Disabilities*, 31, 314–26.

MacMillan, D.L. & Speece D.L. (1999). Utility of current diagnostic categories for research and practice. In *Developmental Perspectives on Children with High-incidence Disabilities*, ed. R. Gallimore, L.P. Bernheimer, D.L. MacMillan, D.L. Speece, & S. Vaughn, pp. 111–33. Mahwah, NJ: Erlbaum.

Mann, L., Davis, C.H., Boyer, C.W., Metz, C.M., & Wolford, B. (1983). LD or not LD that was the question: a retrospective analysis of Child Service Demonstration Centers' compliance with the federal definition of learning disabilities. *Journal of Learning Disabilities*, 16, 14–17.

Monroe, M. (1932). *Children who Cannot Read*. Chicago, IL: University of Chicago Press.

Morgan, B.S. (1914). *The Backward Child*. New York: Putnam.

Morgan, W.P. (1896). A case of congenital wordblindness. *British Medical Journal*, 2, 1378.

Norman, C.A. Jr & Zigmond, N. (1980). Characteristics of students labelled and served in school systems affiliated with Child Service Demonstration Centers. *Journal of Learning Disabilities*, 13, 546–7.

Olson, R.K., Wise, B., Ring, J., & Johnson, M. (1997). Computer-based remedial reading training in phoneme awareness and phonological decoding: effects on the post-training development of word recognition. *Scientific Studies of Reading*, 1, 235–53.

Orton, S.T. (1937). *Reading, Writing and Speech Problems in Children*. New York: Norton.

Pennington, B.F. (1994). Genetics of learning disabilities. *Journal of Child Neurology*, 19 (Suppl.), S69–S76.

Public Law 94–142, Education for All Handicapped Children Act of 1975 (23 August 1977). 10 U.S.C. 1401 et seq. *Federal Register*, 42 (163), 42 474–518.

Richardson, J.G. (1999). *Common, Delinquent, and Special: the Institutional Shape of Special Education*. New York: Faimer.

Rourke, B.P. (1989). *Nonverbal Learning Disabilities: The Syndrome and the Model*. New York: Guilford.

Scarborough, H.S. (1990). Very early language deficits in dyslexic children. *Child Development*, 61, 1728–43.

Schmitt, C. (1921). Extreme retardation in arithmetic. *Elementary School Journal*, 21, 529–47.

Shaywitz, S.E., Shaywitz, B., Fletcher, J.M., & Escobar, M.D. (1990). Prevalence of reading disability in boys and girls: results from the Connecticut Longitudinal Study. *Journal of the American Medical Association*, 264, 998–1002.

Shepard L.A., Smith, M.L., & Vojir, C.P. (1983). Characteristics of pupils identified as learning disabled. *American Educational Research Journal*, 20, 309–31.

Snowling, M. & Hulme, C. (1989). A longitudinal case study of developmental phonological dyslexia. *Cognitive Neuropsychology*, 6, 379–401.

Stanovich, K.E. (1999). The sociopsychometrics of learning disabilities. *Journal of Learning Disabilities*, 32, 350–61.

Sternberg, R.J. & Grigorenko, E.L. (1999). *Our Labeled Children: What every Parent and Teacher needs to know about Learning Disabilities*. Reading, MA: Perseus Books.

Strauss, A.A. & Kephart, N.C. (1955). *Psychopathology and Education of the Brain-injured Child: Vol. II Progress in Theory and Clinic*. New York: Grune & Stratton.

Strauss, A.A. & Lehtinen, L.E. (1947). *Psychopathology and Education of the Brain-injured Child*. New York: Grune & Stratton.

Strauss, A.A. & Werner, H. (1943). Comparative psychopathology of the brain-injured child and the traumatic brain-injured adult. *American Journal of Psychiatry*, 99, 835–8.

Torgesen, J.K. (1998). Learning disabilities: an historical and conceptual overview. In *Learning about Learning Disabilities*, 2nd edn, ed. B. Wong, pp. 3–34. San Diego, CA: Academic Press.

Tropea, J.L. (1987). Bureaucratic order and special children: urban schools, 1890's–1940's. *History of Education Quarterly*, 27, 29–53.

US Office of Education (1994). *Sixteenth Annual Report to Congress on the Implementation of the Individuals with Disabilities Education Act*. Washington, DC: Author.

US Office of Education (1996). *Eighteenth Annual Report to Congress on the Implementation of the Individuals with Disabilities Education Act*. Washington, DC: Author.

Warrington, E.K. (1982). The fractionation of arithmetical skills: a single case study. *Quarterly Journal of Experimental Psychology*, 34A, 31–51.

Wiederholt, J.L. (1974). Historical perspectives on the education of the learning disabled. In *The Second Review of Special Education*, ed. L. Mann & D. Sabatino, pp. 103–52. Philadelphia, PA: JSE Press.

Zigmond, N. (1993). Learning disabilities from an educational perspective. In *Better Understanding Learning Disabilities: New Views from Research and their Implications for Education and Public Policies*, ed. G.R. Lyon, D.B. Gray, J.F. Kavanagh, & N.A. Krasnegor, pp. 251–72. Baltimore, MD: Paul H. Brookes.

2

The Wechsler intelligence scales

Gary Groth-Marnat

The Wechsler intelligence scales are individually administered, composite batteries which measure a wide range of intellectual abilities. Given the diversity of abilities measured, they are often perceived as being well suited for the assessment of learning disabilities. Accordingly, they have become some of the most extensively used and time-honored tools in learning disabilities assessment. In order to evaluate their relevance for this task, it is essential both to provide a complete description of the instruments and, more importantly, to outline clearly Wechsler scale strategies for learning disabilities assessment.

History, development, and goals

During the 1930s, David Wechsler wanted to devise a broad-band intelligence test for adults. He was in part guided by his conception that intelligence is both global in nature and also guided by a wide number of aspects of personality. Specifically, he considered that intelligence involved a person's ability to act purposively, think rationally, and deal effectively with his or her environment. Wechsler also stressed that intellectual assessment must be considered in relation to the person as a whole. This might include nonintellectual aspects of a person's functioning, such as interests, persistence, drive, or need for achievement. Despite this early emphasis on a general or unitary aspect of intelligence, there has been considerable interest and controversy concerning the extent to which the Wechsler scales can measure more specific aspects of a person's functioning (Lezak, 1988; McDermott, Fantuzzo, & Glutting, 1990; Kaufman, 1994; Glutting et al., 1997). Strategies have been designed to organize various Wechsler scores around such areas as distractibility, fluid versus crystallized intelligence, and simultaneous as opposed to sequential styles of processing information (see Kaufman, 1990; Groth-Marnat, 1999). Because learning disability assessment is often concerned with understanding specific difficulties in information processing, the extent to which the Wechsler scales can actually measure these specific abilities is crucial for full evaluation.

Even though Wechsler was guided by his unitary conceptualization of intelligence, he began to design his scale by searching for specific subtests. A number of these were derived from portions of the 1937 Stanford Binet (Comprehension, Arithmetic, Digit Span, Similarities, Vocabulary). Others came from a diversity of previously developed scales, including the Army Alpha (Information, Comprehension), Army Beta (Digit Symbol, Coding), Koh's Block Design (Block Design), Pintner–Patterson Test (Object Assembly), Healy Picture Completion (Picture Completion), and the Army Group Examinations (Picture Arrangement). In 1939 these scales were combined and published as the Wechsler–Bellevue Intelligence Scale. Due to technical difficulties, the Wechsler–Bellevue was revised in 1955 to form the Wechsler Adult Intelligence Scale (WAIS). The WAIS has been revised and updated, once in 1981 (the Wechsler Adult Intelligence Scale–Revised; WAIS–R) and, most recently, in 1997 as the Wechsler Adult Intelligence Scale–Third Edition (WAIS–III). The purpose of these revisions was to insure that the standardization sample was representative of current demographics and performance, to update the subtests, incorporate new subtests, and refine the instructions and test materials (Psychological Corporation, 1997; Sattler & Ryan, 1998). The WAIS–III has also been normed and integrated with the Wechsler Memory Scales–III and the Wechsler Individual Achievement Test (Psychological Corporation, 1997).

The WAIS and each of its revisions have allowed examiners to calculate a Full Scale IQ as well as Verbal and Performance IQs. These subdivisions into verbal and nonverbal (performance) aspects of intelligence are supported by both theoretical formulations and empirical research. Factor analytic studies on the WAIS and WAIS–R have typically found a slightly different clustering of subtests to form Verbal Comprehension and Perceptual Organizational factors, as well as a third factor which has been referred to as Freedom From Distractibility (Kaufman, 1990, 1994; Allen & Thorndike, 1995). When the WAIS–III was developed, three new subtests were added (Symbol Search, Matrix Reasoning, Letter–Number Sequencing; see Table 2.1). These have resulted in the emergence of the following four-factor or 'index' scores: Verbal Conceptualization, Perceptual Organization, Working Memory (previously referred to as Freedom from Distractibility), and Processing Speed. The advantage of these index scores is that they allow test interpreters to evaluate a client's strengths and weaknesses by noting whether or not these indexes are clearly higher or lower relative to one another. This is potentially relevant for assessing learning disabilities in that it has often been suggested that such populations are likely to be lowest in Freedom from Distractibility and Processing Speed.

In order to extend the range of the WAIS, Wechsler also developed the

Table 2.1. Descriptions of WAIS–III and WISC–III subtests

Subtest	Description
Verbal subtests	
Vocabulary*	List of orally and visually printed words; the examinee is requested to provide oral definitions
Similarities	Orally presented pairs of words; examinee explains the similarity between the two words or concepts
Information	Orally presented questions related to common events, objects, places, and people
Comprehension	Series of orally presented questions related to social rules and concepts or solutions to everyday problems
Arithmetic	Series of orally presented arithmetic problems; examinee must solve them mentally and express them orally
Digit Span	Series of orally presented numbers; examinee is requested to repeat them verbatim for Digits Forwards and in reverse for Digits Backwards
Letter–Number Sequencing (WAIS–III only)	Series of orally presented letters and numbers; examinee mentally tracks these and orally presents them with the numbers in ascending order and the letters in alphabetical order
Performance subtests	
Picture Arrangement	Cartoon-type pictures presented in a mixed-up order; examinee must rearrange them to make a logical story sequence
Picture Completion	Set of color pictures or common objects and settings, each picture is missing an important part; the examinee is requested to identify the most important part that is missing
Block Design	Set of blocks; examinee must arrange the blocks to replicate various patterns
Matrix Reasoning (WAIS–III only)	Series of incomplete gridded patterns; examinee answers by indicating which of a possible five patterns is correct
Coding (WISC–III) or Digit–Symbol–Coding (WAIS–III)	Series of numbers which are paired with their own symbol; examinee must match and write down the symbol which corresponds with the number
Symbol Search	Series of paired groups of symbols with each pair representing a target group and a search group; examinee marks the appropriate box to indicate whether the target group symbol appears in the search group
Object Assembly	Set of puzzles of common objects; examinee assembles the pieces to replicate the objects

Adapted from Wechsler (1997a).

*All subtests are on both the WAIS–III and WISC–III unless otherwise indicated.

Wechsler Intelligence Scales for Children (WISC) in 1949. This primarily represented a downward extension of the WAIS subtests in that easier items were included. Norms were developed from children between the ages of 5 years 0 months and 15 years 11 months. However, these early norms included exclusively European American children and over-represented children from middle and upper socioeconomic backgrounds. In 1974, the WISC was restandardized on a more representative sample to form the WISC–R. The age range was also extended up to 16 years 11 months. The most recent (1991) revision (WISC–III) was not only based on a current representative standardization, but also incorporated the new Symbol Search subtest. IQ scores can be calculated for Full Scale, Verbal, and Performance abilities. Similar to the WAIS–III, the following four index scores can also be calculated: Verbal Comprehension, Perceptual Organization, Freedom from Distractibility, and Processing Speed.

In 1967, a downward extension of the WISC was developed in the form of the Wechsler Preschool and Primary Scale of Intelligence (WPPSI). This enabled practitioners to assess children between the ages of 4 years and 6 years 6 months. The WPPSI included simpler items than the WISC, as well as certain types of items unique to the WPPSI itself. The WPPSI was most recently revised in 1989 (WPPSI–R). The subtests between the 1967 and 1989 versions have remained essentially the same, except that the WPPSI–R has emphasized speed of performance more than the WPPSI did.

The psychometric properties of the Wechsler intelligence scales have generally been excellent. They are often used as models for other psychological tests. The following descriptions focus on the most recent versions of the Wechsler intelligence scales (WAIS–III and WISC–III). It should also be noted that the psychometric data reported below are abbreviated. More detailed descriptions can be found in the manuals (Wechsler, 1991, 1997a, 1997b) or various texts (Kaufman, 1990, 1994; Sattler, 2001; Groth-Marnat, 1999; Sattler & Ryan, 1998; Kaufman & Lichtenberger, 1999).

The recent WAIS–III manual (Wechsler, 1997) has reported split half reliabilities for the Full Scale, Verbal, and Performance IQs as .98, .97, and .94 respectively. Test–retest reliabilities over a six-week retesting interval have been slightly lower but still comparable. Split half reliabilities for the index scores have been similarly high (Verbal Comprehension = .96, Perceptual Organization = .93, Working Memory = .88, Processing Speed = .88). For the most part, reliabilities for the subtests have been in the eighties to low nineties. The highest reliabilities have been reported for Vocabulary (split half $r = .93$) and Information (split half $r = .91$). In contrast, relatively low reliabilities have been found for Object Assembly (split half $r = .70$) and Picture Arrangement (split half $r = .74$).

Validity of the WAIS–III will vary, of course, depending on the criteria or strategy used to establish its validity and the purpose for which the test is being used. Typical WAIS–III validation strategies include correlations with the earlier (and well-validated) WAIS–R, correlations with other ability measures, factor analysis, and ability to predict the performance of clients with known cognitive deficits (i.e., Alzheimer's disease). Overall, research findings have been quite supportive. For example, correlations with the earlier WAIS–R were quite high (Full Scale IQ = .93, Verbal IQ = .94, Performance = .86). This suggests that much of the validity established for the WAIS–R is also transferable to the WAIS–III. Thus, it would be expected that the WAIS–III would be equally as good at predicting academic and occupational performance as its predecessors (see Hunter, 1986; Schmidt, Ones, & Hunter, 1992; Neisser et al., 1996). Correlations with other ability measures have also been quite high. These include the Stanford Binet–IV (0.88), Standard Progressive Matrices (with the Performance IQ $r = .79$), and the Wechsler Individual Achievement Test ($r = $ high sixties to high seventies). Factor analyses support the presence of a general intelligence factor (g), as well as the division into both verbal and performance abilities, and the presence of the four indexes (Wechsler, 1997b). Finally, the WAIS–III has been found to be sensitive to cognitive impairments present in various clinical groups. For example, Alzheimer's disease patients were found overall to score lower than controls and to score particularly low on Processing Speed compared to their Verbal Conceptual abilities.

Similar to the WAIS–III, the WISC–III reports excellent psychometric properties. Split half reliability across the 11 different age groups for the Full Scale, Verbal, and Performance IQs are .96, .95, and .91 respectively (Wechsler, 1991). As would be expected, reliabilities for the specific subtests are lower but still generally in the eighties. The highest split half reliability was for Vocabulary (.87), with the lowest for Object Assembly (.69). In general, lower reliabilities were found among the younger age groups. Test–retest reliabilities for the IQs and subtests over a 23-day interval were roughly comparable to the split half reliabilities. For example, test–retest reliabilities for the Full Scale, Verbal, and Performance IQs were .94, .94, and .87. The above data indicate that the WISC is both stable over time and internally consistent.

Strategies to validate the WISC–III include establishing its correlation with the WISC–R, correlating it with external ability measures, factor analysis, and assessing its ability to predict relevant performance. The WISC–III has been found to correlate highly with the earlier WISC–R (Full Scale $r = .89$, Verbal IQ $r = .90$, Performance IQ $r = .81$). This suggests that much of the validity established for the WISC–R can also be generalized to the WISC–III (Dixon & Anderson, 1995). Selected correlations between the WISC–III and external ability measures include the Stanford–Binet–IV (median $r = .78$), Kaufman Assessment Battery for Children (K-ABC; median $r = .70$), Wide Range Achievement Test (r range $= .52–.59$), and the Peabody Individual Achievement Test (median $r = .71$; see Sattler, 1992). Factor analyses support both the presence of generalized intelligence (g) as well as Wechsler's division into verbal and performance abilities. Factors have also emerged supporting the presence and use of the four indexes (Verbal Comprehension, Perceptual Organization, Freedom from Distractibility, and Processing Speed). The WISC–III has also been found to predict relevant performance, such as the .47 correlation with school grades (Wechsler, 1991).

Description of the instruments

The Wechsler intelligence scales are comprised of an administration manual, stimulus materials, and scoring sheets (Fig. 2.1). The WAIS–III also has a technical manual. The administration manuals are clearly laid out and easy to read. They begin with information on how the tests were developed and on standardization, reliability, and validity. They then include clear descriptions of each of the different subtests, followed by detailed administration and scoring instructions. The appendixes include further clarification on administration and scoring, as well as tables that can be used to convert raw scores to the different IQs, indexes, and subtest scaled scores. The manuals have generally been praised as providing sufficient guidelines to work appropriately with and administer the stimulus materials. In some cases, however, deciding on the most appropriate score can be somewhat difficult. In addition, the number of administration and scoring errors made by practitioners is higher than it should be (Slate & Hunnicutt, 1988; Slate, Jones, & Murray, 1991). This underscores the need to follow optimal training guidelines (see Fantuzzo, Blakey, & Gorsuch, 1989; Slate et al., 1991) with well supervised repeated practice administrations.

The stimulus materials for the Verbal subtests (see Table 2.1) are simply words or sentences which are read to the examinee. For example, Information items involve clients answering questions related to their general fund of knowledge, and Vocabulary requires the examiner to read a series of progress-ively more difficult words which the examinee must define. The administration

Fig. 2.1. Wechsler Intelligence Scale for Children–III.

manual clarifies when (or whether) the examiner should repeat the questions or probe for further explanation. Most of the items on the Performance subtests use physical materials that the examinee must somehow manipulate. For example, the Block Design subtest requires examinees to arrange designs using a series of blocks so that they match pictures of designs. Similarly, Picture Arrangement requires examinees to rearrange a cartoon-type series of pictures into a new order so that they make optimal sequential sense. As with the Verbal subtest instructions, the manual provides detailed information on such things as what to say to the examinee and how to arrange the stimulus materials prior to the examinee working on them.

The scoring sheets include space to record the examinee's responses, graphs to allow a profile of the different scores, and tables/figures to assist in calculating IQ, index, and subscale scores. The WAIS–III also includes tables that can be used to calculate the extent to which the index scores vary from one another. Both the more recent WISC–III and WAIS–III scoring sheets allow for more calculations and tables than their previous versions. This is potentially quite useful, because it allows practitioners to have access to a larger amount of potentially useful data. For example, neither the WISC–R nor the WAIS–R allowed for the calculation of index (factor) scores. In contrast, these are standard features on the WISC–III and WAIS–III. This might be particularly useful for assessing clients suspected of having learning disabilities in that wide variations in cognitive abilities would be expected to underlie their difficulties and therefore possibly be reflected on the index scores. However, the greater number of calculations would also be expected to increase the likelihood of clerical errors. This is consistent with the finding that, even with the simpler early Wechsler intelligence scales, the number of clerical errors was worryingly high (Slate & Hunnicutt, 1988; Slate et al., 1991).

Normative and developmental issues

Each of the versions of the Wechsler intelligence scale variations has been standardized on groups that are generally representative of people from different age, ethnic, educational, and geographic groups within the USA. The representativeness has been a particularly prominent feature of the more recent versions. In contrast, the WAIS and WISC somewhat over-represented people from more highly educated populations and did not have a sufficient number of people from ethnic minorities. The various age groups are used to make comparisons of people within certain age groups to develop IQs based on the performance of people within these ages. The scales have also been standardized on various international groups so that the test scores will more accurately reflect patterns within the various countries.

The WAIS–III was standardized on 2450 adults between the ages of 16 and 89. The group represented European Americans, African Americans, and Hispanics according to the 1995 US census. There were more females than males in the higher age brackets, but this is consistent with census data. All geographic regions in the USA were represented and stratified according to different educational levels. There were 200 people within each of the 13 age groups, with the exception of the 80–84 and 85–89 age groups, which had 100 and 150 people respectively.

The standardization sample for the WISC–III was also excellent in that it had a sufficient number of people and was also representative of US census data. A total of 2200 children were included between the ages of 6 and 16 and were divided into 11 age groups. Each group had 100 males and 100 females. The sample was stratified based on age, race/ethnicity, geographic region, and parent education (used to reflect socioeconomic status). The relative proportions closely reflected 1988 US census data. Subjects were also selected to represent different geographical regions within the USA.

Application to diagnosis and treatment of learning disabilities

The assessment of learning disabilities using the Wechsler intelligence scales is intrinsically linked to the strategy of interpreting the scales themselves. Thus, an initial familiarity with Wechsler interpretive strategies is outlined below. Such an interpretation is successive and begins with the more general features of the scales (Full Scale IQ) and gradually proceeds to more specific details (qualitative analysis of unusual responses). It should be stressed that there is more support for interpreting the more global aspects and relatively less support for the more specific details. Thus, a fairly high reliance can be placed on interpretations of IQ and index scores. In contrast, interpretations based on an analysis of various high and low subtests should be considered as hypotheses in need of further confirmation. Some authors even recommend not interpreting individual subtests at all, because the subtests have insufficient reliability, specificity, and validity (McDermott et al., 1990; Glutting et al., 1997). In contrast, others believe that profile analysis not only can but should be performed, in that it allows the clearest representation of a person's intellectual strengths and weaknesses (Lezak, 1988, 1995; Kaufman, 1990, 1994; Groth-Marnat et al., 2000). This is a particularly crucial issue for the assessment of learning disabilities, which typically entails understanding a person's specific strengths and weaknesses as they relate to his or her disability. However, even those who advocate profile analysis emphasize the importance of obtaining additional support, making careful observations of the client, and paying attention to issues of ecological validity (Kaufman, 1994; Sbordone & Long, 1996; Groth-Marnat & Teal, 2000; Kaufman & Lichtenberger, 1999).

Wechsler interpretation typically proceeds along the following five-step process (Table 2.2).

Level I: Full Scale IQ

The Full Scale IQ can be considered the most reliable and valid estimate of a client's overall ability. Extensive research supports the ability of the IQ in predicting academic and occupational performance. The Full Scale IQ can often be more clearly represented as a percentile rank or IQ classification (Very Superior, Superior, High Average, Average, Low Average, Borderline, Extremely Low Range). It is also sometimes useful to include the standard error of measure of an IQ score so that readers of a report are aware that there is an

Table 2.2. Outline of successive, five-level WAIS–III/WISC–III interpretive procedures

---

Level I. Interpret Full Scale IQ

Level II. Interpret Verbal–Performance, Index Scores, and Additional Groupings

   a. Verbal–Performance IQs

   b. Index Scores: Verbal Comprehension, Perceptual Organization, Working Memory/Freedom from Distractibility, Processing Speed

   c. Additional Groupings: Bannatyne's categories, ACID/SCAD profiles, Horn groupings

Level III. Interpret Subtest Variability (Profile Analysis)

Level IV: Analyze Intrasubtest Variability

Level V. Conduct a Qualitative Analysis

Adapted from Groth-Marnat (1997).

expected range of error around the score, but can also be assured that the range of error still clusters fairly closely around the IQ itself. If there is very little variation among Verbal–Performance IQs, indexes, or subtests, then a high degree of reliance can be placed in the Full Scale IQ. However, when variations in these scores do occur, then it means that the Full Scale IQ is likely to be less unitary. It then becomes important to understand the importance and meanings behind these variations.

Level II: Verbal–Performance IQs, Index scores, and additional groupings

Level II interpretation focuses on subdividing different abilities based on various clusters of subtests. The most time-honored cluster is represented by Wechsler's groupings into either Verbal or Performance subtests. A nine-point Verbal–Performance difference on the WAIS–III and a 12-point difference on the WISC–III are generally considered significant at the 0.05 level. If the Verbal IQ is significantly higher than the Performance IQ, it suggests a number of possibilities, including more highly developed verbal comprehension abilities, higher educational level, tendency toward overachieving, difficulty with practical tasks, deficits with performance tasks, the presence of right hemisphere lesions, or either a slow, deliberate work style (resulting in greater penalties on the timed performance subtests) or an impulsive work style (resulting in more errors on the performance subtests). In contrast, a Performance IQ which is significantly higher than Verbal IQ suggests superior perceptual organizational abilities, tendency toward low academic achievement, ability to work well under time pressure, a person from a low socioeconomic background, presence of a language deficit, or left hemisphere lesions.

It should be noted that statistically significant Verbal–Performance differences are not particularly unusual. A full 18% of the WAIS–III and 24% of the WISC–III standardization samples had Verbal–Performance differences of 15 or more points. This means that interpretations should be treated cautiously and always supported by additional sources of information.

A finer distinction in abilities can be found by noting whether or not there are significant differences between index (factor) scores. The WAIS–III and WISC–III profile sheets provide graphs for plotting the index scores, and the significance of the differences can be noted in the administration and scoring manuals. Strengths or weaknesses can be hypothesized by noting significant elevations/lowerings on the following indexes (factors):

Verbal Comprehension: ability to work with abstract symbols, degree of benefit from education, verbal fluency, verbal memory.

Perceptual Organization: ability to integrate perceptual stimuli with relevant motor responses, work in concrete situations, work quickly, assess visuo-spatial information.

Working Memory (WAIS–III)/Freedom from Distractibility (WISC–III): short-term memory, concentration, attention, ability to make appropriate mental shifts, sequencing, ability to attend to stimuli.

Processing Speed: mental and motor speed in solving nonverbal problems; ability to plan, organize, and develop relevant strategies; scores can be lowered due to a slow reflective problem-solving style or poor motivation.

As with differences for Verbal–Performance IQs, interpretations should be made with appropriate caution (including hypothesis testing) and also with an awareness that moderate differences are a fairly frequent occurrence. It should also be noted that the abilities measured by both the Verbal Comprehension and Perceptual Organization indexes are essentially the same as for the Verbal and Performance IQs.

Many of the additional Wechsler intelligence scale groupings have been developed in attempts to assess learning disabilities more fully. These group-ings are objectively described below, but their effectiveness in assessing learn-ing disabilities are evaluated in a later subsection.

One of the earliest attempts at a specific learning disability profile is *Ban-natyne's categories* (Bannatyne, 1974). The theory underlying Bannatyne's re-categorization is that people with learning disabilities would be expected to do best on spatial, holistic tasks which require simultaneous processing. In con-trast, they would be expected to do quite poorly on tasks requiring sequencing, and this would result in poor academic performance, which would be reflected in a low level of acquired knowledge. This led to the following subtest groupings and expected relative magnitudes:

Table 2.3. Summary of Ted's WISC–III results

IQ scores			
Verbal IQ	81		
Performance IQ	89		
Full Scale IQ	83		
Index scores			
Verbal Comprehension	84		
Perceptual Organization	120		
Freedom from Distractibility	72		
Processing Speed	75		
Subtest scores			
Information	6	Picture Completion	9
Similarities	7	Coding	4
Arithmetic	5	Picture Arrangement	10
Vocabulary	7	Block Design	18
Comprehension	8	Object Assembly	16
Digit Span	5	Symbol Search	6

Bannatyne's categories (mean of subtests in each category)

Spatial (14.3) > Verbal Conceptualization (7.3) > Acquired Knowledge (6) > Sequential (4.7)

SCAD profile (converted to IQ equivalent): 66

Spatial (Picture Completion + Block Design + Object Assembly + ?Matrix Reasoning) >
Verbal Conceptualization (Vocabulary + Comprehension + Similarities) >
Sequential (Digit Span + Arithmetic + Coding + ?Letter–Number Sequencing) >
Acquired Knowledge (Information + Vocabulary + Arithmetic).

This can be more simply summarized as follows: Spatial > Verbal Conceptualization > Sequential > Acquired Knowledge (see example in Table 2.3). Question marks appear before Matrix Reasoning and Letter–Number Sequencing because these are new WAIS–III subtests and their appropriateness for Bannatyne's categories has not yet been evaluated. Theoretically, however, they would be expected to be included in the indicated groupings. It should also be noted that sometimes Acquired Knowledge has not been included as one of the categories.

The *ACID, ACIDS,* and *SCAD* profiles are similar recategorizations. They are based on the theory and observation that learning-disabled people tend to do particularly poorly on some subtests as opposed to others (Kaufman, 1990, 1994; Prifitera & Dersh, 1993; Mayes, Calhoun, & Crowell, 1998). The ACID profile was originally developed for the WISC–R (and WAIS–R) and is simply the scores on Arithmetic, Coding, Information, and Digit Span. The WISC–III has included a Symbol Search subtest such that a WISC–III variation on the ACID profile is simply to add Symbol Search to create an ACIDS profile. Kaufman (1994) has recommended a somewhat similar WISC–III SCAD profile, which is also comprised of the newer Symbol Search subtest, along with Coding, Arithmetic, and Digit Span. It should be noted that the ACID/SCAD profiles are somewhat similar to Bannatyne's recategorization in that three of the ACID/SCAD subtests are included in Bannatyne's Sequential category (Arithmetic, Coding, and Digit Span). The subscale scores on the ACID/SCAD profiles can either be combined to form an overall subscale mean, or a formula can be used to calculate an equivalent ACID/SCAD profile 'IQ' (see example in Table 2.3; Kaufman, 1990, 1994; Groth-Marnat, 1999). Because the WAIS–III includes an upward extension of the WISC–III Symbol Search subtest, it would be reasonable to assume that a SCAD profile might also be relevant for the WAIS–III. It might also be speculated that learning-disabled people would do relatively poorly on Letter–Number Sequencing, because this subtest requires sequencing and attentional abilities. However, no research is currently available investigating the relation between learning disabilities and either the WAIS–III Symbol Search or Letter–Number Sequencing subtest.

A final recategorization has been organized around Horn's *fluid intelligence* versus *crystallized intelligence* (Horn & Cattell, 1966), as well as additional categories for retention (on the WAIS–R) and achievement (for the WISC–III). As no research has been conducted on these categories and learning disabilities, the specific subtests used to calculate these categories will not be included, but are available in Groth-Marnat (1999) and Kaufman (1990, 1994).

Level III: interpreting subtest variability

A further strategy is to determine the meaning of outstandingly low or high subtest scores. This process needs to be undertaken with caution, because the individual subtests may not have sufficient specificity or reliability, and a high degree of subtest scatter is a fairly common occurrence. It is likely that many clinicians have regularly overinterpreted the meanings of high or low subtests. In order to guard against such overinterpretation, careful interpretive steps need to be taken (see Kaufman, 1990, 1994; Groth-Marnat, 1999; Kaufman & Lichtenberger, 1999; Groth-Marnat et al., 2000). First, practitioners should determine whether subtest fluctuations are statistically significant. Next, hypotheses should be checked against the meanings of other patterns of high and low subtests. For example, a high Block Design subtest might be the result of good visual abstract reasoning, speed of information processing, or a combination of both. If another subtest that primarily measures visual abstract reasoning (i.e., Matrix Reasoning) was also high, this further supports the importance of visual abstract reasoning. In contrast, if subtests that primarily involved speeded performance were low (i.e., Symbol Search), then it reduces the likelihood that speed was a crucial factor involved in the high Block Design score (and further supports the relative importance of visual abstract reasoning). The final step is to integrate subtest hypotheses with additional information. This step is extremely important and involves considering such factors as the client's level of motivation, school records, reports from teachers, other test results, medical records, or relevant history.

Level IV: intrasubtest variability

The Wechsler subtest items are organized such that there is an even progression from less difficult items to more difficult ones. This means that subjects are likely to miss progressively more items at a fairly even rate. If a client misses early easier items but passes later more difficult ones, this should be investigated further. Possible explanations might include poor attentional abilities, poor motivation, or even motivation to do poorly, which might be consistent with malingering.

Level V: qualitative analysis

Often, clients will make unique responses to the Wechsler items that help to further understand their thought processes and personalities. For example, responses might represent concrete thinking, unusual associations, impulsiveness, or aggressive tendencies. It should be stressed, however, that this level of interpretation is more speculative than the others, relies more on clinical judgment (see Garb, 1998), and should be treated with appropriate caution.

The above review of Wechsler intelligence scale interpretation provides the necessary background and structure for more fully understanding the various strategies used to assess learning disabilities. The first three of these levels have been fairly thoroughly utilized and researched. The results of the strategies and relative support for them can enable practitioners to evaluate the appropriateness of using the Wechsler scales for individual cases.

The Full Scale IQ

The Full Scale IQ is the best overall indicator of a person's ability. As such, it can be used as one of a variety of variables to determine whether someone is achieving at his or her expected level. For example, further investigation needs to be made if a child is performing poorly in school but has a Full Scale IQ in the Superior range. A diagnosis of learning disabilities is one possibility. Other possibilities might include emotional disturbance, little support from his or her family environment, or poor student–teacher relationships. In contrast, a child who is performing poorly but has a Full Scale IQ in the Borderline or Extremely Low Range is more likely to be given a quite different diagnosis (and treatment). In this case, the Full Scale IQ can be used to exclude learning disabilities and, along with relevant measures of adaptive functioning, can be used to diagnose intellectual disabilities (mental retardation).

Usually, the search for learning disabilities proceeds beyond the Full Scale IQ into an understanding of relative cognitive strengths and weaknesses. These discrepancies might theoretically be reflected in variations among the child's subtest scores.

Verbal–Performance discrepancies

Because learning-disabled people typically do relatively poorly in academic areas, it might be expected that their verbal subtests (and Verbal IQ) would be lower relative to their performance abilities. Several studies with the WISC and WISC–R have provided some support for this hypothesis (Anderson, Kaufman, & Kaufman, 1976; Smith et al., 1977). In addition, moderate support has been found for Verbal being lower than Performance IQs for the WISC–III (Daley & Nagle, 1996), in that 27% of a sample of learning-disabled people had discrepancies of 16 points or higher. In contrast, the WISC–III manual reported discrepancies of 16 or more points in only 21.6% of the standardization sample.

The above data suggest that, while there is some support for Performance > Verbal discrepancies among learning-disabled people, this occurrence is not much higher than among the normal population. Although this may not provide much of an argument for the distinctiveness of greater performance abilities among learning-disabled people, the pattern of abilities still may have interpretive significance for an individual case in the same way that it would have interpretive significance for nonlearning-disabled people. Thus, it might help to understand individual cases in more depth. A further point is that while Performance > Verbal may be present for approximately 27% of learning-disabled people, this still means that this pattern did *not* occur in the remaining 73%. Again, even though Performance > Verbal discrepancies occurred in a fairly large proportion of learning-disabled people, the absence of this pattern does not exclude a diagnosis of learning disabilities.

Index (factor) scores

Early research on the WISC/WISC–R indicated that learning-disabled populations typically showed a distinctive profile in which Perceptual Organization > Verbal Comprehension > Freedom from Distractibility (Galvin, 1981; Stanton & Reynolds, 1998). As has been noted, the WISC–III has been found to have the three factors originally found with the WISC/WISC–R as well as a fourth (Processing Speed) factor, which was formed from combining Coding with Symbol Search. Findings with the WISC–III index scores and learning disabilities have been generally supportive of the above pattern. Specifically, some researchers have found that both Processing Speed and Freedom from Distractibility were depressed when compared with Perceptual Organization and Verbal Comprehension (Wechsler, 1991; Prifitera & Dersch, 1993; Mayes et al., 1998). In contrast, Daley and Nagle (1996) found mixed support in that Freedom from Distractibility was lower than either Processing Speed or Perceptual Organization. However, they found no differences between Freedom from Distractibility and Verbal Comprehension. There were also no differences between Verbal Comprehension, Processing Speed, and Perceptual Organization.

Research with the WAIS–III is limited because it has only been recently published. The *WAIS–III/WMS–III Technical Manual* has reported a pronounced pattern for people diagnosed with learning disabilities. The clearest finding was that Verbal Comprehension was significantly higher than Working Memory (7 and 13 points for reading-disabled and math-disabled groups, respectively). A full 41.7% of the learning-disabled group had discrepancies in which Verbal Comprehension was 15 points or more higher than Working Memory (versus only 13% of the WAIS–III standardization sample). Similarly, Perceptual Organization was an average of 7 points higher than Processing Speed. A 15-point or more discrepancy was found in 30.4% of the learning-disabled group (compared with 14% of the standardization sample). At the present time, then, there are data to support the hypothesis that, at least for the WAIS–III, Working Memory and Processing Speed are relatively lower among people diagnosed with learning disabilities. In contrast, research on the WISC–III is more equivocal.

Additional groupings: Bannatyne's categories and ACID/ACIDS/SCAD profiles

Most of the research with the Wechsler scales and learning disabilities has focused on trying to find a distinctive grouping of subtests that would be specific to learning disabilities. Bannatyne's recategorization was one of the earliest formulations, but research with it has received mixed results. In some studies, learning-disabled students have exhibited the expected Spatial > Conceptual > Sequencing > Acquired Knowledge pattern (Kavale & Forness, 1984; Ackerman, McGrew, & Dykman, 1987; Kaufman, 1990, 1994; Katz et al., 1993; Daley & Nagle, 1996). When working with Bannatyne's categories, caution is needed in that even studies with positive findings report that the Bannatyne profile only occurred slightly more frequently among the learning-disabled group than among the normal population. In addition, the majority of learning-disabled people *did not* have the profile. The classic Bannatyne pattern has also frequently been found among other groups, such as juvenile delinquents (Groff & Hubble, 1981; Culbertson, Feral, & Gabby, 1989) and emotionally handicapped children (Thompson, 1981). The above means that the Bannatyne profile is neither specific to learning disabilities, nor does its absence exclude a diagnosis of learning disabilities. However, it is far from useless, in that if the profile does occur in individual cases, it can be used to understand more fully the client's various strengths and weaknesses (see illustrative case).

One caution is that sometimes quite bright, highly motivated people can compensate for their learning disability by developing a high level of acquired knowledge. The result would be that the Acquired Knowledge category might be outstandingly high even though the person might struggle with poor sequencing abilities (low Sequencing; Ackerman et al., 1987). In contrast, many, if not most, learning-disabled people would find academic learning both frustrating and unrewarding. Therefore, they would benefit less than other people, with the result that they would acquire little knowledge (low Acquired Knowledge).

The ACID profile is comprised of those subtests on which learning-disabled people do particularly poorly (Arithmetic, Coding, Information, and Digit Span). This has become an important marker for learning disabilities, which has been supported by numerous studies. Most of these studies indicate that approximately 20% of learning-disabled people exhibit either a partial (three of the four subtests are lowest) or full (all four of the subtests are lowered) ACID profile (Cordoni et al., 1981; Ackerman et al., 1987; Kaufman, 1990, 1994; Wechsler, 1991; Prifitera & Dersh, 1993; Mayes et al., 1998; Stanton & Reynolds, 1998). For example, data presented in the WISC–III manual indicate that 20.2% of learning-disabled people presented with a partial ACID profile, compared to 5.6% of the standardization sample. Similarly, 24% of learning-disabled people on the WAIS–III exhibited a partial ACID profile and 6.5%

exhibited a full ACID profile (Wechsler, 1997a). In contrast, the ACIDS profile (which includes the new Symbol Search subtest) has received less support. Ward et al. (1995), for example, actually found that Symbol Search was one of the highest scoring subtests among their sample of learning-disabled children.

Similar to the ACID subtests, the SCAD grouping is comprised of subtests which emphasize speed of information processing, visual short-term memory, visual–motor coordination (Symbol Search and Coding), along with number ability and sequencing (Arithmetic and Digit Span). A number of studies have found that children with learning disabilities (and also attention deficit disorder) score particularly low on the SCAD subtests (Prifitera & Dersh, 1993; Kaufman, 1994; Mayes et al., 1998). In contrast, Ward et al. (1995) found that the SCAD profile did not occur significantly more in a learning-disabled population than in the WISC–III standardization group (19.6% versus 16.0%, respectively).

Research on each of the above profiles (Bannatyne, ACID, SCADS) seems to come to the same general conclusions. These profiles do seem to occur somewhat more frequently among learning-disabled populations. However, there are other groups that also have these profiles, the frequency of the profiles is not that much higher than in the normal population, and the majority of people diagnosed with learning disabilities still do not exhibit them. A further caution is that learning-disabled six and seven year olds did not have these profiles any more frequently than normal comparison children (Mayes et al., 1998). This is probably due to difficulty in making an accurate diagnosis for children this young, such that probably a large proportion of the 'learning-disabled' group was not actually learning disabled (see Chapter 1 for diagnostic issues).

Subtest variability

The major features of subtest variability have been incorporated into the above sections on patterns of various subtests. However, one hypothesis that has been put forward is that there would be greater overall subtest variability (range between highest and lowest subtests) among people with learning disabilities. This seems plausible, in that learning disabilities might be considered to be the result of a high degree of disparities in abilities. In general, this hypothesis has not been supported by research (Bolen et al., 1995; Bolen, 1998; Mayes et al., 1998).

Intrasubtest variability

Little research has been done investigating the meaning of high intrasubtest scatter. However, Dumont and Willis (1995) did find that there was somewhat more scatter on the WISC–III subtests of Vocabulary, Comprehension, and Block Design among a sample of learning-disabled people. The meaning of this scatter was unclear. Investigation of intrasubtest variation on the WISC–III Coding subtest did not reveal any differences between learning-disabled and other groups (Dumont et al., 1998). Among adult populations, greater intrasubtest scatter has been found among those with cognitive dysfunction (Mittenberg, Hammeke, & Rao, 1989; Kaplan et al., 1991), but this has not been studied in relation to adults with learning disabilities. Dumont and Willis (1995) conclude their study by emphasizing that intrasubtest scatter should not be used to make diagnostic inferences, even though there may be some value in using scatter to describe individual cases. Thus, intrasubtest scatter should not be used to diagnose learning disabilities (or any other condition) but, when it does occur, should be used as a marker which can potentially be used to understand the person.

Summary and conclusions

Given the above review, the following summary points seem warranted.

- The Full Scale IQ can be most appropriately used to estimate the person's overall potential and assist in excluding possible explanations for poor academic performance other than learning disabilities (i.e., intellectual disabilities/mental retardation).
- There is moderate to equivocal evidence that some profiles (relatively low Processing Speed and Working Memory/Freedom from Distractibility, Spatial > Conceptual > Sequential, ACID, SCAD) occur more frequently in learning-disabled populations compared to the general population.
- The above profiles are not unique to learning disabilities, but often occur in other groups as well (juvenile delinquents, attention deficit hyperactivity disorder, emotionally handicapped).
- If a person does have a 'learning-disabled' Wechsler profile (ACID, etc.) it is *consistent with although not necessarily diagnostic of* learning disabilities.
- The majority of learning-disabled people *do not have* Wechsler 'learning-disabled' profiles. Thus, the absence of one of the profiles *does not exclude* a diagnosis of learning disabilities.
- The various patterns of Wechsler subtests can, at times, be used to further understand individual cases of people experiencing learning difficulties (see case illustration).

Illustrative case study

Ted is a 16-year-old, white, right-handed male in his tenth year of high school who was referred by his family practice physician to determine why he was performing poorly in school. His parents reported that four years prior to the current evaluation he had been labeled mentally retarded. They could not recall if any formal testing had been done, and his past records were unavailable. Due to his earlier diagnosis, he had been placed in programs with other intellectually disabled (mentally retarded) people. His parents were somewhat confused that he did poorly in school yet seemed extremely good at practical tasks, such as quickly and efficiently disassembling and reassembling bicycles. He appeared for his assessment casually dressed and seemed motivated to perform well on the tasks presented to him. However, his eye contact was poor and his speech was sometimes halting. He frequently stopped in the middle of his sentences, saying 'um . . . ah,' and then would continue with what he was saying.

As part of his assessment, he was administered a full WISC–III battery (see Table 2.3). His Full Scale IQ of 83 placed him in the Low Average range or 13th percentile when compared with his age-related peers. Thus, his previous diagnosis of mentally retarded was both inappropriate and resulted in decisions which were likely to have been detrimental to his educational development. Differences between his Verbal and Performance IQs were not significant and were therefore not interpreted.

The striking differences in his index and subtest scores enable a more detailed understanding of Ted's learning difficulties. Formal calculations involving his index scores revealed a significant lowering in Freedom from Distractibility (72) and Processing Speed (75) when compared with Perceptual Organization (120) and Verbal Comprehension (84). This suggests that he was experiencing difficulties with short-term memory, sequencing, poor number facility, and speed of processing sequential information. It should be noted that he had extremely high scores on Block Design (18) and Object Assembly (16), both of which are timed tests. This suggests that when working on material involving processing simultaneous, nonverbal information, he can work quite quickly, efficiently, and accurately. In contrast, when processing sequential information he would be likely to perform poorly. This interpretation is consistent with his academic history as well as reports by his parents that he appeared quite adept at fixing everyday objects (repairing bicycles). Poor sequencing was also supported by the observation of reversals in his writing (writing 'was' instead of 'saw').

A partial Bannatyne profile was found in that his Spatial (mean of subtests = 14.3) and Verbal Conceptualization (7.3) were clearly superior to his Sequential (4.7) and Acquired Knowledge (6) subtests. What was particularly striking was the discrepancy between his Spatial and Sequential subtests. This strongly suggests that his ability to process information in an efficient, simultaneous manner is an outstanding strength, particularly when compared with his marked weakness in sequencing. His SCAD profile (IQ equivalent = 66), which is primarily composed of sequencing tests, also supports this interpretation. Thus, information derived from the indexes, additional groupings, as well as other sources of information all help to support the above interpretation of Ted's relative strengths and weaknesses.

The above information was used to confirm a learning-disability diagnosis. He was placed in special education classes, which in part focused on helping him to compensate for his low sequencing abilities. His outstanding abilities in simultaneously processing and problem solving nonverbal information were also used to build his self-esteem by allowing him to develop and demonstrate these strengths. Career counseling similarly focused on his obtaining training and later employment in occupations which emphasized his strengths (i.e., mechanic, bicycle repairs).

REFERENCES

Ackerman, P.T., McGrew, M.J., & Dykman, R.A. (1987). A profile of male and female applicants for a special college program for learning disabled students. *Journal of Child Psychology*, 43, 67–78.

Allen, S.R. & Thorndike, R.M. (1995). Stability of the WAIS-R and the WISC-III factor structure using cross-validation of co-variance structures. *Journal of Clinical Psychology*, 51, 645–57.

Anderson, M., Kaufman, A.S., & Kaufman, N.L. (1976). Use of the WISC-R with a learning disabled population: some diagnostic implications. *Psychology in the Schools*, 13, 381–7.

Bannatyne, A. (1974). Diagnosis – a note on recategorization of the WISC scaled scores. *Journal of Learning Disabilities*, 7, 272–3.

Bolen, L.M. (1998). WISC-III score changes for EMH students. *Psychology and the Schools*, 35, 327–32.

Bolen, L.M., Aichinger, K.S., Hall, C.W., & Webster, R.E. (1995). A comparison of the performance of cognitively disabled children on the WISC-R and WISC-III. *Journal of Clinical Psychology*, 51, 89–94.

Cordoni, B.K., O'Donnell, J.P., Ramaniah, N.V., Kurtz, J., & Rosenshein, K. (1981). Wechsler Adult Intelligence Scale patterns for learning disabled young adults. *Journal of Learning Disabilities*, 14, 404–7.

Culbertson, F.M., Feral, C.H., & Gabby, S. (1989). Pattern analysis of Wechsler Intelligence Scale for Children–Revised profiles for delinquent boys. *Journal of Clinical Psychology*, 45, 651–60.

Daley, C.E. & Nagle, R.J. (1996). Relevance of WISC-III indicators for assessment of learning disabilities. *Journal of Psychoeducational Research*, 14, 320–33.

Dixon, W.E. & Anderson, T. (1995). Establishing covariance continuity between the WISC-R and the WISC-III. *Psychological Assessment*, 7, 115–17.

Dumont, R., Farr, L.P., Willis, J.O., & Whelley, P. (1998). 30-second interval performance on the coding subtest of the WISC-III: further evidence of WISC folklore? *Psychology in the Schools*, 35, 111–17.

Dumont, R. & Willis, J.O. (1995). Intrasubtest scatter on the WISC-III for various clinical samples vs. the standardization sample: an examination of WISC folklore. *Journal of Psychoeducational Assessment*, 13, 271–85.

Fantuzzo, J.W., Blakey, W.A., & Gorsuch, R.L. (1989). *WAIS-R: Administration and Scoring Training Manual*. San Antonio, TX: The Psychological Corporation.

Galvin, G.A. (1981). Uses and abuses of the WISC-R with the learning disabled. *Journal of Learning Disabilities*, 14, 326–9.

Garb, H.N. (1998). *Studying the Clinician: Judgment Research and Psychological Assessment*. Washington, DC: American Psychological Association.

Glutting, J.J., McDermott, P.A., Watkins, M.M., Kush, J.C., & Konold, T.R. (1997). The base rate problem and its consequences for interpreting children's ability profiles. *School Psychology Quarterly*, 26, 176–88.

Groff, M. & Hubble, L. (1981). Recategorized WISC-R scores of juvenile delinquents. *Journal of Learning Disabilities*, 14, 515–16.

Groth-Marnat, G. (1999). *Handbook of Psychological Assessment*, 3rd edition (revised). New York: Wiley.

Groth-Marnat, A., Gallagher, R.E., Hale, J.B., & Kaplan, E. (2000). The Wechsler Intelligence scales. In *Neuropsychological Assessment in Clinical Practice: a Guide to Test Interpretation and Integration*, ed. G. Groth-Marnat, pp. 129–94. New York: Wiley.

Groth-Marnat, G. & Teal, M. (2000). Block Design as a measure of everyday spatial ability: a study of ecological validity. *Perceptual and Motor Skills*, 90, 522–6.

Horn, J.L. & Cattell, R.B. (1966). Refinement and test of the theory of fluid and crystallized intelligence. *Journal of Educational Psychology*, 57, 253–70.

Hunter, J.E. (1986). Cognitive ability, cognitive aptitudes, job knowledge, and job performance. *Journal of Vocational Behavior*, 29, 340–62.

Kaplan, E., Fein, D., Morris, R., & Delis, D. (1991). *Manual for the WAIS-R as a Neuropsychological Instrument*. San Antonio, TX: The Psychological Corporation.

Katz, L., Goldstein, G., Rudisin, S., & Bailey, D. (1993). A neuropsychological approach to the Bannatyne recategorization of the Wechsler intelligence scales in adults with learning disabilities. *Journal of Learning Disabilities*, 26, 65–72.

Kaufman, A.S. (1990). *Assessing Adolescent and Adult Intelligence*. Boston: Allyn & Bacon.

Kaufman, A.S. (1994). *Intelligent Testing with the WISC-III*. New York: Wiley.

Kaufman, A.S. & Lichtenberger, E.O. (1999). *Essentials of WAIS-III Assessment*. New York: Wiley.

Kavale, K.A. & Forness, S.R. (1984). A meta-analysis of the validity of Wechsler scale profiles and recategorizations: patterns or parodies. *Learning Disability Quarterly*, 7, 136–56.

Lezak, M.D. (1988). IQ: R.I.P. *Journal of Clinical and Experimental Neuropsychology*, 10, 351–61.

Lezak, M.D. (1995). *Neuropsychological Assessment*, 3rd edition. New York: Oxford University Press.

McDermott, P.A., Fantuzzo, J.W., & Glutting, J.L. (1990). Just say no to subtest analysis: a critique on Wechsler theory and practice. *Journal of Psychoeducational Assessment*, 8, 290–302.

Mayes, S.D., Calhoun, S.L., & Crowell, E.W. (1998). WISC-III profiles for children with and without learning disabilities. *Psychology in the Schools*, 35, 309–16.

Mittenberg, W., Hammeke, T.A., & Rao, S.M. (1989). Intrasubtest scatter on the WAIS-R as a pathognomonic sign of brain injury. *Psychological Assessment*, 1, 273–6.

Neisser, U., Boodoo, G., Bouchard, T.J. et al. (1996). Intelligence: knowns and unknowns. *American Psychologist*, 51, 77–101.

Prifitera, A. & Dersh, J. (1993). Base rates of WISC-III diagnostic subtest patterns among normal, learning disabled, and ADHD samples. In *Advances in Psychoeducational Assessment: Wechsler Intelligence Scale for Children*, 3rd edition, ed. B.A. Bracken & R.S. McCallum, pp. 43–55. Journal of Psychoeducational Assessment monograph series. Germantown, TN: Psychoeducational Corporation.

Sattler, J.M. (2001). *Assessment of Children*, 4th edition. San Diego: Jerome Sattler Publisher.

Sattler, J.M. & Ryan, J.J. (1998). *Assessment of Children*, 3rd edition, revised and updated WAIS-III supplement. San Diego: Jerome Sattler Publisher.

Sbordone, R.J. & Long, C.J. (eds.) (1996). *Ecological Validity of Neuropsychological Testing*. Odessa, FL: Psychological Assessment Resources.

Schmidt, F.L., Ones, D.S., & Hunter, D.E. (1992). Personnel selection. *Annual Review of Psychology*, 43, 627–70.

Slate, J.R. & Hunnicutt, L.C. (1988). Examiner errors on the Wechsler scales. *Journal of Psychoeducational Assessment*, 6, 280–8.

Slate, J.R., Jones, C.H., & Murray, R.A. (1991). Teaching administration and scoring of the Wechsler Adult Intelligence Scale–Revised: an empirical evaluation of practice administrations. *Professional Psychology*, 22, 375–9.

Smith, M.D., Coleman, J.M., Dokecki, P., & Davis, E.E. (1977). Recategorized WISC-R scores of learning disabled children. *Journal of Learning Disabilities*, 10, 48–54.

Stanton, H.C. & Reynolds, C.R. (1998). Configural frequency analysis as a method of determining Wechsler profile types. Paper presented at the annual meeting of the American Psychological Association, San Francisco, CA.

Thompson, R.J. (1981). The diagnostic utility of Bannatyne's recategorized WISC-R scores with children referred to a developmental evaluation center. *Psychology in the Schools*, 18, 43–7.

Ward, S.B., Ward, T.J., Hatt, C.V., Young, D.L., & Mollner, N.R. (1995). The incidence and utility of the ACID, ACIDS, and SCAD profiles in a referred population. *Psychology in the Schools*, 32, 267–76.

Wechsler, D. (1991). *Manual for the Wechsler Intelligence Scale for Children–Revised*. San Antonio, TX: The Psychological Corporation.

Wechsler, D. (1997a). *WAIS-III Administration and Scoring Manual*. San Antonio, TX: The Psychological Corporation.

Wechsler, D. (1997b). *WAIS-III/WMS-III Technical Manual*. San Antonio, TX: The Psychological Corporation.

Part II

Alternative Cognitive Approaches to Learning Disabilities Assessment and Remediation

3

Application of the Woodcock–Johnson Tests of Cognitive Ability–Revised to the diagnosis of learning disabilities

Nancy Mather and Richard W. Woodcock

The WJ–R is based on a philosophy that the primary purpose of testing should be to find out more about the problem, not to determine an IQ   (Woodcock, 1997a).

The primary objective underlying the development of the tests described in this chapter was to provide clinicians with better and more comprehensive procedures for investigating problems of cognition and learning. The Woodcock–Johnson Tests of Cognitive Ability–Revised (WJ–R COG) (Woodcock & Johnson, 1989) approaches this goal in two ways. First, the WJ–R COG provides a broader array of information about factors that may be related to learning problems than is available through the use of any other single instrument. Second, certain interpretive procedures are especially useful for evaluating the significance and implications of obtained information. Because of these unique features, both the 1977 (Woodcock & Johnson, 1977) and the 1989 WJ–R have been widely used in school and clinical settings for the diagnosis of learning and reading disabilities (Ostertag & Baker, 1984; Dalke, 1988; Cuenin, 1990; Lewis, 1990).

The WJ–R COG is a wide-age-range, comprehensive set of individually administered tests for measuring cognitive abilities, scholastic aptitudes, and oral language that is complemented by the fully co-normed Woodcock–Johnson Tests of Achievement–Revised (WJ–R ACH) (Woodcock & Johnson, 1989). The WJ–R ACH measures important aspects of reading, mathematics, written language, and three areas of academic knowledge (science, social studies, and humanities). The WJ–R ACH has two forms that are matched in content: Form A and Form B. Both the WJ–R COG and WJ–R ACH have direct Spanish language counterparts, the Batería–R COG and the Batería–R ACH (Woodcock & Muñoz-Sandoval, 1996a, 1996b), which contain all of the same tests and interpretive features. A somewhat more compact version of these batteries is the Woodcock Diagnostic Reading Battery (Woodcock, 1997b), which contains the ten most useful WJ–R tests for the diagnosis of reading disorders. The WDRB draws the four reading achievement tests from the WJ–R ACH and six tests from the WJ–R COG. Among the cognitive tests are two measures of phonemic awareness, two measures of oral comprehension, a test of short-term memory, and a test of cognitive processing speed.

Another important feature of these batteries is that they measure intellectual ability and achievement from age 24 months to over 90 years. Special norms are provided for the college/university population. In addition, a computer program designed to assist with writing interpretive reports, Woodcock Scoring & Interpretive Program (Schrank & Woodcock, 1997), includes automated scoring procedures, as well as producing a report based on information from any combination of factors, clusters, or tests. The report may be edited by the examiner in any way desired using a word processing program. Although the greatest advantage derives from using the WJ–R COG and WJ–R ACH together in an evaluation, the focus of this chapter is on the use of the WJ–R COG and the counterpart Batería–R COG.

This chapter begins with a review of the theoretical and clinical foundations of the WJ–R, including an overview of the Cattell–Horn–Carroll theory of cognitive abilities (CHC theory) and the Cognitive Performance Model. Then brief descriptions of the WJ–R COG and Batería–R tests and clusters are provided, as well as information about the technical features of these instruments. Next, the application of these instruments for the diagnosis of learning disabilities is discussed and two illustrative case studies are presented. In the final section, a brief overview of the new WJ III COG is provided (Woodcock, McGrew, & Mather, 2001).

Theoretical and clinical foundations

The original Woodcock–Johnson Tests of Cognitive Ability (WJ COG) (Woodcock & Johnson, 1977) presented a multi-factor approach to test interpretation. At the time of the 1977 publication, the interpretation of the Wechslers was based on a Verbal/Performance IQ dichotomy and the Stanford–Binet provided a single IQ score. The 1977 WJ moved beyond these unitary and dichotomized views of intelligence by presenting a four-factor (Gc, Gf, Gsm, and Gs) interpretive model. For the 1989 WJ–R COG, interpretation is enhanced by the measurement of seven factors that represent major components of human intellectual ability (Reschly, 1990; Ysseldyke, 1990; McGrew, 1994). Two additional factors (*Grw*, a reading/writing factor, and *Gq*, a quantitative ability factor) are measured by the WJ–R ACH. Thus, nine *Gf–Gc* abilities are measured across the WJ–R COG and WJ–R ACH. Table 3.1 lists these nine factors, provides a brief definition for each broad ability, and includes a statement of the possible implications of a deficit. The implications for academic performance are derived from studies that examined the relationships among *Gf–Gc* abilities and achievement across the lifespan (McGrew, 1993, 1994; McGrew & Hessler, 1995; McGrew & Flanagan, 1998).

Theoretical model

The theoretical basis for the WJ–R COG is founded in the CHC theory (Carroll & Horn, personal communication, July 1999). The work of Cattell and Horn is often referred to as *Gf–Gc* theory (Cattell, 1941; Horn, 1965, 1991; Horn & Noll, 1997). At an American Psychological Association conference in 1941, Cattell proposed that human abilities consisted of two types: fluid intelligence (*Gf*) and crystallized intelligence (*Gc*). Based on the research conducted in the last 30 or 40 years, this conceptualization has been expanded into a nine-factor or ten-factor ability structure.

This factor structure has been consistently replicated through the work of Horn, Carroll, and many others. Carroll's work is often referred to as three-stratum theory (Carroll, 1993, 1998), with Stratum III representing a general factor (*g*); Stratum II the broad abilities listed in Table 3.2 (see pp. 62–3); and Stratum I the many narrow abilities. This theory is viewed as dynamic, rather than static, and in the future will be subject to change, probably by the definition and inclusion of more factors (Woodcock, 1990).

One important feature of this theory is the distinction between broad and narrow abilities (i.e., Stratum II and Stratum I in Carroll's writing). Each of the broad abilities is measured by varied tasks, involving several narrower aspects of the ability. These narrow abilities represent finer differentiations of ability (Carroll, 1993). To measure verbal comprehension–knowledge (*Gc*), for example, one could include tests of vocabulary, knowledge of geology, general information, or even street-wiseness. Within individuals, the pattern of scores within the same broad ability may show patterns of strengths and weaknesses. For example, a person could be knowledgeable about geology, but not as knowledgeable about art.

Table 3.1. Description of nine *Gf–Gc* broad abilities

Gf–Gc ability	Description	Sample implications of deficits
Short-term Memory (*Gsm*) Memoria a corto plazo	The ability to hold information in immediate awareness and then use it within a few seconds, also related to working memory	Difficulty in remembering just-imparted instructions or information; easily overwhelmed by complex or multistep verbal directions
Processing Speed (*Gs*) Rapidez en el procesamiento	Speed and efficiency in performing automatic or very simple cognitive tasks	Slow in execution of easy cognitive tasks; slow acquisition of new material; tendency to become overwhelmed by complex events; need for extra time in responding to even well-practiced tasks
Comprehension– Knowledge (*Gc*) Comprensión– Conocimiento	The breadth and depth of knowledge including verbal communication, information, and reasoning when using previously learned procedures	Lack of information, language skills, and knowledge of procedures
Quantitative Ability (*Gq*) Habilidad cuantitativa	The ability to comprehend quantitative concepts and relationships; the facility to manipulate numerical symbols	Difficulty with arithmetic and other numerical tasks; poor at handling money and calculating change
Reading/Writing (*Grw*) Lectura/Escritura	An ability in areas common to both reading and writing; probably includes basic reading and writing skills, and the *skills* required for comprehension and expression (not yet well defined in the literature)	Difficulty with word attack, reading comprehension, or other basic reading skills; writing is inconsistent and characterized by errors of spelling and usage and of poor expression
Visual Processing (*Gv*) Procesamiento visual	Spatial orientation, the ability to analyze and synthesize visual stimuli, and the ability to hold and manipulate mental images	Poor spatial orientation; misperception of object–space relationships; difficulty with art and with using maps; tendency to miss subtle social and interpersonal cues

Table 3.1. (*cont.*)

Gf–Gc ability	Description	Sample implications of deficits
Auditory Processing (*Ga*) Procesamiento auditivo	The ability to discriminate, analyze, and synthesize auditory stimuli; also related to phonological awareness	Speech discrimination problems; poor phonological knowledge; failure to recognize sounds; increased likelihood of misunderstanding complex verbal instructions
Long-Term Retrieval (*Glr*) Recuperación a largo plazo	The ability to efficiently store information and retrieve it later	Difficulty in recalling relevant information and in learning and retrieving names; needs more practice and repetition to learn than peers; inconsistent in remembering previously learned material
Fluid Reasoning (*Gf*) Razonamiento fluido	The ability to reason and solve problems that often involve unfamiliar information or procedures; manifested in the reorganization, transformation, and extrapolation of information	Difficulty in grasping abstract concepts, generalizing rules, and seeing implications; has difficulty changing strategies if first approach does not work

Empirical support

A central feature of CHC theory is that it is not based on any particular test, but rather is derived from the statistical and logical analyses of hundreds of data sets from published and unpublished tests. Eight to ten broad abilities have been identified consistently through factor analyses. For example, Woodcock (1990) presented results from 15 sets of exploratory and confirmatory factor analyses that included a total of 68 variables. All analyses with these variables supported an eight-factor model of CHC theory. Furthermore, the factor structure that has been observed in clinical data also approximates the structure predicted by CHC theory (Woodcock, 1998a; Dean & Woodcock, 1999). The *Gf–Gc* taxonomy appears to be the most comprehensive and empirically supported psychometric framework available for understanding the structure of human cognitive abilities (McGrew & Flanagan, 1998).

The Cognitive Performance Model

The application of CHC theory, as the basis for interpreting the meaning and implications of test scores, can be enhanced by a simple dynamic model called the Cognitive Performance Model (CPM) (Woodcock, 1993, 1998b). The CPM (shown in Fig. 3.1) implies that the various *Gf–Gc* abilities are not autonomous, but fall into several functional categories. The level and quality of an individual's cognitive performance result from the interaction among these three types of cognitive factors: (a) stores of acquired knowledge, (b) thinking abilities, and (c) cognitive efficiency, plus various noncognitive factors known as facilitator-inhibitors.

The stores of acquired knowledge include both procedural and declarative knowledge. Thinking abilities are drawn upon when information cannot be processed automatically and must be processed with some level of intent. Cognitive efficiency factors include speed of processing and short-term memory, which are important prerequisites for smooth, automatic, cognitive processing. Facilitator-inhibitors represent noncognitive factors that impact cognitive performance for better or for worse, often overriding or mediating strengths and weaknesses among cognitive abilities. Facilitator-inhibitors include internal factors (e.g., health, emotional status, or persistence) and external factors (e.g., distractions in the environment or type of instruction). Experienced clinicians know that scores obtained from cognitive tests must be interpreted with caution, because the observed performance may be distorted by environmental and test situation variables. The CPM emphasizes the concept that both cognitive and noncognitive abilities interact to produce performance. In other words, good or poor cognitive performance is rarely the result of a single influence.

The CPM also provides a simple but useful description of certain relationships among the cognitive and achievement measures of the WJ–R COG and WJ–R ACH and is the model followed by the narrative report produced by the Woodcock Scoring & Interpretive Program (Schrank & Woodcock, 1997). Confirmatory factor analysis studies by Keith (1997) and Woodcock (1998b) provide some support for the organization of *Gf–Gc* abilities into the CPM.

Description and features of the WJ–R COG and Batería–R

The WJ–R COG and Batería–R measure the following seven intellectual abilities: Long-term Retrieval (*Glr*), Short-term Memory (*Gsm*), Processing Speed (*Gs*), Auditory Processing (*Ga*), Visual Processing (*Gv*), Comprehension–Knowledge (*Gc*), and Fluid Reasoning (*Gf*). Although somewhat different names may be used from one writer to another, the symbols or abbreviations following the name of each broad ability are similar to the notations found in the literature.

Tests

The WJ–R COG and the counterpart Batería–RCOG are composed of 21 tests. The Standard Battery consists of seven tests, each measuring a different *Gf–Gc* intellectual ability. The Supplemental Battery consists of 14 tests. Tests 8–14 provide another measure of each of the seven intellectual abilities. Tests 15–21 provide additional diagnostic measures. These measures may be used for more in-depth assessments or selectively when further evaluation of a particular factor of cognitive ability is desired. Table 3.2 presents a brief description of these tests.

Clusters

Clusters are the primary interpretive unit in the WJ–R. For the cluster scores, results from two or more tests are combined to provide a measure of a broad ability. The principle of cluster interpretation is that it minimizes the danger of generalizing from a single narrow aspect of behavior, such as oral expressive vocabulary, to a broader multifaceted ability, such as oral language. Clusters are more valid for prediction than individual tests, because they contain two or more qualitatively different indicators of the respective broader ability. This structure parallels the principle that clinical decisions should not be based on a single test measuring an important ability. All cluster score reliabilities are at .90 or higher. Table 3.3 presents a brief description of each WJ–R COG cluster.

Technical characteristics

In-depth information about the technical features of the WJ–R COG is presented in the WJ–R Technical Manual (McGrew, Werder, & Woodcock, 1989). For the purposes of this chapter, a brief discussion of the characteristics of the standardization sample, and a review of the developmental changes in cognitive abilities observed across the life-span are provided.

Standardization

Normative data are based on a single sample administered both cognitive and achievement tests. Over 100 geographically diverse communities were represented. These tests were nationally standardized on 6359 subjects, aged 24 months to 90+ years of age, and include a sample of college and university

Table 3.2. Description of the WJ–R COG tests

Test name	Ability measured
Standard Battery	
1. Memory for Names (*Glr*)	Ability to learn associations between unfamiliar auditory and visual stimuli (auditory–visual association)
2. Memory for Sentences (*Gsm*)	Ability immediately to recall meaningful phrases and sentences
3. Visual Matching (*Gs*)	Ability to locate and circle quickly two identical numbers in a series
4. Incomplete Words (*Ga*)	Ability to identify words with missing phonemes (auditory closure)
5. Visual Closure (*Gv*)	Ability to identify pictured objects that have missing parts, are altered by distortion, or have superimposed patterns
6. Picture Vocabulary (*Gc*)	Ability to name pictured objects
7. Analysis–Synthesis (*Gf*)	Ability to analyze an incomplete logic puzzle and determine the missing components
8. Visual–Auditory Learning (*Glr*)	Ability to pair novel visual symbols (rebuses) with familiar words and then translate the symbols into verbal phrases and sentences (visual–auditory association)
9. Memory for Words (*Gsm*)	Ability to repeat lists of unrelated words in correct sequence
10. Cross Out (*Gs*)	Ability to scan and compare geometric patterns quickly
11. Sound Blending (*Ga*)	Ability to synthesize orally presented syllables and/or phonemes into whole words
12. Picture Recognition (*Gv*)	Ability to recognize a subset of previously presented pictures within a field of distracting pictures
13. Oral Vocabulary (*Gc*)	Ability to state antonyms or synonyms for given words
14. Concept Formation (*Gf*)	Ability to examine a set of geometric figures and identify the rules when shown instances and non-instances of the concept
15. Delayed Recall–Memory for Names (*Glr*)	Ability to recall previously learned auditory–visual associations after 1–8 days
16. Delayed Recall–Visual–Auditory Learning (*Glr*)	Ability to recall names for previously learned visual–auditory associations after 1–8 days
17. Numbers Reversed (*Gsm*)	Ability to repeat a series of digits in reverse order
18. Sound Patterns (*Ga*)	Ability to determine whether or not complex sound patterns differ in pitch, rhythm, or sound content

Table 3.2. (*cont.*)

Test name	Ability measured
19. Spatial Relations (*Gv*)	Ability to select the component parts from a series of visual shapes that are needed to form a whole shape
20. Listening Comprehension (*Gc*)	Ability to listen to a short passage and supply a missing final word
21. Verbal Analogies (*Gf/Gc*)	Ability to complete analogies with words that indicate comprehension of the relationships

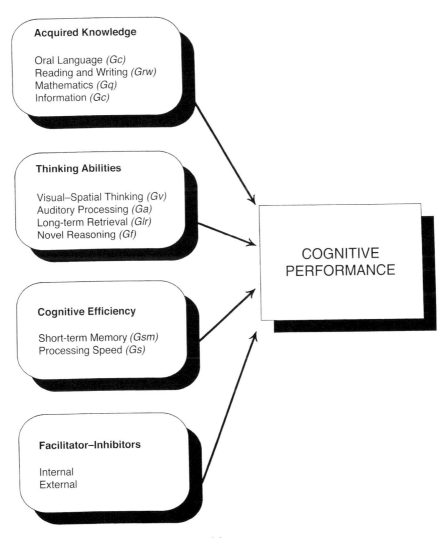

Fig. 3.1. *Gf–Gc* Cognitive Performance Model.

Table 3.3. Description of the WJ-R COG clusters

Cluster	Description
Broad Cognitive Ability (BCA)	
BCA–Early Development	A broad-based measure of intellectual ability appropriate for preschool children or individuals who are low functioning (Tests 1, 2, 4, 5, 6)
BCA–Standard Scale	A broad-based measure of intellectual ability appropriate for subjects at kindergarten level or above (Tests 1–7)
BCA–Extended Scale	A broad-based measure of intellectual ability appropriate for subjects at kindergarten level or above (Tests 1–14)
Cognitive factor clusters	
Long-Term Retrieval (*Glr*)	Effectiveness in storing and retrieving information by association over extended time periods (Tests 1, 8)
Short-Term Memory (*Gsm*)	Apprehension and use of information within a short period of time (Tests 2, 9)
Processing Speed (*Gs*)	Ability on clerical speed-type tasks, particularly under pressure to maintain focused attention (Tests 3, 10)
Auditory Processing (*Ga*)	Analysis and synthesis of auditory patterns and sounds (Tests 4, 11)
Visual Processing (*Gv*)	Perceiving non-linguistic visual patterns, spatial configurations, and visual details (Tests 5, 12)
Comprehension–Knowledge (*Gc*)	Breadth and depth of knowledge and its effective application, including language comprehension (Tests 6, 13)
Fluid Reasoning (*Gf*)	Capability for abstract reasoning in novel situations (Tests 7, 14)
Quantitative Ability (*Gq*)	Ability to comprehend quantitative concepts and relationships, skill in mentally manipulating numerical symbols (Tests 24, 25)
Oral language	
Oral Language	Broad-based receptive and expressive verbal ability (Tests 2, 6, 13, 20, 21)

Table 3.3. (*cont.*)

Cluster	Description
Aptitude clusters	
Reading Aptitude	Predicted reading performance based on the most relevant set of cognitive skills (Tests 2, 3, 11, 13)
Mathematics Aptitude	Predicted mathematics performance based on the most relevant set of cognitive skills (Tests 3, 7, 13, 14)
Written Language Aptitude	Predicted written language performance based on the most relevant set of cognitive skills (Tests 3, 8, 11, 13)
Knowledge Aptitude	Predicted acquired knowledge performance based on the most relevant set of cognitive skills (Tests 2, 5, 11, 14)
Oral Language Aptitude	Predicted oral language performance based on the nonverbal abilities most related to oral language proficiency (Tests 12, 14, 17, 18)

students. Both grade and age norms are available. One advantageous feature of the WJ–R is the use of continuous-year norms for school-age subjects, and year-by-year norms for adult subjects (ages 19–90+). Thus, scores can be compared to those of people of the same age or grade level, rather than to individuals grouped into broad time periods, such as twice during the year (e.g., Spring and Fall norms).

Although CHC theory is used throughout this chapter, an alternate way of classifying these tests can help a clinician determine which set of tests it may be most useful to administer based on the referral question. Four useful categorizations of tests that cut across *Gf–Gc* factors include tests of: (a) attention, (b) memory and learning, (c) language, and (d) reasoning and problem-solving. These categories have particular relevance to the assessment of learning disabilities as these disorders involve many different perceptual and cognitive–linguistic processes.

Tests of attention

In the past several decades, attention has evolved from its conceptualization as a unitary construct to a complex and multidimensional construct. As noted by Barkley (1994, p. 69):

Attention plays a critical role in the neuropsychological assessment of children with developmental, learning, or other neuropsychological problems because it underlies the very capacity of children to undergo any form of psychological testing. Without adequate attention by a child to the tests or tasks given by the examiner, the test results are open to considerable question as to their representativeness of that child's neuropsychological integrity.

Because so many children with learning disabilities also have attention deficit hyperactivity disorder (ADHD), and both of these disorders influence cognitive performance, the issue of comorbidity must be addressed (Fletcher, Shaywitz, & Shaywitz, 1994).

Although the WJ–R COG does not measure all important aspects of this construct, three aspects (selective attention, sustained attention, and attentional capacity) are measured by six WJ–R tests and listed in Table 3.4. Two tests, Visual Matching (*Gs*) and Cross Out (*Gs*), each with a three-minute time limit, require both selective and sustained attention. A third test, Writing Fluency, in the WJ–R ACH, probably requires sustained attention only. This test has a seven-minute time limit and is a factorially mixed measure of *Gs* and *Grw*. Three other WJ–R tests are measures of attentional capacity or the span of auditory short-term memory: Memory for Words (*Gsm*), Memory for Sentences (*Gsm, Gc*), and Numbers Reversed (*Gsm*).

Students with learning disabilities frequently display weaknesses in memory and speed of processing basic symbolic information (Meltzer, 1994). These deficits then interfere with academic performance. The skilled clinician will have to determine if weaknesses on these WJ–R COG tests are more indicative of ADHD, learning disabilities, or both.

Tests of memory and learning

Memory and learning tests constitute a rather broad category of tests in a traditional neuropsychological classification. At least three factorially distinct *Gf–Gc* abilities (*Gsm, Glr, Gc*) fall within this category. The clinical assessment of memory deficits typically involves evaluating the ability to learn and remember new material presented in both auditory and visual modalities. The adequacy of both short-term memory (or immediate recall) and long-term retention (or delayed recall) is typically assessed. Indices of remote memory may also be helpful with people of advanced age and other clinical populations. For individuals with learning disabilities, the interactions among various abilities (automaticity, cognitive flexibility, and working memory) are powerful predictors of

Table 3.4. WJ–R/BAT–R tests of attention

Test	Gf/Gc factor	Description
Sustained and Selective Attention		
3 Visual Matching *Pareo visual*	Gs	Measures the ability to quickly locate and circle the two identical numbers in a row of six numbers: task proceeds in difficulty from single-digit numbers to triple-digit numbers and has a 3-minute time limit
10 Cross Out *Tachar*	Gs	Measures the ability to quickly scan and compare visual information: subject must mark the five drawings in a row of 20 drawings that are identical to the first drawing in the row; examinee is given a 3-minute time limit to complete as many rows of items as possible
Sustained Attention		
35 Writing Fluency *Fluidez en la redacción*	Gs, Grw	Measures the examinee's skill in formulating and writing simple sentences quickly; this subtest has a 7-minute time limit
Attentional Capacity		
9 Memory for Words *Memoria para palabras*	Gsm	Measures the ability to repeat lists of unrelated words in the correct sequence; words are presented by audio tape
2 Memory for Sentences *Memoria para frases*	Gsm, Gc	Measures the ability to remember and repeat simple words, phrases, and sentences presented auditorily by a tape player
17 Numbers Reversed *Inversión de números*	Gsm, Gf	Measures the ability to repeat a series of random numbers backward; number sequences are presented by audiotape; a measure of 'working memory'

Table 3.5. WJ–R/BAT–R tests of memory and learning

Test	Gf/Gc factor	Description
Short-Term Memory		
9 Memory for Words *Memoria para palabras*	Gsm	Measures the ability to repeat lists of unrelated words in the correct sequence; words are presented by audio tape
2 Memory for Sentences *Memoria para frases*	Gsm, Gc	Measures the ability to remember and repeat simple words, phrases, and sentences presented auditorily by a tape player
17 Numbers Reversed *Inversión de números*	Gsm, Gf	Measures the ability to repeat a series of random numbers backward; number sequences are presented by audiotape; a measure of 'working memory'
12 Picture Recognition *Reconocimento de dibujos*	Gv, Glr	Measures the ability to recognize a subset of previously presented pictures within a larger set of pictures
Long-Term Retrieval		
1 Memory for Names *Memoria para nombres*	Glr	Measures the ability to learn associations between unfamiliar auditory and visual stimuli (an auditory–visual association task): task requires learning the names of a series of space creatures
8 Visual–Auditory Learning *Aprendizaje visual–auditivo*	Glr	Measures the ability to associate new visual symbols (rebuses) with familiar words in oral language and to translate a series of symbols presented as a reading passage (a visual–auditory association task)
15 Delayed Recall–Memory for Names *Memoria diferida–Memoria para nombres*	Glr	Measures the ability to recall (after 1–8 days) the space creatures presented in Memory for Names

Table 3.5. (*cont.*)

Test	Gf/Gc factor	Description
Delayed Recall–Visual–Auditory Learning *Memoria diferida–Aprendizage visual–auditivo*	Glr	Measures the ability to recall (after 1–8 days) the symbols (rebuses) presented in Visual–Auditory Learning
Remote Memory		
28 Science *Ciencia*	Gc	Measures the subject's knowledge in various areas of the biological and physical sciences
29 Social Studies *Estudios sociales*	Gc	Measures the subject's knowledge of history, geography, government, economics, and other aspects of social studies
30 Humanities *Humanidades*	Gc	Measures the subject's knowledge in various areas of art, music, and literature

academic performance (Meltzer, 1994). Eleven WJ–R tests are identified in Table 3.5 as good measures of some aspect of memory or learning.

Tests of auditory short-term memory include Memory for Words (*Gsm*), Memory for Sentences (a mixed measure of *Gsm* and *Gc*), and Numbers Reversed (*Gsm*). Numbers Reversed may also be interpreted as a measure of working memory. Picture Recognition (*Gv*) is included in Table 3.6 as it is an indicator of immediate visual recall. The next four tests in Table 3.6 are measures of new learning, long-term retrieval, or associational memory. Memory for Names (*Glr*) is an auditory–visual association learning task, and the next test, Visual–Auditory Learning (*Glr*), is a visual–auditory association learning task. Both tests require learning new associations, with corrective feedback provided whenever the examinee makes an error. A delayed recall version exists for each of these two tests based upon the ability to recall, from one to eight days later, the newly learned associations: Delayed Recall–Memory for Names (*Glr*) and Delayed Recall–Visual–Auditory Learning (*Glr*). The WJ–R

Table 3.6. WJ–R/BAT–R tests of oral language

Test		*Gf/Gc* factor	Description
6	Picture Vocabulary *Vocabulario sobre dibujos*	*Gc*	Measures the ability to name familiar and unfamiliar pictured objects
13	Oral Vocabulary *Vocabulario oral*	*Gc*	Measures knowledge of word meanings: in Part A: Synonyms, the examinee must say a word similar in meaning to the word presented; in Part B: Antonyms, the examinee must say a word that is opposite in meaning to the word presented
2	Memory for Sentences *Memorial para frases*	*Gc, Gsm*	Measures the ability to remember and repeat simple words, phrases, and sentences presented auditorily by a tape player
20	Listening Comprehension *Comprensión de oraciones*	*Gc*	Measures the ability to listen to a short tape-recorded passage and to verbally supply the single word missing at the end of the passage
21	Verbal Analogies *Analogías verbales*	*Gc, Gf*	Measures the ability to complete phrases with words that indicate appropriate analogies; although the vocabulary remains relatively simple, the relationships among the words become increasingly complex

delayed recall tests are among the few clinical memory tests that include standardized and normed delay procedures extending more than 24 hours after initial administration.

Tests of language

The ability to communicate through language is typically assessed by examining both receptive and expressive abilities. As noted, the WJ–R and Batería–R have parallel tests in English and Spanish. This feature allows the clinician to explore issues in regard to language development in both languages, which can help clarify whether or not learning difficulties may be attributed to second language acquisition, as opposed to intrinsic learning problems.

One important aspect of a learning disability evaluation is to distinguish between children whose problems are specific to one or more cognitive domains and those whose problems result from a more pervasive impairment in language skills (which may be more appropriately classified as an oral language disorder: Fletcher et al., 1998). The three broad divisions of language are oral language, reading, and writing. A commonly proposed discrepancy model is a comparison of oral language abilities with reading or writing achievement (Stanovich, 1991a, 1991b). Although there are limitations to this type of procedure as well, many individuals with specific reading and writing impairments have a discrepancy between oral and written language competencies.

The oral language tests are in the WJ–R COG, whereas the reading and writing tests are in the WJ–R ACH. The spectrum of oral language tasks included in the WJ–R ranges from the naming of pictures to verbal reasoning. The five oral language tests listed in Table 3.6 include: Picture Vocabulary (*Gc*), Oral Vocabulary (*Gc*), Memory for Sentences (*Gsm*/*Gc*), Listening Comprehension (*Gc*), and Verbal Analogies (*Gc*/*Gf*).

The four reading tests measure a spectrum of reading abilities from identifying letters and words in isolation to comprehension of written text. The tests are Letter–Word Identification (*Grw*), Word Attack (*Grw*/*Ga*), Reading Vocabulary (*Grw*/*Gc*), and Passage Comprehension (*Grw*). The four tests of writing ability include Dictation (*Grw*), Proofing (*Grw*), Writing Fluency (*Grw*/*Gs*), and Writing Samples (*Grw*).

Tests of reasoning and problem-solving

Problem-solving, or the ability to arrive at solutions in novel and unpracticed situations, involves a complex set of cognitive processes. Some students with learning disabilities have been observed to be inflexible and inefficient in their application of problem-solving strategies (Meltzer, 1991). Abstract thinking and adequate concept formation are required to formulate flexible ideas and strategies and to apply them across a variety of situations. These types of tasks are likely to be more related to academic tasks requiring problem-solving (e.g., reading comprehension) than to those requiring automaticity and efficiency (e.g., basic reading skills). Meltzer (1994) summarized several studies that compared students with learning disabilities to students without such difficulties. For the students with learning disabilities, problem-solving tasks that assessed pattern analysis were the second most important variable for predicting reading comprehension (automatic memory for sight vocabulary was first), as well as math performance (rapid and automatic computation was first).

Table 3.7 lists the tests in the WJ–R COG and WJ–R ACH that measure aspects of reasoning and problem-solving. Two tests are strong measures of abstract reasoning: Analysis-Synthesis (*Gf*) and Concept Formation (*Gf*). Three other tests also measure reasoning, though factorially mixed with other cognitive abilities: Verbal Analogies (*Gc/Gf*), Spatial Relations (*Gv*), and Numbers Reversed (*Gsm*). Carroll (1993) specifies quantitative reasoning as another aspect of reasoning. The only WJ–R ACH test that may be considered a measure of quantitative reasoning is Applied Problems (*Gq*).

Application of the WJ–R and Batería–R to the diagnosis and treatment of learning disabilities

Past research in the field of learning disabilities has often focused upon neuropsychological and information-processing models (Torgesen, 1986). The purpose is to attempt to understand the specific factors that are affecting scholastic or vocational performance, and then to develop appropriate interventions. When viewed from the perspective of a neuropsychological paradigm, the goals of a learning disability and a neuropsychological assessment are similar: to document an individual's intact or preserved functions, as well as to identify the impaired functions or the underlying specificity of the disorder. Both types of assessments are designed to explore cognitive–linguistic processes. The purpose is to uncover the central processing abilities and deficits that predispose an individual to different patterns of social as well as academic learning difficulties (Rourke, 1994).

To uncover specific deficits, the clinician should investigate performance on a wide array of tasks. Rourke notes that a comprehensive neuropsychological assessment should sample tasks involving sensory, perceptual, attentional, linguistic, and problem-solving abilities. In addition, these tests should: (a) vary along a continuum of difficulty, ranging from quite simple to quite complex, (b) vary along dimensions of rote and novel requirements, and (c) vary from tasks that involve processing within one modality to those that involve the coordination of response requirements within several modalities. The WJ–R COG provides a collection of tests that addresses these three dimensions.

Analysis of WJ–R COG results can help practitioners to consider the relationships among abilities, explore how these abilities may affect scholastic performance, and develop a more comprehensive understanding of an individual's needs. As Scarborough (1991, pp. 38–9) so aptly explained:

Table 3.7. WJ–R/BAT–R tests of reasoning and problem-solving

Test		Gf/Gc factor	Description
7	Analysis–Synthesis *Análisis–Síntesis*	Gf	Measures the ability to analyze the components of an incomplete logic puzzle and to determine and name the missing components
14	Concept Formation *Formación de conceptos*	Gf	Measures the ability to identify and state the rule for a concept about a set of colored geometric figures when shown instances and noninstances of the concept
21	Verbal Analogies *Analogías verbales*	Gf, Gc	Measures the ability to complete phrases with words that indicate appropriate analogies; although the vocabulary remains relatively simple, the relationships among the words become increasingly complex
19	Spatial Relations *Relaciones espaciales*	Gf, Gv	Measures the ability to visually match and combine shapes; subject must select, from a series of shapes, the component parts composing a given whole shape
17	Numbers Reversed *Inversión de números*	Gf, Gsm	Measures the ability to repeat a series of random numbers backward; number sequences are presented by audio tape
25	Applied Problems *Problemas aplicados*	Gq	Measures the subject's skill in analyzing and solving practical problems in mathematics; subject must decide not only the appropriate mathematical operations to use but also which of the data to include in the calculation

... instead of casting the preschool characteristics of dyslexic children as 'precursors' and the reading problems of these children as 'outcomes,' it might be more helpful to view both as successive, observable symptoms of the same condition ... Therefore, while the education goal may be to explain reading disability for its own sake, the neuropsychological goal is to define the nature of the fundamental difficulty that manifests itself most evidently, but not solely, as underachievement in reading.

Table 3.8 illustrates the relative contributions of different cognitive abilities for predicting achievement in a simulated referral sample for Grades 1 to 12. All individuals from the normative sample with achievement standard scores below 90 were selected for this analysis. Different patterns of cognitive abilities are associated with poor performance in different areas of achievement. For example, *Ga* abilities show a strong relationship with basic reading but not with reading comprehension, which is highly related to *Gc*. Processing speed (*Gs*) is highly related to math skills but not to math applications, which is more highly related to *Gsm*, and *Gf. Glr* and *Gs* are highly related to written language skills. *Gc*, which is a measure of verbal ability, is highly related to performance in science, social studies, and humanities.

The only ability that does not show up in Table 3.8 as an important predictor of achievement deficits is *Gv*, visual–spatial thinking. This suggests that if the purpose of assessment is to investigate difficulties in school performance, these abilities generally will not be relevant. The table demonstrates again the critical importance of using a comprehensive battery when attempting to describe learning abilities and disabilities.

Neurological basis of learning disabilities

Although many children struggle to learn because of extrinsic factors (e.g., environmental), learning disabilities are believed to be an intrinsic disorder or specific neurological difference that inhibits various facets of performance. Throughout the century, learning disabilities have been associated with central nervous system dysfunctions and described as neurologically based phenomena that result in differences in perceptual, linguistic, and/or cognitive processing. In the 1980s, attempts were made to discredit the neurological roots of this disability, but new insights from cognitive research and advances in neuroimaging have revived the interest in and study of neuropsychological and information processing. For example, O'Donnell (1991) found that 42% of young adults with learning disabilities showed indications of mild cerebral dysfunction on neuropsychological test scores. (See Reitan and Wolfson's thorough discussion of O'Donnell's study in Chapter 10.)

A common premise of many definitions is that an individual with a learning

Table 3.8. Relative contributions of *Gf–Gc* abilities to predicting achievement in a simulated grade 1 to 12 referral sample

Standardized coefficients

Gf–Gc ability		Total Reading < 90 (n = 436)		Total Math < 90 (n = 460)		Total Written Language < 90 (n = 474)		Broad Knowledge < 90 (n = 488)
		Reading skills	Reading comprehension skills	Math skills	Math applications	Written language skills	Written language expression	
Acquired Knowledge								
Verbal Ability	Gc	—	.38**	.09	.14*	—	.15**	.49**
Thinking Abilities								
Visual–Spatial Thinking	Gv	—	—	—	—	—	—	.09*
Auditory Processing	Ga	.28**	—	.08	—	.14**	.12**	.12**
Long-Term Retrieval	Glr	—	—	.11*	.09	.20*	.14**	—
Fluid Reasoning	Gf	—	.11**	.09	.15**	—	—	—
Cognitive Efficiency								
Short-Term Memory	Gsm	.08	.13*	.08*	.20**	.09	—	.16**
Processing Speed	Gs	.15**	.14**	.21**	.11	.18**	.14**	.09*

*p < 0.05.
**p < 0.01.

disability has greater difficulty acquiring, applying, and retaining information than would be predicted from other information about the person (Bateman, 1992). Kirk (1978) stated: 'I like to define a learning disability as a psychological or neurological impediment to the development of adequate perceptual or communication behavior' (p. 617). In other words, children with learning difficulties have significant discrepancies in the development of their psychological processes (e.g., perception, attention, memory). For example, an individual with perceptually based learning disabilities may be successful on tasks that involve higher-order cognitive processes, such as language and reasoning, but have difficulty with tasks that involve lower-order processing, such as processing speed or short-term memory. These developmental disorders then contribute to domain-specific academic deficiencies. Thus, the person described above may have adequate comprehension of text, but a compromised reading rate. In addition, performance is likely to improve when listening to text, rather than reading.

Consult Shepherd (Chapter 1) for a historical analysis of Kirk's definition of specific learning disability in the context of alternate definitions. Also, for an extended discussion of the neurological bases of learning disabilities from a historical and research perspective, see Spreen (Chapter 9), and consult Reitan and Wolfson (Chapter 10) for a summary of neuropsychological research with individuals with specific learning disabilities.

Learning disabilities viewed as a disorder in basic cognitive processes

To diagnose learning disabilities accurately, it is important to differentiate between underachievement caused by neurological differences and that caused by other factors (Adelman, 1992). Although a discrepancy between ability and achievement may be present in an individual with a learning disability, it represents only one manifestation of the disability (i.e., underachievement) (Lewis, 1990), and should, therefore, not be used as the sole, or a necessary, diagnostic criterion (Fletcher et al., 1998; Mather & Healey, 1990). Although a significant cognitive deficit can contribute to the development of an aptitude–achievement discrepancy, a learning or reading disability should not be defined as a discrepancy between aptitude and achievement. To diagnose learning and reading disabilities accurately, the core concept of deficits in cognitive processes needs to be maintained (Torgesen, 1979). As Torgesen (1979, 1986) suggested, the learning disabilities field's problem with psychological processes arose because the idea was ahead of its time.

Although current legal requirements often control the assessment process within public schools in the USA, less restrictive definitions of learning disabilities include three premises: (a) learning disabilities are caused by disorders in processing information; (b) these processing deficits are a reflection of neurological, constitutional, and biological factors; and (c) the deficit depresses specific areas of cognitive and academic functioning (Swanson, 1991). Similarly, the assumption that underlies the concept of dyslexia is that a cognitive deficit exists that is reasonably specific to the reading task (Stanovich, 1991b). The 'garden-variety' poor reader (Gough & Tunmer, 1986) has a general cognitive delay or developmental lag, whereas a reader with a disability has a specific cognitive deficit that contributes to the reading problem but does not extend into all cognitive domains (Stanovich, 1988, 1991a, 1991b). This theme of specificity has permeated the history of the field. In describing 'word blindness' in children, Orton (1925) noted that difficulty memorizing symbols is an isolated disability, not the result of a general mental defect.

The common theme is that learning disabilities arise from a deficiency in basic cognitive processes, which in turn contribute to academic failure (Senf, 1978). These symbol-processing deficits are not maturational lags as they are also present in adults with low reading and spelling skills (Fraunheim & Heckerl, 1983; Read & Ruyter, 1985). In testing the basic literacy of 50 men, Read and Ruyter observed that disabilities resulted from deficits in perception, short-term memory, or analysis of speech. Learning disabilities result from intra-individual differences in patterns of cognition. A pattern of 'islands of excellence' within a 'sea' of disabilities can often have very important neuropsychological significance (Rourke et al., 1983).

Although the diagnosis is not as simple as looking at subtest scatter on a profile to document strengths and weaknesses, the tenet of a specific deficiency in basic cognitive processes is a fundamental concept of learning disabilities. In most instances, it is not the actual test scores that allow clinicians to understand the behaviors, but rather the information that is obtained from an in-depth analysis of the types of errors made by the individual (Morris, 1993).

In other words, the emphasis of a neuropsychological assessment is on a detailed evaluation of the ability structure of the child (Fletcher et al., 1995). Similarly, the goal of a learning disability assessment is to uncover the unique abilities and disabilities of an individual. The WJ–R COG provides information to help the practitioner understand elements of a person's perceptual, cognitive, and linguistic functioning. As noted by Rourke (1994), a comprehensive neuropsychological or learning disability assessment also includes information on what a person can do, as well as what he or she cannot do. In other words, a major goal of the assessment is to identify the areas in which the individual's abilities are intact. This information is critical for designing an appropriate treatment/intervention plan. The WJ–R discrepancy procedures are designed to reveal these intra-ability strengths and weaknesses.

Discrepancy Analysis

The WJ–R provides information on three types of discrepancy (Woodcock, 1984). Type 1, an aptitude–achievement discrepancy, reflects the amount of disparity between certain intellectual capabilities and actual academic performance. It is a unidirectional comparison, with cognitive abilities being used to predict achievement. On the WJ–R COG, the aptitude clusters are composed of the specific abilities that comprise the best predictor of performance. Type 2, an intracognitive discrepancy, is present within individuals who have specific cognitive strengths or weaknesses. For this procedure, an individual's performance on one cognitive factor is compared to his or her average performance on the other six cognitive factors. Analysis of intra-cognitive discrepancies can contribute to an appreciation of the types of tasks that will be easy or difficult for an individual (Woodcock & Mather, 1989). For example, a person with limited comprehension of oral language may struggle with tasks that involve reading comprehension and written expression, but be successful on tasks involving mathematical calculations. Type 3, an intra-achievement discrepancy, is present within individuals who have specific academic strengths and weaknesses. Both intracognitive and intra-achievement discrepancies are bi-directional; equal interest exists in the individual who has a strength in fluid reasoning but a weakness in short-term memory, and in the individual who has a strength in short-term memory, but a weakness in fluid reasoning.

Although each of these discrepancies is useful as part of a comprehensive learning disabilities assessment, an intracognitive discrepancy constitutes the primary disability, whereas the other two types of discrepancies, aptitude–achievement and intra-achievement, are considered to be secondary discrepancies that arise from the deficiencies within cognitive processes (Mather, 1993). Figure 3.2, adapted from Woodcock (1984), depicts the relationships among these three discrepancies.

Consider the following example, which illustrates the interactive relationships among the three types of discrepancies. Ann, a third-grade student, had a significant intracognitive weakness in auditory processing. Performance on all other cognitive factors was within the average range. Ann did not have a significant aptitude–achievement discrepancy in reading, given her cognitive abilities (including the weakness in auditory processing). Ann also had a significant intra-achievement discrepancy. Reading and writing performance were lower than performance in mathematics and acquired knowledge. This

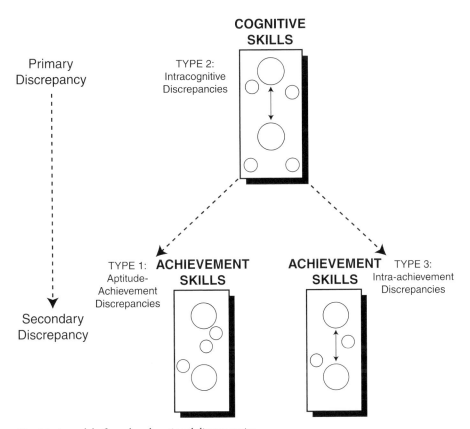

Fig. 3.2. A model of psychoeducational discrepancies.

would be expected because problems in phonological processing will have a greater impact on the development of literacy, rather than numeracy, skills. Even though Ann's reading ability was within the predicted range for others with similar cognitive abilities, the diagnostic question then becomes one of identifying the factors that have contributed to her poor reading performance by examining the cognitive abilities that underlie or support successful reading (e.g., phonological processing). In other words, the focus has shifted from reading ability *per se* to identification of the specific cognitive abilities that have interfered with the acquisition of reading skills. WJ–R COG results can help the clinician understand the factors affecting reading performance.

Part of the confusion has stemmed from the field's lack of clarity regarding use of the terms *category* and *diagnosis* (Mather & Healey, 1990). In the field of learning disabilities, the term 'learning disability' is often used incorrectly to subsume both the category of disability, as well as the presumed causative factor or the diagnosis. The categorical term is learning disability, but the diagnosis needs to be a description of a specific subtype or specific symptoms, such as poor short-term memory or phonological awareness. For the case of Dan, presented later in the chapter, one would say that he has a learning disability (the category) and that the subtype of learning disability performance is poor phonological awareness (the diagnosis). When the diagnosis is not as apparent, one would describe the specific characteristics observed.

Cognitive patterns by types of sample

The WJ–R COG may also be useful for differentiating among various clinical disorders. A pool of clinical data has been assembled for the purpose of documenting and validating neuropsychological applications. The subjects range in age from 6 to 81 years and have a variety of neuropsychological diagnoses, including learning disabilities, ADHD, language disorders, and central auditory processing disorders. Table 3.9 presents the results obtained on the clusters listed by standard score order for selected clinical groups.

Although differences in performance exist, an interesting and consistent pattern of low *Gs* and high *Gv* scores exists across all clinical subgroups. The results suggest that *Gs* scores may be particularly associated with learning disabilities and ADHD, whereas *Gv* abilities appear to be generally unaffected by these conditions (Woodcock, 1998a; Dean & Woodcock, 1999). Fletcher et al. (1995) found similar results when examining the profile performance in nine cognitive domains by three groups of children with reading disabilities. All three groups had particular difficulty on a phoneme deletion task, and moderate difficulties on tasks involving verbal memory, vocabulary, and rapid naming, but performed much better on tasks involving visual–spatial skills.

In addition, specific clinical groups are likely to exhibit different profiles on the WJ–R ACH. As a recent example, Marshall et al. (1999) found that students with ADHD scored lower on the Calculation test than they did on the Applied Problems test, regardless of subtype. When WJ–R ACH results are analyzed for selected clinical groups, different patterns of performance occur. For example, Dictation and Word Attack are two of the highest achievement scores in individuals with mild mental retardation, whereas they are the two lowest achievement scores for students with reading disabilities. Dalke (1988) also found that these two tests were the lowest when examining the profiles of college students with learning disabilities.

This type of information again documents the need to use a cognitive battery that measures the spectrum of abilities that may impact learning. If this spectrum of measurement is not available with a given battery, then an evaluator should supplement the instrument by selecting tests from other sources. This principle is known as *cross-battery assessment* and is most fully developed in the Intelligence Test Desk Reference (McGrew & Flanagan, 1998). Table 3.10 illustrates the breadth of measurement of *Gf–Gc* abilities provided by several commonly used cognitive batteries.

Illustrative case studies

When combined with assessment of academic performance, classroom observations, work samples, and other pertinent information, WJ–R COG results can help the evaluator determine the type and severity of learning disability and the individual's present cognitive status. In other words, WJ–R COG results can help an evaluator understand the manifestations and symptomatology of specific learning disabilities. Observed differences in cognitive processing may be most useful for characterizing different subtypes of learning disabilities (Fletcher et al., 1993).

Although somewhat atypical in the severity of the problem, as well as the circumspect nature of the disability, two illustrative cases with results from the intracognitive discrepancy procedure are provided (Mather, 1993).

Jon

Jon was enrolled in a private school for children with learning disabilities. Table 3.11 presents intracognitive discrepancy data for Jon as a fifth-grade student. When Jon's low performance on the Long-Term Retrieval factor is compared to his average performance on the other six cognitive factors, only 1 out of 1000 (Discrepancy Percentile Rank: 0.1) individuals would have a *Glr* score as low or lower. Conversely, when his high performance on the Fluid Reasoning factor is compared to the average of his other abilities, only 3 out of 1000 subjects (Discrepancy Percentile Rank: 99.7) would obtain a score as high or higher. In regard to academic performance, Jon was struggling with reading and writing tasks, but had high average performance in mathematics, as long as the tasks were not timed.

Error analysis provides additional support for the conclusion of good reasoning and language comprehension, but difficulty in performing learning tasks requiring associative memory, a *Glr* function. For example, Fig. 3.3 illustrates Jon's attempt to solve the following item on the WJ–R ACH Applied Problems test: 'Mr. Roberts lives in a large city. His job is in a suburb thirty-seven miles from his home. How many miles does he travel during a five-day work week driving only to and from his job?'

Jon began by setting up a problem of adding together five 37s. He

Table 3.9. *Gf–Gc* cluster score pattern by type of sample (age = 5–81 years)

Sample	n		BCA	Gf–Gc cluster by standard score order						
				1	2	3	4	5	6	7
Reference samples										
WJ–R norming	5470	Cluster: BCA		Gv	Gc	Gf	Ga	Gs	Glr	Gsm
sample		Mdn:	100	100	100	100	100	100	100	100
Total clinical		SD:	16	16	16	15	15	16	16	16
sample	1315	Cluster: BCA		Gs	Glr	Gc	Ga	Gf	Gsm	Gv
		Mdn:	90	87	91	92	93	93	94	98
Gifted		SD:	18	18	15	18	15	17	18	17
	84	Cluster: BCA		Gv	Gsm	Ga	Glr	Gf	Gs	Gc
		Mdn:	120	105	110	111	112	116	118	120
		SD:	11	13	15	13	16	11	14	13
Clinical samples										
Deficits in Acquired Knowledge										
Knowledge < 70	56	Cluster: BCA		Gc	Gf	Gs	Gsm	Glr	Ga	Gv
		Mdn:	56	58	65	68	70	72	73	76
		SD:	11	10	12	15	12	16	11	16
Math < 70	122	Cluster: BCA		Gs	Gc	Gf	Gsm	Glr	Ga	Gv
		Mdn:	64	68	68	72	77	78	80	82
		SD:	14	15	16	12	14	15	13	16
Oral Language < 70	63	Cluster: BCA		Gc	Gsm	Gf	Gs	Glr	Ga	Gv
		Mdn:	59	60	70	70	71	73	74	77
		SD:	10	10	11	11	12	12	11	15
Reading < 70	133	Cluster: BCA		Gc	Gs	Gsm	Gf	Glr	Ga	Gv
		Mdn:	66	69	72	75	76	77	82	89
		SD:	15	16	13	15	14	13	13	16
Written Language < 70	164	Cluster: BCA		Gs	Gc	Glr	Gsm	Gf	Ga	Gv
		Mdn:	70	75	76	78	78	80	83	89
		SD:	15	14	16	12	15	14	13	16
Anxiety Spectrum Disorders	100	Cluster: BCA		Gs	Glr	Ga	Gc	Gf	Gsm	Gv
		Mdn:	95	91	94	94	96	97	97	100
		SD:	16	17	15	15	17	16	16	15

Table 3.9. (*cont.*)

Sample	n	BCA		Gf–Gc cluster by standard score order						
				1	2	3	4	5	6	7
Attention Deficit/ Hyperactivity Disorders, Mixed	494	Cluster:	BCA	Gs	Glr	Ga	Gc	Gf	Gsm	Gv
		Mdn:	95	90	93	94	96	96	97	100
		SD:	16	17	14	14	16	15	17	15
Brain Tumors, Mixed	32	Cluster:	BCA	Gs	Gc	Glr	Gsm	Ga	Gf	Gv
		Mdn:	90	90	92	93	94	94	96	97
		SD:	15	20	17	12	14	11	14	16
Depressive Spectrum Disorder	150	Cluster:	BCA	Gs	Gc	Gf	Gsm	Glr	Gc	Gv
		Mdn:	95	92	94	96	96	97	98	100
		SD:	16	18	13	14	17	14	17	15
Impulsive/Disruptive Spectrum Disorders	73	Cluster:	BCA	Gs	Gc	Gf	Ga	Gsm	Glr	Gv
		Mdn:	87	86	87	91	90	92	94	98
		SD:	16	19	14	16	14	17	14	17
Language Disorders	48	Cluster:	BCA	Gsm	Gc	Ga	Gs	Gf	Glr	Gv
		Mdn:	78	81	82	82	84	86	88	100
		SD:	15	14	16	11	15	17	15	14
Learning Disorders, Mixed	484	Cluster:	BCA	Gs	Glr	Gc	Ga	Gf	Gsm	Gv
		Mdn:	88	86	89	91	92	93	93	98
		SD:	15	17	14	16	14	15	17	16
Mental Retardation, Mild to Profound	81	Cluster:	BCA	Gc	Gf	Gs	Gsm	Ga	Glr	Gv
		Mdn:	56	62	66	68	71	74	75	80
		SD:	13	12	13	16	13	13	15	17
Motor Impairment	52	Cluster:	BCA	Gs	Glr	Ga	Gf	Gv	Gsm	Gc
		Mdn:	93	90	90	95	96	96	101	102
		SD:	17	16	18	13	16	18	20	18

Key to cluster abbreviations: BCA = Broad Cognitive Ability; Gsm = Short-Term Memory; Gs = Processing Speed; Glr = Long-Term Retrieval; Gv = Visual Processing; Gc = Comprehension–Knowledge; Ga = Auditory Processing; Gf = Fluid Reasoning; Mdn = median; SD = standard deviation.

Table 3.10. *Gf–Gc* composites available in eight cognitive batteries[1]

Gf–Gc ability	WJ–R (1989)	CAS (1997)	DAS (1990)	K-ABC (1983)	KAIT (1993)	SB-IV (1986)	WAIS–III (1997)	WISC–III (1991)
							Cognitive battery	
Gsm	Short-Term Memory	Successive	—	Sequential Processing	—	Short-Term Memory (primarily *Gsm*, some *Gv*)	Working Memory (primarily *Gsm*, some *Gq*)	—
Gs	Processing Speed	Planning Attention	—	—	—	—	Processing Speed	Processing Speed
Gc	Comprehension–Knowledge	—	Verbal Ability	—	Crystallized Scale (primarily *Gc*, some *Grw*)	Verbal Reasoning	Verbal Comprehension	Verbal Comprehension
Gv	Visual Processing	—	Spatial Ability	Simultaneous Processing (primarily *Gv*, some *Gf*)	—	Abstract/Visual Reasoning (primarily *Gv*, some *Gf*)	Perceptual Organization (primarily *Gv*, some *Gf*)	Perceptual Organization (primarily *Gv*, some *Gc*)
Ga	Auditory Processing	—	—	—	—	—	—	—
Glr	Long-Term Retrieval	—	—	—	—	—	—	—

| Gf | Fluid Reasoning | — | Nonverbal Reasoning Ability | — | — | Quantitative Reasoning (primarily Gf, some Gq) | — | Freedom from Distractibility (mixed Gq and Gsm) |

Composites not included above due to mixture of Gf–Gc abilities that impact diagnostic utility

| — | Simultaneous (mixed Gv and Gf) | — | — | Fluid Scale (mixed Gv, Glr, and Gf) | — | — |

[1]Based in part on information from Keith (1997); McGrew & Flanagan (1998); and Woodcock (1990). WJ–R, Woodcock–Johnson Tests of Cognitive Ability–Revised; CAS, Das–Naglieri Cognitive Assessment System; DAS, Differential Ability Scales; K-ABC, Kaufman Assessment Battery for Children; KAIT, Kaufman Adult Intelligence Test; SB–IV, Stanford–Binet, Fourth Edition; WAIS–III, Wechsler Adult Intelligence Scale, Third Edition; WISC-III, Wechsler Intelligence Scale for Children, Third Edition.

Table 3.11. Discrepancy data for Jon

Intracognitive discrepancies	Actual SS	Predicted SS	PR[1]	SD[2] diff
Long-Term Retrieval (*Glr*)	59	100	0.1	−3.33
Short-Term Memory (*Gsm*)	104	92	82	0.92
Processing Speed (*Gs*)	81	97	12	−1.18
Auditory Processing (*Ga*)	99	93	69	0.49
Visual Processing (*Gv*)	100	95	64	0.37
Comprehension–Knowledge (*Gc*)	99	91	76	0.71
Fluid Reasoning (*Gf*)	120	87	99.7	2.80

[1]Discrepancy Percentile Rank (PR): this score represents the percentage of the population that has actual factor ability the same or lower, given the predicted factor ability.
[2]Diff: the difference between the subject's actual and predicted standard scores in units of the standard error of estimate, the appropriate standard deviation statistic for this application.
SS, standard score.

commented that after he added the five numbers, he would double the resulting sum. Jon first attempted to sequence count by sevens. After becoming confused twice, he crossed out these numbers and attempted a new strategy. Analysis of his solution to this problem illustrates systematic application of a strategy but poor retrieval of number facts.

Figure 3.4 illustrates several of Jon's responses from the WJ–R ACH Writing Samples tests. Both spelling and visual–motor difficulties may be observed. Jon commented that sometimes when he is writing, he forgets whether or not he has already started a word. From the assessment results, as well as the informal observations, Jon appears to be a student with average to above-average language comprehension (Oral Language standard score = 115), above-average reasoning abilities, but difficulty with tasks involving rote learning, such as multiplication facts and spelling. His difficulty with school tasks requiring rote learning appears to be related to his poor performance on associational learning tests.

Dan

Table 3.12 presents intracognitive discrepancy data for Dan, a beginning ninth-grade student. Dan had received learning disability services in a self-contained classroom since second grade. Upon transferring to a new high school, Dan was re-evaluated and determined to be ineligible for learning disability services because he no longer showed a significant aptitude–achieve-

TEST 25

Applied Problems Worksheet

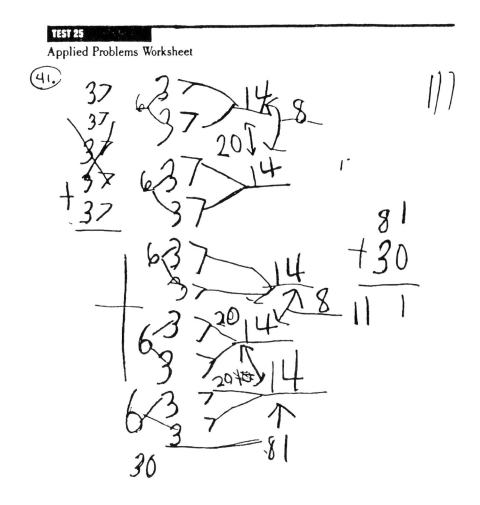

Fig. 3.3. Jon's response to Applied Problems, Form A, Item 41.

ment discrepancy between his Full Scale WISC–III score and his WJ–R Achievement cluster scores.

The nature and severity of Dan's problem with tasks involving phonological processing become apparent when analyzing WJ–R intracognitive discrepancy data. When the Auditory Processing factor (Incomplete Words, Sound Blending) is compared to his average performance on the other six factors, only 1 out of 1000 students would obtain a score as low or lower. Dan's deficit in phonological processing has interfered with his development and progress in both word pronunciation and spelling. Not surprisingly, Dan has failed

Fig. 3.4. Jon's responses on the Writing Sample Test, Form A.

Introductory Spanish twice. Wise and Olson (1991) provide a thorough review of research that suggests that phonological coding skills are the strongest predictor and correlate of reading disabilities, that they are uniquely deficient in most readers with disabilities, and that the deficit is highly heritable.

Although the cases of Jon and Dan are unusual in the severity of the impairment, analysis of their patterns of scores on the WJ–R COG yields information for both diagnostic and instructional purposes. As with the interpretation of any intra-individual differences, a practitioner would want to corroborate these findings with other data sources (McGrew & Flanagan, 1998).

Table 3.12. Discrepancy data for Dan

Intracognitive discrepancies	Actual SS	Predicted SS	PR[1]	SD[2] diff
Long-Term Retrieval (*Glr*)	98	91	72	0.59
Short-Term Memory (*Gsm*)	91	93	44	−0.16
Processing Speed (*Gs*)	109	91	92	1.38
Auditory Processing (*Ga*)	54	100	0.1	−3.54
Visual Processing (*Gv*)	109	91	92	1.38
Comprehension–Knowledge (*Gc*)	101	90	85	1.03
Fluid Reasoning (*Gf*)	95	92	60	0.24

For explanations of abbreviations, see Table 3.11.

Brief description of the new WJ III COG

The WJ III COG (Woodcock, McGrew, & Mather, 2001) will be a revised version of the WJ–R Tests of Cognitive Abilities (Woodcock & Johnson, 1989). Although many of the basic features have been retained, the extensive renorming, as well as several new tests, clusters, and interpretive procedures, improve and increase its diagnostic power as a tool for assessing learning disabilities. The WJ III COG organizational format and interpretive plan have been modified to increase both the breadth and depth of coverage.

Although the WJ III is similar in many respects, the cognitive factor structure has improved construct validity, with several new tests to ensure that each test in a cluster measures a qualitatively different narrow aspect of the broader ability. Other new tests were designed to better measure important information-processing abilities, such as working memory, planning, cognitive fluency, and attention, all of which are relevant to the assessment of learning disabilities. Table 3.13 depicts the tests included in the WJ III COG, as well as the new organizational format. Table 3.14 provides a brief description of the new tests.

The procedures for evaluating aptitude/achievement as well as intra-ability discrepancies have been expanded. In addition to the former intracognitive and intra-achievement procedures, a new intra-individual discrepancy procedure will have particular relevance to the assessment and diagnosis of learning disabilities. This procedure will allow the evaluator to examine simultaneously an individual's strengths and weaknesses across 30 clusters, both cognitive and academic. One new ability/achievement discrepancy procedure will be available in which Oral Language may be used as the measure of aptitude. This

Table 3.13. WJ III COG organization

Test	Standard battery	Extended battery
Verbal ability		
Verbal Comprehension–Knowledge (*Gc*)	1. Verbal Comprehension	11. General Information
Thinking abilities		
Long-Term Retrieval (*Glr*)	2. Visual–Auditory Learning	12. Retrieval Fluency
Visual Processing (*Gv*)	3. Spatial Relations	13. Picture Recognition
Auditory Processing (*Ga*)	4. Sound Blending	14. Auditory Attention
Fluid Reasoning (*Gf*)	5. Concept Formation	15. Analysis–Synthesis
Cognitive efficiency		
Processing Speed (*Gs*)	6. Visual Matching	16. Decision Speed
Short-Term Memory (*Gsm*)	7. Numbers Reversed	17. Memory for Words
Supplemental (*Ga, Gs, Gsm, Gf, Glr*)		
	8. Incomplete Words	18. Rapid Picture Naming
	9. Auditory Working Memory	19. Planning
	10. Visual–Auditory Learning–Delayed	20. Pair Cancellation

ability/achievement procedure may have particular relevance for helping clinicians to distinguish between individuals with adequate oral language capabilities, but poor reading and writing abilities (i.e., specific reading disabilities), versus individuals whose oral language abilities are commensurate with reading and writing performance. In the first case, intervention would focus on reading and writing development; in the second case, intervention would be directed to all aspects of language.

Conclusion

In most instances, a child is referred for a learning disability or a neuropsychological assessment because insufficient information is known about that child in order to develop a treatment plan (Rourke et al., 1983). When used in conjunction with other assessments, interviews, and observations, the WJ–R and the Batería–R are useful tools for helping practitioners determine the type and severity of a learning disability.

Table 3.14. Description of the new tests in the WJ III COG

Test	Description
Test 1: Verbal Comprehension (*Gc*)	Measures verbal ability through four tasks: the first requires naming pictured objects, the second requires providing synonyms, the third requires providing antonyms, and the fourth requires providing analogies
Test 8: Auditory Working Memory (*Gsm*)	Measures aspects of short-term auditory memory span and working memory: the task involves retaining two types of information (words and numbers) that are presented orally in a specified random order and then reordering that information sequentially
Test 12: Retrieval Fluency (*Glr*)	Measures an aspect of ideational fluency: the task measures the ability to list orally as many items as possible in each of three categories (things to eat or drink, first names of people, and animals) in 1 minute
Test 14: Auditory Attention (*Ga*)	Measures an aspect of auditory discrimination: the task measures the ability to differentiate among similar-sounding words with increasing levels of background noise (recorded)
Test 16: Decision Speed (*Gs*)	Measures an aspect of conceptual reasoning speed: the task measures the ability to scan a row of pictures and then circle the two drawings that are most related
Test 18: Rapid Picture Naming (*Gs*)	Measures aspects of lexical retrieval and fluency: the task requires the subject to name common objects rapidly
Test 19: Planning (*Gv, Gf*)	Measures an aspect of spatial scanning and planning: the task requires the subject to use forward thinking by planning a tracing route that covers as many segments of a visual pattern as possible without retracing or lifting the pencil
Test 20: Pair Cancellation (*Gs*)	Measures an aspect of sustained attention: the task measures the ability to scan and circle a repeated pattern in several rows of pictures

When conducting an assessment of learning disabilities, it is important to keep several factors in mind. The focus of the evaluation should be on determining how, or if, specific cognitive impairments are affecting school or vocational performance. Individuals with learning disabilities do not display a single, unitary pattern of neuropsychological assets and deficits (Rourke, 1994). In addition, when considering a comprehensive assessment of learning disabilities, it is important to integrate a perspective of learning disabilities as discrete processing deficits into broader paradigms that recognize that learning disabilities are heterogeneous, developmental, and comprise a multiplicity of interacting characteristics (Meltzer, 1994).When evaluated with diagnostic information from other sources, information from psychological assessments can contribute to an understanding of etiology, as well as to the design of effective instructional programs.

Individuals with learning disabilities vary significantly in regard to linguistic and cognitive characteristics. Tests that provide only a few broad-based scores ignore the significant research advances made over the last decade (Share, McGee, & Silva, 1991). Current notions of intelligence focus on multiple abilities where each type of intelligence represents specific abilities or processing capacities that are related to solving different types of problems (Fletcher et al., 1998). In order to assess these specific abilities or processing capacities, a clinician should use a battery that addresses these factors or move to the more complex alternative of cross-battery assessment.

REFERENCES

Adelman, H.S. (1992). LD: the next 25 years. *Journal of Learning Disabilities*, 25, 17–22.

Barkley, R.A. (1994). The assessment of attention in children. In *Frames of Reference for the Assessment of Learning Disabilities: New Views on Measurement Issues*, ed. G.R. Lyon, pp. 69–102. Baltimore, MD: Paul H. Brookes.

Bateman, B. (1992). Learning disabilities: the changing landscape. *Journal of Learning Disabilities*, 25, 29–36.

Carroll, J.B. (1993). *Human Cognitive Abilities: A Survey of Factor-Analytic Studies*. Cambridge: Cambridge University Press.

Carroll, J.B. (1998). Human cognitive abilities: a critique. In *Human Cognitive Abilities in Theory and Practice*, ed. J.J. McArdle & R.W. Woodcock, pp. 5–23. Mahwah, NJ: Erlbaum.

Cattell, R.B. (1941). Some theoretical issues in adult intelligence testing. *Psychological Bulletin*, 38, 592.

Cuenin, L.H. (1990). Use of the Woodcock–Johnson Psycho-Educational Battery with learning disabled adults. *Learning Disabilities Focus*, 5, 119–23.

Dalke, C. (1988). Woodcock–Johnson Psycho-Educational test battery profiles: a comparative study of college freshmen with and without learning disabilities. *Journal of Learning Disabilities*, 21, 567–70.

Dean, R.S. & Woodcock, R.W. (1999). *The WJ-R and the Batería-R in Neuropsychological Assessment*, Research Report Number 3. Itasca, IL: Riverside.

Fletcher, J.M., Francis, D.J., Rourke, B.P., Shaywitz, S.E., & Shaywitz, B.E. (1993). Classification of learning disabilities: relationships with other childhood disorders. In *Better Understanding Learning Disabilities: New Views from Research and their Implications for Education and Public*

Policies, ed. G.R. Lyon, D.B. Gray, J.F. Kavanagh, & N.A. Krasnegor, pp. 27–55. Baltimore, MD: Paul H. Brookes.

Fletcher, J.M., Francis, D.J., Shaywitz, S.E. et al. (1998). Intelligent testing and the discrepancy model for children with learning disabilities. *Learning Disabilities Research and Practice*, 13, 186–203.

Fletcher, J.M., Shaywitz, B.A., & Shaywitz, S.E. (1994). Attention as a process and as a disorder. In *Frames of Reference for the Assessment of Learning Disabilities: New Views on Measurement Issues*, ed. G.R. Lyon, pp. 103–16. Baltimore, MD: Paul H. Brookes.

Fletcher, J.M., Taylor, H.G., Levin, H.S., & Satz, P. (1995). Neuropsychological and intellectual assessment of children. In *Comprehensive Textbook of Psychiatry*, ed. H. Kaplan & B. Sadock, pp. 581–601. Baltimore, MD: Basic Books, Williams & Wilkins.

Fraunheim, J.G. & Heckerl, J.B. (1983). A longitudinal study of psychological and achievement test performance in severe dyslexic adults. *Journal of Learning Disabilities*, 16, 339–46.

Gough, P. & Tunmer, W. (1986). Decoding, reading, and reading disability. *Remedial and Special Education*, 7, 6–10.

Horn, J.L. (1965). Fluid and crystallized intelligence. Unpublished doctoral dissertation, University of Illinois, Urbana-Champaign.

Horn, J.L. (1991). Measurement of intellectual capabilities: a review of theory. In *WJ–R Technical Manual*, ed. K.S. McGrew, J.K. Werder, & R.W. Woodcock, pp. 267–300. Itasca, IL: Riverside.

Horn, J.L. & Noll, J. (1997). Human cognitive capabilities: *Gf–Gc* theory. In *Contemporary Intellectual Assessment: Theories, Tests, and Issues*, ed. D.P. Flanagan, J.L. Genshaft, & P.L. Harrison, pp. 53–91. New York: Guilford.

Keith, T.Z. (1997). Using confirmatory factor analysis to aid in understanding the constructs measured by intelligence tests. In *Contemporary Intellectual Assessment: Theories, Tests, and Issues*, ed. D.P. Flanagan, J.L. Genshaft, & P.L. Harrison, pp. 373–402. New York: Guilford.

Kirk, S.A. (1978). An interview with Samuel Kirk. *Academic Therapy*, 13, 617–20.

Lewis, R. (1990). Educational assessment of learning disabilities: a new generation of achievement measures. *Learning Disabilities: A Multidisciplinary Journal*, 1(2), 49–55.

Marshall, R.M., Schafer, V.A., O'Donnell, L., Elliott, J., & Handwerk, M.L. (1999). Arithmetic disabilities and ADD subtypes: implications for the DSM-IV. *Journal of Learning Disabilities*, 32, 239–47.

Mather, N. (1993). Critical issues in the assessment of learning disabilities addressed by the Woodcock–Johnson Psycho-Educational Battery–Revised. *Journal of Psychoeducational Assessment*. Monograph Series: Advances in psychoeducational assessment: Woodcock–Johnson Psycho-Educational Battery–Revised, pp. 103–22.

Mather, N. & Healey, W.C. (1990). Deposing aptitude–achievement discrepancy as the imperial criterion for learning disabilities. *Learning Disabilities: A Multidisciplinary Journal*, 1, 40–8.

McGrew, K.S. (1993). The relationship between the WJ–R *Gf–Gc* cognitive clusters and reading achievement across the lifespan. *Journal of Psychoeducational Assessment*. Monograph Series: Advances in psychoeducational assessment: Woodcock–Johnson Psycho-Educational Battery–Revised, pp. 39–53.

McGrew, K.S. (1994). *Clinical Interpretation of the Woodcock–Johnson Tests of Cognitive Ability–Revised*. Boston: Allyn and Bacon.

McGrew, K.S. & Flanagan, D.P. (1998). *The Intelligence Test Desk Reference (ITDR): Gf–Gc Cross-Battery Assessment*. Boston: Allyn and Bacon.

McGrew, K.S. & Hessler, G.L. (1995). The relationship between the WJ–R *Gf–Gc* cognitive clusters and mathematics achievement across the life-span. *Journal of Psychoeducational Assessment*, 13, 21–38.

McGrew, K.S., Werder, J.K., & Woodcock, R.W. (1989). *WJ–R Technical Manual*. Itasca, IL: Riverside.

Meltzer, L.J. (1991). Problem-solving strategies and academic performance in learning disabled students: do subtypes exist? In *Subtypes of Learning Disabilities*, ed. L.V. Feagans, F.J. Short, & L.J. Meltzer, pp. 163–88. Hillsdale, NJ: Lawrence Erlbaum Associates.

Meltzer, L.J. (1994). Assessment of learning disabilities: the challenge of evaluating cognitive strategies and processes underlying learning. In *Frames of Reference for the Assessment of Learning Disabilities: New Views on Measurement Issues*, ed. G.R. Lyon, pp. 571–606. Baltimore: Paul H. Brookes.

Morris, R. (1993). Issues in empirical versus clinical identification of learning disabilities. In *Better Understanding Learning Disabilities: New Views from Research and their Implications for Education and Public Policies*, ed. G.R. Lyon, D.B. Gray, J.F. Kavanagh, & N.A. Krasnegor, pp. 73–93. Baltimore, MD: Paul H. Brookes.

O'Donnell, J.P. (1991). Neuropsychological assessment of learning-disabled adolescents and young adults. In *Neuropsychological Foundations of Learning Disabilities: A Handbook of Issues, Methods, and Practice*, ed. J.E. Obrzut & G.W. Hynd, pp. 331–53. San Diego: Academic Press.

Orton, S.T. (1925). Word-blindness in school children. *Archives of Neurology and Psychiatry*, 14, 581–615.

Ostertag, B.A. & Baker, R.E. (1984). *A Follow-up of Learning Disabled Programs in California Community Colleges*. Sacramento, CA: Community College Chancellor's Office.

Read, C. & Ruyter, L. (1985). Reading and spelling skills in adults of low literacy. *Remedial and Special Education*, 6(6), 43–52.

Reschly, D.J. (1990). Found: our intelligences: what do they mean? *Journal of Psychoeducational Assessment*, 8, 259–67.

Rourke, B.P. (1994). Neuropsychological assessment of children with learning disabilities. In *Frames of Reference for the Assessment of Learning Disabilities: New Views on Measurement Issues*, ed. G.R. Lyon, pp. 475–514. Baltimore, MD: Paul H. Brookes.

Rourke, B.P., Bakker, D.J., Fisk, J.L., & Strang, J.D. (1983). *Child Neuropsychology: An Introduction to Theory, Research, and Clinical Practice*. New York: Guilford.

Scarborough, H.S. (1991). Antecedents to reading disability: preschool language development and literacy experiences of children from dyslexic families. In *Reading Disabilities: Genetic and Neurological Influences*, ed. B.F. Pennington, pp. 31–45. Dordrecht: Kluwer.

Schrank, F.A. & Woodcock, R.W. (1997). *Woodcock Scoring & Interpretive Program*. Itasca, IL: Riverside.

Senf, G.M. (1978). Implications of the final procedures for evaluating specific learning disabilities. *Journal of Learning Disabilities*, 11, 11–13.

Share, D.L., McGee, R., & Silva, P.A. (1991). The authors reply. *Journal of the American Academy of Child and Adolescent Psychiatry*, 30, 697.

Stanovich, K.E. (1988). Explaining the differences between the dyslexic and the garden-variety poor reader: the phonological-core-variable-difference model. *Journal of Learning Disabilities*, 21, 590–604, 612.

Stanovich, K.E. (1991a). Conceptual and empirical problems with discrepancy definitions of reading disability. *Learning Disability Quarterly*, 14, 269–80.

Stanovich, K. (1991b). Discrepancy definitions of reading disability: has intelligence led us astray? *Reading Research Quarterly*, 26, 7–29.

Swanson, H.L. (1991). Operational definitions and learning disabilities: an overview. *Learning Disability Quarterly*, 14, 242–54.

Torgesen, J.K. (1979). What shall we do with psychological processes? *Journal of Learning Disabilities*, 12, 514–21.

Torgesen, J.K. (1986). Learning disabilities theory: its current state and future prospects. *Journal of Learning Disabilities*, 19, 399–407.

Wise, B.W. & Olson, R.K. (1991). Remediating reading disabilities. In *Neuropsychological Foundations of Learning Disabilities: A Handbook of Issues, Methods, and Practice*, ed. J.E. Obrzut & G.W. Hynd, pp. 631–58. San Diego, CA: Academic Press.

Woodcock, R.W. (1984). A response to some questions raised about the Woodcock–Johnson. *School Psychology Review*, 13, 355–62.

Woodcock, R.W. (1990). Theoretical foundations of the WJ-R measures of cognitive ability. *Journal of Psychoeducational Assessment*, 8, 231–58.

Woodcock, R.W. (1993). An information processing view of *Gf–Gc* theory. *Journal of Psychoeducational Assessment*. Monograph Series: Advances in psychoeducational assessment: Woodcock–Johnson Psycho-Educational Battery–Revised, pp. 80–102.

Woodcock, R.W. (1997a). The Woodcock–Johnson Tests of Cognitive Ability–Revised. In *Contemporary Intellectual Assessment: Theories, Tests, and Issues*, ed. D.P. Flanagan, J.L. Genshaft, & P.L. Harrison, pp. 230–46. New York: Guilford Press.

Woodcock, R.W. (1997b). *Woodcock Diagnostic Reading Battery*. Itasca, IL: Riverside.

Woodcock, R.W. (1998a). *The WJ-R and Batería-R in Neuropsychological Assessment*, Research Report 1. Itasca, IL: Riverside.

Woodcock, R.W. (1998b). Extending *Gf–Gc* theory into practice. In *Human Cognitive Abilities in Theory and Practice*, ed. J.J. McArdle & R.W. Woodcock, pp. 137–56. Mahwah, NJ: Erlbaum.

Woodcock, R.W. & Johnson, M.B. (1977). *Woodcock–Johnson Psycho-Educational Battery*. Allen, TX: DLM.

Woodcock, R.W. & Johnson, M.B. (1989). *Woodcock–Johnson Psycho-Educational Battery–Revised*. Itasca, IL: Riverside.

Woodcock, R.W. & Mather, N. (1989). WJ-R Tests of Achievement: examiner's manual. In *Woodcock–Johnson Psycho-Educational Battery–Revised*, ed. R.W. Woodcock & M.B. Johnson. Itasca, IL: Riverside.

Woodcock, R.W., McGrew, K.S., & Mather, N. (2001). *Woodcock–Johnson Tests of Cognitive Abilities, III*. Itasca, IL: Riverside.

Woodcock, R.W. & Muñoz-Sandoval, A.F. (1996a). *Batería Woodcock–Muñoz: Pruebas de aprovechamiento–Revisada*. Itasca, IL: Riverside.

Woodcock, R.W. & Muñoz-Sandoval, A.F. (1996b). *Batería Woodcock–Muñoz: Pruebas de habilidad cognitiva–Revisada*. Itasca, IL: Riverside.

Ysseldyke, J.E. (1990).Goodness of fit of the Woodcock–Johnson Psycho-Educational Battery–Revised to the Horn–Cattell *Gf–Gc* theory. *Journal of Psychoeducational Assessment*, 8, 268–75.

4

The Kaufman tests – K-ABC and KAIT

Elizabeth O. Lichtenberger

This chapter provides a context in which to understand how two instruments developed by Alan and Nadeen Kaufman may be utilized in the diagnosis and treatment of learning disabilities. The theoretical underpinnings of both of the measures are described, as well as the process of their development and standardization. To clarify how these instruments may be applied to the diagnosis and treatment of learning disabilities, case studies are presented. The Kaufman Assessment Battery for Children (K-ABC, Kaufman & Kaufman, 1983) and the Kaufman Adolescent and Adult Intelligence Test (KAIT; Kaufman & Kaufman, 1993) are the two featured intelligence tests.

History, development, and goals of the K-ABC and KAIT

In development of their two tests of intelligence, the K-ABC and the KAIT, the Kaufmans stepped away from the common conception of intelligence as an overall global entity (known as *g*). Both of the batteries were developed with the intention of improving upon existing individually administered tests of intelligence. Unlike the Wechsler tests, both the K-ABC and the KAIT were developed on the basis of neuropsychological theories and theories of cognitive psychology, as well as on the basis of available research.

K-ABC theory and development

The K-ABC is based on a theory of sequential and simultaneous information processing. This theoretical perspective focuses on *how* children solve problems rather than *what type* of problems they must solve (e.g., verbal or nonverbal). An updated version of a variety of theories provides the framework for the sequential and simultaneous processing model that underlies the K-ABC (Kamphaus et al., 1995). Both the information-processing approach of Luria (1966) and the cerebral specialization theory of Sperry (1968, 1974), Bogen (1975), Kinsbourne (1978), and Wada, Clarke, and Hamm (1975) provide the theoretical and experimental foundation for the sequential and simultaneous framework.

The observations of those such as Alexander Luria (1966, 1973) and Roger

Sperry (1968), coupled with the psychoeducational research of J.P. Das (1973; Das, Kirby, & Jarman, 1975, 1979; Naglieri & Das, 1988, 1990) and Nadeen and Alan Kaufman's psychometric research (1983) supply the origins of the neuropsychological processing model. The strengths of the neuropsychological processing model include the following: (1) it provides a unified framework for interpreting a wide range of important individual difference variables; (2) it rests on a well-researched theoretical base in clinical neuropsychology and psychobiology; (3) it presents a processing, rather than a product-oriented, explanation for behavior; and (4) it lends itself readily to remedial strategies based on relatively uncomplicated assessment procedures (Kaufman & Kaufman, 1983; McCallum & Merritt, 1983; Perlman, 1986).

Individuals utilize two distinct types of processes to organize and process information, according to the neuropsychological processing model. One of these types of processes is successive or sequential and the other type is holistic or simultaneous processing (Levy & Trevarthen, 1976; Luria, 1966). These two processes are similar to the problem-solving strategies of the right hemisphere of the brain (gestalt–holistic) and the left hemisphere (analytic–sequential) (Sperry, 1968). These processes are also represented in Luria's (1966) theory as 'coding' processes – part of the 'Block 2' functions.

With all of these theoretical models taken together, when individuals process information using a sequential or serial order, they are using successive processing. In processing information in this manner, the total system, or the 'big picture,' is not available at any one point in time. In contrast, when individuals process information by synthesizing separate elements into groups, they are using simultaneous processing. Using a simultaneous mode to process information, any part of the result may be looked at individually without dependence on its position in the whole. An assumption of these two types of processing is that they are both available to an individual; they are not mutually exclusive. At any given time, individuals may use successive or simultaneous processing depending on the demands of the task and what their habitual mode of processing is (Das et al., 1979). It is thought that an individual's habitual mode of processing is determined by sociocultural and genetic factors (Das et al., 1979).

In applying the sequential and simultaneous processing model to the scales of the K-ABC, simultaneous processing refers to the ability to mentally integrate information all at once to solve a problem. Spatial, analogic, or organizational abilities are commonly used in simultaneous processing (Kaufman & Kaufman, 1983; Kamphaus & Reynolds, 1987). On tasks requiring simultaneous processing, there is often a visual aspect to the problem, requiring visual imagery to solve it. A K-ABC subtest that exemplifies the simultaneous process-ing mode is Triangles. Like the Block Design subtest of Wechsler's tests, in Triangles a child must see the entire design in his or her mind and integrate the individual pieces to form the whole.

The other mental processing scales on the K-ABC are the Sequential Process-ing scales. These scales emphasize the ability to arrange stimuli in sequential or serial order. There is a linear or temporal relationship between each of the stimuli, which creates a form of serial interdependence within the stimulus (Kaufman & Kaufman, 1983). The subtests of the K-ABC assess sequential abilities via many modalities. For example, some subtests require visual input and a motor response (Hand Movements), others involve auditory input and a vocal response (Number Recall), while others involve auditory input and a simple motor response (Word Order). Because different modes of input and output are utilized in the Sequential Processing subtests of the K-ABC, the examiner can assess sequential abilities in many different ways.

One of the ways in which the K-ABC is dramatically different from existing tests of intelligence, such as the Wechsler scales, is that its mental processing subtests do not include subtests found on the Verbal Scale of the WISC–III (Wechsler, 1991) or on similar tests of intelligence. Instead, an Achievement scale of the K-ABC was developed by Kaufman and Kaufman (1983) that includes subtests that require children to assimilate information from their cultural and school environment. The K-ABC thereby distinguishes problem-solving tasks from those that require knowledge and facts. On many other IQ tests, an individual's acquired factual knowledge and applied skills greatly affect the obtained IQ; however, in the development of the K-ABC, these skills were kept separate from tasks that measure IQ (Kaufman & Kaufman, 1983).

KAIT theory and development

The KAIT is based on the theory of Horn and Cattell (1966), but other theories also guided the development of the KAIT. Piaget's theory of formal operations (Inhelder & Piaget, 1958; Piaget, 1972) and Luria's model of planning ability (Luria, 1973, 1980) helped in the development of high-level, decision-making tasks for adults on the KAIT. The notion of planning ability, as described by Luria (1980), involves decision making, evaluation of hypotheses, and flexibil-ity. Planning ability is associated with the tertiary areas of the prefrontal region of the brain and represents the 'highest levels of development of the mam-malian brain' (Golden, 1981, p. 285).

The formal operations concept described by Piaget also depicts a hypotheti-cal–deductive abstract-reasoning system. This system is capable of generating and evaluating hypotheses through the testing of propositions. Formal operational thought is believed to emerge around ages 11 to 12 (Piaget, 1972), which is approximately the same time that the prefrontal areas of the brain (associated with planning ability) mature (Golden, 1981). The theories of Luria and Piaget seem to converge with respect to the ability of individuals to deal with abstraction. This convergence provided the rationale for the KAIT's lower age boundary being set at age 11 and for attempting to measure decision making and abstract thinking with virtually every task on the test (Kaufman & Kaufman, 1993).

Although the theories of Luria and Piaget were instrumental in the development of many of the KAIT's tasks, Kaufman and Kaufman (1993) relied on the Horn–Cattell theory for organizing and interpreting their test. The Horn–Cattell model distinguishes fluid from crystallized intelligence. Fluid intelligence (Gf) refers to novel tasks that tap problem-solving and the ability to learn. Crystallized intelligence (Gc) involves acquired skills, knowledge, and judgments that have been systematically taught or learned through acculturation. Gc often reflects cultural assimilation and is influenced by formal education. Although there are 'purer' versions of Gf and Gc in Horn's expanded and refined version of the Horn–Cattell fluid–crystallized theory (Horn, 1989; Horn & Hofer, 1992), the KAIT does not utilize these 'pure' abilities that are measured by the expanded and refined Horn theory. Rather, the KAIT subtests attempt to measure the complex nature of adult intelligence, which the Kaufmans believe calls for a small number of clinically useful scales rather than many specific scales (Kaufman & Kaufman, 1997a). Thus, in the KAIT, some of the Crystallized subtests also have a Gf component, and some of the Fluid subtests also require memory processes (e.g., Horn's short-term apprehension and retrieval; SAR). Combining some of these processes allows the subtests to measure complex cognitive processes, rather than simple ones.

It is important to note that the crystallized–fluid construct split is not the same as the verbal–nonverbal split on Wechsler's (1974, 1981, 1991) scales. Although the Crystallized subtests of the KAIT seem to measure the same ability as the Wechsler Verbal IQ, the KAIT's Fluid IQ does not correspond well to the Wechsler Performance IQ. The evidence for the dissociation between scales comes from a factor analytic study using the WISC–R, WAIS–R and KAIT subtests (Kaufman & Kaufman, 1993). In a sample of 118 people administered the KAIT and WISC–R and 338 people administered the KAIT and WAIS–R, the exploratory and confirmatory factor analyses were examined. Kaufman and Kaufman (1993) reported that the KAIT Crystallized and Wechsler Verbal subtests loaded on the same factor, but the KAIT Fluid subtests and the Wechsler Performance subtests for the most part loaded on separate factors. The KAIT Memory for Block Designs subtest loaded on the Perceptual Organization factor as well as the Fluid factor, which is understandable given the visual–spatial coordination needed for this Fluid subtest. The Wechsler Arithmetic subtest also loaded meaningfully on the Fluid factor, which, too, is understandable as it emphasizes reasoning (a component of Gf). The dissociation between the KAIT Fluid subtests and the Wechsler Performance subtests is not surprising given that the KAIT subtests minimize the role played by visual–spatial ability and visual–motor speed for correct responding, but they stress reasoning and verbal comprehension.

Description of the K-ABC and KAIT

Structure of the K-ABC

The K-ABC is a battery of tests designed to measure the intelligence of children aged $2\frac{1}{2}$ to $12\frac{1}{2}$. It yields scores on four scales: Sequential Processing, Simultaneous Processing, Mental Processing Composite (Sequential and Simultaneous together), and Achievement. An additional Nonverbal Scale score comprised of portions of the Sequential and Simultaneous Processing scales may also be obtained. Each of the scales yields a standard score with a mean of 100 and a standard deviation of 15. The individual K-ABC subtests yield scaled scores with a mean of 10 and a standard deviation of 3. A description of the subtests (Kaufman & Kaufman, 1983) is provided in Table 4.1.

K-ABC psychometric properties

The K-ABC has strong psychometric properties (Lichtenberger, Kaufman, & Kaufman, 1998). Split-half reliability coefficients for the K-ABC global scales range from .86 to .93 (mean = .90) for preschool children, and from .89 to .97 (mean = .93) for children aged 5 to $12\frac{1}{2}$ years (Kamphaus et al., 1995). The range of split-half reliability coefficients for individual mental processing subtests administered to preschoolers was .72 to .78 (mean = .80), and for school-age children the coefficients ranged from .71 to .85 (mean = .80). Test–retest reliability data were provided from a study of 246 children tested after a two–four-week interval. The research revealed a developmental trend, with the stability of the test being stronger as the children got older. The stability coefficients for the Mental Processing Composite were .83 for children aged 2 years 6 months to 4 years 11 months; .88 for ages 5 years through 8 years; and .93 for ages 9 years through 12 years 5 months. On the Achievement scale, the

Table 4.1. Description of K-ABC subtests

Mental Processing Scale			
Sequential Processing Scale		Simultaneous Processing Scale	
Subtest (Age administered)	Description	Subtest (Age administered)	Description
Hand Movements (Ages $2\frac{1}{2}$ to $12\frac{1}{2}$)	Child imitates a series of hand movements in the same sequence that the examiner performed them	Magic Window (Ages $2\frac{1}{2}$ to 4)	Child identifies a picture that the examiner has exposed by passing it through a narrow slit, making the picture only partially visible at any one time
Number Recall (Ages $2\frac{1}{2}$ to $12\frac{1}{2}$)	Child repeats a series of digits in the same order as they were said by the examiner	Face Recognition (Ages $2\frac{1}{2}$ to 4)	Child selects, from a group photograph, the one or two faces that were shown briefly in a preceding photograph
Word Order (Ages $2\frac{1}{2}$ to $12\frac{1}{2}$)	Child touches a series of pictures in the same sequence as they were named by the examiner, with more difficult items involving a color interference task	Gestalt Closure (Ages $2\frac{1}{2}$ to $12\frac{1}{2}$)	Child names an object or scene pictured in a partially completed drawing
		Triangles (Ages 4 to $12\frac{1}{2}$)	Child assembles several identical blue and yellow triangles to match a model
		Matrix Analogies (Ages 5 to $12\frac{1}{2}$)	Child selects the meaningful picture or abstract design which best completes a visual analogy
		Spatial Memory (Ages 5 to $12\frac{1}{2}$)	Child is required to recall the location of the placement of pictures on a page exposed briefly
		Photo Series (Ages 6 to $12\frac{1}{2}$)	Child places photographs of an event in chronological order

Table 4.1. (*cont.*)

Achievement Scale			
Subtest (Age administered)	Description	Subtest (Age administered)	Description
Expressive Vocabulary (Ages $2\frac{1}{2}$ to 4)	Child names an object pictured in a photograph	Riddles (Ages 3 to $12\frac{1}{2}$)	Child names an object or concept described by a list of three characteristics
Faces & Places (Ages $2\frac{1}{2}$ to $12\frac{1}{2}$)	Child names a well-known person, fictional character, or place pictured in a photograph or drawing	Reading Decoding (Ages 5 to $12\frac{1}{2}$)	Child has to name letters and read words
Arithmetic (Ages 3 to $12\frac{1}{2}$)	Child demonstrates knowledge of numbers and mathematical concepts through a series of questions	Reading Understanding (Ages 7 to $12\frac{1}{2}$)	Child is required to act out commands given in a written sentence

test–retest coefficients for the same age groups were .95, .95, and .97, respectively (Kamphaus et al., 1995).

Validity data were obtained through many studies on the K-ABC (Kaufman & Kaufman, 1983; Kamphaus & Reynolds, 1987). The K-ABC Mental Processing Composite and the WISC–R Full Scale IQ (Wechsler, 1974) were found to correlate .70 in a sample of 182 normally developing children. In samples of exceptional children, the K-ABC and WISC–R overall IQs are found to have correlations ranging from .57 to .74. With the sizable, yet not perfect, correlations, the K-ABC and WISC–R seem to overlap a good deal, but yet show some independence (Kamphaus et al., 1995).

Structure of the KAIT

The KAIT is an individually administered intelligence test for individuals aged 11 through 85 and older. It provides three global IQ scores: Fluid, Crystallized, and Composite, each a standard score with a mean of 100 and a standard deviation of 15. The KAIT structure includes a Core Battery (three Crystallized and three Fluid subtests) and an Expanded Battery (including the Core Battery

Table 4.2. Description of KAIT subtests

Core Battery	
Crystallized subtests	Fluid subtests
Definitions. Examinees work out a word by studying the word shown with some of its letters missing and hearing or reading a clue about its meaning	*Rebus Learning.* Examinees learn the word or concept associated with a particular rebus (drawing) and then 'read' phrases and sentences composed of these rebuses
Auditory Comprehension. Examinees listen to a recording of a news story and then answer literal and inferential questions about the story	*Logical Steps.* Examinees attend to logical premises presented both visually and aurally, and then respond to a question by making use of the logical premises
Double Meanings. Examinees study two sets of word clues and then think of a word with two meanings that relates closely to both sets of clues	*Mystery Codes.* Examinees study the identifying clues associated with a set of pictorial stimuli and then figure out the code for a novel pictorial stimulus
Expanded Battery	
Auditory Delayed Recall. Examinees answer literal and inferential questions about news stories that they heard approximately 25 minutes earlier during Auditory Comprehension	*Rebus Delayed Recall.* Examinees 'read' phrases and sentences composed of rebuses they learned about 45 minutes earlier during Rebus Learning
Famous Faces. Examinees name people of current or historical fame, based on their photographs and a verbal clue about them (alternate Crystallized subtest)	*Memory for Block Designs.* Examinees study a printed abstract design that is exposed briefly, and then copy the design from memory using six yellow and black wooden blocks and a tray
Supplemental subtest	
Mental Status. Examinees answer simple questions that assess attention and orientation to the world	

plus two supplementary subtests, and two measures of delayed recall). An eleventh subtest, Mental Status, may also be administered, but it does not contribute to the calculation of the IQ. Each of the subtests, except Mental Status, yields an age-scaled score with a mean of 10 and a standard deviation of 3. Table 4.2 provides a description of each of the KAIT subtests.

KAIT psychometric properties

Like the K-ABC, the KAIT has strong psychometric properties. The mean split-half reliability coefficients for the Crystallized, Fluid, and Composite IQs were .95, .95, and .97, respectively (Kaufman & Kaufman, 1993). For the ten

Table 4.3. Oblimin factor loadings of KAIT subtests on Crystallized and Fluid factors for the total standardization sample

KAIT subtest	Crystallized	Fluid
Crystallized Scale		
Definitions	**.80**	.07
Auditory Comprehension	**.69**	.15
Double Meanings	**.69**	.15
Famous Faces	**.84**	.11
Fluid Scale		
Rebus Learning	.23	**.55**
Logical Steps	.13	**.66**
Mystery Codes	.05	**.71**
Memory for Block Designs	.09	**.76**

Source: Kaufman & Kaufman (1993, Table 8.8).

Note. Loadings of .50 or greater are shown in bold.

individual subtests, the mean split-half reliability coefficients ranged from .71 on Auditory Delayed Recall to .93 on Rebus Learning (median = .90). Mean test–retest reliability coefficients, based on 153 identified normal individuals in three age groups (11–19, 20–54, and 55–85+ years), retested after a one-month interval, were .94 for Crystallized IQ, .87 for Fluid IQ, and .94 for Composite IQ. Mean test–retest reliability values for each of the ten individual subtests ranged from .63 on Auditory Delayed Recall to .95 on Definitions (median = .78).

The construct validity of the Crystallized and Fluid scales was supported by exploratory and confirmatory factor analysis. Two-factor solutions were identified for the total standardization sample as well as for separate groups of whites, African Americans, and Hispanics, and males and females (Gonzales et al., 1995; Kaufman, McLean, & Kaufman, 1995). Table 4.3 shows the oblique factor solution for the total standardization sample (*n* = 2000).

The construct validity of the KAIT was further demonstrated through its correlations with other measures of adolescent and adult intelligence (Kaufman & Kaufman, 1993). In four samples between the ages of 16 and 19, 20 and 34, 35 and 49, and 50 and 83, the Composite IQ of the KAIT correlated from .83 to .88 with the Full Scale IQ of the Wechsler Adult Intelligence Scale–Revised (WAIS–R; Wechsler, 1981). In a sample of 79 adolescents and adults, the KAIT Composite IQ was found to correlate .87 with the Stanford Binet–Fourth

Edition (SB–IV; Thorndike, Hagen, & Sattler, 1986). In a sample of 124 normal 11–12 year olds, the KAIT composite was found to correlate .66 with the K-ABC Mental Processing Composite, but showed a stronger correlation ($r = .82$) with the K-ABC Achievement Scale (Kaufman & Kaufman, 1993).

Normative and developmental issues

K-ABC standardization

The K-ABC was standardized on a sample of 2000 children, stratified to match the 1980 US census data according to gender, age, geographic region, community size, socioeconomic status, race or ethnic group, parental occupation and education, and educational placement of the child. The sample included a number of children (proportionate with the number in the general population) with speech impairment, learning disabilities, mental retardation, emotional disturbance, and gifted and talented capabilities. Each six-month age group between the ages of $2\frac{1}{2}$ and $12\frac{1}{2}$ in the standardization sample was comprised of 100 children (50 female and 50 male). In addition to these children, 496 black children and 119 white children were tested for the sociocultural norming program that was used to develop sociocultural norms by race and parental educational level.

Developmental trends on the K-ABC

Some developmental trends were noted in the K-ABC standardization data. As mentioned above in the Normative and Developmental Issues section, the preschool children tended to have less stable scores on the K-ABC than the school-age children. However, this trend is consistent with the known variability over time that characterizes preschool children's standardization test performance in general (Kamphaus & Reynolds, 1987). Another difference in the scales as development progresses has to do with the factor structure. In evaluating the factor structure of the K-ABC, Kaufman and Kamphaus (1984) concluded that the K-ABC produces only two meaningful factors at ages two and three, with the third (achievement) factor beginning to emerge at age four. It appears that the achievement factor becomes even more distinct shortly after the onset of formal schooling.

Analyses of the K-ABC data from preschool children between the ages of two and a half and five years show sequential and simultaneous factors when all mental processing and achievement subtests are factor analyzed. The Sequential and Simultaneous Processing subtests show the highest loadings on these factors, and even when a third factor is extracted for ages four and five, the sequential and simultaneous dimensions remain robust (Kaufman & Kamphaus, 1984). At ages four and five, the K-ABC Achievement subtests have an average loading above 0.50 on the achievement factor, and in school-age children the achievement factor is even more robust. Thus, the three-scale structure of the K-ABC is well supported for children who have reached their fourth birthday (Lichtenberger & Kaufman, 2000). For children younger than age four, the following achievement subtests are best interpreted as measures of simultaneous processing: Expressive Vocabulary, Faces and Places, and Riddles. However, the Arithmetic subtest may be interpreted primarily as a sequential subtest.

Specific K-ABC subtests were also noted to be apparently measuring different modes of processing at different developmental stages. For example, for children aged four and younger, the Hand Movements subtest was a potent measure of Sequential Processing, but for children aged five and above, this subtest also had a decided Simultaneous component (Kaufman & Kaufman, 1983). It was hypothesized that the processing demands required for the longer series of hand movements were different from those required for the shorter series.

KAIT standardization

The KAIT normative sample was comprised of 2000 adolescents and adults between the ages of 11 and 94 years. The sample was stratified to match 1988 US census data on the variables of gender, geographic region, socioeconomic status, and race or ethnic group. For the socioeconomic variable, parental education was used for subjects aged 11 to 24 and self-education was used for those aged 24 to 94. Between 100 and 250 subjects were tested at each age level of the sample. The sample matched US census data well on the variables of race, gender, and educational attainment. The matches for geographic region were close for the North Central and South regions, but the sample was underrepresented in the Northeast and overrepresented in the West (Kaufman & Kaufman, 1993).

Developmental trends on the KAIT

Crystallized abilities have been noted to be fairly well maintained throughout the lifespan, but fluid abilities are not as stable, peaking in adolescence or early adulthood before dropping steadily through the lifespan (Horn, 1989; Kaufman, 1990; Kaufman & Lichtenberger, 1999). To analyze age trends in the KAIT standardization data, a separate set of 'all-adult' norms was developed to provide the means by which to compare performance on the KAIT subtests and

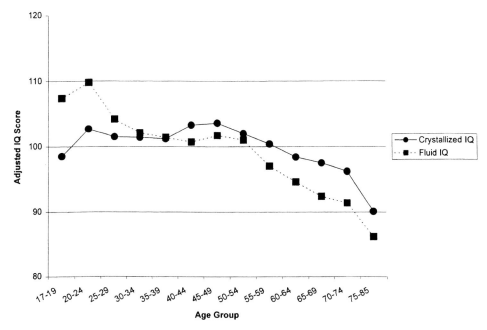

Fig. 4.1. Crystallized and Fluid IQ across the age span on the KAIT (Kaufman & Kaufman, 1993, Fig. 8.3).

IQ scales (Kaufman & Kaufman, 1993). Data from 1500 individuals between the ages of 17 and 85+ were merged to create the all-adult norms. The IQs from this new all-adult normative group were also adjusted for years of education, so that this would not be a confounding variable in analyses.

Analyses of the Crystallized and Fluid scales across ages 17 to 85+ produced results that generally conformed to those reported in previous investigations. As shown in Fig. 4.1, the crystallized abilities generally increase through age 50, but do not drop noticeably until age 75 and older. The fluid abilities, on the other hand, do appear to peak in the early 20s, then plateau from the mid-20s through the mid-50s, and finally begin to drop steadily after age 55 (see Fig. 4.1). These findings were consistent for males and females (Kaufman & Horn, 1996). Kaufman and Kaufman (1997a) hypothesize that the fluid aspects of some of the KAIT Crystallized subtests may have contributed to the accelerated age-related decline in scores on these subtests.

Application to diagnosis and treatment of learning disabilities

The diagnosis of a learning disability requires assessment of both intellectual ability and achievement. Thus, a comprehensive battery of tests is typically required to assess adequately for a learning disability. The K-ABC provides a measure of both of these parts of a learning disabilities assessment battery, which is beneficial in the process of diagnosis. However, all areas of achievement ability are not tapped by the K-ABC Achievement Scale. The KAIT provides measures of cognitive aptitude, and begins to give a sense of how well developed an individual's base of school-learned knowledge is (through the Crystallized Scale), but a formal measure of achievement is not part of the KAIT battery.

In light of the fact that the K-ABC lacks tests of certain achievement skills, examiners may find that they need to supplement the K-ABC with other instruments that tap verbal expression and additional areas of achievement aptitude. For example, the subtests of the WISC–III (Wechsler, 1991) Verbal Scale require much more verbal expression than the K-ABC, and can be used to obtain data about a child's abilities in this area. In fact, the amount of verbal expression required on the K-ABC was purposefully minimized during the development of the instrument in order to lessen the role of language in assessment of IQ and to provide simple objective scoring systems (Kaufman & Kaufman, 1983). The K-ABC Achievement Scale also does not provide subtests that assess areas such as written expression, spelling, and written mathematical computation. Thus, other tests of achievement such as the Peabody Individual Achievement Test–Revised (PIAT–R; Markwardt, 1989, 1997), the Kaufman Test of Educational Achievement (Kaufman & Kaufman, 1985, 1997b), or the Woodcock–Johnson Tests of Achievement–Revised (Woodcock & Johnson, 1989) may be useful supplements to the K-ABC battery. Standardized tests of achievement for adults are not as plentiful as those for children. Thus, when assessing for learning disabilities in adults, obtaining a measure of achievement abilities can be a bit more challenging. The Woodcock–Johnson Tests of Achievement–Revised (Woodcock & Johnson, 1989) are normed through adulthood, and the Kaufman Functional Academic Skills Test (K-FAST; Kaufman & Kaufman, 1994) may be used to measure the reading and mathematical skills of adolescents and adults.

Another area that is not well covered in the K-ABC or the KAIT that typically needs to be measured as part of a learning disability assessment is visual–motor reproduction. Tests such as the Developmental Test of Visual Motor Integration (VMI; Beery, 1997), the Coding subtest of the WISC–III or WAIS–III, or informal drawings such as Draw-a-Person tests may be used to obtain information of visual–motor skill. Additional factors that should be ruled out in diagnosing problems related to learning include memory and attention. The Children's Memory Scale (CMS; Cohen, 1997), the Wechsler Memory Scale–

Third Edition (Wechsler, 1997b), Wide Range Assessment of Memory and Learning (WRAML; Sheslow, & Adams, 1990), the Test of Memory and Learning (TOMAL, Reynolds & Bigler, 1994), or the Working Memory Index of the WAIS–III (Wechsler, 1997a) can be useful tools in examining memory and attention.

In the process of diagnosis, information must be obtained from multiple test scores on the various tests administered, in addition to information from the client's developmental, medical, educational, and psychological history. Before interpreting the scores, examiners must evaluate observations that have been made of the client's behavior during testing and in other settings. It is only in the context of these behaviors and obtained history that the test scores can be appropriately interpreted. Keeping in mind the philosophy that multiple bits of data must be used to support a hypothesis is important. This philosophy is one that is strongly advocated by Kaufman and others (e.g., Kaufman, 1994; Kaufman & Lichtenberger, 1999).

Although each child or adult with learning disabilities will show a unique pattern of scores in his or her K-ABC or KAIT profile, there are some general patterns that have appeared in the literature. On the K-ABC, there has been mixed evidence supporting a significant discrepancy between the Sequential and Simultaneous Processing scales in favor of the Simultaneous Scale for children who have been diagnosed with reading or learning disabilities. Some of the studies which report group discrepancies favoring Simultaneous Processing for students with learning disabilities include Obrzut, Obrzut, and Shaw (1984), Kempa, Humphries, and Kershner (1988), Rethazi and Wilson (1988), Smith et al. (1988), and Kaufman and Kaufman (1983). However, there is also a body of evidence which has found a pattern of either equivalent Simultaneous and Sequential Processing or differences in favor of Sequential Processing for children with learning disabilities (Naglieri & Haddad, 1984; Klanderman, Perney, & Kroeschell, 1985; Bain, 1993). The reason for the inconsistency in the literature is not clear. It may be due in part to the different selection criteria for learning disabilities used in the various studies. Table 4.4 provides a summary of some of the research on children with learning disabilities on the K-ABC. When interpreting the K-ABC profile of a child with a potential learning disability it is important to keep in mind that the literature has not definitively shown a certain pattern of processing to be present amongst all children with learning disabilities.

On the KAIT, profiles of individuals with learning disabilities have not been as heavily researched or as clear cut as on the K-ABC. Kaufman and Kaufman (1993) reported in a small sample of 14 adolescents with reading disabilities that there were no differences between this sample and matched controls. However, they did report that a trend was evident, with the Fluid Scale being significantly higher than the Crystallized Scale.

In a study comparing the performance of 30 college students with learning disabilities with that of 30 students without learning disabilities on the KAIT and WAIS–R, interesting nonsignificant differences were found (Morgan et al., 1997). The participants with learning disabilities had been previously diagnosed with a learning disability. Morgan and colleagues found that there were no differences between the learning-disabled group and the group without learning disabilities on the following: WAIS–R Full Scale IQ, Verbal IQ, and Performance IQ, and KAIT Composite, Crystallized, and Fluid Scale. However, when comparing the scales of the KAIT to the scales of the WAIS–R, one significant difference was found. In both the groups (those with and those without learning disabilities), the WAIS–R Performance IQ was significantly higher than the KAIT Fluid IQ. Possible explanations for the differences between these two scales include: (1) the KAIT has newer norms, and (2) the Fluid subtests are more novel than the Performance subtests (Morgan et al., 1997). Because these results demonstrate that the KAIT offers comparable results to those obtained with the WAIS–R, the new format of the KAIT, which has less emphasis on expressive language, appears to be a valuable addition to a learning disabilities assessment battery.

Differential diagnosis

In making a differential diagnosis between learning disabilities and other disorders such as psychiatric disorders, it is important to examine not only a person's scores but also clinical symptoms. In children, for example, the behavioral manifestation of a learning disability may be confused with oppositional defiant disorder, conduct disorder, attention-deficit hyperactivity disorder, or being lazy (Culbertson & Edmonds, 1996). Because of the struggles in school that children with learning disabilities have, it is not surprising that secondary emotional difficulties and adjustment problems often develop. When symptoms of a behavioral or emotional disorder are present, it is important to determine whether the symptoms are primary or secondary to the learning disability. Silver (1993) discusses in detail some responses that children with learning disabilities exhibit, such as withdrawal, regression, somatic complaints, paranoia, depression, clowning, or impulsiveness.

Learning disabilities can be more subtle in adults than in children, because, after years of struggling with the disability, individuals often develop compensatory strategies. For example, an adult with a learning disability may be aware

Table 4.4. Summary of research on K-ABC with students with learning disabilities

Other instruments utilized	Sample	n	K-ABC mean scores				Other IQ measure			Achievement measure		Reference
			MPC	Seq.	Sim.	Ach.	V-IQ or Verbal Reasoning	P-IQ Abstract Reasoning	FS-IQ or Composite	Math	Reading	
WISC–R	MR	33	78	78	82	70	71	84	75	—	—	Naglieri (1985)
	LD	34	96	92	100	86	93	103	97	—	—	
	Normal	34	109	109	107	104	106	110	108	—	—	
WISC–R PIAT	LD Referrals	86	96	95	97	87	94	97	95	93	91	Clarizio & Bennett (1987)
WISC–R	LD	43	95	91	99	88	96	103	99	—	—	Rethazi & Wilson (1988)
	Normal	27	104	101	109	108	—	—	—	—	—	
—	LD	94	81	89	79	—	—	—	—	—	—	Bain (1993)
SB–IV	LD	30	86	89	89	77	81	93	84	—	—	Knight, Baker, & Minder (1990)
WISC–R	LD	32	80	78	85	72	77	86	80	—	—	Obrzut, Obrzut, & Shaw (1984)
PPVT	LD Referrals	47	87	88	89	84	90[a]	—	—	—	—	D'Mato, Gray, & Dean (1987)
WISC–R	LD	198	92	91	93	87	93	96	94	—	—	Kaufman & McLean (1986)
WISC–R	LD	32	94	90	98	90	94	101	97	—	—	Smith et al. (1988)
	LD Referrals	35	98	96	100	94	102	99	101	—	—	

| WISC–R | LD | 44 | — | 93 | 92 | 88 | 92 | 97 | 94 | — | — | Klanderman, Perney, & Kroeschell (1985) |

Note. All values have been rounded to the nearest whole number. MPC = Mental Processing Composite; Seq. = Sequential Processing Scale; Sim. = Simultaneous Processing Scale; Ach. = Achievement Scale; MR = mentally retarded; LD = learning disabled; WISC–R = Wechsler Intelligence Scale for Children–Revised; PIAT = Peabody Individual Achievement Test; SB–IV = Stanford Binet–Fourth Edition; PPVT = Peabody Picture Vocabulary Test; V-IQ = Verbal IQ; P-IQ = Performance IQ; FS-IQ = Full Scale IQ.

[a]The PPVT is a measure of receptive vocabulary.

that he or she is prone to making numerous spelling errors or confusing letters such as *b* and *d*, but yet when homework is handed in to a college professor, there are very few errors. Clinically, what needs to be noted is that the person has spent an inordinate amount of time with a dictionary or computerized spell-check. The process by which he or she arrived at a nearly flawlessly spelled paper was laborious and exhausting. That same person may be hesitant or dysfluent in reading or may take extra time before being able to respond to a test item (Culbertson & Edmonds, 1996). Not only may the adult's academic history reflect poor performance in academic areas affected by the learning disability, but tests of intellectual ability may also reflect the learning disability. On tests like the Wechsler scales, the Verbal IQs would be expected to be low; on the K-ABC, the Achievement Scale would be low; and on the KAIT, the Crystallized Scale may be low. Many tests of cognitive ability are confounded with school-learned knowledge to some extent, as mentioned earlier. Adults with learning disabilities often show a history of underachievement that is reflected in their cognitive test scores.

KAIT illustrative case study

Wechsler Adult Intelligence Scale–Revised (WAIS–R)

Scale	IQ	90% confidence interval	Percentile rank
Verbal Scale	82	±5	12
Performance Scale	71	±9	3
Full Scale	76	±5	5

Subtest	Scaled score	Age-scaled score	Age-scaled score percentile rank
Information	3	(5)	5
Digit Span	10	(11)	63
Vocabulary	5	(7)	16
Arithmetic	7	(8)	25
Comprehension	4	(5)	5
Similarities	7	(9)	37
Picture Completion	3	(4)	2
Picture Arrangement	6	(5)	5
Block Design	6	(6)	9
Object Assembly	3	(3)	1
Digit Symbol	9	(9)	37

Kaufman Adolescent and Adult Intelligence Test (KAIT)

Composites	Standard score ± 90% confidence interval	Percentile rank
Fluid Scale	87 ± 5	20
Crystallized Scale	84 ± 5	15
Total Composite Scale	85 ± 4	15

Subtests	Scaled scores	Percentile rank
Fluid Scale		
Rebus Learning	5	5
Logical Steps	9	37
Mystery Codes	9	37
Memory for Block Designs	4	2
Crystallized Scale		
Definitions	7	16
Auditory Comprehension	9	37
Double Meanings	5	5
Famous Faces	9	37
Delayed Recall		
Rebus Delayed Recall	5	5

Kaufman Functional Academic Skills Test (K-FAST)

Subtest	Standard score	90% confidence interval	Percentile rank
Arithmetic	81	74–90	10
Reading	80	72–90	9
Composite	80	75–87	9

Kaufman Test of Educational Achievement (K-TEA): Comprehensive Form

	Standard score ± 90% confidence interval	Percentile rank
Composite		
Reading Composite	93 ± 6	32
Mathematics Composite	82 ± 6	12
Battery Composite	91 ± 4	27
Subtest		
Mathematics Applications	75 ± 8	5
Reading Decoding	103 ± 7	58
Spelling	110 ± 8	75
Reading Comprehension	85 ± 8	16
Mathematics Computation	91 ± 8	27

Peabody Picture Vocabulary Test–Revised (PPVT–R)

	Standard score	Percentile rank
PPVT–R	74	4

Wechsler Individual Achievement Test (WIAT)

Subtest	Standard score	Percentile rank
Written Expression	80	9

Developmental Test of Visual–Motor Integration (VMI)

	Standard score	Percentile rank
VMI	86	18

Woodcock–Johnson–Revised Tests of Cognitive Ability (WJ–R) profile

Subtest	Standard score	Percentile rank
Visual Closure	93	32
Memory for Names	107	68
Analysis–Synthesis	73	3

Woodcock–Johnson Revised: Tests of Achievement (WJ–R) profile

	Standard score	Percentile rank
Broad Knowledge	66	1
Science	77	6
Social Studies	75	5
Humanities	61	0.5

Reason for referral

Leo M. was referred for assessment of learning disability at the age of 17 years. He was referred for an evaluation because of his parents' concern about the presence of a possible learning disability. His parents also wanted information to determine if there was any way to help Leo get into college, and to succeed once he entered college. Mr and Mrs M. stated that Leo has difficulty with 'comprehension of written passages, processing information and coming out with an appropriate response, vocabulary, and self motivation.' Leo's parents developed questions about his ability and a potential learning disability after he received low scores on the SAT exam he had recently taken (Verbal 260, Math 260). Leo stated that he can remember vocabulary for a test, but cannot remember it later. He also stated concern over the fact that it is sometimes difficult for him to concentrate well enough to comprehend fully what he is reading.

Background information

Leo is the youngest of three children in his family. He currently lives alone with his parents, as his two sisters are attending college out-of-state. Mr and Mrs M. both work in the computer industry.

Mrs M. reported that Leo's prenatal and birth histories were unremarkable. She had a normal, full-term pregnancy, and gave birth to Leo through a normal delivery. Leo weighed 7 pounds 3 ounces at birth and was 19.75 inches long. According to his mother, Leo's medical history includes having tubes placed in his ears at the age of 33 months, due to repeated ear infections. He also had chicken pox at the age of five, and is currently affected mildly by hay fever. No other major illnesses or injuries were reported. His parents indicated that he has a physical examination annually for his participation in school athletics.

With the exception of his speech development, Mr and Mrs M. reported that all of Leo's developmental milestones were reached within the normally expected time frame. He sat up at age 3.5 months, walked at 13 months, and was completely toilet trained by around the age of three. Leo's parents reported that, in his early language development, his language was very 'indistinct.' Thus, he received language therapy from the age of three to five. His parents stated that the language difficulty was remediated through this treatment.

Leo's educational history began when he entered preschool at the age of two and a half. He attended preschool until he was five years old, and his parents reported that he enjoyed it. In first grade Leo participated in a special language program to help him with vocabulary and comprehension. His parents stated that they thought this program helped him because he tested too high at the end of the year on a test to qualify to continue in the program.

Leo has attended his high school since ninth grade. He is currently on summer vacation and will be beginning the twelfth grade in less than one month. According to his report card, his overall grade point average is just under a 'B,' at 2.79. Leo reported that he does not like math and science, but he does like history. The lowest grades he has obtained in high school have been in Spanish, English, Biology, and Chemistry.

He is an active participant in extracurricular sports such as soccer and basketball. Leo and his parents both report that they hope he may be able to receive an athletic scholarship for college. Mr and Mrs M. stated that sports take up much of Leo's time after school. To complete all of his homework, his parents indicated that they must help motivate him or push him to do it. They stated that he seems to do better when he has an example in front of him from which to work.

Appearance and behavioral characteristics

Leo is an athletic-looking 17 year old, of husky stature. He is a tall young man, with short blonde hair. He dressed comfortably and appropriately for each of the evaluation sessions, wearing shorts, a T-shirt, and tennis shoes. Leo was responsible for making appointments and getting himself to each of his evaluation sessions. He demonstrated his responsibility by his prompt arrival at the clinic after driving himself to each of his appointments.

Upon initially meeting the examiner, Leo did not seem nervous or anxious, but was somewhat apprehensive about the testing process. He was a bit quiet at first, but always responded to questions asked by the examiner. As rapport developed through initial conversation with the examiner, he began to elicit conversation more spontaneously, and even shared with the examiner what some of his concerns were about his ability. During the testing itself, he was very focused on the task at hand and seldom initiated dialogue, unless asked a question by the examiner.

Leo's face and body were rather expressionless during the evaluation. He rarely smiled, frowned, grinned, or grimaced, and he sat still in his chair with no excess body movement. Occasionally, when he was presented with a problem that he thought looked difficult, his initial response before attempting to solve it was, 'whew' or 'wow.' He never took breaks offered to him by the examiner; he just wanted to keep going through each part of the evaluation. Leo was socially appropriate, pleasantly friendly, and cooperative.

Leo showed a strong ability to concentrate and focus on each task presented to him. His attention never drifted, even on tasks that were somewhat boring for him to do. He also demonstrated stamina and persistence working on tasks that were quite challenging for him. For example, on a task that required him to recreate an example of a geometric design with colored blocks, Leo had difficulty making the correct design, but kept on trying and attempted to complete the design. On other tasks, if he did not know the answer to a problem he said, 'I don't know,' but would not let his inability to answer one question interfere with his attempting the next question.

While attempting more school-related tasks, Leo stated occasionally, 'I know that answer, I learned it in school . . . I can't remember.' He appeared momentarily frustrated, but then just continued on with the next problem. Leo appeared to try his hardest on each item. When asked by the examiner whether his performance was an accurate assessment of his abilities, he agreed that it was. Because of his level of motivation to do his best, and his aforementioned behaviors and good concentration, the results of this evaluation are considered a valid estimate of his current cognitive and academic abilities.

Tests administered
Developmental Test of Visual–Motor Integration (VMI).
Kaufman Adolescent and Adult Intelligence Test (KAIT).
Kaufman Functional Academic Skills Test (KFAST).
Kaufman Test of Educational Achievement (K-TEA) – Comprehensive Form.
Kinetic Family Drawing.
Peabody Picture Vocabulary Test–Revised (PPVT–R).
Wechsler Adult Intelligence Scale–Revised (WAIS–R).
Wechsler Individual Achievement Test (WIAT): Selected Subtest.
Woodcock–Johnson–Revised (WJ–R): Tests of Achievement: Selected Sub-
    tests.
Woodcock–Johnson–Revised (WJ–R): Tests of Cognitive Ability: Selected Sub-
    test.

Test results and interpretation

Cognitive abilities

Leo was administered both the Wechsler Adult Intelligence Scale–Revised (WAIS–R) and the Kaufman Adolescent and Adult Intelligence Test (KAIT), which are individually administered tests of a person's intellectual ability and cognitive strengths and weaknesses. The WAIS–R groups an individual's abilities into two global areas: Verbal IQ and Performance IQ. Leo's Verbal IQ of 82 ± 5 (12th percentile; Low Average Range) was significantly higher than his Performance IQ of 71 ± 9 (3rd percentile; Borderline Range), indicating that he is able to solve problems better when they are presented auditorily and require a verbal response, such as answering a question or defining a word, than when problems are presented visually and require a nonverbal or motor response, such as manipulating objects. However, it is important to note that there is a significant amount of variability in both Leo's verbal and nonverbal abilities. For example, on the Verbal Scale, his scores showed discrepant abilities, with subtest scores ranging from the 5th percentile to the 63rd percentile, and on the Performance Scale, his subtest scores ranged from the 1st percentile to the 37th percentile. Leo's Full Scale IQ of 76 ± 5 is rendered meaningless because it only represents the numerical average of these many very discrepant abilities. Because of the significant amount of variability within his scores, it is more meaningful to look at his individual strengths and weaknesses to gain a better understanding of his cognitive abilities. His cognitive strengths and weaknesses will be discussed in detail later in the report.

Another measure of Leo's cognitive abilities was obtained through the KAIT. The KAIT groups an individual's cognitive abilities into two global areas: Fluid and Crystallized. Leo obtained a scaled score of 87 ± 5 (20th percentile) on the Fluid Scale, which measures one's ability to solve novel problems, and he earned a scaled score of 84 ± 5 (15th percentile) on the Crystallized Scale, which measures one's ability to solve problems that are dependent on schooling and acculturation for success. His individual subtest scores on each of the two scales were not unusually variable, and the two global scales were not significantly different from one another. Thus, his ability to solve new problems and his ability to solve problems using school-learned knowledge are equally well developed. His overall KAIT Composite standard score of 85 ± 5 (15th percentile; Below Average) represents the average of all his abilities.

One of Leo's relative cognitive strengths is in the area of rote memory and recall. He performed well on a WAIS–R task that required him to concentrate, remember, and repeat sequences of numbers that were presented to him auditorily (63rd percentile). He also performed well on another WAIS–R task which required him to copy a code of symbols (37th percentile). On both of these tasks, Leo used his strong attention and incorporated his rote memory and sequencing abilities to succeed. Similarly, his good short-term memory abilities were evident in a Woodcock–Johnson–Revised Test of Cognitive Ability (WJ–R) task that required him to learn and remember the unusual names of numerous visually presented cartoon space creatures, such as 'Plik' and 'Delton.' Leo performed at the 63rd percentile on this task by using his memory and rote recall abilities.

Another relative cognitive strength of Leo's was his ability to use planning and reasoning. Such reasoning is used when different premises are presented and a logical conclusion is found from them. This strength was evident on two KAIT tasks, one which required Leo to respond to a question by making use of logical premises (37th percentile), and another which required him to figure out the code of a novel pictorial stimulus (37th percentile). In a separate, but related, logic task on the WJ–R, Leo did not perform as well. On this task, in which Leo had to complete a logic puzzle, he scored at only the 3rd percentile. His lower performance on this task in comparison to the two KAIT reasoning tasks seemed to be due to the fact that he had difficulty when the task quickly became more and more complex. Leo could reason-out the one-step problems, but had much more difficulty when he had to integrate more steps to solve the problems.

Leo demonstrated some relative cognitive weaknesses in the verbal realm. His basic fund of general information, including knowledge obtained through formal schooling and knowledge obtained through acculturation and general awareness of one's environment, is low compared to his other abilities and others his age (5th percentile). This weakness was further supported by three Achievement subtests of the Woodcock–Johnson–Revised (WJ–R ACH). On subtests measuring his knowledge in the areas of science, social studies, and humanities, Leo obtained scores in the 6th, 5th, and 0.5th percentiles, respectively. In contrast to this, on a KAIT task measuring knowledge of general factual information from history, literature, sports, entertainment, science, and art, which one acquires through television, magazines, and newspapers, Leo scored higher (37th percentile). The difference appears to be in the way the information was presented to Leo. He performed better on the task that presented a verbal cue about a famous face shown, which he had to identify, than on tasks which simply required him to answer questions about facts. The use of verbal and pictorial clues encourages integration of facts and concepts, and makes the task more of a problem-solving exercise than just purely a long-term memory task. Thus, it appears that Leo is not adequately able to use purely his long-term memory to retrieve the broad base of general information that is presented to him in and out of academic settings.

Leo also demonstrated a relative weakness in verbal comprehension. For example, on a WAIS–R task that required him to listen to a verbally presented question involving common sense and judgment, and respond verbally, he had difficulty (5th percentile). This difficulty was paralleled by his performance on the Reading Comprehension subtest of the Kaufman Test of Educational Achievement (K-TEA). This subtest required him to read short passages and answer brief questions about what he had read. He performed at the Below Average Level (16th percentile) on this task. Similarly, on a task from the Kaufman Functional Academic Skills Test (K-FAST) that required Leo to understand written material used in everyday situations, such as signs, labels, recipes, and abbreviations, his difficulty was apparent as he earned a score at the 9th percentile. However, in contrast to these difficulties, he performed at the Average Level (37th percentile) on a related KAIT task that required him to listen to a mock radio news broadcast, and answer questions about it. The differences in his performance on these different verbal comprehension tasks may be two-fold. First, on tasks that are more school-like, requiring reading and answering questions, rather than listening to news on the radio, he has less confidence and weaker ability. Second, on tasks that require him to make inferences or use more than just basic rote recall about what he has heard or read, he has more difficulty.

Related to his difficulties in verbal comprehension, Leo demonstrated a weakness in word storage and retrieval through paired associate learning. On a KAIT task that simulates reading and is like learning a new language, Leo scored at the 5th percentile. This is similar to his performance on a WAIS–R vocabulary task and KAIT task of word knowledge and concept formation, in which he earned scores at the 16th percentile. In addition, Leo earned a standard score of 74 (4th percentile) on the Peabody Picture Vocabulary Test–Revised (PPVT–R), which is a test of receptive vocabulary.

Visual–motor abilities
Overall, Leo's abilities to perceive and visually organize material are weaker than his global verbal abilities. This was evident on most of the WAIS–R Performance Scale subtests, including those requiring him to identify the missing part of a picture, arrange picture cards in the correct sequential order, copy a geometric design with blocks, and solve a puzzle. His scores on these tasks ranged from the 1st to 9th percentiles. Supportive evidence for his perceptual organization and visual organization difficulties was present in a

similar KAIT task of replicating a design with blocks, from memory (he earned a score at the 2nd percentile). Likewise, on a task of visual–motor skill, he performed at a below average level (VMI standard score of 86; 18th percentile). To rule out a potential deficit in simultaneous processing, or holistic processing, a WJ–R subtest was administered. This subtest required Leo to identify a drawing or picture that is distorted, has missing lines, or has a superimposed pattern. His performance was higher (32nd percentile) on this task than on perceptual organizational tasks previously mentioned, indicating that his difficulties are not likely to be due to a weakness in holistic processing.

Achievement abilities

Leo's achievement abilities were thoroughly evaluated, in addition to his cognitive abilities. Some of his achievement scores have been discussed previously in conjunction with his cognitive abilities, but all achievement scores will be discussed in detail in the following paragraphs. Leo was administered multiple separate tests of achievement, to assess his reading ability, both comprehension and decoding, his mathematics computation and applied abilities, his written expression ability, his receptive vocabulary, his spelling ability, and his basic knowledge skills. In general, his achievement abilities were at a level commensurate with his cognitive abilities, with the exception of his spelling and reading decoding, which were higher than would be predicted from his cognitive scores. This indicates that Leo does not have a learning disability and, in fact, it is clear that he works very hard to achieve at the level he does, academically, as evidenced by his current grade point average (GPA) of 2.79.

On the Kaufman Test of Educational Achievement – Comprehensive form (K-TEA), Leo earned Spelling and Reading Decoding scores at the 75th and 58th percentiles, respectively. Given his overall performance on the tests of cognitive ability and intelligence (KAIT and WAIS–R), ranging from the 3rd percentile on WAIS–R Performance IQ to the 20th percentile on KAIT Fluid IQ, he appears to be overachieving in these particular areas. On closer inspection, it seems that Leo is using his strong rote memory abilities to perform strongly on spelling words and on word pronunciation. He appears to have a good understanding and memory of the phonics involved in word pronunciation, which enables him to sound-out words with which he may not be familiar.

Leo's low score on the SAT Verbal exam (260), reported by his parents, was paralleled by his K-TEA Reading Comprehension score at the 16th percentile, his KFAST Reading score at the 9th percentile, and his PPVT–R receptive vocabulary score at the 4th percentile. Commensurate with these verbal scores is his written expression ability (Wechsler Individual Achievement Test (WIAT), 9th percentile). On this task of written expression, points may be earned in the areas of vocabulary, organization, ideas and development, sentence structure, grammar, and capitalization and punctuation. His achievement abilities on this testing also appear to be in line with his lower grades obtained at school in English and Spanish.

Like his SAT Math score (260), in the area of mathematics, Leo earned significantly lower scores on tasks that were applied and required problem-solving in everyday situations, than in the computation of written mathematics problems. On the K-TEA Mathematics Applications and KFAST Arithmetic, he earned scores at the 5th and 10th percentiles, respectively. However, on the K-TEA Mathematics Computation he earned a higher score, at the 27th percentile. This discrepancy is analogous to his performance on the aforementioned reasoning tasks, on which he was able to solve simple, one-step problems, but had much more difficulty with increasingly complex problems, as are the applied math problems.

Summary and diagnostic impressions

Leo M. is a 17-year-old student, who is about to enter his senior year in high school. He was referred for an evaluation because of his parents' concern about his academic abilities and a possible learning disability. This evaluation was performed to answer Mr and Mrs M.'s questions about whether there is any way to help Leo with the academic difficulties he has, which may aid him once he enters college. Cognitive, achievement, and supplemental tests were administered over the course of four sessions. Leo demonstrated good concentration and attention during the entire evaluation. He was persistent and motivated to try his best, even on very challenging tasks. Detailed behavioral observations of the testing, as well as information provided by a clinical interview with Leo and his parents, and academic records gave further insight into Leo's strengths and weaknesses.

Leo's cognitive abilities were assessed by two instruments, the WAIS–R and the KAIT. On the WAIS–R, Leo performed significantly better on tasks requiring answering questions verbally than on solving problems that are presented visually and require a nonverbal, or motor response. He earned a Verbal IQ of 82 ± 5 (Low Average Range) and a Performance IQ of 71 ± 9 (Borderline Range). Because of the significant variability within these different scales, Leo's cognitive abilities are most meaningfully represented by his individual strengths and weakness on the WAIS–R. On the KAIT, Leo's performance did not show a significant amount of variability, indicating that his measured abilities were evenly developed. He earned a Fluid IQ of 87 ± 5 (Below Average Range) and a Crystallized IQ of 84 ± 5 (Below Average Range), indicating that he solves problems equally well whether they are novel problems or whether they are problems dependent on schooling and acculturation for success.

Leo's relative cognitive strengths were evident in two areas: his rote memory and recall abilities, and his ability to use planning and reasoning in problem-solving of uncomplicated, one-step problems. However, when more complex reasoning is involved in problems requiring the integration of multiple steps, Leo has much more difficulty. Overall, Leo generally had more difficulty on tasks that required visual organization and perceptual organization than on those that required only verbal abilities. Specific areas of weakness were found in Leo's general fund of knowledge. It appears that Leo's ability to learn, store, and retrieve information from his long-term memory is below average. Leo has less difficulty when he can use pictorial or visual cues in addition to verbal cues, but has much more trouble when he is required to answer questions about facts that are presented in a written or oral format, such as is most commonly done in an academic setting. Leo also demonstrated a weakness in verbal comprehension of both academic-type material and written material used in everyday situations. In comprehension, Leo again was found to perform much better when he was able to use basic rote memory, but is quite challenged when required to utilize more complex processes, such as making an inference from what he hears or reads.

There were no significant discrepancies between Leo's cognitive abilities, indicated by his IQ scores, and his Achievement abilities, indicated by his achievement standard scores, which demonstrates that he does not have a learning disability. Leo's scores on the individually administered Achievement tests were commensurate with his scores on the SAT exam. In two areas, word pronunciation and spelling words, Leo achieved scores that were better than would have been predicted by his global IQ. It seems that in these two areas, Leo is able to use his strong rote memory to succeed. Similar to what was found in the cognitive testing, Leo performed significantly better on math problems that involved only calculation of written problems than on applied problems which were more complex and involved multiple steps. Leo's achievement in the verbal area ranged from the 4th percentile in Receptive Vocabulary, to the 9th percentile in Written Expression, to the 16th percentile in Reading Comprehension.

Leo's high-school grade point average of just under a 'B'-average, seems to be quite representative of the diligence, effort, and persistence that he shows in his academic work. It is likely that academic work is more difficult for Leo than for other students of his age. Through his performance at school, as evidenced by his grades and comments by his teachers, such as 'conscientious worker and excellent attitude,' it appears that Leo is able to compensate well for his weaknesses.

Recommendations

The following recommendations have been made to assist Leo and his parents to best utilize his strengths in areas that are more challenging for him, both in and out of academic settings.

1. As Leo was found not to have a learning disability, he will not qualify for special academic programs at a college or university to help with learning problems. However, Leo may still find that he will have difficulty with college courses that are more complex and challenging than high school work. Because such advanced courses may be harder for him than for other students, it is recommended that he and/or his parents look into academic programs that offer tutoring support. This may include peer tutoring or teaching by advanced students. Information may be obtained by telephoning or writing to student affairs or student services departments of various universities or community colleges.

2. In choosing a college or university, Leo and his parents may want to consider the size of classes. In making the transition to higher education, sometimes students who struggle academically get lost in big lecture courses that are often found at large universities. Leo will probably benefit from a smaller class size where one-on-one interaction with the professor/teacher is possible. This will allow him easier access to someone who will answer his questions, and place him at lower risk for just being lost in the crowd of students.

3. If Leo decides to enter a school for pursuing his athletic interests, such as football, he will want to consider how rigorous the athletic schedule will be. In college, he will have to set his own study schedule, and the time taken by athletic practice and games should be factored in as a potential conflict. Choosing a program that allows enough time for studying and tutoring, if necessary, will be critical to Leo's academic success beyond high school.

4. As Leo demonstrated difficulty in tasks that rely on general knowledge, it is recommended that he gains more enrichment from his environment. This may include activities such as watching documentary movies, going to museums and concerts, trying new things such as following a recipe to cook a meal, or other such activities.

5. Leo has difficulty retrieving information that is stored long term. To help him

better remember such information, several things are recommended. Leo may benefit from taping lectures and listening to them more than once. He will also benefit from having new information presented in such a way that he can both hear and see what he is expected to learn. This may be made possible by talking to his professors and asking if they can use overheads or videos in addition to lecture. He will also benefit from gaining information through other channels such as touch and movement. Using actual objects to illustrate concepts will be beneficial. Thus, when available, Leo will benefit from laboratory classes, or classes that provide hands-on work.

6.   Learning new information is easier if it is clearly associated with something you already know. Therefore, Leo will benefit from forming relationships, organizing information, and integrating information with prior knowledge. For example, when reading a new text on a scientific concept such as gravity, Leo will benefit form visualizing a familiar object, like a baseball being pitched, to problem solve how the new concept is applied. Thus, using various strategies, such as visualization, can help increase retention of information.

7.   Leo reported that he has difficulty staying focused on reading for an extended period of time and remembering and comprehending what he has already read. He may benefit from reading a passage by breaking it down into smaller parts, making sure that he understands each small part as he goes along. He should periodically stop and ask himself questions about what he has read. Highlighting important text and taking notes in the margin are also effective strategies for enhancing comprehension. He should allow himself extra time while reading so he may take breaks to avoid fatigue and boredom.

Liz Lichtenberger, PhD
Carren Stika, PhD

K-ABC illustrative case study

Kaufman Assessment Battery for Children (K-ABC)

Subtest/scale	Standard score	Percentile rank
Sequential Processing	89 ± 8	23
Simultaneous Processing	121 ± 8	92
Mental Processing Composite	1·7 ± 7	68
Achievement	105 ± 6	63

Sequential Processing	Scaled score	Percentile rank
Hand Movements	8	25
Number Recall	10	50
Word Order	7	16

Simultaneous Processing	Scaled score	Percentile rank
Gestalt Closure	15	95
Triangles	12	75
Matrix Analogies	12	75
Spatial Memory	13	84

Achievement Subtest	Standard score	Percentile rank
Faces & Places	111 ± 13	77
Arithmetic	104 ± 10	61
Riddles	109 ± 11	73
Reading Decoding	96 ± 7	39

Woodcock–Johnson–Revised Tests of Cognitive Ability (WJ–R): Early Development Scale

Subtest	Scaled score	Percentile rank	Grade equivalent
Memory for Names	82 ± 5	12	K.0 [12]
Memory for Sentences	87 ± 5	19	K.0 [24]
Incomplete Words	110 ± 5	75	K.5
Visual Closure	101 ± 6	54	K.2
Picture Vocabulary	101 ± 7	53	K.2
Broad Cognitive Ability			
Global Score	95 ± 4	38	K.0 [43]

Developmental Test of Visual–Motor Integration (VMI)

Subtest	Standard score	Percentile rank	Age equivalent
VMI	116	86	6.0

Wechsler Preschool and Primary Scale of Intelligence (WPPSI)

Subtest	Scaled score	Percentile rank
Comprehension	11	63

Reason for referral

Abby R. is a 5 year old attending a local preschool. She was referred to the clinic by her teacher for assessment of her readiness to begin kindergarten and to determine whether she may be showing early signs of a learning disability. Abby's teacher administered Early Screening Profiles (ESP) to her prior to this evaluation. From the results obtained on the ESP, questions were raised about Abby's visual processing ability and her overall level of maturity. The results of this evaluation will be used to determine if there are any difficulties that may be problematic for Abby when she begins kindergarten next autumn.

Background information

Abby lives at home with her parents, Mr and Mrs R., and her 8-year-old brother, Jake. Mr R. is self-employed and Mrs R. is a full-time homemaker. Mr R. stated that Abby's brother currently receives a 'low dose of Ritalin because he is mildly ADD.' In Abby's prenatal history, Mrs R. reported that she experienced premature dilation at 36 weeks, which required her to be on medication. She indicated that there were no other difficulties with her pregnancy and Abby was born at 38 weeks after 12 hours of labor, weighing 7 pounds and 1 ounce. According to her parents, Abby has had no major illnesses or hospitalizations. About one year ago, Abby was evaluated by a pediatric ophthalmologist. Mr R. indicated that Abby was prescribed eyeglasses for 'vision problems' and difficulty with a 'stray eye.' Abby wears her glasses daily.

According to her parents, Abby reached all of her developmental milestones within the normally expected time limits. She sat up at six months, said her first words at nine months, walked at 14 months, and completed toilet training at 30 months. Her parents noted that, because of 'nodules on her vocal cords,' she had difficulty with her speech and they therefore took her to a speech therapist.

Abby was in speech therapy for approximately one year. The speech therapist stated that, through various exercises practiced at home and during speech therapy, the nodules on Abby's vocal cords were eliminated. According to the therapist, Abby had difficulty pronouncing several sounds such as, 'L,' 'R,' 'Sh,' 'Ch,' and 'J.' After approximately four months of speech therapy, Abby's difficulty pronouncing 'L' was cleared up. The speech therapist reported that Abby still has difficulty pronouncing 'R,' 'Sh,' 'Ch,' and 'J' sounds, which she felt 'may lead to problems and frustration for Abby in learning phonics in school.'

Abby has attended preschool since she was 18 months of age. Her mother reported that, during the first year of preschool, Abby attended just one day a week, and since the age of two and a half, she has attended three days a week. Abby's current school includes approximately 30 preschoolers, with classroom size varying depending on the children's activity. Abby was observed during a typical day at preschool, with activities including music, story reading, art activities, free time, and show-and-tell. Abby was observed to interact well with her peers. She showed the ability to share and cooperate. She allowed other children to help her complete a puzzle she was working on, and at another point allowed a student to play with blocks that she was already playing with. At times Abby demonstrated spurts of excessive energy. For example, she twirled around for a couple of minutes at one time and inappropriately scattered puzzle pieces at another point. However, she was able to quiet herself down quickly and behaved overall very appropriately. Abby demonstrated the ability to work independently on a puzzle for a reasonable amount of time. She was quite persistent and patient in her work on solving the puzzle. She was quiet and attentive when her teacher read a story, and was comfortable participating verbally when asked questions. Abby appeared self-confident as she presented four toys she had brought for 'show-and-tell.'

According to her parents, Abby and her brother get along well, they 'play together a lot, and are nice to each other.' Abby's interests include playing with stuffed animals, Polly Pocket and her new puppy. Her parents describe Abby as 'feminine, petite, and a little immature.' Abby reportedly follows her parents' directions at least 50% of the time, but they indicate that she can be 'stubborn with certain issues.' Overall, Mr and Mrs R. characterize Abby as an 'easy child.'

Appearance and behavioral characteristics

Abby is a very petite 5-year-old girl, who wears small, pink eyeglasses and small earrings. She speaks with slight speech articulation immaturities (difficulty, especially, articulating 'R' and 'Th'), which makes her sound slightly younger than she is. For example, she pronounced *world* as 'wald' and *three* as 'free.' Her speech, along with her diminutive size, give the impression that Abby is younger than her chronological age. She was tested on three separate occasions. Initially, she was quite shy and requested that her mother join her in the testing room. During each of the sessions her mother escorted her to the room. Abby appeared more at ease once she was occupied by drawing with markers. She slowly warmed up to the examiner, first answering questions with nonverbal nods while still drawing and then progressing to short, quick, verbal responses. Abby appears to be more comfortable expressing herself through nonverbal rather than verbal communication. After a short period with her mother present in the room, Abby agreed that she was comfortable being left alone and seemed indifferent when mother did leave the room. She demonstrated a good ability to use fantasy play while interacting with the examiner and also appeared to have a good sense of humor.

Abby tended to have a short attention span during many of the subtests. Tests which provided visual stimulation or manipulation of objects held her attention much more than tests which were purely auditory in nature. Her inattention was accompanied by much fidgeting, resistance, and difficulty following directions. Her fidgeting was evident when she kicked the table, played with pages of the easel, and picked her nose. Abby was resistant when she was tired of a task. This was exhibited in her attempts to close the pages of the examiner's easel, when she sank down in her chair until she was underneath the table, when she pulled her dress over her face, and when she made statements such as 'This is the end' and 'I wanna be done.' Following directions was problematic for Abby during a task which required her to copy a design with triangular-shaped blocks. She wanted to reconstruct the design her way, which was standing the triangles up on their side, instead of flat on the table as the examiner had instructed. After multiple redirection, Abby was still able to follow directions only about 50% of the time.

Abby appears to enjoy tactile, visual, and kinesthetic stimuli, but seems to find auditory stimulation less exciting. She repeatedly attempted to provide additional self-soothing stimulation for herself by sucking her thumb, putting the examiner's easel in her mouth, or by feeling the weight of the easel on her head. She enjoyed manipulating small rubber triangles with her hands and repeatedly asked to play with these items during other subtests. Abby was able to attend to auditory tasks better when she could occupy herself with physical objects. For example, she was fidgeting and having difficulty attending to a task requiring her to listen to an incomplete word and then identify the complete word. However, when she was allowed to hold onto and manipulate a stopwatch during the auditory task, she was able to calm down and focus her attention better. Similarly, she was allowed to play with small rubber triangles during an auditorially presented social comprehension task, and this seemed to allow her to redirect her attention so she was free to listen and respond appropriately.

Although Abby preferred visual stimuli, at times she became overwhelmed when the stimulus field was too crowded. This happened during two separate subtests. On one auditory–visual association task, she was shown a picture of a space creature and told the space creature's name. Then she was required to point out the space creature from a group of others. When the number of creatures became too great for Abby, she could not remember any and just pointed to them all. She had similar difficulty on a different task requiring her to look at a page with two to five pictures on it, and then point on a blank page to where those pictures had been located. When the page was crowded with too many items for Abby (four to five), she was unable to respond and just randomly pointed to multiple spots on the page.

When faced with too much challenge, Abby responded with a decreased interest and effort and often responded in a silly manner. During a task which required her to repeat a series of hand gestures demonstrated by the examiner, she began to make up her own creative gestures when the items became difficult. Similarly, during more challenging items on a number recall task, she began to say any random number that came to her mind. When encouraged by the examiner on other tasks to try a little harder to give a 'real' instead of 'silly' answer, she often came up with the correct answer. For example, on a task requiring Abby to identify a distorted picture, she identified one item as a 'blood head,' but after encouragement from the examiner, responded with the correct answer, 'train.' On challenging items Abby tends to give up easily. She responded to some items by saying they were 'too hard' before even attempting to answer. She did not appear overly concerned or anxious about her performance and demonstrated low frustration tolerance. Her random or silly responses were compensations that helped her deal with this frustration.

Abby tended to be quick to respond when she definitely knew the answer to a problem, but was able to slow herself down to think about more difficult problems. During a design copying task, she initially responded very rapidly, but as the designs became more difficult, she slowed down and took time to study the designs more carefully before copying them. She appeared to enjoy tasks that were administered quickly, and responded to the problems in a similarly quick manner. Abby had difficulty with items that required a sequential problem-solving style. She had difficulty remembering a sequence of verbally presented numbers and a sequence of visually presented hand movements. Once each of the sequences got too long, she lost all of the information presented to her. On one auditory–visual sequencing task, she was required to listen to a verbally presented list of objects and then point to the correct sequence of pictures on a page. Abby at times verbalized the correct order of items in the sequence, but then would not be able to point them out correctly.

Tests administered
Kaufman Assessment Battery For Children (K-ABC).
Developmental Test of Visual–Motor Integration (VMI).
Woodcock–Johnson–Revised (WJ–R): Tests of Cognitive Ability (Early Development Scale).
Wechsler Preschool and Primary Scale of Intelligence–Revised (WPPSI–R): selected subtest.

Test results and interpretation
On the K-ABC, Abby earned a Sequential Processing standard score of 89 ± 8, a Simultaneous Processing standard score of 121 ± 8, a Mental Processing Composite standard score of 107 ± 7 (68th percentile), and an Achievement standard score of 105 ± 6 (63rd percentile). These global scores classify her cognitive abilities within a wide range from the Low Average level of functioning to Superior. The 32-point difference between her Sequential Processing (23rd percentile) and her Simultaneous Processing (92nd percentile) standard scores is statistically significant and unusual and suggests that she performs better when solving problems by integrating many stimuli at once than when solving problems in a linear, step-by-step fashion. However, the substantial difference between her two processing styles was largely affected by Abby's high level of distractibility during the testing. Thus, the discrepancy in favor of Simultaneous Processing may be an overestimate of the processing difference because the Sequential Processing scale subtests are quite susceptible to the effects of distractibility. Because of the large discrepancy and the negative effect of her distractibility, the Composite score should not be used as an indication of her overall ability. Rather, her score on the Simultaneous Processing scale should be considered the best estimate of her intellectual potential.

On the three subtests comprising the Sequential Processing scale, Abby scored at the 16th, 25th, and 50th percentiles. Abby's difficulty attending, as noted in the behavioral observations, significantly affected these subtests. During a test requiring her to repeat with her hands a sequence of hand gestures, she had difficulty remembering a sequence of more than two gestures. On a test that requires recalling a sequence of verbally presented numbers, Abby had difficulty remembering a sequence of more than three numbers. On a task calling for integration of a verbally presented sequence of words and a response of pointing to the pictures of these objects, she could not remember a sequence of more than two items. Each of these subtests required a short period of sustained attention and the ability to recall the information presented. It appears that the most critical factor affecting her relatively lower scores was her inability to remember due to her high distractibility when the stimuli were presented. Two subtests on the WJ–R Cognitive Battery also confirmed that her difficulty remembering may have been affected by her problem sustaining attention for an entire test. On a WJ–R auditory–visual association task measuring long-term retrieval, Abby scored at the 12th percentile. On a WJ–R task requiring short-term retrieval, she had difficulty remembering and repeating single words and phrases, scoring at the 19th percentile.

On tasks that are more resistant to the effects of distractibility, Abby performed much better. Most of these tasks required holistic processing rather than sequential processing. For example, one of Abby's strengths was shown on a K-ABC subtest requiring her to look at a partially completed inkblot drawing and name or describe that drawing. She scored at the 95th percentile on this test of perceptual closure and inference. On a similar WJ–R subtest requiring Abby to identify a picture which is distorted, has missing lines, or a superimposed pattern, she scored in the Average range (54th percentile). Other well-developed areas for Abby include her visual organization, her alertness to her environment and visual detail. Her visual–motor skills were also shown to be well developed on the Developmental Test of Visual–Motor Integration (VMI). On this design copying task, Abby scored at the 86th percentile, equivalent to a child a full year older than her own chronological age.

Abby also showed a well-developed ability to determine the relationship between a whole and its parts. When presented with a word with one or more phonemes missing, she was quickly able to identify the complete word. She scored at the 75th percentile on this WJ–R auditory closure task. On a K-ABC task that required Abby to infer the name of a concrete or abstract verbal concept when given several of its characteristics, she demonstrated similar ability to determine the part–whole relationship, as she scored at the 73rd percentile. Abby demonstrated the ability to infer part–whole relationships with visual stimuli during a K-ABC task of assembling several rubber triangles to match a picture of an abstract design (75th percentile). The K-ABC and WJ–R visual closure tasks mentioned above also provide confirming evidence of this well-developed synthesizing ability (she received scores at the 95th and 54th percentiles).

Abby's academic achievement, as measured by the K-ABC Achievement subtests, was in the Average range. She scored at the 77th percentile on a test measuring her fund of general information by asking her to name pictures of fictional characters, famous people, or well-known places. On the Arithmetic subtest, which measured Abby's ability to identify numbers, count, compute, and demonstrate understanding of mathematical concepts, she scored at the 61st percentile. Abby's reasoning, verbal comprehension, and fund of word knowledge were measured in a task requiring her to solve verbally presented riddles (73rd percentile). On a WJ–R test of receptive vocabulary, she also scored in the Average range (53rd percentile). An additional subtest measuring her verbal comprehension, as well as common sense, social judgment, and social maturity, again showed her ability to achieve in the Average range (63rd percentile). The only area of weakness for Abby within the Achievement subtests was her ability to identify letters and read and pronounce words (39th percentile). Abby could only recognize an 'A' and a 'Y', but did know that they were letters in her name.

Summary and diagnostic impressions

Abby R. is a 5-year-old girl who was referred for an evaluation to determine whether she may be exhibiting early signs of a learning disability and to determine her level of readiness for kindergarten. After being given a preliminary screening test by her teacher, questions were raised about her visual processing ability and level of maturity. During the evaluation, Abby was highly distractible, demonstrated low frustration tolerance, and had difficulty following directions. She was able to focus better on auditory tasks if she had an object to manipulate, which allowed her to redirect her attention.

The assessment shows Abby's abilities to encompass a wide range of intellectual functioning (Low Average to Superior). Her Simultaneous Processing ability significantly outweighed her Sequential Processing ability, but this difference is probably exaggerated because her inattention negatively impacted many of the Sequential subtests. She had weaknesses in remembering sequences of visual and auditory stimuli. Correspondingly, she performed below average on a test of long-term retrieval of auditory–visual information and on a test of short-term retrieval of words and phrases. Abby had strengths in holistic processing, visual organization, attention to visual detail, and alertness to her environment. Her performance on Achievement subtests showed her to have average acquisition of learned material in all areas, with the exception of low-average ability to identify letters and pronounce words.

Overall, Abby is a self-confident, strong-willed young girl, who lacks strong concentration skills and motivation to keep on trying when a situation becomes challenging to her. She likes to take control of situations and can take several minutes to redirect if her behavior is problematic. Although she can be highly inattentive, she can become more focused if she is occupied with a physical object while attempting a more abstract auditory or visual task. From these test results, it does not appear that Abby has any visual processing difficulties, as earlier hypothesized from an initial screening. However, her ability to decode written material is significantly lower than would be expected given her cognitive potential. The 25-point discrepancy between her Reading Decoding and Simultaneous Processing standard scores indicates that this area should be closely monitored for the potential development of a learning disability as she enters school. As she has not yet entered a formal academic setting, diagnosis of a learning disability would be premature at this time. She is also somewhat immature for her age, which is accentuated by her attentional problems, but does not possess any severe cognitive or academic deficits which would cause difficulty for her in a kindergarten setting. There is a possibility that Abby is demonstrating signs of a mild attention deficit, or she may merely be a bit younger developmentally in her self and impulse control.

Recommendations

1. Given Abby's attentional problems and level of maturity, it will be important to find an experienced kindergarten teacher for her, who is willing to make some accommodations for her in the classroom. For example, when the class is expected to listen quietly to the teacher reading, Abby may need also to have her hands occupied with a small object, or may need to doodle while listening.
2. Abby will benefit from being instructed through the use of hands-on activities. She enjoys feeling and manipulating objects and will probably stay focused longer with a task that allows her to do so.
3. Because of Abby's short attention span, lessons should be kept as brief as possible. Planned interruptions when longer lessons are given will be useful. For example, Abby may need to get up and get some more supplies after part of a lesson is complete. Incorporation of quiet activities and active ones within a lesson will also help to keep her attention.
4. Abby's stronger simultaneous processing style than sequential processing style should be recognized in teaching her. Knowledge of her good visual organization and attention to visual detail may also be useful in instructing her.
5. Abby will benefit from practicing letters and numbers at home as much as possible. Such practice can be quite enjoyable, through the use of various games or enjoyable computer programs.

6.   Given Abby's low tolerance for frustration and desire to do things her way, it will be useful for her teacher and her parents to set realistic behavioral goals for her, and follow through with reinforcement when she does what is expected and with consequences when she does not follow these behavioral expectations. Reinforcement may be in the form of tangible or intangible rewards. For example, when appropriate behavior is demonstrated, classroom privileges, free time, and helping the teacher may be given as tangible rewards. Smiles, pats on the back, and praise may be given as intangible rewards.

7.   It is recommended that if Abby's distractibility and attentional difficulties become unmanageable in the classroom, a referral be made to a medical specialist for an evaluation to determine if she would benefit from a trial dose of Ritalin.

Liz Lichtenberger, PhD
Nadeen L. Kaufman, EdD

REFERENCES

Bain, S.K. (1993). Sequential and simultaneous processing in children with learning disabilities: an attempted replication. *The Journal of Special Education, 27*, 235–46.

Beery, K.E. (1997). *The Beery–Buktenica Developmental Test of Visual–Motor Integration Administration Scoring and Teaching Manual.* Parsippany, NJ: Modern Curriculum Press.

Bogen, J.E. (1975). Some educational aspects of hemispheric specialization. *UCLA Educator, 17*, 24–32.

Clarizio, H.F. & Bennett, D.E. (1987). Diagnostic utility of the K-ABC and WISC–R/PIAT in determining severe discrepancy. *Psychology in the Schools, 25*, 309–14.

Cohen, M. (1997). *Children's Memory Scale.* San Antonio, TX: The Psychological Corporation.

Culbertson, J.L. & Edmonds, J.E. (1996). Learning disabilities. In *Neuropsychology for Clinical Practice: Etiology, Assessment, and Treatment of Common Neurological Disorders,* ed. R.L. Adams, O.A. Parsons, J.L. Culbertson, & S.J. Nixon, pp. 331–408. Washington, DC: American Psychological Association.

D'Mato, R.C., Gray, J.W., & Dean, R.S. (1987). Concurrent validity of the PPVT–R with the K-ABC for learning problem children. *Psychology in the Schools, 24*, 35–9.

Das, J.P. (1973). Structure of cognitive abilities: evidence for simultaneous and successive processing. *Journal of Educational Psychology, 65*, 103–8.

Das, J.P., Kirby, J.R., & Jarman, R.F. (1975). Simultaneous and successive syntheses: an alternative model for cognitive abilities. *Psychological Bulletin, 82*, 87–103.

Das, J.P., Kirby, J.R., & Jarman, R.F. (1979). *Simultaneous and Successive Cognitive Processes.* New York: Academic Press.

Golden, C.J. (1981). The Luria–Nebraska Children's Battery: theory and formulation. In

Neuropsychological Assessment of the School-age Child, ed. G.W. Hund and J.E. Obrzut, pp. 277–302. New York: Grune and Stratton.

Gonzales, J., Adir, Y., Kaufman, A.S., & McLean, J.E. (1995). Race and gender differences in cognitive factors: a neuropsychological interpretation. Paper presented at the meeting of the international Neuropsychological Society, Seattle.

Horn, J.L. (1989). Cognitive diversity: a framework of learning. In *Learning and Individual Differences*, ed. P.L. Ackerman, R.J. Sternberg, & R. Glaser, pp. 61–116. New York: Freeman.

Horn, J.L. & Cattell, R.B. (1966). Refinement and test of the theory of fluid and crystallized intelligence. *Journal of Educational Psychology*, 57, 253–70.

Horn, J.L. & Hofer, S.M. (1992). Major abilities and development in the adult period. In *Intellectual Development*, ed. R.J. Sternberg & C.A. Berg, pp. 44–99. New York: Cambridge University Press.

Inhelder, B. & Piaget, J. (1958). *The Growth of Logical Thinking from Childhood to Adolescence*. New York: Basic Books.

Kamphaus. R.W., Beres, K.A., Kaufman, A.S., & Kaufman, N.L. (1995). The Kaufman Assessment Battery for Children (K-ABC). In *Major Psychological Assessment Instruments*, 2nd edition, ed. C.S. Newmark, pp. 384–99. Boston: Allyn & Bacon.

Kamphaus, R.W. & Reynolds, C.R. (1987). *Clinical and Research Applications of the K-ABC*. Circle Pines, MN: American Guidance Service.

Kaufman, A.S. (1990). *Assessing Adolescent and Adult Intelligence*. Boston, MA: Allyn & Bacon.

Kaufman, A.S. (1994). *Intelligent Testing with the WISC–III*. New York: Wiley.

Kaufman, A.S. & Horn, J.L. (1996). Age changes on test of fluid and crystallized ability for females and males on the Kaufman Adolescent and Adult Intelligence Test (KAIT) at ages 17 to 94 years. *Archives of Clinical Neuropsychology*, 11, 97–121.

Kaufman, A.S. & Kamphaus, R.W. (1984). Factor analysis of the Kaufman Assessment Battery for Children (K-ABC) for ages $2\frac{1}{2}$ through $12\frac{1}{2}$ years. *Journal of Educational Psychology*, 76, 623–37.

Kaufman, A.S. & Kaufman, N.L. (1983). *Interpretive Manual for the Kaufman Assessment Battery for Children*. Circle Pines, MN: American Guidance Service.

Kaufman, A.S. & Kaufman, N.L. (1985). *Kaufman Test of Educational Achievement*. Circle Pines, MN: American Guidance Service.

Kaufman, A S. & Kaufman, N.L. (1993). *Manual for Kaufman Adolescent & Adult Intelligence Test (KAIT)*. Circle Pines, MN: American Guidance Service.

Kaufman, A.S. & Kaufman, N.L. (1994). *Manual for Kaufman Functional Academic Skill Test (K-FAST)*. Circle Pines, MN: American Guidance Service.

Kaufman, A. S. & Kaufman, N.L. (1997a). The Kaufman Adolescent and Adult Intelligence Test (KAIT). In *Contemporary Intellectual Assessment: Theories, Tests, and Issues*, ed. D.P. Flanagan, J.L. Genschaft, & P.L. Harrison, pp. 209–29. New York: Guilford.

Kaufman, A.S. & Kaufman, N.L. (1997b). *Kaufman Test of Educational Achievement/NU*. Circle Pines, MN: American Guidance Service.

Kaufman, A.S. & Lichtenberger, E.O. (1999). *Essentials of WAIS-III Assessment*. New York: Wiley.

Kaufman, A.S. & McLean, J.E. (1986). K-ABC/WISC–R factor analysis for a learning disabled population. *Journal of Learning Disabilities*, 19, 145–53.

Kaufman, A.S., McClean, J.E., & Kaufman, J.C. (1995). The fluid and crystallized abilities of white, black, and Hispanic adolescents and adults, both with and without an education covariate. *Journal of Clinical Psychology*, 51, 637–47.

Kempa, L., Humphries, T., & Kershner, J. (1988). Processing styles of learning disabled children on the Kaufman Assessment Battery for Children (K-ABC) and their relationship to reading and spelling performance. *Journal of Psychoeducational Assessment*, 6, 242–52.

Kinsbourne, M. (Ed.) (1978). *Asymmetrical Function of the Brain*. New York: Cambridge University Press.

Klanderman, J.W., Perney, J., & Kroeschell, Z.B. (1985). Comparisons of the K-ABC and WISC-R for LD children. *Journal of Learning Disabilities*, 18, 524–7.

Knight, B.C., Baker, E.H., & Minder, C.C. (1990). Concurrent validity of the Stanford–Binet, Fourth Edition, and Kaufman Assessment Battery for Children with learning-disabled students. *Psychology in the Schools*, 27, 116–25.

Levy, J. & Trevarthen, C. (1976). Metacontrol of hemispheric function in human split-brain patients. *Journal of Experimental Psychology: Human Perception and Performance*, 2, 299–312.

Lichtenberger, E.O. & Kaufman, A.S. (2000). The assessment of preschool children with the Kaufman Assessment Battery for Children. In *The Psychoeducational Assessment of Preschool Children*, 3rd edition, ed. B.A. Bracken, pp. 103–23. Boston: Allyn & Bacon.

Lichtenberger, E.O., Kaufman, A.S., & Kaufman, N.L. (1998). The K-ABC: theory and application. In *Advances in Cross-cultural Assessment*, ed. R.J. Samuda, pp. 20–55. Thousand Oaks, CA: Sage Publications.

Luria, A.R. (1966). *Higher Cortical Functions in Man*. New York: Basic Books.

Luria, A.R. (1973). *The Working Brain: An Introduction to Neuro-psychology*. London: Penguin Books.

Luria, A.R. (1980). *Higher Cortical Functions in Man*, second edition. New York: Basic Books.

Markwardt, F.C. (1989). *Peabody Individual Achievement Test–Revised*. Circle Pines, MN: American Guidance Service.

Markwardt, F.C. (1997). *Peabody Individual Achievement Test–Revised/Normative Update*. Circle Pines, MN: American Guidance Service.

McCallum, R.S. & Merritt, F.M. (1983). Simultaneous–successive processing among college students. *Journal of Psychoeducational Assessment*, 1, 85–93.

Morgan, A.W., Sullivan, S.A., Darden, C., & Gregg, N. (1997). Measuring the intelligence of college students with learning disabilities: a comparison of results obtained on the WAIS–R and the KAIT. *Journal of Learning Disabilities*, 30, 560–5.

Naglieri, J.A. (1985). Use of the WISC–R and K-ABC with learning disabled, borderline mentally retarded and normal children. *Psychology in the Schools*, 22, 133–41.

Naglieri, J.A. & Das, J.P. (1988). Planning–Arousal–Simultaneous–Successive (PASS): a model for assessment. *Journal of School Psychology*, 26, 35–48.

Naglieri, J.A. & Das, J.P. (1990). Planning, Attention, Simultaneous, and Successive (PASS) cognitive processes as a model for intelligence. *Journal of Psychoeducational Assessment*, 8, 303–37.

Naglieri, J.A. & Haddad, F.A. (1984). Learning disabled children's performance on the K-ABC. *Journal of Psychoeducational Assessment*, 2, 49–56.

Obrzut, A., Obrzut, J.E., & Shaw, D. (1984). Construct validity of the Kaufman Assessment Battery for Children for children with learning disabled and mentally retarded. *Psychology in the Schools*, 21, 417–24.

Perlman, M.D. (1986). Toward an integration of a cognitive–dynamic view of personality: the relationship between defense mechanisms, cognitive style, attentional focus, and neuro-psychological processing. Unpublished doctoral dissertation, California School of Professional Psychology, San Diego.

Piaget, J. (1972). Intellectual evolution from adolescence to adulthood. *Human Development*, 15, 1–12.

Rethazi, M. & Wilson, A.K. (1988). The Kaufman Assessment Battery for Children (K-ABC) in the assessment of learning disabled children. *Psychology in the Schools*, 25, 383–91.

Reynolds, C.R. & Bigler, E.D. (1994). *Test of Memory and Learning*. Austin, TX: Pro-Ed.

Sheslow, D. & Adams, W. (1990). *Wide Range Assessment of Memory and Learning: Administration Manual*. Wilmington, DE: Jastak Assessment Systems.

Silver, L.B. (1993). The secondary emotional, social, and family problems found with children and adolescents with learning disabilities. *Child and Adolescent Psychiatric Clinics of North America*, 2, 295–308.

Smith, D.K., Lyon, M.A., Hunter, E., & Boyd, R. (1988). Relationship between the K-AC and WISC–R for students referred for severe learning disabilities. *Journal of Learning Disabilities*, 21, 509–13.

Sperry, R.W. (1968). Hemisphere deconnection and unity in conscious awareness. *American Psychologist*, 23, 723–33.

Sperry, R.W. (1974). Lateral specialization in the surgically separated hemispheres. In *The Neurosciences: Third Study Program*, ed. F.O. Schmitt & F.G. Worden, pp. 723–33. Cambridge, MA: MIT Press.

Thorndike, R.L., Hagen, E.P., & Sattler, J.M. (1986). *Stanford–Binet Intelligence Scale–Fourth Edition*. Chicago, IL: Riverside.

Wada, J., Clarke, R., & Hamm, A. (1975). Cerebral hemisphere asymmetry in humans. *Archives of Neurology*, 37, 234–46.

Wechsler, D. (1974). *Manual for the Wechsler Intelligence Scale for Children–Revised (WISC–R)*. San Antonio, TX: Psychological Corporation.

Wechsler, D. (1981). *Manual for the Wechsler Adult Intelligence Scale–Revised (WAIS–R)*. San Antonio, TX: Psychological Corporation.

Wechsler, D. (1991). *Manual for the Wechsler Intelligence Scale for Children–Third Edition (WISC–III)*. San Antonio, TX: Psychological Corporation.

Wechsler, D. (1997a). *Manual for the Wechsler Adult Intelligence Scale–Third Edition (WAIS–III)*. San Antonio, TX: Psychological Corporation.

Wechsler, D. (1997b). *Manual for the Wechsler Memory Scale–Third Edition (WMS–III)*. San Antonio, TX: Psychological Corporation.

Woodcock, R.W. & Johnson, M.B. (1989). *The Woodcock–Johnson Tests of Achievement–Revised*. Chicago, IL: Riverside.

5

Using the Cognitive Assessment System (CAS) with learning-disabled children

Jack A. Naglieri

Introduction

The Wechsler scales have dominated the field of intelligence testing for some time and the test continues to be the most widely used measure (Wilson & Reschly, 1996). It is important to consider, however, that the Wechsler approach to measuring intelligence represents a tradition in psychological assessment that began with the publication of the Wechsler–Bellevue Scales in 1939. Wechsler developed the Wechsler–Bellevue Scales largely on the basis of the methods described in the book *Army Mental Testing* (Yoakum & Yerkes, 1920), which were used by the US military in the early part of the twentieth century. Wechsler borrowed many of the tests and converted them from group administration to the individually administered format used today. The technology has withstood the test of time, but recent research has suggested that this general intelligence approach has considerable limitations when exceptional children are evaluated, especially those with learning disabilities (Naglieri, 2000). The utility of the Wechsler scales for the evaluation of those specific intellectual problems associated with learning-disabled children's academic failure has led some to consider alternative perspectives (Kaufman & Kaufman, 1983; Sternberg, 1988; Das, Naglieri, & Kirby, 1994). There have been advances in psychology (especially cognitive and neuropsychology), which occurred after the development of the Wechsler scales, that have relevance to the evaluation of children with learning problems.

One of the most important developments in the field of psychology that has considerable relevance to the evaluation of children with learning disabilities is the cognitive revolution. This revolution in thinking was initiated by cognitive psychologists who studied cognition, neuropsychology, neuroscience, and higher mental processes. The revolution described, for example in the book *Plans and the Structure of Behavior* by Miller, Galanter, and Pribram (1960), had a substantial influence on both applied and theoretical psychologists and educators. These and other researchers encouraged a move from the behavioral approach, which focused psychology on observable events, to a willingness to make inferences about behaviors associated with internal cognitive processes. Among the cognitive and neuropsychological researchers who helped stimulate this revolution was A.R. Luria, the 'most frequently cited Soviet scholar in American, British, and Canadian psychology periodicals' (Solso & Hoffman, 1991, p. 251). Luria's works included *Human Brain and Psychological Processes* (1966), *Higher Cortical Functions in Man* (1980), *The Working Brain* (1973), and *Language and Cognition* (1982), which were some of his most significant works that helped stimulate the cognitive revolution. The cognitive revolution also influenced how intelligence was conceptualized and measured.

The impact of the cognitive revolution on the assessment practices of psychologists was apparent with the publication of the Kaufman Assessment Battery for Children (K-ABC; Kaufman & Kaufman, 1983). This test reflected the authors' conceptualization of intelligence according to cognitive and neuropsychological perspectives rather than the general intelligence approach that dominated the field since the early part of the twentieth century. The Kaufmans' reliance on the works of neuropsychologists such as Luria (1966), Gazzaniga (1975), and Kinsborne (1978), and of cognitive psychologists such as Neisser (1967) and Das, Kirby, and Jarman (1975, 1979), placed that test within the cognitive revolutionary perspective and marked a significant point in the evolution of intelligence tests. The K-ABC model of Sequential–Simultaneous processes differed substantially from the general intelligence and factor analytic approach to theory and test building. Importantly, this test was the first of its kind to redefine intelligence as cognitive processes and thereby question the makeup of traditional IQ tests. The idea that IQ tests could be improved through modification and redefinition based on cognitive processes with elimination of achievement from the measure of ability was, and still is, a revolutionary concept.

Many scientific advances are rooted in the work of those that have come before. The K-ABC provided a cognitive frame within which the next alternative to psychometric approaches (e.g., Wechsler, Stanford–Binet, Woodcock–Johnson, and Differential Ability Scales) would be placed. That test is the Cognitive Assessment System (CAS), which I published with my colleague J.P. Das (Naglieri & Das, 1997a). This test was developed according to a specific theory of ability redefined as Planning, Attention, Simultaneous, and Successive (PASS) cognitive processes (Naglieri & Das, 1997a), based largely on the neuropsychological work of A.R. Luria (1966, 1973, 1980, 1982). In addition to being grounded on a specific theory of cognitive processes the CAS was designed to measure more components than had ever been included in a test of ability. Das and I used the PASS theory with its roots in the same cognitive revolutionary thinking that led to the K-ABC, but we focused more directly on the neuropsychological work of A.R. Luria.

The CAS, like the K-ABC, takes a cognitive processing approach to theory building rather than a factor analytic one, and puts more emphasis on the specific components of intelligence, rather than on IQ scores. In fact, the four PASS scales represent the basic psychological processes, described in Individuals with Disabilities Education Act (IDEA 1997; see Naglieri & Sullivan, 1998), which are used, for example, in the definition of a specific learning disability. These basic psychological processes can be used to gain an understanding of how well the child thinks and to discover strengths and needs of children which can then be used for effective differential diagnosis, to make appropriate instructional decisions, and to select or design appropriate interventions. The CAS can achieve these goals because of the important role PASS processes have in academic performance.

Description of the PASS theory and CAS

PASS theory

Naglieri (1999) states that Planning, Attention, Simultaneous, and Successive cognitive processes are the basic building blocks of human intellectual functioning. These four processes form an interrelated system of functions that interact with an individual's base of knowledge and skills. According to this theory, human ability includes four components:

Planning is a mental activity that provides cognitive control, use of processes, knowledge and skills, intentionality, and self-regulation.

Attention is a mental activity that provides focused, selective cognitive activity over time and resistance to distraction.

Simultaneous is a mental activity by which the child integrates stimuli into groups.

Successive is a mental activity by which the person integrates stimuli in a specific serial order to form a chain-like progression.

Planning

This process provides the means to solve problems of varying complexity and may involve attention, simultaneous, and successive processes as well as knowledge and skills. Planning is central to all activities for which the individual has to determine how to solve a problem, including self-monitoring and impulse control as well as plan generation. Success on CAS Planning tests requires the child to develop a plan of action, evaluate the value of the method, monitor its effectiveness, revise or reject a plan to meet the demands of the task, and control the impulse to act without careful consideration. All of the CAS Planning subtests require the use of strategies for efficient performance and the application of these strategies to novel tasks of relatively reduced complexity. The involvement of strategies to solve CAS Planning tests is amply documented by Naglieri and Das (1997b).

Attention

Attention is a mental process by which the individual selectively focuses on particular stimuli while inhibiting responses to competing stimuli presented over time. All CAS tests included on the Attention scale demand focused, selective, sustained, and effortful activity. Focused attention involves directed concentration toward a particular activity, and selective attention is important for the inhibition of responses to distracting stimuli. Sustained attention refers to the variation of performance over time, which can be influenced by the different amount of effort required to solve the test. All CAS Attention subtests present children with competing demands on their attention and require sustained focus.

Simultaneous processing

Simultaneous processing gives the individual the means to integrate separate stimuli into a single whole or group. An essential aspect of simultaneous processing is the need to see how all of the separate elements are interrelated into a whole. For this reason, Simultaneous Processing tests have strong spatial and logical aspects. The spatial aspect of simultaneous processing includes perception of stimuli as a whole. For example, simultaneous processing is involved in grammatical statements that demand the integration of words into a whole idea. This integration involves comprehension of word relationships, prepositions, and inflections so the person can obtain meaning based on the whole idea. Simultaneous Processing tests in the CAS require integration of parts into a single whole and understanding of logical and grammatical relationships. These processes are used in tests that involve nonverbal and verbal content, and recall of the stimuli, but the essential ingredient is simultaneous processing.

Successive processing

The essence of successive processing is the organization of stimuli into a specific serial order that forms a chain-like progression. Successive processing is required when a person must arrange things in a strictly defined order, where each element is only related to those that precede it and these stimuli are not interrelated. Successive processing involves both the perception of stimuli in sequence and the formation of sounds and movements in order. For this reason, successive processing has strong sequential components and is involved with the syntax of language, for example. All CAS Successive tests demand use, repetition, or comprehension based on order.

PASS processes

The four PASS processes are not unrelated constructs that function in isolation, but, instead, the opposite is assumed. Luria (1973) stated this when he wrote, 'each form of conscious activity is always a complex functional system and takes place through the combined working of all three brain units, each of which makes its own contribution. The well established facts of modern psychology provide a solid basis for this view' (p. 99). This conception means that the four PASS processes can be thought of as a functional system, or a 'working constellation' (Luria, 1966, p. 70) of cognitive activity, thus permitting individuals to perform the same task with the contribution of various processes and the participation of the knowledge and skills. Although effective functioning is accomplished through the integration of all PASS processes as demanded by the particular task, not every process is equally involved in every task. For example, tests like those included in the CAS subtests may be heavily weighted, or influenced, by a single PASS process. In fact, one of the goals in development of the CAS was to efficiently measure each of the four processes.

Description of the CAS

The development of the CAS was based on a systematic effort to develop efficient measures of the processes included in the PASS theory and to provide an individually administered instrument for assessing these important cognitive functioning. The PASS theory was used to guide the construction of the CAS and the content of the test was not constrained by previous approaches to intelligence. CAS reflects the merging of high psychometric qualities and a specific theory of cognitive processing within the context of providing a user-friendly, practical test. Thus, CAS was developed to integrate both theoretical and applied knowledge in psychology.

There were several assumptions and goals that were used during the development of the CAS, which are as shown below.

1. A test of intelligence should be based on a sound theory.
2. A theory of intelligence should be based on modern cognitive and neuro-psychological constructs.
3. A theory of ability should be based on the view that intelligence is best described as cognitive processes rather than the concept of general ability.
4. A theory of cognitive functioning should have a sizeable research base and have been proposed, tested, modified, and shown to have several types of validity.
5. The term 'cognitive processes' should replace the term 'intelligence.'
6. A theory of cognitive processes should inform the user about those specific abilities that are related to academic successes and failures.
7. A theory of cognitive processes should have relevance to differential diagnosis.
8. A theory of cognitive processes should provide guidance to the selection and/or development of effective programming for intervention.
9. A test of cognitive processing should follow closely from the theory of cognition on which it is based.
10. A test of cognitive processing should evaluate an individual using items that are as free from acquired knowledge as possible.

Development of CAS subtests

CAS subtests were developed specifically to operationalize the PASS theory of cognitive processing over a period of about 25 years (summarized in three sources: Das et al., 1979, 1994; Naglieri & Das, 1997b). Selection of tests was not dictated or constrained by psychometric theories of human abilities (e.g., Carroll, 1993) or by the content of traditional tests of intelligence. The sole criterion for inclusion was each subtest's correspondence to the theoretical framework of the PASS theory. Development of the CAS subtests was accomplished following an experimental sequence involving item generation, data analysis, test revision, and re-examination until the instructions, items, and other dimensions were refined through a series of pilot tests, research studies, national tryouts, and national standardization. This process allowed for the identification of subtests that provide an efficient way to measure each of the processes (Das et al., 1994; Naglieri & Das, 1997b).

The CAS is organized according to the PASS theory and, for that reason, is comprised of four scales. The Planning, Attention, Simultaneous, and Success-ive scales are derived from the sum of subtests included in each respective scale. Like the Full Scale score (derived from the sum of all subtests), each PASS scale has a normative mean of 100 and a standard deviation of 15. The PASS scales

Table 5.1. Structure of the CAS scales and subtests

Full Scale	Scales	Subtests
	Planning	
	*	Matching Numbers
	*	Planned Codes
		Planned Connections
	Simultaneous	
	*	Nonverbal Matrices
	*	Verbal–Spatial Relations
		Figure Memory
	Attention	
	*	Expressive Attention
	*	Number Detection
		Receptive Attention
	Successive	
	*	Word Series
	*	Sentence Repetition
		Speech Rate (ages 5–7 years) or Sentence Questions (ages 8–17 years)

*Subtests included in the Basic Battery.

represent a child's cognitive functioning and are used in the identification of specific strengths and weaknesses in cognitive processing. There are two combinations of subtests used to obtain PASS Scale and Full Scale scores. One is called the Basic Battery and the other the Standard Battery. The Basic Battery includes eight subtests (two per PASS scale), the Standard Battery includes all 12 subtests.

The CAS subtests and scales to which they are assigned are shown in Table 5.1. Each subtest scaled score is set at a mean of 10 and a standard deviation of 3. The CAS subtests are intended to be measures of the specific PASS process corresponding to the scale on which they are found rather than specific abilities. They do, however, have varying content (some are verbal, some not; some involve memory, others not, etc.), but the most important point is that each is an effective measure of a specific PASS process. Each subtest is described below.

Planning Scale

Matching Numbers consists of four pages, each with eight rows of numbers, six numbers per row. Children are instructed to underline the two numbers in each row that are the same. Numbers increase in length across the four pages from one digit to seven digits, with four rows for each digit length. Each item has a time limit. The subtest score is based on the combination of time and number correct for each page.

Planned Codes contains two pages, each with a distinct set of codes and arrangement of rows and columns. A legend at the top of each page shows how letters correspond to simple codes (e.g., A, B, C, D correspond to OX, XX, OO, XO, respectively). Each page contains seven rows and eight columns of letters without codes. Children fill in the appropriate codes in empty boxes beneath each letter. On the first page, all the As appear in the first column, all the Bs in the second column, all the Cs in the third column, and so on. On the second page, letters are configured in a diagonal pattern. Children are permitted to complete each page in whatever fashion they desire. The subtest score is based on the combination of time and number correct for each page.

Planned Connections contains eight items. The first six items require children to connect numbers appearing in a quasi-random order on a page in sequential order. The last two items require children to connect both numbers and letters in sequential order, alternating between numbers and letters (for example, 1-A-2-B-3-C). The items are constructed so that children never complete a sequence by crossing one line over the other. The score is based on the total amount of time in seconds used to complete the items.

Attention Scale

Expressive Attention uses two different sets of items, depending on the age of the child. Children aged eight years and older are presented with three pages. On the first page, children read color words (i.e., BLUE, YELLOW, GREEN, and RED), presented in quasi-random order. Next, they name the colors of a series of rectangles (printed in blue, yellow, green, and red). Finally, the words, BLUE, YELLOW, GREEN, and RED, are printed in inks of a different color from the colors the words name. The child is instructed to name the color of ink the word is printed in, rather than to read the word. Performance on the last page is used as the measure of attention. The subtest score is based on the combination of time and number correct.

Number Detection consists of pages of numbers that are printed in different formats. On each page, children are required to find a particular stimulus (e.g., the number 1, 2, and 3 printed in an open font) on a page containing many distractors (e.g., the same numbers printed in a different font). There are 180 stimuli with 45 targets (25% targets) on the pages. The score reflects the ratio of accuracy (total number correct minus the number of false detections) to total time for each item summed across the items.

Receptive Attention is a two-page paper-and-pencil subtest. On the first page, letters that are physically the same (e.g., TT but not Tt) are targets, but on the second, letters that have the same name (e.g., Aa not Ba) are targets. Each page contains 200 pairs of letters with 50 targets (25% targets) and the same set of distractors. The score reflects the ratio of accuracy (total number correct minus the number of false detections) to total time for each page, summed across pages.

Simultaneous Scale

Nonverbal Matrices is a 33-item subtest that utilizes shapes and geometric designs that are interrelated through spatial or logical organization. Children are required to decode the relationships among the parts of the item and choose the best of six options to occupy a missing space in the grid. Each matrix item is scored as correct or incorrect. The subtest score is based on the total number of items correctly answered.

Verbal–Spatial Relations is composed of 27 items that require the comprehension of logical and grammatical descriptions of spatial relationships. Children are shown items containing six drawings and a printed question at the bottom of each page. The items involve both objects and shapes that are arranged in a specific spatial manner. For example, the item, 'Which picture shows a circle to the left of a cross under a triangle above a square?' includes six drawings with various arrangements of geometric figures, only one of which matches the description. The examiner reads the question aloud and the child is required to select the option that matches the verbal description. Children must indicate their answers within a 30-second time limit. The subtest score reflects the total number of items correctly answered.

Figure Memory is a 27-item subtest. The child is shown a two-dimensional or three-dimensional geometric figure for five seconds. The figure is then removed, and the child is presented with a response page that contains the original design embedded in a larger, more complex geometric pattern. The child is asked to identify the original design embedded within the more complex figure. To be scored correct, all lines of the design have to be indicated without any additions or omissions. The score reflects the total number of correct items.

Successive Scale

Word Series requires the child to repeat words in the same order as stated by the examiner. The test consists of the following nine single-syllable, high-frequency words: Book, Car, Cow, Dog, Girl, Key, Man, Shoe, Wall.

There are 27 items that the examiner reads to the child. Each series ranges in length from two to nine words, presented at the rate of one word per second. Items are scored as correct if the child reproduces the entire word series. The score is based on the total number of items correctly repeated.

Sentence Repetition requires the child to repeat 20 sentences that are read aloud. Each sentence is composed of color words (e.g., 'The blue is yellowing'). The child is required to repeat each sentence exactly as it was presented. Color words are utilized so that the sentences contain little semantic meaning, to help reduce the influence of Simultaneous Processing and accent the demands of the syntax of the sentence. Each item is scored correct if the sentence is repeated exactly as presented. The subtest score reflects the total number of sentences correctly repeated.

Sentence Questions is a 21-item subtest that uses the same type of sentences as those in Sentence Repetition. Children from ages 8 to 17 are read a sentence and then asked a question about the sentence. For example, the examiner says, 'The blue is yellowing,' and asks the following question: 'Who is yellowing?' The correct answer is 'The blue.' Responses are scored correct if the child successfully answers the question regarding the sentence. The subtest score reflects the total number of questions answered correctly.

CAS scale reliabilities

The CAS subtests and scales have high reliability and meet or exceed minimum values suggested by Bracken (1987). The Full Scale reliability coefficients for the Standard Battery range from a low of .95 to a high of .97 and the average reliabilities for the Standard Battery PASS scales are .88 (Planning and Attention scales) and .93 (Simultaneous and Successive scales). The Basic Battery reliabilities are as follows: Full Scale = .87, Planning = .85, Simultaneous = .90, Attention = .84, and Successive = .90.

Normative and validity studies of CAS

CAS standardization

The CAS was standardized on a large representative group of children aged 5–17 years using a stratified random sampling plan which resulted in a sample that closely matches the US population. Children from both regular education and special education settings were included in their appropriate proportions. During the standardization and validity study data collection program, a total of 3072 children were administered the CAS. Of that sample, 2200 children made up the normative sample and an additional 872 children participated in reliability and validity. A subsample of 1600 of the entire standardization group was also administered a group of achievement tests. The CAS standardization sample was stratified on the basis of: age (5 years 0 months through 17 years 11 months); gender (female, male); race (black, white, Asian, Native American, other); Hispanic origin (Hispanic, Non-Hispanic); Region (Midwest, Northeast, South, West); community setting (urban/suburban, rural); classroom placement (full-time regular classroom, part-time special education resource, full-time self-contained special education); educational classification (learning disability, speech/language impairment, social–emotional disability, mental retardation, giftedness, and non-special education); and parental educational attainment level (less than high school degree, high school graduate or equivalent, some college or technical school, four or more years of college) The methods used to collect the data were designed to yield high-quality data on a sample that closely represents the US population (Naglieri & Das, 1997b). For details on the representativeness of the sample, see the CAS interpretive handbook (Naglieri & Das, 1997b).

Validity

Naglieri and Das (1997b) and Naglieri (1999) provide considerable information about the validity of the CAS. Naglieri (1999) shows that the CAS offers many advantages, but there are three important dimensions of validity that are particularly relevant to the discussion of the use of this test with learning-disabled children. The first point involves different PASS profiles found for children with reading disabilities and attention deficit hyperactivity disorders. Second, the CAS is more strongly related to achievement than similar tests. Finally, the CAS has been shown to have direct links to intervention. Each of these three points will be more fully discussed below.

PASS profiles

Naglieri (1999) provides a discussion of cognitive profiles for children with attention deficit and learning disabilities for the Wechsler Intelligence Scale for Children, Third Edition (WISC–III), Woodcock–Johnson Tests of Cognitive Ability–Revised (WJ–R) Cognitive, and CAS taken from the test manuals and a recent publication by Woodcock (1998). In the WISC–III manual, Wechsler (1991) provides three studies involving children with learning disabilities ($n = 65$) and attention deficit hyperactivity disorder ($n = 68$). The resulting profiles of WISC–III Index scores for the two groups of children were essentially the same. Similarly, Woodcock (1998) reported profiles for the seven *Gf–Gc*

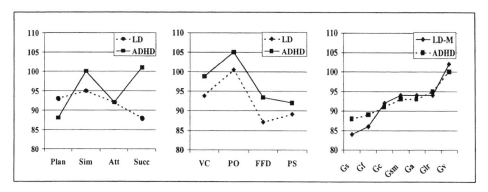

Fig. 5.1. Profiles of Ability scores on the CAS, WISC–III, and WJ–R Cognitive Test batteries. (LD, learning disabled; ADHD, attention deficit hyperactivity disorder; Plan, Planning; Sim, Simultaneous; Att, Attention; Succ, Successive; VC, Verbal Comprehension; PO, Perceptual Organization; FFD, Freedom from Distractibility; PS, Processing Speed.)

clusters for children with learning disabilities ($n = 62$) and attention deficit disorders ($n = 67$). His results also showed similar profiles for the groups. Therefore, the seven-factor Gf–Gc, like the WISC–III four Index level scores, does not yield distinctive profiles of scores for the learning disabilities and attention deficit hyperactivity disorder samples used. In contrast are the results for the CAS. In the studies reported by Naglieri and Das (1997b), children with reading disorders ($n = 24$) and attention deficit ($n = 66$) earned PASS scores that show a different pattern. The attention deficit hyperactivity disorder children were poor in Planning and somewhat lower in Attention, whereas the reading disorders sample was poor in Successive Processing. Thus, the profiles for the various tests (shown in Fig. 5.1) were different from those obtained for the Wechsler and Woodcock.

The comparative results for the WISC–III, WJ–R, and CAS illustrate how different the effectiveness of these instruments are in sensitivity to the problems children with learning disabilities have. The failure of the Wechsler accurately to identify learning-disabled children is well documented, despite the widespread use of scale and subtest interpretive methods (Kavale & Forness, 1984; McDermott, Fantuzzo, & Glutting, 1990). Naglieri (2000) has proposed that subtest analysis is problematic because the Wechsler scales do not measure ability broadly enough, nor does that test differentiate ability into important parts. This is why repeated attempts to validate Wechsler profile analysis have met with failure. Moreover, there is no evidence that reanalysis of the Wechsler subtests, for example using the cross battery approach advocated by McGrew and Flanagan (1998), offers an advantage. In fact, the data in Fig.

5.1 show that the *Gf–Gc* approach utilized by Woodcock was also diagnostically ineffective. This is consistent with discussions of the validity evidence on *Gf–Gc* provided by McGrew et al. (1997) and Horn and Noll (1997), which provide no evidence of differential profiles for exceptional children.

Relationships to achievement

Because the CAS was constructed using an alternative method to the Wechsler scales, one important test of the theory's utility is to examine how well it correlates with achievement. Naglieri (1999) conducted a study of the relationships between several tests of ability and achievement and found that the correlation between the Full Scale of the CAS and achievement was highest among the major intelligence tests. This finding is especially important for two reasons. First, one of the most important dimensions of validity for a test of cognitive ability is the relationship to achievement (Brody, 1992; Cohen, Swerdlik, & Phillips, 1992). Second, the CAS, unlike the Wechsler scales, does not include subtests that are highly reliant on acquired knowledge (e.g., Arithmetic, Information, Vocabulary).

Naglieri (1999) summarized several studies involving large numbers of children and several important tests. It was found that median correlation between the WISC–III (Wechsler, 1991) Full Scale Intelligence Quotient (FSIQ) and all Wechsler Individual Achievement Test (WIAT) achievement scores (Wechsler, 1992) is .59 for a sample of 1284 children aged 5–19 years from all regions of the country, different racial and ethnic groups, and each parental educational level. A similar correlation of .60 was found between the Differential Ability Scales (Elliott, 1990), General Conceptual Ability, and Achievement in Basic Number Skills, Spelling, and Word Reading is for a sample of 2400 children included in the standardization sample. Using the Woodcock–Johnson Revised Broad Cognitive Ability Extended Battery Score (which is comprised of seven *Gf–Gc* factors) and Woodcock–Johnson–Revised Achievement Test Batteries (reported by McGrew, Werder, & Woodcock, 1991), the median was .63 ($n = 888$ children aged 6, 9, and 13 years). This value is virtually the same as the median correlation between the K-ABC Mental Processing composite (MPC) and the K-ABC Achievement, Woodcock Reading Mastery Test, and KeyMath Diagnostic Math Test reported by Kaufman and Kaufman (1985), which is .63 for 2636 for children aged $2\frac{1}{2}$ through $12\frac{1}{2}$ years. Importantly, the K-ABC only has two scales, and content that does not include verbal/achievement content like that found in the first three tests. Finally, the median correlation between the CAS Full Scale and the WJ–R Test of Achievement (Naglieri and Das, 1997b) was .70 (for a representative sample of 1600 children aged 5–17 years

Table 5.2. Relationships between achievement and ability as measured by several intelligence tests

Ability test	n	Correlation	Percentage variance
WISC–III	1284	.59	35
Differential Ability Scale	2400	.60	36
Woodcock–Johnson Cognitive	888	.63	40
K-ABC	2636	.63	40
CAS	1600	.70	49

who closely match the US population). These results are presented in Table 5.2.

The correlations between the various ability tests and achievement summarized by Naglieri (1999) illustrated that the CAS Full Scale score was the most powerful predictor of achievement, accounting for considerably more variance in achievement than any of the measures included. These findings, in conjunction with separate profiles for hyperactivity disorder attention deficit and reading-disabled children and the intervention implications of PASS performance (discussed later in this chapter), provide strong support for the validity of the CAS. Additionally, they cast doubt on statements by McGrew et al. (1997) that the *Gf–Gc* theory is the 'most useful framework for understanding cognitive functioning' (p. 194). Instead, these data beg the question: why would seven *Gf–Gc* scales be needed if two on the K-ABC (Sequential and Simultaneous) are just as effective for prediction of achievement and if four from CAS (PASS) predict even higher? Moreover, given the differences between learning-disabled and attention deficit hyperactivity disorder children on PASS, this scale appears to be well suited for analysis of the cognitive problems children with learning disabilities may have.

Intervention

Two approaches to the translation of CAS results into intervention for children with learning problems are discussed in this chapter. The first is the PASS Remedial Program (PREP by J.P. Das, 1999), and the second is the Planning Facilitation Method described by Naglieri (1999). Both of these approaches are based on PASS and use information from the theory to build an intervention method. In addition, both have been shown to be effective: PREP for reading decoding, and Planning Facilitation for math calculation.

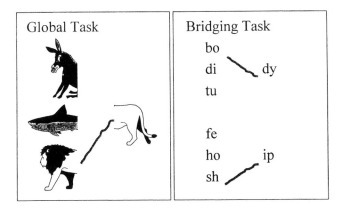

Fig. 5.2. Illustration of PREP Global and Bridging tasks.

PREP Remedial Program

The PREP program has its roots in the early research of Brailsford, Snart, and Das (1984), Kaufman and Kaufman (1979), and Krywaniuk and Das (1976). These researchers showed that students trained to use simultaneous and successive processes more efficiently, 'improved their performance on that process and some transfer to specific reading tasks also occurred' (Ashman & Conway, 1997, p. 169). The current version of PREP (Das, 1999) makes more explicit the connection between successive and simultaneous cognitive processes and reading. The training program includes more tasks that focus on successive processing than simultaneous processing. Each task has two forms, called global and bridging.

The PREP global tasks are nonacademic in content and specifically designed to illustrate the concept. The bridging tasks are similar to reading, but repeat the same conceptual point. For example, Fig. 5.2 shows an illustration of a successive global and bridging task in PREP. In this example, the child is being taught about a two-step sequence using the beginnings and endings of pictures of animals. To extend this to the beginnings and endings of words, the second bridging task is provided. Similar tasks are used to teach the children to work effectively with longer sequences.

The PREP program has been examined in recent research studies, with good results. Carlson and Das (1997) and Das, Mishra, and Pool (1995) conducted studies of the effectiveness of PREP for children with reading decoding problems in the USA. The Carlson and Das (1997) study involved Chapter 1 children who received PREP ($n = 22$) or regular reading program (control $n = 15$) and were tested before and after intervention using the measures of Word Attack and Word Identification. The intervention was conducted in two 50-minute

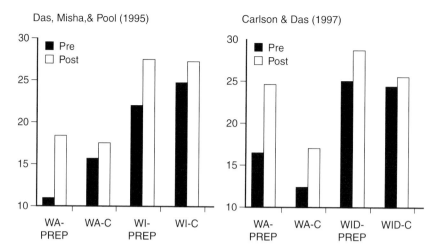

Fig. 5.3. Research report of two experiments on the effectiveness of PREP. (WA-PREP, Word Attack PREP group; WA–C, Word Attack control group; WI-PREP, Word Identification PREP group; WI-C, Word Identification control group.)

sessions each week for 12 weeks. Similarly, the Das et al. (1995) study involved 51 reading-disabled children who were divided into a PREP ($n = 31$) and control ($n = 20$) group. There were 15 PREP sessions given to small groups of four children. Word Attack and Word Identification tests were administered pre-treatment and post-treatment. In both studies, PREP groups outperformed the control groups. These findings (summarized in Fig. 5.3) 'suggest that process training can assist in specific aspects of beginning reading' (Ashman & Conway, 1997, p. 171).

Planning Facilitation

The way in which the CAS scores on PASS can be applied to interventions for children with learning disabilities was closely examined in a series of papers. These intervention studies focused on planning and math based on similar research by Cormier, Carlson, and Das (1990) and Kar et al. (1992). These researchers developed a method that stimulated children's use of planning, which had positive effects on performance. The method was based on the assumption that planning processes should be facilitated rather than directly instructed, so that children discover the value of strategy use without being specifically told to do so. Both the Cormier et al. (1990) and Kar et al. (1992) investigations demonstrated that students differentially benefited from a verbalization technique intended to facilitate planning. They found that participants who initially performed poorly on measures of planning earned significantly higher scores than those with good scores in planning. The verbalization method encouraged a well-planned and organized examination of the demands of the task and this helped those children who needed to do this the most (those with low planning scores). These studies were the basis for three experiments by Naglieri and Gottling (1995, 1997) and Naglieri and Johnson (2000), which focused on improving math calculation performance. The first two research studies by Naglieri and Gottling demonstrated that an intervention that facilitated planning led to improved performance on multiplication problems for those with low scores in planning, but minimal improvement was found for those with high planning scores. Thus, learning-disabled students benefited differentially from the instruction based on their cognitive processing scores; matching the instruction to the cognitive weakness of the child was shown to be important.

A description of the Planning Facilitation intervention

The Planning Facilitation method used in these studies has been applied to individual or groups of children. In the most recent studies, teachers provided instruction to the students about two to three times per week and consulted with the school psychologists on a weekly basis to assist in the application of the intervention, monitor the progress of the students, and consider ways of facilitating classroom discussions. Students completed mathematics work sheets in a sequence of about seven baseline and 21 intervention sessions over about a two-month period. In the intervention phase, the students were given a ten-minute period for completing a mathematics page, a ten-minute period was used for facilitating planning, and a second ten-minute period for mathematics. All students were exposed to the intervention sessions that involved the three ten-minute segments of mathematics/discussion/mathematics in 20-minute instructional periods. During the group discussion, self-reflection and discussion were facilitated so that the children would understand the need to plan and use an efficient strategy when completing the mathematics problems. The teachers provided probes which facilitated discussion designed to encourage the children to consider various ways to be more successful. When a student provided a response, this often became the beginning point for discussion and further development of the idea.

Teacher probes included statements like 'How did you do the math?', 'What could you do to get more correct?' or 'What will you do next time?' The teachers made no direct statements like, 'That is correct,' or 'Remember to use that same strategy,' nor did they provide feedback on the accuracy on previous pages, and they did not give mathematics instruction. The role of the teacher

Table 5.3. Summary of research investigations of the percentage of change from baseline to intervention for children with good or poor Planning scores

Study	High Planning (%)	Low Planning (%)	Difference (%)
Cormier, Carlson, & Das (1990)	5	29	24
Kar et al. (1992)	15	84	69
Naglieri & Gottling (1995)	26	178	152
Naglieri & Gottling (1997)	42	80	38
Naglieri & Johnson (2000)	11	143	132
Median values across all studies	15	84	69

was to facilitate self-reflection and, therefore, encourage the students to plan so that they could complete the work sheets. In response to teacher probes, students made statements such as, 'I have to remember to borrow,' 'I have to keep the columns straight or I get the wrong answer,' and 'Be sure to get them right not just get it done.' Interested readers should see Naglieri (1999) for more details on the Planning Facilitation intervention method and results from these studies.

The use of the Planning Facilitation method is perhaps best illustrated in an investigation by Naglieri and Johnson (2000) following procedures similar to those used by Naglieri and Gottling (1995, 1997), but with a larger sample and with children with learning problems. Because the purpose of their study was to determine if children with specific PASS profiles would show different rates of improvement, children were selected to form groups based on their CAS scores. Children with a cognitive weakness (an individual PASS score significantly lower than the child's mean and below 85) in Planning, Attention, Simultaneous, and Successive scales were selected to form contrast groups. The contrasting groups of children responded very differently to the intervention. Children with a cognitive weakness in Planning improved considerably over baseline rates, whereas those with no cognitive weakness improved only marginally. Similarly, children with cognitive weaknesses in Simultaneous, Successive, and Attention also showed substantially lower rates of improvement. Thus, these studies (summarized in Table 5.3) illustrate that PASS processes are relevant to intervention for children with learning disabilities.

In summary, the results of the studies on PREP and Planning Facilitation illustrate how CAS can be used to help determine if children evidence a PASS cognitive processing weakness that has relevance to intervention selection or design. Determination of a child's PASS profile is also useful for diagnostic and eligibility decisions. The latter is discussed in the next section.

How CAS can be used for learning disabilities diagnosis

The reauthorization of the Individuals with Disabilities Education Act Amendments of 1997 (IDEA 1997) requires that a child suspected of having a specific learning disability (SLD) must be assessed in all areas related to the suspected disability, including intelligence and academic performance. An evaluation must include technically sound instruments that meet the prescribed standards, including protections against racial, ethnic, language, or other bias. IDEA 1997 includes the definition of children with SLD that follows (p. 46):

A disorder in one or more of the basic psychological processes involved in understanding or in using language, spoken or written, which may manifest itself in an imperfect ability to listen, speak, read, write, spell, or do mathematical calculations. Such term includes such conditions as perceptual disabilities, brain injury, minimal brain dysfunction, dyslexia, and developmental aphasia. Such term does not include a learning problem that is primarily the result of visual, hearing, or motor disabilities, or mental retardation, of emotional disturbance, or of environmental, cultural, or economic disadvantage.

This definition of SLD has been operationalized in different ways (see Shepherd's thorough historical discussion of the issue of SLD definition in Chapter 1). Professionals have traditionally determined eligibility on the basis of an ability–achievement discrepancy or identification of a cognitive processing deficit. These concepts can be integrated into a more complete approach to the identification of children with SLDs based on psychological processing (e.g., PASS) cognitive problems. PASS processes can be used as a means to define the 'basic psychological processes' described in IDEA 1997 (Naglieri, 1999), and practitioners and researchers can use the CAS to obtain scores that represent these basic psychological processes. The CAS scores can be applied to detect disorders in one or more of the basic psychological processes and within the widely used discrepancy model.

The discrepancy approach to the identification of SLD children became popular, in part, because the most widely used IQ tests (Wechsler scales) were not developed to measure basic psychological processes, but rather were designed according to the concept of general intelligence. Thus, the Wechsler provided a convenient way to assess discrepancies. In order to assess SLD on the basis of a processing disorder, something other than a traditional general intelligence IQ test is required. Fortunately, in recent years such tests have become available. The K-ABC is one example that provides a test to measure

Sequential and Simultaneous processes which can be used within the guidelines set forth in the IDEA 1997. Another test, for example the Woodcock–Johnson Tests of Cognitive Ability (Woodcock & Johnson, 1989b), has a few scales described as measures of processing (Visual Processing and Auditory Processing) which could offer another option. However, the test is largely built on factor analysis rather than on a comprehensive theory of basic psychological processes, and to date no empirical evidence substantiates the use of specific *Gf–Gc* ability scores in making diagnostic (or treatment) recommendations (see McGrew et al., 1997, for a discussion of these points). Thus, it appears that the K-ABC and CAS are the best options for the assessment of basic psychological processes within the guidelines provided in IDEA 1997. In the following section, the procedures for the identification of weaknesses in basic psychological processes are discussed, along with methods to relate these weaknesses to academic failure.

Identification of a basic psychological processing disorder

Naglieri and Sullivan (1998) provide guidelines for how the CAS can be used to identify SLD children with a disorder in basic psychological processes as defined in IDEA 1997. Analysis begins with an examination of an individual child's PASS profile to determine if there exists a relative or cognitive weakness. A relative weakness is found when at least one PASS Scale standard score is significantly lower than the child's mean PASS score. Because the PASS scores are compared to the individual child's average (and not the normative mean of 100), this tells us about 'relative' strengths or weaknesses. For example, if a child has scores of 114 (Planning), 116 (Simultaneous), 94 (Successive), and 109 (Attention), the Successive score, which is 14.25 points below the child's mean of 108.25, is a 'relative weakness.' This approach has been used in intelligence testing (see Sattler, 1988; Naglieri, 1993; Kaufman, 1994) for some time. In contrast, a dual criterion is used to determine whether there is a 'cognitive weakness.' This includes a relative weakness and the lowest score has to be below average.

Naglieri (1999) suggests that a child who has a disorder in one of the four PASS basic psychological processes should have evidence of a 'cognitive weakness' because only in this case is the child's weakness below normal expectations. That is, a PASS relative weakness could still be within the average range, but a cognitive weakness demands poor performance relative to age-mates. The child with a cognitive weakness is likely to have significantly lower achievement scores and more likely to have been identified as exceptional (Naglieri, 2000).

Relating basic psychological processing weakness to academics

The view that a learning-disabled child has a disorder in a basic psychological process and a similarly low academic score is an integral part of the definition of SLD in IDEA 1997. One way to evaluate if a child's scores are consistent with this definition is to use the approach described by Naglieri (1999), which is summarized here. When a child has a cognitive weakness, it will be important to determine the differences between the separate PASS Scale scores and achievement. To do so, compare all of the PASS scores to the academic score. If the high PASS scores are significantly different from achievement, but the PASS cognitive weakness is not significantly different from an academic area, then an important finding is uncovered. That is, there is a cognitive weakness in PASS, and the weak PASS score is consistent with the poor academic score(s). This is called a Discrepancy/Consistency Approach by Naglieri (1999).

To apply the discrepancy/consistency method, first compare each of the PASS and Full Scale scores to achievement. Naglieri (1999) provides tables of the size of the differences needed for significance when comparing CAS to all achievement scores. For example, if a child has scores presented in Fig. 5.4, it is found that the Successive score of 71 is significantly lower than the child's PASS mean of 91.8. Similarly, the child has a low achievement test score in Letter–Word Identification (84) and Word Attack (82). These scores are significantly lower than the Planning, Simultaneous, and Attention scores but not significantly lower than the Successive score. In this case there is both a discrepancy between Planning, Attention, and Simultaneous scales with Successive, and between Planning, Attention, and Simultaneous scales with achievement. The lack of a significant difference between Successive and Reading Decoding (a relationship anticipated from previous research summarized in Das et al., 1994) provides an explanation for the academic problem. That is, because a strong relationship between word decoding and successive processing is reported in the literature (Kirby & Williams, 1991; Das et al., 1994), this connection is warranted.

The data in Fig. 5.4 are graphically organized into groups in Fig. 5.5. Figure 5.5 shows the relationship among the cognitive and academic measures. At the base of the triangle are the weaknesses, those in achievement (Word Attack and Letter–Word Identification) and one in cognitive processing (Successive). At the top of the triangle are the child's high scores. These include the Planning, Simultaneous, and Attention scales as well as areas of achievement that are relatively good for the child. When this relationship is found, the practitioner has an important perspective on the child. This child has a cognitive weakness and associated academic weakness that warrant intervention.

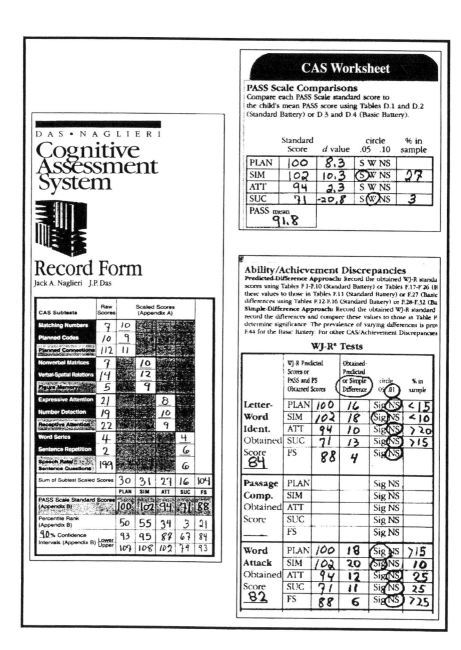

Fig. 5.4. CAS results.

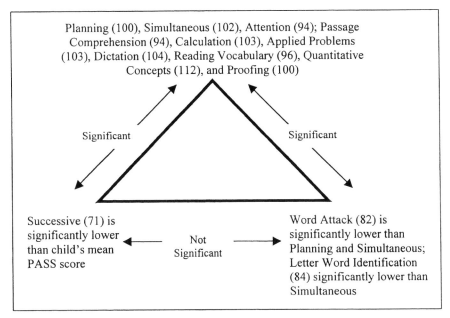

Planning (100), Simultaneous (102), Attention (94); Passage Comprehension (94), Calculation (103), Applied Problems (103), Dictation (104), Reading Vocabulary (96), Quantitative Concepts (112), and Proofing (100)

Significant

Significant

Successive (71) is significantly lower than child's mean PASS score

Not Significant

Word Attack (82) is significantly lower than Planning and Simultaneous; Letter Word Identification (84) significantly lower than Simultaneous

Fig. 5.5. CAS–Achievement test discrepancy and consistency results for an illustrative case study.

The most important advantage of using a cognitive processing perspective to uncover a disorder in basic psychological processing with academic failure is the explanatory power the view gives. In the current illustration, the child's low score in Successive Processing and reading failure give an explanation about why the child has had such difficulty. In this case, the child's difficulty with successive processing (dealing with things in specific order) is related to similar demands of reading. In particular, successive processing is important in assembling the sounds in the correct order to make words, ordering letters and groups of letters to spell, sounds blending, etc. This example also illustrates a case in which the PREP intervention would be appropriate, because it teaches children to focus on the sounds of events in order and helps them to apply these processes to reading. The steps needed to interpret this case are provided in the next section.

Case examples of interpretation of PASS theory and CAS

Case illustration 1

The data provided in Fig. 5.4 are for a girl aged 7 years 6 months included in the CAS standardization sample. The case is shown to illustrate how the CAS can be used to uncover PASS cognitive weakness and how the weakness can be related to academic performance. This illustration is not intended to show a full evaluation of a child, but rather, the use of CAS. The steps required for interpretation and the implications of these results are as follows:

1. The PASS and Full Scale standard scores are obtained and examined. It is found that the child has three out of the four PASS scales that fall in the Average Range but the Successive Scale standard score is very low (in the Below Average classification from Naglieri & Das, 1997b, p. 193).

2. The four PASS scores are compared using the ipsative method and it is found that the Successive Scale standard score is 20.8 points lower than the child's mean of 91.8. This difference is significant and unusual, only occurring in about 3% of children in regular educational settings. The Simultaneous Scale standard score is a relative strength, but the difference of 10.3 points is not unusual, occurring in about 27% of children in regular educational settings.

3. Examination of the Achievement Test results indicates that the child earned average or higher scores in the WJ–R Achievement subtests Passage Comprehension (94), Calculation (103), Applied Problems (103), Dictation (104), Reading Vocabulary (96), Quantitative Concepts (112), and Proofing (100), but her Word Attack and Letter–Word Identification standard scores were 82 and 84, respectively. For a child at this age, the low Successive Processing score and low Reading scores reflect the connection between basic psychological processing and use of sounds in order. Given the age of the child and the extent of the Successive Processing deficit, the child does have a disorder in one of the basic psychological processes involved in understanding or in using written language, as demonstrated by her low reading test scores. This provides supportive evidence that the child may meet regulations for identification as Specific Learning Disabled under IDEA 1997.

Case illustration 2

Sam, aged eight years and three months, is in second grade at Bailey Elementary School in Columbus, Ohio. According to his teacher, Mrs Corso, Sam has had difficulty with reading since his kindergarten year, when he began the Reading Recovery program. Sam has continued in Reading Recovery through the current year. In addition to the Reading Recovery program at school, Sam's parents provide instruction in reading and spelling each night. Unfortunately, despite the efforts at home and at school, Sam continues to have problems with reading and spelling (Table 5.4).

Sam's mother, Mrs D., reported that he was diagnosed with Arnold–Chiari 1 malformation, which is a rare neurological disorder in the brainstem. This malformation can lead to spinal cord fluid flow difficulties, which result in

Table 5.4. Case illustration: Sam, aged 8 years 3 months

Scale	Standard score	95% confidence interval	Percentile rank	Difference from child's mean
CAS				
Planning	96	88–105	39	−2.0
Simultaneous	114	105–121	82	16.0*
Attention	84	77–95	14	−14.0*
Successive	98	90–106	45	0.0
Full Scale	97	91–103	42	NA
DSMD scales				
Conduct	54	50–57	69	4.3
Attention	63	54–68	91	13.3
Anxiety	43	37–52	31	−6.7
Depression	43	38–51	35	−6.7
Autism	44	39–51	39	−5.7
Acute Problems	51	43–58	81	−1.3
DSMD composites				
Externalizing	59	55–62	83	9.3
Internalizing	43	39–48	30	−6.7
Critical Pathology	47	42–53	55	−2.7
PIAT–R				
General Information	118	112–125	88	NA
Reading Recognition	83	80–87	13	NA
Reading Comprehension	78	71–86	7	NA
Total Reading	80	76–83	9	NA
Mathematics	95	85–106	37	NA
Spelling	82	76–89	12	NA
Total test	88	84–91	21	NA

Note: Child's mean PASS score was 98.0. Differences that are significant from the child's mean ($p = 0.05$) are noted with an asterisk. DSMD is the Devereux Scales of Mental Disorders. Child's mean DSMD Scale T-score is 51.3 and the mean composite T-score is 49.7.

headaches. A recent surgical procedure was performed to remove a growth and this operation seems to have alleviated the effects of the problem. Sam continues to have academic problems, however.

Sam stated that he has lots of problems with reading and spelling, but loves math and science and is very good at them both. For example, Sam reported that he recently misspelled the word grape on his spelling test because he left off the 'e.' When asked why, he stated that he did not write it because he 'didn't remember seeing it before.' Thus, it appears that he has not focused his attention on the details of words. Despite Sam's stated desire to do better in reading and spelling, he finds these subjects very difficult and reported that he has trouble concentrating when studying.

Clinical observations

Sam was cooperative and friendly throughout the testing session, and engaged in appropriate social interactions with the examiner. Although he typically responded well to the questions, Sam appeared anxious when he could not easily answer some of them. At those times it was clear that he lost focus on the task and avoided interacting with the examiner. He also stated that he begins to 'sweat if the question is really hard' and in these situations 'it gets hard for me to concentrate.' Difficulty with focus of attention was also apparent on several occasions when he was provided with a multiple-choice test. For example, during a math test Sam responded verbally with the correct choice (e.g., 12.1), but chose an incorrect option, in this example 121. Additionally, on other tests with multiple options that were similar, he often chose an answer that was close to the correct option, but not completely correct. He apparently did not notice the similarity of the options.

Selected tests

Cognitive Assessment System (CAS).
Devereux Scales of Mental Disorders (DSMD).
Peabody Individual Achievement Test–Revised (PIAT–R).

Test results and interpretation

Sam's performance on various measures of ability, achievement, and behavior varied considerably and provided important insight into his current levels of functioning. He earned a CAS Full Scale score of 97, which falls in the Average range and ranks him at the 42nd percentile rank when compared to other children of his age. There is a 95% probability that his true Full Scale falls within the range of 91–103. However, because there was significant variation among the four scales that comprise the CAS Full Scale, the score of 97 should not be considered a good overall description of his performance. In fact, his scores on the separate PASS scales of the CAS varied considerably, from 84 (Attention Scale) to 114 (Simultaneous Scale). Sam's Attention score is a cognitive weakness and his Simultaneous score is a relative strength. Like the PASS scales, his Achievement test results on the PIAT–R also showed variability, with scores in

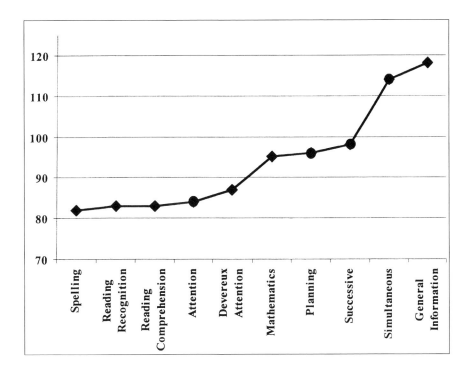

Fig. 5.6. Case illustration 2: graphic representation of Sam's test results.

the low 80s in Reading and Spelling but Average and Above Average scores in Math and General Information, respectively. Similarly, Sam's Devereux Scales of Mental Disorders (DSMD) Total Scale T-score was Average (T-score of 49, 58th percentile), but included scores that ranged from the Average classification (Anxiety, Depression, Autism, and Acute Problems) to the Elevated classification (63 in Attention). These scores indicate that the behaviors rated by Sam's father suggest significant problems with attention. The scores on tests of ability, behavior, and achievement all reflect the difficulty Sam has with attention (Fig. 5.6).

Sam's attention was formally assessed in two ways, using the CAS Attention Scale and a behavior rating scale (DSMD) completed by his father. Sam earned a score that falls in the Low Average range and is ranked at the 14th percentile on a cognitive measure of attention. This means that Sam did only as well as or better than 14% of children of his age on the subtests that make up the CAS Attention Scale. His attentional processing was measured by tests on the CAS that required him to respond only to particular stimuli and not to respond to distracting stimuli. He had problems both finding the correct targets and avoiding responding to the stimuli that were designed to be distracting. Although he tried his best during these tasks, he was anxious and frustrated with his inability to respond and often said, 'I just can't concentrate on this!'. Thus, it appeared that his poor performance was a combination of difficulty finding targets and resisting distractions. These findings are consistent with poor scores on the DSMD items dealing with distractibility, paying attention, and concentration. Thus, Sam earned very poor scores (in the Elevated range, T-score of 63 and percentile of 91) on the DSMD's Attention Scale and the CAS (behavioral and cognitive measures, respectively).

Attention processing problems can influence academic achievement in many ways. For Sam, choosing the incorrect answer instead of the option that is almost correct but not completely correct (a distractor option) was an indication of his difficulty with attention, as demonstrated by poor scores on the CAS Attention and DSMD Attention scales. Sam's scores on tests of achievement dealing with the decoding of words were significantly lower than his performance on all of the other academic tests. He earned a PIAT–R Spelling standard score of 82 (12 percentile, 95% confidence range of 76–89), a Reading Recognition score of 83 (13th percentile, 95% range of 80–87), and Reading Comprehension score of 78 (7th percentile, range of 71–86). Throughout these tests, Sam overemphasized phonetic rules and often chose options that were close to, but not exactly, the correct answers. He also made many comprehension errors because he misread the statements. For example, one question required him to understand the statement, 'The monkey is holding a rocket with it tail,' and Sam chose an answer that showed a monkey holding a rock with its tail. His failure to attend to the detail of the sentence (rocket not rock) and his failure to note the similarity of the two options led to poor performance on this academic task and others. Similarly, Sam lost points on the PIAT–R Mathematics subtest because he chose options that were close but not correct. These findings are consistent with his poor scores on the CAS Attention Scale and problems reported on the Devereux Attention Scale.

In contrast to Sam's poor performance on cognitive, behavioral, and academic tasks that involved attention, he performed very well on tests that demanded simultaneous processing. The tests that measure simultaneous processing required Sam to integrate several pieces of information into a whole or group. His score of 114 on the CAS Simultaneous Scale falls in the High Average range and is ranked at the 82nd percentile (range = 105–121). Not only is this a high score relative to his age-mates, but it is higher than his overall PASS score. These results suggest that Sam can perform well when he is asked to see relationships or patterns among things and to see how parts fit within a larger whole.

Sam earned Average scores on successive processing tests. He earned a score of 98 (45th percentile, 95% range = 90–106) on the Successive Scale of the CAS. Successive processing was measured by tests that required information to be arranged in a specific linear order in which each step was related only to the previous one. For example, Successive tests require the retention of the order of words spoken by the examiner and comprehension of the syntax of oral statements. Sam successfully remembered up to four unrelated words at a time.

Sam performed within the Average range on tests that demand planning processing. He earned a 96 on the Planning Scale of the CAS, which falls at the 39th percentile (range of 88–105). Sam's score on the Planning Scale reflects his ability to generate and use efficient and effective strategies for solving problems, self-monitoring, and self-regulation. For example, on a test that required him to connect numbers and letters serially on a page, Sam utilized a combination of efficient strategies by repeating the alphabet and number series to himself, scanning the page for the next number or letter, and lifting his hand off the page in order to see better.

Summary

Sam earned scores on measures of cognitive processing, behavior, and academic achievement that varied considerably. His scores fall in the Below Average (CAS Attention Scale, Devereux Attention Scale, PIAT–R Reading and Spelling), Average (CAS Planning and Successive scales, Devereux scales), and Superior (CAS Simultaneous Scale, PIAT–R Math and General Information) classifications. Sam's cognitive weakness on the CAS Attention Scale (84 standard score) and poor score on the Attention Scale of the DSMD indicate considerable difficulty when he was asked to identify correct targets (focus his attention) and avoid responding to the stimuli that are distracting (resist distraction). Thus, these two different approaches to measuring attention suggest that Sam has considerable difficulty with concentration, paying attention, and dealing with distractions. Sam's scores in attention are commensurate with his scores in reading (PIAT–R Reading Comprehension score of 78 and Reading Recognition score of 83) and spelling (PIAT–R Spelling score of 82). These scores indicate that Sam's difficulty with attention is a disorder in one of the basic psychological processes involved in understanding and using written language which manifested itself as significant problems with reading and spelling.

Sam exhibited a strength on the Simultaneous Processing Scale of the CAS (score of 114, which falls within the High Average classification). This high score indicates that he can perform well when asked to see relationships or patterns among things and determine how parts fit within a larger whole. Sam also earned average scores on the CAS Planning Scale (score of 96), which indicates that he developed and used efficient solutions to problems he was presented with. Similarly, he earned an Average score on the Successive Processing Scale of the CAS (score of 98), indicating that he effectively dealt with information that was presented or arranged in specific linear order. In summary, Sam was found to have a strength; average performance; and cognitive, behavioral, and academic weakness related to attention.

Recommendations

1. Sam's difficulty with the CAS Attention Scale and DSMD Attention rating, along with his poor academic performance, indicate that his problems with attention are related to the specific areas of academic difficulty. One way to help him improve his attention is to utilize a cognitive training program designed to help children better understand their attention difficulty and overcome it through a variety of compensatory skills. The Douglas Cognitive Control Program should be implemented to help teach Sam strategies for paying attention to his work through providing successful experiences and teaching him general rules on how to approach tasks. The program is described in the book *Learning Problems: A Cognitive Approach* by Kirby and Williams (1991) on pages 152–6 and in the handout at the end of this report.

2. Sam's strength in simultaneous processing should be utilized to teach him to recognize and spell words better. For example, a technique called 'Word Sorts' should be attempted to help Sam learn to spell. This technique draws on the similarities among word spellings and encourages children to see the patterns of spelling and sound/symbol association needed for reading decoding. Because Sam is so good at Simultaneous Processing, it will be easy for him to see these interrelationships and work with words in this manner. For example, the teacher may give a list of words such as grape, he, tree, knee, save, and tube and request that Sam sort them according to how the e at the end of the word sounds (e.g., grape, save, and tube all have silent e, whereas he, be, and knee all end in long e sound). This approach is appropriate for Sam because it has an emphasis on Simultaneous Processing, which is his strength. A summary of how Word Sorts works is provided in the intervention below.

Pam Gutter
Jack A. Naglieri

INATTENTION HANDOUT

From: J.R. Kirby & N.H. Williams (1991). *Learning Problems: A Cognitive Approach*.

This handout outlines methods to increase children's ability to attend and resist distraction. The present summary is based on the discussion Kirby and Williams (1991) provide in Chapter 11 about how to improve attention. The goal of the intervention is to help children learn to improve cognitive control of attention and resist distraction.

Overview of the Douglas's Cognitive Control Program (citation: Douglas, V.I. (1980). Treatment and training approaches to hyperactivity: establishing internal or external control. In *Hyperactive Children: The Social Ecology of Identification and Treatment*, C.K. Whalen & B. Hencker, New York: Academic Press.)

Level I: Help children understand the nature of their deficits including:
1. Attention, resistance to distraction, and control of attention
2. Recognition of how these deficits affect daily functioning
3. That the deficit can be overcome
4. Basic elements of the control program.

Level II: Improve motivation and persistence
1. Promote success via small steps
2. Ensure success at school and at home
   - Allow for oral responses to tests
   - Circumvent reading whenever possible.
3. Teach rules for approaching tasks
   - Define tasks accurately
   - Assess child's knowledge of problems
   - Consider all possible solutions
   - Evaluate value of all possible solutions
   - Checking work carefully is required
   - Correct your own test strategy (see Pressley & Woloshyn, 1995, p. 140).
4. Discourage passivity and encourage independence
   - Teacher should only provide as much assistance as is needed
   - Discourage exclusive use of teacher's solutions
   - Child needs to
     - take responsibility for correcting own work
     - see the difference between careless errors and those that reflect problems with knowledge
     - be self-reliant (Scheid, 1993).

5. Help children avoid
  - Excessive talking
  - Working fast with little accuracy
  - Giving up too easily
  - Sloppy, disorganized papers.

Level III: Teaching specific problem-solving strategies
1. Model and teach strategies that improve attention and concentration
  - Child must recognize if he is under or over attentive
  - Teach the use of verbal self-commands (e.g., 'OK, calm down and think about what the question is.')
  - Teach the use of organized and exhaustive scanning techniques
  - Teach focusing strategies such as checking for critical features
  - Careful listening for basic information
  - Teach a few strategies but teach them well (Pressley & Woloshyn, 1995).
2. Teach strategies that increase inhibition and organization
  - Encourage the use of date books
  - Encourage the use of special notebooks for keeping papers organized
  - Teach the child to stop and think before responding
  - Teach the child to count to 10 before answering.
3. Teach strategies to increase alertness
  - Teach the child to be aware of levels of alertness
  - Teach the child to use calming self statements
  - Encourage planned breaks.
4. Teach other relevant strategies
  - Teach rehearsal and mnemonic devices (Mastropieri & Scruggs, 1991)
  - Teach reading or math strategies (Pressley & Woloshyn, 1995).

INTERVENTION HANDOUT

Word Sorts Intervention for Spelling and Reading Decoding

This handout outlines a method called Word Sorts, which is designed to help children learn spelling and sound/symbol associations needed for reading decoding that has an emphasis on simultaneous processing. The goal of the intervention is to help children see the interrelationships among spelling rules and letter patterns that are associated with different sounds. The summary is based on the paper: Zutell, J. (1998). Word sorting: a developmental spelling approach to word study for delayed readers. *Reading & Writing Quarterly: Overcoming Learning Difficulties*, 14, 219–38.

Overview

Word sorting is an intervention in which 'students organize words printed on cards into columns on the basis of particular shared conceptual, phonological, orthographic, and meaning-related features' (Zutell, 1998, p. 226). This teaches students to generate concepts and generalizations about the features of how words are spelled, and it helps them connect new words to ones they already know (Pinnell & Fountas, 1998). The technique involves careful analysis of the students' current methods for spelling (Barnes, 1989) and involves a series of activities conducted for about 10 minutes each day. The basic system and different ways of sorting words are explained below.

1. Teach children about Word Sorts
   - There are many ways that words can be sorted according to their spelling. This includes sorts by sound (long e) or silent letters (w in the word wrist).
   - Example of a word sort activity:
     - Give children the following words: wrap, white, wren, what, wrist, write, would, when, whistle, wrong.
     - Two options:
       Closed sorts – the teacher chooses the category of silent versus nonsilent W in the words. Children are then taught to sort the words in the two groups according to the rule. Closed sorts are helpful in that they can be used to focus the child's attention on a specific word characteristic that may help with word recognition and production (Zutell, 1998).
       Open sorts – the teacher instructs the children to categorize the words based on shared features that the students discover (Pinnell & Fountas, 1998). This type of sort may be useful because it allows the students to display how they think about words (Zutell, 1998). Regardless of the students' level, it is important that they discuss the words while they are sorting them because the discussion will help with the internalization of the principles and it promotes under-standing (Pinnell & Fountas, 1998).
     - There are many different categories of words, sounds, patterns, etc. that can be used in word-sorting activities. These categories can help students' sound and letter patterns and get past regular, easy letter–sound correspondence, allowing for students to learn how to find complex patterns (Pinnell & Fountas, 1998).

2. How to apply the technique
   - The Word Sorts instruction should be a daily activity that lasts about 10

minutes and can be done in groups, pairs, or individually. Because the English language has many dimensions, an unlimited number of sorts can be used and discovered.

Conclusions

This chapter began with the assumption that intelligence tests have not changed appreciably since the beginning of the twentieth century and that advances in cognitive psychology and neuropsychology have provided the opportunity for change in this field. Tests like the K-ABC and CAS offer cognitive processing alternatives to the general intelligence model. The CAS and its base, the PASS theory, offer a strong alternative to traditional tests, as evidenced by three important findings. First, children's PASS profiles are relevant to differential diagnosis and especially helpful for those with learning disabilities and attention deficits. Second, the CAS is an excellent predictor of achievement, despite the fact that it does not contain verbal and achievement-based tests like those found in traditional measures of IQ. Third, the CAS provides information that is relevant to intervention and instructional planning.

REFERENCES

Ashman, A.F. & Conway, R.N.F. (1997). *An Introduction to Cognitive Education: Theory and Applications*. London: Routledge.

Barnes, W. (1989). Word Sorting: the cultivation of rules for spelling in English. *Reading Psychology: An International Quarterly*, 10, 293–307.

Bracken, B.A. (1987). Limitations of preschool instruments and standards for minimal levels of technical adequacy. *Journal of Psychoeducational Assessment*, 5, 313–26.

Brailsford, A., Snart, F., & Das, J.P. (1984). Strategy training and reading comprehension. *Journal of Learning Disabilities*, 17, 287–90.

Brody, N. (1992). *Intelligence*. San Diego: Academic Press.

Carlson, J. & Das, J.P. (1997). A process approach to remediating word decoding deficiencies in Chapter 1 children. *Learning Disabilities Quarterly*, 20, 93–102.

Carroll, J.B. (1993). *Human Cognitive Abilities: A Survey of Factor-analytic Studies*. New York: Cambridge University Press.

Cohen, R.J., Swerdlik, M.E., & Phillips, S.M. (1992). *Psychological Testing and Assessment*. Mountain View, CA: Mayfield.

Cormier, P., Carlson, J.S., & Das, J.P. (1990). Planning ability and cognitive performance: the compensatory effects of a dynamic assessment approach. *Learning and Individual Differences*, 2, 437–49.

Das, J.P. (1999). *PASS Reading Enhancement Program*. Deal, NJ: Sarka Educational Resources.

Das, J.P., Kirby, J.R., & Jarman, R.F. (1975). Simultaneous and successive syntheses: an alternative model for cognitive abilities. *Psychological Bulletin*, 82, 87–103.

Das, J.P., Kirby, J.R., & Jarman, R.F. (1979). *Simultaneous and Successive Cognitive Processes*. New York: Academic Press.

Das, J.P., Mishra, R.K., & Pool, J.E. (1995). An experiment on cognitive remediation or word-reading difficulty. *Journal of Learning Disabilities*, 28, 66–79.

Das, J.P., Naglieri, J.A., & Kirby, J.R. (1994). *Assessment of Cognitive Processes*. Needham Heights, MA: Allyn & Bacon.

Elliott, C.D. (1990). *Differential Ability Scales: Introductory and Technical Handbook*. San Antonio, TX: The Psychological Corporation.

Gazzaniga, M.S. (1975). Recent research on hemispheric lateralization of the human brain: review of the split-brain. *UCLA Educator*, 17, 9–12.

Horn, J.L. & Noll, J. (1997). Human cognitive capabilities: *Gf–Gc* theory. In *Contemporary Intellectual Assessment: Theories, Tests and Issues*, ed. D.P. Flanagan, J.L. Genshaft, & P.L. Harrison, pp. 53–91. New York: Guilford.

Kar, B.C., Dash, U.N., Das, J.P., & Carlson, J.S. (1992). Two experiments on the dynamic assessment of planning. *Learning and Individual Differences*, 5, 13–29.

Kaufman, A.S. (1994). *Intelligent Testing with the WISC–III*. New York: Wiley.

Kaufman, D. & Kaufman, P. (1979). Strategy training and remedial techniques. *Journal of Learning Disabilities*, 12, 63–6.

Kaufman, A.S. & Kaufman, N.L. (1983). *Kaufman Assessment Battery for Children*. Circle Pines, MN: American Guidance Service.

Kaufman, A.S. & Kaufman, N.L. (1985). *Kaufman Assessment Battery for Children*. Circle Pines, MN: American Guidance Service.

Kavale, K.A. & Forness, S.R. (1984). A meta-analysis of the validity of the Wechsler Scale profiles and recategorizations: patterns or parodies? *Learning Disability Quarterly*, 7, 136–51.

Kinsborne, M. (1978). *Asymmetrical Function of the Brain*. Cambridge, UK: Cambridge University Press.

Kirby, J.R. & Williams, N.H. (1991). *Learning Problems: A Cognitive Approach*. Toronto: Kagan and Woo.

Krywaniuk, L.W. & Das, J.P. (1976). Cognitive strategies in native children: analysis and intervention. *Alberta Journal of Educational Research*, 22, 271–80.

Luria, A.R. (1966). *Human Brain and Psychological Processes*. New York: Harper & Row.

Luria, A.R. (1973). *The Working Brain: An Introduction to Neuropsychology*. New York: Basic Books.

Luria, A.R. (1980). *Higher Cortical Functions in Man*, 2nd edition. New York: Basic Books.

Luria, A.R. (1982). *Language and Cognition*. New York: Wiley.

Mastropieri, M.A. & Scruggs, T.E. (1991). *Teaching Students Ways to Remember*. Cambridge, MA: Brookline Books.

McDermott, P.A., Fantuzzo, J.W., & Glutting, J.J. (1990). Just say no to subtest analysis: a critique on Wechsler theory and practice. *Journal of Psychoeducational Assessment*, 8, 290–302.

McGrew, K.S. & Flanagan, D.P. (1998). *The Intelligence Test Desk Reference: Gf–Gc Crooss-battery Assessment*. Boston, MA: Allyn & Bacon.

McGrew, K.S., Keith, T.Z., Flanagan, D.P., & Vanderwood, M. (1997). Beyond g: the impact of Gf–Gc specific cognitive abilities research on the future use and interpretation of intelligence tests in the schools. *School Psychology Review*, 26, 189–210.

McGrew, K.S., Werder, J.K., & Woodcock, R.W. (1991). *WJ–R Technical Manual*. Chicago, IL: Riverside.

Miller, G., Galanter, E., & Pribram, K. (1960). *Plans and the Structure of Behavior*. New York: Henry Holt and Company.

Naglieri, J.A. (1993). Pairwise and Ipsative WISC–III IQ and Index Score comparisons. *Psychological Assessment: A Journal of Consulting and Clinical Psychology*, 5, 113–16.

Naglieri, J.A. (1999). *Essentials of CAS Assessment*. New York: Wiley.

Naglieri, J.A. (2000). Can profile analysis of ability test scores work? An illustration using the PASS theory and CAS with an unselected cohort. *School Psychology Quarterly*, 15, 419–33.

Naglieri, J.A. & Das, J.P. (1997a). *Cognitive Assessment System*. Chicago, IL: Riverside Publishing Company.

Naglieri, J.A. & Das, J.P. (1997b). *Cognitive Assessment System Interpretive Handbook*. Chicago, IL: Riverside Publishing Company.

Naglieri, J.A. & Gottling, S.H. (1995). A cognitive education approach to math instruction for the learning disabled: an individual study. *Psychological Reports*, 76, 1343–54.

Naglieri, J.A. & Gottling, S.H. (1997). Mathematics instruction and PASS cognitive processes: an intervention study. *Journal of Learning Disabilities*, 30, 513–20.

Naglieri, J.A. & Johnson, D. (2000). Effectiveness of a cognitive strategy intervention to improve math calculation based on the PASS theory. *Journal of Learning Disabilities*, 33, 591–7.

Naglieri, J.A. & Sullivan, L. (1998). IDEA and identification of children with specific learning disabilities. *Communiqué*, 27, 20–1.

Neisser, U. (1967). *Cognitive Psychology*. New York: Appleton-Century-Crofts.

Pinnell, G. & Fountas, I. (1998). *Word Matters: Teaching Phonics and Spelling in the Reading/Writing Classroom*. Portsmouth, NH: Heinemann.

Pressley, M.P. & Woloshyn, V. (1995). *Cognitive Strategy Instruction that really Improves Children's Academic Performance*, 2nd edition. Cambridge, MA: Brookline Books.

Sattler, J.M. (1988). *Assessment of Children*, 3rd edition. San Diego, CA: Jerome M. Sattler.

Scheid, K. (1993). *Helping Students Become Strategic Learners*. Cambridge, MA: Brookline Books.

Solso, R.L. & Hoffman, C.A. (1991). Influence of Soviet scholars. *American Psychologist*, 46, 251–3.

Sternberg, R.J. (1988). *The Triarchic Mind: A New Theory of Human Intelligence*. New York: Viking.

Wechsler, D. (1991). *Wechsler Intelligence Scale for Children, Third Edition*. San Antonio, TX: The Psychological Corporation.

Wechsler, D. (1992). *Wechsler Individual Achievement Test*. San Antonio, TX: The Psychological Corporation.

Wilson, M.S. & Reschly, D.J. (1996). Assessment in school psychology training and practice. *School Psychology Review*, 25, 9–23.

Woodcock, R.W. (1998). *The WJ–R and Bateria–R in Neuropsychological Assessment: Research Report Number 1*. Itasca, IL: Riverside Publishing Company.

Woodcock, R.W. & Johnson, M.B. (1989a). *Woodcock–Johnson Revised Tests of Achievement: Standard and Supplemental Batteries*. Itasca, IL: Riverside Publishing.

Woodcock, R.W. & Johnson, M.B. (1989b). *Woodcock–Johnson Revised Tests of Cognitive Ability: Standard and Supplemental Batteries*. Itasca, IL: Riverside Publishing.

Yoakum, C.S. & Yerkes, R.M. (1920). *Army Mental Tests*. New York: Henry Holt and Company.

Ysseldyke, J., Dawson, P., Lehr, C., Reschly, D., Reynolds, M., & Telzrow, C. (1997). *School Psychology: A Blueprint for Training and Practice II*. Bethesda, MD: NASP.

Zutell, J. (1998). Word sorting: a developmental spelling approach to word study for delayed readers. *Reading & Writing Quarterly: Overcoming Learning Difficulties*, 14, 219–38.

6

Application of the Differential Ability Scales (DAS) and British Ability Scales, Second Edition (BAS II), for the assessment of learning disabilities

Colin D. Elliott

Introduction and overview

Two decades have passed since what was then a new test battery – the British Ability Scales (BAS; Elliott, Murray, & Pearson, 1979) – was introduced to the stable of tests for assessing cognitive abilities in children. The battery has since been further developed, resulting in the publication of the Differential Ability Scales (DAS; Elliott, 1990a) and the British Ability Scales, Second Edition (BAS II; Elliott, 1997a), which have achieved widespread acceptance and popularity in the USA and UK, respectively.

The BAS II and DAS represent an advance in cognitive assessment. In a review of the original BAS, Embretson (1985) stated: 'The BAS is an individual intelligence test with greater scope and psychometric sophistication than the major American individual tests. The test development procedures and norms are laudatory' (p. 232). In another review, Wright and Stone (1985) stated that the BAS 'is a significant advance in mental measurement . . . Its form and function are a model for contemporary test builders and a preview of the future of test construction' (p. 232). Kamphaus (1993), in reviewing the DAS, wrote: 'There is every indication that the developers of the DAS erred in the direction of quality at every turn. The manual is extraordinarily thorough, the psychometric properties are strong, and the test materials are of high quality' (pp. 320–1). Similarly, Anastasi and Urbina (1997), in a review of the DAS in the seventh edition of *Psychological Testing*, write that 'the DAS is a "state of the art" instrument of its type, as yet unsurpassed in the possibilities and advantages it affords to users' (p. 232). Sound theory, technical sophistication, and high-quality norms all characterize the BAS II and the DAS, and are essential qualities in a good cognitive assessment instrument. Perhaps even more importantly, the instruments are also engaging for children, time-efficient for the examiner, and yield a range of subtest and composite scores that are reliable, interpretable, relevant to children's learning and development, and have much to offer the clinician in translating assessment results into practical recommendations.

History, development, and goals

History

The initial stages of the development of the BAS were set against a background of increasing provision for children with special needs and an expansion of the role of educational psychologists. Until the 1960s, psychologists in Great Britain had used adaptations of scales published in the USA, such as the various Wechsler scales or editions of the Stanford–Binet. These instruments met many of the needs of British users, yielding credible estimates of general ability and useful predictions of school achievement. At the same time, however, these scales were criticized along several lines. For example, some test questions with specifically American content were considered unsuitable for use in Great Britain. The lack of British norms was also an important issue, although the results of a Scottish standardization of the Wechsler Intelligence Scale for Children (WISC; Wechsler, 1949) in the mid-1960s were extremely close to the US norms (Scottish Council for Research in Education, 1967).

Psychologists also criticized the available intelligence scales in more general terms. Concerns over ethnic and social-class bias in test scores fuelled research and provoked controversy. Some test users were dissatisfied with scales whose purposes were primarily to produce a summary score (IQ) and only secondarily to yield multiple subscores with known diagnostic implications. Furthermore, in the 1960s, researchers inspired by Piagetian theory were exploring several dimensions of early cognitive development that were not measured by existing ability-test batteries.

All of these concerns amplified the need for a new intelligence battery constructed and standardized in Great Britain. In the late 1950s, the British Psychological Society convened a committee of specialists to produce a plan for such a battery. The British Government's Department of Education and Science provided a substantial grant to the British Psychological Society to support the development of the new scale, to be called the 'British Intelligence Scale.' In turn, this grant made possible the establishment of a research unit at the University of Manchester, which began its work in 1965 under the direction of Professor F.W. Warburton.

Initial item development and trialling went ahead until 1969, with the untimely death of Frank Warburton coinciding with the cessation of the initial funding. The project restarted in 1973, with additional funding, under the direction of the present author. The purpose of the battery was reconceptualized, primarily emphasizing its development as an instrument measuring ability profiles rather than having its primary emphasis as a measure of 'intelligence.' This reconceptualization resulted in the change of name to the 'British Ability Scales.' The period 1973 to 1978 was spent in restructuring the battery, writing many new items and developing new subtests, carrying out a national standardization, and preparing the battery for publication.

Following initial publication, analytic work continued, together with the further development of some scales to rectify a number of weaknesses, including lack of sufficient items at particular age levels and procedural problems with the scoring. Thus, after completion of this work in 1982, a revised edition was published in 1983. Also in 1983, The Psychological Corporation in the USA started a project to develop a version of the BAS tailored for North America, which became the DAS, published in 1990. This version dropped six of the original BAS scales, and developed four additional scales (or subtests).[1] Other major revisions were made that are described by Elliott (1990c).

Finally, the changes made to the DAS were incorporated in the BAS II, published in 1997. In addition, the BAS II included one subtest not in the DAS, as well as a number of revisions to other subtests.

Development and goals

Two principles – self-evident truths to many practitioners – drove the development of the DAS and the BAS II. The first is that professionals assessing children with learning and developmental disabilities need information at a finer level of detail than an IQ score. IQ tests in the past have had a primary, disproportionate focus on global composite scores. The second principle is that psychometric assessment has much to offer the practitioner: psychometric tests of cognitive abilities not only have well-established qualities of reliability, validity, time efficiency, objectivity, and lack of bias, but often give us information critical to our understanding of a child's learning styles and characteristics.

The first principle led to the major priority in the development of the DAS and BAS II: to produce a battery in which subtests would be sufficiently reliable and measure sufficiently distinct cognitive functions to make them individually interpretable. While it was expected that meaningful composites would be derived from the subtests, the primary focus in test development was at the subtest level. This emphasis distinguishes the DAS and BAS II from most other batteries. Although some (usually the critics of the whole psychometric enterprise) may misleadingly characterize the DAS and BAS II as 'IQ tests,' in truth they are not. They downplay the importance of the general composite, and do not even call that composite 'IQ.' Indeed, the terms 'intelligence' and 'IQ' are rejected: they have been so vaguely and variously defined as to have become scientifically meaningless. Back in 1927, Spearman also expressed the same view when he described intelligence as 'a word with so many meanings that finally it has none' (p. 14). Thus, the goal for the DAS and BAS II is to measure a range of cognitive abilities. The term 'cognitive ability' refers to a more specific and narrower domain of human cognition than the term 'intelligence.'

Spearman's g has not been lost, however. For all age levels from 3 years 6 months upwards, six subtests, measuring a number of cognitive abilities, form an overall composite score reflecting the general factor g. Psychometric g is defined as 'the general ability of an individual to perform complex mental processing that involves conceptualization and the transformation of information' (Elliott, 1990c, p. 20). From this definition comes the term used to describe the most general DAS and BAS II composite score: General Conceptual Ability (GCA).

If one is to produce a test battery that measures profiles of children's strengths and weaknesses across a range of distinct cognitive abilities, it is necessary to have lower-order composites and subtests with sufficiently high specificity and reliability as to allow the clinician to interpret each as measuring something unique and distinct from the others. The purpose of this enterprise is that the creation of a reliable profile of a child's cognitive strengths and weaknesses will lead to a better understanding of his or her learning difficulties and ultimately to practical recommendations to classroom teachers about remediation (Elliott, 1990c).

The DAS and BAS II were not developed solely to reflect a single model of cognitive abilities, but may be interpreted from a number of theoretical perspectives. Their content is designed to address processes that often underlie children's difficulties in learning, and what we know of neurological structures underlying these abilities. As Carroll (1993) has shown, there are considerable similarities in the factor structures of cognitive batteries. A general factor (g) is an inescapable reality. It pervades all measures of ability and all relationships between cognitive abilities of any kind. It must therefore be represented in any test battery structure and in its theoretical model. In reviewing the many theories of the structure of abilities, it was apparent that no single theory is entirely persuasive and certainly no single theory has universal acceptance among theoreticians or practitioners. Even the proponents of what has now become known as the Cattell–Horn–Carroll (CHC) theory, currently the most popular factor theory of the structure of abilities, are not all agreed on the number of factors in the model or the precise nature of each factor (McGrew, 1997).

Despite the fact that no single theory or model has universal acceptance, there is a common core of theory and research that is supportive of a number of propositions on which the development of the DAS and BAS II was based:

Human abilities are not explainable solely in terms of a single cognitive factor (g) or even in terms of two or three lower-order factors.

Human abilities form multiple dimensions on which individuals show reliably observable differences (Carroll, 1993), and which are related in complex ways with how children learn, achieve, and solve problems.

Human abilities are interrelated but not completely overlapping, thus making many of them distinct (Carroll, 1993).

The wide range of human abilities represents a number of interlinked subsystems of information processing.

Subsystems of information processing have structural correlates in the central nervous system, in which some functions are localized and others are integrated.

The last two of these points will be elaborated later in this chapter.

Description of the BAS II and DAS

The BAS II and the DAS are individually administered cognitive test batteries, standardized for children between the ages of 2 years 6 months and 17 years 11 months.

Structure of the batteries

The structure of the BAS II and DAS assumes a hierarchical organization of cognitive ability (Elliott, 1990b). Subtests, or specific measures of distinct abilities, make up the base of this structure. However, because all ability measures are intercorrelated, these subtests will tend to group together in clusters at a second higher level. These clusters, in turn, are interrelated, thereby yielding an estimate of psychometric g which is at the apex of this hierarchical structure. It seems possible, from the analyses of standardization data, that this hierarchy becomes more differentiated as a child develops.

The preschool and school-age batteries are similar in structure. Subtests in the two instruments are designated as either 'core' or 'diagnostic.' Core subtests are those that are the most highly g loaded, and thus measure more complex mental processing. They are used in the estimation of the Cluster

Table 6.1. Number of BAS II and DAS subtests and composites at each age level

Age level	Number of subtests	General composites	Cluster scores
Lower preschool level Age 2:6–3:5 (Extended age 2:6–4:11)	4 core 2 diagnostic	1. GCA 2. Special Nonverbal	
Upper Preschool level Age 3:6–5:11 (Extended age 3:6–6:11)	6 core BAS II: 6 diagnostic DAS: 5 diagnostic	1. GCA 2. Special Nonverbal	BAS II: 1. Verbal Ability 2. Pictorial Reasoning Ability 3. Spatial Ability DAS: 1. Verbal Ability 2. Nonverbal Ability
School-Age level Age 6:0–17:11 (Extended age 5:0–17:11)	6 core BAS II: 5 diagnostic DAS: 4 diagnostic Both instruments: 3 achievement	1. GCA 2. Special Nonverbal	1. Verbal Ability 2. Nonverbal Reasoning Ability 3. Spatial Ability

scores, the GCA score, and the Special Nonverbal Composite (SNC). On the other hand, diagnostic subtests are intended to measure more specific or distinct skills, such as aspects of short-term memory or speed of information processing. They have a lower correlation with g and measure less complex mental processing. The overall structure is summarized in Table 6.1.

The BAS II and the DAS each comprise essentially two cognitive test batteries. The first is geared to preschool and early school-age children from age 2 years 6 months through 5 years 11 months. This preschool battery is further subdivided into an upper and lower preschool level. The lower level is specifically designed for children from 2 years 6 months to 3 years 5 months. The upper preschool level is used for assessing children from 3 years 6 months to 7 years 11 months. The second cognitive battery is designed for school-age children from age 5 years 0 months to 17 years 11 months. Although the nominal age ranges of the two batteries have a dividing point at 6 years, they were completely co-normed across the age range 5 years 0 months through 7

Table 6.2. Subtests of the BAS II and DAS Preschool Cognitive Batteries, showing abilities measured (and relation of measures to Cattell–Horn factors) and their contribution to composites

Subtest	Abilities measured	Contribution to composite
Core subtests		
Block Building[1]	Visual–perceptual matching, especially of spatial orientation, in copying block patterns (*Gv*)	GCA
Verbal Comprehension	Receptive language: understanding oral instructions using basic language concepts (*Gc*)	GCA Verbal
Naming Vocabulary	Expressive language: knowledge of names (*Gc*)	GCA Verbal
Picture Similarities	Nonverbal Reasoning: matching pictures that have a common element or concept (*Gf*)	GCA Special Nonverbal BAS II: Pictorial Reasoning DAS: Nonverbal
Pattern Construction	Nonverbal, spatial visualization in reproducing designs with colored blocks and flat squares (*Gv*)	GCA Special Nonverbal BAS II: Spatial DAS: Nonverbal
Copying	Visual–spatial matching and fine-motor coordination in copying line drawings (*Gv*)	GCA Special Nonverbal BAS II: Spatial DAS: Nonverbal
Early Number Concepts[2]	Knowledge of pre-numerical and numerical quantitative concepts (*Gq*)	GCA BAS II: Pictorial Reasoning
Diagnostic subtests		
Matching Letter-Like Forms	Visual discrimination of spatial relationships among similar shapes (*Gv*)	
Recall of Digits Forward (DAS: Recall of Digits)	Short-term auditory–sequential memory for sequences of numbers (*Gsma*)	
Recall of Objects	Short-term and intermediate-term learning and verbal recall of a display of pictures (*Glr*) (BAS II also has spatial recall)	

Table 6.2. (*cont.*)

Subtest	Abilities measured	Contribution to composite
Recognition of Pictures	Short-term, nonverbal visual memory measured through recognition of familiar objects (*Gsmv, Gv*)	
Recall of Digits Backward (only in BAS II)	Short-term auditory–sequential working memory for sequences of numbers recalled in reversed order (*Gsma*)	

[1] Used only for the GCA composite at the Lower Preschool level. Used as a diagnostic subtest at the upper Preschool level.

[2] Not used for either cluster score, because it has similar factor loadings on both the Verbal and Nonverbal factors.

years 11 months, and may be used equivalently in that age range. Thus, the school-age battery may be used appropriately to assess relatively gifted five year olds. Most importantly for the majority of clinicians, the preschool battery may be used to assess six and seven year olds, for whom the school-age materials are developmentally less appropriate. There is also a brief achievement test battery for school-age children in each instrument.

Subtest composition

The component subtests for the Preschool Cognitive, School-Age Cognitive, and Achievement batteries are listed and described in Tables 6.2, 6.3, and 6.4. In each cognitive battery table, the subtests are grouped according to whether they are designated 'core' subtests or 'diagnostic' subtests. Each subtest has a brief description of the abilities it measures, including its relation to the CHC factors. Subtests have normative scores in a T-score metric (mean = 50; SD = 10).

Tables 6.2 and 6.3 also show the composites that can be derived from the core subtests, and the subtests that contribute to those composites. Two types of composite are provided, all in a standard score metric (mean = 100; SD = 15). First are lower-order cluster scores. There are three of these at the Upper Preschool level for the BAS II: Verbal, Pictorial Reasoning, and Spatial, for children aged 3 years 6 months to 5 years 11 months. At the same age level there are two cluster scores for the DAS: Verbal and Nonverbal. For both instruments, there are three cluster scores at the School-Age level (Verbal,

Table 6.3. Subtests of the BAS II and DAS School-Age cognitive batteries, showing abilities measured (and relation of measures to CHC factors) and their contribution to composites

Subtest	Abilities measured	Contribution to composite
Core subtests		
Word Definitions	Expressive language: knowledge of word meanings (*Gc*)	GCA Verbal
Verbal Similarities (DAS: Similarities)	Verbal, inductive reasoning and verbal knowledge (*Gc*)	GCA Verbal
Matrices	Nonverbal, logical reasoning: perception and application of relationships among abstract figures (*Gf*)	GCA Special Nonverbal Nonverbal Reasoning
Quantitative Reasoning (DAS: Sequential and Quantitative Reasoning)	Detection of sequential patterns or relationships in figures or numbers (*Gf*)	GCA Special Nonverbal Nonverbal Reasoning
Recall of Designs	Short-term recall of visual–spatial relationships through drawing abstract figures (*Gv, Gsmv*)	GCA Special Nonverbal Spatial
Pattern Construction	Nonverbal, spatial visualization in reproducing designs with colored blocks and flat squares (*Gv*)	GCA Special Nonverbal Spatial
Diagnostic subtests		
Recall of Digits Forward (DAS: Recall of Digits)	Short-term auditory–sequential memory for sequences of numbers (*Gsma*)	
Recall of Objects	Short-term and intermediate-term learning and verbal recall of a display of pictures (*Glr*) (BAS II also has Spatial recall)	
Speed of Information Processing	Speed in performing simple mental operations (*Gs*)	
Recall of Digits Backward (only in BAS II)	Short-term auditory–sequential working memory for sequences of numbers recalled in reversed order (*Gsma*)	

Table 6.4. BAS II and DAS Achievement tests

Achievement test	Skills measured
Basic Number Skills	Knowledge and written recall of spellings; includes diagnostic performance analysis on items
Spelling	Recognition of printed numbers and performance of arithmetic operations; includes diagnostic performance analysis of errors
Word Reading	Recognition and decoding of printed words

Nonverbal Reasoning, and Spatial). Note that at the Lower Preschool level (ages 2 years 6 months to 3 years 5 months) there are no cluster scores.

Second are the higher-order composites. For most children, the most general composite will be the GCA score. For children for whom it is judged that the verbal component of that score is inappropriate, a SNC is provided. For both instruments at the Upper Preschool age level, this is formed from three subtests. Also for both instruments, the SNC for the School-Age battery is formed from the four subtests in the Nonverbal Reasoning and Spatial clusters.

Table 6.4 lists the three achievement tests. The normative scores on these tests are in a standard score metric (mean = 100; SD = 15), to facilitate comparison with composite scores from the cognitive battery. The achievement and cognitive batteries were fully co-normed. Discrepancies between ability (as measured by GCA or SNC) may be evaluated taking either (a) the *simple difference* between the achievement score and the composite, or (b) the *difference between predicted and observed achievement*, with predicted achievement being based on the GCA or SNC score. The BAS II and DAS handbooks provide information on both the statistical significance (or reliability) of discrepancies, and their frequency of occurrence (or unusualness) in the standardization sample.

In considering the composition of the subtests of the BAS II and the DAS, one of their greatest advantages is their high appeal for all children, and particularly preschoolers. For a test to provide a reliable and valid assessment when used with young children, it must not only have good psychometric characteristics, but also look interesting enough so that they want to participate in the assessment and keep going when the work starts becoming difficult. The instruments include many activities at all age levels for children to do with their hands. Many psychologists who work with preschoolers have lamented the loss from many newer instruments of the little toys and activities from the Stanford–Binet L-M (Terman & Merrill, 1960), which have generally been replaced by a much greater requirement for the child to focus on looking at pictures.

The DAS restores the Stanford–Binet L-M approach to working with preschool children.

Another important feature of the instruments is that administration time for the core subtests is significantly shorter than that typically needed for competitors like the Stanford–Binet or the Wechsler scales. An experienced examiner can complete the core subtests of the DAS and obtain a reliable and valid estimate of clusters and GCA in about 30 to 40 minutes. Most professionals report that the Stanford–Binet, Fourth Edition, the Wechsler Intelligence Scale for Children, Third Edition (WISC–III) and the Wechsler Preschool and Primary Scale of Intelligence–Revised (WPPSI–R) take about 15 to 30 minutes longer than the DAS to obtain a similar estimate. This is a critical advantage in working with populations not distinguished for their lengthy attention spans.

Psychometric properties

The psychometric properties of the BAS II and the DAS are given in detail in their respective technical handbooks (Elliott, 1990c, 1997a). A brief review of the major features is therefore given below, and, unless otherwise stated, all data are quoted from the respective technical handbooks.

Tailored assessments

The use of item response theory in the development of the subtests has resulted in what is called an 'item set' approach to assessment. For most children on most subtests, it is unnecessary to start each subtest at the first and easiest item and then progress to a traditional ceiling level – say, five consecutive failures before discontinuing. In the BAS II and the DAS, smaller sets of items from each subtest are given. For most subtests, if the child has three passes and three failed items, that item set gives a reliable estimate of the child's ability.

The great advantages of this approach are reduced time spent in testing for both the child and the examiner, and a reduced exposure to failure on items for the child. Indeed, in the Pattern Construction subtest, it is possible for a valid estimate of ability to be obtained from eight or ten items which may *all* be passed by the child. In the Standard method of administration, items carry several points each, depending on the time taken to make the pattern correctly. The examiner may stop testing at a given decision point if the child has failed to get a maximum score on any three items in the set. The advantages are obvious: the subtest is often completed in less than five minutes, and many children have no experience of failure whatsoever. The technical basis for this new approach to subtest administration is explained in the technical handbooks for the instruments (Elliott, 1990c, 1997a).

Reliability

Unsurprisingly, the BAS II and the DAS have similar psychometric characteristics. Internal reliability is high at the level of the GCA and cluster scores. The mean GCA reliabilities for the BAS II and DAS, respectively, are .89 and .90 at the Lower Preschool level, .93 and .94 at the Upper Preschool level, and .96 and .95 for the School-Age batteries. The mean reliability of the SNC is a point or two lower. Both instruments show SNC mean reliability at .89 at the Upper Preschool and .94 at the School-Age level. Mean cluster score reliability ranges from .85 to .93 for the BAS II and from .88 to .92 for the DAS. Internal consistency at the subtest level is also relatively strong, with some exceptions, with mean reliability coefficients ranging from .70 to .92. For the BAS II, of the 27 possible mean internal reliability coefficients for subtests, 19 are .8 or greater and, of these, seven are .90 or greater. Similarly, for the DAS, of the 26 possible mean internal reliability coefficients for subtests, 17 are .8 or greater, and of these, four are greater than .9.

The assessment of test–retest reliability was accomplished using three age groups for the BAS II and four age groups for the DAS. Results showed that GCA and cluster scores are very stable. For the BAS II, GCA test–retest scores correlated between .90 and .95, with a range of .74 to .96 for cluster scores. For the DAS, the range was .89 to .94 for the GCA and .79 to .90 for the clusters. Four DAS subtests, which require a significant amount of clinician judgment to score, were examined for interrater reliability. Coefficients were found to be .9 or above.

Specificity

BAS II and DAS scores were also evaluated in terms of specificity or how much of the score variance is reliable and unique to that measure. The higher the specificity of a measure, the more confident the clinician can be about interpreting the score as measuring something unique from the other tests in the battery. McGrew and Murphy (1995) argue that specificity is high when it accounts for 25% or more of the test's total variance and when it is greater than the error variance. Every cluster score in both instruments, every subtest in the DAS, and every subtest but one[2] in the BAS II, meets this criterion of high specificity.[2]

For the BAS II at the Preschool level, specificities for subtests range from .38 to .57, with cluster specificities of .34 to .55. At the School-Age level, BAS II subtest specificities range from .24 to .82, with cluster specificities of .45 to .57. For the DAS, subtest specificities at the Preschool level range from .31 to .65, with cluster specificities of .35 and .45. At the School-Age level, DAS subtest specificities range from .30 to .82, with cluster specificities from .39 to .49. Elliott (1997b) presents these data in more detail, together with data showing that the DAS has approximately one-third more reliable specificity than other widely used cognitive batteries, including the Wechsler scales. The data on the specificity of the BAS II, published subsequent to the preparation of the Elliott (1997b) article, show that the conclusion about the heightened specificity of the DAS also applies to the BAS II.

Validity

Construct validity for both the BAS II and the DAS is supported by confirmatory and exploratory factor analyses (Elliott, 1990c, 1997a). For both instruments, results support a one-factor model at the Lower Preschool level. At the Upper Preschool level, the BAS II results support a three-factor model. In the British standardization data, Early Number Concepts was slightly more highly correlated with Picture Similarities than in the US data on the DAS. Thus, these two subtests formed a separate cluster named Pictorial Reasoning. This left Copying and Pattern Construction to form an easily interpretable Spatial cluster. By way of contrast, the DAS results supported a two-factor (Verbal/ Nonverbal) model at the Upper Preschool level. In this solution, Early Number Concepts loaded equally on both factors, so this subtest is not used in the DAS as a component of any cluster score, although (because it has a high *g* loading) it is used in the calculation of the GCA score. Both instruments had data clearly supporting a three-factor (Verbal/Nonverbal/Spatial) model for school-age children (Elliott, 1990c, 1997a). Keith's (1990) independent hierarchical confirmatory factor analyses of DAS data reported consistent results that Elliott (1997b) found were essentially in agreement with the DAS data analyses given in the test handbook (Elliott, 1990c). Importantly, Keith's (1990) analyses demonstrated that the *g* factor, as measured by the GCA, is indistinguishable in the Preschool and School-Age batteries of the DAS. In a similar study, Elliott (1997a) reported a correlation of approximately 1.0 between the underlying general factors derived from the Preschool and School-Age batteries of the BAS II.

Elliott (1997b) also reports a joint factor analysis of the DAS and Wechsler Intelligence Scale for Children–Revised (WISC–R; Wechsler, 1974), which supports a Verbal/Nonverbal Reasoning/Spatial factor model for school-age children. Interestingly, the results of this study show that the DAS Matrices and Sequential and Quantitative Reasoning subtests do not relate strongly to any of the Wechsler subtests. The Wechsler Performance subtests appear to measure Spatial Ability (or *Gv* in the CHC models), the Verbal subtests measure Verbal

Ability (or *Gc*), and no Wechsler subtests appear to be strong measures of Fluid Reasoning (*Gf*). A study on 38 children who had been assessed using the BAS II and the WISC–III, reported by Elliott (1997a), showed very similar findings, although the sample size precluded any factor analyses.

Evidence for the concurrent validity of the BAS II and DAS is provided by studies (Elliott, 1990c, 1997a; Wechsler, 1991) showing consistently high correlations between the GCA and the composite scores of other cognitive batteries, such as the WISC–III (Wechsler, 1991), WPPSI–R (Wechsler, 1989), and the Stanford–Binet Intelligence Scale, Fourth Edition (Thorndike, Hagen, & Sattler, 1986). High correlations were also found between the DAS achievement tests and other group or individual achievement tests as well as with actual student grades (Elliott, 1990c, 1997a).

Bias

Extensive effort was put into ensuring the fairness of the BAS II and DAS across culture. For both instruments, test items were first reviewed for possible bias by a panel representing women and several ethnic minority groups and, based on their recommendations, a number of items were changed or dropped from the test. To aid statistical analyses of bias in the DAS, an additional 600 Hispanic and African American children were tested along with the standardization sample in order that each test item could be analyzed for differential item difficulty across culture. The children in this bias oversample also assisted in ensuring that test scoring rules reflected possible culture-specific responses from minority children.

Item bias analyses were conducted on the standardization data for both instruments. A small number of items that proved to be biased despite the earlier expert reviews were deleted from the final published versions of the tests at this stage. Studies of prediction bias were also reported. In the case of the BAS II, three samples of 39 'White,' 27 'Black,' and 54 'Pakistani/ Bangladeshi' children in Year 3 at school were given the BAS II and the Suffolk Reading Scale (Hagley, 1987). Results showed that the GCA score predicted Suffolk Reading scores in the same way for different ethnic groups, indicating no prediction bias. This result is supported by a much larger study conducted using the DAS. This study employed samples of 125 'Black,' 133 'Hispanic,' and 467 'White' children who had taken the DAS, group-administered achievement tests, and the Basic Achievement Skills Individual Screener (BASIS; Psychological Corporation, 1983). Once again, results showed that there was no unfair bias against minority children in the ability of the DAS GCA score to predict school achievement (Elliott, 1990c).

Further analyses of these data have examined construct bias in the DAS (Keith et al., 1999). This study was accomplished by conducting hierarchical, multi-sample confirmatory factor analysis of the DAS standardization data, including data from the bias oversample. Results showed that the DAS measures the same constructs for all three ethnic groups (Black, White, Hispanic) across the entire age range of the 2 through 17 years. Thus, it was concluded that the DAS shows no construct bias across groups.

Profile analysis

A particularly strong feature of the BAS II and the DAS is the support provided to the clinician in the process of interpreting test results (Elliott, 1990c, 1997a). The clinician is guided through a systematic plan of attack for interpreting DAS test scores as well as a clear rationale for this approach. To enable significantly high and low scores to be identified, the test Record Forms indicate differences between scores that are statistically significant at the 0.05 level. Such differences are adjusted to take into account the fact that the psychologist is making multiple comparisons. Differences that are detected at this level of significance are by definition reliable; that is, they are unlikely to have arisen due to measurement error.

Encouragement is given to checking first for significant differences between the cluster scores themselves and then between the cluster scores and the GCA. The method also evaluates whether core subtests within clusters are significantly different, and whether any subtest is significantly higher or lower than the child's own mean of the core subtests. With the availability of scoring software for both instruments (Elliott et al., 1998), this detailed analysis, including an analysis of cognitive processes underlying subtest scores, is made easy.

Detailed analyses of subtest relative strengths and weaknesses are not encouraged unless a significant difference is found between scores. This approach should significantly reduce the risk of Type I error during subtest analyses. The technical handbooks for the two instruments provide guidance on the clinical interpretation of cluster and subtest profiles, including tables of the frequency, or unusualness, of score differences as well as of their statistical significance.

Normative and developmental issues

Standardizations

The standardization samples for both instruments were intended to be representative of the normal range of children and students within the population.

They drew children from publicly funded school and from private schools, without respect to special education status. The samples only excluded children in special schools (a very small percentage of the child population in both the USA and Great Britain), which in practice meant that only children with severe intellectual deficits or with severe emotional problems were excluded. Children receiving special educational provision in ordinary schools were eligible to be drawn for the sample.

The DAS was standardized between 1987 and 1989 on a sample of 3475 children selected to match the 1988 US census on the stratification variables of age, gender, ethnicity, geographic location, and parent education level. The preschool sample was further stratified to match the census data according to the proportion of children who had attended a preschool educational program. Detailed census records were used in order that at each age-level of the test the standardization sample matched the population at that particular age-level in terms of the *joint distributions* of ethnicity, geographic location, and parent education level.

This is an unusually stringent constraint in sampling, and far more difficult to achieve than representative distributions on each stratification variable taken singly. This, and other procedural refinements in sampling, made the DAS unique in its sampling accuracy (Elliott, 1997b). A sample of 175 children was utilized for each six-month age interval at the preschool range, and a sample of 200 children was utilized at each age-level of the school-age range (Elliott, 1990c).

The BAS II was standardized in 1995 on a sample of 1689 children. Apart from a shortfall of cases at the upper and lower extreme age groups, the number of children at each year level was generally in excess of 100. For preschool children, appropriate quotas of children were obtained who spent their daytime hours in certain environments such as nursery classes, play-groups, with childminders, or full-time at home. For school-age children, information was gathered on their schools – their type, size, region, and relative number of children receiving free school meals. Information on individuals in the sample was also gathered on ethnicity, parent education level, family type and size, and child's birth order in the family. On these variables, the standardization samples provided a good match to 1994 population distributions.

Child development considerations

The work of many clinicians is concerned with children with learning difficulties or those whose development is delayed in one or more cognitive areas. The DAS offers great flexibility in choosing an individually tailored assessment battery for children with developmental disabilities. Also, it offers much greater sensitivity than many cognitive batteries to the differential diagnosis of severe and profound mental retardation. Sometimes, too, psychologists need to assess gifted children, whose development is advanced compared to average children of their age. For such children, four major features of the design of the BAS II and the DAS are aimed at providing clinicians with resources to be able to test children with appropriate tasks whatever their developmental level.

Separate and overlapping Preschool and School-Age batteries

As described earlier, the cognitive batteries of the two instruments are each divided into two levels, for preschool and school-age children. The two levels of the cognitive batteries were deliberately designed to be developmentally appropriate and engaging for preschool and school-aged children, respectively. By contrast, the practice of other test developers (for example in the Wechsler and Woodcock–Johnson scales) to push tasks originally designed for adults or older children into the preschool domain was considered to be undesirable. Such a practice leads to tasks that are less intrinsically interesting for pre-schoolers, resulting in poorer motivation and greater difficulty for the examiner in maintaining rapport.

The Preschool and School-Age levels of the cognitive batteries were fully co-normed for children in the age range of 5 years 0 months to 7 years 11 months. This provides a major advantage for the professional examiner, who has the option of choosing which battery is most developmentally appropriate for a given child in this age range.

Out-of-level testing

The design of the BAS II and the DAS, by incorporating the concept of out-of-level testing, makes tests normally used within a given age range available for assessing exceptional children who are often older, and sometimes younger, than the usual age range. To make this possible, a number of subtests were standardized across a wider age range than the usual one for certain subtests. For example, Block Building is focused mainly on the Lower Pre-school children, being a core subtest at this level. However, it is standardized through age 5 years 11 months in the BAS II and 4 years 11 months in the DAS, enabling it to be used as a supplementary diagnostic subtest for older pre-schoolers. Similarly, Naming Vocabulary is a Preschool level subtest, but is standardized through 7 years 11 months in the BAS II and 8 years 11 months in the DAS, enabling it to be used as an alternate subtest to Word Definitions if a young school-aged child is unable or unwilling to respond appropriately. The most broadly standardized subtest that is used out-of-level for school-aged children is Recognition of Pictures, standardized in both instruments through the entire age range to 17 years 11 months. This is an excellent supplementary diagnostic test of visual short-term recognition memory for children whose abilities in that domain are average to below-average.

Special Nonverbal Composite

If a clinician judges, either prior to or during testing, that it will not be fair to include verbal tasks as components of the GCA, the SNC can be used as an alternative assessment of the general factor *g*. For older preschool children, the Special Nonverbal scale consists of three subtests (Picture Similarities, Pattern Construction, and Copying). At the school-age level, the four subtests in the Nonverbal Reasoning and Spatial clusters are used to form the Special Nonverbal scale. The directions for all the subtests included in this composite can, if necessary, be conveyed through gestures. It is expected that the composite will be used by clinicians assessing a range of children such as shy preschoolers, elective mutes, children suspected of hearing loss, and those from home environments lacking in verbal stimulation or where the primary language is not English. However, it should be noted that if the SNC is used, this does not mean that the verbal subtests will not be administered. They will often give valuable information about the child's current level of verbal skills.

Downward extension of GCA scores

Both of the instruments allow for the estimation of *extended* GCA scores for children with moderate to severe levels of mental retardation. The normal range of GCA scores runs from 50 to 150. However, situations sometimes arise in which a child very low in ability earns *T*-scores of 20 on several of the core subtests; or when a retarded individual needs to be given the Preschool subtests even though he or she may be 12 or 13 years old and the subtests are not normed to that age level. For such individuals, extended GCA norms are provided, based on an equating of the scales across ages. These norms enable users to assess children with moderate to severe developmental delays using developmentally appropriate tasks, yielding GCA scores as low as about 25.

The relationship between cognitive abilities and neurological structure

The relationship between cognitive abilities and neurological structure has for long exercised the discipline of psychology, because although it has been known for many years that there are cause-and-effect relationships, their nature has not been clear. The following section of this chapter briefly outlines some links between the factor structure of abilities and the neuropsychological evidence concerning the nature of structures underlying verbal and spatial abilities, fluid or general intelligence, and some aspects of memory. BAS II and DAS measures (both subtests and composites) will be mapped onto this structure.

Broad verbal and visual–spatial abilities

Two of the major ability clusters in the BAS II, DAS, and other cognitive batteries, reflect two major systems through which we receive, perceive, remember, and process information. These systems are linked to the auditory and visual modalities. Factorially, the systems are represented by verbal and visualization/spatial factors – Gc and Gv in the CHC theory. Neuropsychologically, there is strong evidence for the existence of these systems. They tend to be localized in the left and right cerebral hemispheres, respectively, although there are individual differences in areas of localization of function. Moreover, the systems are doubly dissociated – that is, they represent two distinct, independent systems of information processing (Springer & Deutsch, 1989; McCarthy & Warrington, 1990). In the BAS II and DAS, the *verbal* factor is measured by the Verbal cluster in both the Preschool and School-Age cognitive batteries. At the Preschool level, the Verbal cluster is formed by the Naming Vocabulary and Verbal Comprehension subtests, and at the School-Age level it is formed by Verbal Similarities (in the DAS, 'Similarities') and Word Definitions. The *visualization* or *spatial* factor is measured by the Spatial cluster at the School-Age level (consisting of the Pattern Construction and Recall of Designs subtests), and by the Pattern Construction, Block Building and Copying subtests at the Preschool age level.

Integration of complex information processing

For normal cognitive functioning, the auditory–verbal and visual–spatial systems operate in an integrated fashion. Integration of the visual and auditory information processing systems (and information from all subsystems) is probably a necessary underpinning for complex mental activity. Factorially, this integrative system is represented by the Fluid Reasoning (Gf) factor in the CHC theory. Measures of Gf typically require integrated analysis of both verbal and visual information. Neuropsychologically, it seems that the integrative function of frontal lobe systems is central to complex mental functioning (Luria, 1973, discussed by McCarthy and Warrington, 1990, pp. 343–64), and it is therefore reasonable to hypothesize that it provides a structural correlate for Gf. In the BAS II and DAS, the Gf factor is measured in the School-Age battery by the Nonverbal Reasoning cluster. Both subtests require integrated analysis and transformation of both visual and verbal information. For example, in the Matrices subtest, verbal mediation is critical for the solution of visually presented problems for most individuals. At the Preschool age level, the Picture Similarities subtest provides a measure of fluid reasoning.

There is considerable evidence that *Gf* forms the basis of the higher-order general factor (*g*). Although there are many factors at a lower order of generality that are related to *g*, the three that have the greatest contribution to defining *g* are the *Gf*, *Gv*, and *Gc* factors, discussed above. Carroll (1993) puts it this way: 'There is abundant evidence for a factor of general intelligence . . . that dominates factors or variables that can be mastered in performing induction, reasoning, visualization, and language comprehension tasks' (p. 624). The central importance of *Gf* is also emphasized by Gustafsson (1988, 1989) and Härnqvist et al. (1994), whose research indicates that the loading of *Gf* on *g* has been found consistently to be unity, which implies that *g* is equivalent to fluid intelligence. The hierarchical factor analyses of the DAS standardization data by Keith (1990), referred to earlier in this chapter, provide further support for this position. In the BAS II and the DAS, *g* is measured by the GCA composite. Because it is estimated from only those subtests that are the best estimators of *g* (that is, those that measure *Gf*, *Gc*, and *Gv*), the GCA is a purer measure of *g* than the composites of most other batteries that include all cognitive subtests in the composite, irrespective of their *g* loading.

Verbal and visual short-term memory systems

Some cognitive tests, such as the Stanford–Binet Intelligence Scale, Fourth Edition (SB-IV; Thorndike et al., 1986), and the Woodcock–Johnson Psychoeducational Battery–Revised (WJ–R; Woodcock and Johnson, 1989), represent memory by a single factor. The CHC theory of the structure of mental abilities also does not distinguish between separate, modality-related memory systems. However, there is much evidence from cognitive psychology and from neuropsychology that verbal and visual short-term memory systems are distinct and are doubly dissociated (Hitch et al., 1988; McCarthy & Warrington, 1990, pp. 275–95). The BAS II and the DAS keep visual and auditory short-term memory tasks as distinct measures, and do not treat short-term memory as unitary. Visual short-term memory is represented at the Preschool level by Recognition of Pictures and at the School-Age level by Recall of Designs and Recognition of Pictures (this being out-of-level for ages eight and over: It is a reliable and valid measure for older children of average to below-average ability). Auditory short-term memory is represented across the entire age range by Recall of Digits, a subtest designed to be a purer measure of this function than the Digit Span subtest of a number of other batteries. Also, in the BAS II at the School-Age level (age six years and upwards), Recall of Digits Backwards provides an additional verbal short-term memory task.

The intermediate-term memory factor (*Glr* in the CHC model) is typically measured by tests that have both visual and verbal components. In the BAS II and DAS Recall of Objects subtest, for example, pictures are presented, but they have to be recalled verbally. McCarthy and Warrington (1990, p. 283) call this 'visual–verbal' short-term memory, and conclude that it is underpinned by another distinct information processing system. In the BAS II and DAS, the Recall of Objects subtest, which provides a measure of this factor, is for children of four years and older.

Application to diagnosis and treatment of learning disabilities

As previously discussed, the BAS II and DAS were created with the intention of providing a profile of a child's cognitive strengths and weaknesses, with the hope that this profile would lead to a better understanding and more effective remediation of possible learning difficulties. Major texts on assessment with children emphasize the importance of a careful examination of the patterns of performance on the various subtests of an instrument (Sattler, 1992; Kamphaus, 1993; Kaufman, 1994). Kaufman (1994) states that the composite scores tell us about the 'what' of a child's abilities, whereas the subtests bring to light the 'how.' However, it will be argued that the instruments' lower-order composites (Verbal, Nonverbal Reasoning, and Spatial) are also particularly important in illuminating the 'how.'

Controversy surrounding the analysis of cognitive test profiles

In recent years, the analysis of subtest profile patterns to give a better understanding of a child's learning strengths and weaknesses has been controversial, and McDermott, Glutting, and colleagues (e.g., McDermott, Fantuzzo, & Glutting, 1990; McDermott et al., 1992; McDermott & Glutting, 1997; Glutting et al., 1997, 1998; Youngstrom, Kogos, & Glutting, 1999) have been very active in questioning such procedures. At the beginning of the last decade, McDermott et al. (1990) made a general statement advising 'that psychologists just say "no" to subtest analysis.' This was on the basis of a critique of practice using the Wechsler, but the recommendation came to be perceived as generalized to all cognitive tests. One of their concerns centers on the relatively lower reliability and stability of subtest scores in comparison with composites. They argue that, because subtests typically have lower reliability and stability than composites, it is likely that the pattern of strengths and weaknesses among subtests that appear one day might not be there the next. Another concern relates to the use of ipsative scores in profile interpretation. Ipsative scores are produced by subtracting the child's average normative score across various subtests from each individual subtest score, thereby removing the mean elevation of scores (i.e., variance associated with g). We emphasize that, although they have applied these critiques to the DAS, they do not constitute a major threat to BAS II or DAS profile interpretations for the following reasons.

- Interpretation of high and low subtest and composite scores is only recommended when differences between scores are statistically significant. This takes account of the reliability of the measures being compared. Relatively lower reliability results in larger differences being required for significance. Moreover, the BAS II and DAS method adjusts significant differences for multiple comparisons: because several comparisons are being made, differences required for significance are greater than for a simple comparison of two scores. This conservative approach is designed to ensure that only reliable differences, not attributable to measurement error, are reported.

- McDermott and Glutting's negative conclusions about the value of profile analysis using ipsative scores do not apply to the BAS II and DAS, which use direct comparisons of normative subtest and composite scores. The only time scores are 'ipsatized' is when the mean standardized T-score for the core subtests is subtracted from individual subtest scores for the purpose of evaluating whether that subtest score is, overall, significantly high or low. The ipsatized score (or the difference score, to put it another way) is never reported: once a subtest score is identified as significantly high or low, the unadjusted T-score itself is reported. Also, note that the composite scores are never ipsatized in the BAS II and DAS procedure.

Glutting et al. (1997) have also made the point that the interpretation of a profile should be done with reference to *base rate* information. Base rates refer to the frequency with which a particular profile is found in the population. Glutting et al. (1997) correctly assert that statistically significant differences (those that are reliable, unlikely to have arisen because of measurement error) can be quite common and ordinary, even though very 'significant.' To address this problem, Holland and McDermott (1996), using hierarchical multistage cluster analyses of the DAS standardization sample, identified seven core profile types in this sample, which was representative of the child population. Five of these profiles, shown by a total of 71% of the sample, were flat in terms of their scores on the DAS core subtests (although there was some variation among the diagnostic subtests). The differences between the groups were defined mainly by variation in general ability. In other words, the profiles varied in the altitude rather than in the pattern of their scores. The remaining two core profile types were defined by (a) 16% of students who had relatively high Verbal *versus* low Spatial subtest scores, and (b) 13% of students who had relatively high Spatial *versus* low Verbal subtest scores. The Verbal and Spatial cluster scores were ten points different in both cases. These two profile types are discussed more fully in the next section of this chapter.

Attempts to show the utility of profile analyses with the BAS II and DAS have previously concentrated mostly on children with learning disabilities and in particular on children with reading disabilities. Readers may refer to studies by Elliott (1990c, 1997a), Kercher and Sandoval (1991), Shapiro, Buckhalt, and Herod (1995), McIntosh and Gridley (1993), and McIntosh (1999). In these studies, a variety of cluster and subtest profiles was reported. It seems common, both in studies of a normal population and in studies of children with disabilities, to find some groups with flat cluster and/or subtest profiles. Looking only at cluster scores, some studies have found groups with relatively high Verbal *versus* Spatial scores, relatively high Spatial *versus* Verbal scores, and relatively low Nonverbal Reasoning *versus* Verbal and Spatial scores. In most studies, there was considerable variability among the diagnostic subtests.

The study described below attempts to address most of the issues raised by critics of profile interpretation, and also aims to identify a number of distinct profiles of BAS II and DAS cluster scores among groups of normal and exceptional children.

Profiles of samples of dyslexic and learning-disabled children

This study is principally based on an examination of patterns of cluster scores, measuring Verbal, Nonverbal Reasoning, and Spatial abilities. Four major sources of data are used, as follows.

1.   DAS standardization sample. This consists of 2400 children aged 6 years 0 months through 17 years 11 months. A total of 353 poor readers were identified in this total sample. Poor readers are defined as those with DAS Word Reading standard scores below 85. These poor readers were further subdivided into two subsamples:

Poor Readers with No Significant Discrepancy: 86 poor readers whose observed Word Reading score was not significantly lower than that predicted from their GCA.

Poor Readers with Significant Discrepancy: 267 poor readers whose observed Word Reading score was significantly lower than that predicted from their GCA.

This sample provides data constituting a baseline against which results from the other two samples may be evaluated.

2.   DAS dyslexic sample.[3] This sample comprises 160 children identified as dyslexic by psychologists of the Dyslexia Institute in England. This sample has the major advantage from a research perspective that the DAS had *not* been used in the original diagnostic process to identify these individuals as dyslexic. No information is available as to how much time elapsed between their initial identification and the subsequent DAS assessment. It seems likely that many would have received a considerable period of intervention for their reading difficulties before their DAS assessment. The sample was divided into two subsamples, as follows:

Dyslexics with DAS Word Reading standard scores below 85.

Dyslexics with DAS Word Reading scores between 85 and 100.

3.   Learning disabilities sample.[4] This sample comprises 53 children identified as learning disabled, with the WISC–III used as the initial assessment battery. Once again, this sample has the major advantage that the DAS had *not* been used in the original diagnostic process to identify these individuals as learning disabled. The sample was re-evaluated on the DAS three years after initial assessment. Full details of the sample, the procedure, and initial findings are reported by Dumont et al. (1996).

4.   BAS II dyslexic sample.[3] This sample comprises 287 children referred to the Head of Psychology at the Dyslexia Institute in England for assessment as possibly dyslexic. All children were asssessed by the same psychologist. As in the case of the DAS dyslexic sample, this sample was divided into two subsamples, as follows:

Dyslexics with BAS II Word Reading standard scores below 85.

Dyslexics with BAS II Word Reading scores between 85 and 100.

Definition of subgroups

Children in all three samples were placed into subgroups based upon the presence or absence of significant discrepancies between scores that were significant at the 5% confidence level, adjusted for multiple comparisons. The differences were obtained from Tables B.4. and B.5. in the BAS II and DAS handbooks (Elliott, 1990c, 1997a), and are similar to the differences indicated on the respective Record Forms.

   The subgroups were defined according to the possible combinations of high and low scores that may be found among the three school-age clusters, and also including subgroups with flat cluster profiles. Even among poor readers with a significant discrepancy between GCA and Word Reading (or, more properly, between observed Word Reading and Word Reading predicted from the GCA), it would be expected that there would be a proportion of children with flat cognitive test profiles. Poor reading has many causes, and there is no reason to believe that children who have failed to read because of lack of exposure to teaching through absences from school, or because of poor teaching, or because of poor motivation, should have anything other than normal (i.e., flat) cognitive profiles. Other poor readers may have verbal or spatial disabilities, both of which are amply reported in the literature (e.g., Rourke et al., 1990; Snow, Burns, & Griffin, 1998). Finally, we may find some whose Nonverbal Reasoning ability is lower than both their verbal and spatial abilities. Such a group had been identified by McIntosh and Gridley (1993). The present author has also received many questions and comments during the past several years from psychologists who had observed LD children showing this profile pattern. Finally, there may be some individuals who show the reverse pattern, with Nonverbal Reasoning ability higher than both verbal and spatial, although no research studies have identified such a subgroup. The subgroups are therefore as follows.

Flat cluster profile: No significant differences among the three DAS cluster scores.

Low Spatial, High Verbal: Verbal cluster significantly higher than Spatial cluster. Possibly nonverbal learning disability.

Low Verbal, High Spatial: Verbal cluster significantly lower than Spatial cluster. Typically reported pattern for poor readers (e.g., Snow et al., 1998; British Psychological Society, 1999).

High Nonverbal Reasoning: Nonverbal Reasoning cluster higher than both the Verbal and Spatial scores, and significantly higher than at least one of them. Interpreted as signifying good ability to process complex auditory–visual information.

Low NVR: Nonverbal Reasoning cluster lower than both the Verbal and Spatial scores, and significantly lower than at least one of them. Interpreted as having difficulty in processing complex auditory–visual information.

Results

Tables 6.5 and 6.6 show the frequency and percentages of children with each profile in the standardization sample and in the dyslexic/LD samples. Chi-square tests showed that:

there is no significant difference between the two DAS dyslexic groups (Word Reading below 85 and Word Reading 85–100; $\chi^2 = 5.13$; $df = 4$; N.S.);

there is no significant difference between the two BAS II dyslexic groups (Word

Table 6.5. Number of students drawn from DAS standardization sample with various profiles: normative baseline data

Type of profile	Poor Readers with no discrepancy	Poor Readers with discrepancy	Total DAS standardization sample
Flat cluster profile	57	121	1203
	66.3	**45.3**	**50.1**
Low Spatial, High Verbal	6	16	257
	7.0	**6.0**	**10.7**
Low Verbal, High Spatial	8	63	239
	9.3	**23.6**	**10.0**
High Nonverbal Reasoning	8	28	355
	9.3	**10.5**	**14.8**
Low Nonverbal Reasoning	7	39	346
	8.1	**14.6**	**14.4**
Column totals	86	267	2400

Column percentages are shown in bold type. The subsamples in the first two columns form 14.7% of the total standardization sample.

Reading below 85 and Word Reading 85–100; $\chi^2 = 5.49$; df $= 4$; N.S.);

there is no significant difference between the combined DAS dyslexic groups and Dumont's LD sample ($\chi^2 = 1.337$; df $= 4$; N.S.);

there is a significant difference between the combined DAS dyslexic groups and the combined BAS II dyslexic groups ($\chi^2 = 17.92$; df $= 4$; $p < 0.01$). This difference is largely attributable to differences between the two samples in the proportion of children with a Low Nonverbal Reasoning profile.

As might be expected from inspection of Tables 6.5 and 6.6, there is a highly significant difference between the frequencies for each profile for the dyslexic and LD samples, on the one hand, and the standardization sample, on the other. Comparison of the frequencies for each profile for the combined dyslexic/LD sample and the Poor Readers with Discrepancy, taken from the standardization sample, yields a chi-square of 28.09 (df $= 4$; $p < 0.001$). Similarly, comparison of the combined dyslexic/LD sample and Total standardization sample yields a chi-square of 102.76 (df $= 4$; $p < 0.001$). The differences that account for the highest chi-square values are for children with the Low Nonverbal Reasoning profile.

Table 6.6 shows estimated base rates of each profile in the school-age

Table 6.6. Number of dyslexic and LD students with various profiles

Type of profile	DAS: dyslexic with Word Reading below 85	DAS: dyslexic with Word Reading 85–100	Dumont et al. LD sample	BAS II: dyslexic with Word Reading below 85	BAS II: dyslexic with Word Reading 85–100
Flat cluster profile	28	28	20	48	78
Low spatial,	4	12	5	7	10
High Verbal	**4.9**	**15.2**	**9.4**	**6.0**	**5.8**
Low Verbal,	10	7	6	26	28
High Spatial	**12.3**	**8.9**	**11.3**	**22.4**	**16.4**
High Nonverbal	5	4	1	5	18
Reasoning	**6.2**	**5.1**	**1.9**	**4.3**	**10.5**
Low Nonverbal	34	28	21	30	37
Reasoning	**42.0**	**35.4**	**39.6**	**25.9**	**21.6**
Column totals	81	79	53	116	171

Column percentages are shown in bold type.

population. Fifty percent of the total standardization sample had a flat cluster profile. However, 66.3% of the poor readers who had no discrepancy between observed and predicted reading had a flat cluster profile. The range of GCA scores in this particular group is quite restricted, ranging from 54 to 84, the group therefore including children who may be mildly to moderately mentally retarded. The larger group of poor readers with a significant discrepancy between observed and predicted reading have, as would be expected, larger variance in GCA scores, ranging from 46 to 118. Compared with the total standardization sample, a slightly smaller percentage (45.3%) of these poor readers with a discrepancy showed flat profiles. Also, about a quarter of this subgroup (23.6%), as might be expected, had significantly lower Verbal than Spatial ability. Other percentages were unremarkable: in the total standardization sample, 10% of children had Low Spatial and High Spatial scores, and 14–15% showed Low and High Nonverbal Reasoning profiles.

Table 6.6 shows the results for the dyslexic and LD samples. They are remarkably similar for the three samples, despite the data being gathered in different countries and in different settings. About one-third to nearly one-half of these samples had *flat cluster profiles*, fewer than in the standardization sample but still a substantial proportion. Both the *DAS* dyslexic sample with Word

Reading below 85 and the Dumont sample had 11–12% in the Low Verbal, High Spatial subgroup. This is about half the frequency of Low Verbal children in the comparable subgroup from the standardization sample who were poor readers with ability–achievement discrepancies. One wonders whether Low Verbal children tend not to be identified as dyslexic or LD. It seems possible that many such children may be found in inner-city and poor socioeconomic environments. They may thereby get special educational services from other sources (for example Title 1 funding in the USA). Such children may often be considered to be 'garden-variety' poor readers, to use Stanovich's (1988) term, rather than dyslexic or LD. However, the BAS II sample of children referred as possibly dyslexic, and who had Word Reading scores of 85 and below, had a very similar proportion of Low Verbal children to the base-rate group from the standardization sample of Poor Readers with Discrepancy. Further research is needed to clarify these issues concerning the proportion of Low Verbal children referred and later identified as dyslexic or LD. Turning to the Low Spatial, High Verbal subgroup, the dyslexic and LD samples showed a similar proportion, compared to the base rate, of students with this profile. It is possible that a number of children with this profile have a Nonverbal Learning Disability (Rourke et al., 1990).

Apart from the BAS II-tested dyslexics with Word Reading scores greater than 85, few dyslexic or LD children had a High Nonverbal Reasoning profile – considerably fewer than the proportion in the total DAS sample. However, more than one-third of the DAS-tested dyslexic and LD samples and about a quarter of the BAS II-tested sample fell into the Low Nonverbal Reasoning subgroup. Although the number of BAS II-tested children with this profile is significantly lower than for the other dyslexic and LD groups, it is still substantially greater than the base rate. Considering the different times and settings when these data were gathered, the results are remarkably similar, providing mutual cross-validation of these findings. The mean profile for the combined dyslexic and LD children who are in this subgroup ($n = 83$) is shown in Fig. 6.1. The differences between the mean scores are dramatic: Nonverbal Reasoning is lower than both Verbal and Spatial means by more than one standard deviation.

Why should children with reading disabilities score poorly on the two DAS subtests measuring Nonverbal Reasoning? The answer seems most plausibly to lie in the nature of the tasks of reading and 'nonverbal' reasoning. Reading requires a high level of visual/verbal integration in order to convert visual printed codes into sounds and words. For fluent reading, and for recognition of common words or letter strings, an individual needs information in the

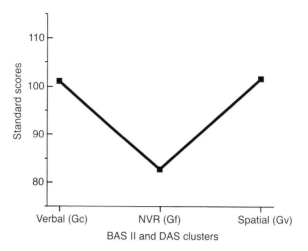

Fig. 6.1. Mean scores on BAS II and DAS clusters for dyslexic and LD children in the Low Nonverbal Reasoning (NVR) subgroup.

auditory/verbal and visual processing systems to be effectively integrated. Similarly, to perform well on the DAS Nonverbal Reasoning tasks (or, indeed, any good measures of fluid reasoning), one needs good integration of the visual and verbal processing systems. These tasks are presented visually – hence the term 'nonverbal' that describes them – but to solve the problems effectively, the use of internal language to label and to mediate the solution of the problems is generally essential. Even if an individual has excellent verbal and spatial abilities, if the two brain processing systems specialized for those abilities do not 'talk' to each other effectively, this may have an adverse effect on performance, both in reasoning and in reading acquisition.

Readers may wonder why these striking findings, on two independent samples, have not been reported previously for other test batteries. The simple and short answer (as there is insufficient space to elaborate on it) is that all other psychometric batteries used with children, with one exception, do not have three separate measures of Verbal ability (Gc), Spatial ability (Gv), and Nonverbal Reasoning ability (Gf).[5]

A brief account of the case of Mike (age 7 years 11 months) may serve to illustrate a typical dyslexic or reading-disabled student with a Low Nonverbal Reasoning profile. Mike was referred for assessment because, despite being self-evidently bright verbally and very capable in visual–motor tasks, he had had persistent problems since starting school in learning to read fluently and to spell accurately. His scores on the DAS are shown in Table 6.7.

There are no significant differences between Mike's scores on the two

Table 6.7. DAS subtest, cluster, and achievement scores for Mike

DAS subtest or cluster	Score
Core subtests	*(T-score)*
Word Definitions	53
Similarities	49
Matrices	40
Sequential and Quantitative Reasoning	47
Recall of Designs	59
Pattern Construction	61
Diagnostic subtests	
Recall of Digits	40 (L)
Recall of Objects (Immediate)	50
Speed of Information Processing	61 (H)
Clusters	*(Standard score)*
Verbal	101
Nonverbal Reasoning	88 (L)
Spatial	116 (H)
GCA	102
Achievement tests	*(Standard score)*
Word Reading	79 (L)
Spelling	87 (L)
Basic Number Skills	91 (L)

In the score column, (L) denotes a statistically significant low score, and (H) a statistically significant high score. These are explained more fully in the text.

Verbal, the two Nonverbal Reasoning, or the two Spatial subtests. However, his Nonverbal Reasoning cluster score is significantly lower than his Spatial cluster score, and is lower than his Verbal score (this difference falling just short of statistical significance). Nevertheless, his Nonverbal Reasoning score is well below both the Verbal and Spatial scores, making his profile fit the Low Nonverbal Reasoning subgroup. His Nonverbal Reasoning and Spatial scores are also significantly lower and higher than his GCA score, respectively, and are consequently marked 'L' and 'H'. As discussed earlier, it seems probable that whereas Mike is fluent verbally, and has good spatial skills, he has problems in auditory–visual integration that arguably have influenced his acquisition of reading skills.

Turning to the diagnostic subtests, Mike's score on Recall of Digits is significantly low, in comparison with his mean T-score derived from the six core subtests. His score on Speed of Information Processing is significantly high. He therefore appears to have a significant weakness in auditory short-term memory, in addition to his relative weakness in auditory–visual integration. His parents and teacher also commented that Mike often quickly forgets verbally given instructions. They put this down to inattention, but an alternative hypothesis is a relative weakness in short-term verbal processing. On the other hand, his speed of visual information processing is relatively high, supporting his good spatial ability.

On the three DAS achievement tests, Mike's obtained scores on Word Reading, Spelling, and Basic Number Skills are all significantly lower than the scores predicted from his GCA score (Word Reading and Spelling have predicted scores of 101; Basic Number Skills has a predicted score of 102). The difference of 22 points between Mike's observed and predicted scores on Word Reading is found in fewer than 5% of children.

So, what would appropriate intervention recommendations be for a boy like Mike? For many years, teachers of dyslexic children have actively advocated multi-sensory teaching methods, despite research evidence that appeared to discredit auditory–visual integration as a cause of poor reading acquisition (e.g., Bryant, 1968). Teachers appear to have long held to the view that dyslexic children have difficulty integrating visual and verbal information. The reader will recall that it is hypothesized that a relative weakness in this ability underlies the Low Nonverbal Reasoning profile found in the samples of dyslexic and LD children, reported earlier. Thus, it was recommended that a multi-sensory teaching method should be used with Mike. His poor auditory short-term memory should also be taken account of through (a) minimizing the length of verbal instructions; (b) using repetition where necessary; and (c) using his above-average visual short-term memory to compensate for his relatively poor auditory short-term memory, perhaps by keeping a notebook of things to remember. Useful references to multi-sensory teaching approaches are given by Thomson and Watkins (1998), Augur and Briggs (1992), and Walker and Brooks (1993). The 40% of dyslexic and LD children found in this study with a Low Nonverbal Reasoning profile may well benefit from such an approach.

Illustrative case study: Benjamin W.

The case presented here illustrates the use of the BAS II in investigating the abilities of a child referred because of concern about his basic school attainments. Ben was assessed on the BAS II at the age of 8 years 1 month. He did not show a dramatically spiky cognitive profile on the BAS II. The case study shows how various hypotheses may be tested and evaluated in conjunction with careful observation and information from home and school, and illustrates how the conclusions drawn are then used to develop recommendations about appropriate interventions.

Introduction

Ben's parents had approached his teacher and head teacher at school, as they were somewhat concerned about his progress at school in basic skills. He was showing little interest in reading for pleasure, and was resistant to doing small homework tasks in spelling, reading, writing, or maths. The teacher had also noticed that Ben would do the bare minimum that she set him to do, and would often be inattentive in class. The school then referred him for assessment. The psychologist focused on the area of basic skills, and confirmed the teacher's comments after observing him in class. He was not strongly engaged in classroom tasks that focused on basic skills, but was clearly a fluent thinker and speaker in conversation. He was enthusiastic about physical activities and creative tasks in art. Socially, he mixed well with other children and with adults.

The BAS II was used to assess Ben's cognitive abilities. All tests were completed in a single session. Ben cooperated well, maintaining attention and interest until near the end of the session.

Summary of test results

Ben's test results on the BAS II are summarized in Table 6.8. The table starts with the core scales, from which the composite scores are derived, then presents the diagnostic scales, measuring aspects of short-term memory and speed of information processing, and concludes with the school achievement tests.

Discussion and interpretation

Cognitive abilities

Ben's cognitive abilities are almost uniformly above average: he is within the top 15% of children of his age. His scores on the core scales of the BAS II are very similar indeed, with no significant scatter. Thus, his Verbal, Nonverbal Reasoning, and Spatial abilities are 113, 112, and 115 respectively. He has a flat profile on the core subtests and cluster scores.

On the diagnostic scales, he again performed at a similar level to his performance on the core scales. He scored exceptionally well on Speed of Information Processing, within the upper 1% of children of his age. His short-term memory abilities also appear to be above average.

The single exception to his succession of above-average scores was his significantly low score (when compared to his own scores on other scales) on

Table 6.8. Ben's scores on the BAS II

	Score	Percentile	Descriptive category
Core Scale scores[a]			
(Mean = 50, SD = 10)			
Word Definitions	61	86	
Verbal Similarities	55	69	
Matrices	62	88	
Quantitative Reasoning	53	62	
Recall of Designs	59	82	
Pattern Construction	59	82	
Diagnostic Scale scores			
(Mean = 50, SD = 10)			
Recall of Objects (Verbal Recall of Pictures)	61	86	
Speed of Information Processing	74	99	Significantly high
Recall of Digits Forward (Auditory Memory)	61	86	
Recall of Digits Backward (Auditory Memory)	49	46	Significantly low
Recognition of Pictures (Visual Memory)	59	82	
Composite scores			
(Mean = 100, SD = 15)			
Verbal Ability	113	81	Above Average
Nonverbal Reasoning Ability	112	79	Above Average
Spatial Ability	115	84	Above Average
General Conceptual Ability (GCA)	116	86	Above Average
Achievement scale scores			
(Mean = 100, SD = 15)			
Word Reading	100	50	Significantly low[b]
Spelling	98	45	Significantly low[b]
Number Skills	109	73	

[a]There are no significant differences among the core scale scores.

[b]These scores are significantly lower than the scores that are predicted by his GCA score. For children such as Ben, with a GCA score of 116, scores on the Word Reading and Spelling tests are both predicted to be 109.

Recall of Digits *Backward*. This test requires a child to repeat, in reverse order, a string of single-digit numbers presented verbally at the rate of two digits per second (for example 3, 9, 7, 8, 2). The test is considered to be a measure of verbal working memory, requiring the child to hold and manipulate the numbers before producing a response. This was the last test given to Ben after a long session, and his relatively low score may simply be attributable to tiredness, particularly because he was able to do the Recall of Digits *Forward* task at an above-average level (repeating digit strings in the same order as presented). Ben's score on Recall of Digits Backward was *relatively* low in comparison with his own scores on other scales. However, in comparison with other children of his age, his score was average. On balance, therefore, the psychologist did not consider this score to be important in the overall assessment of Ben's abilities, and concluded that, with a flat profile across a wide range of cognitive abilities, Ben showed no evidence that cognitive processing difficulties accounted for his relatively poor attainments. In other words, he does not have a specific learning disability.

Basic school achievement

On all three tests, Ben's scores fell into the average range for his age. Although Ben's scores were within the average range on Word Reading and Spelling, both of these scores were significantly lower than the achievement scores that would be expected from his cognitive abilities, and specifically from his GCA score. Based on that score, Word Reading and Spelling scores of 109 would be expected. His actual scores on Word Reading and Spelling are very consistent. His actual score of 100 on Word Reading places him at the 50th percentile, and his score of 98 on Spelling places him at the 45th percentile. However, his expected position is around the 73rd percentile. Such discrepancies are found in about 20–25% of children with GCA scores of 116. However, although not unusual, the results do support the concerns expressed by his parents and teacher.

An observation of both his reading and spelling strategies suggests that Ben reads and spells familiar words quickly when he knows them. When faced with an unfamiliar word, however, he has few systematic strategies to decode them (if reading) or encode them (if spelling). Thus, his *errors in reading* show signs of undue dependence on strategies of visual recognition and a nonuse of systematic phonetic strategies to solve unfamiliar words. Unknown words therefore tend to be guessed quickly rather than being slowly and systematically broken down.

In spelling, he clearly has a vocabulary of (for him) irregular words, such as 'come' and 'eight.' For words he does not know, his *errors in spelling* tend to be of a simple phonetic type. He has not yet developed *orthographic strategies* for longer words (strategies that show he is developing hypotheses that a word might belong to a 'family' of letter combinations). His visual strategies are not efficient enough to allow him to recognize illegal letter combinations. Some examples from the Spelling test are as follows:

Cue word	Ben's spelling	Comment
work	werk	Simple phonetic
walk	work	Simple phonetic – didn't recognize that this said 'work'!
soil	soal	Illegal combination ('oa' never spells the sound 'oi')
friend	frend	Simple phonetic
know	no	Simple phonetic – hasn't learnt this homonym
catch	cach	Simple phonetic with an illegal ending
worse	wers	As above
circle	calcale	No systematic phonetic mapping of sounds. Some visual resemblance

Such spelling errors are, of course, very common in young children. Although his absolute levels of reading and spelling are just average for his age, this assessment indicates that his literacy skills need improvement, and are below expectation, based upon his cognitive development across verbal, spatial, and fluid reasoning areas.

Intervention suggestions

Whilst Ben's reading and spelling performance is around average for his age, and does not require specialist remedial resources at this time, the results of this assessment indicate that Ben does have the cognitive ability to do significantly better. At the age of eight years, he should be developing systematic phonetic and orthographic strategies for reading and spelling.

In observing Ben's reading, both in this assessment session and in general at school and at home, it appears that there are two major issues. The first is that he needs to learn a larger range of systematic decoding and encoding skills that are essential foundations of literacy. The second key issue is motivation: he will need a lot of encouragement.

At school, the following steps are recommended.

1. Hear Ben read daily.
2. Systematically teach a range of phonetic and orthographic strategies.
3. Note his common errors and use these as a focus for teaching decoding and encoding skills.
4. Reading and writing tasks, whether in the form of a phonics programme or in the form of books to read or written expression of ideas, should have a high interest level for him wherever possible.
5. Try to develop reading speed provided his reading is accurate (i.e., fluency). Perhaps have a longer passage and divide it up into chunks of, say, five lines, with Ben reading a piece each day under timed conditions and charting his progress (number of words read in, say, 60 seconds, or time taken to read, say, five lines). Ben enjoys the challenge of doing things quickly, and trying to beat his previous time!

    At home, the following steps are recommended.
1. Mum or Dad should hear Ben read for ten minutes each day. Books should be selected for pleasure or interest. If possible, choose books that he can read reasonably fluently, so that he experiences success. If he sticks on a word, help him break it down, if it is reasonably regular. If it isn't anything he could reasonably decode at this stage, say the word, and get him to repeat it. At the *end* of the session, go back to two or three words (maximum) that he got wrong (but you think he should know them), and get him to read them again.
2. Give Ben a 'quiet time' of maybe 30 or 45 minutes each day. Give him the choice of doing reading or writing, as well as the choice of what he reads (keep drawing pictures to a minimum – it's an easy diversion!). Have someone check periodically to make sure he's not just daydreaming.
3. Ration the time he spends watching TV or doing computer and video games! Maybe give time on them as a reward for constructive reading or writing.
4. Have a star chart system for recording good work each day, with associated rewards (could be extra TV time, pocket money, etc.).

Follow-up

Ben's basic skills achievements were followed up six months after this assessment. His teacher and parents reported that they had put the recommendations into practice systematically. Ben had made excellent progress in reading, spelling, and written expression. He was enjoying these activities, and his test scores had increased as follows: Word Reading 115, Spelling 110. Now the concern of his teacher and his parents is his number skills!

ENDNOTES

1 Individual subtests in the two instruments are called 'subtests' in the DAS and 'scales' in the BAS II. For the sake of clarity, they are referred to as 'subtests' in this chapter.

2 The exception is the Word Definitions subtest, which has a specificity of .24, thereby narrowly failing the .25 criterion.

3 The data for this sample have been very kindly provided by Martin Turner, Head of Psychology, Dyslexia Institute, Staines, England.

4 The data for this sample are used by kind permission of Dr Ron Dumont, Director, MA and PsyD Programs in School Psychology, Farleigh Dickinson University, Teaneck, New Jersey, USA.

5 The one exception is the Woodcock–Johnson Tests of Cognitive Ability–Revised (WJ–R; Woodcock & Johnson, 1989). A lack of research evidence on such difficulties with fluid reasoning tasks for dyslexic and learning-disabled children may be due to one of two possible reasons: (a) a lack of research with substantial samples; or (b) a problem with the subtests that purport to measure Gv and Gf. For example, the correlation between the two WJ–R subtests measuring Gv (Visual Closure and Picture Recognition) is very low: .22 at age six years, .30 at age nine years, and .29 at age 13 years. Such low correlations beg the question of whether the composite formed from such a weak pairing measures anything meaningful. In comparison, the correlations between the two DAS measures of Gv (Recall of Designs and Pattern Construction) are .56, .54, and .61 for the same age groups.

REFERENCES

Anastasi, A. & Urbina, S. (1997). *Psychological Testing, Seventh Edition*. Upper Saddle River, NJ: Prentice Hall.

Augur, J. & Briggs, S. (eds.) (1992). *The Hickey Multisensory Language Course*, 2nd edition. London: Whurr.

British Psychological Society (1999). *Dyslexia, Literacy and Psychological Assessment*. Report by a working party of the Division of Educational and Child Psychology. Leicester, England: British Psychological Society.

Bryant, P.E. (1968). Comments on the design of developmental studies of cross-modal matching and cross-modal transfer. *Cortex*, 4, 127–37.

Carroll, J.B. (1993). *Human Cognitive Abilities: A Survey of Factor Analytic Studies*. New York: Cambridge University Press.

Dumont, R., Cruse, C.L., Price, L., & Whelley, P. (1996). The relationship between the Differential Ability Scales (DAS) and the Wechsler Intelligence Scale for Children–Third Edition (WISC–III) for students with learning disabilities. *Psychology in the Schools*, 33, 203–9.

Elliott, C.D. (1990a). *Differential Ability Scales*. San Antonio, TX: The Psychological Corporation.

Elliott, C.D. (1990b). The nature and structure of children's abilities: evidence from the Differential Ability Scales. *Journal of Psychoeducational Assessment*, 8, 376–90.

Elliott, C.D. (1990c). *Differential Ability Scales: Introductory and Technical Handbook*. San Antonio, TX: The Psychological Corporation.

Elliott, C.D. (1997a). *British Ability Scales, 2nd edition*. Windsor, England: NFER-Nelson.

Elliott, C.D. (1997b). The Differential Ability Scales. In *Contemporary Intellectual Assessment: Theories, Tests, and Issues*, ed. D.P. Flanagan, J.L. Genshaft, & P.L. Harrison, pp. 183–208. New York: Guilford Press.

Elliott, C.D., Dumont, R., Whelley, P., & Bradley, J. (1998). *Scoring Assistant for the Differential Ability Scales*. San Antonio, TX: The Psychological Corporation.

Elliott, C.D., Murray, D.J., & Pearson, L.S. (1979). *British Ability Scales*. Windsor, England: National Foundation for Educational Research.

Embretson, S. (1985). Review of the British Ability Scales. In *Ninth Mental Measurements Yearbook*, ed. J.V. Mitchell, pp. 231–2. Lincoln, NE: University of Nebraska Press.

Glutting, J.J., McDermott, P.A., Konold, T.R., Snelbaker, A.J., & Watkins, M.W. (1998). More ups and downs of subtest analysis: criterion validity of the DAS with an unselected cohort. *School Psychology Review*, 27, 599–612.

Glutting, J.J., McDermott, P.A., Watkins, M.W., Kush, J.C., & Konold, T.R. (1997). The base rate problem and its consequences for interpreting children's ability profiles. *School Psychology Review*, 26, 176–88.

Gustafsson, J.-E. (1988). Hierarchical models of individual differences in cognitive abilities. In *Advances in the Psychology of Human Intelligence*, Vol. 4, ed. R.J. Sternberg, pp. 35–71. Hillsdale, NJ: Erlbaum.

Gustafsson, J.-E. (1989). Broad and narrow abilities in research on learning and instruction. In *Abilities, Motivation, and Methodology: The Minnesota Symposium on Learning and Individual Differences*, ed. R. Kanfer, P.L. Ackerman, & R. Cudeck, pp. 203–37. Hillsdale, NJ: Erlbaum.

Hagley, F. (1987). *The Suffolk Reading Scale*. Windsor, England: NFER-Nelson.

Härnqvist, K., Gustafsson, J.-E., Muthén, B.O., & Nelson, G. (1994). Hierarchical models of ability at individual and class levels. *Intelligence*, 18, 165–87.

Hitch, G.J., Halliday, S., Schaafstal, A.M., & Schraagen, J.M.C. (1988). Visual working memory in young children. *Memory and Cognition*, 16, 120–32.

Holland, A.M. & McDermott, P.A. (1996). Discovering core profile types in the school-age standardization sample of the Differential Ability Scales. *Journal of Psychoeducational Assessment*, 14, 131–46.

Kamphaus, R.W. (1993). *Clinical Assessment of Children's Intelligence*. Boston: Allyn & Bacon.

Kaufman, A.S. (1994). *Intelligent Testing with the WISC–III*. New York: Wiley & Sons.

Keith, T.Z. (1990). Confirmatory and hierarchical confirmatory analysis of the Differential Ability Scales. *Journal of Psychoeducational Assessment*, 8, 391–405.

Keith, T.Z., Quirk, K.I., Schartzer, C., & Elliott, C.D. (1999). Construct bias in the Differential Ability Scales? Confirmatory and hierarchical factor structure across three ethnic groups. *Journal of Psychoeducational Assessment*, 17, 249–68.

Kercher, A.C. & Sandoval, J. (1991). Reading disability and the Differential Ability Scales. *Journal of School Psychology*, 29, 293–307.

McCarthy, R.A. & Warrington, E.K. (1990). *Cognitive Neuropsychology: An Introduction*. San Diego, CA: Academic Press.

McDermott, P.A., Fantuzzo, J.W., & Glutting, J.J. (1990). Just say no to subtest analysis: a critique of Wechsler theory and practice. *Journal of Psychoeducational Assessment*, 8, 290–302.

McDermott, P.A., Fantuzzo, J.W., Glutting, J.J., Watkins, M.W., & Baggaley, A.R. (1992). Illusions of meaning in the ipsative assessment of children's ability. *Journal of Special Education*, 25, 504–26.

McDermott, P.A. & Glutting, J.J. (1997). Informing stylistic learning behavior, disposition, and achievement through ability subtests – or, more illusions of meaning? *School Psychology Review*, 26, 163–75.

McGrew, K.S. (1997). Analysis of the major intelligence batteries according to a proposed comprehensive Gf–Gc framework. In *Contemporary Intellectual Assessment: Theories, Tests, and Issues*, ed. D.P. Flanagan, J.L. Genshaft, & P.L. Harrison, pp. 151–79. New York: Guilford Press.

McGrew, K.S. & Murphy, S. (1995). Uniqueness and general factor characteristics of the Woodcock–Johnson Tests of Cognitive Ability–Revised. *Journal of School Psychology*, 33, 235–45.

McIntosh, D.E. (1999). Identifying at-risk preschoolers: the discriminant validity of the Differential Ability Scales. *Psychology in the Schools*, 36, 1–10.

McIntosh, D.E. & Gridley, B.E. (1993). Differential Ability Scales: profiles of learning-disabled subtypes. *Psychology in the Schools*, 30, 11–24.

Psychological Corporation (1983). *Basic Achievement Skills Individual Screener*. New York: Psychological Corporation.

Rourke, B.P., Del Dotto, J.E., Rourke, S.B., & Casey, J.E. (1990). Nonverbal learning disabilities: the syndrome and a case study. *Journal of School Psychology*, 28, 361–85.

Sattler, J.M. (1992). *Assessment of Children*, 3rd Edition–Revised. San Diego, CA: Sattler.

Scottish Council for Research in Education (1967). *The Scottish Standardisation of the Wechsler Intelligence Scale for Children*. London: University of London Press.

Shapiro, S.K, Buckhalt, J.A., & Herod, L.A. (1995). Evaluation of learning disabled students with the Differential Ability Scales (DAS). *Journal of School Psychology*, 33, 247–63.

Snow, C.E., Burns, M.S., & Griffin, P. (eds.) (1998). *Preventing Reading Difficulties in Young Children*. Washington, DC: National Academy Press.

Spearman, C. (1927). *The Abilities of Man*. London: Macmillan.

Springer, S.P. & Deutsch, G. (1989). *Left Brain, Right Brain*, 3rd edition. New York: Freeman.

Terman, L.M. & Merrill, M.A. (1960). *Stanford–Binet Intelligence Scale: Manual for the Third Revision, Form L-M*. Boston, MA: Houghton-Mifflin.

Thomson, M.E. & Watkins, E.J. (1998) *Dyslexia: A Teaching Handbook*, 2nd edition. London: Whurr.

Thorndike, R.L., Hagen, E.P., & Sattler, J.M. (1986). *Technical Manual for the Stanford–Binet Intelligence Scale: Fourth Edition*. Chicago, IL: Riverside.

Walker, J. & Brooks, L. (1993) *Dyslexia Institute Literacy Programme*. London: James and James.

Wechsler, D. (1949). *Wechsler Intelligence Scale for Children*. New York: The Psychological Corporation.

Wechsler, D. (1974). *Wechsler Intelligence Scale for Children–Revised*. San Antonio, TX: The Psychological Corporation.

Wechsler, D. (1989). *Wechsler Preschool and Primary Scale of Intelligence–Revised*. San Antonio, TX: The Psychological Corporation.

Wechsler, D. (1991). *Wechsler Intelligence Scale for Children–Third Edition*. San Antonio, TX: The Psychological Corporation.

Woodcock, R.W. & Johnson, M.B. (1989). *Woodcock–Johnson Psycho-Educational Battery–Revised*. Chicago, IL: Riverside.

Wright, B.D. & Stone, M.H. (1985). Review of the British Ability Scales. In *Ninth Mental Measurements Yearbook*, ed. J.V. Mitchell, pp. 232–5. Lincoln, NE: University of Nebraska Press.

Youngstrom, E.A., Kogos, J.L., & Glutting, J.J. (1999). Incremental efficacy of Differential Ability Scales factor scores in predicting individual achievement criteria. *School Psychology Quarterly*, 14, 26–39.

7

Is dynamic assessment compatible with the psychometric model?

Reuven Feuerstein and Raphael S. Feuerstein

Avtalyon said: Scholars, be careful with your words! You may incur the penalty of exile and be banished to a place of evil waters and the disciples who follow you into exile are likely to drink of them and die . . . (Ethics of the Fathers, I, 11).

This paper, presenting our stance towards dynamic assessment, is dedicated to two of our most devoted colleagues and supporters: Dr David Krassilovsky, MD, *z'al*, renowned psychiatrist, former head of Talbieh Hospital, a founding member and long-time Associate Director of the International Center for the Enhancement of Learning Potential, and Mr Shimon Tuchman, *z'al*, former Deputy Director General of Youth Aliyah who was deeply involved in the development of the center. They both contributed to making our experimental, clinical, and empirical work possible. May this paper keep their memory alive and be a blessing to the continuation of our work.

Summary

The purpose of this chapter is to examine the risks involved in using the psychometric model in shaping the dynamic assessment of cognitive development. It is shown that the psychometric definition of intelligence as a stable trait classifies individuals as a function of their manifest level of functioning. By contrast, the definition of intelligence as a cluster of states that governs the Learning Propensity Assessment Device and the theory of Structural Cognitive Modifiability which underlies it evaluates an individual's propensity for modifiability. Conventional psychometric conceptions and tools constitute a barrier to the evaluation of the modifiability of the individual's states, and hinder our ability to assess and ultimately raise the level of low functioning individuals, so that they can benefit from education towards higher levels of adaptability and more efficient levels of functioning.

IQ revisited

> How can individual differences in the results be accounted for? There is no satisfactory answer but it may be assumed in all likelihood that different mental processes are tapped by the different tasks and that these processes are not identical across all children.

Who is the author of this very modern statement on the interpretation of intelligence tests? Strangely enough, it is the inventor of the procedure himself, Alfred Binet, writing in *Les Idées Modernes sur les Enfants* [*Modern Ideas on Children*, 1909], two years before his death in 1911. Nearly a century ago, when Binet was studying in Paris, psychology as a field was heavily influenced by Darwinism. Binet, like his mentor Broca, studied craniometry (measurement of the skull), which was designed to rank races according to their intelligence (e.g., skull size) and hence create a criterion for the superiority of some segments of humanity over others. In one experiment, Binet measured the skulls of students defined by their teachers as either the most or the least capable. Fortunately for the history of psychology, Binet only found small differences in skull size (1 mm), and some weak students even had larger skulls. The conclusion Binet drew from the failure of these experiments was that the paradigm itself was wrong: rather than searching for a global definition of intelligence, psychologists should not exclude the individual differences they obtain through measurement, but rather focus on these. The way, according to Binet, would be to discard the psychophysical description of simple processes (and the psychophysical crutch of a physical measure for each mental state) and base psychology on the study of higher processes. To achieve this goal, Binet himself was assisted by two factors. The first was his longitudinal study of the development of his two daughters, begun in 1890, a highly differential account of their cognitive development which curiously prefigures Piaget's precise analysis of cognitive behavior.[1] The second was the commission from the French Ministry of Public Education in 1904 to develop a method to screen abnormal from normal children in public schools.

Alfred Binet's major theoretical breakthrough was the idea to associate the metric of development – age – to the scores obtained on his tests of mental ability. By associating a measurable quantity (age) with another measurable quantity (score), he provided a solution to the problem Broca and others had tried to solve by using an external criterion such as skull size as a dimension of intelligence. As Zazzo points out, 'the failures of his predecessors arose from their inability to truly disengage themselves from laboratory instruments and the philosophy implicit to these instruments – but also their inability to find a measure common to the diversity of mental phenomena.' (1962, p. 13).

Nevertheless, Binet's true paradigm-breaking insights either went unnoticed or were deliberately disregarded by those who were too eager to bend the notion of mental age to their own purposes. What did Binet himself intend his test to measure?

Our goal, when we have a child in front of us, is to measure his intellectual capacities in order to determine whether he is normal or retarded. For this purpose we should study his current state and this state only. Neither his past nor his future should concern us; hence we ignore his etiology and in particular we make no distinction between acquired retardation and congenital retardation; and above all we will avoid all considerations as to anatomical pathology which could account for his intellectual deficit. As regards the future, the same abstention holds: we are neither attempting to establish nor prepare a prognosis and we leave unanswered the question of whether his retardation is curable or not, subject to improvement or not. We restrict ourselves to gathering the truth on his current state.[2]

Further, Binet warned that intelligence was a composite notion and could not be reduced to a linear measure:

This scale serves, not strictly speaking as a measure of intelligence, since intellectual qualities cannot be measured like lengths, they are not superposable – but rather as a classification, a hierarchy between diverse intelligences.

Binet warned that the use of an age scale itself calls for special interpretation because a difference in age is relative to total age. A given developmental delay, say a two-year delay, does not mean the same thing at age 15 as it does at age five. Finally, Binet foresaw the social misuse of his scales and clearly attempted to show that his scale could be influenced by social factors:

Take children of the rich, it is absolutely certain that they will answer better on the average and will be a year, two years ahead, of our little primary schools students. Take children from the countryside, maybe they will answer less well? Take children from Belgium in areas where they speak both French and Walloon, the lower class children will answer even less well in particular on the language tasks. Our colleague Rouma, professor at the Charleroi Teachers' College drew our attention to these astounding inequalities in intelligence which he observed using our tests, and which are dependent on background (Binet, 1909, p. 138).

Perhaps because Binet's untimely death prevented him from expanding upon his theories, his efforts at developing a measure of current state of performance and his care in restricting his interpretation of his findings were shunted aside. His real intentions were misinterpreted and the notion of mental age became a reified IQ measure based on a rank order, leading psychometricians to a classification and categorization resulting in the prediction of the future of human beings according to their current manifest level of functioning.

However, as early as 1934, Professor André Rey[3] decried the ills of categorization and labeling of manifest levels of functioning as measured by psychometric tests. As he once pointed out, if we were asked to compare the behavior of two dogs, one of which had received training to produce a conditioned reflex and the other had not, we would view the request as absurd, because we do not compare animals that are different on the basis of an acquired characteristic. The right question would have been whether the second dog after training could also display the conditioned reflex. Yet conventional psychometric approaches, Rey argued, regard intelligence as fixed and immutable and have a tendency to include environmental factors as themselves reflecting certain endogenous parameters. (Rey, 1934, cited in Feuerstein et al., 1979, p. 28.)

Impact of the psychometric model on the concept of intelligence

For many years now, this narrow misinterpretation of mental age has been recognized as a source of injustice to individuals, groups, and to the psychology of intelligence itself. Clearly, there are great dangers associated with this misinterpretation, the major one being the belief that inherited IQ serves to distinguish people and groups and destines these people for a given 'station in life', i.e., that the differences across groups are the outcome of heredity and that differences in quality of life have little or no impact on IQ. I will not address the fallacies of the genetic analysis of IQ scores because it has been dealt with comprehensively elsewhere (see, for instance, Gould, 1996).

There is a greater consensus today that a low score on any given IQ subtest can be attributed to a variety of socioeconomic as well as genetic factors. The issue as regards intelligence scores is hence one of interpretation of these results and the use made of this interpretation. The first of these issues is the role of isolated performance on the test itself. It has been argued that 'problem solving strategies differ not only because various individuals possess various "abilities" but also because individuals' strategies are different under various conditions and because level of performance in any decision making task may depend on different processes' (Gitmez, 1971). Thus, beyond spurious genetic claims, socioeconomic handicap such as a lack of exposure to a certain type of educational conditions and/or skills required for adaptation negatively affect performance on an IQ (or any other) test.

This is one of the reasons why some behavioral scientists, primarily in the 1950–1960s, sought to correct the verbal nature of the IQ tests to make it more 'culture free,' primarily by using pictorial or visual devices. Culture 'fair' tests, such as the Davis–Eells Games (1953), which integrated games non-mainstream children were familiar with, were developed in an attempt at 'positive discrimination.' Anastasi (1961, p. 268) commented, nevertheless, that 'lower class children perform as poorly on these tests as they do on other intelligence tests.' The poor outcomes of these culture-free and culture fair tests led researchers to conclude that rendering aseptic an intelligence test would not solve the problem of differences in performance, or the readiness to respond appropriately to a test situation itself.

Similarly, researchers rejected the predictive value of 'clean' tests: 'What could it predict? Covering up differences in this way does not erase test bias. Rather it delimits drastically the kinds of information one can gather about problem solving strengths and weaknesses associated with groups as well as individuals.' (Masland, Saranson, & Gladwin, 1958, p. 723). In the 1960s, Wesman rejected the 'gold mine' approach to intelligence testing, in which intelligence is a reified substance that must be rooted out from underneath layers of classifiable performance (speed, length, weight, etc.): 'Because [these objects] can be measured does not mean that they are substances. We need not accept the converse notion that if something is measurable it is necessarily a substance' (1968, p. 267).

Later attempts at correcting for differences in background within the framework of psychometrics were also unsuccessful. One such attempt was made by Mercer (1979), who developed the SOMPA (System of Multicultural Pluralistic Assessment). The SOMPA suggested compensating for relative sociocultural and educational level by a point system. Although the intent was praiseworthy, the scores corrected by the individual's level of socioeconomic disadvantage were of little value to educators because they provided no indications as to what remediational intervention was possible and what path to follow. The incorporation of this point system within the Wechsler battery served merely to return the system to its inherent psychometric roots and weaknesses.

The awareness that psychometric assessment does not respond satisfactorily to the fact that certain socioeconomic groups are overrepresented in specialized schools has prompted a search for other assessment instruments, both within the psychometric tradition and in reaction to it, in the form of dynamic assessment (for an overview, see Neisser et al., 1996). Over the last 40 years, interest in dynamic assessment has developed as a response to the inability of static psychometric tests to characterize non-mainstream, culturally different, socioculturally disadvantaged, deprived, and genetic–chromosomal-impaired children.

In the early 1960s, the first author introduced the principles behind the

Learning Propensity Assessment Device (LPAD) in relation to work with culturally different children. Dynamic assessment, whose principles began to evolve in the early 1950s, arose from the need to assess culturally different and deprived children whose level of functioning was such that they were classified as mentally retarded at varying degrees of severity. Dynamic assessment has spread, and is now used by researchers who have been inspired by the original LPAD notions or have developed models of their own.[4] The test–teach–test model has served many of those who were inspired by Vygotsky (1962) and Feuerstein et al. (1979, 1980, 1987, 1988, 1997). The general principle guiding all dynamic approaches to assessment is the introduction of a learning phase within the assessment procedure itself.[5] This feature has major implications for the content of learning, the role of the examiner, the interpretation of change scores, and, obviously, for the theory of learning behind the procedure. Some forms of dynamic testing maintain psychometric properties for purposes of preserving the statistical power required for norming these tests. Many misconceptions arise from attempts to force dynamic assessment into a psychometric mold when the theory of modifiability of the learner is at odds with these concepts. In particular, the LPAD and the theory of Structural–Cognitive Modifiability have often been viewed through a psychometric prism and have hence been diluted of much of their explanatory impact and intent. The next section reviews the development of the LPAD in an attempt to clarify these issues.

Children of the Ashes

In the early 1950s, Israel was faced with the enormous task of the immigration and absorption of child victims of the Holocaust and adolescents from vastly different ethno-cultural, economic, and social backgrounds (Yemen, Cochin, North Africa, Europe, etc.). In addition to the hardships of displacement, these children and adolescents often came from broken and poverty-stricken families. Standard psychometric tests classified some of them as below normal. How could these individuals be integrated into technological Israeli society? The moral issues underlying the necessity of aid to these adolescents were coupled with the theoretical problem of the assessment of their real abilities – so as to do justice to their needs for schooling and cognitive and educational growth.

The LPAD was the dynamic assessment tool that emerged from these experiences. Over the last 50 years, the LPAD has been expanded upon to deal with children and adults with a variety of etiologies of learning disorders. The LPAD (1979) and the theory of Structural–Cognitive Modifiability which is at its core make it clear that a number of concepts linked to the psychometric model have become totally outdated and irrelevant to the dynamic model. If human beings have a prime option of becoming modified and this modifiability is not merely a change in the quantity of knowledge or skills but represents a real change in the mental structure of the organism, the following concepts will need to be recast.

1. The shift from the concept of 'trait' as representative of the stable and immutable characteristics of the individual to the concept of 'state' reflecting the modifiability of the human condition. The trait concept should be replaced by the concept of states. Intelligence is a state in which the individual behaves in a given way for a more or less extensive period of time in a seemingly permanent way depending on what has produced this state. A state is defined as the product of a constellation of conditions in which bio-neurological and sociocultural, experiential factors play a combined role. Further, state is a concept that describes a modal type of receptivity of the organism. It can be extended to a wide range of modalities of human functioning, including some pathological manifestations. For instance, schizophrenia must not be seen as a 'trait' that will persist forever. It is a *state* that may appear or disappear. Dyslexia, to use another example, is viewed by some as a state existing even after its manifestations have long since vanished – for instance the professor who considers himself to be dyslexic after having written 40 books and read many hundreds more.

2. The concept of measurement should be replaced by the terms assessment/ evaluation. Measurement as a concept has been used legitimately when referring to a trait as a stable entity, similar to the stability we attribute to an object, because the reification of human characteristics legitimates the concept of IQ measurement if IQ itself is seen as a reified entity. However, measurement is no longer relevant to the concept of state because a state is highly volatile, dynamic, and not amenable to measurement, unlike a trait. Measurement must be replaced by other concepts such as assessment or evaluation; these in turn must be the product of methodologies different from those used for measurement. This implies looking for something other than hard-wired reiterative dimensions, which are usually the goal of measurement.

3. The issue of predictability. If the essence of human existence is formed by states rather than traits, and as a consequence states are perceived as modifiable, then predictability may no longer be an option. Can we predict the development of certain states on the basis of their manifestations at a given point in time in the individual, given that states are determined by life, and individuals are exposed to meaningful change in these conditions?

Predictability can only be defined as a condition of generalization of the measures, functions, and stability of traits over time, and variations of the functions to which measures are applied. Predictability is impossible if the assessed 'state' is highly unstable and modifiable. However, certain states may become more permanent through the effects of long-term presence in the life of the individual, the socioeconomic conditions of an individual's state, or by the creation of an internal self-image that will consolidate certain modes of behavior. The fact that some individuals can escape these 'states' suggests that certain types of intervention or even changes in conditions of life are effective, and can thus overcome conditions of resistance to change. These individuals will require more massive types of intervention to restore the level of flexibility and plasticity necessary to become modified.

4.   Validity and reliability of measurement must be reconsidered. Reliability of measurement ensures that what is measured indeed reflects a stable reiterable condition, which is observable under many changed circumstances and conditions. Yet, does the IQ of a three-year-old girl stay the same with age, despite the enormous increase in speech and skills and modality of function? The stability of the IQ is due to the reliability of the measurement, which, despite the changes in content and substance of the measured function, will nevertheless not budge. Anyone familiar with test construction knows how to achieve this type of reliability. Namely, there is deliberate elimination from the measurement scale of all of the items that exhibit a certain degree of sensitivity to the changed conditions of the individual, such as mood, level of functioning, skills, attitude, etc. Sensitive items are eliminated in order to gain as high a reliability coefficient as possible. The left-overs – the strong habits – affect it, and reliability, in fact, measures the most hard-wired traits or characteristics of the individual.

The case of Alex is relevant to this point. Alex is an 18-year-old adolescent suffering from Sturge–Weber syndrome. He was totally nonverbal until the age of nine. His first words appeared only after he underwent left hemispherectomy. His initial IQ of 35 went up to approximately 52 after surgery and onset of speech. His greatest progress started after he was referred to us by his mother at the age of 15, about six years after surgery. We assessed Alex with the LPAD in order to evaluate his modifiability. The treatment staff in London was very skeptical about the possibility of modifying his level of functioning, in particular as regards reading, writing, and higher-order thinking, which he could not master, despite attempts made by teachers and specialists. The process observed during the LPAD showed a high level of flexibility and learning propensity. Alex mastered and applied a large number of operations and strategies for learning. Yet repeated measures on conventional IQ tests were totally insensitive to the considerable changes in his level of functioning, achieved over a period of three years of Mediated Learning Experience and Instrumental Enrichment, and remained stable and fixed on the level of 50 to 52. Alex learned to read and write in a highly functional way. He became proficient in solving analogies in verbal, figural, and numerical modalities. He became a well-motivated learner and showed readiness to continue his studies beyond the level he had reached.

Paradoxically, the application of the Wechsler Adult Intelligence Scale (WAIS) at the age of 18 showed a considerable increase in IQ, from 50 on the Wechsler Intelligence Scale for Children (WISC) administered at the same time, to 80 on the WAIS. A functional analysis of his problem-solving behavior indicated that even the IQ of 80 did not reflect the level of operational functioning Alex exhibited in his cognitive behavior. The WISC as well as the WAIS are tests with a high level of reliability. They are constructed and applied in such a way as to stay insensitive to the changes that occur in the individual following diverse forms of activity, experiences, and interventions. We will not enter into the lengthy discussion as to the determinants of the insensitivity of psychometrically constructed instruments and test situations. However, it is our firm contention that the use of instruments with high orders of reliability is radically opposed to the very concept of assessment of modifiability. Tests which are constructed to show reliability and construct validity cannot be sensitive to the dynamics of development and the change inherent to this process and therefore are inadequate to assess modifiability.

The theory of Structural–Cognitive Modifiability

The theory of Structural–Cognitive Modifiability postulates that modifiability is an option available to all human beings, irrespective of the etiology, the age at which the option becomes empowered through intervention, or severity of condition. The emphasis on the cognitive element is based on the belief that it plays a crucial role in the plasticity and flexibility of the human mental structure. This postulate represents somewhat of a de-emphasis of the role of emotional factors, which are viewed (as Piaget did) as the energetic rather than the structural dimension of human behavior.

The ontogeny of human development is considered to be dual (as suggested by Rom Harré (1989), as an extension of Vygotsky), and is made up of:
Biological ontogeny, which is defined as a community of cells interacting among themselves and the outside world, and

Sociocultural ontogeny, which defines the individual as the product of cultural transmission acting on his or her life.

The impact of biological and sociocultural ontogeny on each other may vary greatly at different ages, states, and under different conditions. Thus, the biological and the social remain in a permanent state of dynamic tension and disequilibrium.

The basic tenet of the theory of Structural–Cognitive Modifiability is that the human being is in a constant state of evolvement toward new states and structures, which develop as a result of processes and confrontation with activities requiring new structures and the adjustment of old ones. This is consonant with Piaget's three-pronged definition of structure. Briefly, the part–whole relationship in the structure of modifiability means that the changes in one part will result in a change in the whole to which the changed part belongs. Structural change produces transformations that are sustained beyond the constancy of a process. Finally, structural change is marked by a condition of self-perpetuation and continuity of the process of change initiated by an external action. This continuity and self-perpetuation is in response to the quality of the total field, i.e., the particular need system affected by the change.

Modifiability is an option for all individuals, irrespective of the variables acting as obstructive agents. The theory of Structural–Cognitive Modifiability views modifiability as an option even when the etiology is related to endogenous inherited or chromosomal organic deficiencies which are normally viewed as part of the fixed and immutable nature of the organism. The barriers produced by etiology can be overcome under specific conditions of intervention provided to the individual. Modifiability is also considered as an option irrespective of the age at which intervention takes place or at which the conditions for change are created. The conditions for change exist at any time in one's life. The severity of the condition as a barrier to change is also considered likely to change provided certain characteristics of the intervention respond to resistance produced in the organism over time.

The major aim of assessment is not to measure or detect a particular trait or characteristic. Rather, the question is whether a state, condition, or structure can be brought into existence. The focus is thus on the modifiability of the condition, rather than the existence and scope of the condition. In other words, does the propensity for modifiability (and change) exist and can it be brought to existence and increased? How resistant is the state to attempts to produce changes? What is the best way to produce changes? What is the quality of change in state we hope to achieve? How permanent and generalizable is this change? How transferable is it to other situations? What will be the effect of the changes so produced on other states that will emerge in the repertoire of the individual?

Based on the theory of Structural–Cognitive Modifiability, the LPAD assessment procedure examines the process of change as it becomes manifest through observation of the examinee's adaptability to increasingly and progressively new situations, as compared to situations in which he or she has learned via mediation to adapt him or herself. These changes are achieved through the LPAD by using the test–mediate–retest model, although the test phases are not necessarily sharply delineated from the mediation and post-test phases. The flexibility of the Mediated Learning Experience is designed to adapt itself to the individual's condition. The means used to overcome the barriers and resistance preclude any rigorous standardized application of the intervention such as those necessary for normative comparable psychometric models.

Principles of the LPAD

There are four meaningful shifts required to turn regular conventional psychometric measures, or certain adaptations of the LPAD suggested by other authors, into the dynamic LPAD assessment. These changes represent a crucial departure from the measurement approach. Wherever these changes are not included, one may have doubts as to the dynamic nature of the assessment.

1.   Changes in the nature, structure, and content of the instruments used for the dynamic assessment and evaluation.
2.   Changes in the test situation by restructuring the interaction between the examiner and examinee.
3.   The shift from product to process.
4.   Changes in the interpretation of the results.

Changes in the instrument

To produce reiterative comparable measurement, the measurement tool in conventional psychometric assessment must demonstrate an accepted level of reliability, i.e., it must guarantee that the results obtained at a given point in time on a given individual or situation will repeat themselves at the next point of measurement. One of the greatest successes of psychometrics was to produce high instrument reliability. However, where they did not succeed is in rendering the object of their measurement sufficiently reliable. Conventional tests are constructed to measure reiterable, structural consistency, which is unalterable. Nevertheless, a great deal of reliability and validity are the product of measurement itself, because the treatment and intervention generated by measurement determine to a large extent the often-observed self-fulfilling prophesy.

By contrast, the LPAD dynamic battery of tests is designed to create samples of change, and evaluates these changes as indicative of the modifiability of the individual. The battery addresses itself primarily to fluid intelligence rather than to crystallized intelligence, which requires extensive investment in time in order to be modified. Further, crystallized intelligence is less amenable to transfer and generalization because it is based on habit formation in a restricted area of activity. Many psychometric tests base their data on crystallized functioning rather than on fluid intelligence (Rey, 1934) because they attempt to evaluate intelligence on the basis of what has been learned, rather than what can be learned, using a repertoire which they equate with intelligence, i.e., the person's capacity to learn as manifested by what he or she knows.

The LPAD assesses fluid intelligence because an assessment of modifiability must be based on tasks in which generalization and transfer will be eased by the small distances the individual must go to apply the newly acquired rules, cognitive structures, and needs for elaboration. This is why we have developed a number of tasks that include variations of the problems that the examinee has to solve. We look for the way in which the previous exposure to a process – the learning of previous tasks – affects the individual's readiness, and propensity (*not capacity*) to solve the problem at hand.

The mediational process is formulated in such a way as to include transcendence. We build the orientation toward transfer and generalization into the mediational interaction. The evaluator also takes into account (*does not count, does not measure*) the amount of mediation necessary until an adequate response is produced. This is a crucial component in the evaluation of the amount and nature of intervention needed to achieve a higher level of functioning. The assessment as a whole is oriented toward evaluation of the effects of producing a sample of the mental, cognitive, and performance behavior on tasks which will become progressively more distant and more complex from the tasks used for training. This is illustrated schematically by the Cylinder Model in Fig. 7.1.

Changes in the test situation

The second change is the shift from a static measurement model of human intelligence to a dynamic one, and is achieved by a complete change in the test situation. Briefly, the nomothetic nature of static tests requires highly standardized forms of presentation which are only feasible if the test conditions are rigorously standardized to guarantee the comparability of the results obtained on one individual to his or her normative group. This standardization excludes

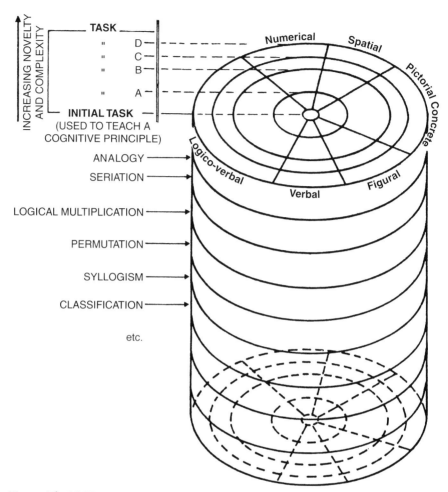

Fig. 7.1. The LPAD cognitive map.

any attempt on the part of the psychologist or examiner to provide the examinee with the amount and nature of the instructions needed to perform the task. It forbids any feedback to the examinee as to the nature of his or her answers, for fear that the responses which will follow will not be viewed as spontaneous and representing the present level of functioning. It requires a neutral attitude from the examiner and, in many cases, a demeanor that can be misleading to the examinees, making them believe that their answer was appropriate. Thus, in many cases, the examinees will not learn from the task about the nature of their responses. The opposite is true of the test situation in dynamic assessment whose pivotal principle is the Mediated Learning Experience. The Mediated Learning Experience is not only used to generate in the individual the data needed to solve the problem in the appropriate way, but also includes transcending elements that will enable the individual to apply the newly acquired modes of functioning and transfer them to new tasks.

The test situation incorporates carefully planned steps of mediation, which vary with the particular needs of the individual. These needs become observable to the examiner over the course of interaction with the examinee and/or become available from information that he or she has gathered on the examinee's level of functioning, or problems experienced by the examinee in other areas of activity.

One of the most important goals is to correct the deficient functions that have been found by the examiner to impair the functioning of the examinee (Table 7.1).

The examiner keeps in mind a series of deficient cognitive functions on the level of Input, Elaboration and Output. She or he will intervene to correct the deficiencies and observe the effects of intervention on future functioning of the individual on the parts of the test where the same deficiencies are likely to reappear. Attempts will be made to see whether these deficiencies have been corrected to the point that they are absent from the repertoire of the examinee, and the way the correction of the specific deficiency affects the individual's efficiency of functioning. On the Input level, blurred perception often hampers the child's activities. Similarly, the unsystematic search for data makes the individual neglect certain elements needed to solve the problem at hand, as do the lack of use of additional sources of information, and the lack of use of temporal and spatial dimensions to define the observed objects or stimuli. On the elaborational level, deficient functions are characterized by a lack of readiness to define the problem and egocentric and inadequate, imprecise, impulsive forms of behavior, lack of comparative behavior, lack of the need for logical evidence, etc. All these will become the focus of intervention by the examiner during the test situation.

Through the Mediated Learning Experience, the examiner will endow the student with the verbal, conceptual, operational tools needed to solve the problems at hand. The prime goal is to enrich and orient the examinee towards insightful activity so that the process of change can become the major locus of contemplation, namely:

How did I change?

Why did I do better?

Why did I fail?

All these will be the products of a mediational interaction whose goal is to make the individual aware of the ongoing processes as changes are occurring.

Table 7.1. List of deficient functions

Deficient functions at the Input Phase

1. Blurred and sweeping perception.
2. Unplanned, impulsive, and unsystematic exploratory behavior.
3. Lack of, or impaired, receptive verbal tools that affect discrimination (e.g., objects, events, and relationships are not appropriately labeled).
4. Lack of, or impaired, spatial orientation and lack of stable systems of reference by which to establish organization of space.
5. Lack of, or impaired, temporal concepts.
6. Lack of, or impaired, conservation of constancies (e.g., size, shape, quantity, color, orientation) across variations in one or more dimensions.
7. Lack of, or deficient, need for precision and accuracy in data gathering.
8. Lack of capacity for considering two or more sources of information at once. This is reflected in dealing with data in a piecemeal fashion rather than as a unit of facts that are organized.

Deficient cognitive functions at the Elaboration Phase

1. Inadequacy in the perception of the existence of a problem and its definition.
2. Inability to select relevant as opposed to irrelevant cues in defining a problem.
3. Lack of spontaneous comparative behavior or the limitation of its application by a restricted need system.
4. Narrowness of the mental field.
5. Episodic grasp of reality.
6. Lack of need for the education or establishment of relationships.
7. Lack of need for and/or exercise of summative behavior.
8. Lack of, or impaired, need for pursuing logical evidence.
9. Lack of, or impaired, inferential hypothetical ('iffy') thinking.
10. Lack of, or impaired, strategies for hypothesis testing.
11. Lack of, or impaired, planning behavior.
12. Lack of, or impaired, interiorization.
13. Nonelaboration of certain cognitive categories because the verbal concepts are not a part of the individual's verbal inventory at a receptive level, or because they are not mobilized at the expressive level.

Deficient cognitive functions at the Output Phase

1. Egocentric communication modalities.
2. Difficulty in projecting virtual relationships.
3. Blocking.
4. Trial and error responses.
5. Lack of, or impaired, verbal or other tools for communicating adequately elaborated responses.
6. Lack of, or impaired, need for precision and accuracy in the communication of one's responses.
7. Deficiency in visual transport.
8. Impulsive, random, unplanned behavior.

Equally crucial, mediation creates a need for intrinsic motivation, by providing the individual with an awareness of the meaning of his or her activity and a meaning of the change produced. Finally, a crucial subgoal in mediational interaction is to render the individual aware of his or her role as a generator of new information, rather than the mere recipient or reproducer of information provided ready made by others.

The mediational process adheres to the parameters of the Mediated Learning Experience in an active and interactive way, permitting the examiner to see the types of changes 'in vitro' along with the cooperative reporting of the examinee about the changes which have occurred in the structure of his or her modal behavior. The readiness to create an interactive mode of assessment, during which feedback and insightful activities take place, endows the individual with the necessary tools for adequate functioning. This enables individuals to repeat the successfully mastered tasks to achieve a certain degree of solidification and crystallization of their recently acquired behavior. All these processes are meant to produce samples of change in the examinee, which will then be interpreted as indicators of modifiability.

The level of permanency of these changes may not be high, but is sufficient to serve as an indicator of the amount, nature, extension, and, to a certain degree, the durability of change produced. The differential levels of change in areas of perceptual, logical, and verbal functioning etc., will also point to the areas of greater or lesser resistance to change. By the same token, they also provide information on the amount and nature of intervention (mediational or otherwise) needed to produce a given result, thus fulfilling a key requirement of the LPAD – namely, to create a strong link between the assessment and planning of the intervention needed to produce change. The test situation is clearly the pivotal aspect of the LPAD. It is obvious that applying the test this way will disqualify it for conventional reliability measures. Further validity is not based on a score (a product), but rather on the process which has made the observed results possible.

The shift from product to process

The major focus is on the process of assessment. Limited interest, if any, is devoted to the product. In other words, a test result which indicates a high level of functioning will be of very little value in attempting to explain the difficulties the examinee has encountered in academic functioning. The test product, which may be the outcome of certain capacities, may totally conceal these difficulties, which will come to the fore once the individual is called upon to apply these functions in a particular learning or functioning situation. This is the case for the gifted underachiever, who, indeed, may show giftedness in certain types of tasks but fails to recognize the deficiencies or processes underlying his or her results. A product-based test has very little significance if it cannot shed light on the discrepancies between good test results and failure in areas of academic or other types of achievement. The value of the LPAD lies in the identification of the process underlying an individual's functioning or dysfunctioning. Even when an individual has proven able to respond adequately on some particular task, it may have been solved by compensating for difficulties by using certain hypertrophied functions that cover up those deficiencies which suppress his or her functions as they come to the fore in other situations.

The analysis of the cognitive behavior of the individual on a given task may enable us to answer such questions as to what extent success or failure of this individual is due to content specific to this task. Is this content familiar or unfamiliar to the individual, enabling problem solution without requiring investment or actively testing adaptation to the task? Or to what extent is the language of the task responsible for the failure of the individual to interact successfully with the task? Language is known to act as a source of disadvantage for certain minority populations, but also for certain individuals who may have different language backgrounds or priorities as to the language through which they interact best. The same is true for the level of abstraction, the level of task complexity, and the level of elaboration required on one of the three phases of the mental act (Input, Elaboration, and Output). The Cognitive Map may answer such questions as what level of efficiency is required for this task to be successfully performed. We define efficiency as the rapidity–precision complex, to which we add an imponderable dimension – namely, the level of mobilization and energetic investment needed to solve a given task. Efficiency, or lack of efficiency, which may be totally extraneous to the true propensity of the individual to learn, may be a major source of failure for a particular individual when there is inability to respond to the level of efficiency required by a specific task. For instance, imagine you need to dial a telephone number with 50–60 digits within a certain lapse of time in order to connect. Inefficiency, a lack of rapidity, etc. may cause the individual to fail, and repeated failures can make the individual reluctant to become involved in such activities except when absolutely essential (the same is true for reading). Efficiency is too low and the failure to connect will not be relevant to the cognitive level of the individual but rather to the rapidity of processing. Hence, thorough understanding of the two conceptual tools (Deficient Functions and the Cognitive Map) helps characterize both the process of functioning and the types of changes being produced in the individual as he or she becomes involved in the production of samples of change. This is associated with the fourth change in perspective from conventional testing.

A change in the interpretation of the results

The shift to a dynamic modality of interpretation of the results obtained in the LPAD is best illustrated by our attempt to produce a profile of modifiability which is based on the observed process of change. The profile uses the data that were gathered during the assessment of the three dimensions which are dealt with during the mediational intervention.

I. The dimension of *content*: what are the contents that have required correction and needed to become modified in order to increase the operations, functions, and efficiency of the individual? This dimension is assessed in four major areas.

(a) Deficient functions: to what extent have they been corrected and where?

(b) The acquisition of higher-order operations, relations (verbal, visual–motor, other modes of operation) needed for the intervention to be acquired and applied on the tasks.

(c) Changes in the emotional, attitudinal, and affective responsiveness of the examinee.

(d) Level of efficiency acquired during the mediational and experiential exposure to the intervention.

II. The dimensions of the profile deal with the *definition* of the nature of the observed changes.

(a) The permanence of the observed change, the degree of resistance to the task (novelty, complexity, lack of meaning).

(b) Lack of motivation.

(c) Generalization and transfer of newly acquired functions.

III. The third dimension is the *evaluation of the change in the amount and nature of mediational experience* needed to produce a particular change in the performance level of the individual. This degree of reduction in need for mediation reflects the level of independence the individual has acquired in dealing with certain tasks compared to the degree of dependence manifested in his or her functioning in the initial stages of assessment. This dimension is extremely close to the Vygotsky and Luria formulation of the assessment of effects of support given to the examinee for independent functioning.

Thus, instead of an index, or a coefficient based on the number of successfully mastered tasks, the results should express the dynamics of a process which can be observed as it changes across time, across tasks, across different modalities of interaction, across different tasks and contents. The interpretation takes into account the preferential mode of functioning initially observed in the individual, which can exhibit meaningful changes. Dimensions such as those suggested by A. and N. Kaufman such as the Kaufman Adolescent and Adult Intelligence Test (KAIT) certainly tap very important and interesting styles, experiences, and types of activities in terms of their presence in the repertoire of the individual, the access he or she has to them, and his or her efficiency in using them. However, the focus of the LPAD is on the extent to which such preferential functions are amenable to change if and when necessary. The real issue is the interpretation of mediational interaction and observations of processes during which such changes can be produced. The same holds true for a variety of other attempts to see individuals from the point of view of their most preferred areas of functioning, as found in Gardner's seven dimensions and Sternberg's Triarchic Intelligence. We do not deny that such preferential forms of function do, indeed, exist. Our question concerns the adaptability of the individual to situations requiring changes in style and preferences in order to succeed and survive, by adapting to changes he or she is confronted with. The interpretation of the results in the LPAD takes into account the nature of resistance encountered by the individual during involvement in an active mediational process, and the amount of mediation needed to affect him or her differentially in one of these areas to create a profile of change. This enables the LPAD examiner to define the nature, features, and magnitude of change produced in the examinee and to evaluate them in terms of the nature of intervention necessary in order to produce a particular level of modifiability in the various areas of functioning.

This is a complex procedure. This level of complexity may lend itself poorly to a statistical elaboration or to an attempt to create the necessary processes of reliability. Yet the validity may well be substantiated by a variety of criteria whenever processes of change are available to assessment and the meaning of change is substantiated in areas of the individual's adaptation. These features are examined in the next section.

Principles of construction of the LPAD test battery

The battery of tests which was chosen for structuring the LPAD has its rationale in the following dimensions.

1.   The instruments which evaluate fluid thinking may provide insight into the processes leading to the evolvement of samples of change. The LPAD test battery is drawn from specially structured material or from other tests on the basis of the functions which they require from the examinee. The tasks are

aimed at fluid types of cognitive functions and operations rather than crystal-lized functions, because the latter require automatization based on solidifi-cation through repetition and exposure to the task. Fluid thinking is preferred, because it lends itself better to the process of generalization and transfer on a variety of other types of tasks which serve as indicators of modification in the individual.

There is little interest within the framework of the LPAD in producing samples of crystallized functions because of the time limits, which do not permit the amount of intervention necessary to produce automatized modes of functioning. If crystallized functions emerge despite the brevity of intervention, they can be interpreted as a positive learning quality of the individual.

2.　All the functions lend themselves to mediated intervention. The second cri-terion for the choice of the test instrument is accessibility to mediation and the meaningful increase in the functioning of the individual following the Mediated Learning Experience. Not all tasks required from the individual can benefit from mediation in the sense of intentionality, transcendence, and meaning. Some tasks are simply informative by nature and call for the retrieval and enrichment of the informational repertoire of the individual, where the learner at best acts as the recipient of information communicated to him or her by the mediator. The types of teaching which may affect the individual's repertoire of functioning may be restricted to the focus of the particular content. For these reasons, the choice of LPAD tasks are those which lend themselves to as many parameters of mediation as possible; in other words, those tasks that will affect the cognitive, emotional, and behavioral aspects of the cognitive structure of the examinee. The results of these tasks will then be used to draw up a profile of modifiability based on the produced samples of change. The tasks call on the examinee to contribute in a very direct and active way to the organization and fulfillment of the task. Here, mediational interaction, even though varied to correspond to the diversity of populations it will address itself to, will allow us to view the samples of change that are directly linked to the nature of mediation. For instance, Raven's B8–12 task, which even high-functioning individuals find difficult to solve,[6] may be mediated to very low-functioning children with no familiarity with summative mathematical behavior or pro-cedures to discover conceptual forms of negative and positive numbers and even less experience operating with them volitionally and consciously. Never-theless, because of the nature of the task and because we can induce an orientation in the child to look for transformations occurring on each of the three lines, we can make the child discover the rule, which becomes obvious by following the transformation that was present in the first line, confirmed by the

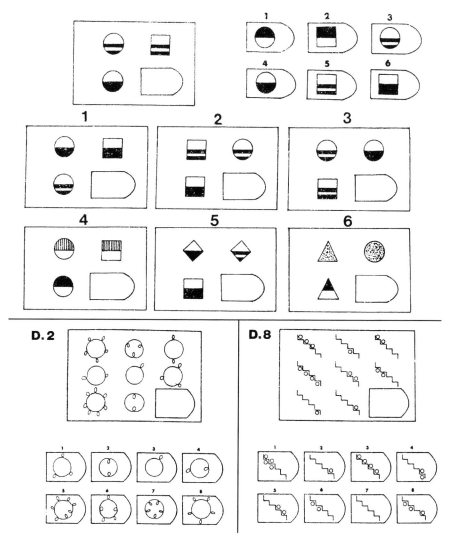

Fig. 7.2. Raven's B-8 and six LPAD variations.

second line, and then reapplied to the third line. Once the rule discovery procedure has been established, many low-functioning children succeed and prove their propensity by applying the rule to variations requiring its rediscovery across changes in the nature and the form of the task (Fig 7.2).

By choosing similar high-level cognitive functions, we create a sample of modifiability in areas not considered accessible to low-functioning individuals. It also provides us with a rare opportunity to observe learning style, define deficient functions displayed in action, determine the amount and nature of intervention necessary for functioning and giving meaning to changes produced by the intervention in order to make the individual modifiable.

3. The test instruments are structured in such a way as to study the effects of mediation even when they emerge in a very minimal way. The LPAD has developed tasks which act as a 'tightly knit net' through which even the most minimal changes in the structure of focusing, learning, thinking, and comprehension in the examinee can be observed 'in vitro' and are accessible to interpretation as reflecting propensity for change. The Cylinder Model serves as a basis for constructing the test material for the LPAD because it is fine tuned to detect any change produced by intervention and interaction with the task, and the effects of these changes on the individual's functioning in other situations. This makes it possible to assign approximate attributes to the diverse determinants such as task management, mediation, repetition, and prior experience. The most minimally detected change is seen as representative of a universe of possible changes which can be produced in a similar constellation. The key target of observation is change in the level of modifiability of the examinee.

4. The test instruments can be used to interpret functions implemented and assessed in other studies. The criteria for task selection are both theoretical and practical. The choice of tests previously used for static measurement was made both to benefit from previous studies, and to challenge their results by introducing mediational interaction. Because the LPAD is based on theory and practice to a large extent at variance with other theoretical and practical methodologies, we choose some of the tasks from the existent repertoire of tests that have been found satisfactory to the psychometrician from the standpoint of reliability and validation. Thereby, we are able to rely on these designed materials and interpret our results with the help of attributes of meaning, significance, functions, etc. Raven's analysis of the B8–12 task, as quoted above, is based on a large set of data. We chose his conclusion that low-functioning individuals are unable to solve the analogies as a target for our intervention to challenge his claim. We designed a special interventional, mediational format for the structuring of thought processes in children classified as very low functioning, trainable mentally retarded (IQ 35–50). One of the great and gratifying surprises was that the children were not only able to grasp the analogy but also could generalize it through the necessary mediation to solve variations on the analogy with great success.

5. The results can be compared to the body of existing data. In interpreting the results, comparison with data produced by other researchers helps attribute a general value to the findings (in particular, the processes underlying them).

Furthermore, the results are analyzed on the seven dimensions of the Cognitive Map, which evaluates the task as to the level of abstraction, complexity, and efficiency required from the individual to reach out to the particular functions required by the task.

Finally, many of the tasks chosen from existent data have been adapted dynamically. Changes were made in the task itself, by producing variations, and/or by changing the modality of presentation, application, or interpretation. The box below presents the tests as they cluster around particular functions, although the tasks can be elaborated in a variety of ways.

LPAD instrument clusters

Perceptual–Motor Functions organized by Cognitive Components
Organization of Dots – Complex Figure Drawing Test – Diffuse Attention Test (Lahi) – Reversal Test

Memory with a Learning Component
Positional Learning Test – Plateaux Test – Functional Associative Recall (functional reduction and part–whole) – Word Memory

Higher-Order Cognitive Processes and Mental Operations
Raven's Colored Progressive Matrices, Raven's Standard Progressive Matrices, Set Variations I, II – Representational Stencil Design Test – Numerical Progressions Organizer

---

The mosaic nature of these tests enables us to respond to highly diverse populations who are in need of dynamic assessment and display deficiencies on a wide spectrum of levels. Two recent developments in the test instrument now broaden the reach of the LPAD. The first is a downward extension of the LPAD using three-dimensional materials in the form of puzzles for nonverbal children and some adults. The downward assessment material is designed for children with acquired or developmental deficiencies which preclude them from responding to verbal or operational types of thinking or have deteriorated through certain pathological adverse conditions. The mosaic nature of the downward extension is preserved by introducing learning tasks in a variety of dimensions (spatial, temporal, numerical, logical–verbal, and dialogic).

The second development is an upward extension to high-functioning individuals who need to be assessed for their propensity to be involved in the processes of change in areas where they are experiencing difficulty despite their high level of functioning. In particular, we have designed a dynamic assessment battery measuring readiness to learn for people who need to change jobs and learn a new technology.

Conclusion

The LPAD thus described has been applied since the mid-1950s and has proven to be useful for a variety of populations whose level of academic, occupational, and personal functioning required an evaluation of the modifiability of the individual for purposes other than classification, categorization, or labeling. Over the last five decades, the LPAD has proven itself to be the crucial, vital, and decisive methodology to assess the modifiability of the culturally different and societally disadvantaged, and to convince, parents, teachers, and the children themselves of the legitimacy of the fight to education within a mainstream environment. Such placement entails the definition of goals for these individuals and the use of appropriate means to reach them.

The application of the LPAD has proven itself highly useful to tens of thousands of youngsters in their struggle to become integrated into society through adequate education. Children who were classified as only accessible to menial tasks in terms of their manifest level of functioning as measured by IQ tests demonstrated processes of change following dynamic assessment. Many of these children received mainstream placement. For these youngsters, dynamic assessment resulted in a dramatic change in the course of their lives. Our greatest success has been with Down's syndrome children, who have been able to change radically the stereotyped view that the child with Down's syndrome could not have an IQ over 70. Here, our dynamic assessment findings have been able to show that the Down's syndrome child is eligible for full integration into high school, sometimes can finish high school, and exhibits the higher mental functions required for further studies.

The most striking recent application of the LPAD is to Ethiopian child immigrants to Israel. These children were defined as the most extremely culturally different group to be absorbed by a Western culture, because their integration required efficient literacy, and they were children whose tradition of pre-literacy goes back over tens of generations. In particular, their integration called for a transition to a language based on conceptual superordinate concepts. Many other assessments using conventional tests (culture fair, culture free, developmental tests, operational tests) indicated that these children could only be placed in special education classes. Some 5000 children and youngsters were administered a group LPAD battery, and about 1000 whose level of functioning on the group test was not satisfactory had to be assessed individually. The results literally saved them from placement in special education and the typical watered-down program offered to children whose manifest level of functioning suggests they cannot be placed in mainstream education. Only some 15–20% had to be placed in a special preparatory program, where they were given mediated intervention for 15 hours a week, including reading, math, and Instrumental Enrichment, while integrated into classes with normal children for the rest of the school day. This resulted in the possibility of fully integrating the great majority of the children after they had acquired the basic school and thinking skills in a regular class three to nine months later.

The shift from a static, conventional, psychometric model to a dynamic approach to the assessment of cognitive modifiability is, today more than ever, a pervasive need. Our dynamic approach, seeking those states in the individual that are modifiable, is based on three major assumptions, which have found increasing confirmation in research and practice.

1. The definition of modal behaviors of the human being as *states*, rather than being defined as characteristics, traits, or other forms of hard-wired conditions of the person. A state is, by definition, modifiable, whereas a trait represents a stable and immutable condition of the individual.

2. The understanding that the human organism is the product of a double ontogeny – biological and sociocultural. The relationship between the two sources of development is a constant process of equilibration, with the sociocultural factor being in many instances dominant and producing changes in the individual which enable the organism to bypass biologically determined limits. If we consider the condition of the child with Down's syndrome as determined to a very large extent by chromosomal conditions, a sociocultural interference with the biological condition clearly accounts for the enormous changes now evident in level of functioning, which were not considered accessible to these children because of their biological condition. The statement often expressed in relationship to our work, that 'chromosomes do not have the last word,' illustrates this critical relationship between the biological and sociocultural factors as an option for the development of all individuals irrespective of their biological conditions.

3. The plasticity of the brain and its responsiveness to certain types of activities imposed upon it that may affect the brain's structure in a very meaningful way – and not only as was previously believed – the structure of behavior.

As these three sources of evidence for human modifiability are becoming accepted, the LPAD should become the major tool for evaluating modifiability, its condition, extent, meaning, level of permanence, degree of generalizability, and transfer, and the modalities by which such modifiability can best be achieved. It is obvious that dynamic assessment requires a certain degree of liberation from the psychometric mode of thinking, which adheres to the measurement of certain traits as they are reified by the process of measurement itself. Dynamic assessment calls for freedom of the evaluation process from those dimensions shaped by the psychometric model in order to respond to the concept of intelligence as an object, and promotes educability as a condition that is immutable and essentially unchangeable in the individual. This refers to the concepts of reliability of the test instruments, the fact that the validity of test results is tightly related to the type of intervention, and recommendations that arise from the results of the psychometrically oriented process. The tendency of some researchers who have criticized the concept of IQ, the *g* factor, and other static concepts of intelligence, but have attempted to introduce a 'dynamic' teaching factor to comply with their need to preserve the rigor of the psychometric approach, are actually eliminating the major benefits of the dynamic assessment process as embodied in the LPAD.

How dynamic can an assessment be if it must be done with reliable tests, where reliability means that the individual must stay the same in order to keep the process reliable? What kind of dynamics can one attribute to a test situation where the relationship between the task and the individual is kept sterile and everything is done to insure that no change occurs except the one that the assessor has rigorously attempted to produce?

The attempt to create a dynamic assessment which will maintain a rigorous, limited, or predetermined form of measurement (for instance how many times the examinee was cued, what kinds of scripted prompts were used, what levels of failure were experienced, etc.) is a contradiction in terms. The LPAD is, of necessity, based on the use of Mediated Learning Experience, which must adapt to the needs of the individual in order to produce maximal samples of change which the individual can produce at a given point in his or her interaction.

This chapter has attempted to respond to some of the questions that have been raised by colleagues, many of whom have become convinced of the need for Mediated Learning Experience, but who feel it necessary to constrict themselves by adhering to some of the 'rules of the game' required by the scientific (psychometric) measurement approach. The position taken here is that there is a need to free ourselves of this approach and produce a profile of change with the means that are at the disposal of the examiner as a mediator. This is the essence of the LPAD as a dynamic assessment process. Indeed, this way has been strongly advocated by some of those who have adhered to and accepted our interpretation of dynamic assessment. The first author of this chapter admits to have been himself searching for modalities to bridge static and dynamic assessment by looking for psychometric tools which could be compatible with the LPAD. During the author's many discussions with Professor L. J. Cronbach, he requested help from this eminent statistician and methodologist in shaping the instruments of the mediational process and the interpretation of the results in such a way as to make it consonant with the psychometric model and yet not offensive to the dynamic nature of the LPAD. Cronbach argued against this, stating that the use of a psychometric tool would neutralize and eventually dilute the true meaning of the LPAD and thus prevent it from attaining its goals. During this dialogue, the author again expressed his desire to establish some kind of convergence with psychometrics from which the use of samples of behavior representing a larger universe of functions could have been preserved. Yet again, no way was found to establish a language which would be common to the psychometric model in the appropriate modes for shaping test instruments and information. This request was made to Cronbach because of his development of the Aptitude–Treatment–Interaction (ATI), which seemed to provide a potential structure to bridge between the two modes. After listening to the arguments and request, Professor Cronbach rose up from his chair, threw his hands into the air, and exclaimed: 'I cannot advise you to use it . . . I am more Feuerstein than Feuerstein!'

ENDNOTES

1 In one experiment, Binet used tokens of different sizes and asked his daughter (aged four) to compare groups numerically. Binet showed that the child used the size of the tokens (amount of space the larger tokens took up) rather than numeration to determine which group of tokens was mathematically larger. (See Zazzo, 1962, for a description.)

2 Binet, Alfred, *Année Psychologique*, Volume XI, 1905, p. 191, quoted in Zazzo, 1962, p. 47. Note the use made by Binet of the concept of 'state,' which we consider as the only way to define many of the conditions of the human being. As shown later, the concept of state is contrasted by the authors with the concept of trait or characteristic. Binet's concept of 'état' may not have been coupled on the other pole with the concept of trait, but his use of the term comes very close to the opposition used here between state as modifiable, and trait as a stable characteristic.

3 Rey's belief in 'éducabilité' and his view that classification was of limited value because intelligence arises from varying educational and environmental interactions had a profound impact on the development of the Learning Potential Assessment Device (Feuerstein, Rand, & Hoffman, 1979). The fact that Rey's 1934 paper on this subject only came to the attention of

the first author and many other students after Rey's death highlights the pressure on behavioral scientists to conform to the dominant genetic–heredity belief system concerning the origins of intelligence – both then and now, because Rey's public position was psychometric.

4 A lecture by Reuven Feuerstein at the New York Medical College in 1963 came to the attention of Milton Budoff, who then adapted dynamic principles to his own research.

5 For a critical presentation of current models of dynamic assessment, see, in particular, Grigorenko and Sternberg, 1998.

6 'A high-grade intellectually defective person remains throughout life characteristically incapable of solving the more difficult problems of Set B . . .' (Raven, 1965, p. 25).

REFERENCES

Anastasi, A. (1961). *Psychological Testing*. New York: Macmillan.

Binet, A. (1909). *Les idées modernes sur les enfants*, Flammarion, Paris, quoted in Zazzo, Rene, *Conduites et Conscience*, p. 139.

Eells, K., Davis, A., Havighurst, R.J., Herrick, V.E., & Tyler, R.M. (1951). *Intelligence and Cultural Differences*. Chicago, IL: University of Chicago Press.

Feuerstein, R., Feuerstein S., & Schur Y. (1997). Process as content in regular education and in particular in education of the low functioning retarded performer. In *Envisioning Process as Content; Towards a Renaissance Curriculum*, ed. A.L. Costa & R.M. Leibmann. Thousand Oaks, CA: Corwin Press.

Feuerstein, R., Rand, Y., & Hoffman, M. (1979). *The Dynamic Testing of Retarded Performers: The Learning Potential Assessment Device: Theory, Instruments and Techniques*. Baltimore, MD: University Park Press.

Feuerstein, R., Rand, Y., & Hoffman, M. (1980). *Instrumental Enrichment*. Baltimore, MD: University Park Press.

Feuerstein, R., Rand, Y., Jensen, M.R., Kaniel, S., & Tzuriel, D. (1987). Prerequisites for testing of learning potential: the LPAD Model. In *Dynamic Testing*, ed. C.S. Lidz, pp. 35–51. New York: Guilford Press.

Feuerstein, R., Rand, Y., & Rynders, J.E. (1988). *Don't Accept Me as I am: Helping 'Retarded' People to Excel*. New York: Plenum Press.

Gitmez, A.S. (1971). Instructions as determinants of performance: the effect of information about the task on problem solving efficiency. NATO Conference on Cultural Factors in Mental Test Development, Turkey.

Gould, S.J. (1996). *The Mismeasure of Man*. New York: W.W. Norton.

Grigorenko, E.L. & Sternberg, R.J. (1998). Dynamic testing. *Psychological Bulletin*, 124(1), 75–111.

Harré, R. (1989). Metaphysics and methodology: some prescriptions for social psychological research. *European Journal of Social Psychology*, 19, 439–53.

Masland, R.L., Saranson, S.B., & Gladwin, T. (1958). *Mental Subnormality*. New York: Basic Books.

Mercer, J.R. (1979). *Technical Manual, SOMPA.* New York: Psychological Corporation.

Neisser, U., Boodoo, G., Bouchard,T. et al. (1996). Intelligence, knowns and unknowns. *American Psychologist*, 51(2), 77–101.

Raven, J.C. (1965). *Guide to Using the Colored Progressive Matrices, Sets A, Ab, and B.* London: H.K. Lewis.

Rey, A. (1934). D'un procédé pour évaluer l'éducabilité, quelques applications en psycho-pathologie. *Archives de Psychologie*, XXIV, 96, 326–37.

Vygotsky, L.S. (1962). *Thought and Language.* Cambridge, MA: MIT Press.

Wesman, A.G. (1968). Intelligence testing. *American Psychologist*, 23(4), 267–74.

Zazzo, R. (1962). *Conduites et Conscience, Psychologie de l'Enfant et Methode Génétique.* Neuchatel, Switzerland: Delachaux et Niestle.

8

Multi-perspective, clinical–educational assessments of language disorders

Elisabeth H. Wiig

History, development, and assessment objectives

Assessment and intervention paradigms

The intention of this chapter is to present selected issues associated with the assessment of primary language disorders and language-based learning disabilities, and to discuss a multi-perspective assessment process for obtaining and interpreting language test results. In these discussions, there are assumptions and premises. The first is that to implement equitable assessments of language and communication in today's global society, multi-cultural and multi-linguistic factors must be considered. Secondly, the process must embrace multi-dimensional and multi-perspective approaches. The use of norm-referenced and standardized tests is considered to be an integral component of multi-perspective assessment. The instruments should be complemented by naturalistic and authentic procedures. The objectives of a multi-dimensional and multi-perspective assessment process are many. One objective, however, stands out. It is to arrive at interpretations and decisions that reflect educational and social, as well as clinical perspectives.

In the USA, the inclusion movement (Will, 1986; Biklen, 1992) provided a forceful impetus for collaboration among regular and special educators, such as speech–language pathologists. Public Law 94-142 started this movement by mandating that special education services should be provided in the least restrictive environment. As a result, students with language disorders have been integrated in regular education classrooms with adequate and appropriate support from teachers, specialists, and related services. Traditional pull-out therapy programs in speech–language pathology were modified in many different ways, among others by moving language intervention from 'closets' to the classrooms.

Among tangible outcomes are that models have been presented for developing team-based assessment and intervention for inclusion. The *Ohio Handbook for the Identification, Evaluation, and Placement of Children with Language Problems* (Ohio Department of Education, 1991) is one example. At the same time, the objectives, content, strategies, and formats for language intervention have changed. The intervention objectives for students with language disorders were traditionally deficit driven and reactive. In contrast, they are now strength driven, curriculum based, and proactive in nature.

In the past, the emphasis in language assessment was on clinically based testing to establish a diagnosis and determine eligibility for speech and language services. Several norm-referenced language tests respond to this emphasis (e.g., Wiig, Secord, & Semel, 1992b; Semel, Wiig, & Secord, 1995, 1998). The 1997 Individuals with Disabilities Education Act (IDEA) (Public Law 105-17) has initiated significant changes in language assessment and intervention in the USA, the extent of which is not yet clear. Among stated IDEA mandates are to:

(a)   use the primary language of the child – not necessarily that of the parents;
(b)   provide alternative assessments for children who cannot participate in state or district-wide assessments;
(c)   give a child access to assistive technology as needed;
(d)   evaluate a child's strengths and communication needs, parental concerns, and need for assistive technology to develop an Individualized Education Plan (IEP) that is followed by periodic review and revision;
(e)   describe how a child's language disorder affects educational performance;
(f)   link intervention objectives and annual goals to the curriculum.

Speech–language pathologists now develop profiles of language and communication strengths and weaknesses based on data from a variety of sources, and they use a variety of approaches to assessment. This has led to the development of, for example, criterion-referenced tests and observational scales for language and learning disabilities (Wiig, 1990; Semel, Wiig, & Secord, 1996; Hammill & Bryant, 1998). The scope of assessment has broadened, and the process is designed to provide opportunities to obtain authentic indicators of performances in the real-world settings of classrooms, family, communities, and work. The recommended approaches to language assessment are contextual, interactive, and performance and real-world oriented. Norm-referenced tests for assessing language are often discredited or considered irrelevant, a point of view that is not taken here.

The model for a multi-perspective language assessment process in this chapter advocates the inclusion of norm-referenced language tests and standardized measures. Other methods, such as criterion-referenced instruments and behavioral ratings of language and communication behaviors in natural contexts, are also discussed. The premise for all discussions is that the child or student is a multi-faceted entity with language and communication behaviors that change and impact other performances differently with age, cognitive development, and external demands.

Language-assessment objectives

The objectives for language assessment should combine clinical as well as educational perspectives. From a clinical perspective, the primary purposes are to establish evidence of a primary language disorder, determine causal factors, and establish the degree and general nature of the disorder. From an educational perspective, the objectives are to (a) develop profiles of language and communication strengths and weaknesses, (b) identify language-learning needs, (c) establish interfaces between deficit areas and academic performance, (d) determine eligibility for special services, and (e) develop a curriculum-related intervention plan for implementation in the least restrictive environment. In a multi-perspective, collaborative language assessment process, there should be no conflict in meeting both clinical and educational objectives. Moreover, there should be no conflict in developing the most appropriate intervention plan and sequence of implementation, if there is an understanding that some syndromes or symptoms are best managed with medical intervention, whereas others are best managed with educational intervention, or with a combination of these. Constraints in financial or human resources for medical and/or educational interventions may cause the system to fail in fully meeting a given child's or student's needs.

Causal factors

Advances in probing neurological functions, systems, and interactions have revolutionized our understanding of brain–behavior relationships (Reid Lyon & Rumsey, 1996; Chin & Marx, 1997). It is accepted that working memory capacity contributes to language comprehension and acquisition, verbal and nonverbal reasoning, and intelligence (Wickelgren, 1997). It is also accepted that auditory processing deficits, attention deficit disorders, and dysnomia are neurobehavioral disorders (Tallal, 1983; Rourke, 1989; Korhonen, 1991, 1995; Goodglass & Wingfield, 1997; Wolf, Bowers, & Biddle, 2000).

Deficits in auditory and phonological processing, speed of processing, and short-term verbal memory are considered to be central to primary language disorders (Tallal et al., 1996). This is supported by evidence from brain imaging, indicating that anatomical asymmetry of the auditory cortex, observed as primarily H-planar asymmetry, contributes to the prediction of deficits in phonological awareness (Leonard et al., 1996). Investigations of students with dyslexia identify auditory processing and speed of naming deficits as two distinct, contributing factors (Ackerman, Dykman, & Gardner, 1990; Torgesen et al., 1990; Shankweiler et al., 1995).

Post-hoc analyses of data from research with students with dyslexia point to the alternative that an underlying, precise timing mechanism, shared by language and motor functions, may be deficient, resulting in reduced continuous-naming speed (Wolf et al., 2000). There is evidence for the existence of three clinical subgroups among dyslexic readers. The largest, single-deficit, subgroup contains children with modest reading impairments and primarily phonological deficits. A second single-deficit subgroup contains children with primary naming-speed deficits. A smaller, double-deficit, subgroup contains children in whom naming-speed and phonological-processing measures are significantly lowered and reading is most impaired. This indicates that deficits in naming speed and phonological processes can occur concomitantly or independently.

In a related study, Wiig, Zureich, and Chan (2000) report that, in a group of more than 300 children with primary language disorders, about 50% exhibit significant reductions in continuous naming speed for color–shape combinations. Nearly all (97%) in the naming-deficit group exhibited severe receptive–expressive language disorders. Naming-speed deficits, either independently or in combination with phonological-processing deficits, are hypothesized to be contributing factors in primary language disorders, as well.

Damage to the prefrontal areas is detrimental to planning and goal-directed behavior (Krasnegor, Reid Lyon, & Goldman-Rakic, 1997, pp. 211–378). These areas play a central role in regulating cognitive and emotional behaviors, executive functions, working memory, and aspects of language decoding and encoding. Electrical stimulation of the left anterior frontal lobe results in disruption of naming, reading, and sequencing orofacial movements (Ojemann, 1983; Stuss & Benson, 1984). Retrieval from memory seems to be disrupted, especially when the inferior and orbital sections are involved. In a similar vein, Warkentin et al. (1991) measured regional blood flow during associative naming with a modified version of the Word Fluency Test (Benton & Hamsher, 1977). Blood-flow values were significantly higher in the left anterior and inferior frontal areas, and lower in the left central and anterior parietal areas during the test condition than during resting. The findings support the idea that the disruptions result from blockage of a precise timing mechanism involved in controlling language decoding and encoding.

Developmental patterns

One objective for language assessment is to identify patterns of strength and weakness. Examiners are looking for evidence of language and communication behaviors that are common deficits in children with language disorders. This section gives a short review of research findings that indicate what the expectations might be.

Language and communication disorders cause primary as well as secondary adaptive problems for students during childhood and adolescence, and may persist in adulthood (Bashir, Wiig, & Abrams, 1987; Gerber, 1993; Ratner & Harris, 1994; Owens, 1995). During the preschool and early school years, the child's language impairments result in problems in acquiring and using basic language skills for social interaction, academic learning, and performance. In the middle and upper school years, the adaptive problems are often reflected in inadequacies in using language for reasoning, problem solving, and communication in academic, vocational, and social contexts. The impact of a language disorder can be far reaching and may interfere with common sense, life-long learning, and social adjustment in adolescence and adulthood.

Word and concept knowledge are excellent measures of cognitive–linguistic growth, learning potential, and academic performance (Gardner, 1991). Among students with language disorders, early spontaneous concepts, such as *bus* or *angry*, may be adequately developed, whereas abstract and scientific concepts, such as *liquid* or *idealism*, may not. Students with limited, fragmented, or episodic word and concept knowledge remain 'concrete' in thinking and do not tend to think in logical, sequential terms or to use cause–effect reasoning. They may, therefore, not make the transition from concrete to abstract thinking and conceptualization spontaneously (Piaget & Inhelder, 1969; Feuerstein et al., 1980). They are likely to plateau in word and concept knowledge at fifth grade level, limiting the ability to access the language of classroom instruction and learning materials (Wiig & Secord, 1992; Wiig, Freedman, & Secord, 1992a; Nippold, 1993). These deficits commonly co-occur with difficulties in interpreting and using verbal analogies and figurative language, resulting in concrete, literal communications.

Linguistic rules for forming words and sentences give structure and predictability to language. In the early school years, students with language disorders may attract attention due to word formation problems (e.g., saying 'writed' for 'wrote'). In the later school years, problems in forming complex sentences with, for example, subordinated and relative clauses and achieving grammatical and logical consistency (e.g., using appropriate conjunctions and transition words) are more likely to attract attention (Wiig & Secord, 1992; Semel et al., 1995). Limitations in linguistic-rule acquisition are often reflected in breakdowns and inefficiencies in communicating knowledge and intents, exchanging and discussing information, participating in conversation, and producing written language.

The acquisition of pragmatic rules and social conventions for communication in context is usually deficient among students with language disorders. Classroom listening, speaking, reading, and writing are often compromised (Kamhi & Catts, 1988; Gerber, 1993; Owens, 1995). Deficits in using language for communication in context may reflect, among other things, inadequate linguistic-rule acquisition, lack of cognitive and linguistic flexibility, or problems in perspective taking.

Language provides a sequential code for internalizing scripts, creating higher-order abstractions (schemata), and organizing communication. It is a valuable code for guiding categorization, a productive approach to organization, task management, and developing mental models (Lakoff, 1987). During the school years, difficulties in acquiring metalinguistic abilities seem to contribute to the academic and adaptive problems of students with language disorders. They may not be able to analyze and talk about language, or use language as a tool, or interpret jokes, sarcasm, or metaphors. Inadequacies in the acquisition of metacognitive abilities and problem-solving processes are also evident among these students (Stone & Forman, 1988; Wansart, 1990; Ellis Weismer, 1992; Meltzer, 1993). The resulting difficulties may be reflected in problems with, for example: (a) planning and organizing language for extended speaking and writing; (b) making inferences and forming hypotheses from text; (c) developing and selecting among communication options for speaking or writing; and (d) monitoring, correcting, or editing language in use. Students with language disorders must often depend on auditory and working memory functions that may be inadequate for the task demands. Deficits in aspects of language and communication, inner language, and verbal mediation, unfortunately, also make effective compensation difficult.

Primary language disorders among children and adolescents are heterogeneous in nature. This dictates that language assessment must be broad in scope and content, probe multiple dimensions of language use, and reflect multiple perspectives to catch individual symptoms, syndromes, and behavioral variations. The assessment process must incorporate a diversity of methods and measures (e.g., norm-referenced, standardized, informal, authentic, and descriptive) and should include self-assessment (Reif, 1990; Roffman, Herzog, & Wershba-Gershon, 1994). To meet educational objectives for language assessment, the diagnostician must consider the constraints and demands placed on language and communication by different academic subjects and settings in which a student is required to function. Interactions among a student's inherent strengths and weaknesses and external constraints and demands must also be considered.

Assessment perspectives and methods

Student–clinician perspectives

Older students with language disorders bring up common themes. They feel they have little or no control of their lives and often do not understand what went wrong. Many emphasize that they performed well in the lower grades and still do well in subjects such as math and sciences. They often have little awareness of how a language disorder impacts learning and socialization. They may not understand how a disorder affects academic performance in reading, writing, and other language-based subjects. They feel that others place unreasonable demands on them and they show evidence of low self-esteem.

Students with language disorders often say that their primary concern is to find out what hampers academic performance. Many students are direct in commenting on the role they see for themselves in the evaluation and intervention process. Older students feel they must participate in assessing language, planning intervention, and evaluating outcomes. They also comment that clinicians should not define a complex language deficit in simplistic terms, such as saying that dysnomia means that words are trapped inside. They want insight into language strengths and weaknesses to empower them in handling problems over the long term. They want concrete examples of difficulties that may be caused by a primary language disorders.

The professional perspective of students with language disorders is increasingly holistic (Vygotsky, 1962) and it is applied to assessment and intervention (Gerber, 1993; Shames, Wiig, & Secord, 1998). Clinicians accept that language disorders may persist into adolescence and even adulthood (Bashir et al., 1987; Lapadat, 1991; Bashir & Scavuzzo, 1992; Gerber, 1993; Nippold, 1993; Capute, Accardo, & Shapiro, 1994). They recognize that language disorders co-occur with other deficits such as attention deficit disorders, dyslexia, or nonverbal learning disabilities, and that the symptoms take new forms with changes in academic, vocational, and social demands.

Despite broadened understanding, a given language evaluation may not meet a student's most urgent needs. This may reflect the realities of a clinic or school system, where time, financial, and staff resources for testing are often limited. Clinicians must, therefore, select assessment instruments and approaches carefully to obtain reliable and valid data for a student.

Multi-perspective and collaborative assessments

The evolution of language assessment has turned attention to the settings in which a student is taught and learns (Wiig, Secord, & Hutchinson, 1997).

Teachers, parents, and students have become legitimate observers and raters of language, communication, and other prerequisite behaviors for successful learning. Norm-referenced testing is complemented by authentic, descriptive, and other qualitative assessments, such as checklists, behavioral ratings, and self-evaluations to assess a child's potential for learning in the regular classroom.

The ability to learn and perform in school may be compromised by factors other than a child's inherent language disorder. There may be a 'mismatch' between the instructional language, classroom, and curriculum demands, and the student's ability to respond to these. Competencies required for reasoning and thinking, emotional control, and self-control, and interacting socially with others may be compromised and must be evaluated. A multi-perspective approach to assessment can help put together the puzzle of a given student's language strengths or weaknesses. It can suggest how the demands of different settings or tasks impinge on the student to cause either success or failure. Students with language disorders form a heterogeneous group, and every approach to assessment has assets and limitations in the face of this heterogeneity. Furthermore, communication contexts, demands, and personal perceptions of adequacy vary among individuals and within individuals over time.

In a multi-perspective assessment process, clinicians evaluate the inherent abilities and behaviors the child brings to the process of learning and also how she or he interacts with educational and social demands. Among variables to explore are abilities required for listening, speaking, reading, and writing, interpersonal interaction and socialization, and personal awareness and management. Aspects of the child's culture, language, and family backgrounds must also be taken into account. Figure 8.1 shows a conceptualization of what needs to be assessed in a student-centered evaluation to probe inherent as well as external dimensions and factors.

Multi-perspective assessment probes a child's language and communication from several points of view, as shown in Fig. 8.2. It uses quantitative as well as qualitative assessment tools. It engages clinicians, teachers, parents, students, and others in the process (Semel et al., 1996; Wiig et al., 1997). This implies that the assessment is a collaborative process of detection and fact finding about the child.

The student's language and communication strengths and weaknesses provide the inputs to the process. The clinician explores the target situation through multi-dimensional, multi-perspective data collection by using norm-referenced or standardized tests, observations, interviews, records of previous evaluations, and other appropriate means. The clinician and others then

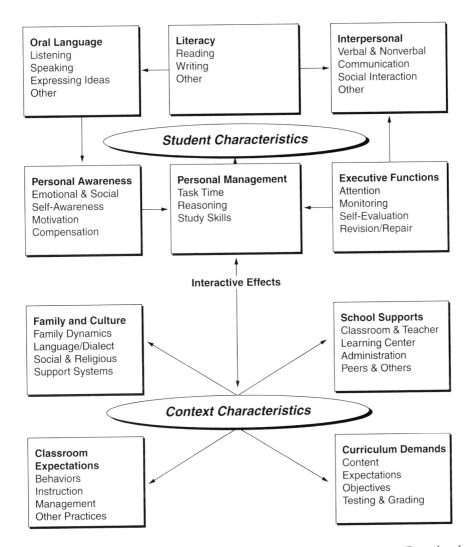

Fig. 8.1. Overview of dimensions of student-centered, multiperspective assessment. (Reproduced with permission from Wiig et al., 1997.)

address critical issues or questions. The data are subjected to analysis, evaluation, and synthesis to arrive at a holistic view of the child's current status. This usually leads to a process of reframing the child's situation, in which issues such as priorities and options for intervention are addressed. At the conceptual level, data and interpretations are integrated to evaluate the child's potential for regular-classroom inclusion and to develop a long-term clinical or educational intervention plan. The final step in the process is to address issues related to evaluating the student's progress and the efficacy of intervention over time. To

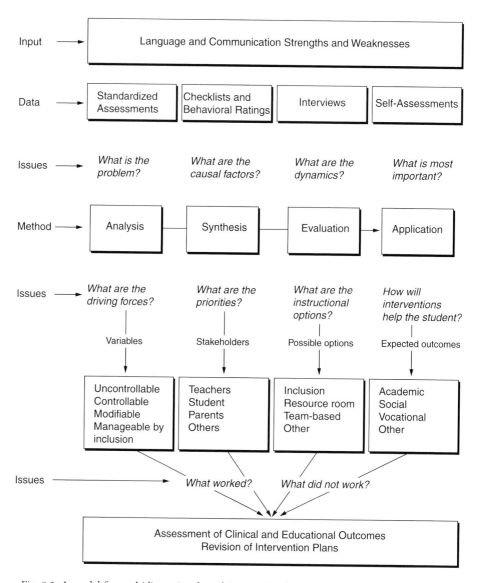

Fig. 8.2. A model for multidimensional, multiperspective language assessment. (Adapted from Wiig, 1994.)

bridge the transition from assessment to intervention, staff and other resources are identified, and the functions, roles, and responsibilities of each participant in the intervention plan are delineated. As in all collaborative ventures, all participants share available resources, responsibilities, risks, and rewards.

Norm-referenced language assessments

The use of norm-referenced tests to obtain quantitative measures of a child's language and communication has been questioned, and not without cause (Damico, 1993). However, there are many justifiable reasons for using norm-referenced tests for evaluating the language of students in schools (Hutchinson, 1996; Sabers, 1996). One asset of a norm-referenced test is the time and care invested in the development. A second is that the statistical characteristics of the instrument (e.g., internal consistency, test–retest reliability, concurrent validity, standard error of measurement) are controlled and available for evaluation.

Norm-referenced language tests may be focused or broad in scope. Tests of vocabulary and auditory comprehension of language (Dunn & Dunn, 1997; Carrow-Woolfolk, 1999) are among examples of focused, norm-referenced instruments. The administration of a language test with a specific focus does not provide the measures necessary for diagnosing a primary language disorder, even though test scores may correlate significantly with scores from broader-based language tests. Language tests with a narrow scope cannot identify or predict deficits in language abilities beyond the scope of their content, and are best used to explore a specific problem such as articulation, vocabulary development, or word finding.

Norm-referenced language tests, which are broad in scope and content, are designed with the objective of identifying and diagnosing a language disorder in a statistical comparison with performances by the student's age-level peers. This includes tests such as the Clinical Evaluation of Language Fundamentals – Preschool (CELF–P) (ages 3–7), Clinical Evaluation of Language Fundamentals–3 (CELF–3) and CELF–3 Spanish Edition (ages 6–21) (Wiig, Secord, & Semel, 1992b; Semel, Wiig, & Secord, 1995, 1997), the Test of Language Development – Primary (TOLD–P:3) (ages 3–10) and Intermediate (TOLD–I:3) (ages 7–14), and the Test of Adolescent Language (TOAL–3) (Hammill et al., 1994; Hammill & Newcomer, 1997; Newcomer & Hammill, 1997). These tests can determine the degree, extent, and nature of a language disorder. The composite standard scores can identify whether a language disorder is primarily receptive, primarily expressive, or mixed in nature. They can also identify areas or modalities of relative strength or weakness in the interpretation or use of language content or structure by comparing scores. Norm-referenced language tests are a component of the evaluation process to establish a child's eligibility for (a) language intervention, either through individualized therapy or language adaptations and interventions in the classroom; (b) using alternative technologies for completing classroom work; or (c) taking classroom and other tests without time limits (Wiig & Secord, 1991).

Design features and interpretation

Most broadly based language tests follow a standard design. This is the case for the CELF (CELF–P, CELF–3, and CELF-Spanish), TOLD (TOLD–P:3, TOLD–I:3), and TOAL–3 tests. A number of content-related test items, usually from 20 to 30 or more, are grouped into the major subtests, usually from four to six. Each subtest represents a dimension of the ability tested. Subtests are clustered into composites that measure a specific theoretical construct, for example primarily receptive versus primarily expressive language abilities. The CELF–3 features supplementary subtests that focus on associative naming, rapid naming, and understanding spoken paragraphs. Scores from the supplementary subtests are not included in forming the total, receptive, or expressive language scores that are used for diagnostic decision making.

Two language tests for infants and preschool children, the Preschool Language Scale (ages 3–6) (Zimmerman, Steiner, & Pond, 1992) and the Test of Early Language Development–3 (ages 3–7) (Hresko, Reid, & Hammill, 1999), differ in design. The latter contains subtests, whereas the former does not. Despite this difference, they both allow for the calculation of total, receptive, and expressive language scores.

In norm-referenced language tests, the total language score reflects a general performance construct. It is usually the most reliable single measure of the collective set of tasks and constructs. The receptive and expressive language composites reflect modality differences in the tasks and constructs. For diagnostic purposes, the total, receptive, and/or expressive language scores should be used for diagnosing the degree and general nature of a language disorder. Rather than basing the diagnosis on the actual standard score earned, the confidence interval for the 90% level of confidence should be used. This is the interval within which the 'true' score can be expected to fall if the child is tested repeatedly with the same test. Diagnostic categorization and decisions relating to eligibility for services should generally be based on the total language score. An exception occurs when the receptive and expressive language scores differ significantly or the 90% confidence intervals for the two scores do not overlap. Subtest or linguistic content-based standard scores should not be used to determine a diagnosis. These scores can point to relative strengths or weakness in language content or structure. They can also suggest areas for follow-up evaluation with criterion-referenced tests, observational rating scales, and other descriptive or performance-based measures.

Scope, content, and development

Norm-referenced language tests vary in the scope of content and task formats and in the underlying models for subtests and theoretical constructs. The CELF tests contain subtests that address linguistic skills and the interactions between linguistic skills and auditory memory, retrieval, and recall (Wiig et al., 1992b; Semel et al., 1995). Other broad-based, norm-referenced tests reflect an underlying model which is primarily linguistic in nature and evaluates primarily linguistic skills in the areas of semantics and syntax (Hammill & Newcomer, 1997; Newcomer & Hammill, 1997) or using these for listening, speaking, reading, or writing (Hammill et al., 1994). The widely used norm-referenced language tests employ essentially similar procedures for normative sampling, standardization, establishing validity, reliability, and error of measurement, and analyzing for item bias.

Relatively few norm-referenced language tests evaluate the transitions from linguistic-skill to metalinguistic-ability acquisition and communication strategy use. The Test of Language Competence – Expanded (TLC–E) (Wiig & Secord, 1989) is an example of a language test designed to explore the development of metalinguistic abilities. It includes a supplementary subtest for assessing working memory that probes the recall of word pairs in two sequential presentations. TLC–E can be helpful in a comparison to evaluate whether a language deficit encompasses linguistic skills, metalinguistic abilities, and communication strategies. Norm-referenced language tests that probe metalinguistic and strategic aspects of language use are appropriate for first-time evaluations of adolescents or for establishing outcomes after language intervention in elementary and secondary school students.

Norm-referenced language tests can combine a specific focus with a broad content. The Test of Word Knowledge (TOWK) (Wiig & Secord, 1992) is an example of a focused yet broadly based test of semantics. It evaluates the acquisition of referential (e.g., receptive and expressive vocabulary), relational (e.g., word definitions, synonyms, and antonyms), and metalinguistic aspects of word knowledge (e.g., multiple contexts, figurative usage, conjunctions, and transition words). In a heterogeneous sample of students with learning disabilities, deficits in word and concept knowledge were found in 60–75% of the subjects (Wiig, Jones, & Wiig, 1996). Fortunately, intervention to expand word knowledge and foster concept formation is readily instituted in classrooms and appears effective in improving a student's academic achievement (Wiig et al., 1992a).

Commonly used norm-referenced language tests have gone through an extensive developmental process, which may be described in the technical manual (Wiig et al., 1992b; Secord et al., 1995), starting with a statement of objectives and conceptualization for the design of subtests and items. The pilot version is submitted to several studies, followed by extensive statistical analyses and revisions. The process ends with large-scale normative testing, statistical analyses, standardization, and publication. The statistical characteristics of a test can support or cause us to question the use of a given norm-referenced language test. Among characteristics to evaluate in any norm-referenced test are whether or not (a) the language content, dimensions evaluated, design of tasks, and age-norms are appropriate; (b) the test is well standardized, valid, and reliable, with a relatively small Standard Error of Measurement (SEM); and (c) the results can reveal performance patterns or syndromes or lead to hypotheses or conclusions that are not easily arrived at through informal testing (Hutchinson, 1996).

Relationships to IQ

There are several indications of the relationships clinicians can expect between broadly based, norm-referenced measures of language (standard scores) and intelligence (IQ) (Table 8.1). During standardization of CELF–Preschool (Wiig et al., 1992b), two tests of intelligence – Wechsler Preschool and Primary Scale of Intelligence–Revised (WPPSI–R) (Wechsler, 1989b) and the Differential Ability Scales (DAS) (Elliot, 1990) – were co-administered to a group of over 50 children. The correlation between the CELF–Preschool Total Language Score and Verbal IQ is clearly stronger than that for Performance IQ. The pattern of correlations between the CELF–Preschool and DAS scores was similar.

In the standardization of CELF–3 (Semel et al., 1995), the third edition of the Wechsler Intelligence Scale for Children (WISC–3) (Wechsler, 1989a) was co-administered to a sample of 203 students. The pattern of correlations support the CELF–3 as a measure of general verbal ability.

The Wechsler Intelligence Scale for Children–Revised (WISC–R) (Wechsler, 1974) was co-administered with the TLC–E (Wiig & Secord, 1989). The correlation between the TLC–E Total Language Score and WISC–R Verbal IQ was significantly stronger than that with Performance IQ for both levels of the test.

Across CELF–Preschool, CELF–3, and TLC–E, a pattern emerges for the relationship between the standard scores for total language ability and intelligence. The correlations between the Total Language Scores and Full Scale IQ are significant, but moderate (.71 to .75). The correlations with Verbal IQ or the DAS Verbal Cluster are consistently higher (.70 to .78) than those with Performance IQ or the DAS Nonverbal Cluster (.12 to .60).

Table 8.1. Correlations for standard scores on language and intelligence tests

Language	Mean (SD)	Intelligence	Mean (SD)	Correlation
CELF–P		WPPSI–R		
Total Language	101.5 (14.0)	Full Scale	101.7 (14.0)	$r = .71$
		Verbal	101.0 (12.6)	$r = .72$
		Performance	102.1 (14.9)	$r = .58$
		DAS		
		General Conceptual	102.7 (13.6)	$r = .68$
		Verbal	102.6 (13.4)	$r = .70$
		Nonverbal	101.7 (14.7)	$r = .58$
CELF–3		WISC–III		
Total Language	102.0 (15.8)	Full Scale	103.7 (15.2)	$r = .75$
		Verbal	102.4 (15.3)	$r = .75$
		Performance	104.8 (15.5)	$r = .60$
TLC–E Level 1		WISC–R		
Composite	77.7 (12.2)	Full Scale	93.4 (13.8)	$r = .46$
		Verbal	88.7 (13.1)	$r = .70$
		Performance	102.9 (14.6)	$r = .12$
TLC–E Level 2		WISC–R		
Composite	73.1 (9.9)	Full Scale	95.3 (12.5)	$r = .75$
		Verbal	89.3 (12.7)	$r = .78$
		Performance	103.4 (14.1)	$r = .53$

Limitations

An often-cited limitation of language norm-referenced tests is that they are, by their nature, biased against some individuals and minorities. This bias can be minimized during development by obtaining expert bias reviews and using statistical procedures to identify items with significant bias and eliminate them. It can also be minimized by giving separate norms for selected minorities or directives for interpretation within a multi-lingual, multi-dialectic, or multi-cultural framework. As examples, the family of CELF tests (CELF–P and CELF–3) (Wiig et al., 1992b; Semel et al., 1995) underwent extensive reviews and statistical analyses with different procedures for bias. Items that showed gender or minority bias were deleted or redesigned. The CELF tests also give examiners extensive guidelines for scoring and interpreting the effects of linguistic or dialectic variations. Recently, the incorporation of item-bias analyses has become more common. Clinicians who feel that a norm-referenced test is too easy or too difficult for their population can create local or special population norms by following guidelines (Bryant, 1992) or using software programs (Pinsach, 1992; Sabers, Hutchinson, & Mobley, 1992).

Misuses

Norm-referenced language tests can be misused or abused. These transgressions may reflect: (a) inappropriate use of test norms; (b) using single subtests to develop a diagnosis, (c) using subtest results for developing skill-based IEP objectives, and (d) implementing interventions that respond only to the specific test content or tasks. Clinicians may make the erroneous assumption that by providing intervention that focuses on the child's language and communication deficits, the inherent difficulties can be reduced or eliminated. Teaching to items in a test develops splinter skills and invalidates further use of the same test to evaluate progress. It must be avoided.

Another source exists when a clinician interprets an exact language score rather than the expected range of scores to establish a diagnosis. Norm-referenced tests usually provide an index, the SEM, of the size of measurement error to be expected. Statistically, a given child's 'true score' should fall within a range that is determined by the size of the SEM. All important decisions – diagnosis, nature, degree, and eligibility for services – should be made based on interpreting confidence intervals at 90% for the total, receptive, and expressive language scores. Subtest scores can only suggest areas of strengths or weaknesses. Major clinical or educational decisions about a child should be based on interpreting confidence intervals for the total language score or the receptive or expressive composite scores, if there is a significant discrepancy between these.

Cross-cultural and linguistic issues

Language is an inherently biased tool for exchanging information and interacting socially in which the vocabulary (semantics) and rules for using language in context (pragmatics) are modified in an evolving process. The rules for what, how, and when to communicate in different contexts vary and reflect, among other things, authority, religion, and social status within a culture or language community. Cultural and linguistic diversities play out in language, communication, and social interaction at many levels.

Some of these issues emerged in the standardization of the Clinical Evaluation of Language Fundamentals – Spanish, developed to respond to the needs of a large Hispanic population in the USA (Semel, Wiig, & Secord, 1997). In the development, the visual stimuli were modified to reflect the norms of a Hispanic community. Subtests and items were changed or modified, starting with the identification of Spanish language characteristics that could be sensitive in identifying language impairments. One of the CELF–3 English subtests, Sentence Assembly, requires the student to make two sentences with different meanings or intents (e.g., statement versus a question) with the same given words. This format proved of limited diagnostic value due to the many combinatorial choices in Spanish and was left out.

Language clinicians in metropolitan settings serve children from a variety of cultural and linguistic backgrounds. There may be no norm-referenced or criterion-referenced tests for a given child's primary language. When this is the case, it is important to determine possible points of conflict between a child's primary language and English. A comparison of the cultural and linguistic features of the primary and the instructional language (English) can assist clinicians in predicting problem areas. Parents or other competent adult speakers from the child's primary language community can provide the information for a comparison of the vocabulary, morphology, and syntax.

Criterion-referenced assessments

Criterion-referenced assessments are standard in format and administration and generally use tasks or test probes with narrowly focused content. These assessments may result in raw scores that can be compared to age-level criteria for performance, as is the case for tests of articulation (Goldman & Fristoe, 1986; Hodson, 1986) and rapid automatic naming (Wolf, 1986; Semel, Wiig, & Secord, 1995). They may also result in percentage scores that can be compared to performance levels based on age, grade, rate of growth, or other criteria for language acquisition (Wiig, 1990; Sanclemente et al., 1998; Wiig & Wilson, 1999).

Several criterion-referenced tests evaluate functions associated with rapid, automatic naming deficits. The Stroop Color–Word Test is the classical example (Stroop, 1935). There are a number of more recent continuous rapid-naming tasks that are criterion-referenced and predict dyslexia and interference with fluency in language production (Denckla & Rudel, 1976; Wolf, 1986, 1991; Semel et al., 1995).

Rapid automatic naming (RAN) tasks are used for diagnostic purposes by, among others, aphasiologists, neuropsychologists, speech–language pathologists, and psychoeducational specialists. RAN tests that are diagnostically sensitive to naming deficits appear to require rapid perceptual or conceptual shifts from one dimension or semantic field to another (Wiig et al., 2000; Wolf et al., 2000).

From a clinical perspective, the rationale for administering continuous rapid-naming tasks is to identify whether a naming deficit might be a contributing factor in a primary language disorder or dyslexia. The CELF–3 RAN tasks (Semel et al., 1995) and the Rapid Alternating Stimuli (RAS) naming test (Wolf, 1986) are well suited for co-administration for clinical and educational diagnostic purposes. The clinician may want to analyze a spontaneous language sample for additional evidence of dysnomia (German, 1991) if a rapid-naming deficit is established.

Criterion-referenced language inventories

Speech–language pathologists are getting reacquainted with criterion-referenced measures for evaluating language (McCauley, 1996). Criterion-referenced measures can probe, among other things, linguistic content, skill and rule acquisition, and use of language in social contexts or for meeting curriculum objectives (Starlin & Starlin, 1973; Wilson, 1980; Wiig, 1990; Wiig & Wilson, 1999). Criterion-referenced language inventories can be used to validate norm-referenced test results, behavioral ratings, and observations of error patterns, to determine baselines and targets for intervention, and to evaluate growth and educational outcomes.

Criterion-referenced language inventories usually contain a series of probes, each with ten related items, to evaluate specific language and communication skills, rules, or objectives. Items within a given language probe test the same ability at different levels of difficulty or complexity, or in different contexts.

The use of ten items in a language probe allows for easy conversion to a percentage-correct level for the performance. This percentage can establish a student's level of success or failure compared to some standard of judgment. Seventy percent accuracy is often accepted to indicate adequate acquisition of the content or skill tested (Wilson, 1980). This overlooks the fact that language acquisition progresses at a slowed-down rate among students with language disorders and that over-learning is beneficial for these students (Wiig, 1990; Sanclemente et al., 1998; Wiig & Wilson, 1999). Examiners are therefore advised to use variable criteria for determining a student's performance level and intervention needs. An example of a variable criteria performance scale for language assessment is summarized in Table 8.2.

The Wiig Criterion-Referenced *Inventory of Language* (CRIL) probes language content (semantics), form (morphology and syntax), and use (pragmatics) in three separate modules (Wiig, 1990). In the morphology and syntax module,

Table 8.2. Variable performance criteria for criterion-referenced language assessment

Mastery (80% or above correct)	Reflects *Mastery* and ability to perform independently in most contexts
Transition (60–79% correct)	Reflects a transition to independent performance (*Mastery*) Opportunities for practice, modeling, coaching, and other support is sometimes needed
Emergence (40–59% correct)	Reflects a need for instruction with scaffolding, guided questioning, and other facilitators (*Emergence*)
Random Performance (below 39% correct)	Reflects trial-error responding (*Random Performance*) and a critical need for direct intervention to establish basic concepts, skills, rules, or strategies

Source: adapted from Wiig & Wilson (1998).

for example, a probe for English morphology focuses exclusively on forming noun plurals; another focuses on forming past tense of regular verbs. An examiner can select probes from the language inventory according to criteria for linguistic content or rule acquisition, age and development, or grade-level curriculum objectives. The inventory can serve as a long-term resource for selecting age-level or grade-level probes. Specific probes can be readministered to track a child's progress in a specific area of using linguistic content, rules, or conventions for oral communication. In the broader context of literacy, CRIL can evaluate the adequacy of oral-language prerequisites for language content, rule, and use systems.

The efficacy of interpreting the results of criterion-referenced assessments depends on selecting the appropriate probe content for educational objectives and evaluating responses against the child's primary cultural–linguistic background. A Spanish-language inventory (Sanclemente et al., 1998) broadens the application of criterion-referenced assessment to bilingual, Spanish–English, students. The Spanish-language inventory reports growth curves for children in Spain. Parallel probes in the English and Spanish language inventories can be used as a resource for educators who want to compare performance levels for Spanish–English bilingual students. Table 8.3 shows an example of a parallel language probe.

Wiig and Wilson (1994, 1999) use criterion-referenced measures to evaluate text comprehension in the classroom. The assessment component features two grade-level appropriate passages for each of Grades 2 to 7. Each passage features ten test questions, designed according to *Bloom's Taxonomy of Educational Objectives* (Kratwohl, Bloom, & Masai, 1964). The questions are grouped

Table 8.3. Comparison of a bilingual, English/Spanish language probe

English Spatial prepositions	Spanish Locativo
Where is Misty (a cat) sleeping? (in)	¿Donde duerme Moni?
Where is Misty sitting? (on)	¿Donde esta sentado Mino?
Where is Misty hiding? (under)	¿Donde esta escondido Mino?
Where is Misty hiding now? (behind)	¿Donde esta ahora Mino?
Where is Misty sitting? (in front of)	¿Donde esta escondido ahora Mino?
Where is Misty sitting? (between)	¿Pero donde se ha colocado Mino?
Where is Misty standing? (by)	¿Donde esta parado?
Where is Misty sleeping? (outside)	¿Donde esta durmiendo Mino?
Where is Misty going? (inside)	¿Hacia donde va Mino?
Where is Misty playing? (in the middle)	¿Donde juega Mino?

Source: adapted from Wiig (1990), and Sanclemente et al. (1998).

to probe two broad levels of comprehension and facilitate scoring and interpretation. Five questions measure recalling and using given information (i.e., knowledge, analysis). Five other questions probe the ability to go beyond the given information (i.e., comprehension, application, synthesis). The resulting measures differentiate students with language disorders from their normally developing age-level and grade-level peers (Wiig & Wilson, 1994).

Descriptive assessments

Checklists and behavioral ratings

Observational checklists and interviews are rich sources of information that can validate language, communication, and literacy difficulties (Wiig & Secord, 1991; Damico, 1992; Westby & Erickson, 1992). There are many checklists available for evaluating language and communication behaviors (Nelson, 1992, 1993; Secord, Wiig, & Damico, 1994a; Secord et al., 1994b). However, only a few observational rating scales of language abilities are standardized and tested for diagnostic validity (Semel et al., 1996).

The descriptive procedures and ratings in checklists are not necessarily designed to differentiate students by diagnostic categories. The item content of language checklists can be relatively narrow or encompassing in content and scope (Semel et al., 1996; Wiig et al., 1997). Checklists can explore different dimensions of language (e.g., content, form, and structure) and language-based performance (e.g., listening, speaking, reading, and writing) from different perspectives (e.g., teacher, parent, and student). The data provide valuable information for identifying language strengths and weaknesses, learning needs, and planning interventions.

Behavioral checklists can be administered in self-administered or other-administered formats, interviews, or computer-administered procedures. This adds flexibility for the user and the opportunity for dynamic interaction. The behavioral ratings can be completed by teachers, parents, or educational specialists. Older students can complete a checklist in a self-evaluation procedure.

Checklists with observational ratings can be valid sources for identifying language disorders. This has been supported in a standardization and validation study of the CELF–3 Observational Rating Scales (ORS) (Semel et al., 1996). The research edition probed and rated 42 listening, speaking, reading, and writing behaviors. The checklist questions were stated in the negative to elicit deficit ratings. The frequency of occurrence was rated on a four-point scale and assigned a score in which *Never* was assigned 1 point, *Sometimes* 2, *Often* 3, and *Always* 4 points. The final version of CELF–3 ORS contains 40 items distributed in four categories: Listening, Speaking, Reading, and Writing. The Learning Disabilities Diagnostic Inventory (Hammill & Bryant, 1998) provides similar as well as complementary measures. It targets characteristics commonly associated with dyslexia and learning disabilities.

Standardization of ORS indicated that the sum of the frequency ratings 'Often' (3 points) and 'Always' (4 points) differentiated students with primary language disorders with a high degree of accuracy (90%). Correlations between the behavioral rating scores by teachers and CELF–3 diagnostic language test scores were negative and in the low range (−0.35 to −0.43). These correlations lead to two conclusions. First, a behavioral rating scale does not provide the same diagnostic data as a broadly based diagnostic language test. Second, a clinician can obtain a greater diversity of data for determining intervention objectives by the combined administration of a norm-referenced language test (e.g., CELF–3) and a behavioral rating scale (e.g., CELF–3 ORS).

A single, student-centered perspective for behavioral observation and rating overlooks the fact that children are subjected to varying academic and social demands for language and communication. Teachers, curriculum objectives, subject areas, and social situations impose different constraints and demands that must be met for effective communication. For these reasons, Wiig et al. (1997) recently developed a large-scale database of categorized checklist items for observing, questioning, and rating speech, language, communication, and language-based aspects of literacy in different academic and social contexts and in dyadic interaction.

The Diagnostic Speech and Language Profile (DSLP) (Wiig et al., 1997) is a performance-based system for monitoring language and communication from the initial identification through management and long-term progress evaluation. DSLP contains more than 1000 categorized items that, together with the software system which operationalizes the database, give the user flexibility in selecting, adapting, and administering checklist probes. It is a comprehensive, naturalistic tool for rating observations of language behaviors in action. The behavioral ratings can come from a variety of observers, including teachers, parents, and students. DSLP can also identify points of agreement and/or conflict between the student's inherent language abilities and teacher, classroom, or curriculum demands. One section of probes focuses on the student and the inherent language abilities she or he brings to the classroom. A second focuses on dyadic interactions between the student and the teacher, classroom context, instructional language, and curriculum demands. An example of a dyadic language probe is presented in Table 8.4.

The DSLP items are written in a positive voice to focus on strengths. A rating scale with four labels is used to develop qualitative ratings and assign point scores for quantitative analyses. The quantitative ratings can be used to develop local or regional statistical information or norms for expected performances at different age or grade levels. The DSLP database and software system can assist in developing and managing appropriate, individualized intervention objectives based on naturalistic measures. It can also assist schools in developing interfaces with curriculum objectives, and tracking educational outcomes to conform to new Federal Regulations in the USA (IDEA *Amendments to Public Law 105-17*, 1997).

Interviews

Interviewing the teacher, parents, or student is a time-tested option for obtaining information about a child or for administering checklist items or probes. The interview can be individualized and modified based on answers and other feedback (e.g., nonverbal communication cues). The procedure has many assets, among them that the interviewer can build strong working relationships with parents and students. Interviewing can also strengthen collaboration and consultation with professionals and consumers. Ethnographic interviews typically take more time than using checklists with behavioral ratings. However, the added time can yield unexpected information.

One purpose of an interview may be to complete a checklist to explore the

Table 8.4. Illustrative checklist probe for classroom demands and expectations for questioning and answering questions. Probe 3. Teacher questions and student responses

The teacher	The student
• Asks questions for content (i.e., factual or quiz-like)	• Responds well to questions for content
• Asks open-ended, WH-questions	• Responds well to WH-questions
• Asks questions for feelings or reactions	• Responds well to questions for feelings or reactions
• Asks questions for prior experience and knowledge	• Responds well to questions for past experience and knowledge
• Asks questions for evaluation/opinion (e.g., right, wrong, neutral)	• Responds well to questions for evaluation or opinion
• Asks implications or inference questions (i.e., causes–effects)	• Responds well to questions for implications or inference
• Asks exploration or probing questions	• Responds well to questions that explore or probe for information
• Repeats student's answers to verify (e.g., *You said . . .*)	• Accepts or corrects teacher's repetition of answers
• Encourages questions for clarification	• Asks questions for clarification as needed
• Elaborates on comments, opinions, or views	• Learns from teacher's elaborations of students' comments or opinions

Source: Wiig & Secord (1999), reprinted with permission.
WH-questions: Who? What? Where? When? Why? How?

frequency of occurrence of behavioral strengths and weaknesses. There are other purposes for interviewing, among them to gain understanding of the child's cultural and linguistic background, family constellation and dynamics, and available support systems. When an exploratory interview has been completed, an evaluation team should review the responses, summarize the findings in terms of language and communication strengths and weaknesses, clarify any questions or concerns, and integrate all findings.

Self-assessments

Many educational specialists use self-assessments with late elementary and secondary-level students, college students, and adults (Gerber et al., 1990; Reif, 1990; Roffman et al., 1994). The importance of allowing an older child (ages eight and up) to assess him or herself as part of an evaluation cannot be minimized. The student feels empowered, assumes ownership, and takes charge of language and learning difficulties, and becomes his or her own advocate. Self-assessment allows students to describe academic, emotional, and social strengths and weaknesses. It may probe a student's perception of language, academic, and social performances, emotional impacts, use of coping and compensation strategies, motivation, and future goals.

Self-assessments can use, among other things, interview procedures, checklists, anecdotal accounts, or exchanges of letters or notes. Each procedure has assets, demands, and limitations that must be discussed before a specific approach is chosen collaboratively. Self-assessments can assist in analyzing and evaluating norm-referenced and ethnographic data, perceptions and reactions by self and others, and identifying instructional difficulties and needs. They can help professionals, parents, and students in reframing all input from testing to arrive at an overall strategy for educational management in the least restrictive environment.

Computer-based assessments and analyses

Advances in microcomputer technology have had a drastic, if localized, influence on educational practices and programs (Thomas, Sechrest, & Estes, 1994). In speech–language pathology, these technologies are used, for example, for: (a) client management; (b) spontaneous language-sample analysis; (c) scoring and interpreting norm-referenced test results; (d) assessing aspects of language; and (e) providing direct, interactive language intervention (Long, 1991; Ferguson, 1993; Fitch, 1993; Long & Masterson, 1993; Wiig & Wiig, 1993; Tallal et al., 1996; Semel, Wiig, & Secord, 1998). There are still areas where microcomputer technologies have not yet been exploited, such as for broad-based, interactive, or self-administered language assessments.

Spontaneous language sample analysis is a commonly used tool for evaluating early expressive language and story-telling abilities (Miller & Chapman, 1991; Hedberg & Westby, 1993). Recent procedures analyze and rate spontaneous language samples beyond the early developmental stages (Miller & Chapman, 1991; Dollaghan, 1992). There are now procedures for, among other things, computerized analysis of structural features and of frequency and types of disruptions (e.g., 'mazes,' repetitions) (Dollaghan & Campbell, 1992; Miller et al., 1992).

Today's microcomputer technologies can provide multi-media presentations, text-to-speech and speech-to-text transformations, and interactive communication. Students can select a keyboard, mouse, or touch screen for responding. Wiig, Jones, and Wiig (1996) used some of these features in computer-based, self-administered adaptation of the Test of Word Knowledge (TOWK) (Wiig & Secord, 1992). Correlations between the results from the computer-administered version and a standard oral administration of TOWK were moderately high. This suggested that aspects of language assessment can be conducted in supervised interaction between students and microcomputers linked to a mainframe. It can give students and teachers freedom to schedule testing at a convenient time and place, if the required technologies are available. Observational checklists and criterion-referenced language probes can be stored in a database within an interactive software system. This can allow teachers to customize probes and teachers and students to enter behavioral ratings directly. Automatic scoring routines could be developed, and the learning difficulties and needs of a student could be identified by computerized profiling. Computer-based language evaluations with appropriate adaptations may also ensure equity of access to assessment for students with handicapping conditions or who rely on computers for communication.

Illustrative case history

Introduction

This case study focuses on a child with language and communication disorders who received individual language intervention, enhanced by an approach called conceptual mapping (Wiig & Wilson, 1998, 2000; Wiig & Kusuma-Powell, 1999). In conceptual mapping, visual diagrams are combined with cognitive mediation to develop critical thinking skills and build mental models for language and communication. The child, Jane, was evaluated before and after one year of therapy (Wilson & Wiig, 1998). She was born in the USA as the second child of a highly educated, bilingual family. English is Jane's primary language, and she speaks only a basic form of her parents' native language.

Jane was referred for language assessment by a teacher in grade 4. The teacher reported that Jane's classroom behaviors changed drastically during the academic year. She became discouraged, depressed, and serious looking, and hardly looked up from her materials during instruction. Her behavior was tenacious, with a high degree of motivation and an overwhelming desire to achieve and please her parents. When asked to do a task, Jane was hyperfocused and kept saying 'I want to do well. I have to stay at my school.' The referral mentioned classroom difficulties in listening, paying attention, following directions, reading comprehension, and staying on task. Her parents indicated that Jane cried easily, when frustrated or discouraged, and did not express her feelings verbally.

Table 8.5. CELF–3 and TOWK–Level 2 standard scores and 90% confidence intervals (in parentheses) before and after language intervention

	Pre-intervention	Post-intervention
CELF–3		
• Total	78 (72–84)	102* (96–108)
• Receptive	69 (61–77)	102* (94–110)
• Expressive	90 (83–97)	102 (95–109)
TOWK–Level 2		
• Total Score	89 (82–96)	97 (90–104)
• Receptive	86 (79–93)	100* (93–107)
• Expressive	93 (86–100)	93 (87–99)

*Indicates a significant difference at the 0.05 level.

Source: Wilson & Wiig (1998), reprinted with permission.

Pre-intervention and post-intervention assessments

On intake, Jane (aged 10 years 1 month) was evaluated to determine:

- Reading achievement (Woodcock–Johnson Psycho-Educational Battery: Part 2: Tests of Achievement);
- Intellectual ability (Wechsler Intelligence Scale for Children–III and Matrix Analogies Test–Expanded Form, MAT–EF);
- Language and communication (Clinical Evaluation of Language Fundamentals–3, CELF–3 Observational Rating Scale, and Test of Word Knowledge–Level 2).

Jane obtained a Woodcock–Johnson Reading-Cluster Age-Level score of 495, a Letter–Word Identification score of 171, a Word Attack score of 163, and a Passage Comprehension score of 161. The results indicated that Jane read words and nonsense syllables and comprehended paragraphs at levels below average for her age. Jane's WISC–III Full Scale IQ was 99, Verbal IQ 110, and Performance IQ 87. The difference of 23 points between Verbal and Performance IQ was significant. Jane's total MAT–EF score was 89.

The CELF–3 and TOWK–Level 2 composite language scores are shown in Table 8.5. The CELF–3 Receptive Language score falls within the moderate to severe deficit range before intervention, while the Expressive Language score falls within the average-normal range. The TOWK Total, Receptive and Expressive scores indicate performances within the average-normal range. The difference between the Expressive (10) and Receptive Vocabulary (3) standard score was significant. A standard score of 3 on the supplementary subtest, Conjunctions and Transition Words, indicated severe difficulties in integrating semantics and syntax. The CELF–3 ORS identified consistent difficulties in the areas of Listening, Reading, and Writing, and selected difficulties in Speaking. The observational ratings supported the areas of difficulty identified by norm-referenced tests of language and reading.

After one year of intervention, the CELF–3, CELF–3 ORS, and TOWK–Level 2 were readministered. The pre-intervention and post-intervention test results indicate significant progress in all areas of language (Table 8.5).

Conclusion

In conclusion, the assessment of language disorders in children of school age is a complex task. It requires a clinician to evaluate what the student brings to the learning context in terms of linguistic and metalinguistic repertoires and strategies. It also requires assessment of the adequacy of neuropsychological and neurolinguistic functions that support speed and accuracy of auditory processing, and language comprehension and production to differentiate language delays and differences from specific language disorders. The clinical assessments must be complemented by contextual, performance-based evaluations to determine how the characteristics of a specific language disorder manifest themselves under academic and social constraints and demands. This chapter discusses formats, assets and limitations of, among others, norm-referenced and criterion-referenced tests, behaviour ratings of language in action, and developing structured, multidimensional assessment profiles (S-MAP) of portfolio samples. The case history was introduced to illustrate that focused language intervention can result in observable and educationally significant changes in a student's language and communication. The design and implementation of appropriate interventions are, after all, the end-goals for all language assessments.

REFERENCES

Ackerman, P.T., Dykman, R.A., & Gardner, M.Y. (1990). Counting rate, naming rate, phonological sensitivity, and memory span: major factors in dyslexia. *Journal of Learning Disabilities*, 23, 3257.

Bashir, A.S. & Scavuzzo, A. (1992). Children with learning disabilities: natural history and academic success. *Journal of Learning Disabilities*, 25, 53–65.

Bashir, A.S., Wiig, E.H., & Abrams, J.C. (1987). Language disorders in childhood and adolescence: implications for learning and socialization. *Pediatric Annals*, 16, 145–58.

Benes, F. (1997). Corticolimbic circuitry and the development of psychopathology during childhood and adolescence. In *Development of the Prefrontal Cortex: Evolution, Neurobiology, and Behavior*, ed. N.A. Krasnegor, G. Reid Lyon, & P.S. Goldman-Rakic, pp. 211–39. Baltimore, MD: Paul H. Brookes.

Benton, A.L. & Hamsher, K. (1977). *Multilingual Aphasia Examination*. Iowa City: University of Iowa.

Biklen, D. (1992). *Schooling Without Labels: Parents, Educators, and Inclusive Education*. Philadelphia, PA: Temple University Press.

Bryant, B.R. (1992). Creating local or special norms for norm-referenced tests. *LD Forum*, 17, 22–4.

Capute, A.J., Accardo, P.J., & Shapiro, B.K. (eds.) (1994). *Learning Disabilities Spectrum: ADD, ADHD, & LD*. Timonium, MD: York Press.

Carrow-Woolfolk, E. (1999). *Test of Auditory Comprehension of Language, Third Edition*. Austin, TX: Pro-Ed.

Chin, G.J. & Marx, J. (eds.) (1997). Cognitive neuroscience. *Science*, 275, 1579–610.

Damico, J.S. (1992). Descriptive/nonstandardized assessment in the schools. *Best Practices in School Speech–Language Pathology*, Vol. 2. San Antonio, TX: The Psychological Corporation.

Damico, J.S. (1993). Language assessment in adolescents: addressing critical issues. *Language, Speech, and Hearing Services in Schools*, 24, 29–35.

Denckla, M.B. & Rudel, R.G. (1976). Rapid 'automatized' naming (R.A.N.): dyslexia differentiated from other learning disabilities. *Neuropsychologia*, 14, 471.

Dollaghan, C.A. (ed.) (1992). Analyzing spontaneous language: new methods, measures, and meanings. *Topics in Language Disorders*, 12(2).

Dollaghan, C.A. & Campbell, T.F. (1992). A procedure for classifying disruptions in spontaneous language samples. In Analyzing spontaneous language: new methods, measures, and meanings, ed. C.A. Dollaghan. *Topics in Language Disorders*, 12(2), 56–68.

Dunn, L.M. & Dunn, L. (1997). *Peabody Picture Vocabulary Test, Third Edition*. Circle Pines, MN: American Guidance Services.

Elliot, C.D. (1990). *Differential Ability Scales*. San Antonio, TX: The Psychological Corporation.

Ellis Weismer, S. (1992). Hypothesis-testing abilities of language impaired children. *Journal of Speech and Hearing Research*, 34, 1329–38.

Ferguson, M.L. (1993). Computer technology: use in public schools. *American Speech–Language–Hearing Association*, 35(9), 46–7.

Feuerstein, R., Rand, V., Hoffman, M., & Miller, R. (1980). *Instrumental Enrichment: An Intervention Program for Cognitive Modifiability*. Baltimore, MD: University Park Press.

Fitch, J.L. (ed.) (1993). Computer technology. *American Speech–Language–Hearing Association*, 35(9), 35–51.

Gardner, H. (1991). *The Unschooled Mind: How Children Think and How Schools Should Teach*. New York: Basic Books.

Gerber, A. (1993). *Language-related Learning Disabilities: Their Nature and Treatment*. Baltimore, MD: Paul H. Brooks.

Gerber, P.J., Schneiders, C.A., Paradise, L.V., Reiff, H.B., Ginsberg, R.J., & Popp, P.A. (1990). Persisting problems of adults with learning disabilities: self-reported comparisons from their school-age and adult years. *Journal of Learning Disabilities*, 23, 570–3.

German, D.J. (1991). *Test of Word Finding in Discourse*. Austin, TX: Pro-Ed.

Goldman, R. & Fristoe, M. (1986). *Goldman–Fristoe Test of Articulation*. Circle Pines, MN: American Guidance Service.

Goodglass, H. & Wingfield, A. (1997). *Anomia: Neuroanatomical and Cognitive Correlates*. San Diego, CA: Academic Press.

Hammill, D.D., Brown, V.L., Larsen, S.C., & Wiederholt, J.L. (1994). *Test of Adolescent and Adult Language*, 3rd edition. Austin, TX: Pro-Ed.

Hammill, D.D., & Bryant, B.R. (1998). *Learning Disabilities Diagnostic Inventory*. Austin, TX: Pro-Ed.

Hammill, D.D. & Newcomer, P.L. (1997). *Test of Language Development – Intermediate*, 3rd edition. Austin, TX: Pro-Ed.

Hedberg, N.L. & Westby, C.E. (1993). *Analyzing Storytelling Skills*. San Antonio, TX: Communication Skills Builders.

Hodson, B.W. (1986). *The Assessment of Phonological Processes*, revised edition. Danville, IL: Interstate Printers and Publishers.

Hresko, W.P., Reid, K., & Hammill, D.D. (1999). *Test of Early Language Development, Third Edition*. Austin, TX: Pro-Ed.

Hutchinson, T.A. (1996). What to look for in the technical manual: twenty questions for users. *Language, Speech, and Hearing Services in Schools*, 27, 109–21.

IDEA Amendments to Public Law 105-17. (1997). Washington, DC: US Congress.

Kamhi, A. & Catts, H. (1988). *Reading Disabilities: A Developmental Language Perspective*. Austin, TX: Pro-Ed.

Korhonen, T.T. (1991). Neuropsychological stability and prognosis of subgroups of children with learning disabilities. *Journal of Learning Disabilities*, 24, 48–57.

Korhonen, T.T. (1995). The persistence of rapid naming problems in children with reading disabilities: a nine-year follow-up. *Journal of Learning Disabilities*, 28(4), 232–9.

Krasnegor, N.A., Reid Lyon, G., & Goldman-Rakic, P.S. (eds.) (1997). *Development of the Prefrontal Cortex: Evolution, Neurobiology, and Behavior*. Baltimore, MD: Paul H. Brookes.

Kratwohl, D.R., Bloom, B.S., & Masai, B.B. (1964). *Taxonomy of Educational Objectives: The Classification of Educational Goals. Handbook II: Affective Domain*. New York: David McKay.

Lakoff, G. (1987). *Women, Fire, and Dangerous Things*. Chicago, IL: University of Chicago Press.

Lapadat, J. (1991). Pragmatic language skills of students with language and/or learning disabilities: a quantitative synthesis. *Journal of Learning Disabilities*, 24, 147–58.

Leonard, C.M., Lombardino, L.J., Mercado, L.R., Browd, S.R., Breier, J.I., & Agee, O.F. (1996). Cerebral asymmetry and cognitive development in children: a magnetic resonance imaging study. *Psychological Science*, 7, 89–94.

Leonard, P. (1997). Language and the prefrontal cortex. In *Development of the Prefrontal Cortex: Evolution, Neurobiology, and Behavior*, ed. N.A. Krasnegor, G. Reid Lyon, & P.S. Goldman-Rakic, pp. 141–66. Baltimore, MD: Paul H. Brookes.

Long, S. (1991). Integrating computer applications into speech and language assessments. *Topics in Language Disorders*, 11, 1–17.

Long, S. & Masterson, J.J. (1993). Computer technology: use in language analysis. *American Speech–Language–Hearing Association*, 35(9), 40–7.

McCauley, R.J. (1996). Familiar strangers: criterion-referenced measures in communication disorders. *Language, Speech, and Hearing Services in Schools*, 27, 122–31.

Meltzer, L.J. (ed.) (1993). *Strategy Assessment and Intervention for Students with Learning Disabilities.* Austin, TX: Pro-Ed.

Miller, J. & Chapman, R. (1991). *SALT: Systematic Analysis of Language Transcripts.* Madison, WI: University of Wisconsin Press.

Miller, J.F., Freiberg, C., Rolland, M., & Reeves, M.A. (1992). Implementing computerized language sample analysis in the public school. *Topics in Language Disorders*, 12(2), 69–82.

Nelson, N.W. (1992). Targets of curriculum-based language assessment. *Best Practices in School Speech–Language Pathology*, 2, 73–86.

Nelson, N.W. (1993). *Childhood Language Disorders in Context: Infancy through Adolescence.* Boston, MA: Allyn & Bacon.

Newcomer, P.L. & Hammill, D.D. (1997). *Test of Language Development – Primary*, 3rd edition. Austin, TX: Pro-Ed.

Nippold, M. (1993). Developmental markers in adolescent language: syntax, semantics, and pragmatics. *Language, Speech, and Hearing Services in Schools*, 24, 21–8.

Ohio Department of Education (1991). *Ohio Handbook for the Identification, Evaluation, and Placement of Children with Language Problems.* Columbus, OH: Ohio Department of Education.

Ojemann, G.A. (1983). The intrahemispheric organization of human language derived from electrical stimulation techniques. *TINS*, 184–9.

Owens, R. (1995). *Language Disorders: A Functional Approach to Assessment and Intervention*, 2nd edition. Boston, MA: Allyn & Bacon.

Piaget, J. & Inhelder, B. (1969). *The Psychology of the Child.* New York: Basic Books.

Pinsach, J.R. (1992). *Diseño de Tests.* Barcelona, Spain: Idea Investigacion y Desarrollo, S.A.

Ratner, V. & Harris, L. (1994). *Understanding Language Disorders: The Impact on Learning.* Eau Claire, WI: Thinking Publications.

Reid Lyon, G. & Rumsey, J.M. (eds.) (1996). *Neuroimaging.* Baltimore, MD: Paul H. Brookes.

Reif, L. (1990). Finding the value in evaluation: self assessment in a middle school classroom. *Educational Leadership*, 47, 2.

Roffman, A.J., Herzog, J.E., & Wershba-Gershon, P.M. (1994). Helping young adults understand their learning disabilities. *Journal of Learning Disabilities*, 27, 413–19.

Rourke, B.P. (1989). *Nonverbal Learning Disabilities: The Syndrome and the Models.* New York: Guilford Press.

Sabers, D.L. (1996). By their tests we will know them. *Language, Speech, and Hearing Services in Schools*, 27, 102–8.

Sabers, D., Hutchinson, T., & Mobley, M. (1992). *User Norms Software.* Chicago, IL: Applied Symbolix.

Sanclemente, M.P., Wiig, E.H., Pinsach, J.R., & Perez, A.S. (1998). *Bateria de Lenguaje Objectiva y Criterial*. Barcelona, Spain: Masson.

Secord, W.A., Wiig, E.H., & Damico, J.S. (1994a). *Classroom Communication Assessment: Evaluating Performance in Context*. Chicago, IL: Applied Symbolix.

Secord, W.A., Wiig, E.H., Damico, J.S., & Goodin, G.L. (1994b). *Classroom Communication and Language Assessment*. Chicago, IL: Applied Symbolix.

Semel, E.M., Wiig, E.H., & Secord, W.A. (1995). *Clinical Evaluation of Language Fundamentals–3*. San Antonio, TX: The Psychological Corporation.

Semel, E.M., Wiig, E.H., & Secord, W.A. (1996). *CELF–3: Observational Rating Scales*. San Antonio, TX: The Psychological Corporation.

Semel, E., Wiig, E.H., & Secord, W.A. (1997). *Clinical Evaluation of Language Fundamentals–Spanish*. San Antonio, TX: The Psychological Corporation.

Semel, E.M., Wiig, E.H., & Secord, W.A. (1998). *Clinical Evaluation of Language Fundamentals – 3. Scoring Assistant*. San Antonio, TX: The Psychological Corporation.

Shames, G.H., Wiig, E.H., & Secord, W.A. (1998). *Human Communication Disorders*, 5th edition. Boston, MA: Allyn & Bacon.

Shankweiler, D., Crain, S., Katz, L. et al. (1995). Cognitive profiles of reading-disabled children: comparison of language skills in phonology, morphology, and syntax. *Psychological Science*, 6, 149–56.

Starlin, C. & Starlin, A. (1973). *Guides for Continuous Decision Making*. Bemidgi, MN: Unique Curriculum Unlimited.

Stone, C.A. & Forman, E.A. (1988). Differential patterns of approach to a complex problem solving task among learning disabled students. *Journal of Special Education*, 22, 167–85.

Stroop, J.R. (1935). Studies of interference in serial verbal reactions. *Psychological Monographs*, 50, 38–48.

Stuss, D.T. & Benson, D.F. (1984). Neuropsychological studies of the frontal lobes. *Psychological Bulletin*, 95, 3–28.

Tallal, P. (1983). A precise timing mechanism may underlie a common speech perception and production area in the peri-Sylvian cortex of the dominant hemisphere. *The Behavioral and Brain Sciences*, 6, 219–20.

Tallal, P., Miller, S.L., Bedi, G. et al. (1996). Language comprehension in language-learning impaired children improved with acoustically modified speech. *Science*, 271, 81–4.

Thomas, M., Sechrest, T., & Estes, N. (eds.) (1994). Deciding our Future: technological imperatives for education, Vol. 2. Proceedings of the 11th International Conference on Technology in Education, London.

Torgesen, J.K., Wagner, R.K., Simmons, K., & Laughon, P. (1990). Identifying phonological coding problems in disabled readers: naming, counting, or span measures? *Learning Disability Quarterly*, 13, 236–43.

Vygotsky, L.S. (1962). *Thought and Language*. Cambridge, MA: MIT Press.

Wansart, W.L. (1990). Learning to solve a problem: a microanalysis of the solution strategies of children with learning disabilities. *Journal of Learning Disabilities*, 23, 164–70.

Warkentin, S., Risberg, J., Nilsson, A., Karlson, S., & Graae, E. (1991). Cortical activity during speech production: a study of regional cerebral blood flow in normal subjects performing a word fluency task. In *Brain Dysfunction in Psychosis*, ed. S. Warkentin, pp. 11–39. Lund, Sweden: Departments of Psychiatry and Psychogeriatrics, University Hospital and Department of Psychology, University of Lund.

Wechsler, D. (1974). *Wechsler Intelligence Scale for Children–Revised*. San Antonio, TX: The Psychological Corporation.

Wechsler, D. (1989a). *Wechsler Intelligence Scale for Children–Third Edition*. San Antonio, TX: The Psychological Corporation.

Wechsler, D. (1989b). *Wechsler Preschool and Primary Scale of Intelligence–Revised*. San Antonio, TX: The Psychological Corporation.

Westby, C. & Erickson, J. (eds.) (1992). Changing paradigms in language-learning disabilities: the role of ethnography. *Topics in Language Disorders*, 12(3), 1–87.

Wickelgren, I. (1997). Getting a grasp on working memory. *Science*, 275, 15 580–2.

Wiig, E.H. (1990). *Wiig Criterion Referenced Inventory of Language*. San Antonio, TX: The Psychological Corporation.

Wiig, E.H. (1994). *A Multi-dimensional Assessment Model*. Working Paper. Arlington, TX: Knowledge Research Institute.

Wiig, E.H., Freedman, E., & Secord, W.A. (1992a). Developing words and concepts in the classroom: a holistic–thematic approach. *Intervention in School and Clinic*, 27, 278–85.

Wiig, E.H., Jones, S.S., & Wiig, E.D. (1996). Computer-based assessment of word knowledge in teens with LD. *Language, Speech and Hearing Services in Schools*, 27, 21–7.

Wiig, E.H. & Kusuma-Powell, O. (1999). *Visual Tools for Critical Thinking in Classrooms*. (Prepublication version.) Arlington, TX: Schema Press.

Wiig, E.H. & Secord, W.A. (1989). *Test of Language Competence–Expanded*. San Antonio, TX: The Psychological Corporation.

Wiig, E.H. & Secord, W.A. (1991). *Measurement and Assessment: A Marriage Worth Saving*. Chicago, IL: Riverside.

Wiig, E.H. & Secord, W.A. (1992). *Test of Word Knowledge*. San Antonio, TX: The Psychological Corporation.

Wiig, E.H. & Secord, W.A. (1999). *Diagnostic Speech and Language Profiler. Experimental Edition*. Arlington, TX: Schema Press.

Wiig, E.H., Secord, W.A., & Hutchinson, T. (1997). *Diagnostic Speech and Language Profiler, Experimental Edition*. Chicago, IL: Applied Symbolix.

Wiig, E.H., Secord, W.A., & Semel, E. (1992b). *Clinical Evaluation of Language Fundamentals–Preschool*. San Antonio, TX: The Psychological Corporation.

Wiig, E.H. & Wiig, E.D. (1993). *Test of Word Knowledge Computer-based: Experimental*. Arlington, TX: Schema Press.

Wiig, E.H. & Wilson, C.C. (1994). Is a question a question? Differential patterns in question answering by students with LLD. *Language, Speech, and Hearing Services in Schools*, 25, 250–9.

Wiig, E.H. & Wilson, C.C. (1998). *Visual Tools for Language and Communication*. Chicago, IL: Applied Symbolix.

Wiig, E.H. & Wilson, C.C. (1999). *Ladders to Interpretation: Assessing and Developing Text Comprehension*. Arlington, TX: Schema Press.

Wiig, E.H. & Wilson, C.C. (2000). *Map it Out! Visual Tools for Thinking, Organizing and Communicating*. Eau Claire, WI: Thinking Publications.

Wiig, E.H., Zureich, P., & Chan, H-N.H. (2000). A clinical rationale for assessing rapid, automatic naming in children with language disorders. *Journal of Learning Disabilities*, 33(4), 359–74.

Will, M. (1986). Educating students with learning disabilities: a shared responsibility. *Exceptional Children*, 52, 411–15.

Wilson, C.C. & Wiig, E.H. (1998). *Language Intervention with Conceptual Mapping: A One-year Case Study*. Working Paper. Arlington, TX: Knowledge Research Institute.

Wilson, R. (1980). *Test Service Notebook 37: Criterion-referenced Testing*. San Antonio, TX: The Psychological Corporation.

Wolf, M. (1986). Rapid alternating stimulus naming in the developmental dyslexias. *Brain and Language*, 27, 360–79.

Wolf, M. (1991). Naming speed and reading: the contribution of the cognitive neurosciences. *Reading Research Quarterly*, 26, 123–41.

Wolf, M., Bowers, P.G., & Biddle, K. (2000). Naming-speed processes, timing, and reading: a conceptual review. *Journal of Learning Disabilities*, 33(4), 387–407.

Zimmerman, I.L., Steiner, V.G., & Pond, R.E. (1992). *Preschool Language Scale*. San Antonio, TX: The Psychological Corporation.

Part III

Neuropsychological Approaches to Learning Disabilities Assessment and Remediation

Learning disabilities and their neurological foundations, theories, and subtypes

Otfried Spreen

This chapter deals with two separate, but linked, lines of research. First, is the historic relationship between neuropsychology and learning disability (LD): the accumulating evidence of neurological impairment is reviewed, as well as theories about the role of neurological deficit. Second, the question of subtypes of LD is discussed. Surprisingly, subtype research has, for the most part, proceeded in isolation from the search for a neurological substrate of LD. An attempt is made to show that a convergence of these two types of research may contribute greatly to our knowledge of the field.

The relationship between neuropsychology and LD is built into most definitions. For example, the National Joint Committee on Learning Disabilities (1998) describes LD as a 'heterogeneous group of disorders manifested by significant difficulties in the acquisition and use of listening, speaking, reading, writing, reasoning, or mathematical skills . . . These disorders are intrinsic to the individual, presumed to be due to central nervous system dysfunction.'

The stress is on 'presumed.' In contrast, detailed descriptions, assessments, and often also treatment protocols have been developed for many childhood disorders of neurological origin, but LD are still based on a *presumed* neurological origin – the same is true for pervasive developmental disorders and attention deficit hyperactivity disorder (ADHD).

As Benton (1982) wrote in a review of child neuropsychology 18 years ago: 'Much of the research and clinical and educational service that we categorize as neuropsychological is, in fact, purely behavioural in nature . . . It is neuropsychological only because of my assumption, which is derived from observations of adult patients with demonstrable brain disease.' Oscar Parsons (1977) put it even stronger, by calling the search for brain correlates of psychological impairment without independent physiological or anatomical confirmation 'the new phrenology.' The question remains: have we learned more about this relationship or does it still remain an assumption? Also, what contribution does

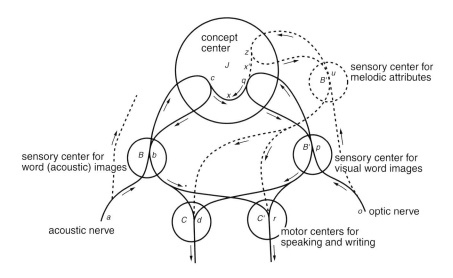

opqpr = optic-motoric pathways for written language
qpr = pathways for writing down thoughts

Fig. 9.1. Kussmaul's model of Spoken and Written Language (1877).

the knowledge of a 'neurological connection' make to the treatment of the individual dyslexic?

History

Even before the description of the first cases of acquired dyslexia, Adolf Kussmaul in Heidelberg (1877) provided an outline of the brain processes involved in reading (Fig. 9.1). In the tradition of the diagram makers, he described the connection between the optic nerve and the 'sensory center for visual word images' connecting to a 'sensory center for melodic attributes,' leading to the crucial 'concept center,' perhaps not too different from Wernicke's area. He proposed further connections to the 'optic–motoric pathway for written language' and a 'pathway for writing down thoughts.' The concept center was also connected to the 'sensory center for word (acoustic) images,' and to the acoustic nerve.

In 1892, Dejerine, using the classical connectionist model, confirmed that the lesion for *acquired* word-blindness was probably located in the left angular gyrus area and extended to the occipital horn of the lateral ventricle.

The history of the relationship between neuropsychology and *developmental* dyslexia starts in 1896, when Pringle Morgan, a general practitioner in Seaford, England, presented a first case of congenital 'word-blindness' in the *British*

Medical Journal. The year before, James Hinshelwood in Scotland had published a case of 'acquired word-blindness' after injury to the angular gyrus.

Hinshelwood, an ophthalmological surgeon in Glasgow, responded in the same journal and accepted Morgan's suggestion of a congenital form of the disorder. He and other physicians in Europe and North America followed quickly with reports of 14 cases of their own, so that Hinshelwood, in his 1917 monograph entitled *Congenital Word Blindness*, was able to present the accumulated evidence of a well-established disorder. But Hinshelwood warned that the term should be reserved for cases that were marked by (a) the 'gravity of the defect,' and (b) the 'purity of symptoms,' that is, that they should resemble closely the cases of acquired word-blindness with lesions in the angular gyrus area. 'Cases where children simply lag somewhat behind their fellows in acquiring the visual memories of letters or words' should not be described by this term.

The discovery of dyslexia as a special condition with neurological causes set the direction for most subsequent research. In the 1930s, Samuel Orton (1928, 1937), a neurologist, used the term 'strephosymbolia' as well as 'developmental alexia,' and added another significant dimension, namely lateralization, to the 'presumed' substrate: his language areas involved in reading are not too different from those hypothesized by Kussmaul. His diagram includes the angular gyrus, Wernicke's and Broca's area, and parts of the motor strip (Fig. 9.2). But Orton also did away with Hinshelwood's stringent definition: 'Our experience in studying and retraining several hundred such cases has convinced us that they form a *graded series including all degrees of severity* of the handicap.' Orton accepted the notion of the origin of dyslexia in the angular gyrus region, but stressed that it may not originate from a specifically deviant development of that region, but 'from a deviation in the process of establishing *unilateral brain superiority* in individual areas while taking into account hereditary facts.' He further wrote that 'such disorders should respond to specific training if we become sufficiently keen in our diagnosis, and if we prove ourselves clever enough to devise proper training methods to meet the need *for each particular case.*'

This is a surprisingly modern statement, in view of the current research on subtypes and training methods. Orton also suggested what could be called the first attempt at subtyping LD: he described developmental alexia, developmental agraphia, developmental word-deafness, developmental apraxia (abnormal clumsiness), and combined mixed syndromes.

Incidentally, dyscalculia, the other major form of LD, has a similar early history, but was not described in further detail until much later.

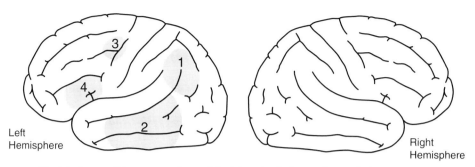

Fig. 9.2. A map of the outer surfaces of the left and right hemispheres of a human brain, showing the 'critical' language areas. This diagram shows the conditions as they exist in a right-handed individual, with the critical areas for language in the left hemisphere only.

Orton's theory remained a theory until, in 1947, Strauss and Lehtinen called attention to the frequent appearance of neurological signs in learning-disabled children. Much has been written about the presence of neurological signs in learning-disabled populations, particularly about the so-called 'soft,' 'pastel,' or 'non-focal' signs, i. e., signs with dubious or nonfocal significance. Studies of such signs have been available since the 1950s. An increased incidence of soft neurological signs in learning-disabled children was reported by Hertzig (1983) and in six other studies in the 1970s and 1980s. One criticism is that these signs are 'developmental,' and therefore disappear with time. The Victoria study with 203 learning-disabled children (Spreen, 1988), however, compared the occurrence of each sign at ages 8 to 12 years and in a follow-up at age 25: they did not disappear with time, but tended to persist or even increase in number. The other problem with such signs is that they rarely point to specific locations in the cortex. For this reason, they have limited use in pursuing the relationship between LD and neurological abnormalities. In an attempt to relate specific signs to the outcome of LD in young adulthood, only a general factor of motor integrity was found, which had a direct bearing on outcome (Spreen, 1989a, 1989b). After a critical evaluation of the many contradictory findings in the literature, Rie (1987) concluded that 'the child who fails in school, who is otherwise psychologically healthy, and who manifests one or more of the more complex soft signs is highly likely to suffer from a learning disability.' However, soft neurological signs have also been found in children with hyperactivity, autism, affective disorders, and schizophrenia. It is suggested that these signs may be explored as expressions of central nervous system abnormality, of subtle malfunction, maldevelopment, or malformation, which may or may not contribute to LD.

An interesting parallel to Hertzig's findings is the observation by Waldrop and collaborators about minor physical anomalies (Waldrop, Pedersen, & Bell, 1968; Waldrop, Bell, & Goering, 1976) in LD. Single anomalies without physical or cosmetic significance, like attached ear lobes, single palmar crease, and furrowed tongue, are not uncommon in a child population, but Waldrop found that multiple physical anomalies are more common in children with psychiatric or academic difficulties, and a recent study reported a high incidence in autism. In fact, two studies (Willems, Noel, & Evrard, 1972; Paulson & O'Donnell, 1980) reported an increased number of minor physical anomalies in children with soft neurological signs, and one study related these anomalies to atypical cerebral lateralization (Yeo et al., 1997). Again, these abnormalities are nonfocal; they are also not specific to dyslexia – they have been found in schizophrenics, but not in their siblings or in bipolar disorders (Green et al., 1994a; Green, Satz, & Christenson, 1994b).

Since the late 1960s, new and more specific evidence for the relationship between dyslexia and neurological impairment has been presented in macroscopic studies. The first evidence came from the autopsy study of a dyslexic child by Drake in 1968, and later from five further autopsies published by Galaburda and Kemper (1978), and Humphreys, Kaufmann, and Galaburda (1990). The autopsy studies showed microdysgenesis with ectopias and dysplasias bilaterally along the Sylvian fissure frontally and along the planum temporale, in the left more than in the right hemisphere. Whereas normal brains show only one or two ectopias, the dyslexics' brains had 30 to 100 ectopias (nests of neurons in layer 1). The occurrence of ectopias is assumed to be due to increased survival of neurons during corticogenesis at mid-gestation. These studies add a first piece of real evidence of neurological abnormalities.

Since the late 1970s, further evidence of a number of structural abnormalities from computerized tomography (CT) and magnetic resonance imaging (MRI) has become available.

Asymmetry of lobes and ventricles

The first CT study by Hier and collaborators in 1978 showed abnormal reversal of the typical normal posterior leftward asymmetry (Fig. 9.3), although a later CT study by Denckla, LeMay, and Chapman (1985) found such asymmetries in only a small number of dyslexics. A later study by Larsen et al. (1990) found a higher proportion of symmetrical plana. The results of ten other studies are contradictory in part. Adjustments for age and gender are necessary in such studies. Schultz and collaborators (1994) found no difference between 17 dyslexics and 14 nonimpaired children in a variety of areas, especially in surface areas and in the planum temporale, and reported that 'apparent differences in

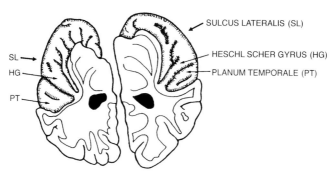

Fig. 9.3. Normal asymmetry of the human brain. Note the increased size of the planum temporale and of Heschl's gyrus on the left, and of the frontal area on the right side.

the size of the left hemisphere structures and symmetry of the planum temporale between dyslexics and controls were not reliable after controlling for age and overall brain size.' Both Beaton (1997) and Morgan and Hynd (1998; see also Clinton et al., 1998), in recent reviews, note that symmetry or abnormal asymmetry of the plana has not been consistently found in dyslexics, that they are not sufficient to produce dyslexia, and that such findings have also been reported in children with specific language impairment, not just dyslexia.

Corpus callosum

Rumsey and collaborators (1996) and Duara et al. (1991) found enlargement of the area of the isthmus and the splenium of the corpus callosum in 21 adult dyslexics. They suggested that this could be interpreted as a sign of greater number of crossing fibers, thicker fibers, denser myelination, or greater packing density. This, in turn, could lead to increased communication between hemispheres, resulting in decreased lateralization of language or increased inhibition of one hemisphere by the other. Temple, Reeves, and Villaroya (1990) related dysgenesis of the corpus callosum to the phonological aspects of dyslexia. In a Dutch study, Njiokiktjien (1993; Njiokiktjien & de Sonneville, 1994) focused only on one type of dyslexia, the 'dysphasic–dyslexic syndrome.' They looked at the mid-callosal size in 110 children, and found the size to be normal in dyslexic/dysphasic children *without* a family history of such disorders, but thicker in children with *familial* dysphasia/dyslexia. Other findings have been contradictory, which may be explained by the confounding factor of age: the corpus callosum has been shown to show linear and robust growth between the ages of 4 and 18 in 114 normal subjects, specifically in the posterior and mid-regions (Giedd et al., 1996). In a recent review, Beaton (1997) concluded that 'it is clearly too early to draw firm conclusions regarding callosal morphology in dyslexia' (p. 304).

Reviewing the evidence from all CT studies, Rumsey (1996) concluded cautiously that the studies so far show that 'subtle developmental anomalies may constitute the substrate of dyslexia,' but that they 'are not strictly localized to any small portion of the cortex. Rather, cortical anomalies may be variably distributed, and additional subcortical structures (e.g., thalamus) may be affected' (p. 73).

Functional abnormalities

Most recently, studies have looked at the functional rather than structural abnormalities in children with learning disabilities. Positron emission tomography (PET), single-photon emission tomography (SPECT), and functional MRI (fMRI) measure local changes in hemodynamic responses that are correlated with changes in neuronal activity. fMRI has been most promising because it is noninvasive and can therefore be used in larger numbers of subjects. Investigators generally measure changes in blood flow and blood oxygenation in one experimental condition relative to another condition. Unfortunately, the findings are not as clear as one would hope, because most studies use very few subjects, and these subjects show a lot of behavioral heterogeneity, and because comorbidity, especially with general LD and low IQ, and with ADHD, is high. As might be expected, the type of task selected as a reading test also plays an important role, e.g., whether the child or adult reads aloud or silently, reads for meaning, for phonology, or for orthography, whether accuracy or rate of reading is stressed: the activated regions, therefore, are participating but not necessarily critical for reading.

As an example, Fig. 9.4 (Rumsey, 1996) shows results during rhyme detection for words and for a tonal memory task in the lower panels. It also shows that rhyme detection registers mainly in the left hemisphere, and tonal memory in the right. In dyslexics, on the right panels, both tasks show underactivation of several areas.

With the advent of these techniques in the 1990s, a host of new studies concentrated on the question of what areas are involved in reading and what areas are impaired in dyslexia. Rumsey (1996) reviewed 13 anatomical and eight functional neuroimaging studies on developmental dyslexia. Twelve additional studies have appeared since.

Not surprisingly, a considerable number of areas of the brain show activation during *normal* reading: the left temporo-parietal region is primarily involved in phonological processing (Table 9.1). Phonological processing was also related to left inferior frontal and temporal sites. Lexical–semantic processing activated middle and superior temporal areas, whereas orthographic processing activated

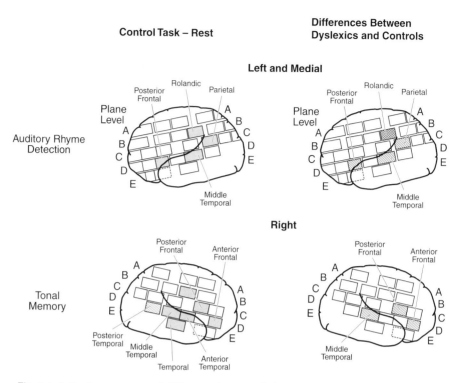

Fig. 9.4. Activation patterns and differences between dyslexic men and control associated with auditory rhyme detection and tonal memory tasks. Black and grey areas indicate activation; stippled areas indicate underactivation. Dyslexic men failed to activate the left temporoparietal cortex during rhyme detection and activated fewer right frontotemporal areas during tonal memory tasks. (Reproduced with permission from Rumsey, 1996.)

the left extrastriate area and the peri-insular cortex bilaterally. In addition, the occipital extrastriate cortex was found to be involved in the processing of visual word forms. However, conclusions and results from these studies differ to some extent. Although Shaywitz and the Haskins group confirmed the locations for phonologic and orthographic processing, they found confusing evidence for semantic processing locations, whereas the National Institute of Health (NIH) group confirmed the temporal location. Whereas the Haskins group stressed phonological and simultaneous processing as the core component of reading, the NIH group (Rumsey et al., 1997a, 1997b) offers a multifocal serial processing model and ascribes the 'sometimes conflicting results' to the 'heterogeneity in the neuropsychological deficits associated with dyslexia.' Activation is primarily on the left side in men, but bilateral in women. Bookheimer and Lapretto (1996) point out that the participation of the frontal areas is primarily dependent on task demands, i.e., 'oral word generation

Table 9.1. Component processes of reading and corresponding brain areas

Type of processing	Brain areas involved
Phonological processing Non-word rhyme judgment	Inferior–frontal (Brodman 44/45, Shaywitz, Pugh, Liberman); left in men, bilateral in women
Pseudoword pronunciation Sensitivity to stimulus-length effects Picture naming, especially with polysyllabic or low-frequency words	Superior temporal–parietal (Petersen, Borkheimer), angular–supramarginal, planum temporale (Rumsey)
Lexical–semantic processing (meaning) Semantic category judgment	Middle/superior temporal (Shaywitz–Pugh) (Wernicke) Frontal
Orthographic–visual processing Letter-case recognition Visual word form recognition Visual motion	Occipital–striate–extrastriate (Galaburda, Shaywitz–Pugh, Rumsey, Petersen, Eden) Visual, oculomotor system (Raghavar)
Auditory processing Speech–sound discrimination	Medial geniculate nuclei, Heschl's gyrus (Galaburda)

produces strong increases in several frontal lobe regions . . . in the primary motor cortex (mouth area),' whereas silent reading does not.

Another source of information about the brain areas involved in reading is the studies by Ojemann (1989) using electrical stimulation of the exposed surface of the brain during epilepsy surgery. As Fig. 9.5 shows, stimulation of a large number of frontal, temporal, and parietal areas resulted in disruption of reading and/or naming in a total of 55 patients. The participation of other areas is probably limited by the restricted operating field during epilepsy surgery. Ojemann stressed in his interpretation that there was a large amount of individual variability, i.e., that the areas disrupted in one patient were not necessarily the same as in another.

In *dyslexics*, Rumsey and collaborators (1994) tested 17 adult men and 14 controls, and found altered patterns of activation in the mid to posterior temporal cortex bilaterally and in the left inferior parietal cortex, but normal activation of the left inferior frontal areas, suggesting bilateral involvement of the posterior temporal and parietal cortex in dyslexia. They interpreted this as a failure to activate the left temporo-parietal cortex during phonological processing, a sign of dysfunction of the cortical language area in severe dyslexia, and report that dyslexics 'differed primarily in magnitude rather than location.' Similar findings were reported by Gross-Glenn et al. (1990) and by Kaneko and collaborators (1998) for familial dyslexics. Decreased activity was also found in

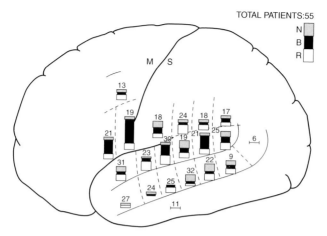

Fig. 9.5. Individual variability in areas of electrical stimulation evoking changes in Naming (N), Sentence Reading (R) or both (B). In each zone the number of patients with one or more sites creating errors in that zone is indicated by a bar graph. (Reproduced with permission from Ojemann, 1989.)

the extrastriate and the peri-insular cortex. Not included in Table 9.2 is the cerebellar area, proposed by Nicolson and Fawcett (1999) of the Sheffield group, because its presence remains theoretical at this time.

In addition, a number of studies of evoked potentials have investigated the difference between dyslexic and normal readers. Remschmidt, Schulte-Körne, and Henninghausen (1998; Henninghausen, Remschmidt, & Warnke, 1994) found some consensus that, for at least a subgroup of more severe dyslexics, the N1 component was lacking, suggesting a delayed pattern of visual information processing. Of course, evoked potentials, electrical stimulation and fMRI do not point to actual defects of the brain itself, only to abnormal or absent processing in certain areas of the brain, which may be due to the lack of practice in reading.

Unfortunately, in all studies, the description of the dyslexic population under study often leaves much to be desired and includes wide ranges of age, of ability, and of areas of learning. As Hynd and Semrud-Clikeman (1989) also noted, reports of possible comorbidity and of academic performance measures other than the task used during functional measurements are entirely missing.

Theories

The first autopsy findings on dyslexics led Norman Geschwind to develop a major explanatory theory about the origin of the relationship between learning disabilities and neurological abnormalities in the 1970s. Geschwind (1984) and

Table 9.2. MRI, CT and fMRI study results in dyslexics

Frontal	Normal frontal asymmetry (larger on right)
	Smaller and symmetrical frontal areas (Hynd)
	Shorter insulae
	fMRI: left inferior frontal activation normal (Rumsey)
	left inferior frontal overactivated (Shaywitz)
Temporal	Reversal of left-dominant ventricular asymmetry
	Reversal of asymmetry or symmetry of planum temporale
	(increase of area on right side, Rumsey; Morgan; Hynd;
	Semrud-Clikeman; Larsen)
	Extent of asymmetry related to severity of dyslexia (Duara)
	Left asymmetry of temporal bank (Leonard)
	fMRI: left mid-posterior temporal activation reduced (Rumsey)
Parietal	Right asymmetry of parietal bank
	fMRI: left mid-parietal and inferior parietal activation
	(Wernicke, angular gyrus, striatum) reduced (Shaywitz)
	No difference after adjustment of data for age and sex
Occipital	fMRI: poor activation of cortical visual system (magnocellular
	subsystem)
Corpus callosum	Splenium and isthmus enlarged (Duara, Rumsey)
	Splenium and isthmus reduced (Semrud-Clikeman, Temple)
	Mid-callosum thicker in familial dyslexics only (Njiokiktjen)
	Mid-callosum *reduced* in ADHD (confounding factor, Beaton)
Medial geniculate nuclei	Smaller on left side (Galaburda)

Geschwind and Galaburda (1993) reviewed the evidence and concluded that the common denominator in these cases was anomalous cerebral dominance due to defective neuronal migration and assembly, especially in the left cortex, leading to dysplasias, ectopias, and arteriovenous malformations or lateralized developmental arrest. They wrote that 'it is precisely this type of "minor" developmental pathology that is responsible for many of the learning disabilities and related disorders and psychiatric conditions' (p. 445). In a much-cited theoretical design, the authors interpreted the concept of anomalous dominance, originally first raised by Orton, in terms of its relevance not only for LD, but also for handedness, special giftedness, emotional disorders, immune deficiencies, other disorders, and even hair color. Without going into details here, the male fetus, in particular, develops in an estrogen-saturated environment and produces the genetically determined androgenic hormone testosterone and related hormones not only to develop into a male, but also to alter the formation of brain structures, specifically to slow down left hemisphere development or, according to a later reappraisal, to promote the growth of the right (Galaburda et al., 1985; Galaburda, 1993); and altering brain functioning. Cerebral dominance, according to this theory, is inversely related to the size and density of the corpus callosum. Faulty composition of the hormonal environment, as well as a variety of teratogenic factors, contribute to these disorders of cell migration and are the ultimate cause of a variety of disorders.

Geschwind and Galaburda have provided one possible framework for the predisposition to LD as well as to emotional disorders. They propose a clear relationship between a number of symptoms and a cause. In fact, Geschwind considered the disturbance of the birth process to be a consequence of 'the hormonal atmosphere of pregnancy' (1984, p. 681). Geschwind and Galaburda's work was a milestone in taking us from speculation to the actual mechanisms of predisposition, which may ultimately have its origin in environmental as well as genetic causes.

Unfortunately, their theoretical framework provides only for one general mechanism and does not allow for the occurrence of specific types of emotional disorder or specific types of LD. Congenital brain dysfunction of the type proposed by Geschwind and Galaburda does not allow the description of a clear-cut relationship between focus of lesion and form of psychopathology; in fact, one may go so far as to say that, based on this model, a clear relationship between form of damage and form of disorder cannot even be expected, particularly if one considers the numerous and complex compensation mechanisms of the embryonic and infant brain (Prechtl, 1978; Spreen, Risser, & Edgell, 1995).

During the last 20 years, several critical appraisals of the Geschwind–Galaburda concept and studies to confirm the theory have been published (Van Strien, Bouma, & Bakker, 1987; Satz, Soper, & Orsini, 1988; Soper et al., 1988; Bryden, McManus, & Bulman-Fleming, 1994; St. Marseille & Braun, 1994; Biederman et al., 1995; Flannery & Liederman, 1995; Bulman-Fleming, Bryden, & Wise, 1996). One recent registry-based field study of 2202 LD adults by Smith et al. (1996) found no support for Geschwind's lateralization theory; this study and others (Hugdahl, Synnevagt, & Satz, 1990; Hugdahl, 1993; Jariabkova, Hugdahl, & Glos, 1995) also found only marginal association between some immune disorders and left-handedness in dyslexics and negative associations in others. In addition, a total of 12 different studies failed to confirm the associations proposed in the model, or found only limited support for one association but not for others.

Most of the studies reviewed so far and the Geschwind theory do not attempt to 'split' the LD into subgroups, let alone split the dyslexics into subtypes. As Rourke (1990) argued, 'lumping' LD children into a single group may be counterproductive in that it obscures the hypothetical relationship with neurological evidence. Since the late 1960s, is has been suspected that LD is not a homogeneous classification, and several unique forms of dyslexia as well as degrees of severity may exist (Hynd, Hooper, & Takahashi, 1992). If this is correct, then the theoretical framework for the neurological basis of LD must be expanded. There are three theories that suggest a strong relationship between subtypes and specific neurological abnormalities.

1. The first subtype theory relating to a neurological basis was developed by Bakker (1979). His theory proposed two types of dyslexia: the slow but accurate reader (which he called the P type) who uses a right hemisphere strategy, and the fast and sloppy reader (which he called the L type) who uses a left hemisphere strategy. The P type relies heavily on the early methods of dealing with script, i.e., spatial–temporal exploration; the L type relies prematurely on linguistic skills, bypassing the early exploratory stage. Bakker suggested that a hemispheric imbalance could be demonstrated by dichotic listening and evoked potential techniques, and developed a hemisphere-specific training method (Bakker, Licht, & Kappers, 1995) to correct the imbalance by exposing letters to the right or left visual and tactile fields. Bakker did not specify what specific areas of the brain are impaired, merely that there is a hemispheric imbalance. However, it was the first theory to propose specific substrates for two different forms of LD and a first formula for type-specific treatment.

   A critical appraisal of Bakker's model (Hynd et al., 1992) points out that subtypes evolve over time, and that subtypes are more complex than indicated by the model. Few independent investigators have replicated Bakker's work. Grace and Spreen (1994) tried to replicate it, but found that the distinction between L and P type is very difficult to make, because in most poor readers there is a continuum of both characteristics proposed by Bakker. In the Victoria study, the attempt to select students who best fitted Bakker's model and to train them in the suggested fashion also showed little success. When placebo training was used, all students improved moderately, regardless of typology. Similar results were found in a recent British study and inconsistent results in another (Van den Honert, 1977). Other studies lacked untreated controls. Van der Vlugt (1998) suggested that the P and L types correspond roughly to two of five subtypes isolated in two studies. Van der Leij, van Daal, and Vieijra's (1998) critical appraisal finds little support for Bakker's theory other than that it stimulated the development of a new form of treatment research.

2. Satz (1990, 1991) proposed a somewhat similar theory, involving both hemispheres. Reviewing the remarkable recovery from aphasia due to a shift in language dominance in early childhood, he argued that similar compensation mechanisms should be available for lesions causing dyslexia. Therefore, we

need to think of the neurological substrate of dyslexia in terms of *bilateral* damage. Subtypes similar to Bakker's may exist, depending on which hemisphere sustained the more severe damage. Satz proposed that

... in cases of predominant left-hemisphere anomaly one might expect to find the characteristic language-disorder subtype ... This is also compatible with Bakker's P-type which is characterized by over-reliance on perceptual strategies because of the delay or impairment in linguistic processing. In cases of predominant right-hemisphere anomaly, one might expect to find the visuo-spatial subtype ... This subtype is also compatible with Bakker's L-type, which is characterized by over-reliance on left-hemisphere strategies because of the delay or impairment in abstracting perceptual features from script. In cases of predominant bifrontal lobe anomaly, one might expect to find some of the attentional and disinhibition difficulties observed in some dyslexic children with attention-deficit disorders (Satz, 1991, p. 108).

Incidentally, this typology is very similar to the types proposed by Lovett (1984) – the rate-disabled and the accuracy-disabled reader – and to Boder's (1973) dysphonetic and dyseidetic dyslexics. Unfortunately, there has been no follow-up on Satz's heuristic formulation.

3. Whereas Bakker's theory focused mainly on dyslexia, a third theory, by Rourke, focused mainly on one form, the nonverbal learning disability. In 1985, Rourke described an unusual complex of cognitive and emotional deficits which resembles a pattern first mentioned by Myklebust in 1975. According to Rourke's (1995) theory, *right*-hemisphere brain dysfunction (primarily frontal) is 'etiologically' related to nonverbal learning disorder, e.g., clumsiness, poor spatial thinking, difficulties in the organization of mathematical problems and knowledge of time of day, poor handwriting, estimation of size, distance, and weight, losing the place on the page while reading. Based on their experience with 29 such cases, Hernadek and Rourke (1994) described this subtype of LD as 'non-verbal perceptual–organizational–output disability' (NPOOD). They found that psychopathology was frequent in these children, characterized by psychotic trends, depression, withdrawal, anxiety, and poor socializing ability, summarized as 'personality deviance' and 'internalized psychopathology.' Rourke explained this specific disability as 'poor performance on measures ordinarily thought to be subserved primarily by the right hemisphere' (1985, p. 173), although damage to 'either hemisphere will disrupt arithmetic learning in the child.' In a further extension and revision of this hypothesis, Rourke (1987, p. 215) proposed that 'dysfunction of white matter necessary for inter-modal integration' is the main basis of this syndrome, whereas right-hemisphere lesions may constitute a 'sufficient, but not necessary condition.' The specification of the involvement of white matter is based on the notion that the

right hemisphere has more long myelinated fiber connections than the left and therefore is more involved in integrative processing.

However, replication or confirmation of the proposed white matter abnormalities has shown mixed results. A total of 14 papers failed to find evidence for the proposed right-hemisphere or white matter damage in nonverbal LD and related disorders. In a recent paper, Rourke and Conway (1997) stated that 'no entirely satisfactory statement of the relationship between arithmetic and brain function has yet emerged.'

Clearly, Rourke has called attention to an important, though rare, subtype of LD. He is also one of the few authors who addressed the complex area of developmental dyscalculia. (See the related discussion of Rourke's work in Chapter 10, where Reitan and Wolfson focus primarily on Rourke's neuropsychological research investigations and their implications.)

Subtypes

To study whether subtypes are related to neurological findings, a subtype analysis was attempted of the learning-disabled children in our study, based on test variables at the time of referral (Spreen & Haaf, 1986). We used cluster analysis, and replicated five clusters frequently reported in the literature: (1) minimally impaired, (2) primarily arithmetic disabled, (3) specific reading disabled, (4) visuo-perceptually impaired, and (5) linguistically impaired (Table 9.3). In addition, we found groups of normal learners and children who were impaired in all areas. However, none of these subtypes was related to specific soft or hard neurological signs.

This list of subtypes is not presented here as a definite solution to the subtyping problem, but to illustrate that some consensus appears to be emerging from older and more recent subtyping studies. A similar, though not identical, solution has been proposed in a recent study by van der Vlugt (1998) and in a very comprehensive analysis by Fletcher et al. (1997) and Morris et al. (1998), which reported a nine-cluster solution with two near-normal, two severely and generally impaired groups – a typical finding in cluster analysis. In addition, they found five specific subtypes, which they labelled according to the deficits found in phonological, lexical, rate, and memory aspects of reading. There is strong similarity, also, with subtypes proposed in earlier studies. The differences are most likely to be due to differences in test selection.

There is no shortage of subtypes suggested by various authors, based on clinical experience and/or on empirical or statistical analyses, but without reference to a specific neurological basis. Boder (1973) suggested a dysphonetic,

Table 9.3. Changes in subtypes of learning disability over a 15-year period

	Percentage of subjects in study	
	Aged 8–12 years	Aged 25 years
1. Nearly normal in all areas or minimally impaired	7	8
2. Arithmetic disabled	7	20
3. Auditory–linguistic–dysphonetic, phonologic	12	13
4. Visuo–perceptual–spatial–dyseidetic	17	14
5. Linguistic–semantic (similarities, vocabulary)	9	—
6. Graphomotor–visuomotor (coding)	17	4
7. Graphomotor–sequencing (block design, coding, right–left orientation, sequencing	12	14
8. Globally impaired in all areas	18	27

From Spreen & Haaf (1986).

dyseidetic, and mixed type, a typology that is still the most frequently used, and is somewhat similar to Lyon's (Newby and Lyon, 1991) typology. Marshall and Newcomb (1973) suggested a visual (word-form), surface, and deep dyslexia, based mainly on studies of acquired alexia, later replicated in dyslexics by Castles and Coltheart (1993) and by Stanovich et al. (1997) as surface and phonological subtypes. Mattis, French, & Rapin (1975) suggested a linguistic, articulo-graphomotor, and visuo-perceptual type (based on post-hoc data analysis, but confirmed by others). Denckla (1977) proposed similar types plus a dysphonemic sequencing disorder. Decker and DeFries (1981) suggested a typology based on factor scores, including impairment of spatial reasoning, coding speed, and reading impairment only. Doehring and Hoshko (1977) used Q-type factor analysis to develop three types of dyslexia: associative, sequential, and oral. But, despite the many different and confusing terms and disagreements between these theoretical and empirical typologies, and at the risk of oversimplification, a certain consensus appears to be emerging, as indicated in Table 9.4. A similar consensus was also noted in reviews by Newby and Lyon (1991), Hynd et al. (1992), and Cohen, Campbell, & Yaghmai (1989). For example:

1. Satz, Boder, Lyon, Bakker, Lovett, Rourke, and Morris all describe what could be called an auditory–linguistic subtype, also described as a 'phonological' form of dyslexia.

Table 9.4. Subtypes of learning disabilities based on cluster analysis (Spreen & Haaf, 1986) and similar subtypes proposed by other authors

	Morris	v.d Vlugt	Satz	Rourke	Bakker	Doehring	Denckla	Mattis	Marshall	Lovett	Boder	Lyon
1. Near normal in all areas or minimally impaired	X	X	X	X								
2. Arithmetic disabled	X	X	X	X								
3. Auditory–linguistic–dysphonetic, phonologic	X	X	X	X	X	X		X	X	X	X	X
4. Visuo–perceptual–spatial–dyseidetic	X	X	X	X	X	X	X	X	X	X	X	X
5. Linguistic–semantic (similarities, vocabulary)		X	X	X			X	X	X		X	X
6. Graphomotor–visuomotor (coding)	X	X	X	X			X		X	X		X
7. Graphomotor–sequencing (block design, coding, R–L orientation)			X	X			X	X				
8. Globally impaired in all areas	X	X	X							X	X	

2.   Lyon, Tallal, Boder, Bakker, and Satz describe a visual–perceptual type.
3.   Satz, Lyon, Morris, and most other authors describe a language-deficit subtype.
4.   All authors describe one or more global or mixed impairment types as well as one or more minimally impaired subtypes appearing in their analysis.

There is no agreement as to whether these are discrete subtypes, or whether, as Lyon suggested, these subtypes lie on continuous dimensions of verbal or visual impairment.

Stability and outcome of subtypes

Another persisting problem is the lack of stability of subtypes. That dyslexia persists into adulthood is now generally accepted and has also been shown by the finding of structural and functional changes in adult dyslexics. But, as Jan Rispens (1998) in a recent Dutch book points out, the prediction of dyslexia of any kind from kindergarten or grade 1 to grade 6 has been notoriously poor. For example, the Connecticut study found that only 28% of 414 children classified as learning disabled in grade 1 received the same classification in grade 3 (Shaywitz et al., 1992, 1998), and Jorm et al. (1986) found only 6 of 25 children classified as LD with the same classification in grade 2. Furthermore, the question of changes of subtypes over longer periods and of adult outcome has not been addressed in most studies. Perhaps one should expect the most serious or bilateral anomalies in those subtypes that have the poorest outcome. There are four studies that describe the fate of subtypes as the child grows older. In the Victoria Study (Spreen & Haaf, 1986) and in other studies, a subgroup of LD characterized as language impaired at the time of referral at age ten, showed the poorest outcome at adult age: nearly all changed from group 5 to group 8, the globally impaired type. This is consistent with findings in several other studies that children with early language impairment frequently show LD persisting into adulthood. Denckla (1993) referred to a similar group of adult LD subjects, suggesting that the core of their disability may have shifted to an 'executive dysfunction,' and that the focus on academic disabilities at this age 'masks a more general dishevelment in the patient's life.' Membership in other subtypes in our study remained constant for 36%, but changed for a large number of subjects from age 10 to age 25.

Conclusions

Although the neurological explanation has been widely accepted (Gaddes & Edgell, 1993), the nagging feeling that we are 'neurologizing' in an important field of education remains, especially among special educators, who, perhaps rightly, suggest that a neurological explanation leads to educational pessimism. Colleagues in behavioral psychology often suggest that causes do not really matter, and only delay and hinder remedial efforts (Reschly & Gresham, 1989).

This chapter has tried to review the evidence for the relationship between LD and neuropsychology. The 'neurological connection' was first based on cases analogous to brain-damaged adults with acquired alexia. This parallel has launched and propelled research in the field for the past 100 years. Yet it remained an analogy until recently. The neurological basis is no longer 'presumed,' although it is not always confirmed, and less specific than we would like it to be.

There are three conclusions to be drawn from the material presented.

1. We now know a lot more about the component processes of reading and, to some extent, of arithmetic. It is clear from that evidence that a consensus is emerging about the areas of the brain that are involved in reading. We cannot expect a single location, such as the angular gyrus, to be the only critical component of dyslexia. Which of these areas is of critical importance or whether there are several areas remains to be determined. Instead, we must focus on the subtype approach, with different forms of LD and several different locations.

2. Several theories about the neurological substrate of LD have been presented. None of them has found unanimous support in subsequent studies. One reason for this is that the currently offered theories do not take into account the large individual variability found in neuroanatomical, neurophysiological, and functional studies of normal and abnormal readers.

3. The majority of studies suggest that LD is persistent over the school years and into adulthood. However, the Victoria study suggests that the outcome of specific subtypes may differ as the children grow into adulthood. How specific subtypes fare over the course of development of the child, is another field of studies, with important consequences for remediation that need to be addressed in future research. For example, Joschko and Rourke (1985) implied that the adult form of the ACID (Arithmetic–Coding–Information–Digit Span deficit on the Wechsler Intelligence Test) subtype shows poor prognosis in all areas, and our and other studies show poor outcome for the language-impaired subtype.

4. The search for subtypes of LD has been continuing since the 1960s in apparent isolation from studies of the neurological substrate of LD. A fair degree of consensus between different subtype systems is noted, and differences appear to be mostly related to the use of different areas of assessment. In addition, the subtype classification appears to be subject to age-related changes. It is argued

that careful selection of subjects for functional and neuroanatomical research along the lines of subtypes, on the one hand, and subtype research using the available literature on the neuroanatomical substrate of LD, on the other, may be of mutual benefit and result in a clearer picture of LD which will eventually aid the training and treatment of children with LD.

The situation in the neighboring fields of autism and ADHD is not very different from that in LD. The search for an underlying neurological substrate has produced many studies, but with contradictory or spurious results (Piven et al., 1990; Ozonoff & Miller, 1996; Baron-Cohen et al., 1999). fMRI studies even suggest that areas similar to those implicated in LD are involved, e.g., superior temporal gyrus and prefrontal areas in 'social intelligence.' Here, again, the suggestion of subtype analysis has been proposed, and may lead to more convincing evidence. If we move into sophisticated analyses of various neurological or neuroradiological techniques, the psychologist selecting the subjects should be equally sophisticated: we should be sure that our group of subjects is well defined, in terms of age, of severity, and of subtype. This would seem to be the most important program for the future.

REFERENCES

Bakker, D.J. (1979). Hemispheric specialization and stages in the learning to read process. *Bulletin of the Orton Society*, 23, 84–100.

Bakker, D.J., Licht, R., & Kappers, E.J. (1995). Hemisphere stimulation techniques in children with dyslexia. In *Advances in Child Neuropsychology*, Vol. 3, ed. M.G. Tramontana & S.R. Hooper, pp. 144–77. New York: Springer.

Baron-Cohen, S., Ring, H.A., Wheelwright, S. et al. (1999). Social intelligence in the normal and autistic brain: an fMRI study. *European Journal of Neuroscience*, 11, 1891–8.

Beaton, A.A. (1997). The relation of the planum temporale asymmetry and morphology of the corpus callosum to handedness, gender, and dyslexia: a review of the evidence. *Brain and Language*, 60, 255–322.

Benton, A.L. (1982). Child neuropsychology: retrospect and prospect. In *Perspectives on Child Study*, ed. J. de Wit & A.L. Benton, pp. 41–6. Lisse, Netherlands: Swets & Zeitlinger.

Biederman, J., Milberger, S., Faraone, S.V., Lapey, K.A., Reed, E.D., & Seidman, L.J. (1995). No confirmation of Geschwind's hypothesis of associations between reading disability, immune disorders, and motor preference in ADHD. *Journal of Abnormal Child Psychology*, 23, 545–52.

Boder, E. (1973). Developmental dyslexia: a diagnostic approach based on three atypical reading–spelling patterns. *Developmental Medicine and Child Neurology*, 15, 663–87.

Bookheimer, S.Y. & Lapretto, M. (1996). Functional neuroimaging of language in children. In

Developmental Neuroimaging: Mapping the Development of Brain and Behavior, ed. R.W. Thatcher, G.R. Lyon, J. Rumsey, & N. Krasnegor, pp. 65–77. San Diego, CA: Academic Press.

Bryden, M.P., McManus, I.C., & Bulman-Fleming, M.B. (1994). Evaluating the empirical support for the Geschwind–Behan–Galaburda model of cerebral lateralization. *Brain and Cognition*, 26, 1–65.

Bulman-Fleming, M.B., Bryden, M.P., & Wise, D.M. (1996). Associations among familiar sinistrality, allergies, and developmental language disorders. *International Journal of Neuroscience*, 87, 257–65.

Castles, A. & Coltheart, M. (1993). Varieties of developmental dyslexia. *Cognition*, 47, 149–80.

Clinton, A.B., Kroese, J.M., Morgan, A.E., & Hynd, G.W. (1998). Reversed planum temporale asymmetry associated with language impairment? *Journal of the International Neuropsychological Society*, 4, 59–60 (Abstract).

Cohen, M., Campbell, R., & Yaghmai, E. (1989). Neuropathological abnormalities in developmental dysphasia. *Annals of Neurology*, 25, 567–70.

Decker, S.N. & DeFries, J.C. (1981). Cognitive ability profiles in families of reading-disabled children. *Developmental Medicine and Child Neurology*, 23, 217–27.

Dejerine, J. (1892). Contribution á l'etude anatomic–pathologique et clinique des différentes variétés de cécite verbale. *Comptes Rendus des Seances et Memoires de la Societé de Biologie et de Ses Filiales*, 44, 61.

Denckla, M.B. (1977). Minimal brain dysfunction and dyslexia: beyond diagnosis by exclusion. In *Topics in Child Neurology*, ed. M.E. Blaw, I. Rapin, & M. Kinsbourne, pp. 243–62. New York: Spectrum.

Denckla, M.B. (1993). The child with developmental disabilities grows up: adult residuals of childhood disorders. *Neurologic Clinics*, 11, 105–25.

Denckla, M.B., LeMay, M., & Chapman, C.A. (1985). Few CT scan abnormalities found even in neurologically impaired learning disabled children. *Journal of Learning Disabilities*, 18, 132–6.

Doehring, D.G. & Hoshko, I.M. (1977) Classification of reading problems by the Q-technique of factor analysis. *Cortex*, 13, 281–94.

Drake, W.E. (1968). Clinical and pathological findings in a child with developmental learning disability. *Journal of Learning Disabilities*, 1, 9–25.

Duara, B., Kushch, A., Gross-Glenn, K. et al. (1991). Neuroanatomical differences between dyslexic and normal readers on magnetic resonance imaging scans. *Archives of Neurology*, 48, 410–16.

Flannery, K.A. & Liederman, J. (1995). Is there really a syndrome involving the co-occurrence of neurodevelopmental disorder, talent, non-right handedness, and immune disorder among children? *Cortex*, 31, 503–15.

Fletcher, J.M., Morris, R., Lyon, G. et al. (1997). Subtypes of dyslexia: an old problem revisited. In *Foundations of Reading Acquisition and Dyslexia. Implications for Early Intervention*, ed. B.A. Blachman, pp. 95–114. Mahwah, NJ: Lawrence Erlbaum.

Gaddes, W.H. & Edgell, D. (1993). *Learning Disabilities and Brain Function: a Neuropsychological Approach*, third edition. New York: Springer.

Galaburda, A.M. (ed.) (1993). *Dyslexia and Development: Neurobiological Aspects of Extra-ordinary Brains*. Cambridge, MA: Harvard University Press.

Galaburda, A.M. & Kemper, T.L. (1978). Cytoarchitectonic abnormalities in developmental dyslexia: a case study. *Annals of Neurology*, 6, 94–100.

Galaburda, A.M., Sherman, G.F., Rosen, G.D., Aboitiz, F., & Geschwind, N. (1985). Developmental dyslexia: four consecutive patients with cortical abnormalities. *Annals of Neurology*, 18, 222–33.

Geschwind, N. (1984). Cerebral dominance in biological perspective. *Neuropsychologia*, 22, 675–83.

Giedd, J.N., Rumsey, J.M., Castellanos, F.X. et al. (1996). A quantitative MRI study of the corpus callosum in children and adolescents. *Brain Research and Developmental Brain Research*, 91, 274–80.

Grace, G.M. & Spreen, O. (1994). Hemisphere-specific stimulation of L- and P-types: a replication study and a critical appraisal. In *The Balance Model of Dyslexia. Theoretical and Clinical Progress*, ed. R. Licht & G. Spyer, pp. 133–81. Assen, Netherlands: Van Gorcum.

Green, M.F., Bracha, H.S., Satz, P., & Christenson, C.D. (1994a). Preliminary evidence for an association between minor physical anomalies and second trimester neurodevelopment in schizophrenia. *Psychiatry Research*, 53, 119–27.

Green, M.F., Satz, P., & Christenson, C. (1994b). Minor physical anomalies in schizophrenia patients, and their siblings. *Schizophrenia Bulletin*, 20, 433–40.

Gross-Glenn, K., Duara, R., Yoshii, F. et al. (1990). PET scan studies: familial dyslexics. In *Perspectives on Dyslexia*, Vol. 1, ed. G.Th. Pavlidis, pp. 109–18. New York: Wiley.

Henninghausen, K., Remschmidt, H., & Warnke, A. (1994). Visual evoked potentials in boys with developmental dyslexia. *European Child and Adolescent Psychiatry*, 3, 72–81.

Hernadek, M.C.S. & Rourke, B.P. (1994). Principal identifying features of the syndrome of nonverbal learning disabilities in children. *Journal of Learning Disabilities*, 27, 144–54.

Hertzig, M.E. (1983). Temperament and neurological status. In *Developmental Neuropsychiatry*, ed. M. Rutter, pp. 164–80. New York: Guilford Press.

Hier, D.B., LeMay, M., Rosenberger, P.B., & Perlo, V.B. (1978). Developmental dyslexia: evidence of a subgroup with reversal of cerebral asymmetry. *Archives of Neurology*, 35, 90–2.

Hinshelwood, J. (1895). Word-blindness and visual memory. *Lancet*, 2, 1564–70.

Hinshelwood, J. (1917). *Congenital Word Blindness*. London: H.K. Lewis.

Hugdahl, K. (1993). Functional brain asymmetry, dyslexia, and immune disorders. In *Dyslexia and Development: Neurobiological Aspects of Extra-Ordinary Brains*, ed. A.M. Galaburda, pp. 133–54. Cambridge, MA: Harvard University Press.

Hugdahl, K., Synnevagt, B., & Satz, P. (1990). Immune and autoimmune disease in dyslexic children. *Neuropsychologia*, 28, 673–9.

Humphreys, P., Kaufmann, W.E., & Galaburda, A.M. (1990). Developmental dyslexia in women: neuropathological findings in three cases. *Annals of Neurology*, 28, 764–74.

Hynd, G.W. (1992). Neurological aspects of dyslexia: comment on the balance model. *Journal of Learning Disabilities*, 25, 110–12.

Hynd, G.W., Hooper, S.R., & Takahashi, T. (1992). Dyslexia and language-based learning disabilities. In *Textbook of Pediatric Neuropsychiatry*, ed. C.E. Coffey & R.A. Brumback, pp. 186–205. Washington, DC: American Psychiatric Press.

Hynd, G.W. & Semrud-Clikeman, M. (1989). Dyslexia and brain morphology. *Psychological Bulletin*, 106, 447–82.

Jariabkova, K., Hugdahl, K., & Glos, J. (1995). Immune disorders and handedness in dyslexic boys and their relatives. *Scandinavian Journal of Psychology*, 36, 355–62.

Jorm, A.F., Share, D.L., Maclean, R., & Matthews, R. (1986). Cognitive factors at school entry predictive of specific reading retardation and general reading backwardness: a research note. *Journal of Child Psychology and Psychiatry*, 27, 45–54.

Joschko, M. & Rourke, B.P. (1985). Neuropsychological subtypes of learning-disabled children who exhibit the ACID pattern on the WISC. In *Neuropsychology of Learning Disabilities. Essentials of Subtype Analysis*, ed. B.P. Rourke, pp. 65–88. New York: Guilford Press.

Kaneko, M., Uno, A., Kaga, M., Matsuda, H. et al. (1998). Cognitive neuropsychological and regional cerebral blood flow of a developmentally dyslexic child. *Journal of Child Neurology*, 13, 457–61.

Kussmaul, A. (1877). *Die Störungen der Sprache. Versuch einer Pathologie der Sprache*. Leipzig: Vogel.

Larsen, J.P., Hien, T., Lundberg, I., & Odegaard, H. (1990). MRI evaluation of the size and symmetry of the planum temporale in adolescents with developmental dyslexia. *Brain and Language*, 39, 289–301.

Lovett, M.W. (1984). A developmental perspective on reading dysfunction: accuracy and rate criteria in the subtyping of dyslexic children. *Brain and Language*, 22, 67–91.

Marshall, J.C. & Newcomb, F. (1973). Patterns of paralexia: a psycholinguistic approach. *Developmental Medicine and Child Neurology*, 2, 175–99.

Mattis, S., French, J.H., & Rapin, J. (1975). Dyslexia in children and young adults: three independent neuropsychological syndromes. *Developmental Medicine and Child Neurology*, 17, 150–63.

Morgan, A.E. & Hynd, G.W. (1998). Dyslexia, neurolinguistic ability, and anatomical variations on the planum temporale. *Neuropsychology Review*, 8, 79–93.

Morgan, P. (1896). A case of congenital word-blindness. *British Medical Journal*, 2, 1378.

Morris, R.D., Stuebing, K.K., Fletcher, J.M. et al. (1998). Subtypes of reading disability: variability around a phonological core. *Journal of Educational Psychology*, 90, 347–73.

Myklebust, H.R. (1975). Nonverbal learning disabilities: assessment and intervention. In *Progress in Learning Disabilities*, Vol. 3, ed. H.R. Myklebust, pp. 85–121. New York: Grune & Stratton.

National Joint Committee on Learning Disabilities (1998). Operationalizing the NJCLD definition of learning disabilities for ongoing assessment in schools. *Learning Disabilities Quarterly*, 21, 186–93.

Newby, R.F. & Lyon, G.R. (1991). Neuropsychological subtypes of learning disabilities. In *Neuropsychological Foundations of Learning Disabilities*, ed. J.E. Obrzut & G.W. Hynd, pp. 355–86. San Diego, CA: Academic Press.

Nicolson, R.J. & Fawcett, A.J. (1999). Developmental dyslexia: the role of the cerebellum. In *Dyslexia: Advances in Theory and Practice*, ed. I. Lundberg, F.E. Tonnessen, & I. Austad, pp. 54–68. Dordrecht, Netherlands: Kluwer.

Njiokiktjien, C. (1993). Neurological arguments for a joint developmental dysphasia–dyslexia syndrome. In *Dyslexia and Development: Neurobiological Aspects of Extra-Ordinary Brains*, ed. A.M. Galaburda, pp. 205–36. Cambridge, MA: Harvard University Press.

Njiokiktjien, C. & de Sonneville, L. (1994). Callosal size in children with learning disabilities. *Behavioral and Brain Research*, 64, 213–18.

Ojemann, G.A. (1989). Some brain mechanisms in reading. In *Brain and Reading*, ed. C. van Euler, I. Lundberg, & G. Lennarstrand, pp. 47–59. New York: Stockton Press.

Orton, S.T. (1928). Specific reading disability – strephosymbolia. *Journal of the American Medical Association*, 90, 1095–9.

Orton, S.T. (1937). *Reading, Writing, and Speech Problems in Children*. New York: Norton.

Ozonoff, S. & Miller, J.N. (1996). An exploration of right-hemisphere contributions to the pragmatic impairments of autism. *Brain and Language*, 52, 411–34.

Parsons, O. (1977). Human neuropsychology: the new phrenology. *Journal of Operational Psychiatry*, 8, 47–56.

Paulson, K. & O'Donnell, J.P. (1980). The relationship between minor physical anomalies and 'soft signs' of brain damage. *Perceptual and Motor Skills*, 51, 402–10.

Piven, J., Berthier, M.L., Starkstein, S.E., Nehme, E. et al. (1990). Magnetic resonance imaging evidence for a defect of cerebral cortical development in autism. *American Journal of Psychiatry*, 147, 734–9.

Prechtl, H.F.R. (1978). Minimal brain dysfunction syndrome and the plasticity of the nervous system. *Advances in Biological Psychiatry*, 1, 96–115.

Remschmidt, H., Schulte-Körne, G., & Henninghausen, K. (1998). What is specific about specific reading disorder. In *Perspectives on the Classification of Specific Developmental Disorders*, ed. J. Rispens, T.A. van Iperen, & W. Yule, pp. 126–32. Dordrecht, Netherlands: Kluwer.

Reschly, D.J. & Gresham, F.M. (1989). Current neuropsychological diagnosis of learning problems: a leap of faith. In *Handbook of Clinical Child Neuropsychology*, ed. C.R. Reynolds & E. Fletcher-Jantzen, pp. 503–20. New York: Plenum Press.

Rie, E.D. (1987). Soft signs in learning disabilities. In *Soft Neurological Signs*, ed. D.E. Tupper, pp. 201–24. Orlando, FL: Grune & Stratton.

Rispens, J. (1998). The validity of the category of specific developmental reading disorder. In *Perspectives on the Classification of Specific Developmental Disorders*, ed. J. Rispens, T.A. Van Yperen, & W. Yule, pp. 12–20. Dordrecht, Netherlands: Kluwer.

Rourke, B.P. (1985). *Neuropsychology of Learning Disabilities. Essentials of Subtype Analysis*. New York: Guilford Press.

Rourke, B.P. (1987). Syndrome of nonverbal learning disabilities: the final common pathway of white-matter disease/dysfunction? *Clinical Neuropsychologist*, 1, 209–34.

Rourke, B.P. (1990). Learning disability subtypes: a neuropsychological perspective. In *Perspectives on Dyslexia*, Vol. 1, *Neurology, Neuropsychology, and Genetics*, ed. G.T. Pavlidis, pp. 27–46. New York: Wiley.

Rourke, B.P. (ed.) (1995). *Syndrome of Nonverbal Learning Disabilities. Neurodevelopmental Manifestations*. New York: Guilford Press.

Rourke, B.P. & Conway, J.A. (1997). Disabilities of arithmetic and arithmetic reasoning: perspectives from neurology and neuropsychology. *Journal of Learning Disabilities*, 30, 34–46.

Rumsey, J.M. (1996). Neuroimaging in developmental dyslexia: a review and conceptualization. In *Neuroimaging: a Window to the Neurological Foundations of Learning and Behavior in Children*, ed. G.R. Lyon & J.M. Rumsey, pp. 57–77. Baltimore: Brookes.

Rumsey, J.M., Casanova, M., Mannheim, G.B. et al. (1996). Corpus callosum morphology, as measured with MRI, in dyslexic men. *Biological Psychiatry*, 39, 769–75.

Rumsey, J.M., Horwitz, B., Donahue, B.C., Nace, K., Maisog, J.M., & Andreason, P. (1997a). Phonological and orthographic components of word recognition: a PET–rCBF study. *Brain*, 120, 739–59.

Rumsey, J.M., Nace, K, Donahue, B., Wise, D., Maisog, J.M., & Andreason, P. (1997b). A positron emission tomography study of impaired word recognition and phonological processing in dyslexic men. *Archives of Neurology*, 54, 562–73.

Rumsey, J.M., Zametkin, A.J., Andreason, P. et al. (1994). Normal activation of frontotemporal language cortex in dyslexia, as measured with oxygen 15 positron emission tomography. *Archives of Neurology*, 51, 27–38.

Satz, P. (1990). Developmental dyslexia: an etiological reformulation. In *Perspectives on Dyslexia*, Vol. 1, *Neurology, Neuropsychology, and Genetics*, ed. G.T. Pavlidis, pp. 3–26. New York: Wiley.

Satz, P. (1991). The Dejerine hypothesis: implications for the etiological reformulation of developmental dyslexia. In *Neuropsychological Foundations of Learning Disabilities*, ed. J.E. Obrzut & G.W. Hynd, pp. 99–112. San Diego, CA: Academic Press.

Satz, P., Soper, H.V., & Orsini, D.L. (1988). Human hand preference. Three nondextral subtypes. In *Brain Lateralization in Children: Developmental Implications*, ed. D.L. Molfese & J.S. Segalowitz, pp. 281–7. New York: Guilford Press.

Schultz, R.T., Cho, N.K., Staib, L.H. et al. (1994). Brain morphology in normal and dyslexic children: the influence of sex and age. *Annals of Neurology*, 35, 732–42.

Shaywitz, S.E., Escobar, M.D., Shaywitz, B.A., Fletcher, J.M., & Makuch, R. (1992). Evidence that dyslexia may represent the lower tail of a normal distribution of reading ability. *New England Journal of Medicine*, 326, 145–50.

Shaywitz, S.E., Shaywitz, B.A., Pugh, K.R. et al. (1998). Functional disruption in the organization of the brain for reading in dyslexia. *Proceedings of the National Academy of Science, Neurobiology*, 95, 2636–41.

Smith, S., Branford, D., Collacott, R.A., Cooper, S.A., & McGrother, C. (1996). Prevalence and cluster typology of maladaptive behaviors in a geographically defined population of adults with learning disabilities. *British Journal of Psychiatry*, 169, 219–27.

Soper, H.V., Cicchetti, D.V., Satz, P., Light, R., & Orsini, D.L. (1988). Null hypothesis disrespect in neuropsychology: dangers of alpha and beta errors. *Journal of Clinical and Experimental Neuropsychology*, 10, 255–70.

Spreen, O. (1988). *Learning Disabled Children Growing Up*. New York: Oxford University Press.

Spreen, O. (1989a). The relationship between learning disability, emotional disorders, and neuropsychology: some results and observations. *Journal of Clinical and Experimental Neuropsychology*, 11, 117–40.

Spreen, O. (1989b). Learning disability, neurology, and long-term outcome: some implications for the individual and for society. *Journal of Clinical and Experimental Neuropsychology*, 11, 389–408.

Spreen, O. & Haaf, R.G. (1986). Empirically derived learning disability subtypes: a replication attempt and longitudinal patterns over 15 years. *Journal of Learning Disabilities*, 19, 170–80.

Spreen, O., Risser, A.H., & Edgell, D. (1995). *Developmental Neuropsychology*, 2nd edition. New York: Oxford University Press.

St. Marseille, A. & Braun, C.M. (1994). Comments on the immune aspects of the Geschwind–Behan–Galaburda model and of the article of Bryden, McManus, and Bulman-Fleming. *Brain and Cognition*, 26, 281–90.

Stanovich, K.E., Siegel, L.S., Gottardo, A. et al. (1997). Subtypes of developmental dyslexia: differences in phonological and orthographic coding. In *Foundations of Reading Acquisition and Dyslexia. Implications for Early Intervention*, ed. B.A. Blachman, pp. 115–42. Mahwah, NJ: Lawrence Erlbaum.

Strauss, A. & Lehtinen, L. (1947). *Psychopathology and Education of the Brain-injured Child*. New York: Grune & Stratton.

Temple, C.M., Reeves, M.A., & Villaroya, O.O. (1990). Reading in callosal agenesis. *Brain and Language*, 39, 235–53.

Van den Honert, D. (1977). A neuropsychological technique for training dyslexics. *Journal of Learning Disabilities*, 10, 21–7.

Van der Leij, A., van Daal, V.H.P., & Vieijra, J.P.M. (1998). Neuropsychological treatment of dyslexia: a critical appraisal. In *Child Neuropsychology, Reading Disability and More. A Tribute to Dirk J. Bakker*, ed. R. Licht, A. Bouma, W. & W. Koops, pp. 145–60. Delft, Netherlands: Eburon.

Van der Vlugt, H. (1998). Balancing the scale of the balance. In *Child Neuropsychology: Reading Disability and More*, ed. R. Licht, A. Bouma, & W. Koops, pp. 127–44. Delft, Netherlands: Eburon.

Van Strien, J.W., Bouma, A., & Bakker, D.J. (1987). Birth stress, autoimmune disease, and handedness. *Journal of Clinical and Experimental Neuropsychology*, 9, 775–80.

Waldrop, M.F., Bell, R.Q., & Goering, J.D. (1976). Minor physical anomalies and inhibited behavior in elementary school girls. *Journal of Child Psychology and Psychiatry*, 17, 113.

Waldrop, M.F., Pedersen, F.A., & Bell, R.C. (1968). Minor physical anomalies and behavior in school children. *Child Development*, 39, 391–9.

Willems, G., Noel, A., & Evrard, P. (1972). L'examen neuropediatrique des fonctions d'apprentic-age chez l'enfant en age prescolaire. *Revue Francaise d'Hygiene et de Medicine Scolaire et Universitaire*, 32, 3–18.

Yeo, R.A., Gangestad, S.W., Thoma, R., Shaw, P., & Repa, K. (1997). Developmental instability and cerebral lateralization. *Neuropsychology*, 11, 552–61.

10

The Halstead–Reitan Neuropsychological Test Battery: research findings and clinical application

Ralph M. Reitan and Deborah Wolfson

The term *learning disabilities*, as a categorical entity, is attributed to Samuel Kirk (Kirk & Bateman, 1962), although there had been many earlier studies of academic underachievers. The history of neuropsychology, with its emphasis on brain damage or impairment as a basis for limiting higher-level abilities, made it reasonable to postulate a biological basis for learning disabilities. It must be recognized, however, that a host of factors (including genetic and maturational variables, auditory and/or visual impairments, differences in rates of development, conflicts in handedness and footedness, variations in cognitive style, deviant patterns of cerebral dominance, emotional and psychiatric problems, and, perhaps the most common cause, poor teaching) have been implicated. Aware of these many possible etiological influences, Spreen (1976) favored a 'multiple cause – multiple outcome interaction model.' Learning disabilities obviously represent a complex condition, and many factors can be contributory.

Rourke's research program

The first systematic program of investigation based on a modern neuro-psychological approach was instituted by Rourke (1975). (See Spreen's related discussion of Rourke's work in Chapter 9, where the focus is on Rourke's theory rather than on his research methodology.) From the beginning, Rourke included subjects who were performing very poorly in one or more academic subjects, but excluded children with mental retardation, emotional disturbances, cultural deprivation, and defective hearing or vision as *primary* factors, despite poor academic progress. McCarthy and McCarthy (1969), following the predisposition to presume cerebral dysfunction as a critical factor in producing learning disabilities, had recommended the use of exclusionary procedures. They believed that cerebral dysfunction was implicated if other possible etiological factors could be eliminated. Rourke, however, felt that scientific standards required positive criteria to identify the behavioral or neuropsychological characteristics of children with learning disabilities. In his studies, he used subjects with definitive evidence of cerebral disease or damage, even though they might be academically impaired, for comparison with learningdisabled children who did not have evidence of brain damage. Thus, Rourke's aim was to produce research results that characterized children with learning disabilities as a relatively unique category, distinct from other etiologies that might affect a child's academic capability.

In order to place this research in a neuropsychological frame of reference, Rourke utilized investigative tests and measures that had established sensitivity to cerebral damage or dysfunction and met methodological criteria for demonstrating brain-related (neuropsychological) deficits. He recognized the need for comprehensive neuropsychological testing in order to assess the entire range of functions to characterize a category (learning disability) that was undoubtedly complex and variable from one subject to another. The test battery Rourke routinely used included a pertinent version of Wechsler's scales to evaluate general intelligence, the Halstead–Reitan Neuropsychological Test Battery for Older Children (HRNTB–OC), the Reitan–Indiana Neuropsychological Test Battery for Young Children, the Kløve–Matthews Motor Steadiness Battery, and measures of academic achievement.

Rourke was also concerned that the research battery he used be susceptible to analysis using various methods of inference to identify brain damage. Reitan (1966), in describing his research program investigating the neuropsychological effects of brain lesions in human beings, described four methods of inference (or techniques for deducing brain damage) which he felt it was necessary to use in a complementary manner to draw valid inferences about individuals. Rourke was also concerned that the research battery he used would produce research data that related explicitly to individual children (as contrasted with research findings that stood alone as separate points of information). As Reitan (1967) had noted earlier, Rourke made it quite clear that an individual's level of performance on any test needed to be supplemented by additional approaches. One of these approaches, or methods of inference, utilized tests that could produce pathognomonic signs (indications of impaired performance) that occurred essentially only among people with cerebral damage. Rourke realized that even though these signs did not occur among normal subjects, they might also fail to occur among a number of children with brain damage. However, if a child did demonstrate a pathognomonic sign, it would be a reliable indication of brain impairment. In the test batteries that he developed for both older and younger children, Reitan had explicitly included a number of tests that are able to elicit pathognomonic signs.

Reitan, recognizing that brain-damaged children might be significantly impaired in one area of function as compared with other areas, included another method of inference that assesses intra-individual deviations among test results. This method, sometimes referred to as the differential score approach, has a long history in the evaluation of the effects of brain damage among adults (Babcock, 1930; Hunt, 1943). A final method of clinical neuropsychological inference that Rourke wished to investigate also concerned intra-individual differences. This approach used sensory–perceptual and motor tasks to evaluate comparative performances on the two sides of the body. The brain is 'wired' in such a manner that one side of the brain principally controls both input (sensory function) and output (motor function) of the opposite side of the body. Many people who sustain brain impairment have a differential degree of damage on one side of the brain or the other and, correspondingly, a greater degree of impairment on one side of the body than the other. A striking degree of intra-individual disparity in sensory–perceptual and motor functions serves almost as a pathognomonic sign of brain damage in both adults and children (Reitan & Wolfson, 1992, 1993). Rourke and his colleagues (1973b) studied children with learning disabilities who were selected because of poor performances on one side of the body or the other, and Rourke (1975) drew the following conclusion from these studies:

The results of these studies indicate that when children with learning disabilities are separated into groups solely on the basis of patterns of lateralized deficits on a complex psychomotor task, their performances are, in many respects, similar to those exhibited by adult subjects with well-documented cerebral lesions.

Rourke and his colleagues also performed a series of studies using the differential score approach to identify patterns that characterize children with learning disabilities. In one series of studies (Rourke & Telegdy, 1971; Rourke, Young, & Flewelling, 1971; Rourke, Dietrich, & Young, 1973a), children with learning disabilities were divided into groups according to their patterns of performance on the Wechsler Intelligence Scale for Children (WISC). These investigators found that older children (in the 9–14-year age range) with learning disabilities demonstrated Verbal IQ/Performance IQ discrepancies that were 'quite similar to that which would be expected (on the basis of adult data) if they were experiencing the effects of cerebral dysfunction' (p. 916). Younger children, however, did not show these same clear-cut patterns of ability deficits.

Rourke and Finlayson (1975) investigated differential levels of performance on Parts A and B of the Trail Making Test, having noted that Reitan and Tarshes (1959) had published findings indicating that adults with left cerebral lesions performed quite poorly on Part B as compared with their own performances on Part A, whereas the reverse relationship occurred with right cerebral lesions.

The approach used by Rourke and Finlayson was to establish three groups of learning-disabled children in accordance with their differential performances on the two parts of the Trail Making Test. Thus, there was one group of children who performed normally on both Parts A and B, a second group of children who performed normally on Part A but did poorly on Part B, and a third group of children who performed poorly on both Parts A and B. Rourke and Finlayson compared these three groups and reported that the children 'demonstrated rather clearly that specific patterns of performance on the Trail Making Test were related to consistent differences on a number of verbal, auditory–perceptual, visual–spatial, and psychomotor abilities' (p. 916). In addition, children who performed poorly on Part B of the Trail Making Test demonstrated deficiencies on other measures that would imply left cerebral dysfunction, whereas children who performed poorly on Part A showed, in general, a pattern of relatively deficient right cerebral functions.

Rourke and his colleagues carried these research efforts much further, always being careful to investigate the applicability of research findings to the interpretation of results for individual children. These research results, and their application in individual cases, have been extensively reported (Rourke et al., 1983; Rourke, 1985, 1989, 1991; Rourke, Fisk, & Strang, 1986; Rourke & Fuerst, 1991). These articles report on the identification of subtypes of children with learning disabilities and explore differential adaptational capabilities and problems in psychosocial functioning of children with learning disabilities.

In one of these reports, Rourke (1989) describes in detail a category of children with nonverbal learning disabilities. Because our orientation to learning is so heavily weighted toward academic deficiencies and verbal limitations, this may well seem to be a very surprising category. However, children who have principally nonverbal deficits that limit their academic development constitute a very important category, and demonstrate: (1) the broad base of dysfunction (in contrast to a delimited area of deficit corresponding with involvement of the language area of the cerebral cortex) that would be expected to occur when adverse circumstances cause brain impairment or damage; and (2) the integrative nature of abilities dependent upon the biological condition of the brain, even to the extent that basic impairment of nonverbal abilities may have a generalizing effect and influence many other aspects of adaptive skills, including academic progress.

Dean's research program

Dean and his colleagues (Batchelor & Dean, 1991) also developed and pursued a research program aimed toward gaining an improved understanding of learning disabilities. They pointed out that the National Joint Committee for Learning Disabilities noted that the learning disorders 'are intrinsic to the individual and presumed to be due to a central nervous system dysfunction' (Hamill et al., 1981). Dean and his colleagues felt that development of knowledge that would be sufficient to diagnose learning disorders would require identification of brain-related neuropsychological functions. Their research program was conceptualized and implemented on this basis.

Dean and his associates felt that it was necessary to administer a standardized battery of tests to all children in their studies in order to develop a replicable research program. They selected the HRNTB–OC, the Wechsler Intelligence Scale for Children–Revised (WISC–R), the Wide Range Achievement Test (WRAT), and Reitan's Lateral Dominance Examination. All of their subjects had evidence of learning disabilities, but no subject was included who had diagnosed neurologic or psychiatric disorders. Learning disability was established in accordance with criteria stated in Public Law 94-142, based on decisions made by a multidisciplinary team of educational specialists.

The principal areas of investigation in the research program conducted by Dean and his associates included the nature of the relationship between severity of academic achievement deficits and neuropsychological dysfunctions, the influence of intelligence and age on neuropsychological measures, and the neuropsychological correlates of functional capabilities in reading, spelling, and arithmetic. These researchers also investigated the possibility of establishing subgroups of children with learning deficits. They used two approaches: (1) to establish subtypes on the basis of clinical observations and patterns of relationships among test scores, and (2) to subject a range of neuropsychological measurements to various statistical techniques such as Q-factor analysis and cluster analysis.

Using the first approach, Batchelor, Dean, and Williams (1989) formed groups of learning-disabled children in accordance with discrepancies between expected grade-equivalent performances and actual grade-equivalent scores earned on each of the three WRAT subtests. Children were grouped according to three levels: current grade level or higher, grade level one year below expected grade-equivalent performance, and grade level more than one year below expected grade-equivalent performance. A range of neuropsychological variables was then used in a discriminant analysis to predict group membership for each individual. This procedure was successful in predicting only 32% of the cases, with false-positives and false-negatives occurring in each of the three groups (which were composed according to differences between WRAT scores and grade level). The results appeared to be of little clinical use in characterizing subgroups of children with learning problems.

As a second step in this study, the investigators reorganized the subjects according to the severity of their deficits (marginal to mild, moderate, and severe) in reading, spelling, and arithmetic. A discriminant function analysis accurately classified 64% of the children with severe deficiencies and 63% of the children with moderate deficiencies; however, only 25% of the marginally to mildly deficient subjects were identified correctly. These results suggested that when severity of deficits was considered (as contrasted with type of deficit), neuropsychological dysfunction correlated more closely with academic deficits (Davis, Dean, & Krug, 1989).

A host of studies have used statistical methods to group either tests or subjects according to neuropsychological findings, but the results of these investigations have been characterized by a considerable degree of variability. Reasons for variability are not unexpected, considering differences in the groups of children evaluated, variations in tests, and differences in statistical procedures. In addition, however, there is a significant question concerning the degree to which any resulting subgroups of learning-disabled children who have been identified using these statistical procedures would actually fit clinically meaningful categories.

Batchelor, Kixmiller, and Dean (1990) used a multiregression procedure to analyze data from the HRNTB–OC, the WISC–R, and the WRAT. A canonical analysis of the data from the same tests was performed by Batchelor and Dean (1989). These studies showed a similarity among tests that predicted reading and spelling performance. The tests that demonstrated a significant predictive value for both Reading and Spelling Achievement scores fell in the areas of verbal attention and short-term memory, remote verbal memory, symbolic language integration, nonverbal concept formation, and motor skills involving strength of the dominant upper extremity and fine-motor speed and dexterity of the nondominant upper extremity. Additional analyses, however, suggested that when reading and spelling performances were combined into a single score, the neuropsychological relationships with performances in these academic areas were diminished (Batchelor et al., 1990). The authors concluded that reading and spelling, from a neuropsychological point of view, should be viewed as separate functions which share some common elements.

These investigators also studied the neuropsychological aspects of arithmetic deficits, concentrating not only on adequacy of performance, but also on differences and similarities in results when data were based upon verbal arithmetic performance (WISC–R performances) and written arithmetic (WRAT performances). A number of neuropsychological abilities was significantly linked with both oral and written arithmetic performance, but written arithmetic performance was most closely related to measures of nonverbal attention and immediate spatial memory. Verbal arithmetic tasks, however, appeared to depend more heavily upon verbal facility, abstract verbal reasoning, nonverbal short-term memory, and nonverbal concept formation. These investigators concluded that both verbal and nonverbal functions are required to solve arithmetic problems, and that both verbal and written arithmetic performances appear to involve the functions of both the right and left cerebral hemispheres.

It is interesting to consider these results with relation to findings reported on adult subjects who had the advantage of normal development through childhood and then sustained a lateralized cerebral lesion in adulthood. Children with learning disabilities develop academic abilities using brain functions that may be deviant in certain respects, even though there is no frank evidence of neurological disease or damage. In a study of adult subjects with lateralized cerebral lesions, Wheeler and Reitan (1962) found that about 75% of those who demonstrated dyscalculia had left hemisphere lesions and 25% had right hemisphere lesions.

These findings would still suggest that both hemispheres may be involved in arithmetical processes, but when one hemisphere is damaged, the great preponderance of patients with dyscalculia are those with left hemisphere damage. It is entirely possible that the organization of behavioral capabilities in the brains of learning-disabled children is different, at least to an extent, from that in the brains of people who have had a normal brain in the developmental years. This seems clearly to be the case among children who have sustained lateralized lesions early in life (see Reitan & Wolfson, 1992).

O'Donnell's research program

O'Donnell (1991) and his colleagues instituted a program oriented toward producing both research and clinical findings in the investigation of learning disabilities in adolescents and young adults. O'Donnell noted that early postulates, based on studies of patients with acquired aphasia, suggested that focal left cerebral lesions might be responsible for the difficulty encountered by children in acquiring reading, spelling, and computational skills. However, most children with learning disabilities did not demonstrate any positive findings on the physical neurological examination or show any evidence of major focal lesions of the brain on imaging procedures. A second hypothesis related to 'developmental lag,' which suggested that children with academic problems were only a little delayed in the development of their abilities to master academic subject matter, and that they could, in time, outgrow their academic difficulties.

O'Donnell pointed out that many studies, based upon longitudinal evaluations as well as other procedures, have indicated quite clearly that many children with learning disabilities have difficulties that persist into adulthood. In their study of individuals who had learning disabilities in young adulthood, O'Donnell, Kurtz, and Ramanaiah (1983) interpreted their results as reflecting the same kind of psychological deficits noted by Selz and Reitan (1979a) among children with learning disabilities. For these reasons, O'Donnell and his associates felt that comprehensive research and evaluation of adolescents and young adults with learning disabilities were required.

O'Donnell elected to adopt the HRNTB for Adults as his basic procedure for collecting neuropsychological test data, essentially for the same reasons as those cited by Rourke and Dean. As contrasted with the use of an individual test, or even a series of individual tests, there is a great advantage in understanding a person's comparative abilities on a series of tests to determine that person's comparative strengths and weaknesses, and to use this information to develop a remediation program that is appropriate for the individual. O'Donnell indicated that there were four purposes that were of significance for his research program:

1. To determine whether the HRNTB, together with some additional tests, would provide evidence of neuropsychological functions that might be relevant to the academic and learning deficiencies of young adults.

2. To determine whether these neuropsychological measures could differentiate among (a) normal young adults, (b) young adults who had been diagnosed as having learning disabilities, and (c) young adults who had sustained significant head injuries, in order to establish the validity of inferences about neuropsychological impairment in young adults with learning disabilities.

3. To determine whether the test results provided a basis for differentially identifying subgroups of learning-disabled young adults that might be of value in planning individually appropriate interventions.

4. To determine whether socioemotional factors are significant in determining the adjustmental status of young adults with learning disabilities.

O'Donnell and his colleagues studied a group of 233 applicants to a college support program for students with learning disabilities. These applicants had been independently diagnosed in primary or secondary grades as having learning disabilities, and these diagnoses appeared to have been continuingly relevant through high school. Although each subject met federal government criteria for the diagnosis of learning disabilities, the subjects were not all consistently impaired on objective measures of academic achievement. Full Scale IQ had been used as a standard with respect to scores earned on the WRAT, and 79% of these subjects had at least one score (Reading, Spelling, or Arithmetic) that was 15 or more standard-score points below his or her own Full Scale IQ. In this group, 83% had at least one WRAT score that was below the 20th percentile.

O'Donnell pointed out that this group might not be typical generally of young adults who have learning disabilities. Only 35% of the group had a WRAT Reading subtest score that was less than the 20th percentile, whereas 83% had deficient Spelling scores, and 72% had deficient Arithmetic scores. None of the subjects had a history of brain injury, seizures, sensory deficits, drug abuse, or severe emotional problems. The subjects had a mean age of 18.6 years and a mean Wechsler Adult Intelligence Scale (WAIS) Full Scale IQ of 103.4 (SD 9.6).

O'Donnell conducted a factor analysis of the tests that were administered (essentially the HRNTB for Adults plus a few additional tests) to determine whether the emerging factors had any significant relevance to learning disabilities. Six factors accounted for 92.3% of the total variance, although the last two factors were not sufficiently supported to be subject to interpretation. O'Donnell interpreted the first factor as 'possibly characterized by nonverbal reasoning.' The second factor 'seemed to reflect deficits in auditory processing abilities.' The third factor, based principally on tests that reflected motor functions, was clearly a motor-abilities factor. The fourth factor received significant loadings from measures of sensory–perceptual skills plus a measure of visual–motor abilities and was interpreted as representing a sensory–motor factor. O'Donnell interpreted these results as suggesting that the measurements in the neuropsychological test battery were relevant to deficiencies demonstrated by people with learning disabilities.

The next step in the analysis of the research data concerned intercorrelations of measures from the neuropsychological test battery and scores from the WAIS and the WRAT. Scores were correlated for each of the six factors, scores from the Verbal and Performance subtests of the WAIS, and standard scores from the WRAT. These correlations were minimal, suggesting that the WAIS and WRAT measures were relatively independent of the neuropsychological test scores. However, correlation of a combined score for the six factors with a combined score for Picture Completion, Picture Arrangement, Block Design, and Object Assembly subtests from the WAIS yielded a correlation of .60.

Correlations between WRAT scores and scores for factors one through six were generally minimal, except for a correlation of .46 between Reading and the factor representing Nonverbal Reasoning, and a correlation of .40 between Spelling and the same factor of Nonverbal Reasoning. Correlations between the WRAT Arithmetic score and factors one through six were minimal.

The major findings of interest in O'Donnell's report concerned the sensitivity of the neuropsychological tests in differentiating between groups of normal, learning-disabled, and head-injured young adults. O'Donnell had noted that in previous studies both learning-disabled and brain-damaged children had lower IQs than normal children, and felt that it would be advantageous to equate IQ values in the groups that he studied. It should be noted, however, that Wechsler IQ values have repeatedly been found to be dependent variables with relation to brain damage and, in all probability, represent part of the picture of neuropsychological impairment. Thus, elevating IQ values for learning-disabled people and brain-damaged people would, to the extent that these variables were correlated with neuropsychological measures, diminish the differences between the groups in terms of neuropsychological test findings as well. Nevertheless, even though O'Donnell's normal, learning-disabled, and head-injured groups were matched for Full Scale IQ, he found very striking differences between the groups on neuropsychological measures. O'Donnell performed a linear discriminant function analysis in evaluation of the test scores for subjects representing these three groups, and found that 92% of *all* subjects were correctly classified. A breakdown among the three groups indicated that correct classification occurred in 100% of the normal subjects, 93% of the learning-disabled subjects, and 80% of the head-injured subjects. Seven percent of the learning-disabled subjects and 7% of the head-injured subjects were misclassified as normal, whereas 13% of the head-injured subjects were classified as learning disabled. The Halstead Impairment Index was particularly effective in differentiating subjects among the three groups. Using an Impairment Index of 0.4 as a cut-off point, 97% of normal subjects were below this point and 97% of the head-injured subjects were above it. Using this same cut-off point, 42% of the learning-disabled subjects scored in the impaired range. The learning-disabled subjects therefore occupied an intermediate position between the normal subjects and the subjects with significant traumatic brain injuries, with a substantial proportion of the learning-disabled subjects experiencing a degree of neuropsychological impairment.

O'Donnell summarized the results of Phillips' (1986) doctoral dissertation in which she cluster-analyzed the test protocols of 163 subjects (143 men and 20 women) who were applicants for the Learning Disability College Support Program. This analysis was based principally upon tests included in the HRNTB, with the addition of a few other tests. Her analysis yielded five clusters: (1) normal test scores, (2) auditory processing deficits, but normal results on visual–spatial measures, (3) spatial processing deficits, but normal results on auditory and language measures, (4) global deficits, and (5) language-processing deficits.

These results suggest that adults with learning disabilities demonstrate a variety of neuropsychological patterns, emphasizing the diversified nature of this condition as it is reflected in neuropsychological functions. Although a number of categories may be identified through the use of statistical analytical processes, our contention is that every individual with learning disabilities, if examined over a sufficient range of functions, will show a unique configuration of test scores that must be respected. Statistical methods of categorization may have investigational or heuristic value, but we must never forget that every human being is an individual, and the full range of individuality should be recognized in dealing clinically and therapeutically with each person.

O'Donnell also summarized the findings of Leicht (1987), who used Lanyon's Personality Screening Inventory (PSI) (Lanyon, 1978) to evaluate the personality and social functioning of normal young adults and young adults with learning disabilities.

Comparisons of the normal and learning-disabled subjects, using linear discriminant function analyses of the PSI data, showed that the profiles for the two groups were significantly different ($p < 0.001$). The learning-disabled group consistently had higher scores on the PSI scales, but the accuracy with which the test scores allocated subjects to their appropriate groups was only moderately satisfactory, with a correct classification of 72.7% of the normal and 67.1% of the learning-disabled subjects. The PSI severity index correctly classified 74.4% of the normal, but only 52% of the learning-disabled subjects.

Leicht also performed a cluster analysis of the PSI scores for the learning-disabled subjects, which yielded six clusters. These findings therefore suggested that learning-disabled young adults fall into a range of categories with respect to personality/social problems. The first cluster suggested the presence of impulsive, socially dominant behavior with a disregard for social conventions (extroverted, social nonconformists). The second cluster included people who tended to deny negative feelings and view themselves as well-adjusted (defensively adjusted). The third category included people whose test results suggested that they were overly sensitive, had poor interpersonal skills, and were anxious and dissatisfied with the world (alienated, anxious nonconformists). The fourth cluster was composed of people with no clinically significant scores (normal subjects). The fifth and sixth clusters were determined by a single high-scaled score, with the fifth cluster suggesting a degree of social isolation and the sixth cluster being similar to the first cluster, with profiles that suggested extroverted, anxious nonconformists. As might be expected, these results indicated that young adults with learning disabilities tended to show a degree of personality and social problems, but problems of this type appear to be rather diversified.

Individuals who fell into these various clusters were also studied in relation to evidence of academic skill deficits, and no meaningful differences between the groups were found. The neuropsychological subtypes previously found by Phillips (1986) were also compared to the PSI severity index, and analysis of the data yielded no differences in neuropsychological subtests with respect to personality and social problems.

With regard to his findings in studying young adults with learning disabilities, principally using the HRNTB, O'Donnell said:

> The present results showed that the neuropsychological test battery defines academically relevant constructs, it accurately discriminates LD from normal young adults, it shows that a proportion (perhaps as many as 40%) of LD young adults exhibit mild neuropsychological dysfunction, and it shows that the dysfunctional LD fall into defined subgroups (Phillips' Subtypes III and IV) with predictable educational deficits. Although some LD were maladjusted (Leicht's Subtypes III and V), these maladjustments were unrelated to academic skills or to neuropsychological status. In other words, the present research seems to support the continued viability of the neurological hypothesis.

O'Donnell went on to say that 'the present findings confirm the validity of the Halstead–Reitan Neuropsychological Test Battery in the assessment of young adults with learning disabilities.'

Reitan and Wolfson's research program

Research and clinical work on the neuropsychology of children with learning and academic problems was begun by Reitan shortly after the HRNTB–OC was completed in 1955 (Reitan, 1974). The HRNTB was initially developed according to the model later enunciated by Reitan and Wolfson (and described below), being driven by the deficits actually shown by children with brain disease or damage. Thus, in a very real sense, the model of neuropsychological functions proposed by Reitan and Wolfson represents a conceptual framework that was not merely derived theoretically, but instead was determined by empirical observation, testing, and clinical work with brain-damaged children. In fact, each child enrolled in every research study was also treated as a clinical case in order to promote the prospect of transferring research findings into clinically meaningful and applicable information.

Because the Reitan–Wolfson model was also the framework within which our studies of academic and learning deficits were performed, it is necessary to provide the reader with a description of the model (which applies to adults as well as children) before proceeding with discussion of research and clinical findings in the area of learning disabilities.

The Reitan–Wolfson model of neuropsychological functioning provides a conceptual framework that is implemented using the Halstead–Reitan Battery for individual assessment complemented by REHABIT, an extensive set of cognitive rehabilitation materials for remediation of the neuropsychological deficits. As descriptions and integration of the Reitan–Wolfson model with assessment procedures using the Halstead–Reitan Battery and brain-retraining procedures have been discussed in detail in other publications (Reitan & Wolfson, 1988a, 1988c, 1992), this model will be described only briefly at this point.

As noted in Fig. 10.1, the initial aspect of this model is concerned with input of sensory information to the brain. The neuropsychological response cycle first requires input to the brain from the external environment via one or more of the sensory avenues. Primary sensory areas are located in each cerebral hemisphere, indicating that this level of central processing is widely represented in the cerebral cortex, and involves the temporal, parietal, and occipital areas particularly.

Once information reaches the brain, the first step in central processing is the 'registration phase,' and represents alertness, attention, continued concentration, and the ability to screen incoming information with relation to prior experiences (immediate, intermediate, and remote memory). Alertness and concentration are necessary for all types of problem-solving, and appear to be generally distributed throughout the brain.

After initial registration of incoming material, the brain proceeds to process verbal information in the left cerebral hemisphere and visual–spatial information in the right cerebral hemisphere. At this point, the specialized functions

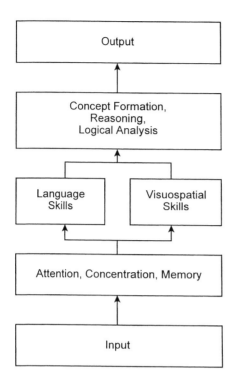

Fig. 10.1. A simplified graphic representation of the Reitan–Wolfson model of neuropsychological functioning.

(left-brain/right-brain) of the two cerebral hemispheres become operational.

The left cerebral hemisphere, as it develops neuropsychological capabilities, is particularly involved in speech and language functions, or the use of language symbols for communication purposes. It is important to remember that deficits may involve quite simple kinds of speech and language skills or, conversely, may involve the sophisticated higher-level aspects of verbal communication. It must also be recognized that language functions may be impaired in terms of expressive capabilities, receptive functions, or both.

Right cerebral functions particularly center on spatial abilities (mediated principally by vision, but also by touch and auditory function) and manipulatory skills. Again, it must be kept in mind that an individual may be impaired in the expressive aspects or receptive aspects of visual–spatial functioning, or both. It must also be remembered that we live in a world of time and space as well as in a world of verbal communication. People with impairment of visual–spatial abilities are often severely handicapped in terms of efficiency of functioning in a practical, everyday sense, and this type of impairment may have general effects which impinge on learning and development of academic skills.

In the Reitan–Wolfson model, the highest level of central processing is represented by abstraction, reasoning, concept formation, and logical analysis skills. Research evidence indicates that these functions are generally represented throughout the cerebral cortex (Doehring & Reitan, 1962). The generality and importance of abstraction and reasoning skills may be suggested biologically by the fact that these skills are distributed throughout the cerebral cortex rather than being limited as a specialized function of one cerebral hemisphere or a particular area within a cerebral hemisphere. Generalized distribution of abstraction abilities throughout the cerebral cortex may also be significant in the interaction of abstraction with more specific abilities (such as language) that are represented more focally.

Impairment at the highest level of central processing has profound implications for the adequacy of neuropsychological functioning. People with such deficits have lost a great deal of the ability to profit from experience in a meaningful, logical, and organized manner. In casual or superficial contact, however, such people may appear to be relatively intact, because the nature of their deficits is general rather than specific. Because of the close relationship between organized behavior and memory, these individuals often complain of memory problems and are grossly inefficient in practical, everyday tasks. They are not able to organize their activities properly, and frequently direct their energy to elements of a situation that are not appropriate to the nature of the problem. In everyday behavior, deficits of this kind augment any weaknesses that the child may have in areas of attention and focused concentration.

This nonappropriate activity, often followed by an eventual withdrawal from attempting to deal with problem situations, also constitutes a major component of what is frequently (and imprecisely) referred to as a 'personality' change. Upon clinical inquiry, such changes are often found to consist of erratic and poorly planned behavior, deterioration of personal hygiene, a lack of concern and understanding for others, etc. When examined neuropsychologically, it is often discovered that these behaviors are largely represented by cognitive changes at the highest level of central processing and are misclassified as primary emotional problems.

Finally, in solving individual problems or expressing intelligent behavior, it is important to recognize that the sequential element from input to output frequently involves an interaction of the various aspects of central processing. Visual–spatial skills, for example, are closely dependent upon registration and continued attention to incoming material of a visual–spatial nature, but analysis and understanding of the problem also involve the highest element of central processing, represented by concept formation, reasoning, and logical analysis. Exactly the same kind of relationship between areas of functioning in the Reitan–Wolfson model determines one's effectiveness in using verbal and language skills. In fact, the speed and facility with which an individual carries out such interactions within the content categories of central processing probably in themselves represent a significant aspect of efficiency in brain functioning.

The final aspect of the model is represented by output, or the motor response that is required to implement the input (observation of the problem) and central processing (analysis of the problem). It must be remembered that the motor response, in and of itself, is not usually the critical element of neuropsychological efficiency or adaptability. The central processes, which guide the response, usually represent the critical competencies. Thus, the child with learning disabilities may have adequate sensory function and adequate muscular function to perform, but the limiting competencies lie in the linkage between these two areas, namely central processing capabilities. The HRNTB was devised to provide an understanding of these immensely complex linkages as they exist for the individual child.

Some basic principles of neuropsychology

If impairment of brain functions, even though subtle and perhaps relatively mild in most cases of learning disability, is a factor in producing limited aptitude for academic achievement, it is important to review certain basic principles that have been learned through the study of children with known damage of the brain.

Principle 1

The field of child neuropsychology has been plagued for many years by what is referred to as the Kennard principle. This principle states that, because of the plasticity of the immature brain, and the great potential for recovery of functions, the effects of cerebral damage in infancy or early childhood are far less impairing than the effects of brain damage sustained in adulthood (following maturation of brain–behavior relationships).

The Kennard principle was based on the work of Margaret Kennard in the late 1930s and early 1940s (Kennard, 1936, 1938, 1942). Kennard imposed brain lesions in infantile and adult monkeys and found, in general, that there was a lesser degree of deficit and greater recovery of motor functions in the infantile monkeys. Although Kennard herself did not generalize this finding to human beings, and even recognized that the findings did not apply perfectly in differentiating infantile and adult monkeys, there was a strong tendency among psychologists and neuroscientists to generalize the principle. In fact, Rudel (1978) cited the well-known neuropsychologist Hans-Lukas Teuber as having commented during a major conference on the effects of head trauma in the 1960s that if one were to sustain a brain injury, it would be wise to have the head injury in childhood rather than in adulthood in order to escape deleterious and impairing effects.

Reitan and Wolfson (1992) reviewed, in considerable detail, the literature concerning the effects of infantile versus adult brain damage, and found that although a number of neuroscientists had begun to question its applicability to humans, a rather pervasive belief in the Kennard principle continued to exist in the 1980s. Reitan and Wolfson concluded that the Kennard principle, instead of being a rule to follow, is in most cases quite misleading with respect to human beings. Evaluations of children who had sustained infantile brain damage provide evidence of quite significant and serious neuropsychological impairment, apparently resulting from the fact that the child's impaired brain provided an equally impaired potential for developing normal intellectual and cognitive abilities. In order to evaluate the generally impairing effects of early cerebral damage, Reitan and Wolfson (1992) performed a very simple test. They identified the first ten children in their files who had a brain injury that dated back to the time of the child's birth. Their IQ values, when tested as older children, were as follows: 34 (estimated), the next child was too impaired to test, 91, 46, 82, 46, 52, 73, 57, and 50. Omitting the child who was so impaired that it was not possible to test him, these values yield a mean Full Scale IQ of 59 (mean Verbal IQ, 63.56; mean Performance IQ, 60.44).

Although many neuroscientists have emphasized the plasticity of the immature brain and the potential for recovery (based upon neurophysiological and neurochemical studies at the cellular level as well as investigations using lower animals), it would appear to be more pertinent to direct the question to the actual development of human beings. The results of such inquiries indicate that development of higher-level intellectual and cognitive functions is generally difficult to achieve for children with damaged brains, particularly if the damage is substantial.

Principle 2

One factor that is significant in determining neuropsychological test results for individual children relates to the age at which brain damage was sustained (and the reciprocal factor, the duration of cerebral damage).

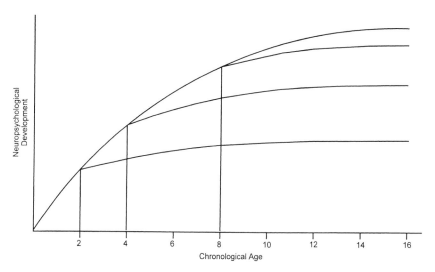

Fig. 10.2. Schematic illustration of a theoretical postulate regarding the effect on neuro-psychological development of cerebral damage sustained at different ages.

The earlier brain damage has been sustained (other factors being equal), the more severe the neuropsychological impairment (see Reitan & Wolfson, 1992, for a more complete discussion). If neuropsychological development is essentially complete before brain damage is sustained, the limitation of future development of neuropsychological function is less significant. However, in this latter case the child comes closer to the typical situation of adults who sustain cerebral damage – he or she suffers impairment of previously developed abilities.

Figure 10.2 provides an illustration of the general effects of cerebral damage and the developmental consequences with relation to the age at which the damage was sustained. This graph obviously represents a simplification and generalization of these relationships. For example, neuropsychological development undoubtedly is not a single or unitary factor. Some research has indicated that verbal abilities and skills mature considerably more slowly than abilities related to abstraction and logical reasoning. Nevertheless, if a brain lesion of fairly significant proportions is sustained at the age of two years, the consequences appear to be relatively severe, because the child is put on a generally different course of development as compared with the normal child. If damage is sustained at the age of four years, a greater degree of normal development has preceded the occurrence of cerebral damage and, even though the child is put on a reduced general course of neuropsychological development, his or her eventual level of abilities is somewhat higher. It must be remembered that a fairly substantial brain lesion is necessary to produce the type of effects noted in Fig. 10.2, that other factors are also of influence, and that individual variation is to be expected.

Figure 10.2 has very practical significance for those psychologists involved in the longitudinal assessment of individual children. For example, it is not uncommon for a child with cerebral damage to show progressively lower IQs as he or she grows older. In some instances, this apparent decline in intelligence has caused concern about the possibility of some type of progressive deterioration of brain functions. It must be remembered, however, that a brain-damaged child does not usually have the basic brain functions to develop neuropsychological abilities at the same rate as a normal child, even though their chronological ages progress at exactly the same rate. Thus, the ratio between mental age and chronological age fails to follow the normal progression and the fraction decreases, resulting in a lower IQ.

Principle 3

The age at which brain damage is sustained has a significant influence on neuropsychological development, and this influence interacts with impairment of abilities that have already been acquired.

In general, the younger the child at the time brain damage is sustained, the greater the influence of age at the time of brain damage in limiting future development, and the lesser the influence of loss or impairment of pre-existing abilities (see Reitan & Wolfson, 1992, for a more complete discussion). With older children, however, specific and selective impairment of previously acquired abilities is a factor of increased significance, and the brain's potential to acquire additional neuropsychological abilities assumes a lesser role.

It is important to recognize that the interaction of these variables influences the pattern of neuropsychological deficit for the individual child. Brain damage early in life, which limits potential for development, has a generalized effect on neuropsychological abilities, and tends to produce a picture of generalized impairment regardless of the lateralization or location of the lesion. However, in older children who have already acquired brain-related abilities, a lateralized lesion may produce more specific deficits (for example, in an older child, a loss of Performance intelligence may result from right cerebral damage). As time progresses following the brain lesion, even with older children and adults, the acute effects (selective impairment) of focal or lateralized lesions tend to diminish, yielding to a picture of more generalized higher-level deficits.

The inferential approach concerned with comparisons of identical performances on the two sides of the body (such as finger tapping and tactile finger localization) tends not to be influenced by developmental factors to the extent and in the same manner as higher-level neuropsychological functions. Sensory–perceptual and motor functions are heavily dependent upon the anatomical pathways by which they are mediated. For example, a lesion of the right cerebral hemisphere occurring early in life is likely to produce sensory–perceptual and motor deficits on the contralateral side of the body regardless of the child's age, even though higher-level abilities (such as Verbal and Performance intelligence) are both impaired and may not show any substantial difference.

The above three principles cannot be expected to apply perfectly to children with learning disabilities, inasmuch as these children generally show little evidence of structural damage of the brain tissue. Thus, they would, in all probability, differ in a number of neuropsychological aspects from children with known brain damage. However, if biological impairment of brain functions is a relevant factor in producing learning disabilities, these children may also be similar in a number of neuropsychological aspects to children with known brain damage, and particularly to those children who sustain brain damage early in life.

Research finding comparing normal, learning-disabled, and brain-damaged children

There have been extensive studies validating the HRNTB–OC as a battery that significantly differentiates between brain-damaged and normal children (Reed, Reitan, & Kløve, 1965; Boll, 1974). Additional investigations included children with academic deficiencies and learning disabilities for comparison with the above two groups.

Selz and Reitan (1979a) conducted a detailed study that compared neuropsychological test results of three groups: 25 control children, 25 learning-disabled children, and 25 brain-damaged children. The purpose of this study was to identify the unique neuropsychological features of children with learning disabilities compared with control and brain-damaged children. However, these investigations also demonstrated the striking and consistent differences between control children and brain-damaged children, and identified certain consistent characteristics that were relatively unique to the group with learning disabilities.

The 25 control subjects in the Selz and Reitan studies were volunteers from two school systems; 15 children came from a small-town school and ten were from a suburban school. None of these children had evidence of brain dysfunction, and all were functioning normally without any academic problems or complaints. Obviously, this does not mean that every child was performing ideally, but none of the children had evidence of past or present cerebral disease or damage and all were progressing adequately within their normal class placements. The mean age of this group was 128.16 months (SD 13.08).

Nine of the children with learning disabilities attended city schools, four attended suburban schools, and 12 were enrolled in schools in small towns. The subjects for this group were referred for neuropsychological testing primarily on the basis of school-related deficient performance. All of these children had significant academic deficits; discipline or more general school problems were also noted in the records of five subjects. Four children had been held back one year in school, one child was held back two years, and one child had repeated three grades. In addition, scores on the WRAT indicated that 22 of the children showed a year or more retardation in reading and/or spelling. The three children who did not show deficient WRAT performances were from professional families, and had well-documented evidence of significant learning problems. None of the subjects with learning disabilities had a Full Scale IQ below 80. All of the children were given a complete physical neurological examination, and any child who had positive past or present evidence of clinically significant cerebral disease or damage was excluded from the group. There were 19 boys and six girls in this group, with a mean age of 134.88 months (SD 14.79).

Among the brain-damaged children, nine attended city schools, seven attended suburban schools, and nine were enrolled in schools in small towns. The subjects were selected on the basis of compelling evidence derived from their neurological examination (including specialized neurological diagnostic procedures), and each child had independent and documented evidence of structural brain damage or a clinically significant brain disorder. Selection of these children was entirely independent of psychological test performances. No attempt was made to select brain-damaged children according to location, type, or severity of cerebral damage, and the total group therefore represented heterogeneous brain involvement. The diagnoses of this group included intracranial tumor, both open and closed head injuries, arteriovenous malformation, encephalitis, cerebral abscess, idiopathic epilepsy, and birth injury. The mean age of the brain-damaged group was 133.80 months (SD 17.31).

In this study, the dependent variables included Verbal IQ, Performance IQ, Full Scale IQ, and the results of ten tests included in the HRNTB–OC. Multivariate analysis of variance indicated that the mean values were not the same for all three groups, yielding a highly significant difference. Using the three diagnostic categories, a discriminant analysis based on 13 measures correctly classified 23 of the 25 controls, 19 of the 25 children with learning disabilities, and 18 of the 25 children with brain damage.

Four of the children with brain damage were very mildly impaired and, from the statistical analysis, appeared to be control subjects. A certain degree of overlap of this kind is to be expected, but the results indicated quite clearly that the test results, generally considered for the children in the three groups, permitted differential classification into their appropriate categories. This study demonstrated that children with learning disabilities tended to have neuro-psychological test scores that were intermediate to the other two groups.

The outstanding finding of this investigation, however, was that the children with cerebral damage performed much more poorly than the control subjects. In fact, among the three groups, discriminant analysis yielded an overall correct classification of 80%. When the group with learning disabilities was deleted from consideration, differentiation between the control and the brain-damaged subjects was achieved with a hit-rate of about 87% correct classifications.

This study provided an unequivocal answer to the first question that must be asked: does the HRNTB–OC provide a valid and sensitive procedure for differentiating between children with normal brains and children with damaged brains? This is a question that is critical to the utilization of the test battery, and the answer, clearly, was positive. Secondly, the statistical analyses also separated the learning-disabled children from both the normal controls and the brain-damaged children. Even with Full Scale IQ statistically controlled, the neuropsychological measures differentiated the three groups at a high level of statistical significance.

The significance of this study lies in the fact that an approach oriented toward adequacy of brain–behavior relationships was relevant not only in differential classification of the group with definite brain damage, but also of subjects with learning disabilities. The results give strong support to the postulate that neuropsychological disabilities underlie many instances of academic failure. This finding is especially interesting in consideration of the fact that the learning disabilities group was carefully screened on the basis of neurological (medical) findings, and the learning-disabled children were indistinguishable from the control subjects in this respect. Thus, it would seem possible to conclude that neuropsychological deficits or deviations, in the absence of medical neurological abnormalities, may be relevant in a substantial proportion of children with learning disabilities.

The next question concerned the prospect of developing a method for classifying individual children correctly into their appropriate groups. The same three groups (normal controls, children with learning disabilities, and children with brain damage) were used for this purpose.

First, entirely separate groups of 19 children were composed in each of the three categories. Using results of the HRNTB–OC alone, we developed 37 rules for generating a score for any child who had been given the battery of tests. Raw scores were converted to scaled scores, with a score of zero representing a performance in the normal to superior range. A score of 1 indicated a performance that was still in the normal range, but not quite as good as may have been expected. A score of 2 was somewhat below normal limits, and a score of 3 corresponded with definite impairment. Whereas the scores for the pilot group were used as the basis for determining these score-ranges, the actual cut-off points were based on our extensive clinical experience rather than upon arbitrary statistical procedures. The system of rules was not only based on level of performance, but also included differences in scores for the two sides of the body, patterns of scores, and pathognomonic deficits on certain simple tests.

The rules were then tested (Selz & Reitan, 1979b) with the three groups, each of which included 25 subjects. A total score could be obtained for each subject, and the means for the three groups were strikingly different (10.60 for the controls; 24.44 for the group with learning disabilities; and 40.60 for the brain-damaged children), with probability levels far exceeding 0.001 in comparison of any pair of groups.

In total, the rules system correctly classified 73.3% of the 75 children: 24 (96%) of the controls, 14 (56%) of the children with learning disabilities, and 17 (68%) of the brain-damaged children. Obviously, the rules system was conservative in identifying children as non-normal, although it must also be recognized that some learning-disabled children, and even some children with mild initial brain damage who have largely recovered, might be expected to fall in the normal range of neuropsychological functions.

These results indicate that, in general, entirely objective data represented by neuropsychological test scores can differentiate normal, learning-disabled, and brain-damaged groups of children, with the learning-disabled groups occupying an intermediate position with respect to the degree of impairment. Details for scoring the 37 rules are provided in the original publication (Selz & Reitan, 1979b), but considering the error-rate noted above, we recommend that the scores be used only as a guideline for further evaluation.

Because the learning-disabled group consisted of children who had normal results on the physical neurological examination, it is apparent that many children who have a learning disability appear normal on routine neurological evaluation but demonstrate somewhat deviant brain functions on the basis of neuropsychological evaluation.

Because neuropsychological testing appears to be more sensitive to subtle, higher-level cognitive dysfunction than does the neurological exam (Kløve, 1974), it is implied that learning disability represents fairly normal lower-level functions (as represented in the neurological examination), with impairment primarily evident in the higher-level cognitive processes (as indicated in the neuropsychological examination). Furthermore, because all of the learning-disabled subjects were in the normal range according to the physical neurological exam, it follows that neuropsychological screening for learning disability may be far more effective than neurological screening. The rules system provides a convenient method for interpreting test results, and should be helpful in the clinical evaluation of children with learning disabilities.

Developmental dysphasia and its relationship to learning disabilities

A condition in children referred to as *developmental dysphasia* appears to be very similar to learning disabilities, but the literature pertaining to these conditions tends to overlap relatively little. Zangwill (1978) referred to one of the earliest cases of developmental dysphasia to be reported at some length, and this was by Head (1926) in his widely recognized book *Aphasia and Kindred Disorders of Speech*. Thus, developmental dysphasia, as a categorical disorder, far precedes learning disabilities in time.

Wyke (1978) described developmental dysphasia as 'the deficit in the acquisition of normal language functions in children of normal or above normal intelligence and with adequate hearing ability to permit the perception of verbal sounds.' Zangwill (1978) stated that developmental dysphasia denotes 'slow, limited or otherwise faulty development of language in children' who do not have evidence of gross neurological or psychiatric disability, mental retardation, autism, or deafness. He went on to say that the outstanding handicap of such children is social and educational rather than physical, and sensory or motor deficits are rarely evident.

There has been a good deal of debate about whether developmental dysphasia implicates brain impairment biologically or whether it may be due to other factors (Wyke, 1978). Gaddes (1980) espoused a position in which he was unequivocal in relating brain function to the development of language skills. His review of the evidence led him to conclude that the brain is not only generally involved in developmental dysphasia, but is involved specifically in terms of the location and severity of damage in the brain centers necessary for language. He felt that mild dysfunction in the language centers will cause a child to have a specific learning disability, whereas more severe damage in these centers will merit a diagnosis of dysphasia. He stated explicitly that 'it is important to remember that while the child with specific developmental dyslexia is free from gross neurological damage as shown on the neurological examination, this, of course, does not exclude the possibility of very minimal neurological brain dysfunctions. As well, there may be a further possibility of a genetic deficit that somewhat interferes with normal reading' (p. 252). Gaddes and Edgell (1994) also reviewed in detail the neurobiological bases for reading deficits.

It is apparent that the definition of developmental dysphasia, as well as many of the issues surrounding it, is very similar to the definitions of learning disabilities. Considering our interest in both developmental dysphasia (Reitan, 1964, 1985; Reitan & Kløve, 1968) and learning disabilities and the methods that we developed to evaluate dysphasic manifestations (Reitan, 1960, 1984, 1985), we were eager to examine learning-disabled children using the Reitan–Indiana Aphasia Screening Test (Reitan, 1985). This test consists of items that require naming of objects, identification of numbers and letters, simple reading, simple writing, spelling, arithmetic in the form of subtraction and multiplication, repetition of words and sentences, explanation of the meaning of a simple sentence, demonstration of the use of objects, identification of right and left together with identification of body parts, and copying spatial configurations such as a square, cross, and triangle. Failures on items of the test can be translated into dysphasic and related symptoms such as body dysgnosia, visual number and/or letter dysgnosia, auditory verbal dysgnosia, dysnomia, dysgraphia, dyslexia, dyscalculia, spelling dyspraxia, central dysarthria, right–left confusion, and constructional dyspraxia (see Reitan & Wolfson, 1992, 1993, for a more complete description of the Aphasia Screening Test, procedures for administration and scoring, a review of research reports, and illustrations of clinical interpretation). The test usually requires less than 30 minutes for administration.

Reitan and Wolfson (1985) analyzed results on the Reitan–Indiana Aphasia Screening Test for the three groups of children (normal, learning-disabled, and brain-damaged) used by Selz and Reitan (1979b). Results were evaluated by assigning scaled scores to each deficit that was found. A score of 0 was given for performances that fell within the normal range. If a particular deficit was found, it was assigned a score of 1, 2, or 3, depending upon the significance of the deficit for cerebral damage. For example, spelling dyspraxia received a scaled score of 1, whereas dysnomia, which is a more definite and significant indicator of cerebral impairment, received a score of 3.

This particular study included an approach toward validation of the data that is rarely used: we elected to predict the results that would be found in each group and to compare the predicted result with the actual outcome. This procedure was possible because the scoring procedure was based on the 4-point scale described above.

Having had considerable experience with children in each of the groups, we felt that it might be possible to predict the percentage of children in each group who would show each type of deficit. For example, if we expected none of the subjects to demonstrate body dysgnosia, the prediction would be that all 25 of these subjects would have a score of 0 for that variable. If we felt that none of the controls would show evidence of dysnomia, all 25 children would be placed in the normal category. Dysnomia occurs occasionally in brain-damaged children, and we predicted that four of these 25 children (16%) would show this particular deficit. In this manner, predictions were made for each variable in each group without knowledge of the actual results.

It is obvious that any attempt to make predictions of this kind necessarily depends upon having a considerable amount of clinical experience with the broad range of children who fall in each of the three groups being studied, as well as a good deal of knowledge of the types of results that were reflected by the dependent variables. It was therefore possible that such predictions would end up being strikingly deviant from the actual outcome. On the other hand, if the predictions agreed relatively closely with the actual outcome, there would be a very powerful validation of the experimental findings.

As shown in Table 10.1, we predicted that none of the control children would demonstrate the deficits noted, and the actual outcome data indicated that this prediction was correct. We also predicted that none of these deficits would occur among the 25 children with learning disabilities, and this prediction again was confirmed. However, we felt that it was likely that one child in the group of 25 brain-damaged children (4%) would show these deficits. As indicated in Table 10.1, body dysgnosia and auditory verbal dysgnosia were each demonstrated by one child (4%), whereas two children with brain damage (8%) showed evidence of visual number dysgnosia.

Considering the rare occurrence of these particular deficits, one could question why tests for them were even included in the examination. It is important to recognize that, when these particular deficits are present, they have serious implications for impairment of brain functions. From a clinical point of view, it is important to discern deficits of this kind, even though they occur rarely.

The next grouping of deficits from the Aphasia Screening Test was composed of the type of disorders frequently manifested by children with learning

Table 10.1. Predicted and actual incidence of infrequent aphasic symptoms in control children, learning-disabled (LD) children, and brain-damaged (BD) children

Deficit	Control (%)		LD (%)		BD (%)	
	Predicted	Actual	Predicted	Actual	Predicted	Actual
Body dysgnosia	0	0	0	0	4	4
Auditory–verbal dysgnosia	0	0	0	0	4	4
Visual number dysgnosia	0	0	0	0	4	8

Table 10.2. Predicted and actual incidence of aphasic symptoms seen frequently in children with learning disabilities (LD) and children with brain damage (BD)

Deficit	Control (%)		LD (%)		BD (%)	
	Predicted	Actual	Predicted	Actual	Predicted	Actual
Visual letter dysgnosia	0	0	16	12	16	12
Dysnomia	0	0	16	12	16	12
Dysgraphia	4	0	24	24	24	36
Dyscalculia	4	0	40	40	40	36
Central dysarthria	4	4	40	40	40	40

disabilities. As seen in Table 10.2, these deficits included visual letter dysgnosia, dysnomia, dysgraphia, dyscalculia, and central dysarthria. Table 10.2 also shows that we expected none of the control children to demonstrate visual letter dysgnosia or dysnomia, but we estimated that one child in the control group (4%) would show dysgraphia, dyscalculia, and central dysarthria. The outcome results for the control children were just a little better than we had predicted. One child showed evidence of central dysarthria, but none of the control children manifested any of the other difficulties.

Among the children with learning disabilities and brain damage, we felt that these disorders would be more common and comparable in the two groups. As seen in Table 10.2, we predicted an incidence ranging from 16% to 40% for these variables. The actual outcome was very close to the predicted frequencies, confirming our estimates of the more common manifestations of dyscalculia and central dysarthria than of the other deficits.

We elected to treat dyslexia as a separate variable because of its central role

Table 10.3. Predicted and actual incidence of dyslexia

Deficit	Control (%)		LD (%)		BD (%)	
	Predicted	Actual	Predicted	Actual	Predicted	Actual
Dyslexia	4	4	56	52	44	40

LD, learning-disabled children; BD, brain-damaged children.

Table 10.4. Predicted and actual incidence of 'common' symptoms

Deficit	Control (%)		LD (%)		BD (%)	
	Predicted	Actual	Predicted	Actual	Predicted	Actual
Right–left confusion	24	36	48	48	48	28
Spelling dyspraxia	24	12	76	76	68	68

LD, learning-disabled children; BD, brain-damaged children.

among learning-disabled children, and the predicted and actual incidence of dyslexia is shown in Table 10.3. We felt that one of the 25 control children (4%) would show evidence of reading impairment on the Aphasia Screening Test, and this prediction was confirmed. We predicted that reading difficulty would actually be more common among the children with learning-disabilities than among the brain-damaged children, respecting the fact that each child in the learning-disability group had been identified by the classroom teacher as having specific academic deficits which needed evaluation and remediation. Thus, we predicted that 56% of the children in this group would manifest positive findings on the Aphasia Screening Test, and the actual outcome was 52%. Reading difficulties are not uncommon among children with cerebral lesions, and we predicted that 44% of these children would have such evidence. The actual outcome was 40%. Again, the correspondence between predicted and actual values was extremely close.

Table 10.4 presents the predicted and actual results for right–left confusion and spelling dyspraxia, two types of deficits that are fairly common, even among control subjects, in the 9-year through 14-year age range. We predicted that 24% of the control children would manifest right–left confusion and spelling dyspraxia. Our predictions for these variables were rather deviant from the outcome: more children than expected actually demonstrated evidence of

Table 10.5. Predicted and actual incidence of constructional dyspraxia

Deficit	Control (%)		LD (%)		BD (%)	
	Predicted	Actual	Predicted	Actual	Predicted	Actual
Constructional dyspraxia	4	8	32	32	48	52

LD, learning-disabled children; BD, brain-damaged children.

right–left confusion, and fewer children than expected demonstrated spelling dyspraxia.

Our predictions of the frequency of these deficits among the children with learning disabilities turned out to be exactly in accordance with the actual outcome. As we had predicted, children with brain damage also frequently manifest evidence of spelling dyspraxia. However, in this brain-damaged sample, the incidence of right–left confusion was strikingly low, not only deviating from our predicted frequency, but actually being lower than the frequency for the control sample in this study.

The final variable we evaluated was constructional dyspraxia. We expected this deficit to be more common among brain-damaged children than among the subjects with learning disability, and to occur rarely with control children. As shown by the values in Table 10.5, these predictions were essentially confirmed.

After we made predictions about the frequency of each deficit for each group, we were able to compute mean scores for the predictions as well as for the actual outcome results. As seen in Table 10.6, the controls had a predicted mean of 0.64 and an actual outcome of 0.80. This means that the average performance of the control children was nearly perfect on the Aphasia Screening Test, because any type of deficit would have contributed a minimum score of 1. Predictions for the learning-disabled group yielded a mean of 5.88 points; the actual outcome was 5.72 points. The brain-damaged group performed just a little worse than the children with learning disabilities, earning a predicted mean of 6.24 points (which agreed exactly with the actual outcome).

It is apparent from these summarized findings that basic and simple aspects of language abilities are substantially impaired in groups with learning disability or brain damage, but that performances are essentially normal for control children. This observation led us to tally the number of children in each of several categories to determine differences in the distributions for the three groups. These results are shown in Table 10.7.

Table 10.6. Predicted and actual mean scores (based upon ratings from 0 to 3 for each variable) for control children (LD), learning-disabled children, and brain-damaged children (BD)

	Control	LD	BD
Predicted outcome	.64	5.88	6.24
Actual outcome	.80	5.72	6.24

Table 10.7. Performance of groups on the Aphasia Screening Test and classification of subjects based on aphasic deficits

Groups	Total Deficit Score			Correct classification (%)
	0	1	2 or more	
Control	12	11	2	92
Learning-disabled	2	4	19	76
Brain-damaged	2	2	21	84

In total, 23 of the 25 control children (92%) had total scores of 0 or 1. More specifically, 12 of the control children made no errors at all on the entire Aphasia Screening Test. Eleven children demonstrated either spelling dyspraxia or right–left confusion, and two of the 25 children had difficulties which extended beyond this level.

Children with learning disability or brain damage were rarely perfect in their performances, and usually accumulated a substantial number of points, reflecting their deficits. In fact, 19 (75%) of the children with learning disability and 21 (84%) of the brain-damaged children had scores of 2 or more points. These results suggest that the Aphasia Screening Test can be a very valuable screening procedure for identifying children with learning disabilities or brain damage. In addition, the results demonstrate that the Aphasia Screening Test is useful in identifying impairment in the ability to use language and verbal symbols for communication purposes.

Concerning the varying positions reviewed at the beginning of this section about the nature of developmental dysphasia and its relationship to the biological condition of the brain, our results strongly confirm the position of Gaddes (1980), who felt that brain-damaged subjects would perform significantly worse than controls, and that learning disability, at least in most cases, resulted from a more subtle type of cerebral impairment. In turn, these empirical findings argue strongly that (1) a condition such as developmental dysphasia and/or learning disabilities can be identified using even simple techniques and procedures of examination; (2) the deficits manifested by children with developmental and/or learning disabilities are related to cerebral damage; and (3) clinical evaluation using the Aphasia Screening Test can provide very useful information, not only for children with definite cerebral damage, but also for children with learning disabilities.

Research comparisons of brain-damaged, learning-disabled, and control groups using the NDS

Reitan and Wolfson (1992, 1993) developed Neuropsychological Deficit Scales (NDS) for both adults and children. The scales are reported and described fully in books on the HRNTB for adults and children. NDS scores, based on raw scores, can be determined for each variable in the battery (45 variables for older children; 42 variables for adults). The advantage of NDS scores is that they represent four classifications and relate to the clinical significance of raw scores. An NDS score of 0 represents an excellent performance; a score of 1 is a normal score, but not quite as good as it might be. A distinct dividing point occurs between NDS scores of 1 and 2, because scores of 2 fall in the brain-damaged range. NDS scores of 2 correspond with mild to moderate deficits, and NDS scores of 3 represent severe deficits.

Reitan and Wolfson (1988b) used NDS scores to characterize and compare normal, learning-disabled, and brain-damaged children. In this study, 35 children with brain damage, 35 children with normal brain functions, and 23 children with learning disabilities were evaluated. Age differences between the groups did not approach statistical significance.

Although none of the children with learning disabilities showed any evidence of abnormalities on the physical neurological examination, each child demonstrated significant problems in school. In every case these problems had been formally noted in the classroom, and the child was referred for evaluation because of learning deficits. These children also demonstrated retardation of one year or more in Reading and/or Spelling on the WRAT. None of the learning-disabled children had a WISC–R Full Scale IQ below 80.

Raw scores were converted to NDS scores and means were computed for each of the three groups in the following subcategories: (1) Motor Functions, (2) Sensory–Perceptual Functions, (3) Visual–Spatial Skills, (4) Attention and Concentration, (5) Immediate Memory, and (6) Abstraction, Reasoning, and Logical Analysis. A Total Level of Performance score was also obtained by adding the subtotals of these six subcategories. The results for the three groups are depicted in Figure 10.3.

Multivariate analysis of variance yielded highly significant differences between the three groups, with the control children having the best mean scores in every subcategory as well as the best total NDS score. The children with learning disabilities had intermediate scores in every area except Attention and Concentration. On this section, their scores were worse than even the brain-damaged group.

In each of the other subcategories, the brain-damaged group performed most poorly. Comparisons of paired groups for the total NDS score were highly significant in each instance, clearly indicating that when the neuropsychological variables were considered in total, the controls performed best, the group with learning disabilities was intermediate, and the brain-damaged group performed most poorly.

The results of this study demonstrated that differential levels of performance characterized the neuropsychological functions of control children, learning-disabled children, and brain-damaged children. This finding was not particularly surprising, although the quantitative results help to provide guidelines for the clinical interpretation of the protocols of individual subjects.

The striking finding in this study was the severe degree of deficit shown by children with learning disabilities in the area of Attention and Concentration. This result would appear to have definite implications for remedial approaches. Prior research has indicated that impairment in abstraction, reasoning, and logical analysis has constituted a significant problem for children with learning disabilities (Reitan, 1985; Selz & Reitan, 1979a), but the great difficulty that these children have in relation to other areas of neuropsychological functioning is in the area of Attention and Concentration, indicating that they need structured help, focused on developing primary attentional capabilities.

It appears that in addition to abstraction and reasoning deficits, children with learning disability have great difficulty at the first level of central processing, which is concerned with the registration of incoming material to the brain and maintenance of continued attention or concentration. If a child is limited in the ability to register information per unit of time, it is obvious that additional aspects of central processing will suffer. In turn, impairment in basic aspects of Abstraction, Reasoning, and Logical Analysis (the second lowest area for the learning-disabled group) would tend to exacerbate attentional deficits, as mentioned above.

The comparative performances of the three groups of children used in this study – and the strikingly deviant pattern of the learning-disabled group –

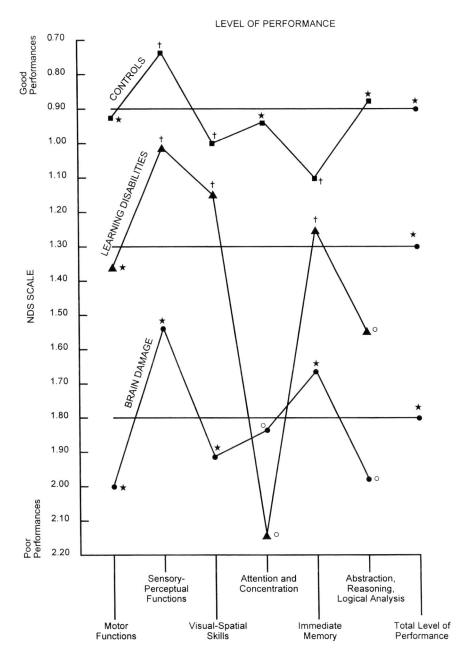

Fig. 10.3. Comparative performance in various neuropsychological areas of normal children, children with learning disabilities, and brain-damaged children in the 9-year through 14-year age range.

would have been much more difficult to discern without the type of scoring provided by the NDS for Older Children. It would therefore appear that the NDS may be particularly advantageous as a basis for grouping test results in research analyses as well as in the clinical interpretation of results for individual children. In clinical evaluation and in planning a program of remediation, it is imperative that both the strengths and weaknesses of the child be fully recognized. Disparities among various aspects of ability structure, as contrasted with overall level of performance, may well be the critical factor in the neuropsychological bases of learning disabilities.

Space limitations do not permit discussion and illustration of the critically significant remaining applications of the HRNTB–OC: (1) clinical evaluation of the individual subject and the value of the information provided by a comprehensive neuropsychological examination, and (2) the integration of a comprehensive examination with the development of a personally appropriate plan for remediation. In order to provide remediation that is maximally effective, it is obviously necessary to identify the deficits that represent stumbling blocks for the individual person. For example, as shown in Fig. 10.3, the major stumbling blocks for most learning-disabled people fall in the areas of attention/concentration and reasoning/abstraction/logical analysis. In individual cases, when these areas of deficiency are remediated, academic progress is achieved with much less effort, and behavioral problems are often resolved. It is necessary, of course, that the remediation (cognitive retraining) program be designed to dovetail with the assessment procedures (in this case, the HRNTB–OC and REHABIT – Reitan Evaluation of Hemispheric Abilities and Brain Intensive Training). The interested reader may gain additional information about the integration of these methods of neuropsychological assessment and cognitive retraining from several sources (Reitan & Wolfson, 1992, 1993, in press).

Finally, we should mention the important matter of the early identification of neuropsychologically based learning deficiencies which, in turn, permits early remediation efforts. Our studies of children aged six through eight years, using the Reitan–Indiana Neuropsychological Test Battery, demonstrated a clear differentiation of groups of control, learning-disabled, and brain-damaged children, with scarcely any overlap of mean scores among the three groups across the full range of tests – including the Wechsler Intelligence Scale for Children (WISC; Reitan & Boll, 1973). 'Blind' clinical evaluation of individual test protocols across the three groups confirmed the significance of the statistical data, with 96% of the brain-damaged children and 80% of the children with learning disabilities showing definite neuropsychological impairment. In contrast, 64% of the controls were judged to be normal neuropsychologically, with

36% showing evidence of mild impairment which appeared to be in genuine need of remediation.

These results suggest that a comprehensive battery of neuropsychological tests, validated individually and as a battery for their sensitivity to cerebral impairment, may serve to identify children who have brain-based problems of learning disabilities that they are unlikely to outgrow through normal maturation, and who therefore are in need of individual remediation and cognitive retraining. We have had excellent results with individual children in whom the deficits have been selective and rather delimited (a weak link in the chain of integrated abilities), whereas our success has been less encouraging with children in whom neuropsychological deficits have been generalized and the entire platform of abilities needed to be raised (Reitan & Boll, 1973).

Our experience with a broad range of individual children has led to an appreciation of the uniqueness of each child, as demonstrated by fully comprehensive neuropsychological testing; the significance of recognizing the individuality of the neuropsychological ability structure of each child; the complex interaction of seemingly unrelated deficits in producing learning disabilities in the individual instance; and the oversimplification, from a clinical and remediational viewpoint, of the outcome of studies aimed toward identifying differential categories or subtypes of learning disabilities.

REFERENCES

Babcock, H. (1930). An experiment in the measurement of mental deterioration. *Archives of Psychology*, 18, 5–105.

Batchelor, E.S. & Dean, R.S. (1989). Empirical derivation and classification of subgroups of children with learning deficits at separate age levels. Unpublished manuscript.

Batchelor, E.S. Jr & Dean, R.S. (1991). Neuropsychological assessment of learning disabilities in children. In *Neuropsychological Foundations of Learning Disabilities*, ed. J.B. Obrzut & G.W. Hynd, pp. 309–29. New York: Academic Press.

Batchelor, E.S., Dean, R.S., & Williams, R. (1989). Severity of neuropsychological functioning in clinically derived groups of learning-disabled children. Paper presented at the annual convention of the National Academy of Neuropsychology, Washington, DC.

Batchelor, E.S., Kixmiller, J., & Dean, R.S. (1990). Neuropsychological aspects of reading and spelling performance in children with learning disorders. Unpublished manuscript.

Boll, T.J. (1974). Behavioral correlates of cerebral damage in children age 9–14. In *Clinical Neuropsychology: Current Status and Application*, ed. R.M. Reitan & L.A. Davison. Washington, DC: Hemisphere Press.

Davis, B., Dean, R., & Krug, D. (1989). Subtests of the Wechsler Intelligence Scale for Children–Revised as predictors of neuropsychological impairment. Unpublished manuscript.

Doehring, D.G. & Reitan, R.M. (1962). Concept attainment of human adults with lateralized cerebral lesions. *Perceptual and Motor Skills*, 14, 27–33.

Gaddes, W.H. (1980). *Learning Disabilities and Brain Function*. New York: Springer-Verlag.

Gaddes, W.H. & Edgell, D. (1994). *Learning Disabilities and Brain Function: A Neuropsychological Approach*, 3rd edition. New York: Springer-Verlag.

Hamill, D.D., Leigh, J., McNutt, G., & Larson, S.C. (1981). A new definition of learning disabilities. *Learning Disabilities Quarterly*, 4, 336–42.

Head, H. (1926). *Aphasia and Kindred Disorders of Speech*, Vol. 1. Cambridge: Cambridge University Press.

Hunt, H.F. (1943). A practical clinical test for organic brain damage. *Journal of Applied Psychology*, 27, 375–86.

Kennard, M.A. (1936). Age and other factors in motor recovery from precentral lesions in monkeys. *American Journal of Physiology*, 115, 138–46.

Kennard, M.A. (1938). Reorganization of motor function in the cerebral cortex of monkeys deprived of motor and premotor areas in infancy. *Journal of Neurophysiology*, 1, 477–97.

Kennard, M.A. (1942). Cortical reorganization of motor function. *Archives of Neurology and Psychiatry*, 48, 227–40.

Kirk, S. A. & Bateman, B. (1962). Diagnosis and remediation of learning disabilities. *The Exceptional Child*, 29, 73–8.

Kløve, H. (1974). Validation studies in adult clinical neuropsychology. In *Clinical Neuropsychology: Current Status and Applications*, ed. R.M. Reitan & L.A. Davison. Washington, DC: Hemisphere Press.

Lanyon, R.T. (1978). *Psychological Screening Inventory: Manual*, 2nd edition. Goshen, NY: Research Psychologists Press.

Leicht, D.J. (1987). Personality/social/behavior subtypes of learning-disabled young adults. Unpublished doctoral dissertation, Southern Illinois University–Carbondale.

McCarthy, J.J. & McCarthy, J.F. (1969). *Learning Disabilities*. Boston, MD: Allyn & Bacon.

O'Donnell, J.P. (1991). Neuropsychological assessment of learning-disabled adolescents and young adults. In *Neuropsychological Foundations of Learning Disabilities*, ed. J.B. Obrzut & G.W. Hynd, pp. 331–53. New York: Academic Press.

O'Donnell, J.P., Kurtz, J., & Ramanaiah, N.V. (1983). Neuropsychological test findings for normal, learning-disabled, and brain-damaged young adults. *Journal of Consulting and Clinical Psychology*, 51, 726–9.

Phillips, F.L. (1986). Subtypes among learning-disabled college students: a neuropsychological multivariate approach. Unpublished doctoral dissertation, Southern Illinois University–Carbondale.

Reed, H.B.C., Reitan, R.M., & Kløve, H. (1965). The influence of cerebral lesions on psychological test performances of older children. *Journal of Consulting Psychology*, 29, 247–51.

Reitan, R.M. (1960). The significance of dysphasia for intelligence and adaptive abilities. *Journal of Psychology*, 50, 355–76.

Reitan, R.M. (1964). Relationships between neurological and psychological variables and their implications for reading instruction. In *Meeting Individual Differences in Reading*, ed. H.A. Robinson, pp. 100–10. Chicago, IL: University of Chicago Press.

Reitan, R.M. (1966). A research program on the psychological effects of brain lesions in human beings. In *International Review of Research in Mental Retardation*, Vol. I, ed. N.R. Ellis. New York: Academic Press.

Reitan, R.M. (1967). Psychological assessment of deficits associated with brain lesions in subjects with normal and subnormal intelligence. In *Brain Damage and Mental Retardation: A Psychological Evaluation*, ed. J.L. Khanna, pp. 137–59. Springfield, IL: Charles C Thomas.

Reitan, R.M. (1974). Psychological effects of cerebral lesions in children of early school age. In *Clinical Neuropsychology: Current Applications*, ed. R.M. Reitan & L.A. Davison, pp. 53–90. Washington, DC: Hemisphere Press.

Reitan, R.M. (1984). *Aphasia and Sensory–Perceptual Deficits in Adults*. Tucson, AZ: Neuropsychology Press.

Reitan, R.M. (1985). *Aphasia and Sensory–Perceptual Deficits in Children*. Tucson, AZ: Neuropsychology Press.

Reitan, R.M. & Boll, T.J. (1973). Neuropsychological correlates of minimal brain dysfunction. *Annals of the New York Academy of Sciences*, 205, 65–88.

Reitan, R.M. & Kløve, H. (1968). Identifying the brain-injured child. In *Clinical Studies in Reading III*, ed. H.M. Robinson & H.K. Smith. Chicago, IL: University of Chicago Press.

Reitan, R.M. & Tarshes, E.L. (1959). Differential effects of lateralized brain lesions on the Trail Making Test. *Journal of Nervous and Mental Disease*, 129, 257–62.

Reitan, R.M. & Wolfson, D. (1985). *The Halstead–Reitan Neuropsychological Test Battery: Theory and Clinical Interpretation*. Tucson, AZ: Neuropsychology Press.

Reitan, R.M. & Wolfson, D. (1988a). The Halstead–Reitan Neuropsychological Test Battery and REHABIT: a model for integrating evaluation and remediation of cognitive impairment. *Cognitive Rehabilitation*, 6, 10–17.

Reitan, R.M. & Wolfson, D. (1988b). Neuropsychological functions of learning-disabled, brain-damaged, and normal children. *The Clinical Neuropsychologist*, 2, 278.

Reitan, R.M. & Wolfson, D. (1988c). *Traumatic Brain Injury*, Vol. II, *Recovery and Rehabilitation*. Tucson, AZ: Neuropsychology Press.

Reitan, R.M. & Wolfson, D. (1992). *Neuropsychological Evaluation of Older Children*. Tucson, AZ: Neuropsychology Press.

Reitan, R.M. & Wolfson, D. (1993). *The Halstead–Reitan Neuropsychological Test Battery: Theory and Clinical Interpretation*, second edition. Tucson, AZ: Neuropsychology Press.

Reitan, R.M. & Wolfson, D. (in press). *Neuropsychological Evaluation of Young Children*. Tucson, AZ: Neuropsychology Press.

Rourke, B.P. (1975). Brain–behavior relationships in children with learning disabilities: a research program. *American Psychologist*, 30, 911–20.

Rourke, B.P. (ed.). (1985). *Neuropsychology of Learning Disabilities: Essentials of Subtype Analysis*. New York: Guilford Press.

Rourke, B.P. (1989). *Nonverbal Learning Disabilities: The Syndrome and the Model*. New York: Guilford Press.

Rourke, B.P. (ed.). (1991). *Neuropsychological Validation of Learning Disability Subtypes*. New York: Guilford Press.

Rourke, B.P., Bakker, D.J., Fisk, J.L., & Strang, J.D. (1983). *Child Neuropsychology: An Introduction* to Theory, Research, and Clinical Practice. New York: Guilford Press.

Rourke, B.P., Dietrich, D.M., & Young, G.C. (1973a). Significance of WISC verbal–performance discrepancies for younger children with learning disabilities. *Perceptual and Motor Skills*, 36, 275–82.

Rourke, B.P. & Finlayson, M.A.J. (1975). Neuropsychological significance of variations in patterns of performance on the Trail Making Test for older children with learning disabilities. *Journal of Abnormal Psychology*, 84, 412–21.

Rourke, B.P., Fisk, J.L., & Strang, J.D. (1986). *Neuropsychological Assessment of Children: A Treatment-oriented Approach*. New York: Guilford Press.

Rourke, B.P. & Fuerst, D.R. (1991). *Learning Disabilities and Psychosocial Functioning: A Neuro-psychological Perspective*. New York: Guilford Press.

Rourke, B.P. & Telegdy, G.A. (1971). Lateralizing significance of WISC verbal–performance discrepancies for older children with learning disabilities. *Perceptual and Motor Skills*, 33, 875–83.

Rourke, B.P., Yanni, D.W., MacDonald, G.W., & Young, G.C. (1973b). Neuropsychological significance of lateralized deficits on the Grooved Pegboard Test for older children with learning disabilities. *Journal of Consulting and Clinical Psychology*, 41, 128–34.

Rourke, B.P., Young, G.C., & Flewelling, R.W. (1971). The relationships between WISC verbal–performance discrepancies and selected verbal, auditory–perceptual, visual–perceptual, and problem-solving abilities in children with learning disabilities. *Journal of Clinical Psychology*, 27, 475–9.

Rudel, R.G. (1978). Neural plasticity: implications for development and education. In *Education and the Brain*, Part 2, ed. J.S. Chall & A.R. Mirsky. Chicago, IL: University of Chicago Press.

Selz, M. & Reitan, R.M. (1979a). Comparative test performance of normal, learning-disabled and brain-damaged older children. *Journal of Nervous and Mental Disease*, 167, 298–302.

Selz, M. & Reitan, R.M. (1979b). Rules for neuropsychological diagnosis: classification of brain function in older children. *Journal of Clinical and Consulting Psychology*, 47, 258–64.

Spreen, O. (1976). Neuropsychology of learning disorders: post-conference review. In *The Neuropsychology of Learning Disorders: Theoretical Approaches*, ed. R.M. Knights & D.J. Bakker, pp. 445–67. Baltimore, MD: University Park Press.

Wheeler, L. & Reitan, R.M. (1962). The presence and laterality of brain damage predicted from responses to a short Aphasia Screening Test. *Perceptual and Motor Skills*, 15, 783–99.

Wyke, M.A. (ed.). (1978). *Developmental Dysphasia*. New York: Academic Press.

Zangwill, O.L. (1978). The concept of developmental dysphasia. In *Developmental Dysphasia*, ed. M.A. Wyke. New York: Academic Press.

11

Developmental assessment of neuropsychological function with the aid of the NEPSY

Marit Korkman, Sarah L. Kemp, and Ursula Kirk

Goals, history, and development of the NEPSY

Children with developmental disorders or learning disabilities often exhibit multiple, overlapping cognitive or visuomotor disorders. For example, verbal learning disorders tend to co-occur with attention disorders (Dykman & Ackerman, 1991; Gilger, Pennington, & DeFries, 1992; Stanford & Hynd, 1994) and with motor coordination and visuomotor problems (Denckla & Rudel, 1978; Denckla, 1985; Korkman & Pesonen, 1994). Even in children with average cognitive capacity, as measured by psychometric tests of intelligence, multiple impairments may be seen. Similarly, multiple or diffuse impairment is also characteristic of children with a medical history associated with neuro-developmental risks, such as fetal alcohol exposure (Conry, 1990; Carmichael Olson et al., 1992; Don & Rourke, 1995) or very low birth weight (Herrgård et al., 1993; Robertson & Finer, 1993).

One important aim of a neuropsychological assessment is to identify all impairments of the child, as well as areas of relative strength. A comprehensive assessment is necessary to identify impairments and to capture the child's pattern of strengths and weaknesses.

Comprehensive sets of psychometrically developed tests can be achieved by using tests from various sources. However, a test profile based on separately standardized tests may reflect differences in test norms, rather than an individual's strengths and weaknesses (Russell, 1986; Wilson, 1992). The ideal is to create and simultaneously standardize a comprehensive set of neuro-psychological tests for children.

An equally important aim of the neuropsychological assessment is that it should lead to an understanding of the nature of the problems of the child.

Insight into the mechanisms of a cognitive disorder makes it possible to develop realistic expectations concerning the child's achievement, and provides a basis for the planning of intervention and remedial teaching. The insight can be obtained through a neuropsychological analysis of the impaired function, by evaluating the subprocesses that contribute to the function in question. For example, in a neuropsychological assessment of poor graphomotor production, different types of motor and visuoperceptual functions need to be assessed to determine the underlying deficit.

Goals

The NEPSY was designed for the following diagnostic aims: (1) to perform a comprehensive scanning and evaluation of neuropsychological functions in children; and (2) to analyze, in depth, disorders of complex functions. In order to achieve a sufficient comprehensiveness, 27 subtests were included. The subtests were selected so as to correspond to important subprocesses or components of complex functions. In the assessment, the components of the impaired function may be assessed one by one and the deficient link in the chain of subprocesses may be determined.

Rationale

The theoretical underpinnings of the NEPSY were derived from two main traditions: (1) Luria's theoretical and clinical frame of reference, and (2) more contemporary traditions of neuropsychological assessment of children with learning disorders or neurological risks or conditions. An overview of the basic concepts of Luria's tradition is presented first, followed by a description of how these concepts were integrated with recent child neuropsychological traditions.

Luria's tradition

One of the advantages of Luria's frame of reference is that it integrates theory with clinical practice. The clinical assessment is guided by the clinician's knowledge of brain–behavior relationships and of neurocognitive disorders. This knowledge incorporates four interconnected levels: the structure of neurocognitive functions, the functional organization of the brain, syndromes and impairments arising in brain disorders, and clinical methods of assessment.

On the functional level, Luria describes cognitive and motor processes as dynamic systems, characterized by a specific aim but carried out, in a dynamic and variable fashion, by many interconnected subprocesses, or components (Luria, 1973, pp. 26–30). The dynamic aspect of functional systems may be illustrated by developmental changes that may be seen in the function of copying a text. A young child needs actively to search, perceive, and produce the graphic characteristics of each letter, whereas an adult automatically verbally codes the written text and transforms it into overlearned motor schemes (Luria, 1973, p. 32). The structure of language, memory, attention, motor performance, and thinking in adults is described in detail by Luria (1973, 1980; see also Korkman, 1999).

On the brain level, Luria specifies the processes of different regions in the brain and relates them to the functional components, in accordance with prevailing traditions in adult neuropsychology. For example, in adults, motor programming of speech is dependent on left precentral and premotor neural systems (Broca's area), whereas decoding speech is dependent on left posterior temporal regions (Wernicke's area). The brain is viewed as 'a functional mosaic,' the different parts of which are brain processes. These brain processes are combined in a flexible and adaptive manner to form various types of cognitive and practical activity (Luria, 1963, 1973).

On the level of symptoms and disorders, Luria describes consequences of impairments of functional components following focal brain damage. For example, a severe impairment of verbal memory span impairs the ability to comprehend verbal passages in speech reception and reading, and may disrupt cognitive processes in general. Luria describes different types of aphasic, amnestic, agnostic, and apraxic disorders in adults, arising as a result of damage to various locations. The descriptions of syndromes include clinical characteristics, primary and secondary deficits, and probable localization of damage. Together, these syndrome descriptions form a comprehensive taxonomy that may guide the diagnostic assessment of adult patients.

On the assessment level (Christensen, 1975), the rationale of Luria's methods is to analyze disorders of complex functions through a systematic assessment of their components, with the aid of focused tasks and observations. This analysis aims at specifying the primary deficits underlying a neurocognitive disorder. For example, when analyzing an aphasic disorder, tests of motor production and articulation of speech, dynamic verbal fluency and ideation, auditory–phonological analysis, comprehension of syntactic structures and conceptual relations, word-finding abilities, and verbal short-term memory are administered. Clinical observations may also give important clues as to the nature of the deficit. For example, different types of speech distortion and misarticulation are characteristic of different types of aphasia (Luria, 1973).

Integrating Luria's approach with contemporary child neuropsychology

Many aspects of Luria's frame of reference are shared by most neuropsychological views. Like Luria's theory, contemporary child neuropsychology views cognitive functions as complex processes consisting of several subprocesses. For example, attention has been viewed as incorporating many different aspects: selective attention, sustained attention, attention span or divided attention, and inhibition and control of behavior (Douglas, 1984; Barkley, 1988; Mirsky, 1989; Cooley & Morris, 1990). Another expression of this view is the attempt to specify subtypes of disorders, such as language disorders (e.g., Bishop & Rosenbloom, 1987; Rapin & Allen, 1988). Thus, the concept of cognitive functions as complex functional systems is probably valid also in child neuropsychology.

However, the exact components that are seen as contributing to cognitive functions in children do not necessarily correspond to those of Luria's syndrome descriptions. In addition, different authors present different views – a consensus does not yet exist concerning the structure and components of neurocognitive functions in children. It seems evident, therefore, that all aspects of Luria's theory cannot be directly applied to children, although many parallels may be found. Table 11.1 summarizes some of the views concerning components of neurocognitive functions in children (for a more extensive review, see Korkman, 1999). Evaluating these components is considered important in a neuropsychological assessment of children. Most of the components are operationalized in the NEPSY, in the form of subtests.

History

The NEPSY is the result of a long development that started with attempts to apply Luria's methods directly to children, and evolved into an instrument that integrates important aspects of Luria's approach with contemporary approaches to the neuropsychological assessment of children. In the 1970s, clinical neuropsychology started to gain recognition as a branch of applied science. Neuropsychological assessments became part of the care of neurological patients. In Finland, neuropsychological methods developed in the USA and Europe were used together with Luria's methods from the Soviet Union. For a long time, this practice remained restricted to adult patients. Corresponding neuropsychological knowledge and clinical instruments had not been developed for children with brain damage or learning disorders. The need for adequate neuropsychological instruments for children eventually led to the construction of a Finnish method of assessment. This first version of the NEPSY was called NEPS (a Neuropsychological Assessment of Children; Korkman, 1980).

Table 11.1. Components of cognitive processes in children

Attention	*Sensorimotor functions*
Selective attention	Sensorimotor differentiation
Attention span	Production of motor series
Activity/hyperactivity	Tactile perception
Sustained attention	Psychomotor speed
Executive functions	*Visuospatial functions*
Planning, strategies	Visual perception
Fluency	Visuospatial judgment
Shift of set	Visuoconstructive performance
Inhibition	Graphomotor production
Search	
Language	*Memory and learning*
Motor production	Visual short-term memory
Verbal expression	Verbal short-term memory
Phonological decoding	Supraspan learning
Verbal comprehension	Name learning
Naming	Long-term memory

Reprinted with permission from Korkman (1999). Applying Luria's diagnostic principles in the neuropsychological assessment of children. *Neuropsychology Review*, 9, 89–105. Copyright 1999 by Kluwer Academic/Plenum Publishers, New York.

The NEPS was a close adaptation of Luria's assessment for use with children. It included a comprehensive series of brief tests, similar in content and format to those of Luria's assessment (Maruszewski, 1971; Christensen, 1975). The items were of a pass–fail type, yielding scores of 0, 1, or 2. No sum scores were calculated. Norms were based on base rates (percentage passing each item) for 5-year-old and 6-year-old children. The level of difficulty of the items was adjusted so that most children passed them in a prescribed manner. A failed item was considered a sign of impairment in the same way as findings in a medical examination.

The NEPS evidently filled a void, and a need to expand the method in terms of age became evident. A revised instrument called NEPS-U in Finnish (NEPS-Uudistettu, i.e., NEPS–Revised) and NEPSY in publications in English was developed and published in Finland for children aged 3 years 6 months to 9 years 6 months (Korkman, 1988a, 1988b, 1995). The NEPSY was also published in Sweden (Korkman, 1990) and Denmark (Korkman, 1993) for a somewhat more restricted age range (see Table 11.2). In these 1988–1993 NEPSY versions, the subtests were modified and psychometrically developed into homogeneous, reliable scales with graduated difficulty. The results of the subtests were expressed as z-scores (−3 to +1), based on age norms.

The revision also provided an opportunity for revisions of the content. New subtests were added, based on test ideas derived from emerging traditions in child neuropsychology (e.g., Boehm, 1969; Venger & Holmomskaya, 1978; Reitan, 1979; Benton et al., 1983). Two tests, the shortened version of the Token Test (DeRenzi & Faglioni, 1978) and the Developmental Test of Visuo–Motor Integration (VMI; Beery, 1983), were used in their original form, and standardized along with the NEPSY subtests.

The NEPSY attracted interest internationally, and plans for an international version took form. Further revisions were undertaken for the new edition in Finland and in the USA. The original subtests were expanded to accommodate a broader age range, from 3 to 12 years, by adding items for younger and for older children. Some subtests were dropped or combined, and new subtests were added or changed (see Korkman, 1999). Most subtests remained basically the same in their content, but were renamed. The revised NEPSY appeared in Finland in 1997 (Korkman et al., 1997) and in the USA in 1998 (Korkman et al., 1998). The 1997 Finnish and 1998 US NEPSY versions correspond closely, except for three subtests which were included in the Finnish NEPSY but not in the American NEPSY. They differ somewhat from the 1988 Finnish NEPSY, especially with respect to age range (see Korkman et al., 1998; Korkman, 1999). A revised Swedish NEPSY, equivalent to the 1997–8 NEPSY, will be published in 2000. An overview of the successive NEPSY versions is presented in Table 11.2.

Description of the NEPSY

Domains and subtests

The NEPSY contains 27 subtests in all. The subtests are organized into five domains: Attention/Executive Functions, Language, Sensorimotor Functions, Visuospatial Functions, and Learning and Memory. This subdivision groups the subtests, according to their content, into categories applied in child neuropsychology (e.g., Mattis, 1992), and also comparable to those in Luria's assessment (Christensen, 1975). The domains should not be seen as definite functional compartments; neither are they comparable to the factors derived from factor analysis. Some tasks are complex and could actually belong to two or even three domains. For example, learning a list of words over many trials taps language functions, memory, and attention and executive functions.

Table 11.2. Published versions of the NEPSY

Year	Age range (years)	Country	Authors	Team responsible for national edition
1980	5 : 0 to 6 : 11	Finland	Korkman	Korkman
1988b	3 : 6 to 9 : 5	Finland	Korkman	Häkkinen, Leppälä, Levänen, Peltomaa, Rissanen, & Vakkuri
1990	4 : 0 to 7 : 11	Sweden	Korkman	Amberla, Andersson, Johansson, Kihlgren, Kvarnevik, & Lindberg
1993	4 : 0 to 7 : 11	Denmark	Korkman	Holm, Frandsen, Jordal, & Trillingsgaard
1997	3 : 0 to 12 : 11	Finland	Korkman, Kirk, & Kemp	Korkman, Klenberg, Barron-Linnankoski, Ginström, Kesti, Lahti-Nuuttila, & Lindblom-Ikonen
1998	3 : 0 to 12 : 11	USA	Korkman, Kirk, & Kemp	Publisher
1999	3 : 0 to 12 : 11	Sweden	Korkman, Kirk, & Kemp	Kihlgren et al.

Attention/Executive Functions

Tower

This subtest is based on a classic test idea (Shallice, 1982), thought to assess planning and monitoring rule-based, problem-solving performance. The child has to place three balls on pegs to form specific patterns shown in pictures. Only a prescribed number of moves is allowed in each task, so the child has to plan the sequence of moves before performing the task.

Auditory Attention and Response Set

This subtest is designed as a continuous performance-type test of attention and mental control. The child listens to a long array of words, presented on audiotape. On the Auditory Attention task, the child takes a red token from a pile of tokens of various colors whenever the word 'red' is said, and drops it into a box . On the Response Set task, the child drops a yellow token in the box whenever the word 'red' is said, a red token whenever the word 'yellow' is said, and a blue token whenever the word 'blue' is said (see Fig. 11.1A).

(A)

(B)

(C)

Fig. 11.1. Examples of NEPSY tasks: (A) The Auditory Attention and Response Set subtest: the child picks up a red square when she hears the word 'yellow' and drops it in the box. (B) The Imitating Hand Positions subtest: the child imitates positions of the examiner's hands. (C) The Block Construction subtest: the child builds block constructions from models.

Visual attention

This subtest is a visual cancellation task. The child marks all of the figures that are identical to target figures presented at the top of the sheet. Three tasks are presented. In the first task (Bunnies; 3–4 year olds), the figures are placed in a linear array. In the second task (Cats; all ages), the figures are placed in a random array, which calls for visual search in addition to attention. In the third task (Faces; 5–12 year olds), the target figures are complex line drawings of faces, and the figures are placed in a linear array.

Statue

This subtest is a motor inhibition task. The child has to stand still for 75 seconds, eyes closed, and inhibit impulses to open them, to make vocalizations, or to move, despite noise distractors such as when the examiner knocks on the table.

Design Fluency (based on Regard, Strauss, & Knapp, 1982)

This subtest is a figural fluency task. The child has to draw designs by connecting dots contained in small squares on a sheet. The child is instructed to generate as many unique designs as possible in one minute.

Knock and Tap

This subtest is a mental control and verbal regulation task. The child inhibits the impulse to do the same thing as the examiner and responds, instead, with another action. For example, the child knocks on the table when the examiner taps and taps when the examiner knocks.

Language

Body Part Naming

This subtest is a naming task for young children (3–4 year olds). Nine body parts are pointed out in pictures and the child is asked to name them.

Phonological Processing

This subtest is a phonological awareness task, consisting of two parts. In the easier tasks, the examiner says a word segment and the child points to the appropriate picture from three alternatives. For example, the examiner says: 'Here, you see a castle, a postcard, and candy. In which word is there a part such as -ost?' More demanding tasks consist of stimulus words that are only orally presented. The child is asked to delete one segment or a phoneme from a word, or exchange it for another, for example: 'Say "changing." Say it again, but change "-ange" to "-omp".'

Speeded Naming

This subtest is a rapid alternating naming task. The child names, as quickly as possible, the size, color, and shape of 20 figures on a sheet. For example, the child says: 'Little red circle, big blue square,' etc.

Comprehension of Instructions

This subtest is a verbal comprehension task. The child responds to verbal directions, for example: 'Show me the figure that is above one cross and beside another cross.'

Repetition of Nonsense Words

The subtest is a complex task that puts demands on auditory–phonemic decoding, articulation, and short-term memory. The child repeats phonologically complex nonsense words, such as 'Incusement' or 'Pledgyfriskree,' presented on audiotape.

Verbal Fluency

This subtest is a word fluency task. The child names as many animals and as many things to eat or drink (semantic fluency) as he or she can generate in one minute. In a second task, the child names as many words beginning with S and F (phonemic fluency) as he or she can generate in one minute.

Oromotor Sequences

This subtest is an oromotor production task. The child repeats phonological sequences or tongue twisters, for example 'Scoobelly doobelly/scoobelly doobelly,' four times.

Sensorimotor functions

Fingertip Tapping (based on Denckla, 1973)

This subtest assesses the tapping speed of each hand. The child taps the tips of the index finger and the thumb together as quickly as possible 32 times. A second task consists of rapidly tapping the tips of the fingers sequentially against the tip of the thumb eight times, as quickly as possible. The score consists of performance time.

Imitating Hand Positions

This subtest assesses the ability to imitate hand positions. The child imitates positions of the hand, such as pointing outward with the thumb and the little finger while keeping the other fingers in a fist (see Fig. 11.1B).

Visuomotor Precision

This subtest assesses visuomotor speed and precision on a paper-and-pencil task. The child draws continuous lines along curvilinear tracks. Crossing the edge of the track is an error.

Manual Motor Sequences

This subtest represents manual motor learning. The child is taught manual motor sequences and repeats them five times. One example is to knock the knuckles of the right hand on the table, then the left-hand knuckles, then tap right palm, then tap left palm.

Finger Discrimination

These two subtests assess finger discrimination based on touch for both hands separately. The child's hand is hidden from his or her view by a shield. The examiner touches one or two fingers at a time. The child points to the finger that was touched.

Visuospatial functions

Design Copying

This subtest is a two-dimensional visuomotor construction type of task. The child copies geometric designs of increasing complexity.

Arrows

This subtest assesses the ability to evaluate the spatial orientation of lines. The stimuli consist of pictures with eight arrows pointing to a target. The child indicates the two arrows in each picture that point to the center of the target.

Block Construction

This subtest is a three-dimensional construction task. The child builds block constructions from models (see Fig. 11.1C).

Route Finding (based on Venger & Holmomskaya, 1978)

This subtest requires visuospatial analysis of directionality as well as visual search. The child locates houses on schematic maps according to a miniature drawing of the route to the house.

Memory and Learning

Memory for Faces

This subtest puts demands on visual memory for faces. The child is shown 16 black-and-white photographs of children. Then 16 pages are presented, each showing one of the previous photographs and two distractors. The child points to the photographs previously seen. Half an hour later, the child is asked to point to the target photographs again among new distractors (delayed recall condition).

Memory for Names

This subtest is a name-learning task. Six (for 5 year olds) or eight (for 6–12 year olds) line drawings of children's faces are presented. Each drawing is named and the child repeats the name. After that the child is shown the drawings and is asked to recall the names. Correct responses are provided when necessary. This procedure is repeated twice. Half an hour after the immediate recognition task, the drawings are shown again and the child is asked to name them (delayed recognition).

Narrative Memory

This subtest assesses the immediate reproduction and recall of a narrative. A story is told to the child. In a free recall condition, the child is asked to tell the story again. In a cued recall condition, questions are asked concerning all details the child omitted in the free recall.

Sentence Repetition

This subtest is a short-term verbal memory task. The child has to repeat, verbatim, progressively longer sentences, starting from two-word sentences, the longest sentence consisting of 19 words.

List Learning

This subtest is a verbal learning task. The child is read a list of 15 unconnected words and repeats as many he or she remembers. The procedure is repeated four more times, after which a new (interference) list is taught once and recalled. The child is, thereafter, asked to recall the first list once more, and again half an hour later.

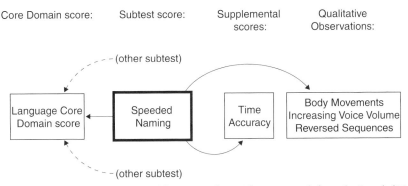

Fig. 11.2. Example of scores derived from one subtest. The main result from the Speeded Naming subtest is the Subtest score. This score may also be included in the Language Core Domain score. In addition, two Supplemental scores, and three Qualitative Observations may be derived.

Psychometric data

Types of scores

For a very comprehensive assessment, the full NEPSY may be administered. However, in clinical practice, time restraints often force examiners to focus on some central problems of the child, and / or to perform a briefer scanning across all domains. The NEPSY provides a pool from which tests may be selected for such purposes. To aid examiners to select subtests, different types of assessments are proposed in the manual (see below). One of these is the orienting, or Core Assessment. Thirteen subtests, two or three from each domain, are administered to provide samples of performance across domains. Expanded Assessments may then be performed by using the other subtests from the domain. Core and Expanded subtests yield subtest scores. In addition, Core Domain scores may be calculated from the Core subtests of each domain.

In addition to the subtest scores, a number of Supplemental scores and Qualitative Observations may be derived. The Supplemental scores are subscores of the subtests, related to different aspects (e.g., performance time, number of correct responses, and errors of different types) or different parts of the subtest. They provide a way to separate particular aspects of performance, in order to provide more specific diagnostic information. The Qualitative Observations represent behaviors or signs, such as tremor, misarticulations, mirror movements, off-task behaviors etc., which may be noted and recorded as the child performs the tasks. Norms are available also for the Supplemental scores and the Qualitative Observations. Examples of the different types of scores are given in Fig. 11.2.

The Core Domain scores are expressed in standard scores with a mean of 100 and a standard deviation of 15, as in the intelligence quotients of the Wechsler intelligence scales (Wechsler, 1989, 1991). The results of the Core Subtests and most of the Expanded Subtests are expressed in standard scores with a mean of 10 and a standard deviation of 3, as in the subtests of the Wechsler tests. Some of the Expanded subtests were not normally distributed in the norm sample, and were, therefore, expressed as percentile ranks. The Supplemental scores and Qualitative Observations are expressed in standard scores (mean = 10, SD = 3), percentages of the standardization sample displaying the behaviors, or means and standard deviations at the different age levels, as appropriate.

Standardization and reliability

The American standardization was performed on a geographically, ethnically, and socially representative sample of children (*n* = 1000), 100 children per age level. Each age group included an equal number of boys and girls. The large norm sample fully reflects the ethnic and social variation of the USA, which renders the normal variation relatively broad. Finnish and Swedish norm groups include 40 and 50 children per age level, respectively.

For the American NEPSY (Korkman et al., 1998) reliability coefficients were calculated for each age level separately. Average (across age levels) internal consistency (split-half) reliabilities are between .70 and .91, with one exception (Design Fluency = .59). The average (across age levels) stability (test–retest) coefficient varies from .52 (Arrows) to .81 (Visual Attention). The interrater agreement for qualitative observations varies from kappa coefficients of .42 (= fair agreement; Misarticulations) to 1.00 (= perfect agreement; Visual Guidance, Incorrect Position, Body Movement). In all, reliability measures were acceptable, adequate, or good.

Developmental issues

Developmental changes in subtest scores

The test norms of the Finnish NEPSY are expressed in tables and, unlike the 1998 US version, also graphically. The norm graphs provide an opportunity to study the developmental curves of the NEPSY subtest scores. It may be assumed that these findings are comparable to data that may be derived from other countries as well. In general, the norm graphs suggest that development is rapid from age three until age eight and nine, but less significant after that. Figure 11.3 presents examples of the results across age levels of six subtest scores. It may be seen that the scores, except one, increase steeply until around age eight, and less steeply after that. The standard deviations tend to decrease

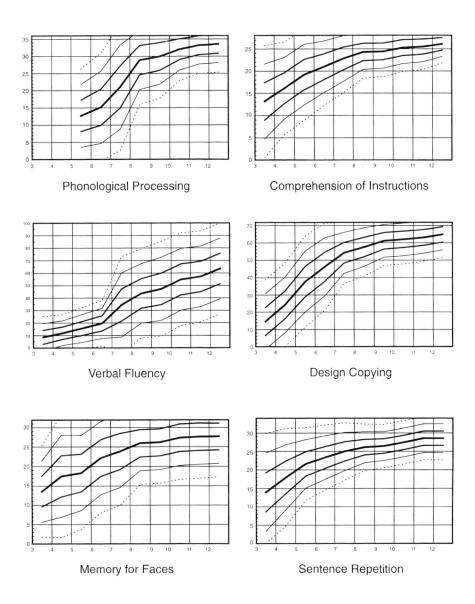

Fig. 11.3. Examples of age-related changes in subtests scores of six NEPSY subtests. The data is derived from the Finnish norm sample ($n = 400$). The bold line represents the means of the age groups ($n \approx 40$), and the lines below and above are drawn at one, two, and three standard deviations below and above the mean. (From *NEPSY. Lasten neuropsykologinen tutkimus*, by M. Korkman, U. Kirk, & S.L. Kemp (1997). Helsinki, Finland: Psykologien kustannus. Copyright 1997. Adapted with permission.)

across age levels, except for the same subtest. This exception is the Verbal Fluency subtest, in which the number of words the child can produce in one minute increases more in the higher age range than in the lower.

The Attention/Executive Functions subtest data of the Finnish norm sample ($n = 400$) was studied in greater detail by Klenberg, Korkman, and Lahti-Nuuttila (in press). This analysis indicated that the subtests of Attention and Executive Functions had somewhat different developmental time tables. The Attention subtests (Auditory Attention and Response Set, Visual Attention) as well as the subtests purported to measure inhibition (Statue, Knock and Tap) developed rapidly in younger age groups and leveled off at ages six to eight years. In the Tower subtest, a task thought to involve planning and monitoring of responses, significant increase in test scores continued somewhat longer. By contrast, the scores on the Design Fluency subtest and the Verbal Fluency subtest continued to show strong developmental trends across the whole age range. Earlier studies (Regard et al., 1982; Vik & Ruff, 1988) have indicated that figural fluency increases throughout adolescence. The difference in developmental trajectories is probably related to the nature of the fluency tasks: the number of words and unique designs that may be produced is, in principle, limited only by performance time. The child's increasing vocabulary and graphomotor skills, and improving strategies for controlled search may interact, producing an exponential (upturned curve, see Fig. 11.3), rather than linear, increase in production.

Figure 11.3 also demonstrates another interesting developmental trajectory in the Finnish data: that of the Phonological Processing subtest score. The score for this subtest in Fig. 11.3 represents the capacity for phoneme deletion and exchanging phonemes of words. The performance of children below the age of five is not shown because these children do not take the more demanding part of the subtest. From age six to age eight years, the developmental curve shows a steep increase in group means. Finnish children go to school at the age of seven, and the sharp increase in this capacity is related to the start of schooling. The acquisition of reading and spelling may enhance their capacity to analyze the sound composition of words and to manipulate the sounds mentally. One aspect of this facilitation may be that the letters and letter combinations provide concrete symbols of the sounds and make it easier to conceptualize and perceive them. These results (Korkman, Barron-Linnankoski, & Lahti-Nuuttila, 1999) conform to those obtained by other authors as well (Bentin, Hammer, & Cahan, 1991; Wimmer et al., 1991; Morrison, Smith, & Dow-Ehrensberger, 1995).

Developmental data from the large US standardization sample are being analyzed at present. Accumulating normative data from different countries will also provide possibilities for cross-cultural studies.

Relationship of cognitive level to test performance

Neuropsychological measures are almost always administered together with measures of general cognitive ability, usually the Wechsler scales (Wechsler, 1989, 1991). The general cognitive capacity is important per se, but can also provide a point of reference for the interpretation of a child's neuropsychological test results. A retarded child cannot be expected to achieve average results on tests of language, motor, visuospatial, and other tasks. In contrast, particular areas of impairment in a child with normal psychometric intelligence are usually seen as indicating specific learning or developmental disorders. For such clinical interpretations it is, however, important to know the extent to which neuropsychological performance is related to psychometric intelligence. Table 11.3 presents the correlations $\geq .30$ of the NEPSY subtests with subtests of the Wechsler Intelligence Scale for Children–Third Edition (WISC–III; Wechsler, 1991). Subjects were children from the US NEPSY norm sample who also performed the WISC–III ($n = 127$). The mean age for this group was 9.87 years (SD = 1.95), mean Verbal IQ was 104.4 (SD = 14.72), and mean Performance IQ 103.4 (SD = 13.74) (Korkman et al., 1998).

The correlations between the Wechsler Preschool and Primary Scale of Intelligence–Revised (WPPSI–R; Wechsler, 1989) IQ values and the NEPSY Core Domain scores in normal 3–6 year olds ($n = 45$), also drawn from the US NEPSY standardization sample, varied between .24 and .60 (Korkman et al., 1998). Preliminary data from a study on 4-year-old children exposed to lead demonstrated even higher correlations between WPPSI–R and the NEPSY Core Domain scores (Chandlee, Tuesday-Heathfield, & Radcliffe, 1999).

Relationship of neurological development to test performance

Neurological risk factors and conditions may affect the child's neurocognitive development, and are frequent indications for referrals for neuropsychological assessments. In general, the neuropsychological sequelae seem to vary less in accordance with the localization or lateralization of a brain insult than with the type of risk factor or insult. The absence of localization and lateralization effects on neuropsychological test performance is particularly conspicuous in children with congenital or early damage to the brain (see below).

One reason for this is that early brain insults or abnormalities tend to be diffuse or multifocal. This is the case, for example, in postasphyxial damage

Table 11.3. Correlations ≥ 0.30 of the NEPSY subtests with the WISC–III subtests

	I	S	A	V	C	DS	PC	Cd	PA	BD	OA	SS	Mz
Attention/Executive Functions													
Tower	0.30					0.31	0.31						
Auditory Attention and Response Set													
Visual Attention													
Design Fluency								0.34					
Statue													
Knock and Tap													
Language													
Phonological Processing	0.43	0.40	0.39	0.41	0.30	0.52							
Speeded Naming	0.32	0.31	0.34	0.39									
Comprehension of Instructions	0.44	0.47	0.42	0.45	0.41		0.41						
Repetition of Nonsense Words	0.38	0.40.	38.		50								
Verbal Fluency	0.38	0.36	0.33	0.35	0.31	0.33							
Oromotor Sequences	0.41	0.57	0.30	0.47	0.31	0.32	0.34						
Sensorimotor													
Fingertip Tapping													
Imitating Hand Positions													
Visuomotor Precision													
Manual Motor Sequences						0.39	0.34						
Finger Discrimination													
Visuospatial													
Design Copying		0.32					0.38			0.35			
Arrows	0.35	0.34	0.31				0.33			0.36	0.38		
Block Construction	0.30						0.33	0.35		0.42	0.40		
Route Finding													
Memory and Learning													
Memory for Faces													
Memory for Names	0.44	0.34	0.30	0.33									
Narrative Memory	0.36	0.34		0.39	0.40								
Sentence Repetition	0.52	0.50	0.50	0.53	0.43	0.55	0.45						
List Learning								0.32					

Adapted with permission from *NEPSY. A Developmental Neuropsychological Assessment*, by M. Korkman, U. Kirk, & S.L. Kemp (1998). San Antonio, TX: The Psychological Corporation. Copyright 1988 by The Psychological Corporation.

I = Information; S = Similarities; A = Arithmetic; V = Vocabulary; C = Comprehension; DS = Digit Span; PC = Picture Completion; Cd = Coding; PA = Picture Arrangement; BD = Block Design; OA = Object Assembly; SS = Symbol Search; Mz = Mazes.

(Truwit et al., 1992; Volpe, 1992; Williams et al., 1993), or alcohol exposure (Miller, 1986; West & Pierce, 1986). However, children with more focal brain damage also fail to demonstrate disorders such as aphasia or neglect, which would be typical of damage to the same brain regions in adults. For example, children with early left-sided damage do not exhibit a significant verbal disadvantage as compared to nonverbal performance (Aram & Ekelman, 1988; Vargha-Khadem & Polkey, 1992; Korkman & von Wendt, 1995). Even in children with acquired damage in childhood, aphasic signs tend to subside rapidly (Hécaen, 1983). Evidently, brain development may adapt to a focal damage.

The functional compensation is probably related to a high degree of neural redundancy in childhood; that is, an early surplus of neurons and synapses, which are gradually reduced to adult levels (Cowan, 1979; Huttenlocher et al., 1982). Neurons and synapses that are not yet functionally committed may be recruited to compensate for lost or undeveloped groups of neurons. One extreme example of plasticity is that of transfer, when language develops in the the right hemisphere in left-sided damage (see, for example, Strauss, Satz, & Wada, 1990). This mechanism has been one explanation of the absence of aphasia in left-sided damage in children. However, other, intrahemispheric forms of neural adaptation probably also operate (Korkman & von Wendt, 1995).

In contrast to these nonspecific findings in children, the literature contains many examples of neuropsychological findings that are characteristic of specific neurological etiologies. In this context, some of the findings obtained with the 1988 Finnish NEPSY are reported.

The absence of lateralization-specific effects was demonstrated in a study by Korkman and von Wendt (1995) comparing children, aged five to nine, with hemiplegia and congenital left-sided brain damage ($n = 17$) or right-sided brain damage ($n = 16$). Only children with normal intelligence were included. The NEPSY subtests were collapsed to four summary scales, representing verbal comprehension, oromotor production, naming, and a visuoconstructive performance. The results were within the average range on all scales. Both groups were most impaired on the Visuoconstructive Scale, but the discrepancy was larger in the children with right-sided damage. However, group differences were not significant. Thus, in children with congenital, unilateral brain damage, no significant impairment was seen. A relative visuoconstructive weakness was, however, evident, especially in children with right-hemisphere damage.

A second study examined the test profiles of Finnish children, aged five to nine years, exposed to alcohol in utero for varying durations. The children were subdivided according to duration of maternal alcohol abuse, as follows: during trimester I ($n = 16$), during trimesters I and II ($n = 16$), and throughout pregnancy ($n = 14$). A control group ($n = 26$) consisted of unexposed children. The group exposed throughout pregnancy was significantly impaired on composite NEPSY scores of Naming, Receptive Language, and Attention, and to a lesser degree on Manual Motor and Visual–Motor Performance. The subtests of Verbal and Visual Memory and Manual Motor Precision did not significantly differentiate the groups. The group exposed during trimester II had precisely the same pattern of findings; however, only the Naming score differed significantly from that of the control group (Korkman et al., 1998).

In contrast to the studies above, a third study on the consequences of perinatal hypoxia did not find any characteristic strengths and weaknesses in the children's neuropsychological test profile. Different kinds of perinatal risks were studied, as follows: (1) children born with very low birth weight ($< 1500\,g$) who were small for gestational age (VLBW–SGA) ($n = 34$); (2) children born with very low birth weight who were appropriate for gestational age (VLBW–AGA) ($n = 43$); (3) children born at term with acute birth asphyxia ($n = 36$); and (4) control children ($n = 45$). Moderately and severely disabled children were excluded. The groups differed with respect to degree but not type of impairment. The VLBW–SGA group had the poorest results. The VLBW–AGA group was somewhat less impaired, whereas the birth asphyxia group performed at a control group level. Group differences were seen in a diffuse pattern on subtests of different types (e.g., VMI, one attention subtest, the 1988 Phonological Processing subtest, Body Part Naming, and Finger Discrimination), with no child demonstrating specific learning or attentional disorder (Korkman, Liikanen, & Fellman, 1996).

These studies indicated that different types of neurological impairment may be associated with characteristic neuropsychological effects: children exposed to alcohol had particularly pronounced verbal and attentional problems; children with hemiplegia tended to have more visuo–constructive than verbal impairment, irrespective of side of lesion, and VLBW children tended to have diffuse impairment.

Applications

Test selection and structure of assessment

The NEPSY is intended for all types of neuropsychological assessments of children aged three to 12 years. The most prevalent referral questions are probably related to learning disorders or attention problems in school-age children, generalized or specific developmental delays, including attention problems and hyperactivity (ADHD), and delayed language or sensorimotor development in young children, and different types of neurological or neuropsychiatric conditions or risks that may have implications for neurocognitive functions in children of all ages. These conditions may include brain trauma, chromosome abnormalities, epilepsy, fetal alcohol exposure, Asperger's syndrome and autistic spectrum disorders, and Tourette's syndrome, to name a few.

Obviously, the needs of these children differ. In some children, for example young children with signs of developmental delay, the task is to evaluate neurocognitive development broadly and determine types and degree of impairments. In other cases, a particular problem such as developmental language disorder or dyslexia may require a thorough analysis of the disorder, as a basis for intervention. In addition to the differences in referral questions, examiners differ with respect to their background and orientation. Also, settings differ, some offering more time and possibilities for in-depth assessments, others demanding assessment of many children in less time.

As was stated previously, the NEPSY was designed to provide a pool from which tests may be selected for various purposes. There are no strict rules concerning how to select the NEPSY subtests. A successful administration of the NEPSY is dependent on the examiner's qualifications rather than on the test itself. However, different types of assessments, performed by using different selections of subtests, were recommended in the manual.

The Full Assessment, using all NEPSY subtests, provides a thorough, comprehensive assessment across all domains of neurocognitive development. The Full Assessment is particularly useful to evaluate the development of the young child with multiple signs of developmental delays. These children often need early intervention, and the neuropsychological survey of assets and impairments is useful as a basis for planning intervention. School-age children who have complex learning disorders also benefit from a thorough assessment at least once in their school career. Other cases in which a Full Assessment is recommended are children with a history of brain insult or significant risks, such as encephalitis, trauma, epilepsy, etc., who need a comprehensive evaluation of brain functions by the neuropediatric team. Further, the Full NEPSY is also often administered as follow-up assessments of treatment effects when the children are receiving certain treatments, such as neuropsychological intervention.

The Core Assessment involves a briefer scanning across domains. The purpose is to perform an overview of all domains, and to evaluate whether there are signs of impairment that will necessitate a more thorough evaluation. The Core subtests of the NEPSY are proposed for this purpose. The choice of Core subtests was based on the psychometric properties of the subtests (a normal distribution was required), as well as on clinical considerations, and previous research findings.

The results of the Core Assessment may be expressed as Core Domain scores. However, preliminary data show that particular Core subtest scaled scores and even the Supplemental scores of the Core subtests may be equally useful as screeners. In a study on 41 children diagnosed with ADHD, the Response Set score from the Auditory Attention and Response Set subtest differentiated the ADHD children from matched control children more significantly ($p = 0.001$) than did the Domain score ($p = 0.002$). Further, Qualitative Observations also discriminated the ADHD children sensitively (Commission Errors on the Response Set part of the Auditory Attention and Response Set subtest: $p = 0.001$; Omission Errors: $p = 0.001$; Number of Rule Violations on the Tower subtest: $p = 0.001$; Huckeba et al., 1998). Thus, the subtest scores, the Supplemental scores, and the Qualitative Observations, obtained from the Core Assessments, should all be considered when deciding about a need for more thorough assessments.

The Core Assessment is followed by Expanded Assessments in areas where signs of impairment have been found, or in accordance with complaints from daily life or reported in the child's history. Children who have attention problems may be given all subtests from the Attention and Executive Functions domain as well as from the Memory and Learning domain. For children with developmental language disorder or reading disorder, as well as those with other types of verbal learning problems, the subtests from the Language and the Memory and Learning domains may be administered. Children with visuomotor problems, in the form of poor drawing, should be administered all subtests from the Sensorimotor and the Visuospatial domains. In other types of disorders, test selection may be guided by characteristics of the particular condition, as reported in the literature, and by what processes may logically be thought to be implicated in an impaired function. For example, in arithmetical operations, executive functions, and working memory are probably involved, in addition to attention, language and visuospatial abilities. To evaluate this complex function in depth, a Full Assessment is advisable (see also the NEPSY manual, p. 49, for an alternative selection). The Core and Expanded subtests for 5–12 year olds are presented in Table 11.4. Three and four year olds perform a slightly different selection of subtests.

A special problem is related to the assessment of attention. Attention tests

Table 11.4. Core and Expanded subtests for 5–12-year-old children

Domain	Subtest	Type of score
Attention/Executive Functions	Tower	Core
	Auditory Attention and Response Set	Core
	Visual Attention	Core
	Design Fluency	Expanded
	Statue	Expanded
	Knock and Tap	Expanded
Language	Phonological Processing	Core
	Speeded Naming	Core
	Comprehension of Instructions	Core
	Repetition of Nonsense Words	Expanded
	Verbal Fluency	Expanded
	Oromotor Sequences	Expanded
Sensorimotor	Fingertip Tapping	Core
	Imitating Hand Positions	Core
	Visuomotor Precision	Core
	Manual Motor Sequences	Expanded
	Finger Discrimination	Expanded
Visuospatial	Design Copying	Core
	Arrows	Core
	Block Construction	Expanded
	Route Finding	Expanded
Memory and Learning	Memory for Faces	Core
	Memory for Names	Core
	Narrative Memory	Core
	Sentence Repetition	Expanded
	List Learning[1]	Expanded

[1]For ages 7–12 only.

tend to yield relatively inconsistent results and to have low hit rates (Halperin et al., 1990; Barkley, 1991; Matier-Sharma et al., 1995). One reason may be that attention in children with ADHD tends to fluctuate from situation to situation, and that it is highly motivation dependent. Children may find the testing situation motivating, and their attention problems may not always become evident on a test level. It is therefore important to be aware that normal test results on the attention subtests do not exclude the possibility of an attention disorder. Despite the sensitivity of the Attention/Executive Functions subtests to ADHD, reported in the study by Huckeba et al. (1998), other types of information, especially rating scales and interviews with parents and teachers, are also essential. In all cases in which attention problems are suspected, an Expanded Assessment of Attention is indicated, irrespective of whether the Attention/Executive Functions Core Domain score is poor or not. A comprehensive assessment of attention is more likely to detect attention problems than only two attention tests. Similarly, when there is reason to suspect other types of impairment – motor, language, perceptual, etc. – Expanded Assessments are also required when the Core Domain score does not give clear evidence of impairment.

Administering a Core Assessment followed by Expanded Assessments is actually an example of a process-oriented approach in Luria's tradition (Christensen, 1984; Kaplan, 1988), and a branching approach as proposed by Cantwell and Baker (1987). Common to these approaches is that the assessment is guided by successive questions and hypotheses. Questions and hypotheses may also arise in the process of interpretation. The examiner may sometimes need to go back and administer additional tests to test the hypothesis. Because there may be a risk that administering additional tests is not possible after the initial assessment, it is always safer to administer the full NEPSY whenever possible.

For a complete neuropsychological assessment, the NEPSY is not sufficient. Other instruments and data may be needed as well. The first question in the evaluation often concerns whether the child's cognitive capacity is normal or not, so a test of cognitive capacity needs to be administered. The next question may be whether or not the child has signs of impairment in any domain. For such a decision, obtaining a thorough history and collecting data from parents, school, and other examinations are essential, in addition to a Core Assessment (see history in the NEPSY manual, Appendix H). A further question may concern the nature of the child's neurocognitive impairments. To answer this question, all subtests from the impaired domain or related to the impaired function need to be administered. In addition, qualitative observations and data concerning how the problems are present in practice are helpful.

In some instances, time restraints, limited cooperation of the child, or other factors may call for a more restricted assessment. The examiner may then choose to analyze the most disturbing problem of the child, ignoring other possible questions for the time being. A need for such Selective Assessments may arise, for example, in children who need intervention for developmental language disorder or dyslexia.

Principles of interpretation

As expressed above, the aims of a NEPSY assessment are: (1) to perform a comprehensive scanning and evaluation of neurocognitive functions; and (2) to analyze, in depth, disorders of complex functions. The interpretation of the results is in accordance with these aims. In contrast, the NEPSY was not primarily constructed to yield diagnostic labels, such as Learning Disorder, Communication Disorder, or Attention-Deficit/Hyperactivity Disorder. Nevertheless, the assessment may aid in assigning such labels, as when the data meet the criteria of the Diagnostic and Statistical Manual of Mental Disorders, fourth edition (DSM IV: American Psychiatric Association, 1994). NEPSY results can also provide support for a diagnosis of various learning disabilities when underlying processes are impaired (e.g., poor phonological processing in reading disorder).

The results according to the first aim of the assessment – to perform a comprehensive evaluation of the child's neurocognitive strengths and weaknesses – can most of the time be expressed in a relatively straightforward and descriptive fashion. Sometimes, however, determining whether weaknesses or impairments are present is not entirely unproblematic. The NEPSY manual provides tables for significances of discrepancies between subtest scores, and between the Core Domain score and specific subtest scores. More important, however, is the pattern of results. In particular, the examiner should look for consistent evidence of an impairment. As a rule of thumb, an impairment may be indicated when two or more subtest scores, Supplemental scores, or Qualitative Observations point in the same direction. For example, at least two Language/Verbal Memory scores significantly below the subtest mean for normal children (< 7), or results significantly below the child's general level of performance, would indicate a language impairment. Expanded NEPSY assessments as well as a consideration of Qualitative Observations (e.g., misarticulations) are often required to obtain sufficient evidence of an impairment. External data, such as data from history, school, or home, or assessment with other instruments, may also support a NEPSY finding.

The second purpose of the assessment is to analyze a stated impairment. This type of analysis is pertinent in disorders of complex functions, such as language disorders, dyslexia, arithmetic disorders, and graphomotor problems. The findings are interpreted by specifying the primary deficit(s) of a disorder, as well as its effects on other complex functions or subcomponents (secondary deficits). The literature on subtypes of disorders or specific deficits underlying disorders is an important source in the forming and testing of hypotheses. This type of interpretation demands some special knowledge in child neuropsychology. Examiners with little experience in child neuropsychology may choose to provide only descriptive interpretations, as described above.

Findings are not always causally related but may, instead, represent comorbid, separate disorders. An example of primary, secondary, and comorbid disorders may be a child with dyslexia whose test profile suggests a deficit of phonological analysis and decoding, as evidenced by impaired results on the Phonological Processing subtest and the Repetition Nonsense Words subtest. These results seem logically consistent with a dyslexia. Secondary deficits found on receptive language tasks and verbal memory and learning tasks would confirm the hypothesis of a primary phonological–receptive deficit. In mild cases, such secondary effects may not occur. If the same child also has poor manual sensorimotor differentiation, as evident on the Imitating Hand Positions and Tactile Finger Discrimination subtest, this problem would be an unrelated, comorbid problem.

It should be pointed out that several different underlying deficits may contribute to a disturbance of the same complex function. Such is the case, for example, when both visuospatial and sensorimotor problems underlie impaired graphomotor production. A special complication is provided by the high prevalence of comorbid disorders in children (see above). If a child has three or more types of impairments, or a generally poor performance level, specifying primary and secondary deficits may not be meaningful.

The final step is to verify the interpretation. The most important way to do this is to check the interpretation for ecological validity. Stated impairments need to correspond to data from history, home, and school. If the assessment points to impairments that have not been suspected before, the examiner needs to double-check that the diagnostic conclusion is based on firm evidence in the NEPSY findings. In verifying the interpretation of primary and secondary deficits, one important source of verification is the literature. If disorders have been described in a similar fashion in the literature, the examiner knows that the interpretation is at least plausible.

Contradictory and unrelated findings are not uncommon in children. Further assessments may sometimes be indicated to yield sufficient data for conclusions. In other cases it may be possible only to suggest potential problems or possible mechanisms of disorder.

The results of the assessment may also be considered with respect to the degree to which they shed light on the particular problems and assets of the child. The value of the assessment depends on the degree to which it provides useful information for child, parents, and school, and serves as a guide for the planning and follow-up of intervention.

NEPSY studies on learning disorders

Dyslexia

Child neuropsychology is relatively young as an applied science, and still lacks a generally accepted taxonomy – classifications and descriptions of subtypes – of disorders. Interpretations of findings may thus vary according to the orientation of the clinicians. One example is the theories concerning dyslexia.

Most authors recognize the importance of phonological analysis and awareness, i.e., awareness of the sound structure in speech, as a main prerequisite for the normal acquisition of reading and writing (e.g., Liberman et al., 1974; Bradley & Bryant, 1985; Stanovich & Siegel, 1994; Torgesen, Wagner, & Rashotte, 1994; Shaywitz, 1998). However, alternative or additional factors have also been emphasized. Some authors emphasize the role of semantic retrieval (naming) (Korhonen, 1991; Wolf & Obregón, 1992), others that of verbal memory processes (Siegel & Ryan, 1989; Douglas & Benezra, 1990; Gathercole & Baddeley, 1990). According to Tallal et al. (Tallal, Miller, & Fitch, 1993; Tallal et al., 1996), slowed auditory processing is the primary deficit in impaired language learning, and may also affect reading acquisition. Galaburda and Livingstone (1993), Lovegrove (1994), and Stein (1994) propose specific types of visual processing problems to be implicated in reading disorders. Deficits contributing to reading disorders may include all of the above.

The validation study of children with reading disorder in the NEPSY manual indicated that these children ($n = 36$) were particularly impaired on the subtests Phonological Processing, Speeded Naming, Oromotor Sequences, Memory for Names, Narrative Memory, and Sentence Repetition. These results point to an underlying language problem. Two of these findings (Speeded Naming and Name Learning) point to problems of semantic retrieval, that is, to dysnomia. The poor score on Phonological Processing may be related to that on the Sentence Repetition. Both may indicate an impairment in the perception and processing of phonological sequences. The poor Narrative Memory score may be related to the poor Oromotor Sequences score, because both are thought to be sensitive to impairments in expressive speech: phonological programming and articulation and production of a narration. Thus, in this reading disorder sample, many children may have impairment in phonological analysis, semantic retrieval, and subtle, maybe compensated, expressive language and speech problems (Korkman et al., 1998).

Some milder but still significant impairments indicated a presence of comorbid problems in the sample of reading disorder children. Visuospatial problems were indicated by poor scores on the Design Copying and Route Finding subtests. Whether or not this impairment may have contributed to the reading problems cannot be concluded. Logically, reversals may be related to poor perception of directionality, but there is little research evidence to verify such a hypothesis. Poor performance on the Manual Motor Sequences subtest corresponds to that on the Oromotor Sequences. Both findings indicate impairment in motor programming. This deficit may also contribute to the poor result in Design Copying.

Developmental language disorder

Language involves many separate subprocesses or components. Not surprisingly, many primary deficits have been proposed as underlying and explaining language disorders. These include a deficit in processing rapidly changing input (Tallal et al., 1996), impaired phonological analysis (Rapin & Allen, 1988; Scarborough, 1990), problems with syntax and morphology (Gopnik & Crago, 1991), impaired verbal short-term or phonological working memory (Gathercole & Baddeley, 1990), a motor programming deficit (see Bishop, 1992), and dysnomic problems (Korkman & Häkkinen-Rihu, 1994). Some authors emphasize one single responsible mechanism, whereas others recognize the possibility of subtypes with different primary deficits. For a thorough treatment of language assessment and the subprocesses of language, see Wiig (Chapter 8).

The study by Korkman and Häkkinen-Rihu (1994) was performed to delineate subtypes of developmental language disorder, and used the Finnish 1988 NEPSY. In 80 children with developmental language disorder, four subgroups were found and validated. The first subgroup was a global subgroup. Children in this category were characterized by global and severe language disorders, evident as impairment on all subtests of language. The second subgroup was a specific verbal dyspraxia subgroup. Children in this subgroup were characterized by impaired scores on the Repetition of Nonsense Words and the Oromotor Sequences subtests. The third subgroup was a specific comprehension subgroup. Common characteristics were problems in tasks demanding comprehension of instructions and concepts, with or without difficulties on the Phonological Processing subtest (only the easier part was administered). The fourth subgroup was a small, specific dysnomia subgroup. This group was characterized by dysnomic problems, including poor performance on the Speeded Naming and Name Learning subtests. At follow-up of part of the sample, three years later, the children from groups one and three were found to be dyslexic. Follow-up data were not obtained for the small dysnomia subgroup, but previous studies (e.g., Korhonen, 1991; Wolf & Obregón, 1992) would predict that this subgroup would also end up being dyslexic.

The finding that phonological processing and dysnomic problems may be separate problems may be relevant also for dyslexia. It may indicate that dyslexia, too, may include subtypes characterized by phonological awareness problems and dysnomic problems, respectively. For a more detailed discussion of subtypes, see Spreen (Chapter 9) and Reitan and Wolfson (Chapter 10).

The study also shows that dyslexia may be predicted on the basis of the NEPSY subtest scores. This finding may have practical implications. Treatment of dyslexia may start preventively before the start of formal reading education. Such preventive treatment was actually provided to a group of children with developmental language disorder, diagnosed with the NEPSY. Preschool training of phonological awareness and preliminary phoneme–grapheme conversions, provided to a group of children with developmental language disorder, resulted in significantly better results on reading and spelling tests at follow-up than those obtained by a control group receiving more traditional forms of treatment (Korkman & Peltomaa, 1993).

Attention disorders

As already mentioned, attention has been viewed as incorporating many different aspects: selective attention, sustained attention, attention span or divided attention, and inhibition and control of behavior (Douglas, 1984; Barkley, 1988; Mirsky, 1989; Cooley & Morris, 1990). Attention disorders have been mainly subdivided into a predominantly hyperactive–impulsive type, a predominantly inattentive type, and a combined type (American Psychiatric Association, 1994).

An attempt to delineate subtypes of and predict attention disorders was made using the Finnish 1988 NEPSY (Korkman & Peltomaa, 1991). A heterogeneous group consisting of 46 kindergarten students at risk for attention problems was administered the NEPSY Attention subtests and the Matching Familiar Figures test (MFFT; Kagan, 1966). The test profiles were grouped into subgroups with the aid of a Q-type factor analysis. Two subgroups had test findings that seemed to predict attention problems at school: poor results on the Attention subtests, including the Inhibition and Control subtest (which included the 1988 version of the Statue and the Knock and Tap subtests), on a subtest called Sustained Concentration (a measure of how long the child was able to go on working on the testing session), and on the MFFT. Subgroup membership predicted attention problems at school with fair accuracy (Cohen's kappa = .41). However, the NEPSY test profiles used in this study did not discriminate between impulsive and inattentive children.

Closely related to attention are executive functions, that is, planning and

Table 11.5. Summary of types of disorders observed with NEPSY

Dyslexia
Phonological analysis deficit
Dysnomic (semantic retrieval) problems
Language disorder (compensated or evident)

Developmental language disorders
Oromotor dyspraxia
Receptive disorder: phonological decoding deficits
                           verbal processing and comprehension deficit
Dysnomia
Global

Attention and executive functions disorders
Deficits of control and inhibition, inattention (ADHD)
Executive functions problems

---

strategy employment, ability to maintain and shift set, organized search, and impulse control (Welsh, Pennington, & Groisser, 1991; Levin et al., 1991). Pennington, Groisser, and Welch (1993) found ADHD children to perform less well than learning-disabled children on tasks of executive functions: the Wisconsin Card Sorting test (see Pennington et al., 1993) and the Tower of London test (Shallice, 1982).

It is not certain, however, that attention and executive functions are inseparable. The study by Klenberg et al. (in press) showed not only that the Attention and the Executive Functions subtest scores had different developmental time tables (see above), but the subtests also loaded on different factors, with the attention and control and inhibition subtests loading on one factor, the fluency subtests (Design Fluency and Verbal Fluency) on a second, and the Tower subtest on a third. It is to be hoped that research will disentangle the relationship of these functions.

A summary of distinctions of types of disorders so far made with the NEPSY is presented in Table 11.5. The overview is to be regarded as preliminary and is not cross-validated. Further distinctions may also be proposed in the future, for example of types of attention disorders. The overview represents an idea of how we may attempt to construct a taxonomy of subtypes of disorders with the NEPSY.

Comorbidity

In accordance with previous studies (e.g., Denckla, 1985; Dykman & Acker-man, 1991; Gilger et al., 1992; Stanford & Hynd, 1994), Korkman et al. (1998) reported a high prevalence of overlapping and comorbid disorders in children with ADHD, reading disorder, and developmental language disorder, as evident on the NEPSY subtests. In addition to their impaired scores on the Attention/Executive Functions Domain score, children with ADHD ($n = 51$) were significantly impaired also on the Language, Sensorimotor, Visuospatial, and Memory and Learning Core Domain scores. The most severe impairment was noted on the language subtests, for which results in all subtests except one were significantly poorer than in a group of matched control children. The manual motor and sensory subtests also showed widespread impairment in the ADHD children. Less impairment was seen on the Visuospatial subtests, for which none of the subtests differed between the groups, despite the significant difference on the Core Domain score. Of the Memory and Learning subtests the Sentence Repetition and the List Learning subtests differed significantly between the groups. Similarly, Huckeba et al. (1998) found significant differences on many Supplemental scores and Qualitative Observations across domains in the same groups of children.

In contrast, children with reading impairment ($n = 36$) were impaired only on the Language and the Memory and Learning Domain scores of the NEPSY, when compared to matched control children. They did, however, differ with respect to the Statue, the Manual Motor Sequences, the Design Copying, and the Route Finding subtests. Children with language disorders ($n = 19$) differed significantly from matched control children on all Core Domain scores except the Visuospatial Core Domain score. The attention subtests were more widely affected than the sensorimotor subtests.

In the studies above, the children had been assigned to the groups on the basis of a diagnosis, and the possibility of comorbid disorders was not explicitly excluded by external measures, such as tests of academic achievement. In a previous study, using the 1988 Finnish NEPSY, Korkman and Pesonen (1994) found children with specific ADHD and no reading disorders to have a relatively good overall performance level, but they performed significantly less well on the Inhibition and Control subtest (see above). Children with reading disorder but no attention disorder performed significantly less well than ADHD children on the 1988 phonological processing-type subtest, a digit span test, and the 1988 memory for narration-type subtest. Children with attention and reading disorder had the same deficits as both the ADHD and the learning-disabled groups. In addition, this group performed poorly on the Visuomotor

Precision test and the VMI as well, which may indicate comorbid graphomotor problems. In addition to the differences between groups, the Memory for Names and the Speeded Naming subtests were poor in both groups. This finding indicated that the attention-impaired children might also have a tendency for language-level problems of name retrieval.

The findings demonstrated the strong tendency for overlapping attention and verbal learning disorders, as well as a tendency for comorbid problems that were particularly pronounced in children diagnosed as attention disordered.

Case study: executive functions and attention disorder

The case that illustrates the application of the NEPSY is that of a girl, Sally, aged 9 years 11 months. This case was chosen because it illustrates the clinical reasoning involved in the application of the NEPSY. Typical of this reasoning is an investigative, process-oriented approach in a Lurian sense. Sally's case also illustrates the principle that NEPSY assessment aims at enhancing our understanding of learning disorders and problems, rather than at attaching diagnostic labels.

Sally was not a typical learning-disabled child and did not have a diagnosis of learning disability. She came to a children's clinic for assessment because her achievement was unexpectedly poor at school. Earlier, she had suffered from epileptic seizures, which were controlled by medication at the time of the assessment. Her cooperation on the assessment was variable, but for the most part good. Her psychometric intelligence was found to be normal (Verbal IQ = 101; Performance IQ = 111). Sally was well dressed and gave the impression of being confident, bright, talkative, and lively. According to school grades and achievement tests, she was not clearly dyslexic, but she did relatively poorly in reading and spelling. In class she did not attend well and had behavior problems and poor peer relations.

Figure 11.4 presents the full NEPSY profile of Sally. As may be seen, most test results were average. On the Attention/Executive Functions assessment, the Tower subtest was discontinued because Sally refused after failing several tasks. The failures were related to impulsive performance – she did not take her time to plan the sequences of moves. Based on her performance before discontinuation, it was evident that this subtest was poorly achieved, but exact results were not obtained. The results on the Auditory Attention and Response Set and the Visual Attention subtests were within normal limits, but supplemental analyses revealed that fast responses compensated for a larger than

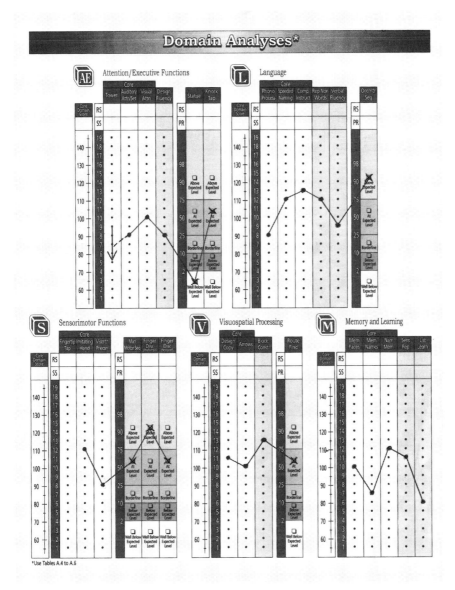

Fig 11.4. NEPSY test profile of Sally, aged 9 years 11 months, with poor school achievement despite average cognitive capacity. Note below-expected scores on Statue and List Learning, and a poor result in relation to average ability on Memory for Names. On the Tower subtests Sally refused to continue after several failures. Supplemental scores on the Auditory Attention and Response Set subtest revealed more errors than expected. Results suggest executive functions problems and attention problems with hyperactivity and impulsivity. (From *NEPSY. A Developmental Neuropsychological Assessment*, by M. Korkman, U. Kirk, & S.L. Kemp (1998). San Antonio, TX: The Psychological Corporation. Copyright 1988 by The Psychological Corporation. Adapted with permission.)

average number of errors. On the Response Set subtest part, Sally made three commission errors, which corresponded to a level below the expected, according to the Finnish norms. Poor impulse control and hyperactivity lowered the score to well below normal on the Statue subtest. Thus, attention problems of a hyperactive and impulsive type were evident.

Deficits typical of dyslexia were not clearly evident, but a relative weakness in phonological processing corresponded to a relatively poor achievement in reading and spelling in school, and may have contributed to the poor overall school performance and motivation. Fingertip Tapping could not be scored as Sally did not follow instructions properly. Poor results were achieved also on the Visuomotor Precision subtest. However, this finding was not confirmed by any other finding, and was contradicted by good results on the Copying Designs subtest as well as by good handwriting, so it was not considered significant. The failure on this subtest was probably caused by too fast and impulsive a performance.

In the Memory and Learning Domain, good results on the Sentence Repetition subtest corresponded to a good performance on Repetition of Nonsense Words subtest, but contrasted with poorer than average scores on the Memory for Names and List Learning. These failures indicated problems with controlled and active memorizing but not with mechanical short-term memory per se. This result, in combination with the problems on the Tower subtest, gave reason to suspect difficulties with organizing and monitoring performance, that is, executive functions problems. In addition, subtle problems in particularly complex tasks of language learning, related to the poor phonological perception, also seemed possible, and may have contributed to the problems in the learning subtests and in school.

In conclusion, Sally seemed to have problems related to executive functions, especially in complex tasks demanding organized activity and effort, and with attention, control, and inhibition. Subtle problems in phonological processing and language learning may have contributed to the difficulties encountered in school. A structuring of the daily routines of schoolwork as well as structuring, supervision, and motivating aids (a timer, keeping records, rewards) to support homework were recommended. In addition, tutoring in reading decoding and spelling was thought to help to improve performance and motivation in school. Assets were good verbal comprehension and rote learning, fast and accurate motor performance, and good visuospatial and visual–constructional abilities.

Conclusion

The basic Lurian frame of reference of the NEPSY is comprised, in a nutshell, as follows: cognitive functions, such as speech, reading, graphomotor performance, learning, paying attention, etc., are all complex systems that incorporate many components. In order to analyze a disordered function, the components need to be assessed one by one. These components are actually brain processes, and therefore a comprehensive neuropsychological assessment is also a scanning of brain functions. The NEPSY subtests aim at assessing the components/brain functions contributing to cognitive and visuomotor functioning.

It was stated previously that a successful assessment using the NEPSY depends more on the examiner's qualifications than on the test itself. However, a comprehensive neuropsychological view was incorporated into the NEPSY and provides a helpful structure to the assessment. Administering the NEPSY may prove to be an educative process. Such an experience was expressed by a young colleague, a novice in neuropsychology, who, after performing her first few assessments using the NEPSY, exclaimed that the NEPSY has taught her a neuropsychological way of thinking.

REFERENCES

American Psychiatric Association (1994). *Diagnostic and Statistical Manual of Mental Disorders, Fourth Edition* (DSM–IV). Washington DC: American Psychiatric Association.

Aram, D.M. & Ekelman, B.L. (1988). Scholastic aptitude and achievement among children with unilateral brain lesions. *Neuropsychologia*, 26, 903–16.

Barkley, R.A. (1988). Attention. In *Assessment Issues in Child Neuropsychology*, ed. M.G. Tramontana & S.R. Hooper, pp. 145–76. New York: Plenum Press.

Barkley, R.A. (1991). The ecological validity of laboratory and analogue assessment methods of ADHD symptoms. *Journal of Abnormal Child Psychology*, 19, 149–78.

Beery, K.E. (1983). *Developmental Test of Visual–Motor Integration*. Cleveland, OH: Modern Curriculum Press.

Bentin, S., Hammer, R., & Cahan, S. (1991). The effects of aging and first grade schooling on the development of phonological awareness. *Psychological Science*, 2, 271–4.

Benton, A.L., Hamsher, K. de S., Varney, N.R., & Spreen, O. (1983). *Contributions to Neuropsychological Assessment*. New York: Oxford University Press.

Bishop, D.V.M. (1992). The underlying nature of specific language impairment. *Journal of Child Psychology and Psychiatry*, 33, 3–66.

Bishop, D.V.M. & Rosenbloom, L. (1987). Classification of childhood language disorders. *Clinics in Developmental Medicine*, 101–2, 16–41.

Boehm, A.E. (1969). *Boehm Test of Basic Concepts*. New York: The Psychological Corporation.

Bradley, L. & Bryant, P.E. (1985). *Rhyme and Reason in Reading and Spelling*. Ann Arbor, MI: University of Michigan Press.

Cantwell, D.P. & Baker, L. (1987). *Developmental Speech and Language Disorders*. New York: Guilford Press.

Carmichael Olson, H., Sampson, P.D., Barr, H., Streissguth, A.P., & Bookstein, F.L. (1992). Prenatal exposure to alcohol and school problems in late childhood: a longitudinal prospective study. *Development and Psychopathology*, 4, 341–59.

Chandlee, L., Tuesday-Heathfield, L., & Radcliffe, J. (1999). NEPSY findings among 4-year-old children with low to moderate lead toxicity. *Journal of the International Neuropsychological Society*, 5, 147.

Christensen, A.-L. (1975). *Luria's Neuropsychological Investigation*. Copenhagen: Munksgaard.

Christensen, A.-L. (1984). The Luria method of examination of the brain-impaired patient. In *Clinical Neuropsychology – a Multidisciplinary Approach*, ed. P.E. Logue & J.M. Schear, pp. 5–28. Springfield, IL: Charles C. Thomas.

Conry, J. (1990). Neuropsychological deficits in fetal alcohol syndrome and fetal alcohol effects. *Alcoholism: Clinical and Experimental Research*, 14, 650–5.

Cooley, E.L. & Morris, R.D. (1990). Attention in children: a neuropsychologically based model for assessment. *Developmental Neuropsychology*, 6, 239–74.

Cowan, W.W. (1979). The development of the brain. *Scientific American*, Sept.-79, 107–17.

Denckla, M. (1973). Development of speed in repetitive and successive finger-movements in normal children. *Developmental Medicine and Child Neurology*, 15, 635–45.

Denckla, M.B. (1985). Development of motor coordination in dyslexic children. In *Dyslexia: a Neuroscientific Approach to Clinical Evaluation*, ed. F.H. Duffy & N. Geschwind, pp. 187–95. Boston, MA: Little, Brown.

Denckla, M.B. & Rudel, R.G. (1978). Anomalies of motor development in hyperactive boys. *Annals of Neurology*, 3, 231–8.

DeRenzi, E. & Faglioni, P. (1978). Normative data and screening power of a shortened version of the Token Test. *Cortex*, 14, 41–9.

Don, A. & Rourke, B.P. (1995). Fetal alcohol syndrome. In *Syndrome of Nonverbal Learning Disabilities. Neurodevelopmental Manifestations*, ed. B.P. Rourke, pp. 372–406. New York: Guilford Press.

Douglas, V.I. (1984). Attentional and cognitive problems. In *Developmental Neuropsychiatry*, ed. M. Rutter, pp. 280–329. Edinburgh, UK: Churchill Livingstone.

Douglas, V.I. & Benezra, E. (1990). Supraspan verbal memory in attention deficit disorder with hyperactivity, normal, and reading-disabled boys. *Journal of Abnormal Child Psychology*, 18, 617–38.

Dykman, R.A. & Ackerman, P.T. (1991). Attention deficit disorder and specific reading disability: separate but often overlapping disorders. *Journal of Learning Disabilities*, 24, 96–103.

Galaburda, A. & Livingstone, M. (1993). Evidence for a magnocellular defect in developmental dyslexia. In Temporal processing in the nervous system, ed. P. Tallal, A.M. Galaburda, R. Liinas, & K. von Euler. *Annals of the New York Academy of Sciences*, 682, 71–82.

Gathercole, S.E. & Baddeley, A.D. (1990). Phonological memory deficits in language disordered children: is there a causal connection? *Journal of Memory and Language*, 29, 336–60.

Gilger, J.W., Pennington, B.F., & De Fries, J.C. (1992). A twin study of the etiology of comorbidity: attention-deficit hyperactivity disorder and dyslexia. *Journal of the American Academy of Child and Adolescent Psychiatry*, 31, 343–8.

Gopnik, M. & Crago, M.B. (1991). Familial aggregation of a developmental language disorder. *Cognition*, 39, 1–50.

Halperin, J..M., Newcorn, J.H., Sharma, V., & Healy, J. (1990). Inattentive and non-inattentive ADHD children: do they constitute a unitary group? *Journal of Abnormal Child Psychology*, 18, 437–49.

Hécaen, H. (1983). Acquired aphasia in children: revisited. *Neuropsychologia*, 21, 581–7.

Herrgård, E., Luoma, L., Tuppurainen, K., Karjalainen, S., & Martikainen, A. (1993). Neuro-developmental profile at five years of children born at =/ < 32 weeks gestation. *Developmental Medicine and Child Neurology*, 35, 1083–96.

Huckeba, W.M., Kreiman, C.L., Korkman, M., Kirk, U., & Kemp, S.L. (1998). Qualitative analysis of NEPSY performance in children with ADHD. Paper presented at the 106th Annual Meeting of APA, San Francisco, CA, August 1998.

Huttenlocher, P.R., de Courten, C., Garey, L.J., & Van Der Loos, H. (1982). Synaptogenesis in human visual cortex – evidence for synapse elimination during normal development. *Neuroscience Letters*, 33, 247–52.

Kagan, J. (1966). Reflection – impulsivity: the generality and dynamics of conceptual tempo. *Journal of Abnormal Psychology*, 71, 17–24.

Kaplan, E. (1988). A process approach to neuropsychological assessment. In *Clinical Neuropsychology and Brain Function: Research, Measurement, and Practice*, ed. T. Boll & B.K. Bryant, pp. 129–167. Washington DC: American Psychological Association.

Klenberg, L., Korkman, M., & Lahti-Nuuttila, P. (in press). Development of attention and executive functions: separate developmental trends? *Developmental Neuropsychology*.

Korhonen, T.T. (1991). Neuropsychological stability and prognosis of subgroups of children with learning disabilities. *Journal of Learning Disabilities*, 24, 48–57.

Korkman, M. (1980). *NEPS. Lasten Neuropsykologinen Tutkimus. Käsikirja* [*NEPS. Neuropsychological Assessment of Children. Manual*]. Helsinki, Finland: Psykologien Kustannus.

Korkman, M. (1988a). NEPSY – an adaptation of Luria's investigation for young children. *The Clinical Neuropsychologist*, 2, 375–9.

Korkman, M. (1988b). *NEPS-U. Lasten neuropsykologinen tutkimus. Uudistettu laitos* [*NEPSY. Neuropsychological Assessment of Children. Revised Edition*]. Helsinki, Finland: Psykologien Kustannus.

Korkman, M. (1990). *NEPSY. Neuropsykologisk undersökning: 4–7 år. Svensk version* [*NEPSY. Neuropsychological Assessment: 4–7 years. Swedish Version*]. Stockholm, Sweden: Psykologiförlaget.

Korkman, M. (1993). *NEPSY. Neuropsykologisk undersøgelse 4–7 år. Dansk vejledning* [*NEPSY. Neuropsychological Assessment: 4–7 years. Danish Manual*]. (Translated from Swedish by K. Holm, K. Frandsen, J. Jordal, & A. Trillingsgaard. Denmark: Dansk Psykologisk Forlag.

Korkman, M. (1995). A test profile approach in the analysis of cognitive disorders in children –

experiences of the NEPSY. In *Advances in Child Neuropsychology*, Vol. 3, ed. M.G. Tramontana & S.R. Hooper, pp. 84–116. New York: Springer-Verlag.

Korkman, M. (1999). Applying Luria's diagnostic principles in the neuropsychological assessment of children. *Neuropsychology Review*, 9, 89–105.

Korkman, M., Autti-Rämö, I., Koivulehto, H., & Granström, M.-L. (1998). Neuropsychological effects at early school age of fetal alcohol exposure of varying duration. *Child Neuropsychology*, 3, 199–212.

Korkman, M., Barron-Linnankoski, S., & Lahti-Nuuttila, P. (1999). Effects of age and reading instruction on the development of phonological awareness, speeded naming, and verbal memory. *Developmental Neuropsychology*, 16, 415–31.

Korkman, M. & Häkkinen-Rihu, P. (1994). A new classification of developmental language disorders (DLD). *Brain and Language*, 47, 96–116.

Korkman, M., Kirk, U., & Kemp, S.L. (1997). *NEPSY. Lasten neuropsykologinen tutkimus* [*NEPSY. A Developmental Neuropsychological Assessment*]. Helsinki, Finland: Psykologien Kustannus.

Korkman, M., Kirk, U., & Kemp, S.L. (1998). *NEPSY. A Developmental Neuropsychological Assessment*. San Antonio, TX: The Psychological Corporation.

Korkman, M., Kirk, U., & Kemp, S.L. (in press). *NEPSY. Neuropsykologisk bedömning* 3:0–12:11år. [*NEPSY. A Developmental Neuropsychological Assessment.*] Stockholm: Psykologiförlaget.

Korkman, M., Liikanen, A., & Fellman, V. (1996). Neuropsychological consequences of very low birth weight and asphyxia at term: follow-up until school-age. *Journal of Clinical and Experimental Neuropsychology*, 18, 220–33.

Korkman, M. & Peltomaa, K. (1991). A pattern of test findings predicting attention problems at school. *Journal of Abnormal Child Psychology*, 19, 451–67.

Korkman, M. & Peltomaa, K. (1993). Preventive treatment of dyslexia by a preschool training program for children with language impairments. *Journal of Clinical Child Psychology*, 22, 277–87.

Korkman, M. & Pesonen, A.-E. (1994). A comparison of neuropsychological test profiles of children with attention deficit-hyperactivity disorder and/or learning disorder. *Journal of Learning Disabilities*, 27, 383–92.

Korkman, M. & von Wendt, L. (1995). Evidence of altered dominance in children with congenital spastic hemiplegia. *Journal of the International Neuropsychological Society*, 1, 251–70.

Levin, H.S., Culhane, K.A., Hartmann, J. et al. (1991). Developmental changes in performance on tests of purported frontal lobe functioning. *Developmental Neuropsychology*, 7, 377–95.

Liberman, I.Y., Shankweiler, D., Fisher, F.W., & Carter, B. (1974). Reading and the awareness of linguistic segments. *Journal of Experimental Child Psychology*, 18, 201–12.

Lovegrove, W. (1994). Visual deficits in dyslexia: evidence and implications. In *Dyslexia in Children. Multidisciplinary Perspectives*, ed. A. Fawcett & R. Nicolson, pp. 113–35. New York: Harvester Wheatsheaf.

Luria, A.R. (1963). *Restoration of Function after Brain Injury* (translated by B. Haigh). Oxford: Pergamon Press.

Luria, A.R. (1973). *The Working Brain* (translated by B. Haigh). London: Penguin Press.

Luria, A.R. (1980). *Higher Cortical Functions in Man*, second edition (translated by B. Haigh). New York: Basic Books.

Maruszewski, M. (1971). Unpublished test material. Personal communication.

Matier-Sharma, K., Perachio, N., Newcorn, J.H., Sharma, V., & Halperin, J.M. (1995). Differential diagnosis of ADHD: are objective measures of attention, impulsivity, and activity level helpful? *Child Neuropsychology*, 1, 118–27.

Mattis, S. (1992). Neuropsychological assessment of school-aged children. In *Handbook of Neuropsychology*, Vol. 6: Child Neuropsychology, ed. I. Rapin & S.J. Segalowitz, pp. 395–415. Amsterdam: Elsevier.

Miller, M.W. (1986). Effects of alcohol on the generation and migration of cerebral cortical neurons. *Science*, 233, 1308–11.

Mirsky, A.F. (1989). The neuropsychology of attention: elements of a complex behavior. In *Integrating Theory and Practice in Clinical Neuropsychology*, ed. E. Perecman, pp. 75–91. Hillsdale, NJ: Lawrence Erlbaum Associates.

Morrison. F.J., Smith, L., & Dow-Ehrensberger, M. (1995). Education and cognitive development: a natural experiment. *Developmental Psychology*, 31, 789–99.

Pennington, B.F., Groisser, D.M., & Welsh, M.C. (1993). Contrasting cognitive deficits in attention deficit hyperactivity disorder versus reading disability. *Developmental Psychology*, 29, 511–23.

Rapin, I. & Allen, D.A. (1988). Syndromes in developmental dysphasia and adult aphasia. In *Language, Communication and the Brain*, ed. F. Plum, pp. 57–74. New York: Raven Press.

Regard, M., Strauss, E., & Knapp, P. (1982). Children's production on verbal and non-verbal fluency tasks. *Perceptual and Motor Skills*, 55, 839–44.

Reitan, R.M. (1979). *Manual for Administration of Neuropsychological Test Batteries for Adults and Children*. Tucson, AZ: Reitan Neuropsychological Laboratory.

Robertson, C.M.T. & Finer, N.N. (1993). Long-term follow-up of term neonates with perinatal asphyxia. *Clinics in Perinatology*, 20, 483–97.

Russell, E.W. (1986). The psychometric foundation of clinical neuropsychology. In *Handbook of Clinical Neuropsychology*, Vol. II, ed. S. Filskov & T.J. Boll, pp. 45–80. New York: Wiley & Sons.

Scarborough, H.S. (1990). Very early language deficits in dyslexic children. *Child Development*, 61, 1728–41.

Shallice, T. (1982). Specific impairments of planning. *Philosophical Transactions. The Royal Society of London B*, 298, 199–209.

Shaywitz, S.E. (1998). Dyslexia. *New England Journal of Medicine*, 338, 307–12.

Siegel, L.S. & Ryan, E.B. (1989). The development of working memory in normally achieving and subtypes of learning disabled children. *Child Development*, 60, 973–80.

Stanford, L.D. & Hynd, G.W. (1994). Congruence of behavioral symptomatology in children with ADD/H, ADD/WO, and learning disabilities. *Journal of Learning Disabilities*, 27, 243–54.

Stanovich, K.E. & Siegel, L.S. (1994). Phenotypic performance profile of children with reading disabilities: a regression-based test of the phonological-core variable-difference model. *Journal of Educational Psychology*, 86, 24–53.

Stein, J. (1994). A visual defect in dyslexics. In *Dyslexia in Children. Multidisciplinary Perspectives*, ed. A. Fawcett & R. Nicolson, pp. 137–56. New York: Harvester Wheatsheaf.

Strauss, E., Satz, P., & Wada, J. (1990). Note. An examination of the crowding hypothesis in epileptic patients who have undergone the carotid amytal test. *Neuropsychologia*, 28, 1221–7.

Tallal, P., Miller, S.L., Bedi, G. et al. (1996). Language comprehension in language-learning impaired children improved with acoustically modified speech. *Science*, 271, 81–4.

Tallal, P., Miller, S., & Fitch, R.H. (1993). Neurobiological basis of speech: a case for the preeminence for temporal processing. In Temporal processing in the nervous system, ed. P. Tallal, A.M. Galaburda, R. Liinas, & K. von Euler. *Annals of the New York Academy of Sciences*, 682, 27–47.

Torgesen, J.K., Wagner, R.K., & Rashotte, C.A. (1994). Longitudinal studies of phonological processing and reading. *Journal of Learning Disabilities*, 27, 276–86.

Truwit, C.L., Barkovich, A.J., Koch, T.K., & Ferriero, D.M. (1992). Cerebral palsy: MR findings in 40 patients. *American Journal of Neuroradiology*, 13, 67–78.

Vargha-Khadem, F. & Polkey, C.E. (1992). A review of cognitive outcome after hemidecortication in humans. *Advances in Experimental Biological Medicine*, 325, 137–51.

Venger, L.A. & Holmomskaya, V.V. (1978). *Diagnostika umst vennogo razvitja doskolnekov [Diagnosing the Cognitive Development of Preschool Children]*. Moscow: Pedagogika.

Vik, P. & Ruff, R.R. (1988). Children's figural fluency performance: development of strategy use. *Developmental Neuropsychology*, 4, 63–74.

Volpe, J.J. (1992). Brain injury in the premature infant – current concepts of pathogenesis and prevention. *Biology of the Neonate*, 62, 231–42.

Wechsler, D. (1989). *Wechsler Preschool and Primary Scale of Intelligence–Revised*. San Antonio, TX: The Psychological Corporation.

Wechsler, D. (1991). *The Wechsler Intelligence Scale for Children–Third Edition*. San Antonio, TX: The Psychological Corporation.

Welsh, M.C., Pennington, B.F., & Groisser, D.B. (1991). A normative–developmental study of executive function: a window on prefrontal function in children. *Developmental Neuropsychology*, 7, 131–49.

West, J.R. & Pierce, D.R. (1986). Perinatal alcohol exposure and neuronal damage. In *Alcohol and Brain Development*, ed. J.R. West, pp. 120–57. New York: Oxford University Press.

Williams, C.E., Mallard, C., Tan, W., & Gluckman, P.D. (1993). Pathophysiology of perinatal asphyxia. *Clinics in Perinatology*, 2, 305–25.

Wilson, B.C. (1992). The neuropsychological assessment of the preschool child: a branching model. In *Handbook of Neuropsychology*, Vol. 6: *Child Neuropsychology*, ed. I. Rapin & S.J. Segalowitz, pp. 377–94. Amsterdam: Elsevier.

Wimmer, H., Landerl, K., Linortner, R., & Hummer, P. (1991). The relationship of phonemic awareness to reading aquisition: more consequence than precondition but still important. *Cognition*, 40, 219–49.

Wolf, M. & Obregón, M. (1992). Early naming deficits, developmental dyslexias and a specific deficit hypothesis. *Brain and Language*, 42, 219–47.

12

Clinical neuropsychological assessment of child and adolescent memory with the WRAML, TOMAL, and CVLT–C

Erin D. Bigler and Wayne V. Adams

Introduction

Central to all aspects of cognition is some facet of memory. Consequently, most neurological and neuropsychiatric disorders disrupt various aspects of normal memory function (see reviews of memory disorders and their assessment in Cullum, Kuck, & Ruff, 1990; Knight, 1992; Reeves & Wedding, 1994; Baron, Fennell, & Voeller, 1995; Gillberg, 1995; Lezak, 1995; Mapou & Spector, 1995; Cytowic, 1996). For example, in cases of traumatic brain injury (TBI), memory disturbances are the most common of all patient complaints (Cronwall, Wrightson, & Waddell, 1990; Golden, Zillmer, & Spiers, 1992; Reeves & Wedding, 1994). Because TBI represents one of the most common sources of childhood injury (Goldstein & Levin, 1990), assessment of memory disorder in children who have sustained a TBI is one of the most frequently explored domains by pediatric neuropsychologists. Similarly, abnormal memory function typically accompanies most learning disorders, the most common referral concerns resulting in psychological assessment of children (Lorsbach, Wilson, & Reimer, 1996; Swanson, Ashbacker, & Lee, 1996; Bull & Johnston, 1997; de Jong, 1998; Nation et al., 1999). Table 12.1 lists the most frequent childhood disorders in which memory and learning are likely to be compromised and should be assessed. Closely allied with assessment is treatment for disordered memory, the primary therapeutic focus in cognitive rehabilitation (Prigatano, 1990), which again underscores the importance of good assessment tools for the evaluation of memory.

Given the ubiquitous nature of memory in everyday life (e.g., academic performance during the school-age years), and the importance of memory in evaluating the functional and the physiological integrity of the brain (Parkin, 1993; Cowan, 1997), it is surprising that the availability of comprehensive memory assessment measures for children and adolescents is a recent phenomenon. This seems particularly odd given the plethora of such tasks available for adults since the 1930s.

Table 12.1. Most frequent childhood disorders in which memory and learning are likely to be compromised

Attention deficit hyperactivity disorder	*In utero* toxic exposure (e.g., cocaine babies, fetal alcohol syndrome)	Neurofibromatosis
Autism and other developmental disorders	Juvenile Huntington's disease	Prader–Willi syndrome
Cancer (especially brain tumors, lung cancer, parathyroid tumors, leukemia, and lymphoma)	Juvenile parkinsonism	Rett's syndrome
Cerebral palsy	Kidney disease / transplant	Schizophrenia
Down syndrome	Learning disability	Seizure disorders
Endocrine disorders	Lesch–Nyhan disease	Tourette's syndrome
Extremely low birth weight	Major depressive disorder	Toxic exposure (e.g., lead, mercury, carbon monoxide)
Fragile X	Meningitis	Traumatic brain injury
Hydrocephalus	Mental retardation	Turner's syndrome
Hypoxic–ischemic injury	Myotonic dystrophy	XXY syndrome
Inborn errors of metabolism (e.g., phenylketonuria, galactosemia)	Neurodevelopmental abnormalities affecting brain development (e.g., anencephaly, microcephaly, callosal dysgenesis)	XYY syndrome

To some extent, memory assessment with children and adolescents must have been viewed as important, because the earliest of modern intelligence tests (the 1905 Binet) and even the venerable Wechsler scales, in their various children's versions, all included one or two brief assessments of immediate recall. Dorothea McCarthy, the noted psycholinguist, was aware of the importance of memory and included a memory index on the then-innovative McCarthy Scales of Children's Abilities (McCarthy, 1972). Koppitz (1977), another pioneer in the assessment of children, noted the need for a more detailed evaluation of children's memory functions and devised the four-subtest Visual–Aural Digit Span Test (VADS).

Nonetheless, the major child neuropsychology texts of the 1970s and 1980s (e.g., Hynd & Obrzut, 1981; Bakker, Fisk, & Strang, 1985) make little reference to memory assessment. In retrospect, this lack in the development of comprehensive measures of memory function in children until recently is particularly puzzling, because, even by 1987, 80% of a sample of clinicians involved in assessment noted memory as a key aspect of cognitive assessment (Snyderman & Rothman, 1987). In contrast, assessment of memory function in children has now become a central focus in discussion of various childhood medical (e.g., Baron et al., 1995) and neuropsychiatric disorders (e.g., Gillberg, 1995) and is a routine topic included in major works on child neuropsychology (Tramontana & Hooper, 1988; Pennington, 1991; Rourke, 1991).

No real attempt at developing a comprehensive assessment of children's memory appears until the introduction of the Wide Range Assessment of Memory and Learning (WRAML) (Sheslow & Adams, 1990). The WRAML, designed for children aged 5 to 17 years, was born from the frustration and dissatisfaction of its authors in not having a sound, comprehensive measure of memory functioning in children (Sheslow & Adams, 1990). Another comprehensive assessment battery designed to evaluate memory function in children is the Test of Memory and Learning (TOMAL) by Reynolds and Bigler (1994b). Although these two comprehensive assessment batteries are the focus of this chapter, a brief review of the basic neurobiology of memory is presented initially to provide a conceptual context in which to view these comprehensive measures. The chapter concludes with a brief overview of the California Verbal Learning Test – Children's Version (CVLT–C) (Delis et al., 1994).

Basic neurobiology of memory

Memory has been the topic of interest within experimental psychology since the beginnings of the discipline (Baddeley, 1990). A comprehensive treatise on the neurobiology of memory is beyond this chapter, particularly in light of excellent reviews on this topic elsewhere (see Diamond, 1990; Scheibel, 1990; Bauer, Tobias, & Valenstein, 1993; Cohen, 1993). Nonetheless, some brief discussion of the apparent memory systems and their associated anatomic structures is important. Obviously, for new learning, some feature of sensation, either singularly or a combination of the senses, is required for initial processing. The way in which initial sensory processing occurs may lay the foundation for the type and modality of memory function. For example, if we invite the reader to think of the space ship Challenger, and the disastrous launch of 1984, what is recalled? The exploding space craft, the three plumes of white, bilious smoke, the stunned look on the faces of the spectators, President Reagan addressing the shocked world, or something else? For many, the recollection of this historical event is primarily mediated through a 'visual memory' because it was initially processed using the visual sense. We all witnessed the dramatic

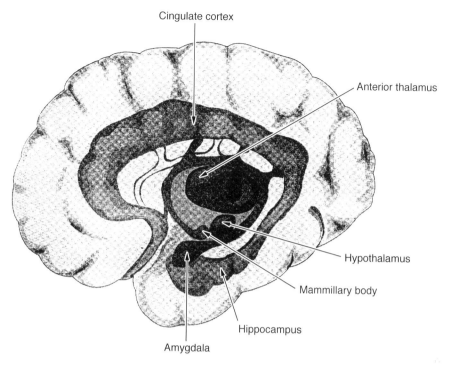

Fig. 12.1. Diagram of the brain highlighting the limbic system, in particular the hippocampus. The hippocampus is located in the temporal lobe and is critical in the process of memory function. (Reproduced with permission from M.T. Banich (1997). *Neuropsychology: the Neural Bases of Mental Function*. Boston: Houghton-Mifflin Co.)

event on the television, or saw the pictures in newsprint. Regardless of how an event is processed – visual, tactile, auditory, gustatory (think of a favorite childhood candy), or olfactory (think of the smell of grandma's house or a favorite food) – memories are established. Although memories are formed and retrieved within any of these modalities, most people process predominantly via the visual, verbal, and auditory senses. Thus, much of what is assessed in the testing of memory focuses upon these three modalities, with a particular emphasis on verbal processing. As discussed below, generally the verbal–visual distinction also aligns with hemispheric specialization: the left hemisphere is more oriented toward verbal and the right toward visual memory (Bigler & Clement, 1997).

Regardless of the type of memory, several critical brain structures partici-pate, in particular the hippocampus, amygdala, fornix, mammillary bodies, various thalamic nuclei, and disseminated regions of the cerebral cortex (Fig. 12.1). The sensory information from any modality, or combination of modalities, inputs to the hippocampus, via pathways that course through the medial–inferior aspect of the temporal lobe on their way to the hippocampus. Although a vast oversimplification, information that has little saliency remains at some momentary sensory register and is never included in the full process of storage and retrieval. Such momentary processing does not access all of these neural structures. Information that has some relevance or saliency may tap all of these structures in the normal process of memory acquisition, storage, and retrieval. It is on this last and more inclusive, aspect of memory that clinical assessment typically concentrates.

Again, an oversimplification, but the hippocampus and its associated structures are critical to the short-term storage of memory that is destined to be available for long-term storage, which, in turn, is dependent on more distributed cerebral cortical functioning. Thus, if the hippocampus is damaged (or its output – fornix, mammillary body, anterior thalamus), then the ability for immediate recall is disrupted, and in severe cases destroyed. Despite hippocampal damage, sensory registration of the information may proceed normally. Thus, if the information to be recalled is a brief stimulus, such as a list of two or three words or numbers, it may be immediately recalled without difficulty. However, for retention of information beyond *immediate* or *short-term memory* span,[1] that is, more than several seconds, additional structures are required. Thus, any delayed recall of information becomes problematic when the hippocampus is damaged, because more complicated information exceeds simple sensory input–processing–registration and recitation. Accordingly, the hippocampus and attendant limbic structures are essential for many aspects of memory that have been traditionally referred to as *long-term memory*.[1]

Given normal brain functioning, information to be retained progresses through a long-term storage process that appears to rely on more distributed functions of the cerebral cortex. Thus, the basic neural systems for memory involve an initial sensory processing (i.e., specific neural pathways that process the sensory information and direct that information to appropriate cortical areas). Next involved is a step to determine the saliency of the information to be recalled. Salient information seems to require processing at the hippocampal level for short-term retention and then within the cerebral cortex for more long-term storage, retention, and retrieval.

Another feature of the neurobiology of memory deals with lateralization of brain function (Stark & McGregor, 1997). Typically, the left hemisphere is more lateralized for language-based functions, whereas the right hemisphere involves more visual and spatial processes. This lateralization sets the stage for assessing differences in memory processes, based on whether the information is processed as a language-based versus spatial-based function. Thus, damage to the left hemisphere, particularly the left temporal lobe, may leave the individual with verbal memory deficits and spared visual–spatial function. Just the opposite may occur with damage to the right hemisphere, particularly the right temporal lobe. Regardless of lateralization, the recall of well-established memories tends to be one of the most robust of neural functions, whereas sustained attention, concentration, and the formation of new memories tend to be the most fragile. This is why memory deficits are so common in neurological disorders.

Finally, no discussion of the neurobiology of memory would be complete without mention of attention. Memory and attention are integral aspects of cognition, and difficult to tease apart within an assessment framework. From the neuroanatomical perspective, there is no specific region that is the exclusive province of attention. Of course, there is the long-known reticular activating and diffuse thalamic projecting systems essential to arousal, but damage to these core structures of the brain typically results in unmistakable deficits in primary arousal (i.e., coma). From the neuropsychological perspective, 'attention' is probably a nonlocalized neural process with major contributions from frontal and temporal lobe regions. However, it is also well known that damage just about anywhere in the cerebral cortex has the capacity to affect attention. Thus, attention may also be considered a whole-brain integrated system and, thereby, attention can be disrupted in a variety of ways when the brain is damaged or made dysfunctional. Disrupted attention may be difficult to distinguish from certain aspects of impaired memory. For example, if sufficient attention is not directed to the stimulus being processed, it will not be processed properly and therefore poorly retained. However, this difficulty with performance is more a deficit in attention than in storage or retrieval.

Currently, assessment of memory has some operationally defined tasks that assess 'attention.' However, as might be expected, 'attention' is rather an ethereal cognitive function that remains problematic whether establishing diagnostic criteria (e.g., DSM-IV) or attempting to operationalize tasks for tests of memory. Essentially, all measures of memory require attention; care, therefore, is always required on the examiner's part to insure that the subject is properly attending to the memory task or stimulus.

Wide Range Assessment of Memory and Learning

Structure

The WRAML (Sheslow & Adams, 1990) was the first comprehensive memory measure for children and adolescents. Until the WRAML was published, most

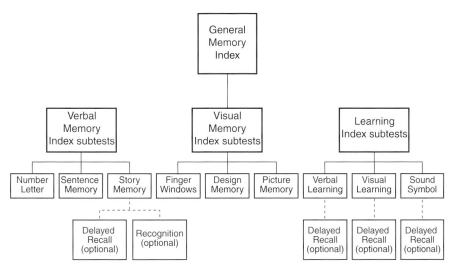

Fig. 12.2. Schematic of the Index and subtest structure of the WRAML.

clinicians wanting to assess memory functions in children had to use various tasks from various sources. The norms associated with these memory tasks were variable in quality, and had been collected on different groups of children. With the publication of the WRAML, clinicians and researchers had a psychometrically sound tool which utilized a broad variety of memory tasks, each of which had a common norm-base, thus allowing meaningful intertask comparisons for the first time.

The WRAML is normed for children aged 5 through 17 years. While administration time depends upon the age and pace of the child as well as on the experience of the examiner, generally, the entire WRAML takes between 45 and 60 minutes to administer. An Examiner Record Form and an Examinee Response Form are utilized in the standard administration.

The structure and hierarchical organization of the instrument are illustrated in Fig. 12.2. The composite General Memory Index is derived from performance in three domains: Verbal Memory, Visual Memory, and Learning. The first two domains, verbal and visual, assess the two dominant information-processing modes of memory for children and adolescents. The third WRAML domain highlights memory within the context of acquiring information over consecutive learning episodes. Such acquisition 'opportunities' are provided for visual, verbal, and dual (visual with verbal) modalities.

The conceptual rationale is similar for the organization of the Verbal and Visual domains. Subtests of each domain provide a gradually increasing amount of information to be immediately recalled. Subtests within both Verbal and Visual domains range from rote memory tasks using minimally meaningful

Table 12.2. Description of each WRAML subtest associated with each WRAML domain

Domain	Subtest name	Subtest description
Verbal Memory	Number/Letter	The child is asked to repeat a series of both numbers and letters verbally presented at a rate of one per second. The subtest begins with an item two units in length (e.g., '1-A') and proceeds until the discontinue rule is satisfied
	Sentence Memory	The child is asked to repeat meaningful sentences. Starting with a three-word sentence, the child attempts to repeat progressively longer sentences, until the discontinue rule is satisfied
	Story Memory	The child is read and then asked to retell a one–two-paragraph story. A second story is then read and again the child is asked to retell the story. Scoring both exact and 'gist' recalled information is recorded
Visual Memory	Finger Windows	The child indicates his/her memory of a rote visual pattern by sequentially placing a finger into 'windows,' or holes, in a plastic card, attempting to reproduce a sequence demonstrated by the examiner. Starting with a sequence of two holes, the child continues until the discontinue rule is satisfied
	Design Memory	A card with geometric shapes is shown to the child for five seconds. Following a ten-second delay, the child is asked to draw what was seen. A blank card with spatial demarcations is provided for the child's drawing. Four different cards are presented in this fashion
	Picture Memory	The child is shown a meaningful scene with people and objects for ten seconds. The child is then asked to look at a second, similar scene. Memory of the original picture is indicated by the child's marking elements which have been altered or added in the second picture. This procedure is repeated with three additional scenes

Table 12.2. (*cont.*)

Domain	Subtest name	Subtest description
Learning	Verbal Learning	The child is read a list of common, single-syllable words and is provided a free recall opportunity. Three additional learning trials are administered in similar fashion. A delayed recall trial is available following an interference task
	Visual Learning	After initially seeing all locations, the child is asked to indicate the specific location of 12 or 14 (depending on age) visual stimuli nested within a 4 × 4 array. Correction of errors occurs. Three additional learning trials follow. A delayed recall trial is also available
	Sound Symbol	The child is presented a paired-associate task requiring him/her to recall which sound is associated with which abstract and unfamiliar symbol shape. Four separate learning trials are administered and a delayed recall trial is also available

content, to tasks making memory demands using quite meaningful content. In this manner, the examiner has the opportunity to observe a child's immediate memory ability on tasks which are modality specific (i.e., verbal or visual) and which vary in meaningfulness.

Three subtests contribute to each of the WRAML's three domains. Each subtest yields a scaled score (mean = 10, SD = 3), and each domain yields a standard score (mean = 100, SD = 15). The scaled scores of all nine subtests are pooled to yield a General Memory Index (mean = 100, SD = 15). The familiar metrics make for easy examiner understanding, and allow easy comparison with other cognitive measures such as intelligence and achievement tests.

In addition to the nine 'core' subtests defining the three major domains, there are 'optional' Delayed Recall components associated with each of the learning-over-trials subtests. One of the Verbal Memory subtests (Story Memory) also provides a Delayed Recall as well as a Recognition Memory option.

Subtest description, rationale, and clinical utility

Table 12.2 provides a description of the subtests within each domain. The narrative that follows provides a rationale for the subtest and some clinical applications that might be derived from a given subtest or subtest combination.

Verbal Memory Scale

The subtests that comprise the Verbal Memory Scale allow the examiner to assess the child's capabilities on a rote, auditory memory task and to compare that performance to that of tasks with more language demands. This allows the examiner to form hypotheses about the child's ability to utilize language as an aide or detractor in remembering. The three subtests can be viewed as demanding increasing amounts of language processing, so that the clinician can also be sensitive to language deficits, which may confound memory assessment within this domain. The three subtests comprising the Verbal Memory Scale are as follows.

Number/Letter

The format of this subtest is familiar to most clinicians. Unlike some such tests, however, only a 'forwards' direction of recall is required in the Number/Letter subtest. Because a backwards recall seems to require a different cognitive skill from forwards recall (Lezak, 1995), the Number/Letter task does not confound these two operations.

Sentence Memory

The 'bits' of information that can be remembered change in this task compared to that in the Number/Letter subtest because of the 'mental glue' language affords. Clinically, because this task requires the ability to remember one or two sentences, it is thought to begin to tap the kind of memory skills required to follow oral directions being given to a child at home or at school.

Story Memory

Two stories are read to the child. The stories differ in developmental level of interest and linguistic complexity. Using two stories permits better sampling than using a single story. It is, then, reasonable to assume that a greater than chance difference between the first and second stories suggests lower verbal intellectual ability, a language disorder, or an inefficient or inconsistent ability to attend to oral information.

Likewise, a child who retells the story in an erratic sequence may have sequencing or organizational problems. By comparing sequencing in Number/

Letter and Sentence Memory with that of Story Memory, one should begin to differentiate between sequencing, organizational, and language deficits. Because of the importance of remembering semantically related information to classroom and social functioning, the clinician may wish to explore whether the child doing poorly on Story Memory remembers the material but cannot reproduce it in a free recall format. Therefore, a Story Recognition subtest is also provided by presenting 15 questions related to the harder story, and using a multiple-choice format to help determine a retention (or storage) versus a retrieval (or expressive language) deficit.

Comparing performance on the Sentence Memory and Story Memory subtests can also be useful. If performance on Sentence Memory is relatively poor, one might conjecture that the rote components of directions would be missed (such as the page number of the assignment). Proportionately better performance on Story Memory would support the notion that the 'gist' of the orally delivered directions (or lecture) would nonetheless be preserved, despite deficits retaining rote details.

Visual Memory Scale

In a manner similar to the Verbal Memory subtests, the Visual Memory subtests vary according to rote memory demands. The three Visual Memory subtests are as follows.

Finger Windows

The Finger Windows subtest is analogous to the Number/Letter subtest within the Verbal Domain, in that discrete and relatively nonmeaningful bits of information are presented, one per second, and immediate recall is required. Retaining a visual trace of a sequence is required.

Design Memory

This subtest introduces a greater degree of meaningfulness than Finger Windows. The child is asked to draw the display of common shapes such as circles, dots, straight lines, rectangles, and triangles. There is a five-second exposure, followed by a ten-second delay before drawing begins. For youngsters who may struggle to reproduce such shapes because of perceptual–motor difficulties, an optional copy task is first administered so that the child's reproduction of each shape becomes the criterion for scoring that shape in the recall phase. Design placement as well as inclusion are scored. Confusions in placement may indicate poor spatial memory, whereas shape omission may indicate poor memory for visual detail. The relatively brief five-second exposure time allowed for each stimulus card is intended to minimize the use of verbal mediation to complete the task. The ecological validity of this task was derived from everyday demands such as copying from a classroom chalkboard, or remembering visual details of a room after leaving it.

Picture Memory

The content of this subtest is quite meaningful in that each of four pictures depicts a scene most children will find familiar. Children with so-called 'photographic memory' will do especially well on this subtest, because task expectations require storage of a scene so that it can be compared from memory to a similar scene in which 20–40% of the visual details have been altered in some way.

Interestingly, it has been discovered that children with attention deficit hyperactivity disorder (ADHD) score as well as or better than a nonreferred sample on the Picture Memory subtest because of a confound created by the scoring procedure (Adams, Hyde, & deLancey, 1995). The subtest's directions indicate that the child is to identify perceived changes in each scene by using a felt-tipped marker, 'marking the things you are sure of.' The examiner is directed to verbally discourage guessing, but not to penalize guessing, instead including only correct responses in the scoring. In their impulsiveness, children with ADHD probably mark some correct details by chance, resulting in a spuriously higher score. What we have found is that children with ADHD between five and eight years of age usually make three incorrect selections per picture, compared to one incorrect selection per picture made by children in this age range within the standardization sample. While the errors-per-picture ratio drops from 3 : 1 to 2 : 1 for the older children with ADHD, the effect remains statistically significant.

Learning Scale

Verbal Learning

The Verbal Learning subtest was adapted from Rey (1958). The child is read a list of 13 or 16 (depending on the child's age) common words, immediately after which the child is asked to recall as many words as possible. This procedure is repeated three more times. Unlike Rey's (1958) procedure, four, rather than five, learning trials are administered on the WRAML, because pre-standardization data demonstrated (similar to Rey's (1958) findings), that a fifth trial contributes little additional information. Also different from Rey (1958), a second list is not used for an interference task following the final list-recall trial, because most children and examiners do not welcome another such a task and, ecologically, most 'real-life' learning is not followed by an almost identical activity serving as interference. Therefore, for economy of administration and to eliminate mounting frustration for some children, the Story Memory subtest follows the Verbal Learning subtest, and serves as the interference task. Following the Story Memory subtest, a delay trial of the Verbal Learning task is administered.

During list-recall opportunities, children will occasionally report words not on the list. These errors, called intrusion errors, occur once or twice over the four trials amongst the standardization sample, especially with younger children. Children with ADHD will, however, average four to five intrusion errors (Adams et al., submitted). There is some feeling that the nature of the intrusion error is relevant, with semantic errors (saying *eye* rather than *ear*) more suggestive of expressive language difficulties, and phonetic errors (saying *bake* rather than *lake*) more suggestive of phonological or auditory processing difficulties.

Visual Learning

Similar to its verbal counterpart, the Visual Learning task requests the child to learn a fixed number of stimuli presented over four trials. To accomplish this, visual designs are presented in a particular location on a 'game' board, and the child is asked to remember the spatial location associated with each design. Immediate feedback for item correctness is provided to promote learning. Similar to the Verbal Learning subtest, a delayed recall trial can be administered following an intervening 'interference' task.

Sound Symbol

This cross-modal learning task resembles demands made in early reading mastery, with both phonological and visual symbolic stimuli utilized. The child is asked to remember a sound that goes with a printed 'nonsense' symbol. In a paired-associated fashion, shapes are presented and the child is asked to say the corresponding 'nonsense' sound; four learning trials of the sound/shape pairs are presented. A delayed recall trial is also available.

While not yet empirically demonstrated, there is considerable anecdotal evidence suggesting that children whose poor performance on the third and fourth trials of this subtest is characterized by responses resembling few of the sounds associated within the subtest, are those children who will experience considerable difficulty learning phonics in their early elementary school grades. If empirically substantiated by a study currently underway, at least one form of a reading disorder might be thought of as a selective memory disorder affecting those subprocesses involved in remembering sound units associated with symbol markings found on a page (see also Swanson, 1987).

Short Form

Administration of the entire WRAML battery may require more time than an examiner has available, and so a 'short form' version was developed to screen memory functions quickly, and thereby help the examiner decide if more in-depth assessment is indicated. Preliminary research yielded four subtests that were varied in content yet highly correlated with the General Memory Composite ($r = .84$). Accordingly, these four subtests were placed first in the WRAML and comprise the Screening Form: Picture Memory, Design Memory, Verbal Learning, and Story Memory. The Short Form, therefore, samples aspects of visual and verbal memory, and verbal learning. The Screening Form requires approximately 10–15 minutes to administer. The psychometric integrity of the norms associated with the Screening Form matches that of the complete WRAML, because the entire standardization sample was utilized to derive the norms, as the first four subtests of the abbreviated scale are the first four subtests of the entire battery. The General Memory Index estimate generated from the Short Form version tends to be about four points higher than the General Memory Index generated from the entire battery (Kennedy & Guilmette, 1997).

Technical information

Standardization

The WRAML was standardized on a population-proportionate sample stratified by age, gender, ethnicity, socioeconomic status, geographic region, and community size. The sample consisted of 2363 children, ranging in age from 5 to 17 years. Details of the standardization procedure and stratification data are provided in the test manual (Sheslow & Adams, 1990).

Reliability

The WRAML subtests and composite indexes show high internal consistency reliability. Item separation statistics ranged from .99 to 1.0. Person separation statistics ranged from .70 to .94. Coefficient alphas ranged from .78 to .90 for the nine individual subtests. For the Verbal Memory Index, the Visual Memory Index, and the Learning Index, the median coefficients are .93, .90, and .91, respectively. The General Memory Index coefficient alpha is .96. Therefore, very good internal consistency is demonstrated by the WRAML.

Using a subgroup of the standardization sample ($n = 153$), a test–retest study was completed. The nature of memory and learning tasks makes them prone to practice effects, so knowing the incremental effect occurring with readministra-

Table 12.3. Correlations of WRAML Index scores and WRAT–R subtests, ages 6 years 0 months–8 years 11 months

	Verbal Memory Index	Visual Memory Index	Learning Index	General Memory Index
Reading	.18	.26*	.40*	.35*
Spelling	.22	.32*	.42*	.39*
Arithmetic	.24	.46*	.40*	.46*

*$p < 0.05$.

tion would be useful information. Generally, a one-point scaled score increase in memory subtests and a two-point increase in learning subtests were found. Over a three-month to six-month interval, there was no correlation between the number of days elapsed and the incremental increase in score. That is, the slight incremental increase in WRAML subtest performance seems to be uniformly obtained throughout a three-months to six-months post-testing interval. Stability coefficients for Index scores ranged from .61 to .84.

Validity

The WRAML manual (Sheslow & Adams, 1990) reports several studies providing evidence that the WRAML is a valid measure of memory functioning. The correlations between the three WRAML indexes and the WISC–R Verbal and Performance IQs ranged from .22 to .51. As predicted, memory, as measured by the WRAML, is related to but not the same as intelligence (most well-constructed intelligence tests yield correlations with each other ranging from .75 to .85). The WRAML General Memory Index correlation with the memory sections of the Stanford–Binet–Fourth Edition and McCarthy scales was .80 and .72 , respectively.

Memory would be expected to be a construct related to school achievement. Further, one might reason that, as children proceed in school, verbal memory would become more predictive of performance than visual memory. Tables 12.3 and 12.4 show this to be the case when WRAML indexes are correlated with measures of reading, spelling, and arithmetic. Interestingly, with children in early elementary school, verbal memory seems to play little role, but visual memory and, especially, learning over trials play a more dominant role. However, by high school, the reverse seems to be true. Thinking about the content demands made by 'typical' school curricula found at these extremes of the formal school experience, these findings make intuitive sense. That is,

Table 12.4. Correlations of WRAML Index scores and WRAT–R subtests, ages 16 years 0 months–17 years 11 months

	Verbal Memory Index	Visual Memory Index	Learning Index	General Index
Reading	.41*	.14	.05	.23
Spelling	.40*	.09	.24	.30
Arithmetic	.34*	.26	.34*	.38*

*$p < 0.05$.

learning to identify letters, numbers, new words, and how to write properly on a page are a major focus of first and second grades. However, history, science, literature, and math classes would make greater verbal memory demands, and proportionately fewer visual memory and rote learning (over trials) demands.

Factor structure

Three-factor Principal Components analyses were performed on the nine WRAML subtests using the full standardization sample of 2363 children. Factors were extracted for two age groupings of children, determined by the test's age division at which slightly different administration procedures and items apply. The results are found in Tables 12.5 and 12.6.

As can be observed, for the younger children, the Visual factor is made up of Picture Memory, Design Memory, and Finger Windows, as expected. However, Visual Learning also loaded with this same factor. More troublesome was the clustering of Sentence Memory and Number/Letter with the Verbal factor, but not Story Memory. This inconsistency continued, with Verbal Learning and Sound Symbol appropriately loading on the so-called Learning factor, but, as noted, Visual Learning not loading on this predicted factor.

A similar pattern of inconsistency occurred with the older sample (see Table 12.3), again calling into question whether a Learning Index score can be justified. Several investigators have reported similar factor analytic results using nonreferred and clinical samples (Aylward et al., 1995; Phelps, 1995; Burton, Donders, & Mittenberg, 1996; Dewey, Kaplan, & Crawford, 1997; Gioia, 1998; Burton et al., 1999). Gioia (1998) has suggested that, based upon the factor analytic results, the WRAML Index scores should not be utilized, but, instead, the subtest scores should be used as the appropriate level of analysis. Some have thought this suggestion a bit extreme, because only two of nine subtests (Story Memory and Visual Learning) loaded inconsistently, not surprising

Table 12.5. Results of Principal Components Analysis with Varimax Rotation of WRAML subtests (completed on children 5 years 0 months through 8 years 11 months of age)

	Factor		
	Visual	Verbal	Learning
Picture Memory	.569	−.148	.320
Design Memory	.669	.078	.259
Finger Windows	.655	.382	−.160
Story Memory	.285	.222	.585
Sentence Memory	.159	.800	.320
Number/Letter	.082	.859	.113
Verbal Learning	.311	.111	.615
Visual Learning	.605	.158	.157
Sound Symbol	−.004	.125	.749

Shading connotes the subtest loaded on the predicted factor.

Table 12.6. Results of Principal Components Analysis with Varimax Rotation of WRAML subtests (completed on children 9 years 0 months through 17 years, 11 months of age)

	Factor		
	Visual	Verbal	Learning
Picture Memory	.674	.012	.221
Design Memory	.720	.023	.277
Finger Windows	.584	.585	−.145
Story Memory	.216	.196	.695
Sentence Memory	.017	.749	.441
Number/Letter	.005	.837	.215
Verbal Learning	.239	.091	.648
Visual Learning	.583	.076	.401
Sound Symbol	.214	.240	.638

Shading connotes the subtest loading on the predicted factor.

Table 12.7. Alternative interpretation of the Principal Components Analysis of WRAML subtests (completed on children 5 years 0 months through 8 years 11 months of age)

	Factor		
	Visual	Verbal	Learning
Picture Memory	.569	−.148	.320
Design Memory	.669	.078	.259
Finger Windows	.655	.382	−.160
Story Memory	.285	.222	.585
Sentence Memory	.159	.800	.320
Number/Letter	.082	.859	.113
Verbal Learning	.311	.111	.615
Visual Learning	.605	.158	.157
Sound Symbol	−.004	.125	.749

Shading connotes the subtest loaded on the predicted factor.

given that the Learning factor clearly consists of visual and verbal memory components, contributing nonorthogonality to the analyses.

Another way to interpret the findings in light of research that followed the publication of the WRAML is to retain the Visual factor, rename the Learning factor as Verbal, and substitute 'Attention' for the original Verbal factor designation. The result of this relatively minor alteration is illustrated in Tables 12.7 and 12.8. This conceptual arrangement continues to group the highly intercorrelated subtests of Sentence Memory and Number/Letter together, but as measures of attention/concentration and not of verbal memory. In research reported below, we learn that children with attention problems consistently do poorly on these two subtests as well as on Finger Windows. Interestingly, for the older children, Finger Windows loads on our relabeled Attention factor and the Visual factor almost equally, suggesting both visual memory skills and attention are involved in succeeding on this task. That would, then, leave Verbal and Visual factors but add a factor of Attention/Concentration. Such a reconceptualization avoids the apparent nonorthogonality of the Learning subtests, and makes for a conceptual 'fit' for all WRAML subtests within the newly configured factors.

Table 12.8. Alternative interpretation of the Principal Components Analysis of WRAML subtests (completed on children 9 years 0 months through 17 years 11 months of age)

	Factor		
	Visual	Verbal	Learning
Picture Memory	.674	.012	.221
Design Memory	.720	.023	.277
Finger Windows	.584	.585	−.145
Story Memory	.216	.196	.695
Sentence Memory	.017	.749	.441
Number/Letter	.005	.837	.215
Verbal Learning	.239	.091	.648
Visual Learning	.583	.076	.401
Sound Symbol	.214	.240	.638

Shading connotes the subtest loading on the predicted factor.

WRAML performance with children with reading disability and attention deficit hyperactivity disorder

Adams et al. (submitted) administered the WRAML to children with high-frequency referral diagnoses: reading disability (RD) and ADHD – combined type. Four groups were utilized: an RD group, an ADHD group, an RD/ADHD group, and a nonclinical comparison group. Children in the clinical groups were selected using traditionally accepted definitions. Therefore, children with RD were those whose Wechsler Intelligence Scale for Children (WISC) Full Scale IQs were 85 or higher, but who had a Reading Achievement score at least 15 points below their Verbal IQ, and whose level of arithmetic achievement was commensurate with their Full Scale IQ. They did not meet criteria for ADHD. The second group was composed of children diagnosed as having ADHD. Each child was diagnosed through a hospital-based ADHD clinic and most scored at least two standard deviations above average on a standard attention rating scale both at home and at school. Children in the ADHD group also had Full Scale IQs > 85 and reading, spelling, and math achievement commensurate with their Full Scale IQs. The third group met criteria for both clinical conditions. Children in each group averaged about ten years of age and none had a history of 'hard' neurological disorder (e.g., seizures, head injury, etc.) or of significant psychological difficulties such as anxiety or depression. The fourth group, a nonclinical comparison group, was

Table 12.9. Canonical Discriminant Functions using WRAML subtest performance

| | Canonical Loadings | |
	Function I	Function II
Number/Letter	.75	−.08
Sound Symbol Learning	.60	.31
Sentence Memory	.51	.33
Finger Windows	.50	−.09
Verbal Learning	.22	.64
Canonical Discriminant Functions (group centroids)		
ADHD	−.5935	.3655
RD	−.6407	−.4762
Nonreferred	.6785	.0087
RD/ADHD	−.8462	.4191

ADHD, attention deficit hyperactivity disorder; RD, reading disabled.

created from the standardization sample, with each child from a clinical group being matched on age, gender, geographic region, urban/rural, and socioeconomic class.

Each child was administered the WRAML. A discriminate function analysis was completed on the WRAML's nine subtest scores. It was found that WRAML scores were able to distinguish between groups (Wilks' lambda = 0.560, $\chi^2 = 115.2$, df = 27), $p < 0.001$). The two significant functions, in succession, accounted for 73.5% and 26.5% of the between-group variability.

Group centroids in the upper part of Table 12.9 reveal that the first function maximally separates the clinical groups (i.e., the ADHD, RD, and RD/ADHD groups) from the nonreferred cohort. The second function best differentiates children with RD from those with ADHD and those who were nonreferred. The pattern of correlations indicates that the first function is defined by appreciable contributions from the subtests Number/Letter, Sound Symbol, Sentence Memory, and Finger Windows. Combining information from the group-centroid comparisons, as well as from the discriminant–function–variable correlations, one would infer that the construct of rote, short-term memory best separates children with ADHD and RD from those without documented symptomatology. Recently, Howes et al. (1999) also demonstrated that readers struggled most with the TOMAL subtests requiring rote oral recall (reciting digits or letters forwards, as well as backwards).

The second function is made up of contributions from the Verbal Learning subtest, which distinguishes the RD from the other three groups. A univariate analysis of the Verbal Learning subtest did show the RD scaled score group mean to be statistically lower than the other groups (mean = 8.8), with the RD/ADHD group mean also lower (9.3), but only tending toward significance ($p < 0.10$), compared to the ADHD (mean = 10.5) and nonreferred (mean = 10.4) group means.

Therefore, children of average IQ who perform poorly on Number/Letter, Sound Symbol Learning, Sentence Memory, and Finger Windows (but do reasonably well on the remainder of the WRAML subtests) are likely to have *some* kind of psychopathology. However, if these children also have low Verbal Learning scores, there is an increased likelihood that the diagnosis is RD. Interestingly, those children who had dual diagnoses could not be well distinguished from single-diagnosis children, which may suggest that there is not an additive negative effect on memory impairment if one has both ADHD and RD.

It is fortunate that different clinical groups were utilized in this investigation. If only children with ADHD (or only children with RD) had been compared to the nonreferred sample, one might have erroneously concluded that lower scores on Number/Letter, Sound Symbol, Sentence Memory, and Finger Windows form a 'diagnostic cluster' helpful in diagnosing ADHD (or RD). Interestingly, preliminary results from an investigation of children being treated for depression are also demonstrating lower scores on the 'pathology' cluster made up of these same four WRAML subtests (Whitney, 1996). Including multiple diagnostic groups in cognitive investigations seems critical in preventing erroneous conclusions that findings are unique to a given clinical population.

WRAML performance and brain injury and other CNS insults

Duis (1998) are concluding an investigation demonstrating that children who have sustained moderate or severe TBI exhibit a significant decrement in all WRAML subtests following a period of rehabilitation and recovery. Table 12.10 lists WRAML subtest means and standard deviations of the ADHD, RD, and TBI groups. The WRAML subtest scores of children with head injuries were generally one standard deviation below average, and those of the children with RD and ADHD were about 0.5 standard deviations below average. Farmer et al. (1999) report a similar degree of decrement for children who have sustained severe TBI. For a sample of children who sustained a mild to moderate injury, poorer performance was noted on only two subtests, Sound Symbol and Design Memory. The WRAML Screening Form has been used

Table 12.10. WRAML subtest means and standard deviations (in parentheses) for children with attention deficit hyperactivity disorder (ADHD), reading disability (RD), and traumatic brain injury (TBI)

Subtests	Groups			
	ADHD	RD	TBI	Nonreferred
Number/Letter	7.3 (2.5)	7.8 (2.5)	7.1 (2.8)	10.1 (2.4)
Sound Symbol	8.5 (3.1)	7.6 (2.1)	7.6 (3.0)	10.3 (2.9)
Sentence Memory	9.1 (2.8)	8.1 (2.9)	7.1 (3.4)	10.6 (3.2)
Finger Windows	8.3 (2.5)	8.7 (3.0)	7.5 (3.2)	10.1 (2.6)
Verbal Learning	10.5 (2.9)	8.8 (2.9)	8.2 (3.1)	10.5 (2.9)
Story Memory	10.1 (2.7)	9.7 (2.8)	7.2 (3.7)	10.1 (2.6)
Design Memory	7.9 (3.1)	9.5 (2.8)	7.2 (3.5)	9.8 (2.9)
Picture Memory	10.1 (2.6)	9.8 (2.3)	8.7 (3.4)	10.1 (3.0)
Visual Learning	9.4 (3.1)	9.7 (3.0)	8.5 (3.1)	10.1 (3.2)

Adapted from Duis (1998).

with TBI patients as well, with the Memory Screening Index (generated by the four screening subtests) correlating significantly with length of coma, and as strongly as the WISC Performance IQ (Woodward & Donders, 1998). Further, those children with severe TBI had significantly lower Screening Indexes than did children with mild or moderate injuries.

Children with seizure disorders seem to show a WRAML subtest pattern different from those with ADHD, RD, or TBI. While performing as a group at a level slightly higher than children with TBI, there was greater subtest variability for the epilepsy sample (Williams & Haut, 1995). Children who had survived childhood lymphoblastic leukemia, having been treated with intrathecal chemotherapy, showed mild but consistent residual deficits on most WRAML Visual and Verbal Memory subtests, as well as on the Visual Learning. This finding corresponded to lower IQ results found in the same sample, compared to healthy, matched controls (Hill et al., 1997).

Case study: Brett

Brett came to a Learning Disorders Clinic, at the age of 7 years 7 months, at the request of both his parents and teachers. He had experienced persistent academic struggles associated with reading and spelling, and behavior problems were starting to emerge during homework times.

Brett was adopted at two months of age. The adoptive parents had been told by the agency assisting with the adoption that Brett's parents were both in college and no significant medical history was associated with either family. Good prenatal care was provided and a recent medical examination was normal.

During infancy, Brett was colicky and did not transition into routines easily. As a toddler, he seemed a bit overactive compared to age-mates. Nonetheless, he had a successful preschool and nursery school experience. However, in first grade he began to experience difficulty by mid-year, but, with 'extra help' being provided at home and school the following spring, Brett's teacher felt that he would be ready to go on to second grade. However, by the end of the first marking period of the new school year, it was evident that Brett was struggling with both reading and spelling assignments. Evening homework sessions were extending beyond two hours, and were becoming increasingly characterized by anger outbursts and defiance. A comprehensive psychoeducational assessment provided the results shown in Table 12.11.

Interpretation

Taken together, the above findings suggest that Brett's academic struggles are not due to ADHD, expressive or receptive language difficulties, visual–spatial weakness, or low intellectual ability. The data do suggest, however, that he is experiencing considerable difficulty remembering sound and symbol associations, a task essential to mastering the phonics skills requisite to fluent reading or spelling abilities. The lower WISC Information score is attributable to the difficulty Brett experienced with temporal concepts (e.g., days of the week, months of the year, etc.), which are given much weight by this subtest at this age. Temporal concepts are found to be difficult for many 'dyslexic' children having trouble with various symbol systems. Rote short-term verbal memory, while a relative weakness, is adequate for classroom 'survival' (as per Digit Span, Number/Letter, and Sentence Memory subtests).

In addition, Brett is experiencing some fairly significant visual–motor problems which seem to be related to both a fine-motor awkwardness (Wide Range Assessment of Visual Motor Abilities, WRAVMA, fine motor score; Adams & Sheslow, 1995) and his ability to remember and graphically reproduce visual gestalts (WRAML Design Memory, WISC Coding, and WRAVMA Visual–Motor Integration scores). Therefore, handwriting is difficult for Brett and some of his spelling errors are due to written letter reversals (e.g., b/d) in addition to his struggle to remember sound–symbol combinations.

Table 12.11. WRAML table case study

Wechsler Intelligence Scale for Children–III	
VIQ = 123	
PIQ = 112	
Information	8
Similarities	14
Arithmetic	13
Vocabulary	12
Comprehension	13
Digit Span	9
Picture Completion	11
Coding	8
Picture Arrangement	12
Block Design	15
Object Assembly	13
Wide Range Achievement Test	
Reading	92
Spelling	84
Arithmetic	111
Wide Range Assessment of Visual–Motor Integration	
Fine-Motor Skills	72
Visual–Spatial Skills	109
Visual–Motor Integration	88
Wide Range Assessment of Memory and Learning	
Verbal Memory	
Number/Letter	10
Sentence Memory	11
Story Memory	16
Visual Memory	
Finger Windows	12
Design Memory	8
Picture Memory	12
Learning	
Verbal Learning	12
Visual Learning	14
Sound–Symbol Learning	6
Delay Task	
Story Memory	14

VIQ = Verbal IQ; PIQ = Performance IQ.

Formidable strengths in reasoning areas can be capitalized upon as Brett is referred to a reading specialist to receive remedial help. At the same time, classroom accommodations must be made so that Brett can remain involved in the content of his classroom science, social studies, and math curricula. Once his decoding skills are improved, reading comprehension should progress (supported by Brett's strong Story Memory results). However, until then, Brett's parents and teachers need to work hard to keep his mastery of content area progressing despite his difficulty in reading. Providing taped textbook chapters and library books (Story Memory results suggest he will have no difficulty with listening comprehension), and allowing taped homework responses will be essential. Avoidance of in-class reading should also be observed in order to reduce Brett's level of frustration.

Comment

This case study illustrates how the WRAML can contribute to a psychoeducational work-up. In this case, results provided the examiner with data to conclude that Brett's struggle has, at least in part, an information-processing basis. The WRAML results would support the notion that there is little or no deficit in the areas of receptive language, short-term visual or verbal rote memory, verbal forgetting rate, or visual sequencing skills. However, perceptual motor inefficiencies and an ability to make sound-to-symbol associations are each areas deserving more investigation. With respect to the latter, an error analysis of the Sound–Symbol subtest might suggest whether looking at auditory discrimination, sound segmentation, or sound sequencing would next be indicated diagnostically.

Test of Memory and Learning

The TOMAL is a comprehensive battery of 14 memory and learning tasks (ten core subtests and four supplementary subtests), normed for use from ages 5 years 0 months through 19 years 11 months (Table 12.12). The ten core subtests are divided into the content domains of Verbal Memory and Nonverbal Memory, which can be combined to derive a Composite Memory Index. A Delayed Recall Index is also available that requires a repeat recall of the first four subtests' stimuli 30 minutes after their first administration.

As noted above, memory performance in any subject may be unique and variable and traditional content approaches to memory may not be the most useful. The TOMAL thus provides alternative groupings of the subtests into

Table 12.12. Core and Supplementary subtests and indexes available for the TOMAL

	M	SD
Core subtests		
Verbal		
Memory for Stories	10	3
Word Selective Reminding	10	3
Object Recall	10	3
Digits Forward	10	3
Paired Recall	10	3
Nonverbal		
Facial Memory	10	3
Visual Selective Reminding	10	3
Abstract Visual Memory	10	3
Visual Sequential Memory	10	3
Memory for Location	10	3
Supplementary subtests		
Verbal		
Letters Forward	10	3
Digits Backward	10	3
Letters Backward	10	3
Nonverbal		
Manual imitation	10	3
Summary scores		
Core indexes		
Verbal Memory Index (VMI)	100	15
Nonverbal Memory Index (NMI)	100	15
Composite Memory Index (CMI)	100	15
Delayed Recall Index (DRI)	100	15
Supplementary indexes (expert derived)		
Sequential Recall Index (SRI)	100	15
Free Recall Index (FRI)	100	15
Associative Recall Index (ARI)	100	15
Learning Index (AI)	100	15
Attention Concentration Index (ACI)	100	15
Factor scores (empirically derived)		
Complex Memory Index (CMFI)	100	15
Sequential Recall Index (SRFI)	100	15
Backwards Recall Index (BRFI)	100	15
Spatial Memory Index (SMFI)	100	15

M = mean; SD = standard deviation.

the Supplementary Indexes of Sequential Recall, Free Recall, Associative Recall, Learning, and Attention and Concentration. To establish these Supplementary indexes, a group of 'expert' neuropsychologists sorted the 14 TOMAL subtests into logical categories . To provide greater flexibility to the clinician, a set of four purely empirically derived factor indexes representing Complex Memory, Sequential Recall, Backward Recall, and Spatial Memory has also been made available (Reynolds & Bigler, 1996).

Table 12.12 summarizes the names of the subtests and summary scores, along with their metric. The TOMAL subtests are scaled to the familiar metric with a mean of ten and a standard deviation of three (range 1 to 20). Composite or summary scores are scaled to a mean of 100 and standard deviation of 15. All scaling was done using the method of rolling weighted averages and is described in detail in Reynolds and Bigler (1994a).

TOMAL subtests

The ten core and four supplementary TOMAL subtests require about 60 minutes for a skilled examiner if the Delayed Recall subtests are also administered. The subtests were chosen to provide a comprehensive view of memory functions (Ferris & Kamphaus, 1995). The subtests are named and briefly described in Table 12.13.

The TOMAL subtests systematically vary the mode of presentation and response so as to sample verbal, visual, motoric (nonverbal), and combinations of these modalities in presentation and in response formats. Multiple trials to a criterion are provided on several subtests, including Selective Reminding, so that learning or acquisition curves may be derived. Multiple trials (at least five are necessary according to Kaplan, 1996, and the TOMAL provides up to eight) are provided on the Selective Reminding subtests to allow an analysis of the depth of processing. In the Selective Reminding format (wherein examinees are reminded only of stimuli 'forgotten' or unrecalled), when items once recalled are unrecalled by the examinee on later trials, problems are revealed in the information transfer from immediate and working memory to more long-term storage. Cueing is also provided at the end of certain subtests to add to the examiner's ability to probe depth of processing, because the difference between cued recall and free recall may be of diagnostic importance for certain neurological disorders.

Well-established memory tasks (e.g., recalling stories) that also correlate well with academic learning are included. In addition, memory tasks more common to experimental neuropsychology that have high (e.g., Facial Memory) and low (e.g., Visual Selective Reminding) ecological salience are included in the

Table 12.13. Description of TOMAL subtests

Core	
Memory for Stories	A verbal subtest requiring recall of a short story read to the examinee; provides a measure of meaningful and semantic recall and is also related to sequential recall in some instances
Facial Memory	A nonverbal subtest requiring recognition and identification from a set of distractors: black-and-white photos of various ages, males and females, and various ethnic backgrounds; assesses nonverbal, meaningful memory in a practical fashion and has been extensively researched; sequencing of responses is unimportant
Word Selective Reminding	A verbal free-recall task in which the examinee learns a word list and repeats it, only to be reminded of words left out in each case: tests learning and immediate recall functions in verbal memory; trials continue until mastery is achieved or until eight trials have been attempted: sequence of recall unimportant
Visual Selective Reminding	A nonverbal analogue to Word Selective Reminding in which examinees point to specified dots on a card, following a demonstration of the examiner, and are reminded only of items recalled incorrectly; as with Word Selective Reminding, trials continue until mastery is achieved or until eight trials have been attempted
Object Recall	The examiner presents a series of pictures, names them, asks the examinee to recall them, and repeats this process across four trials; verbal and nonverbal stimuli are thus paired and recall is entirely verbal, creating a situation found to interfere with recall for many children with learning disabilities but to be neutral or facilitative for children without disabilities
Abstract Visual Memory	A nonverbal task, which assesses immediate recall for meaningless figures when order is unimportant; the examinee is presented with a standard stimulus and required to recognize the standard from any of six distractors
Digits Forward	A standard verbal number recall task; it measures low-level rote recall of a sequence of numbers
Visual Sequential Memory	A nonverbal task requiring recall of the sequence of a series of meaningless geometric designs; the ordered designs are shown, followed by a presentation of a standard order of the stimuli, and the examinee indicates the order in which they originally appeared
Paired Recall	A verbal paired-associative learning task is provided by the examiner; easy and hard pairs and measures of immediate associative recall and learning are provided

Table 12.13. (*cont.*)

Memory for Location	A nonverbal task that assesses spatial memory; the examinee is presented with a set of large dots distributed on a page and asked to recall the locations of the dots in order
Supplementary	
Manual Imitation	A psychomotor, visually based assessment of sequential memory in which the examinee is required to reproduce a set of ordered hand movements in the same sequence as presented by the examiner
Letters Forward	A language-related analogue to common digit span tasks using letters as the stimuli in place of numbers
Digits Backward	This is the same basic task as Digits Forward, except the examinee recalls the numbers in reverse order
Letters Backward	A language-related analogue to the Digits Backward task using letters as the stimuli instead of numbers

TOMAL. Subtests also differ in terms of whether the information to be recalled is based on highly meaningful material (e.g., Memory for Stories) versus more abstract information processing (e.g., Abstract Visual Memory, which uses abstruse complex geometric forms).

Apart from allowing a comprehensive review of memory function, the purpose for including such a factorial array of tasks across multiple dimensions is to allow a thorough, detailed analysis of memory function and the source of any memory deficits that may be discovered. The task of the neuropsychologist demands subtests with great specificity and variability of presentation and response, and that sample all relevant brain functions in order to solve the complex puzzle of dysfunctional brain–behavior relationships. Kaufman (1979) first presented a detailed model for analyzing test data in a comprehensive format (later elaborated: Kaufman, 1994) that likens the task of the clinician to that of a detective. The thoroughness, breadth, and variability of the TOMAL subtests allows the application of this 'intelligent testing' model in the analysis of brain–behavior relationships associated with memory function.

Standardization

The TOMAL was standardized on a population-proportionate stratified (by age, gender, ethnicity, socioeconomic status, region of residence, and community size) random sample of children throughout the USA. Standardization and norming were conducted for ages 5 up to 20 years. Details of the standardization and specific statistics on the sample are provided in Reynolds and Bigler (1994a).

Reliability

The TOMAL subtests and composite indexes show excellent evidence of internal consistency reliability. Reynolds and Bigler (1994a) report coefficient alpha reliability estimates that routinely exceed .90 for individual subtests and .95 for composite scores. Stability coefficients are typically in the .80s.

Validity

The TOMAL scores correlate around .50 with measures of intelligence and achievement, indicating the TOMAL is related to, but not the same as, these measures (Reynolds & Bigler, 1994a), because measures of intelligence typically correlate with one another around .75 to .85 and with measures of achievement around .55 to .65. Similarly, select subtests (i.e., Word Selective Reminding) correlate positively with the previously accepted standard test of verbal (word) memory, the Rey–Auditory Verbal Learning test. Likewise, for older children (16–20 years), the Memory for Stories subtest correlates highly with the venerable adult test, the Wechsler Memory Scale–Revised (see Reynolds & Bigler, 1997).

In contrast to the verbal subtests, the nonverbal sections of the TOMAL are relatively independent of traditional nonverbal memory tests (see Reynolds & Bigler, 1997). The TOMAL nonverbal subtests, unlike a number of other purportedly visual and nonverbal memory tests, are difficult to encode verbally, making them more specific and less contaminated by examinees' attempts at verbal mediation. On the nonverbal or visual memory portions of existing memory batteries, examiners should expect larger differences across tests than on verbal memory measures.

Factor structure of the TOMAL

Based on 1342 children, details of the factor structure, analyses, and indices of the TOMAL have been extensively reviewed by Reynolds and Bigler (1996, 1997) and are beyond but brief mention here. Using the method of principal factors with Varimax and Promax rotations, the correlation matrix for all 14 TOMAL subtests was examined. Factors were extracted for three age groupings (5–8, 9–12, and 13–18) and were found to be consistent across age levels. The analyses reviewed below are based on the full sample of 1342 children. It is worthy of note that those analyses are based on normal, nonreferred children and the factor analyses do not always demonstrate the same results with

exceptional samples, especially samples with central nervous system dysfunction (e.g., see review material by Kamphaus & Reynolds, 1987).

The two-factor solutions of the TOMAL did not support the division of the
subtests into a verbal and a nonverbal scale. Clearly, the structure of the
TOMAL is more complex than is represented by these two simple,
dichotomous groupings. Nevertheless, Reynolds and Bigler (1994b) retained
the verbal/nonverbal distinction because of its clinical utility. There is a general
factor present, much as with the intellectual factor (g), but weaker, that
nevertheless supports the use of a composite score such as the Composite
Memory Index (CMI) with normal populations. Unconstrained, exploratory
factor analyses have also been performed, wherein a four-factor solution (as
presented below) appeared best to capture the clinical composition of the
TOMAL (Reynolds & Bigler, 1997).

- Complex Memory Factor Score (CMF) = Memory for Stories + Word Selective
  Reminding + Object Recall + Paired Recall + Visual Selective Reminding +
  Facial Memory.
- Sequential Recall Factor Score (SRF) = Digits Forward + Letters Forward +
  Visual Sequential Memory + Manual Imitation.
- Backwards Recall Factor Score (BRF) = Digits Backward + Letters Backward.
- Spatial Memory Factor Score (SMF) = Abstract Visual Memory + Memory for
  Location.

The first and strongest factor appearing in the Promax solution appears to be
a reflection of overall memory skills that perhaps represents more complex
memory tasks and cuts across all modalities and memory processes. The
second factor emphasizes sequential recall and attention. The third factor
consists of Digits Backward and Letters Backward, pointing clearly to the need
for separate scaling of backward and forward memory span tasks. Backward
digit recall is known to be a more highly g-loaded task than forward digit recall
and is likely to be more demanding mentally (e.g., see Jensen & Figueroa,
1975). The fourth factor appears to be a nonverbal factor, composed of Abstract
Visual Memory and Memory for Location. This factor seems to tap spatial
memory more strongly than other tasks. The four-factor Varimax solution
resulted in similar findings.

Internal consistency reliability data for the four TOMAL factor indexes at
one-year age intervals fall above 0.90, except for the spatial Memory Factor
Index at the youngest age (five years) when it has a reliability coefficient of .85.
Nearly all of the values are between .94 and .99, with median values of .95 for
the Complex Memory Factor Index and .94 for the spatial Memory Factor
Index. Thus, these reliability coefficients of the empirically derived factor

indexes are quite comparable to the TOMAL Core Indexes and Supplementary Indexes described in the TOMAL manual (Reynolds & Bigler, 1994a).

The presence of high reliability of these factor indexes is thus highly consistent and adds to the armamentarium of the clinician seeking to understand individual cases. Also, these TOMAL factor structure studies suggest that memory as evaluated by this instrument is more process than content driven. Although the verbal–nonverbal memory distinction is clinically useful, especially for those with TBI or with localized lesions, when memory function is examined in normal individuals, process appears to be more salient than item content or modality of presentation.

Subtest specificities

Subtest-specific variance can be derived from factor analysis as well, and represents the proportion of variance of a subtest that is specific to the subtest (not shared with other variables) and that is also reliable. A specificity value of 0.25 has been considered appropriate to support interpretation of an individual subtest score (e.g., see Kaufman, 1979). The values reported by Reynolds and Bigler (1994a, 1994b, 1996) reflect quite high specificities relative to measures of intelligence and achievement, which tend to be more highly interrelated. In all cases, the TOMAL subtests show specificity of 0.40 or higher and each specificity value exceeds the error variance of the subtest. The TOMAL subtests thus demonstrate more than adequate specificity to support their individual interpretation. Thus, when exceptional performance (either high or low) occurs on a subtest (or composite score), that exceptional performance can be trusted as an indication of particular strength or weakness of memory performance in that domain. Procedures for making clinical inferences about such observations are presented in the TOMAL manual (Reynolds & Bigler, 1994a) and are also available through automated interpretation (Stanton, Reynolds, & Bigler, 1995).

Cross-ethnic stability of factor indexes

The TOMAL was standardized and normed with an ethnically diverse population. Very little research has been done with neuropsychological measures and the cultural test bias hypothesis particularly relative to the plethora of bias research on intelligence tests (e.g., see Reynolds, 1995). Several analyses have been performed on the standardization sample with regard to ethnic bias (see Reynolds & Bigler, 1994a, 1996; Mayfield & Reynolds, 1996). These analyses, which should be considered only preliminary, suggested consistency of the factor structures of the TOMAL across race for African-Americans and for Caucasians. This would indicate that the test materials are perceived and reacted to in a highly similar manner for these two groups. Consistent interpretation of performance across race on the TOMAL is thus supported, and changes in interpretation as a function of race do not appear to be appropriate based on current results.

Forward versus backward recall

As alluded to in the introduction, recall of digits in the forward and reverse direction has been a common practice in standardized cognitive testing. However, the number of digits recalled in the forward direction was typically combined with the number recalled in the reverse direction to form a total score of 'digit span.' One feature of the TOMAL was the individual norming of digits and letters recalled in the forward and reverse direction. Ramsay and Reynolds (1995) and Reynolds (1996) have demonstrated that forward and backward memory span tasks should be treated separately. Whereas forward memory span has strong attentional and sequential demands, backward memory span appears to have spatial and/or integrative elements not apparent in forward memory span. Current evidence seems to support forward span tasks as being more simple, perhaps verbally oriented, and strongly sequential, whereas backward memory span invokes more complex processes that require transformations not necessary with forward memory span. Backward recall may also invoke, for many individuals, visuospatial imaging processes, even for ostensibly verbal material such as letters. It is clear that forward and backward memory recall tasks are sufficiently different to be assessed separately for clinical purposes, and are so presented on the TOMAL.

Delayed recall

Delayed recall has always been a component of memory testing. Delayed recall on the TOMAL requires the examinees to recall stimuli from the first four subtests administered (two verbal, two nonverbal), 30 minutes after testing has been initiated. The Delayed Recall Index (DRI) acts as a measure of forgetting. Most examinees will score within about ten points of their CMI on the TOMAL. The TOMAL manual also contains values for assessing the significance of the difference between DRI and CMI, and this is checked automatically by the TOMAL computer scoring program.

DRI scores significantly below the CMI are often an indication of an organically based disturbance of memory, although a variety of neuropsychiatric disorders also disrupt memory (e.g., Grossman et al., 1994). DRI allows the clinician to explore a variety of hypotheses about depth of processing (especially in conjunction with selective reminding, which may show more intermediate forgetting), forgetting, and motivation.

Table 12.14. Means and standard deviations by group for TOMAL indices, WRAT-3 and PPVT scaled scores, and FSIQ score

	Group			
	Control	Mild	Moderate	Severe
TOMAL				
VMI	102 (8)[*]	95 (12)[*]	96 (12)[*]	86 (16)[*a,b,c]
NMI	104 (11)[*]	97 (11)	92 (19)[*a]	89 (14)[*a]
CMI	103 (8)[*]	96 (10)[*]	94 (15)[*a]	87 (14)[*a,b]
DRI	104 (7)[*]	99 (7)[*]	96 (9)[*a]	92 (13)[*a,b]
PPVT–R	106 (12)[*]	99 (14)	98 (21)	94 (18)[*a]
FSIQ	105 (12)[*]	99 (13)	95 (15)	94 (18)[*a]

[*]$p < 0.05$, as examined by post hoc Tukey's HSD procedure.
[a]Reliably different from control group.
[b]Reliably different from mild brain injury group.
[c]Reliably different from moderate brain injury group.
TOMAL = Test of Memory and Learning; VMI = Verbal Memory Index; NMI = Nonverbal Memory Index; CMI = Composite Memory Index; DRI = Delayed Recall Index; PPVT–R = Peabody Picture Vocabulary Test–Revised; FSIQ = Wechsler Full Scale IQ.

Interpretive strategies

The TOMAL manual reviews a basic top-down interpretive strategy that mimics Kaufman's (1979, 1994) basic philosophy of intelligent testing and that requires integration of history and other test data. The additional information presented here and in other papers cited throughout this chapter supplements the strategies given by Reynolds and Bigler (1994a), who also provide data on within-test scatter and the relationship of the TOMAL to the major intelligence scales and to achievement tests as well. Lajiness-O'Neill (1996) examined TOMAL performance in children with traumatic brain injury. Mean index scores from this study are presented in Table 12.14. These children with more severe brain injury had greater memory deficit as assessed by the TOMAL. Howes et al. (1999) examined TOMAL performance in reading-disabled children. Children with reading disorders had significantly lower CMI than matched controls. These studies demonstrate the clinical utility of the TOMAL, as does the following case study.

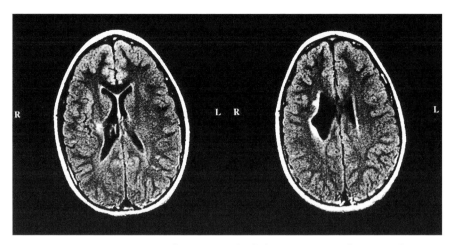

Fig. 12.3. Magnetic resonance scan from Doug. The dark areas represent the ventricular system (internal fluid-filled cavity of the brain), which has significantly enlarged on the right secondary to damage from an intrauterine stroke. The right hemisphere is significantly damaged and there is generalized atrophy of the hemisphere. This has produced prominent left-side motor deficits and impaired non-verbal abilities and visual memory.

Case study: Doug (see Fig. 12.3)

Doug suffered a probable intrauterine right middle cerebral artery stroke, which resulted in significant damage to the right hemisphere (see Fig. 12.1). The lesion was detected at birth when a computerized tomography scan was obtained after it was clinically noted that he had limited spontaneous left-side movement along with abnormal reflexes. He was given extensive physical and occupational therapy as an infant and, by early childhood, could ambulate independently, although general motor skills remained delayed. In contrast, verbal abilities developed normally. Despite 'normal' verbal abilities, he was pronounced to have 'learning problems' in the classroom.

When evaluated at the age of 11 years 8 months, Doug obtained the following scores on the Wechsler Intelligence Scale for Children–III: Verbal IQ = 108, Performance IQ = 57, and Full Scale IQ = 81. His standard score performance on the Peabody Picture Vocabulary Test performance was 108 (70%). Standardized academic testing with the Wide Range Achievement Test–Revised indicated standard scores of 98 (45%) in both reading and spelling, with the math score at 84 (14%). Visuomotor ability on the Beery Visual Motor Integration Test found this child to be capable of performing with a standard score of 70 (2%), indicating significant limitations in visuomotor ability. The neuropsychological interpretation of these findings is consistent with classic right hemisphere involvement disrupting nonverbal, visuospatial,

Table 12.15. TOMAL case study

Wechsler Intelligence Scale for Children–III

VIQ = 108

PIQ = 57

Information	14			
Similarities	12			
Arithmetic	6			
Vocabulary	11			
Comprehension	14			
Digit Span	8			
Picture Completion	2			
Coding	4			
Picture Arrangement	2			
Block Design	3			
Object Assembly	3			

Wide Range Achievement Test

Reading	93
Spelling	98
Arithmetic	84

Beery Test of Visual Motor Integration

Standard Score	70

Test of Memory and Learning

Index scores		Data
	Standard score	%
Verbal Memory	101	53
Nonverbal Memory	79	8
Composite Memory	90	25
Delayed Recall	98	45
Attention/Concentration	85	16

VIQ = Verbal IQ; PIQ = Performance IQ.

and motor functions. However, despite the intactness of verbal abilities, Doug was struggling in school, characterized by inconsistent classroom performance. TOMAL testing demonstrated intact verbal memory but impaired nonverbal memory (Table 12.15). Also, the Attention/Concentration Index was low (16%), particularly in contrast to verbal intellectual abilities (70%). The clinical interpretation of these TOMAL findings indicates deficits in the nonverbal, visual–spatial memory and problematic attention. Teachers were overinterpreting this child's cognitive ability because he could perform so well on verbal tasks. Showing the teachers these TOMAL scores, along with the other nonverbal, visual–spatial deficits, helped in devising an educational plan in which additional time and repetition were given for nonverbal memory. The problems with attention were found to be dominated by Doug becoming distracted by not being able to visually and spatially process information, particularly information presented on the chalkboard or by visual display. Thus, when information was orally presented, he could perform in the average to above-average range. Conversely, if the teacher switched back-and-forth between oral presentation and the chalkboard (or any other visual display format), Doug could not track the information because of the deficits in nonverbal memory. Improved grade performance was achieved when these changes were made in the classroom.

California Verbal Learning Test–Children's Version

The CVLT–C (Delis et al., 1994) is a relatively brief memory task that provides the clinician with a means of evaluating various processes of verbal–auditory learning and recall. Its structure is similar to the California Verbal Learning Test (CVLT) (Delis et al., 1987), the Rey Auditory Verbal Learning Test (Rey, 1958), and the Verbal Learning subtest of the WRAML (Sheslow & Adams, 1990). The CVLT–C is appropriate for children aged 5 to 16 years (the CVLT begins at age 17). The task requests children to learn two lists of familiar and categorized words presented as shopping lists. The authors suggest that this task is relevant to children and may simulate how they might approach a real-world memory situation.

In administering the CVLT–C, the child initially hears and is asked to repeat, in free recall format, a list of 15 words. The child's responses are recorded and the recitation–recall procedure is repeated four additional times. Although not mentioned to the child, the words can be sorted into three categories – clothes, fruits, and toys – with an equal number of words associated with each category.

Following administration of the first list of words, a second 'shopping list' is then presented. The second list consists of 15 different words, which can be sorted into the categories of furniture, fruits, and desserts. Following a single learning/recall trial using the second list, the child is again asked to repeat the first shopping list. Next, the child is told the three categories into which the words of the first list could be grouped. With this cue available, recall for each category is elicited.

A 20-minute delay interval is then introduced, during which other nonverbal testing may be completed. At the end of this interval, the child is again given a free-recall trial of the first list, followed by a cued recall trial. Finally, the child is asked to listen to a list of words that include items from both learning lists as well as distracter words. The child is asked to identify those words from the first shopping list. The entire procedure requires approximately 30 minutes to complete, not including the 20-minute delay.

Care was exercised in determining item inclusion. The words chosen for the shopping lists were selected based on their frequency of occurrence in the English language as well as on how often they were reported by children. To avoid the possibility that children would only report the most common words in a category rather than those learned from the list, the three most commonly used words for each category were not included. The words used for each list were designed to be comparable.

Standardization

The CVLT–C standardization used the 1988 US census to guide subject inclusion. The sample was stratified by age, gender, ethnicity, geographic region, and parent education. Details of the standardization, including sampling statistics, are found in the manual (Delis et al., 1994).

Reliability

Reliability calculations for the CVLT–C are reported as measures of internal consistency, as well as test–retest reliability. Across the five trials for the first shopping list, the average internal consistency correlation is .88, with a range from .84 to .91. Reliability across categories yields an average internal consistency coefficient of .72 for all age groups.

Test–retest measures were obtained. The interval between test periods averaged 28 days. Recall performance on the second CVLT–C administration increased by five, six, and nine words for the 8-year-old, 12-year-old, and 16-year-old age-groups, respectively. Reliability coefficients derived from the first and second administration scores ranged from .31 to .90, which the authors considered acceptable for the nature of this auditory–verbal memory assessment tool.

Clinical utility of the CVLT

The CVLT–C is a relatively short and easy test to administer. Responses are recorded by the examiner and categorized as to their semantic relationship to the original words. In addition, occurrences of perseverations and intrusions are recorded. Various process-oriented scores can be calculated and empirical grounding for qualitative analyses of memory function. These process scores answer questions such as: does the child tend to learn things in categories or randomly? Does the child benefit from a longer delay between new information? Should similar subject areas be separated throughout the day to avoid interference from previously learned tasks? A software program for the CVLT–C is available. It provides computation and multilevel interpretive analyses of the various ways the test results can be considered.

ENDNOTES

1 This chapter does not deal with the ongoing scientific debate over memory nomenclature (Fuster, 1995). There are, in fact, differences between immediate and short-term memory. As a simplification, we have held on to older taxonomy rather than the more recent declarative (or explicit), nondeclarative (or implicit or procedural) and the term working memory. Other memory terms, such as episodic and semantic memory, are not discussed. The older classification of memory fits with how the general clinician deals with the practical conceptualization and implications in memory assessment. For example, in a feedback conference with a parent, teacher and counselor, the use of terms other than immediate, short term and long term becomes confusing.

REFERENCES

Adams, W.V., Hyde, C.L., & deLancey, E.R. (1995). Use of the Wide Range Assessment of Memory and Learning in Diagnosing ADHD in Children. Paper presented at the Child Health Psychology Conference, Gainesville, FL.

Adams, W.V., Robins, P.R., Sheslow, D.V., & Hyde, C.L. (Submitted). Performance of children with ADHD and/or reading disabilities on the Wide Range Assessment of Memory and Learning.

Adams, W. & Sheslow, D. (1995). *Wide Range Assessment of Visual Motor Abilities.* Washington, DC: Wide Range, Inc.

Aylward, G.P., Gioia, G., Verhulst, S.J., & Bell, S. (1995). Factor structure of the Wide Range Assessment of Memory and Learning in a clinical population. *Assessment, 13,* 132–42.

Baddeley, A.D. (1990). *Human Memory: Theory and Practice.* Hove, UK: Lawrence Erlbaum.

Bakker, D.J., Fisk, J.L., & Strang, J.D. (1985). *Child Neuropsychology.* New York: Guilford Press.

Baron, I.S., Fennell, E.B., & Voeller, K.K.S. (1995). *Pediatric Neuropsychology in the Medical Setting.* London: University Press.

Bauer, R.M., Tobias, B.A., & Valenstein, E. (1993). Amnestic disorders. In *Clinical Neuropsychology,* ed. K.M. Heilman & E. Valenstein, pp. 523–602. New York: Oxford University Press.

Bigler, E.D. & Clement, P. (1997). *Diagnostic Clinical Neuropsychology,* 3rd edition. Austin, TX: University of Texas Press.

Bull, R. & Johnston, R.S. (1997). Children's arithmetical difficulties: contributions from processing speed, item identification, and short-term memory. *Journal of Experimental Child Psychology,* 65, 1–24.

Burton, D.B., Donders, J., & Mittenberg, W. (1996). A structural equation analysis of the wide range assessment of memory and learning in the standardization sample. *Child Neuropsychology,* 2, 39–47.

Burton, D.B., Mittenberg, W., Gold, S., & Drabman, R. (1999). A structural equation analysis of the Wide Range Assessment of Memory and Learning in a clinical sample. *Child Neuropsychology,* 5, 34–40.

Cohen, R.A. (1993). *The Neuropsychology of Attention.* New York: Plenum Press.

Cowan, N. (1997). *The Development of Memory in Childhood.* Hove, UK: Psychology Press.

Cronwall, D., Wrightson, P., & Waddell, P. (1990). *Head Injury: the Facts.* Oxford: Oxford University Press.

Cullum, M., Kuck, J., & Ruff, R.M. (1990). Neuropsychological assessment of traumatic brain injury in adults. In *Traumatic Brain Injury,* ed. E.D. Bigler, pp. 129–163. Austin, TX: Pro-Ed.

Cytowic, R.E. (1996). *The Neurological Side of Neuropsychology.* Cambridge, MA: MIT Press.

de Jong, P.F. (1998). Working memory deficits of reading disabled children. *Journal of Experimental Child Psychology,* 70, 75–96.

Delis, D.C., Kramer, J.H., Kaplan, E., & Ober, B.A. (1994). *California Verbal Learning Test – Children's Version.* San Antonio, TX: The Psychological Corporation.

Delis, D.C., Kramer, J.H., Kaplan, J.H., & Kaplan, E. (1987). *California Verbal Learning Test.* San Antonio, TX: The Psychological Corporation.

Dewey, D., Kaplan, B.J., & Crawford, S.G. (1997). Factor structure of the WRAML in children with ADHD or reading disabilities: further evidence of an attention/concentration factor. *Developmental Neuropsychology,* 13, 501–6.

Diamond, M.C. (1990). Morphological cortical changes as a consequence of learning and experience. In *Neurobiology of Higher Cognitive Function,* ed. A. Schiebel & A. Wechsler. New York: Guilford Press.

Duis, S.S. (1998). Differential performances on the Wide Range Assessment of Memory and Learning of children diagnosed with reading disorder, attention-deficit/hyperactivity disorder, and traumatic brain injury. [Dissertation Abstract] Dissertation Abstracts International: Section B. *The Sciences and Engineering,* 58 (7–B), 3919.

Farmer, J.E., Haut, J.S., Williams, J., Kapila, C., Johnstone, B., & Kirk, K.S. (1999). Comprehensive assessment of memory functioning following traumatic brain injury in children. *Developmental Neuropsychology,* 15, 269–89.

Ferris, L.M. & Kamphaus, R.W. (1995). Review of the Test of Memory and Learning. *Archives of Clinical Neuropsychology,* 10.

Fuster, J.M. (1995). *Memory in the Cerebral Cortex.* Cambridge, MA: MIT Press.

Gillberg, C. (1995). *Clinical Child Neuropsychiatry.* Cambridge: Cambridge University Press.

Gioia, G.A. (1998). Re-examining the factor structure of the Wide Range Assessment of Memory and Learning: implications for clinical interpretation. *Assessment,* 5, 127–39.

Golden, C.J., Zillmer, E., & Spiers, M. (1992). *Neuropsychological Assessment and Intervention*. Springfield, IL: Charles C Thomas.

Goldstein, F.C. & Levin, H.S. (1990). Epidemiology of traumatic brain injury: incidence, clinical characteristics, and risk factors. In *Traumatic Brain Injury*, ed. E.D. Bigler, pp. 51–67. Austin, TX: Pro-ed.

Grossman, I., Kaufman, A.S., Mednitsky, S., Scharff, L., & Dennis, B. (1994). Neurocognitive abilities for a clinically depressed sample versus a matched control group of normal individuals. *Psychiatry Research*, 51, 231–44.

Hill, D.E., Ciesielski, K.T., Sethre-Hofstad, L., Duncan, M.H., & Lorenzi, M. (1997). Visual and verbal short-term memory deficits in childhood leukemia survivors after intrathecal chemotherapy. *Journal of Pediatric Psychology*, 22, 861–70.

Howes, N.L., Bigler, E.D., Lawson, J.S., & Burlingame, G.M. (1999). Reading disability subtypes and the test of memory and learning. *Archives of Clinical Neuropsychology*, 14(3), 317–39.

Hynd, G. & Obrzut, J. (1981). *Neuropsychological Assessment of the School-aged Child: Issues and Procedures*. New York: Grune & Stratton.

Jensen, A.R. & Figueroa, R. (1975). Forward and backward digit span interaction with race and IQ: predictions from Jensen's theory. *Journal of Educational Psychology*, 67, 882–93.

Kamphaus, R.W. & Reynolds, C.R. (1987). *Clinical and Research Application of the K-ABC*. Circle Pines, MN: American Guidance Service.

Kaplan, E. (1996). Discussant. Paper presented at the symposium at the annual meeting of the National Association of School Psychologists, Atlanta, GA.

Kaufman, A.S. (1979). *Intelligent Testing with the WISC–R*. New York: Wiley–Interscience.

Kaufman, A.S. (1994). *Intelligent Testing with the WISC–III*. New York: Wiley–Interscience.

Kennedy, M.L. & Guilmette, T.J. (1997). The relationship between the WRAML memory screening and general memory indices in a clinical population. *Assessment*, 4, 69–72.

Knight, R.G. (1992). *The Neuropsychology of Degenerative Brain Diseases*. Hillsdale, NJ: Lawrence Erlbaum.

Koppitz, E.M. (1977). *The Visual Aural Digit Span Test*. New York: Grune & Stratton.

Lajiness-O'Neill, R. (1996). Age at injury as a predictor of memory performance in children with traumatic brain injury. Unpublished Doctoral Dissertation, Department of Psychology, Brigham Young University, Provo.

Lezak, M.D. (1995). *Neuropsychological Assessment*, third edition. New York: Oxford University Press.

Lorsbach, T.C., Wilson, S., & Reimer, J.F. (1996). Memory for relevant and irrelevant information: evidence for deficient inhibitory processes in language/learning disabled children. *Contemporary Educational Psychology*, 21, 447–66.

Mapou, R.L. & Spector, J. (eds.) (1995). *Clinical Neuropsychological Assessment*. New York: Plenum Press.

Mayfield, J.W. & Reynolds, C.R. (1996). Black–white differences in memory test performance among children and adolescents. *Archives of Clinical Neuropsychology*, 11(5), 422–3.

McCarthy, D. (1972). *McCarthy Scales of Children's Abilities*. San Antonio, TX: The Psychological Corporation.

Nation, K., Adams, J.W., Bowyer-Crain, A., & Snowling, M.J. (1999). Working memory deficits in poor comprehenders reflect underlying language impairments. *Journal of Experimental Child Psychology*, 73, 139–58.

Parkin, A.J. (1993). *Memory: Phenomena, Experiment and Theory*. Oxford: Blackwell.

Pennington, B.F. (1991). *Diagnosing Learning Disorders: A Neuropsychological Framework*. New York: Guilford Press.

Phelps, L. (1995). Exploratory factor analysis of the WRAML with academically at-risk students. *Journal of Psychoeducational Assessment*, 13, 384–90.

Prigatano, G.P. (1990). Recovery and cognitive retraining after cognitive brain injury. In *Traumatic Brain Injury*, ed. E.D. Bigler, pp. 273–95. Austin, TX: Pro-Ed.

Ramsey, M.C. & Reynolds, C.R. (1995). Separate digit tests: a brief history, a literature review, and a reexamination of the factor structure of the Test of Memory and Learning (TOMAL). *Neuropsychology Review*, 5, 151–71.

Reeves, D. & Wedding, D. (1994). *The Clinical Assessment of Memory*. Berlin: Springer-Verlag.

Rey, A. (1958). *L'Examen Clinique en Psychologie*. (English translation 1964). Paris: Presses Universitaires de France.

Reynolds, C.R. (1995). Test bias and the assessment of intelligence and personality. In *International Handbook of Personality and Intelligence*, ed. D. Saklofske & M. Zeidner, pp. 545–73. New York: Plenum Press.

Reynolds, C.R. (1996). Forward and backward memory span should not be combined for clinical analysis. *Archives of Clinical Neuropsychology*, 11(5), 440.

Reynolds, C.R. & Bigler, E.D. (1994a). *Manual for the Test of Memory and Learning*. Austin, TX: Pro-Ed.

Reynolds, C.R. & Bigler, E.D. (1994b). *Test of Memory and Learning*. Austin, TX: Pro-Ed.

Reynolds, C.R. & Bigler, E.D. (1996). Factor structure, factor indexes, and other useful statistics for interpretation of the Test of Memory and Learning (TOMAL). *Archives of Clinical Neuropsychology*, 11(1), 29–43.

Reynolds, C.R. & Bigler, E.D. (1997). Clinical neuropsychological assessment of child and adolescent memory with the test of memory and learning. In *Handbook of Clinical Child Neuropsychology*, second edition, ed. C.R. Reynolds & E. Fletcher-Janzen, pp. 296–319. New York: Plenum Press.

Rourke, B.P. (1991). *Neuropsychological Validation of Learning Disability Subtypes*. New York: Guilford Press.

Scheibel, A.B. (1990). Dendritic correlates of higher cognitive function. In *Neurobiology of Higher Cognitive Function*, ed. A. Scheiberl & A. Wechsler. New York: Guilford Press.

Sheslow, D. & Adams, W. (1990). *Wide Range Assessment of Memory and Learning*. Wilmington, DE: Jastak Associates.

Snyderman, M. & Rothman, S. (1987). Survey of expert opinion on intelligence and aptitude testing. *American Psychologist*, 42, 137–44.

Stanton, H.C., Reynolds, C.R., & Bigler, E.D. (1995). *PRO-SCORE: Computer Scoring System for the Test of Memory and Learning*. Austin, TX: Pro-Ed.

Stark, R.E. & McGregor, K.K. (1997). Follow-up study of a right- and left-hemispherectomized child: implications for localization and impairment of language in children. *Brain and Language*, 60, 222–42.

Swanson, H.L. (ed.) (1987). *Memory and Learning Disabilities*. London: JAI Press, Inc.

Swanson, H.L., Ashbacker, M.H., & Lee, C. (1996). Learning-disabled readers' working memory as a function of processing demands. *Journal of Experimental Child Psychology*, 61, 242–75.

Tramontana, M.G. & Hooper, S.R. (1988). *Assessment Issues in Child Neuropsychology*. New York: Plenum Press.

Whitney, S.J. (1996). *The Performance of Children who are Depressed on the Wide Range Assessment of Memory and Learning*. New Brunswick, NJ: Rutgers University.

Williams, J. & Haut, J.S. (1995). Differential performances on the WRAML in children and adolescents diagnosed with epilepsy, head injury, and substance abuse. *Developmental Neuro-psychology*, 11(2), 201–13.

Woodward, H. & Donders, J. (1998). The performance of children with traumatic head injury on the Wide Range Assessment of Memory and Learning – Screening. *Applied Neuropsychology*, 5, 113–19.

Part IV

Integration and Summation

13

Assessment of specific learning disabilities in the new millennium: issues, conflicts, and controversies

Alan S. Kaufman and Nadeen L. Kaufman

Two fields that have embraced controversy from their inception are intelligence testing and specific learning disabilities. This book, with its focus on the assessment of specific learning disabilities (SLDs), unites the two, providing a double dose of controversy. Indeed, one does not need to look very far to understand that professionals differ dramatically in their perceptions about SLDs – causes, definitions, diagnosis, treatment – and about the role that should be played by IQ tests and other standardized neuropsychological tests during the diagnostic process.

Shepherd's insightful history lesson in Chapter 1, rooted in neurology and special education and always oriented toward a pragmatic, educational perspective, delineates the different roads that have been traveled by the pioneers in the field, and enlightens us as to where these paths have led in the present. Yet other histories of learning disabilities also abound in this book, notably Spreen's neurological history (Chapter 9) that emphasizes theory and research, and stresses SLD subtypes; Reitan and Wolfson's history of SLDs from a neuropsychological research perspective (Chapter 10), in which the emphasis is on discriminating SLD individuals from normal and brain-injured individuals, and on understanding each SLD person's unique neuropsychological profile; and Mather and Woodcock's approach (Chapter 3) that cites the historical precedents for interpreting SLDs in terms of 'the common theme . . . that learning disabilities arise from a deficiency in basic cognitive processes, which in turn contribute to academic failure' (see p. 77).

The histories include many of the same names – such as Hinshelwood, Strauss, Orton, Kirk, and Rourke – but they are each distinct in their emphases and interpretations of just what SLDs are, how to diagnose them, and how to treat them. From Shepherd's (Chapter 1) vivid picture of the different pathways that were traveled on the road to contemporary definitions of SLD, and the confusions and contradictions that were (and are) inherent in these perspectives, it is apparent that consensus about SLD cannot easily be achieved, that lack of agreement has consistently led to controversy, and that such controversies are as alive today as they were 30 or 40 years ago.

Contemporary critiques of intelligence tests for SLD assessment

One noteworthy controversy concerns the assessment of SLD. It is currently appearing in the pages of *Journal of Learning Disabilities*, and is demanding the elimination of IQ tests from the SLD assessment process. Stanovich (1999) stated, 'LD advocacy will always be open to charges of "queue jumping" as long as the field refuses to rid itself of its IQ fetishism, refuses to jettison aptitude achievement discrepancy, and fails to free clinical practice from the pseudoscientific neurology that plagued the field in the 1970s' (p. 359). Not to be outdone, Siegel (1999), responding to issues of SLD definition and diagnosis raised by a lawsuit (*Guckenberger v. Boston University*), said, 'Scores on IQ tests are irrelevant and not useful and may even be discriminatory' (p. 304). Vellutino, Scanlon, and Lyon (2000), though generally skeptical about the value of IQ tests for SLD diagnosis, take a less extreme position. They interpret data from their empirical studies of reading as arguing strongly against the use of the IQ–achievement discrepancy as part of the functional definition of reading disability, but do not propose to dismiss IQ tests altogether. Unlike Stanovich (1999) and Siegel (1999), Vellutino et al. (2000, p. 236) give a lukewarm endorsement to IQ tests, conceding that, 'there may be something important about a child's IQ, particularly with respect to how it interacts with that child's emotional and behavioral response to failure.'

The criticisms of IQ tests put forth by Siegel (1999) and Stanovich (1999) are not new. Siegel points out, for example, that some subtests assign bonus points for speed, such that, 'A person with a slow, deliberate style would not achieve as high a score as an individual who responded more quickly' (p. 311). She states further that the SLD in reading is likely to impair performance on an IQ test, especially on tests of vocabulary and similar verbal tasks, and cites other limitations of IQ tests that would preclude the use of an IQ–achievement discrepancy for the diagnosis of SLD. Stanovich echoes Siegel's points, especially the ones that impugn the use of an ability–achievement discrepancy for SLD diagnosis, and also emphasizes the fact that IQ tests do not adequately measure one's 'potential.'

There are a few different (but related) issues here worthy of discussion.

1. Siegel (1999) and Stanovich (1999) link the fallacies inherent in the IQ–achievement discrepancy with the elimination of IQ tests for SLD assessment. Stanovich, in particular, criticizes those who believe that low intelligence *causes*

reading difficulty ('To assume so would make the fundamental reasoning error of inferring cause from . . . correlation,' p. 352). Yet, both professionals make the implicit cause–effect assumption that *if* the discrepancy criterion is eliminated from the definition of SLD diagnosis (a fervent wish of both), *then* IQ tests, with all their imperfections, should be trashed, and deleted from the SLD assessment process. We believe that these issues are separate and that knee-jerk dismissal of IQ tests is not a pertinent response to removal of the discrepancy concept from the SLD definition. Though Vellutino et al. (2000) do not make this same causal inference, they clearly perceive the value of IQ tests to be marginal, more clinical than psychometric (perhaps offering insight into children's response to failure), and more related to people's misperceptions of the value of IQ tests than to any real value. Regarding the latter point, Vellutino et al. (2000, p. 236) argue that IQ is unrelated to reading ability or remedial progress (arguments embraced as well by Siegel and Stanovich), but concede that, 'because of the widespread belief that IQ and reading ability are related, it might well be the case that more resources would be brought to bear to support the reading development of a child who scored high on an intelligence test as compared with a child who scored in the average or low-average range on the test.'

2. All of these authors seem to equate 'IQ test' with 'Wechsler test.' According to Siegel (1999): 'IQ tests consist of measures of factual knowledge, definitions of words, memory, fine motor coordination, and fluency of expressive language; they do not measure reasoning or problem-solving skills' (p. 311). Stanovich (1999) discusses (with apparent disdain) how professionals have argued over whether verbal or nonverbal measures provide the best IQ criterion for evaluating the intelligence of a child with SLD – as if the verbal-nonverbal distinction that characterizes the nontheoretical Wechsler tests is the only one of interest to consider, thereby ignoring the prevalence of non-Wechsler tests that now abound, most of which are derived from theory. Yes, Wechsler's scales are still, by far, the most frequently used IQ tests for SLD diagnosis. But that does not excuse authors for failing to consider the use of alternative measures of intelligence, especially in articles that are passionately calling for the elimination of IQ tests.

3. All of these authors refer to IQ as if it is the unidimensional 'g' factor posited by Spearman (1904) a century ago and supported by Jensen (1998) in the present. They demonstrate no awareness that the 'g' construct is antithetical to most modern theories of intelligence, including Horn's (1989) expansion and elaboration of the Horn–Cattell *Gf–Gc* theory, the theory that has proved to be the most influential model for the development of new and revised intelligence

tests (Woodcock & Mather, 1989; Kaufman, 2000; Woodcock, McGrew, & Mather, 2001) and has greatly influenced the interpretation of Wechsler's scales (Kaufman, 1994; Kaufman & Lichtenberger, 1999, 2000). Furthermore, the authors display some misconceptions about the assumptions that underlie intelligence tests and the IQ construct. One of these misconceptions was mentioned in point 1 regarding Stanovich's (1999) claim that low IQ is attributed to be a cause of reading disabilities. Also, what IQ test developer or psychologist aware of the literature on individual differences and test scatter would agree with Siegel (1999) that, 'One assumption behind the use of IQ tests is that the scores predict and *set limits on academic performance*, so that if a person has a low IQ score, we should not expect much from him or her in the way of academic skills' (p. 311, our italics).

4. The diverse authors seem to be abandoning the concept of SLD altogether, in favor of an approach that lumps all low-achieving students into a single package, without regard to the presence of neuropsychological intactness in unaffected domains. This implicit notion of discrepancy (i.e., that the low achievement in a specific academic area such as reading decoding – which is linked to a cognitive deficit, such as in phonological processing – is inconsistent with measured integrities in other cognitive processes) is absent from these authors' approaches. For example, Siegel (1999) discusses identification of SLDs in terms of what cut-off to use on achievement tests, with no consideration of intra-individual differences in cognitive processes or academic skills. She discusses the merits of identifying as SLD all students who score below the 25th percentile, but notes that the 20th or 15th percentiles might also be acceptable cut-off criteria. She acknowledges that there are some exclusionary criteria, namely, 'ruling out' inadequate education, sensory deficits, serious neurological disorders, and social/emotional difficulties as causes of low academic achievement. Yet, though she perceives these exclusionary criteria as 'reasonable' (p. 311), she is not convinced that they are necessary. She endorses a deficit model that has no room for systematic evaluation of exclusionary criteria or for the need to demonstrate the student's neuropsychological, cognitive, or academic intactness.

We can agree with the suggestion to abandon the psychometric, formulaic IQ–achievement discrepancy, but not with the elimination of the conceptual notion of a discrepancy as one of the hallmarks of any definition of SLD. Certainly, the need for a notable discrepancy between ability and achievement is spelled out clearly in the Individual with Disabilities Education Act (IDEA) of 1997 (PL 105-17) guidelines and in DSM-IV (American Psychiatric Association, 1994) criteria for Reading Disorder (no. 315.00) and other SLDs. Eliminating the use of a rigid formula is defensible; eliminating the discrepancy concept is not.

The IQ–achievement discrepancy

Do we need to have the IQ–achievement discrepancy as an aspect of the SLD definition? From Shepherd's perspective (Chapter 1), the discrepancy is tangential, perhaps irrelevant, to the practical task of placing children in the special education category named 'specific learning disability.' From her own clinical experiences and the experiences of others, data are often put aside when diagnostic decisions are made, supplanted by practical factors such as available resources and the needs of adults (usually parents and teachers). From recent research that Shepherd cites (MacMillan & Speece, 1999), her anecdotal impressions of the way decisions are made conform to the results of empirical study of the dilemma. MacMillan and Speece (1999) reviewed three studies conducted after PL 94-142 was enacted and reported that more than half of the SLD students in each study did not meet relevant diagnostic criteria; these researchers concluded that the appropriate tests were given primarily to conform to legal requirements, but that the data were not systematically used for differential diagnosis. Indeed, low achievement was generally the hallmark of a diagnosis of SLD, apart from the size of the discrepancy or the individual's IQ level (very low IQs were often acceptable for an SLD diagnosis because such a diagnosis is deemed to be more optimistic than a diagnosis of mental retardation).

What a waste! Why bother having trained psychologists to administer 90-minute IQ tests and have other professionals administer time-consuming achievement, adaptive behavior, or processing tests, if these measures are just given so the professionals can cover their own backs? One does not need to weigh the carefully reasoned (though occasionally flawed) arguments of Siegel (1999), Stanovich (1999), or Vellutino et al. (2000) against the use of the IQ–achievement discrepancy for SLD diagnosis. Their attacks on IQ tests, however motivated, are far less impressive evidence for abandoning the IQ–achievement discrepancy than are the apparent everyday realities of differential diagnosis. The discrepancy is often not used when diagnosing SLD, even though the pertinent test data are invariably obtained. Given the realities of clinical practice, at least in schools, why not delete the IQ–achievement discrepancy from the definition of SLD?

As test authors ourselves, that intuitive decision makes sense. Indeed, one of the reasons that we separated intelligence from achievement when we constructed the Kaufman Assessment Battery for Children (K-ABC;

Kaufman & Kaufman, 1983) was because of our deep-seated belief that Wechsler's Verbal IQ was too similar conceptually to conventional tests of achievement to permit meaningful discrepancies to be obtained for SLD diagnosis. We have no problem going one step further and supporting the elimination of the IQ–achievement discrepancy from federal and state guidelines for SLD diagnosis; and we are not the only test authors to endorse this notion. In Chapter 3, Mather and Woodcock, authors of the Woodcock–Johnson Tests of Cognitive Ability–Revised (WJ–R) and Woodcock–Johnson Tests of Cognitive Ability, Third Edition (WJ III), state, 'Although a significant cognitive deficit can contribute to the development of an aptitude–achievement discrepancy, a learning or reading disability should not be defined as a discrepancy between aptitude and achievement' (p. 76). Naglieri (Chapter 5), co-author of the Cognitive Assessment System (CAS), minimizes the importance of the IQ–achievement discrepancy, tracing its emergence to the fact that the popular Wechsler scales were designed according to the 'g' concept, not from any type of processing model, providing an easy and convenient way to measure discrepancies.

But the ease of computing discrepancies is deceiving. Intelligence tests, including Wechsler's, were not built to be used in mathematical formulas or in conjunction with rigid cut-off points to determine eligibility for SLD, mental retardation, or gifted placements. Francis Galton (1869, 1883), half-cousin of Charles Darwin, was strictly a scientist, and attempted to develop an intelligence test that was accurate to the nearest tenth of a point. Though his reliable measures were influential in shaping the world-wide assessment of intelligence at the turn of the twentieth century, later studies of his sensory, motor, and reaction-time tasks challenged their validity as measures of the elusive construct (Kaufman, 2000). Enter Alfred Binet (1903), who insisted that anything as complex as human intelligence demanded complex tasks for its measurement. As Feuerstein and Feuerstein (Chapter 7) explain in their fascinating historical account of the psychometric measurement of intelligence, Binet was indeed influenced by Broca, and studied skull measurements and believed that neither etiology nor future predictions were pertinent when assessing mental ability in the present, and that test performance could not be reduced to a linear measure like length. Also, as the Feuersteins also point out, Binet's major theoretical breakthrough was in his insight that chronological age is systematically related to performance on mental tasks. However, attention also needs to be paid to another of Binet's mentors: the English philosopher John Stuart Mill. To Binet (1903), Mill was his 'only teacher of psychology' (p. 68). Mill (1875) claimed, 'The science of human nature . . . falls far short of the standard of exactness now realized in Astronomy' (p. 432), and that became Binet's guiding principle. By using complex tasks to measure intelligence, Binet and Simon gave us the first modern intelligence test in 1905. Yet, to us, Binet's biggest contribution was his Mill-inspired insistence that one must be willing to accept a certain degree of *measurement error* in order to evaluate human intelligence.

The acceptance of error as a necessary prerequisite for measuring IQ, embraced by David Wechsler, one of the first psychologists to administer the 1916 Stanford–Binet in his role as army psychologist during World War I, has persisted from one century to the next and continues into the new millennium. Error is a fact of assessment life, a fundamental tenet of a psychologist's clinical training, and antagonistic to the use of any discrepancy formulas or cut-off points. Factor in the errors of measurement in the achievement test, and one must contend with two sets of errors instead of one when interpreting IQ–achievement discrepancies, forcing the measurement errors to multiply.

One does not have to be a special educator or learning disabilities specialist to criticize the psychologist's tools. We have historical reasons to acknowledge – even embrace – their limitations. One does not need to read Siegel's (1999) or Stanovich's (1999) criticisms of IQ tests to discover that these measures are imperfect. These tests do have error; different diagnostic results are likely to be obtained if different instruments are used or if different IQs (Wechsler's Verbal, Performance, or Full Scale IQ) are applied in the discrepancy formula; Verbal tasks overlap with the content of achievement tests; process deficits are just as likely to impair performance on IQ tests as on tests of academic skills; neither verbal nor nonverbal measures of IQ are necessarily better or more valid (or valid at all) indicators of the intelligence of an individual with SLD; IQ does not effectively provide a measure of a person's potential; and so forth.

These are criticisms of IQ tests, yes, but they are criticisms that are built in to the measurement of IQ by virtue of Binet's sensible adoption of Mill's philosophy. They are givens. They emerge as offensive problems primarily when IQ tests are used in the wrong way, such as when they are plugged into formulas that are then used to make important life decisions for children and adults. The real problem resides in the federal and state guidelines that mandate the use of these formulas (even if their use is illusory in many real-life situations). As test authors, we have attempted to provide instruments such as the K-ABC (see Lichtenberger's Chapter 4) in an effort to make the comparisons of ability and achievement 'fairer' for students suspected of SLD. Other test authors, such as Mather and Woodcock (Chapter 3), have provided clever, innovative approaches to computing ability–achievement discrepancies, making use of multiple regression methodology to offer specific comparisons (e.g., expected achievement in writing versus predicted writing achievement) instead of comparisons involving global measures of IQ. In that sense, we have bought into the notion of the IQ–achievement discrepancy. But that purchase is really nothing more than an acceptance of the real-world facts of life regarding the practical application of federal and state diagnostic guidelines.

Can we discard the notion of computing formula-based IQ–achievement discrepancies when assessing children, adolescents, or adults for SLD? In a heartbeat. Does the discrepancy have to be included as part of the definition of SLD? Absolutely not. Do we endorse the removal of the IQ test from the SLD assessment process? Not so fast. That is where we diverge dramatically from Siegel, Stanovich, and others, who would click on 'backspace' to delete IQ tests from SLD assessment.

These tests have multiple applications for SLD evaluations, even if the anti-IQ rebels succeed in removing the mandatory IQ–achievement discrepancy from SLD guidelines specified by the Individuals with Disabilities Education Act (IDEA) of 1997 (PL 105-17) and DSM-IV (American Psychiatric Association, 1994) criteria. IQ and related tests have key applications in the diagnostic process, as part of the search for the person's 'spared' neuropsychological assets (in the face of specific academic deficits), as part of the understanding of each referred individual's unique profile of strong and weak cognitive abilities, as part of the quest for process deficits that can lead to academic problems, and as part of the crucial job of remediation. Indeed, the authors of the chapters in the first three parts of this book have made these points abundantly clear concerning the intelligent use of Wechsler's scales (Chapter 2), comprehensive cognitive (usually theory-based) alternatives to Wechsler's scales (Chapters 3, 4, 5, and 6), the evaluation of learning propensity and learning ability (Chapters 7 and 12), the thorough measurement of language abilities (Chapter 8), and in-depth neuropsychological assessment (Chapters 9, 10, and 11).

IQ test ≠ Wechsler test

Despite their continued, widespread popularity for the psychoeducational assessment of SLD, the Wechsler Intelligence Scale for Children–Third Edition (WISC–III; Wechsler, 1991) and Wechsler Adult Intelligence Scale–Third Edition (WAIS–III; Wechsler, 1997) are not the only intelligence tests available to professionals. These tests have an impressive tradition and research history, with an abundance of published empirical research conducted with SLD populations (see Groth-Marnat, Chapter 2). Wechsler did not, however, develop his scales from any theoretical base, relying instead on the selection of intellectual tasks that were already developed to meet practical needs. His Verbal tasks had their roots in the Army Alpha Test, essentially a group-administered Binet Scale constructed to test recruits and officers during World War I. His Performance subtests also had their roots in World War I, with Wechsler selecting subtests from the nonverbal group-administered Army Beta and from the individually administered Army Performance Scale Examination. The latter test was developed, 'To prove conclusively that a man was weak-minded and not merely indifferent or malingering' (Yoakum & Yerkes, 1920, p. 10).

The Army Performance Scale Examination bears a striking resemblance to present-day Wechsler Performance scales. Because the borrowed nonverbal subtests were developed for the low end of the IQ spectrum, rather than for use in the selection of officers, there was no emphasis on constructing high-level thinking tasks that tapped into Piaget's formal operational thought. This lack of 'top' on the Performance subtests was easily solved psychometrically by Wechsler: all he had to do to maintain the reliability of the subtests for adolescents and adults was to add several bonus points for quick perfect performance on numerous nonverbal items. The addition of bonus points for speed also enabled mean test scores to increase from childhood to adolescence and young adulthood; otherwise, mean raw scores tended to plateau at about the age of 11 or 12 years. Those ages correspond to the onset of Piaget's stage of formal operations (Inhelder & Piaget, 1958; Piaget, 1972), and also to the development of the prefrontal cortex of the frontal lobe (Golden, 1981), which is largely responsible for the planning functions that characterize Luria's (1973, 1980) Block 3 (see Naglieri's discussion in Chapter 5). Therefore, because the precursor of Wechsler's Performance Scale was developed from a practical rather than from a theoretical foundation and for the lower end of the ability spectrum, the abstract formal operational skills from Piaget's cognitive–developmental framework and the highly similar planning abilities from Luria's neuropsychological perspective were unintentionally slighted. Yet, Luria's notion of planning ability, involving decision-making, evaluation of hypotheses, and flexibility, 'represents the highest levels of development of the mammalian brain' (Golden, 1981, p. 285).

Furthermore, the array of Performance subtests selected by Wechsler for his original Wechsler–Bellevue (Wechsler, 1939) and continued in his present-day test batteries have a decided emphasis on visual–spatial abilities, giving little weight to the kinds of reasoning and problem-solving abilities that characterize Horn's (1989) definition of fluid intelligence in his expansion and refinement of the Horn–Cattell *Gf–Gc* theory (Horn & Hofer, 1992; Horn & Noll, 1997).

Whether the Performance Scale measures fluid intelligence to a certain extent (Horn & Hofer, 1992; Kaufman, 1994) or not at all (Woodcock, 1990; Flanagan & McGrew, 1997) is open to debate, but it is quite evident that Wechsler's scales emphasize visual–spatial skills, visual–motor coordination, and visual–motor speed to a far greater extent than they stress general reasoning, and fall short of assessing the abstract abilities that are so important to the theories of Piaget and Luria. The addition of Matrix Reasoning to the WAIS–III was an attempt to remedy the situation – this task measures the type of fluid reasoning that Horn considers a prototype of fluid intelligence, does not depend on coordination, and its items are untimed – but that one task does not alter the overall picture substantially.

Consider Siegel's (1999) criticism that IQ tests fail to measure reasoning or problem-solving skills. If one departs from the Wechsler system and examines the available well-constructed, well-designed, theory-driven test batteries (both cognitive and neuropsychological), one finds an abundance of scales or subtests that measure the kinds of abilities that Horn would classify as fluid and Piagetians would consider dependent on formal operational thought. The Woodcock–Johnson Tests of Cognitive Ability-Revised (WJ–R) and WJ III (see Mather & Woodcock, Chapter 3), developed from Horn's expanded theory (now referred to by the test authors as the Cattell–Horn–Carroll (CHC) theory of cognitive abilities), include a Fluid Reasoning cluster, featuring the subtests Analysis–Synthesis and Concept Formation. The Kaufman Adolescent and Adult Intelligence Test (KAIT), whose theoretical roots encompass the models of Luria, Piaget, and Horn–Cattell (see Lichtenberger, Chapter 4), contains a Fluid Scale; the Mystery Codes and Logical Steps subtests are especially good measures of fluid/planning ability. Similarly, the two-subtest British Ability Scales (BAS) II Nonverbal Reasoning Ability First-Order Composite (and the highly similar Differential Ability Scales (DAS) Nonverbal Reasoning Ability Scale) is an excellent measure of Horn's fluid reasoning ability. Naglieri's (Chapter 5) Luria-based CAS includes a Planning Scale intended to measure the skills associated with Block 3, and the Developmental Neuropsychological Assessment (NEPSY), also built from a Luria framework, includes within the domain of Attention/Executive Functions the Tower subtest, a measure of planning ability and rule-based problem-solving performance (see Korkman, Kemp, & Kirk, Chapter 11). The Category Test, from the Halstead–Reitan Neuropsychological Test Battery (see Reitan & Wolfson, Chapter 10), is also an excellent measure of fluid or planning ability.

In addition to the Wechsler tests' shortage of high-level reasoning tasks, the channels of communication measured by the various Wechsler subtests fall into one of only two categories: auditory–vocal (Verbal subtests) and visual–

motor (Performance subtests). These are important channels, but clinicians who evaluate individuals suspected of SLD will often benefit by assessing other channels of communication. For example, the K-ABC includes subtests for school-age children within the auditory–motor channel (Word Order) and the visual–vocal channel (Gestalt Closure, Faces & Places) as well as the two channels measured by Wechsler's scales (see Lichtenberger, Chapter 4). Similarly, the WJ–R (see Mather & Woodcock, Chapter 3) includes two visual–vocal subtests (Picture Vocabulary, Visual Closure) and the CAS (Naglieri, Chapter 5) includes an auditory–motor subtest, Verbal–Spatial Relations. The NEPSY (Korkman et al., Chapter 11) contains the auditory–motor subtests of Auditory Attention and Response Set and Comprehension of Instructions, as well as the visual–vocal subtest of Speeded Naming.

These comments about selected advantages of theory-based tests over Wechsler's scales are illustrative, not exhaustive, and are intended to emphasize the notion that the new breed of tests developed in the 1980s and 1990s are not clones of the Wechsler scales, but offer a variety of advantages to clinicians, including those who evaluate individuals with suspected or known SLD. There is no intention to demean the WISC–III and WAIS–III or to minimize the value of the rich empirical and clinical histories that have accompanied the widespread use of Wechsler's test batteries for more than 60 years. But the time has come for professionals to become fluent with the new wave of instruments, such that psychologists weigh alternative options carefully before automatically choosing a Wechsler scale for inclusion in their assessment battery – and special educators, likewise, consider diverse alternatives before uncompromisingly recommending the deletion of IQ tests from psychoeducational evaluations.

Whereas Wechsler's tests reign supreme in the USA, that circumstance does not necessarily characterize the rest of the world. In Germany and German-speaking countries, for example, the German K–ABC is the number one children's test for psychoeducational, clinical, and neuropsychological assessment, relegating the German WISC–R to the runner-up position (Melchers, 1999). In the UK, according to BAS II and DAS author C.D. Elliott (personal communication, December 10, 1999), the WISC–III and BAS II 'are probably running each other close. My feeling is that BAS and BAS II have been preferred for most large-scale research studies in the UK.'

Misconceptions about the IQ construct

Siegel's (1999) claim that IQ is believed to set limits on academic achievement is not valid. IQ is known to be a good predictor of academic achievement, but it is not a great predictor. Coefficients of correlation in the .50s and .60s are most common for global measures of intelligence, with values peaking at about .70 (see Naglieri's discussion of pertinent research in Chapter 5, pp. 153–4). These are good relationships, strong enough to support the predictive validity of diverse intelligence tests. But the magnitude of these well-known relationships means that only about 25% to 50% of achievement test score variance overlaps with IQ variance. If IQ can be said to account for about one-quarter to one-half of the variance in achievement test scores, that means that up to three-quarters of the variance in achievement scores is due to factors other than IQ, such as motivation, quality of teaching, parental involvement, perseverance, and plain old 'error.' But we are talking about the IQ's ability to predict scores on standardized tests of achievement – not exactly the same thing as predicting school grades. Correlations between IQ and achievement tests are sometimes spuriously high because of overlap in content (e.g., Wechsler's Information and Arithmetic subtests) and because of test-taking ability. Coefficients with teachers' grades are usually notably lower, sometimes in the .20s or .30s. Although the latter finding might relate to the unreliability and subjectivity of the criterion (i.e., teachers' evaluations of students' work), the relevant conclusion from the rich body of empirical research relating global and specific scores on IQ tests to achievement is that *most of the variability in academic achievement is due to factors other than IQ.* That sobering research-based finding makes it ridiculous to claim that IQ is believed to limit students' academic achievement. Furthermore, the vast body of research on test scatter that began to accumulate in the mid-1970s (Kaufman, 1979, 1994) indicates that it is common, for 'normal' as well as for SLD and other exceptional individuals, to differ widely in their test scores on different cognitive tasks. Large differences among cognitive and academic skill areas are the norm, not the exception. It is unreasonable to expect that IQs, in whatever range of ability, would set limits on academic achievement. Abilities and academic skills will differ, with either one higher than the other, simply because scatter is a built-in aspect of cognition and because IQ (as well as subscores on IQ tests) accounts for a minority of the variance in determining one's academic achievement.

Stanovich (1999) states that, 'Intelligence has played a major role in the conceptual muddle surrounding the notion of reading failure. The confusion arises because it makes no sense to say that low intelligence . . . *causes* reading difficulties, given what is currently known about reading disabilities' (p. 352). Why implicate intelligence for this misconception? The whole notion of IQ causing reading difficulties certainly does not come from those who develop intelligence tests or from psychologists who research these tests. The same arguments applied previously to the relationship between IQ and achievement apply here as well. Obviously, if IQ accounts for half or less of the variance in academic achievement, then other variables are even more important, collectively, in predicting either reading success or reading failure. Where do these causation accusations come from? They do not even make sense from a traditional reading disability definition. The whole notion of using IQ–achievement discrepancies for identifying individuals with reading disabilities, a practice that Stanovich decries, is predicated (rightly or wrongly) on the notion that *IQ does not predict reading ability*. That is to say, when looking for a discrepancy as a means of identifying reading-disabled children, one is seeking to identify those individuals whose reading difficulties are specifically *not* predicted by their IQs – otherwise there would be no discrepancy. At the very least, it seems that it is the reasoning of those who advocate the notion that IQ causes reading difficulties that is creating the conceptual muddle referred to by Stanovich. Blaming the concept of intelligence directly, and IQ tests indirectly, is not sensible.

Siegel (1999), Stanovich (1999), and Vellutino et al. (2000) all cite a plethora of research that relates IQ to various reading-related tasks, reading decoding (and occasionally comprehension) tasks, processing mechanisms accounting for word recognition problems, ability to benefit from remediation, and the like. Invariably, the results of these studies show that IQ does not distinguish between groups that it is 'supposed to' discriminate. However, each of these studies reported by the researchers deals with IQ as if the construct is nothing more than 'g' or general intelligence. It is true that Wechsler, himself, was a 'g' theorist, even though he provided three IQs and a multi-subtest profile of scaled scores. But his scales have been interpreted from a variety of theories (see Groth-Marnat, Chapter 2; Kaufman, 1994; Kaufman & Lichtenberger, 1999, 2000) that extend his scores and subscores well beyond general ability. Once again, Wechsler's scales do not define IQ measurement. Would the various subgroups studied by Vellutino et al. (2000), for example, have differed on other IQ-related constructs, even if they did not differ on global IQ (or on Verbal IQ or on Performance IQ)? Might they have differed on the Attention or Planning Scales on the CAS (Naglieri, Chapter 5)? On the Attention/Executive Functions cluster on the NEPSY (Korkman et al., Chapter 11)? In their cognitive modifiability (Feuerstein & Feuerstein, Chapter 7)? In their K-ABC Sequential–Simultaneous discrepancy or KAIT Fluid–Crystallized discrepancy (Lichtenberger, Chapter 4)? In their BAS II or DAS Nonverbal Reasoning Ability–Verbal Ability difference (Elliott, Chapter 7)? On any of the seven Horn-based clusters that comprise the WJ–R or WJ III Tests of Cognitive Ability (Mather & Woodcock, Chapter 3)? On new and forthcoming neuropsychologically based instruments that are designed to go beyond conventional profiles of scores on IQ tests, such as the WISC–III as a Process Instrument (WISC–III – PI) or the Delis–Kaplan Test of Executive Functions?

Furthermore, the empirical research that relates IQ to various reading-related tasks and to remedial progress often treats reading disability as if it, too, is a global construct. Yet, the neuropsychological research on different reading subtypes, as discussed and insightfully interpreted by Spreen (Chapter 9) and Reitan and Wolfson (Chapter 10), cannot simply be ignored or brushed aside. Different results might have been obtained in the Siegel–Stanovich–Vellutino research studies had data been analyzed for homogeneous subtypes of reading-disabled children instead of for heterogeneous samples.

Summarily dismissing IQ tests from the SLD psychoeducational diagnostic and assessment process because global IQ, Wechsler's or otherwise, did not effectively discriminate on reading tasks or ability to be remediated is not reasonable. Tests built upon theories such as Horn's or Luria's – that place no stock at all in the 'g' concept – provide fertile ground for new empirical research with SLD children (such as the exciting intervention research discussed by Naglieri, Chapter 5, with the CAS). These new tests should not merely be included as part of the mass burial in fertile ground that is advocated by those who are primarily interested in eliminating the IQ–achievement discrepancy from the SLD definition.

Discrepancy versus deficit models

The deficit models for identifying individuals with SLD, proposed either explicitly or implicitly by Siegel (1999), Stanovich (1999), and Vellutino et al. (2000), deviate from accepted guidelines for SLD, specifically the ones specified by the Individuals with Disabilities Education Act (IDEA) of 1997 (PL 105-17) and DSM-IV (American Psychiatric Association, 1994). As Shepherd (Chapter 1) indicates, these guidelines give latitude to state education agencies and local school districts, but that latitude is not so great that one can summarily dismiss the notion of a discrepancy from the definition of SLD. Of course, the authors who are arguing for a deficit model that neatly eliminates IQ and other cognitive tests from the equation are all leaders in the SLD field and are well aware of the guidelines. Their hope, apparently, is to change conventional thinking about SLD and convert the definition from focusing on discrepancy to dealing solely with specific achievement deficits.

One of their major arguments for emphasizing deficits instead of discrepancies is the same as their main justification for trashing IQ tests, namely, their documentation of an accumulation of research on children with reading disorders that has demonstrated no differences in these students' performance on reading-related tasks (such as phonological processing), regardless of their IQs. Students with reading problems whose IQs are substantially higher than their reading scores perform no differently on tests such as phonological processing than do reading-disordered students whose IQs are similar in magnitude to their reading scores. The failure of IQ level to differentiate the performance of reading-disordered samples on cognitive processing tests, on other psychometric measures, on remedial gains, and so forth, may have reasonable explanations, as already mentioned. There is more to IQ than Wechsler's notion of IQ and there is more to intelligence than global intelligence.

But suppose we ignore the factors that potentially contaminate the results of many of the reading studies the authors cite and, instead, accept their conclusions about reading disability as valid: all poor readers have the same cognitive deficit, regardless of their IQ level and independent of the size of their IQ–achievement discrepancy. That finding, more than any other, seems to have impelled Siegel (1999) and Stanovich (1999) to react so negatively to IQ tests and to the necessity of an IQ–achievement discrepancy for SLD diagnosis. Yet, that finding is neither astounding nor a compelling reason to abandon a discrepancy model of SLD in favor of a deficit model. We quote some salient points from a letter we received from M.J. Shepherd[1] (personal communication, October 14, 1999):

Siegel and Stanovich's claim that phonological reading disability occurs at all IQ levels is 'déjà vu all over again' – Cruikshank, Kephart et al. claimed that specific learning disability (meaning visual-perceptual deficit) occurred at all IQ levels . . . If we accept the hypothesis that mental activity is specific (unique) to the task being performed it makes sense that all children having difficulty with a particular task (word recognition and spelling) will have similar cognitive deficits. This means (to me) that we will not achieve a full understanding of *specific* learning disabilities by looking at deficits alone. In neuropsychological terms we have to document the cognitive traits that have been 'spared.' This is the point that Stanovich and Siegel aren't making because (a) they insist on working with a limited conception of reading (word recognition) and/or (b) they have a political agenda – protect the poor against the rich.

The curious equating of reading ability to reading decoding by Siegel and Stanovich, with only lip service paid to reading comprehension, may have influenced the outcome of many of the studies cited. Comprehension, much more so than decoding, requires the reasoning and complex thinking skills associated with higher levels of intelligence. Furthermore, Spreen's review (Chapter 9) of the fascinating neurological literature on the use of positron emission tomography (PET), single photon emission computerized tomography (SPECT), functional magnetic resonance imaging (fMRI), evoked potential, and other techniques demonstrates that neurological functioning differs substantially with the type of reading task, for example phonological processing versus lexical–semantic processing (see Spreen's 'History' section, especially the subsection entitled 'Functional abnormalities,' plus his Tables 9.1 and 9.2 and Figures 9.4 and 9.5).

However, even if the results of the various research studies cited by Siegel (1999) and Stanovich (1999), or conducted by Vellutino et al. (2000), are replicated with measures of reading comprehension (or math computation, or math applications), such findings would *not* eliminate the need to identify the individual's neuropsychological integrities in the face of the specific academic deficit. If everyone with a given SLD displays the same cognitive deficit, then it becomes even more important to identify each person's specific cognitive strengths to facilitate a better understanding of the disability and of the most appropriate ways to develop intervention plans.

Comprehensive cognitive and academic assessment, in addition, allows the examiner to understand the individual's array of strengths and weaknesses, aiding in the essential task of identifying the specific cognitive deficits that are causally linked to specific academic deficits. The identification of cognitive competencies also permits the determination of whether the individual has a meaningful discrepancy between ability and achievement (based on professional judgment in interpreting the profile of cognitive and academic scores, not on formulas) to establish the presence of a SLD. Regardless of the accumulated research on reading decoding and the possible irrelevance of global IQ for distinguishing among groups of poor readers, the concept of one or more academic deficits in the face of cognitive integrities – i.e., the notion of a discrepancy – remains the cornerstone of the IDEA and DSM-IV definitions of SLD and is logically necessary for SLD to retain a viable categorization.

The neurological, neuropsychological, neurophysiological, and neuroanatomical variables that distinguish SLD individuals from control samples have been amply documented by the research studies cited by Spreen (Chapter 9), Reitan and Wolfson (Chapter 10), and other chapter authors. As Spreen aptly states, 'The neurological basis is no longer "presumed," although it is not always confirmed, and less specific than we would like it to be' (p. 301). Reitan and Wolfson's reports of research on their Halstead–Reitan and related measures, 'suggest that a comprehensive battery of neuropsychological tests, validated individually and as a battery for their sensitivity to cerebral impairment, may serve to identify children who have brain-based problems of

learning disabilities that they are unlikely to outgrow through normal maturation, and who therefore are in need of individual remediation and cognitive
retraining' (p. 343). Research supports a biological basis for SLD, a disorder that
involves cognitive integrities as well as deficiencies, one that should not be
confused (or lumped together) with simple reading or math deficits. However,
one does not need the extensive research documentation that dominates the
literature and is summarized in this book to conclude that SLD is a 'real'
category. One can simply read Hinshelwood's original documentation of word
blindness in 1917 or the even earlier observations of Pringle Morgan in 1896
(both discussed in some depth by Shepherd in Chapter 1 and by Spreen in
Chapter 9) to realize that SLDs are a discrete disorder. From Morgan's early
paper, the headmaster's statement about Percy, the 14 year old unable to read,
would apply to any number of children throughout history with SLDs: 'he
would be the smartest lad in school if the instruction were entirely oral'
(Shepherd, Chapter 1, p. 19).

From a humanistic standpoint, one cannot argue with Siegel's (1999) dissatisfaction with guidelines that deny various low-achieving students 'the accommodations that are available to students with a learning disability' (p. 311). Her
concern is shared by any layperson or professional who realizes the blatant
unfairness of a legal system that requires categorization and labeling before
funds are available to provide help that is obviously needed. But those are
different issues. They do not speak to the research-supported and history-based
facts that SLD is a meaningful category, one that is different from merely
having deficits that are amenable to remediation, and that the most effective
intervention for individuals with SLD will result from a keen understanding of
the biological bases of SLD, in general, and from knowledge of each individual's specific neuropsychological or psychological profile.

Applications of contemporary instruments for SLD assessment

The previous 12 chapters of this book are concerned, either explicitly or
implicitly (as in the Feuersteins' discussion of cognitive modifiability), with the
use of specific tests or assessment procedures for the evaluation of individuals
known or suspected to have SLD. These tests and procedures are typically
intended to accomplish the following goals: to identify the person's intra-
individual profile of assets and deficits, to facilitate a better understanding of the
person's cognitive/neuropsychological functioning versus academic functioning, to identify the links between the former and the latter types of functioning,
and to translate test profiles to educational intervention.

If standardized tests are given during SLD evaluations primarily to comply with federally or state-mandated rules, but the data are swept into a corner while decisions are made on other bases, as indicated by MacMillan and Speece's (1999) research results and anecdotal sources (Shepherd, Chapter 1), then much time and energy have been wasted. The time has come to release professionals from the burden of using psychometric instruments for purposes that the test authors never intended, and in ways (e.g., plugging obtained scores into uncompromising formulas) that defy a common-sense understanding of psychometrics. Forget the use of an IQ–achievement discrepancy of a given magnitude (you are categorized as SLD in Illinois and Texas, but not in Montana and New Jersey), but do not throw away the concept of a discrepancy, which remains a crucial ingredient to understanding SLDs.

If the need for an IQ–achievement discrepancy of a specific magnitude is eliminated from the SLD definition (but *not* the need to identify the neurological or cognitive integrities that have been 'spared,' despite the specific academic deficit or deficits), that will free examiners to use tests intelligently. The first positive consequence will be for the examiner to have the freedom to choose a test regardless of what it is called or whether it is on some 'acceptable' list of intelligence tests. The second will be for professionals to be able to administer the ability tests based on training and experience rather than on their specific 'label' as psychologist, learning disabilities specialist, and so forth, concerning precisely who is qualified to give specific IQ tests. The third positive consequence will be to allow approaches that are not mainstream and do not necessarily meet specific psychometric guidelines to be used for SLD evaluations; a good example is the unstandardized test–teach–test Learning Propensity Assessment Device (LPAD) described by Feuerstein and Feuerstein (Chapter 7), which can provide valuable information about a person's propensity for learning and responsiveness to feedback, if used by examiners with appropriate training. Interestingly, the Feuersteins do not distinguish SLD from other types of disorders, but emphasize the same philosophy for virtually all cognitive assessments: 'The focus is . . . on the modifiability of the condition, rather than the existence and scope of the condition. In other words, does the propensity for modifiability (and change) exist and can it be brought to existence and increased?' (p. 227).

The ability to use tests for SLD evaluations regardless of their 'type' becomes a huge advantage to examiners who otherwise might routinely administer a Wechsler scale. Certainly, Wechsler's scales provide a wealth of information if they are interpreted intelligently and not just used to produce IQs (see Groth-Marnat, Chapter 2; Kaufman, 1990, 1994; Kaufman & Lichtenberger, 2000). However, examiners should have the choice to administer neuropsychological tests instead, if that is their preference, such as the NEPSY (Chapter 11); Halstead–Reitan (Chapter 10); or a test of memory and learning ability, such as the Test of Memory and Learning (TOMAL), Wide Range Assessment of Memory and Learning (WRAML), or California Verbal Learning Test – Children's Version (CVLT-C) (Chapter 12). Similarly, process-oriented tests like the K-ABC (Chapter 4) and CAS (Chapter 5) – and ability-oriented tests like the WJ–R / WJ III Tests of Cognitive Ability (Chapter 3), KAIT (Chapter 4), DAS (Chapter 6), and BAS II (Chapter 6) – can offer much insight into an individual's intellectual assets and deficits, even if most of these tests avoid the term IQ. Additionally, if examiners are not required blindly to administer a Wechsler scale, they will have the time to obtain a far more thorough evaluation of a person's language abilities than is afforded by Wechsler's Verbal Scale, by administering one or more of the norm-referenced or criterion-referenced language tests developed and/or described by Wiig (Chapter 8).

Indeed, even the label given to a test is sometimes ambiguous or, at least, arguable. Sam Kirk's Illinois Test of Psycholinguistic Abilities (ITPA) came out in 1968, and, as Shepherd (Chapter 1) explained, he had this new type of language test very much in mind when he was coming up with the label 'learning disabilities' at his now-famous 1963 talk. The test was new in its theoretical model (Osgood's theory of communication), its choice of subtests, its names for subtests, and its metrics (mean = 36, SD = 6!). But how different was his subtest Auditory Reception ('Do carpenters kneel?' 'Do barometers congratulate?') from Wechsler's Information or Vocabulary subtests? How different was his measure of Visual Association (picture analogies) from Wechsler's Perceptual Organization subtests? And how different, conceptually, was his auditory–vocal versus visual–motor distinction from Wechsler's Verbal–Performance discrepancy? One might just as well have called the ITPA an IQ test or the WISC a psycholinguistic test. (For an interpretation of WISC–III subtests from the ITPA model, see Kaufman, 1994, pp. 156–8.) Boundaries are similarly fuzzy when thinking of the NEPSY as a neuropsychological test, but the WJ–R / WJ III Tests of Cognitive Ability as a measure of cognitive ability. If the IQ–achievement discrepancy is ever eliminated from the SLD definition, a good next step would be to eliminate artificial distinctions between the names of different types of comprehensive test batteries that all have essentially the same goals of providing a profile of a person's strengths and weaknesses – a profile that, it is to be hoped, will facilitate understanding the relationship of specific process deficits to specific academic deficits (i.e., identifying the learning disability), and will translate to recommendations for educational intervention.

We do not wish to repeat information presented in each of the component chapters of this book, but urge readers to internalize each of the instruments or procedures described in the previous three sections. Each has its own uniqueness, growing body of research, clinical value, and relationship to SLD assessment. The chapters on the WJ–R/WJ III (Mather & Woodcock, Chapter 3) and the CAS (Naglieri, Chapter 5), in particular, deal extensively with the thorny issue of IQ–achievement discrepancies as well as with the need to assess cognitive process deficits and link these weaknesses to specific academic deficits; both of these topics form an integral part of the definition of SLD in IDEA 1997. Most of the chapters on specific tests include one or more case studies to demonstrate the specific application of the test batteries to SLD assessment, especially the translation of test scores to remedial suggestions. The case studies of Leo (KAIT) and Abby (K-ABC) by Lichtenberger (Chapter 4) serve as good illustrations of the intelligent use of cognitive tests (including the integration of data from numerous instruments, several of which are discussed in this book) and the importance of integrating data from cognitive tests with standardized achievement tests for SLD diagnosis.

Even though most chapters discuss one or more specific tests, examiners should not feel compelled to administer an entire comprehensive test battery. That practice is fine for devotees of a particular test or approach, but it may not suit examiners who are oriented toward the assessment of specific domains of functioning, using a variety of carefully chosen tests or subtests that together constitute a hand-picked comprehensive battery. The latter kind of examiner will find a diversity of scales and tasks to choose from in the preceding pages of this book. In Chapter 3, Mather and Woodcock reorganized the WJ–R/WJ III subtests (cognitive and achievement) by domains such as Attention, Language, and Reasoning and Problem Solving. Similarly, we present Table 13.1 (pp. 445–9), organized by the kinds of domains that are commonly assessed when conduct-ing SLD evaluations, instead of by test battery. Whereas Mather and Woodcock's pertinent 'domain tables' are, naturally, limited to WJ–R/WJ III tasks, Table 13.1 includes subtests, scales, and complete tests that are discussed in the chapters in Parts I, II, and III of this book.

The domains we chose and the tests in each category reflect our opinions, and are likely to differ to some extent from the opinions of others; in some cases, we differ from Mather and Woodcock in the categorization of their subtests. That is fine and normal, because consensus is rare in assessment. The table should be considered as food for thought and illustrative of the kinds of ways that tasks from different batteries might be unified into new batteries, unique to each examiner and perhaps unique for each individual tested by a given examiner. We have avoided some categories (even though they are hot topics), such as working memory and executive functioning. The NEPSY (Korkman et al., Chapter 11) includes an Attention/Executive Functioning domain, and the CAS (Naglieri, Chapter 5) includes Attention and Planning scales – all of which are closely associated with current conceptions of executive functioning. However, because many other subtests and scales from diverse tests also require key aspects of executive functioning, we preferred to avoid classifying tests into this complex category. The same reasoning applies to working memory: we preferred to stick to short-term and long-term memory. Yet, even here, there are differences in how to interpret these kinds of memory. From some perspectives, any type of memory task that takes more than 15 or 30 seconds is long-term rather than short-term memory. Mather and Woodcock (Chapter 3) include their subtests Memory for Names and Visual–Auditory Memory, both paired-associate learning tasks, on the WJ–R/WJ III Long-term Memory cluster. However, we prefer Horn's (1989; Horn & Hofer, 1992) stipulation that at least some time – preferably hours or days – elapse for a task to be truly a measure of long-term memory. Therefore, the measures of long-term memory that we list in Table 13.1 are all delayed recall tests that incorporate some type of interference (administration of different tasks) in between stimulus and response. (For a comprehensive discussion of the neurobiology of memory and its assessment, see Bigler and Adams, Chapter 12.)

Summary and conclusions

The fields of SLD assessment and IQ testing are both controversial. These two fields intersect in this book as well as in recent articles appearing in the *Journal of Learning Disabilities* (Siegel, 1999; Stanovich, 1999; Vellutino et al., 2000). The authors of these recent articles are all critical of the use of IQ tests, with all proposing the elimination of the IQ–achievement discrepancy from the definition of SLD, and two (Siegel and Stanovich) proposing that IQ tests should not be used for SLD assessment at all. We find flaws in some of the reasoning of these critics of IQ tests, most notably: (a) eliminating the IQ–achievement discrepancy does not necessarily mean that it is wise to eliminate IQ tests from the SLD assessment process altogether; (b) the Wechsler scales are not the only high-quality IQ tests available; (c) the 'g' approach to IQ that they indirectly espouse does not reflect the approach inherent in most modern theories of intelligence such as Horn's; and (d) they tend to favor an achievement 'deficit' model of SLD instead of a model that incorporates the necessity of demonstrating 'spared' neuropsychological integrities despite specific academic failure.

We have addressed these four reasoning flaws in some depth from a perspective that embraces both the educational and the neurological histories of SLD and that emphasizes the many assessment alternatives to Wechsler's scales that have recently become available as we enter the new millennium. We believe that it is feasible to eliminate the strict, formulaic use of an IQ–achievement discrepancy for the determination of SLD, but that it is essential to retain a definition of SLD that includes the notion of discrepancy. That is to say, there is a long historical precedent, along with an abundance of neurological and neuropsychological research, to support the conceptual definition of SLD as an academic deficit (presumably linked to a specific cognitive process or neuropsychological deficit) that occurs despite the simultaneous presence of 'spared' neurological and cognitive skills. The IQ–achievement discrepancy is expendable, especially in view of empirical and anecdotal evidence that strongly suggests a blatant disregard for such discrepancies when practitioners make their diagnoses of SLD – state-mandated and federal guidelines notwithstanding. But the use of intelligence, neuropsychological processing, learning propensity, and other instruments in the SLD assessment process is not expendable. Indeed, the chapters in this book present a state-of-the-art tableau of the new wave of theory-based and clinically derived instruments that show exceptional promise for the diagnosis and remediation of SLD. Some of these instruments (e.g., WJ–R/WJ III, K-ABC, CAS, BAS II, NEPSY) can be used as comprehensive test batteries to serve as alternatives to Wechsler's scales, whereas others (such as tests of language, memory, learning, and learning propensity) can fill vital adjunct roles alongside comprehensive tests. Another option is to select subtests or scales from several different instruments described in this book to tailor-make comprehensive batteries for SLD assessment, thereby ensuring that most key areas of cognitive and neuropsychological functioning are thoroughly assessed. Table 13.1 is provided to facilitate this multi-battery approach.

Although Wechsler's scales still have much to offer for SLD assessment, as long as the profiles are interpreted intelligently, the new set of alternative instruments includes a variety of subtests that measure essential skills that are covered weakly or not at all by the WISC–III and WAIS–III. These skills include fluid reasoning, learning ability, planning ability, attention, and the measurement of intelligence in channels other than auditory–vocal and visual–motor. Based on the research presented throughout this book, whether specific to the underlying biological mechanisms of SLD or to the interpretation and clinical/educational applications of the tests featured in various chapters, the future of SLD assessment in this new millennium seems quite bright.

ENDNOTE

1 Dr Margaret Jo Shepherd, author of Chapter 1 of this book, played a unique role in our professional development. She was Nadeen's mentor, chairing her doctoral dissertation in the Learning Disabilities program at Teachers College, Columbia University; and her intra-individual approach to test interpretation formed the foundation of the clinical approach to Wechsler interpretation that Alan developed and implemented in his books that promote 'intelligent testing' (e.g., Kaufman, 1979, 1990, 1994).

Table 13.1. Organization of tests, scales, and subtests discussed in this book by domains that might be assessed in SLD evaluations

Global intelligence

WISC–III/WAIS–III Full Scale (Chapter 2)

WJ–R/WJ–III Broad Cognitive Ability (Chapter 3)

K-ABC Mental Processing Composite (Chapter 4)

KAIT Composite (Chapter 4)

CAS Full Scale (Chapter 5)

BAS II General Conceptual Ability Scale (Chapter 6)

DAS General Conceptual Ability Scale (Chapter 6)

Problem-solving ability/reasoning/planning

WJ–R/WJ–III Fluid Reasoning Cluster (especially Analysis–Synthesis, Concept Formation subtests) (Chapter 3)

KAIT Fluid Scale (especially Logical Steps, Mystery Codes subtests) (Chapter 4)

CAS Planning Scale (Chapter 5)

BAS II Nonverbal Reasoning Ability First-Order Composite (Chapter 6)

DAS Nonverbal Reasoning Ability Scale (Chapter 6)

LPAD Raven's Matrices subtest, Representational Stencil Design Test, Numerical Progressions Organizer subtest (Chapter 7)

Halstead–Reitan Category Test (Chapter 10)

NEPSY Tower subtest (Chapter 11)

Language skills

WISC–III/WAIS–III Verbal Scale (Chapter 2)

WJ–R/WJ–III Comprehension-Knowledge Cluster (Chapter 3)

K-ABC Achievement Scale (Chapter 4)

KAIT Crystallized Scale (Chapter 4)

BAS II Verbal Ability First-Order Composite (Chapter 6)

DAS Verbal Ability Scale (Chapter 6)

Clinical Evaluation of Language Fundamentals (CELF–3) (Chapter 8)

Test of Word Knowledge (TOWK) (Chapter 8)

Language skills (*cont.*)

Test of Language Competence – Expanded (TLC-E) (Chapter 8)

Wiig Criterion-Referenced Inventory of Language (CRIL) (Chapter 8)

Test of Adolescent and Adult Language (TOAL) (Chapter 8)

Test of Language Development (TOLD) (Chapter 8)

NEPSY Language Domain (Chapter 11)

NEPSY List Learning subtest (Chapter 11)

WRAML Verbal Memory Scale (Chapter 12)

TOMAL Memory for Stories, Word Selective Reminding, Paired Recall subtests (Chapter 12)

CVLT–C (Chapter 12)

Nonverbal skills

WISC–III/WAIS–III Performance Scale (Chapter 2)

WJ–R/WJ–III Spatial Relations subtest (Chapter 3)

K-ABC Nonverbal Scale (Chapter 4)

CAS Nonverbal Matrices, Figure Memory subtests (Chapter 5)

BAS II Nonverbal Reasoning First-Order Composite (Chapter 6)

DAS Nonverbal Reasoning Ability Scale (Chapter 6)

BAS II Spatial Ability First-Order Composite (Chapter 6)

DAS Spatial Ability Scale (Chapter 6)

BAS II Recognition of Pictures Diagnostic Scale (Chapter 6)

DAS Recognition of Pictures Diagnostic subtest (Chapter 6)

LPAD Raven's Matrices subtest, Representational Stencil Design Test (Chapter 7)

NEPSY Design Fluency, Manual Motor Sequences subtests (Chapter 11)

NEPSY Visuospatial Functions Domain (Chapter 11)

WRAML Visual Memory Scale (Chapter 12)

TOMAL Visual Selective Reminding, Visual Sequential Memory, Manual Imitation, Abstract Visual Memory, Facial Memory, Memory for Location subtests (Chapter 12)

Processing – auditory

WJ–R/WJ–III Auditory Processing Cluster (Chapter 3)

Halstead–Reitan Speech–Sounds Perception Test (Chapter 10)

Halstead–Reitan Rhythm Test (Chapter 10)

NEPSY Language Domain (especially Phonological Processing, Oromotor Sequences, Comprehension of Instructions, Repetition of Nonsense Words subtests) (Chapter 11)

Processing – visual

WISC–III/WAIS–III Picture Completion subtest (Chapter 2)

WJ–R/WJ–III Visual Processing Cluster (Chapter 3)

K-ABC Gestalt Closure, Spatial Memory, Hand Movements subtests (Chapter 4)

CAS Number Detection, Receptive Attention subtests (Chapter 5)

BAS II Recognition of Pictures Diagnostic Scale (Chapter 6)

DAS Recognition of Pictures Diagnostic subtest (Chapter 6)

NEPSY Design Fluency, Arrows subtests (Chapter 11)

Processing – kinesthetic/tactile

Halstead–Reitan Tactual Performance Test, Tactile Finger Recognition Test, Tactile Form Recognition Test, Fingertip Number Writing Perception Test, Sensory Imperception Test (Chapter 10)

NEPSY Finger Discrimination, Imitating Hand Positions subtests (Chapter 11)

Processing – cognitive style

K-ABC Sequential Processing Scale (Chapter 4)

K-ABC Simultaneous Processing Scale (Chapter 4)

CAS Successive Scale (Chapter 5)

CAS Simultaneous Scale (Chapter 5)

Visual–motor coordination/visual–spatial

WISC–III/WAIS–III Performance Scale (Chapter 2)

WISC–III/WAIS–III Perceptual Organization Index (Chapter 2)

WJ–R/WJ–III Spatial Relations subtest (Chapter 3)

K-ABC Simultaneous Processing Scale (Chapter 4)

BAS II Spatial Ability First-Order Composite (Chapter 6)

DAS Spatial Ability Scale (Chapter 6)

LPAD Organization of Dots Test, Complex Figure Drawing Test, Reversal Test (Chapter 7)

Halstead–Reitan Trail Making Test (Chapter 10)

NEPSY Design Fluency subtest (Chapter 11)

NEPSY Visuospatial Functions Domain (Chapter 11)

Motor coordination/functioning (noncognitive)

Halstead–Reitan Tactile Finger Recognition Test, Tactile Form Recognition Test, Fingertip Number Writing Perception Test, Sensory Imperception Test, Grip Strength subtest (Chapter 10)

NEPSY Statue subtest (Chapter 11)

NEPSY Sensorimotor Functions Domain (except Manual Motor Sequences subtest) (Chapter 11)

Attention

WISC–III Freedom from Distractibility Index (Chapter 2)

WAIS–III Working Memory Index (Chapter 2)

WISC–III/WAIS–III Processing Speed Index (Chapter 2)

WJ–R/WJ–III Processing Speed Cluster (Chapter 3)

CAS Attention Scale (Chapter 5)

LPAD Diffuse Attention Test (Chapter 7)

Halstead–Reitan Rhythm Test (Chapter 10)

NEPSY Attention/Executive Functions Domain (especially Auditory Attention and Response Set, Visual Attention subtests) (Chapter 11)

Memory – short-term

WISC–III Freedom from Distractibility Index (Chapter 2)

WAIS–III Working Memory Index (Chapter 2)

WJ–R/WJ–III Short-term Memory Cluster (Chapter 3)

WJ–R/WJ–III Picture Recognition subtest (Chapter 3)

K-ABC Sequential Processing Scale (Chapter 4)

CAS Successive Scale (Chapter 5)

BAS II Recall of Digits Forward, Recall of Digits Backward, Recognition of Pictures, Recall of Objects (Immediate) Diagnostic scales (Chapter 6)

DAS Recall of Digits, Recognition of Pictures, Recall of Objects (Immediate) Diagnostic subtests (Chapter 6)

NEPSY Memory for Faces, Narrative Memory, Sentences Repetition subtests (Chapter 11)

WRAML Verbal Memory Scale (Chapter 12)

WRAML Visual Memory Scale (Chapter 12)

TOMAL Sequential Recall Index (Chapter 12)

TOMAL Backward Recall Index (Chapter 12)

TOMAL Spatial Memory Index (Chapter 12)

TOMAL Memory for Stories, Facial Memory subtests (Chapter 12)

Memory – long-term

WJ–R/WJ–III Delayed Memory for Names, Delayed Visual–Auditory Learning subtests (Chapter 3)

KAIT Delayed Recall subtests (Chapter 4)

BAS II Recall of Objects (Delayed) Diagnostic Scale (Chapter 6)

DAS Recall of Objects (Delayed) Diagnostic subtest (Chapter 6)

NEPSY Delayed Memory for Faces, Memory for Names subtests (Chapter 11)

TOMAL Delayed Recall Index (Chapter 12)

CVLT–C (Chapter 12)

Speed

WISC–III/WAIS–III Processing Speed Index (Chapter 2)

WJ–R/WJ–III Speed Cluster (Chapter 3)

CAS Planning Scale (Chapter 5)

BAS II Speed of Information Processing Diagnostic Scale (Chapter 6)

DAS Speed of Information Processing Diagnostic subtest (Chapter 6)

Halstead–Reitan Trail Making Test, Finger Oscillation Test (Chapter 10)

NEPSY Speeded Naming, Fingertip Tapping subtests (Chapter 11)

Learning ability

WJ–R/WJ–III Analysis–Synthesis, Concept Formation subtests (Chapter 3)

WJ–R/WJ–III Memory for Names, Visual–Auditory Learning subtests (Chapter 3)

KAIT Rebus Learning, Mystery Codes subtests (Chapter 4)

LPAD Positional Learning Test, Plateaux Test, Associative Recall, Word Memory subtest (Chapter 7)

Learning ability (*cont.*)
LPAD (Entire Test) (Chapter 7)
Halstead–Reitan Category Test (Chapter 10)
NEPSY Manual Motor Sequences subtest, Memory for Names, List Learning subtests (Chapter 11)
WRAML Learning Scale (Chapter 12)
TOMAL Word Selective Reminding, Visual Selective Reminding, Object Recall, Paired Recall subtests (Chapter 12)
CVLT–C (Chapter 12)

REFERENCES

American Psychiatric Association (1994). *Diagnostic and Statistical Manual of Mental Disorders, Fourth Edition*. Washington, DC: American Psychiatric Association.

Binet, A. (1903). *L'etude Experimentale de l'Intelligence* (The experimental study of intelligence). Paris: Schleicher.

Flanagan, D.P. & McGrew, K.S. (1997). A cross-battery approach to assessing and interpreting cognitive abilities: narrowing the gap between practice and cognitive science. In *Beyond Traditional Intellectual Assessment: Contemporary and Emerging Theories, Tests, and Issues*, ed. D.P. Flanagan, J.L. Genshaft, & P.L. Harrison, pp. 314–25. New York: Guilford Press.

Galton, F. (1869). *Hereditary Genius: An Inquiry into its Laws and Consequences*. London: Macmillan.

Galton, F. (1883). *Inquiries into Human Faculty and its Development*. London: Macmillan.

Golden, C.J. (1981). The Luria–Nebraska Children's Battery: theory and formulation. In *Neuropsychological Assessment of the School-age Child*, ed. G.W. Hynd & J.E. Obrzut, pp. 277–302. New York: Grune and Stratton.

Hinshelwood, J. (1917). *Congenital Word-blindness*. London: H.K. Lewis.

Horn, J.L. (1989). Cognitive diversity: a framework of learning. In *Learning and Individual Differences*, ed. P.L. Ackerman, R.J. Sternberg, & R. Glaser, pp. 61–116. New York: Freeman.

Horn, J.L., & Hofer, S.M. (1992). Major abilities and development in the adult period. In *Intellectual Development*, ed. R.J. Sternberg & C.A. Berg, pp. 44–99. New York: Cambridge University Press.

Horn, J.L. & Noll, J.G. (1997). Human cognitive capabilities: Gf–Gc theory. In *Contemporary Intellectual Assessment: Theories, Tests and Issues*, ed. D.P. Flanagan, J.L. Genshaft, & P.A. Harrison, pp. 53–91. New York: Guilford Press.

Inhelder, B. & Piaget, J. (1958). *The Growth of Logical Thinking from Childhood to Adolescence*. New York: Basic Books.

Jensen, A.R. (1998). *The g Factor: The Science of Mental Ability*. Westport, CT: Praeger.

Kaufman, A.S. (1979). *Intelligent Testing with the WISC–R*. New York: John Wiley.

Kaufman, A.S. (1990). *Assessing Adolescent and Adult Intelligence*. Boston, MA: Allyn & Bacon.

Kaufman, A.S. (1994). *Intelligent Testing with the WISC–III*. New York: John Wiley.

Kaufman, A.S. (2000). Tests of intelligence. In *Handbook of Intelligence*, ed. R.J. Sternberg, pp. 445–76. New York: Cambridge University Press.

Kaufman, A.S. & Kaufman, N.L. (1983). *K-ABC Interpretive Manual*. Circle Pines, MN: American Guidance Service.

Kaufman, A.S. & Lichtenberger, E.O. (1999). *Essentials of WAIS–III Assessment*. New York: John Wiley.

Kaufman, A.S. & Lichtenberger, E.O. (2000). *Essentials of WISC–III and WPPSI–R Assessment*. New York: John Wiley.

Luria, A.R. (1973). *The Working Brain: An Introduction to Neuro-psychology*. London: Penguin Books.

Luria, A.R. (1980). *Higher Cortical Functions in Man*, second edition. New York: Basic Books.

MacMillan, D.L. & Speece, D.L. (1999). Utility of current diagnostic categories for research and practice. In *Developmental Perspectives on Children with High-incidence Disabilities*, ed. R. Gallimore, L.P. Bernheimer, D.L. MacMillan, D.L. Speece, & S. Vaughn, pp. 111–13. Mahweh, NJ: Lawrence Erlbaum.

Melchers, P. (1999). The German K-ABC – Research and clinical interpretation. In A.S. Kaufman, P. Melchers, & N.L. Kaufman (presenters), The K-ABC and other means of intellectual assessment. APA Level III Workshop and supervision for experienced clinicians. Presented at the German/Dutch Neuropsychological Society: Neuropsychology on the Brink of the Millennium, Cologne, Germany.

Mill, J.S. (1875). *A System of Logic, Ratiocinative, and Inductive, being a Connected View of the Principles of Evidence and the Methods of Scientific Investigation*, ninth edition, Vols. 1 and 2. London: Longmans, Green, Reader and Dyer.

Morgan, P. (1896) A case of congenital word-blindness. *British Medical Journal*, 2, 1378.

Piaget, J. (1972). Intellectual evolution from adolescence to adulthood. *Human Development*, 15, 1–12.

Siegel, L.S. (1999). Issues in the definition and diagnosis of learning disabilities: a perspective on *Guckenberger v. Boston University*. *Journal of Learning Disabilities*, 32, 304–19.

Spearman, C.E. (1904). 'General intelligence,' objectively determined and measured. *American Journal of Psychology*, 15, 201–93.

Stanovich, K.E. (1999). The sociopsychometrics of learning disabilities. *Journal of Learning Disabilities*, 32, 350–61.

Vellutino, F.R., Scanlon, D.M., & Lyon, G.R. (2000). Differentiating between difficult-to-remediate and readily remediated poor readers: more evidence against the IQ–achievement discrepancy definition of reading disability. *Journal of Learning Disabilities*, 33, 223–38.

Wechsler, D. (1939). *Measurement of Adult Intelligence*. Baltimore, MD: Williams & Wilkins.

Wechsler, D. (1991). *Manual for the Wechsler Intelligence Scale for Children, Third Edition (WISC–III)*. San Antonio, TX: The Psychological Corporation.

Wechsler, D. (1997). *Manual for the Wechsler Adult Intelligence Scale–Third Edition (WAIS–III)*. San Antonio, TX: The Psychological Corporation.

Woodcock, R.W. (1990). Theoretical foundations of the WJ–R measures of cognitive ability. *Journal of Psychoeducational Assessment*, 8, 231–58.

Woodcock, R.W. & Mather, N. (1989). WJ–R Tests of Cognitive Ability – Standard and Supplemental batteries: examiner's Manual. In *Woodcock–Johnson Psycho-Educational Battery–Revised*, ed. R.W. Woodcock & M.B. Johnson. Chicago, IL: Riverside.

Woodcock, R.W., McGrew, K.S., & Mather, N. (2001). *Woodcock–Johnson Psycho-Educational Battery, Third Edition (WJ–3)*. Chicago, IL: Riverside.

Yoakum, C.S. & Yerkes, R.M. (1920). *Army Mental Tests*. New York: Henry Holt.

Index

Note: figures and tables are indicated by bold page numbers.